A HISTORY
OF THE BUSINESS MAN

THE MACMILLAN COMPANY
NEW YORK · BOSTON · CHICAGO · DALLAS
ATLANTA · SAN FRANCISCO

MACMILLAN & CO., Limited
LONDON · BOMBAY · CALCUTTA
MELBOURNE

THE MACMILLAN COMPANY
OF CANADA, Limited
TORONTO

A HISTORY

OF THE

BUSINESS MAN

By

MIRIAM BEARD

In the history of mankind, there is a remarkable relationship between Idea and Interest. There is neither an Idea which is independent of interests in its development, nor an Interest which could have remained independent, in its materiality, of ideas.

—Kurt Riezler, "Idee und Interesse
in der politischen Geschichte."

NEW YORK

THE MACMILLAN COMPANY

1938

CONTENTS

v

26162

CONTENTS

PART FOUR

THE INDIVIDUALIST

PART FIVE

THE BIG BUSINESS MAN

A HISTORY
OF THE BUSINESS MAN

INTRODUCTION

THE BUSINESS MAN AND HISTORY

IF IT IS A LITTLE STRANGE that writers have not yet provided a history for the business man, it is still more curious that he himself remains so unconcerned in the matter. For history is a potent weapon, and a man who lacks one nowadays may be said to go unarmed. The conclusion all too readily drawn by the public is that he has a story to hide.

Aristocrats, dictators and priests have long appreciated the beauties and uses of history, for without emphasis on continuity, they would be lost; they need the apparatus of song, emblem, legend and ceremony which connects them with a venerable past, to hallow their persons and sustain their powers. Of late, the technique of historical justification has been refined and turned to the service of parties and institutions, systems, classes, professions. Whole nations may be exalted by an artificial reconstruction like Caesarism and Teutonism, which provide Roman or "Aryan" ancestors for Italians and Germans, or Shintoism, which gives ancient and divine lineage to Japanese. But not only Fascists rely upon "Mythos": Liberals depend on democratic traditions and Communists point to bygone class-struggles. And outside the political sphere, history is adapted for economic and social ends.

Many of the professions have acquired a respectable patina through reinterpretation of the past. Thus physicians are now wrapped in such dignity that the public forgets how recently they occupied the status of barbers. Lawyers have climbed from the family-solicitor relation to a solemn eminence as legal history was composed; art history has made the artist a legitimate successor of the bards and "old masters." Even the poor mountebank, by stepping on the pedestal of the past, has increased his stature. Not so the business man; he still struggles on, unfathered and unhallowed, lacking annals and allegories, a mellowed lineage, a shell of mythos in which to creep. He is his own ancestor and, usually, his memory does not reach back even to the last business crisis.

Although the past of business men is long and crowded, they have come through millennia of strenuous exertions looking as slick and fresh as this year's daisy crop. Their past is of little benefit to their social position or personal morale. Any simple soldier in the rear rank may feel himself a hero because Wellington and Napoleon once lived and triumphed; any attic-aesthete may demand increased respect for himself and his products because Rembrandt and Beethoven cast their mighty shadows behind him. Not so the unfortunate manufacturer of pig-iron, the insurance broker, the peanut magnate, the czars of the corset industry—on *them* falls no glory reflected from Jacques Cœur and Jacob Fugger, the Medici and the Rucellai.

What is the reason for this singular position? An obvious explanation is the sharp break which the Industrial Revolution is commonly supposed to have made in human development: the modern capitalist is assumed to be a wholly new sort of fellow, unrelated to the financiers, shippers, munitioneers and manufacturers of antiquity. Possibly this attitude may change, as the freedom of the unique Victorian Age gives way to renewed State control over industry, and the threads of the past are picked up again. The modern business man may yet learn to look back with more sympathy upon the state-merchants of baroque France or even of far-away Byzance, than upon his own individualistic grandfather.

But there are other reasons for the business man's failure to win the prestige derived from history. His own character has excluded him from orthodox history writing; he could not fit into its conceptions. Though biographies are now written of successful men of commerce, and the story of economic enterprise is being traced, he still remains outside the main stream of history writing, and therefore is not "received," aged and "historified" in the popular estimation. In part, this is due to the fact that the concepts of the older history were formed by Greeks and Romans who despised the trader, and, in modern times, by Germans at a period when business elements were weak in German society. History, as these non-commercial historians conceived it, was the tale of heroes, of institutions, of ideas. But that left out of account the business man, who has not been a hero in the usual sense, who has not served institutions wholeheartedly or been distinguished primarily as a thinker.

The organizer of economic enterprise has generally lacked personality of a sort to capture popular imagination. Remarkable individuals may of course be instanced, far-sighted as William Paterson or Robert Owen, colorful as Schliemann, forceful as Ouvrard or Stinnes; but as a class, business men have been in a sense the victims of their virtues. They have not sacrificed others like tyrants or themselves like saints; through the stormiest ages they were the carriers of morality, the representatives of thrift, temperance, reticence, hard work, domesticity and other qualities which wearied, instead of thrilling readers.

Few really horrid crimes, without rational motive, may be imputed to business men. Seldom have they put out the eyes of competitors with hot irons or burned rival salesmen at the stake. Even early Italian financiers, though they resorted to the stiletto at times when certain industries appeared overcrowded, were cautious and methodical despite their Latin temperament, and did not murder other bankers just for fun, or throw away monopolies for love. To be sure, business men were often drawn into violence as fighters, slavers or pirates, and they did evil in their own way: they robbed widows and orphans and the Indians; they oppressed whole populations with monopolies and usurious practices and cheated the State, by selling it rotten ships, as the Romans did in the Punic Wars or Vanderbilt in the American Civil War, or by outfitting its enemies with arrows or airplanes. But as a class, they were not wanton in barbarity; they have not engaged in the fantastic cruelties, the *crimes passionnels* and massacres for pleasure which endeared other kinds of men to the general public.

As private individuals, moreover, they were quiet and restrained from necessity, for the perverts and maniacs who might succeed as monarchs could never, even in the Renaissance, manage a cloth-factory. True, financiers may have indulged in more eccentricities than wholesalers and manufacturers, but the main body of business men have been too timid, or too busy, or too rationalistic, to cut capers. All down the tempestuous course of history, they are to be found standing aside from the passions that drove their fellows to crusades. They profited from the follies and vices of others and regularly got the better of heroes and prophets. But such steadiness and commonsense exasperated the chivalric-minded; and business men made little attempt to court popularity by witty and memorable remarks, preserving their carefully assumed taciturnity even on their deathbeds. Few "household phrases" have been coined by men of commerce.

Almost the only real controversy which the business man has excited among sociologists and historians is accordingly a dispute over his virtues. The disciples of Max Weber insist that he became a successful capitalist because he was a good Puritan first; the opposing Sombart school maintains that he was always soaked in "bourgeois morality" and was good centuries before Calvin was born. Now obviously, a man who can only stir up a row over the derivation and duration of his good sense is not destined to cut a very fine figure in orthodox history, or to excite the adoration of the throng.

The business man might have been forgiven for his unheroic attitudes and occupations if he had served, with single devotion, some institution or idea that was greater than he was—the State, the Church, Art, Science or Justice. But he lacked significance as well as eccentricity. The most successful attempt to give him this justification has been made in America, where the word Business has attracted a veneration almost equal to that bestowed upon Science. But even this has been only a partial triumph, for the mere addition of the word "big" is enough to ruin the atmosphere—the populace will not hear of Big Business as a suitable aim of supreme human effort.

Other endeavors to portray the business man as the servant of some transcendant idea have also failed. Some, following Kant, have maintained that he fostered peace by linking nations together in commercial bonds; but it is evident that he has financed war as well as peace through the ages. Others have called him, after Addison, the promoter of universalism, but of course he has stood for localism as much as for unity. With his financial network, he helped consolidate the power of the mediaeval Roman Catholic Church, but he also financed the national armies which tore apart this marvelous unity of the Christian world. In our time, he has supported nationalism and internationalism alike.

More persuasively, writers like Sombart have portrayed him as the rationalist, the opponent of the irrational, traditional, emotional forces of agriculture and militarism. But even this theory will not hold water, for the business man does not want the complete rationalization of society. He has not wished, even when he had a chance, to sweep away all feudal vestiges, military or aristocratic or emotional, from human life. He has not offered a planned society; he wants the tooth-and-claw struggle as much as efficiency, or, as Fisher Ames, the American revolutionary business man, phrased it, he demands just "enough order —for others." Consequently, he has not pleased either camp; he has not sided with the emotionalists and the military-religious-aesthetic crowds, nor has he joined the pure rationalists, who would sweep away irrationality, reduce biologic indeterminism to chart, and confine human variability in some sort of scheme, Socialist, Communist or Technocratic.

In short, the business man has steered a veering course. He has favored peace and war, unity and chaos, mystery and science, according to the immediate prospects of profit. Other men, warriors and rulers, may have sought gold more greedily than he, but they could at least pretend to other ends, whereas he was never able to work up a similar, sustained hocus-pocus about his activities, or hold up even an illusory goal. He had no *wohin*, no "whither," no discoverable ultimate purpose.

He did not try to remedy this condition, by creating a legend around his own figure; he did not retain scriveners and bards in his office as Roman and Renaissance captains kept them in their tents. He chose either of two courses: he took over the tradition of some other class, or renounced it entirely. Thus he might creep into the already created shell of sentiment around an aristocracy; by buying titles, castles and blazonry, he merged himself into the purchased background. But when he could not easily win admittance to these higher circles, or when, as in America, he found no tradition to adopt, he repudiated the emotional appeal of heredity and historic glamor. He became, at least in this respect, a hard-headed rationalist, relying upon cold logic and what he called scientific method. Instead of enveloping himself in a mantle of mythos, he depended upon "Nature's law" or the spirit of progress, the psychology of salesmanship, "pep" and the attractive packaging of goods, to see him through. In either case, he developed no independent body of legend and tradition for himself.

To be sure, there have been some limited exceptions to this. Some of the mediaeval German townsmen were on the way toward an independent patrician tradition when their towns were ruined. On the other hand, in the United States, in the Age of Coolidge, much was being done to create a mythos of "service" and "prosperity." But none of this was sufficient to provide the business man with a setting comparable to that enjoyed by princely rulers and warriors.

Not only was the business man careless of history, but he was also continually in opposition to the agrarian-military groups which were the essentially history-conscious elements in society. They stood for continuity, and he stood only for change. They justified themselves by appealing to what Mannheim calls the principle of legitimacy, and traced their lineage in blood or spirit back to heroes, martyrs, demigods, sometimes to the gods themselves. But the business man's few efforts in that direction were worse than futile. As Michels says:

> As is well known, even modern industry surrounds its rise with legends. But the mythology of modern industry is as dry as our science of economics itself. Even in sunny Italy, an attempt was made to tie up the origin of the important textile industry of Biellese with the story of a convict who, after finishing his sentence, appeared on the mountain and acquainted the women of the region with the arts of his prison-work. . . . Nations choose for themselves as founding fathers the great heroes of Hellenic mythology, Hercules, Hector, Æneas or the Jewish favorites of the Gods; great industries content themselves with petty convicts.

Unable to romanticize his lineage, or uninterested in the attempt, the business man has opposed the idea of change to the principle of continuity. A fellow of obscure origins, he excited suspicion from the beginning by his eagerness to traffick with strangers and accept their ideas as well as goods. He moved too continually to acquire a romance, save what his connection with the perilous seas or the treasures of distant lands might win him. He was forever breaking down the fixed attitudes of mind in ordered societies, tempting people to want more than they could pay for, overshadowing the oldest and noblest possessors of the soil by his wealth and ostentation. He dragged high families into debt and bought them out. He demoralized landed gentry; he lived in sensation-hungry cities, fattening upon the land. He was the perpetual parvenu, the everlasting disturber and expander, who had cut himself off from the dark mysteries of blood and soil, the instincts and emotions that sprang from the furrows. He destroyed the fixed, hierarchical and agrarian order of things by introducing temptations and doubts, by outshining the old ruling classes, or overthrowing them in revolution.

Sometimes, over large stretches of time and territory, the business man has been held down by the landed-warrior castes and kept near the bottom of the social and political scale. This was true in India, under the Brahmin caste system, until the coming of a more liberal-democratic wave with Buddhism; in Japan, during the three centuries of his splendid isolation from foreign contacts; in Russia, from the most ancient times down to the modern bolshevist régime. In the Dark Ages of Europe, except in Spain, where Jews and Moors tended commerce, he was sorely oppressed; in Spain, after the Moors and Jews were driven out, he was weakened and weighed down. In Italy in modern times and in modern Germany, he has been comparatively less influential against agrarian-military elements than in England or France.

Often, however, the business man has been able to effect a compromise with his feudal foes. He might remain in the background, wielding invisible power, while the aristocrats and the bureaucratic diplomats strutted in front before the dazzled folk. Modern Britain is the supreme example of such a balance, neatly devised and long maintained, between banking-trading-manufacturing classes and landed-church-navy groups. In France, since the Renaissance, when Italian financiers followed the Medicean queens to Paris, down to the modern banking oligarchy, the moneyed men have kept the saddle under many shifts of political mounts. And other illustrations of compromise are furnished by the Orientals, as in the old Turkish Caliphate, where a set of Christian and Jewish bankers agreed with the warrior-conquerors to divide spheres within the State in an amicable fashion.

While the business man has endured long nights of abasement, and engineered many hours of harmonious agreement, he has known very few and brief periods of genuine triumph. In many centers of antiquity he controlled societies, and in the mediaeval cities of Italy and Germany he enjoyed a limited independence, and, from the tops of his battlements, could look down on the countryside where feudal lords prevailed. One may contend that he reached the apogee of open power in seventeenth-century Holland; there, and only there, he ruled as well as owned a country and dominated the thought as well as the resources of an entire state. Beside this achievement, even the Golden Age of Coolidge appears slightly pale, and must be rated second-best.

Since, with varying degrees of success, the business man stood in opposition to the history-conscious feudal classes, he could not expect to be admitted to *their* history. And he would not make one of his own. The result was that he got scant credit for his operations. Though he was a builder of cities and nations and a welder of international connections; though he was the provider of luxuries, the chief patron of Dutch, German-Gothic, Italian-Renaissance and late-Japanese folk art, and raised multitudes to a new standard of life; though he was the driving force behind so many wars and crusades, such as the Dutch, English, French, Japanese and American rebellions and revolutions—yet as mere business man he remained ignored by reputable writers. It was his antagonism to the history-conscious feudal classes which made history, and at the same time deprived him of a history.

PART ONE
THE HERITAGE OF ANTIQUITY

I

SWORDSMEN AND SALESMEN IN THE HOMERIC AGE

WHEN THE HEROES of myth and saga appear on the Western European scene, they are brandishing weapons supplied them by the agile traders of the Near East. From glancing helmet to well-fitting breastplate, from sharp dagger to ponderous sword or mace, they have been equipped by the business man.

Among these heroes of whom legend tells us, there is only the German Siegfried who possesses sufficient technological skill to make his own armaments. The others disdain crafts. But Siegfried is a very young hero—the "Nibelungenlied" was not written down until 1200 or so after Christ, about two thousand years after the Homeric Age, and by that time the heavy industries had taken root along the Rhine, where Siegfried lived. The other, older warriors of Western heroic saga and story were dependent upon traders who could bring them the refined products of Near Eastern industrial centers.

The business man, thus viewed, was a figure much older than the Western "hero." He had been developing his skill in bargaining and manufacturing long, enormously long, before the first West European heroes of whom we know began to hack their way to fame. Before Greek Achilles or Trojan Hector, Roman Horatius or Cincinnatus, Teuton Siegfried or English Beowulf wielded their mighty swords— thousands of years, in fact, before there were any swords at all—the Eastern trader was well established in the Mesopotamian Valley and was wise with the cunning of untold ages.

Three thousand years before Christ, the Mesopotamian merchant had a very considerable accumulation of technique and experience behind him; he was seasoned in affairs, wary in drawing up contracts, and stout in litigation. By 2500 B.C., he was forming trading-companies for penetration into distant realms; he was trafficking in many kinds of wares, wool, spices, soda, silver, ointments and "fair-skinned slaves," bringing them by caravan or sailing-ship to the cities of Ur, Uruk, Uma and other ancient centers of commerce, which are now being uncovered from the desert sands by the spades of excavators. How far back this development goes, no one can say, but some idea of its antiquity may be obtained by remembering that Ur is as much older than Rome as Rome is older than New York.

Business life was far advanced when the earliest written documents in our possession were made on clay tablets, put into clay jars for safe-keeping and filed for reference in office vaults of these long-buried towns. Laws were in effect covering a wide variety of transactions and regulating market prices; there was a strong tendency toward government control of business. The priest-king, indeed, was the supreme entrepreneur, who let contracts to the trader, or *damkar*. Precious metals were being used as a measure of commodities, not in the shape of coins as yet, but in bars stamped with the guarantee of some temple or its deity. For good "shekels of the Temple of Babylon," many exotic wares could be bought in the bazaars, and those who had no ready cash could offer promissory notes.

Enki, Ni gin, Abu-wakar, Arad-Mardu, and the rest of these ancient damkars can be imagined against a background full of details; we can visualize them dispatching business correspondence, passing notes and signing contracts, forming associations for risky ventures in foreign parts, renting favorable shop-sites, offering to do favors for a customer in search of readymade imported garments, or threatening one another with court action. These were real men, of historic authenticity, whose prosaic deeds are established by documents a thousand, in some cases two thousand and more, years before the legendary heroes of the West found bards to sing their questionable exploits.

Millennia before Homer sang, or the wolf suckled Romulus and Remus, the bustling damkars of Uruk and Nippur and the other cities of the Valley were buckling down to business. Atidum the merchant, in need of enlarged office facilities, was agreeing to rent a suitable location from Ribatum, Priestess of Shamash, for one and one-sixth shekels of silver per year—so much down and the rest in easy installments. Abu-wakar, the rich shipper, was delighted that his daughter had become Priestess of Shamash and could open a real estate office near the temple. Ilabras was writing to Ibi: "May Shamash and Marduk keep thee! As thou knowest, I had issued a note for a female slave. Now the time to pay is come." Ramman-idinna and Arad-Mardu were dissolving their partnership, having agreed from "mouth to money," from the first promise to the final payment, and were going to the gate of the temple of Shamash to turn in their capital and take oath that "neither shall complain, nor go to law with the other. By Shamash and Sippar they swear, that neither shall go to law with the other."

The relations of these agile bargainers were already stretching afar.

Asian colonies have been lately uncovered, revealing piles of correspondence between foreign agents of "dry-goods" firms and their
home offices in Assur. There are anxious inquiries about samples of
Cappadocian cloth; reminders to take enough food for the donkeys
and military protection for the caravan. Here is a letter from the main
office to two traders in Kanish:

> Two talents of lead are with Hura-sanum, two talents with
> Amur-assur, son of Shu-Ishtar, and 100 pieces of stuff are on hand.
> Insist upon good lead. . . . Take the lead and the cloth on short-
> term credit. If you intend to send your money here to buy goods,
> and your written order arrives before the money comes, I will buy
> the wares you designate from my own means and send them to
> you.

It is possible that the efforts of these ambitious traders extended to
the far frontiers of Western Europe. At least, in some manner, the
bronze products of Mesopotamian workshops made their way into the
deep forests where our barbaric forefathers still lived in the primitive
simplicity of the Stone Age, lacking the ingenuity to make anything
better than flint hatchets for flinging at one another's heads. The routes
along which the metal wares from the Near East were brought into
the European wildernesses are traceable today, over the Alps by the
Brenner Pass, to Danube and Elbe and the Scandinavian regions. In a
Pomeranian moor has been found an oaken box, fitted with leather
straps for slinging over the shoulders, which contains specimens of
these goods, a dagger blade, a needle, a sickle; if the conjectures of the
experts are correct, it may have been the sample case of a traveling
salesman in the dawn-age.

These business pioneers were no doubt eagerly welcomed, and received rich freights of honey, wax, furs, slaves, in return for their
sharp knives. Every few centuries, they brought out a new and improved line of goods. They produced excellent axes; in one deposit in
Brittany, four thousand standardized hatchets, neatly bundled together
with wire, have been recovered. Presently, during the period 1800–
1200 B.C., the primitive bayonet was introduced, a dagger on a handle.
Then, as the yet newer metal, iron, was being worked successfully,
around 1000 B.C., the inventive genius of the Mesopotamian industrial
districts achieved a most formidable weapon, broad and long of blade,
true-cleaving and trusty, well fitted to a hero's hand—the Sword.

Calls for defensive armor must have resounded at once from the
depths of the forests, and were met by alert agents from the various
growing centers of the Mediterranean readymade metal garment in-

dustry. Shields, helmets, greaves and other warrior-gear of precious iron went up North, and with such items were sent decorated jars of fiery liquors. In the grave-mounds of savage customers of those days, have been found, with imported armor, the cups and cans and jugs that once held wine of Greece, to judge by the resinous deposits in them.

Thus the civilized trader makes his grand entry into Western Europe—offering arms for sale. He exploits the markets of the frontier and incites the savages with wines and weapons. Probably, he plumes himself upon spreading culture among them. At least an ancient author, Diodorus of Sicily, observes the beneficent results of the traffic in tin upon the unkempt inhabitants of remote Britain. The tin-buyers of Marseilles were accustomed to sailing up the Rhone River, a thirty days' journey, shipping to Britain, and procuring the precious ingredient of bronze from the natives who, says Diodorus, are fast becoming "more cultivated owing to their intercourse with foreign merchants."

Oddly enough, British business men in the eighteenth century justified their slave-trade in Africa by pointing to the parallel with antiquity. In a parliamentary discussion of the British African Company's ventures, in 1777, it was urged that expansion would be desirable in order to procure more of the Gold Coast Negroes, who were laborious and used to living on little, instead of the Congo slaves who "are of a more soft, voluptuous and effeminate nature . . . so that being transplanted to the hardships of our sugar colonies, they commit suicide." This business enterprise would ultimately civilize the Africans, said Temple Luttrell, pointing to the ancient Phoenicians who opened up the wilderness of Britain so long ago, and "found us Britons . . . full as barbarous as we now see the most disgusting figures among them [the Africans]; we dwelt in huts made of mud and . . . went stark naked . . . we besmeared and lacquered our carcasses with grease and various colors."

Possibly the ancient Babylonian, and the Phoenician and Greek traders imagined themselves to be conferring the benefits of superior culture upon our brawny ancestors. But even they must have seen at length the disquieting aspect of such traffic. For after they had impartially distributed sharp iron swords and fire water to the wild men of the woods, these strenuous customers became exhilarated and, swinging their new-bought blades, began to cleave their way to fame. The heroes of the epics, armed so well by the trader, emerged at last from obscurity.

The deep peace which authorities in such matters believe existed in the prehistoric age, 1800–1200 B.C., in northern Europe, came to an end. Unavoidably, in view of the arms traffic situation, European history began.

SWORDSMEN AGAINST SALESMEN

This was to the disadvantage of the trader, who now found himself attacked by the men he had so well equipped. Sea-pirates began to infest the waters and lie in wait for merchant vessels. Along coasts and far inland, as remains still show, forts were constructed, strongholds of primitive robber-barons who planned to live by easing the trader's burdens and taking toll of his casks and sacks. Caesar tells us of the chieftain, Dumnorix, who was one of the successful toll-gatherers, but the practice is older than Caesar. King Minos, builder of the labyrinth in which the ravenous Minotaur lived, was such a baron. Corinth began as a site of pirates. Troy was a nest of robbers who dominated the Dardanelles and fed upon the commerce of Phoenicians with Black Sea regions, source of masts and tar for ships, as well as tunafish, grain and wax. The Greeks battled with the Trojans for valuable strategic positions.

To all these godlike heroes of Homeric song, the trader is the despicable stranger, the crafty Phoenician, their natural prey. The trader cheated them in horse-deals and stole their daughters to sell in slave-markets; they sought revenge upon him. They were *peiratai*, pirates, a term admirable in Greek, denoting adventurers. Pirate societies were recognized by Greek maritime law without opprobrium.

To the Homeric heroes it was insulting to suggest that they might in any way be contaminated with useful commerce. When Odysseus was saved by the fair Nausicaa and led to her kingly father, a nobleman in the court, Euryalus, mocked at him. Odysseus seemed so weak and pensive that he might be a merchant, insinuated Euryalus: "No, truly, stranger, I do not think thee at all like a skilled sportsman, but rather like a merchant . . . one with a memory for his freight, or that hath got the charge of a cargo homeward bound, and of greedily gotten gains."

To repudiate the allegation that he might be a tired business man, Odysseus "looked fiercely on him" and lifted up a monstrous stone, bigger than any man there could raise, and hurled it to a great distance. Since he proved himself so strong, Euryalus made a handsome apology, gave him a sword of bronze, and called him "father." Thereupon King Alcinous, recognizing the stranger as no merchant but the social equal of pirates, invited him to share the feast. He fed Odysseus with a piece of chine from a noble boar, "rich with fat" and fit for a hero's digestion. The people of that island were seamen and fighters, not careworn, calculating tradesmen: "Dear to us ever is the banquet, and the harp, and the dance, and changes of raiment, and the warm bath, and love and sleep."

Even in the Homeric world, therefore, the distinction was clearly drawn between the merry fighting men, with their naïve strength and conceit, who drank deep, slumbered well and lived gaily according to custom, and the cautious, anemic business man, who was worn down by the weighing of profit and loss and the care of cargoes. Already, according to the predominance of the one type or the other in societies, there developed trader-communities and warrior-communities. The hostility between the two was fiercely maintained; it was a fundamental fact of ancient history, although little understood by classic historians on the side of the warriors.

The struggle between the trader and warrior, beginning some time around the flooding of the market with iron swords, circa 1000 B.C., went on with undiminished ferocity, and was not decided until 146 B.C., when warrior-Rome leveled to earth the two great trading cities, Corinth and Carthage. A mighty and merciless duel continued over almost a millennium, between the period when the trader furnished swords to the barbarians, and the terrible hour when the trader succumbed to his armed customers.

In the Homeric Age of ceaseless combat, the trader had to move warily, hiring convoys for his vessels or caravans, ready for disasters that might await him at any turn. In a time of perpetual war, the trader might find his next port blockaded, or the city of his destination a smoking ruin. Having slight arrangements for news, he moved by guess. If he made his way safely to harbor, he might find himself in the midst of an unexpected civic convulsion, one of those periodic remissions of debts which threatened the propertied classes at all times; the tariff might be boosted 50 per cent without warning; very likely, the coinage would be changed. It was of course possible to realize handsome profits from calamity. Perhaps as he voyaged with sword and sample, the trader might make a scoop by smuggling armaments to a pirate-king or assisting some nomad rustler to get rid of his booty. He might arrive with a cargo of grain in the nick of time for a famine-stricken city, and receive, besides a high profit, a crown of leaves and a seat of honor at a play by Æschylus.

In this warring world, as in the late Dark Ages in Europe, there was a certain safety in the shadow of religious buildings. As the cathedral offered sanctuary to the mediaeval trader, who held market before it on festival days, so the Greek and Asian temples afforded some guarantee of law and order. In temples, gold might be deposited and treaties filed. Priests acted as caretakers and judges in disputes. The Babylonian Shamash was one of the market-gods; originally, too, Jehovah was market-god of the Tribe of Levi, at whose yearly festivals men of all tribes gathered to barter; Jehovah's priests were judges if altercation arose. The temple of Jerusalem was the center of a financial network in the Near East somewhat similar to that cast over Western Europe by the later Christian Church.

Such sacred marketplaces were numerous. In the very midst of the lawless Scythian shepherds, merchants assembled to trade at a spot so holy that no weapons of war were needed; fugitives might find asylum there and umpires adjusted quarrels. The temple of Apollo at Delphi was one of the gold-deposits of antique times and a credit-giving institute as well; the interests of this temple-bank were on the side of peace, and frequently the Pythia, the priestess of Apollo, sought to bring order among striving communities. If, as Goethe says, War, Trade and Piracy are triune and indivisible, it is also true that Religion, Law and Trade have been bound together from primordial times, and one evidence of this remains in the Corinthian pillars on bank buildings of Paris, New York, London and Yokohama.

Notwithstanding all difficulties, swarms of wandering traders came "like the birds" in summer, when the sea was navigable, as the ancient dramatist says. Steadily they forced their way into closed societies, tempting people with rarities, bringing the notion of metal as the measure of all goods, and with this money-madness much wisdom as well. According to a Greek philosopher, invisible cargoes of mental wares accompanied material goods: weights and measures, technical arts, sciences, the idea of Time, which came from the East to the happy children of Homeric Greece, who had had no notion of an hour, much less of a minute, or of money either, and hence no suspicion that time could be money.

TRADING TOWNS

Gradually, the trader mounted in wealth, skill and power. Great trading communities were formed. The richest bloom of the cities around the rim of the Mediterranean was in the period 800–450 B.C., when the trader had shaken off the domination of the Oriental despot and yet not fallen under the sway of the Roman landlords. In this golden age, he was his own master.

Not always, to be sure, is it possible to distinguish the warrior from the trader with respect to ethics or methods. The warrior might on occasion sell cargoes of wine and oil from his fields; the trader might engage in plundering forays, carrying off infants for the slave-trade or "hijacking" some fellow-merchant on the high seas. There was little to choose between them for cruelty and treachery. And we do not know in all cases which cities were commercial, or to how large an extent. The difference was one of emphasis: in some places, at Athens most of the time, in Sparta, and later in Rome, the predominant interest was agrarian, traders were excluded from the high councils of state and their occupation was stamped with the disapproval of the community. In other places, the trader rose to political power; he might have to share it with landlords and generals, or he might invest in agriculture and engage in many occupations, but at least he was not stigmatized but heard and heeded.

The Egyptians, the Athenian and Spartan Greeks, and the Romans were the agrarian peoples, among whom trade was associated with dishonor. The Egyptians successfully shut out a money economy longer and more stubbornly than did even Japan. The Spartans, pure warriors for long, resisted commercial contacts which might have brought enervating luxury to their midst. The Athenians, though they might supplement their incomes by shopkeeping or handwork or, if rich, by lending to sea-traders, remained agrarian in vision. Sea-trading was not carried on by Athenians but by foreigners who lived at the port of Piraeus and were kept in a subordinate status, as non-citizens, *metoike*, forbidden to marry a citizen's daughter, own land or conduct lawsuits in their own right. In Egypt and Athens, a mere trader could only break into political circles by owning land; in Egyptian Thebes, by abstaining from market transactions for ten years, he could become eligible for office; in Athens, occasionally, a period of elegant rustication would render respectable an ex-slave such as the banker Pasion. But prevailing prejudices were all against the trader. If he rose socially, it was by renouncing his ignominious occupation.

The Athenian agrarian view was summed up in the "Republic" of her great philosopher Plato. In the most perfect form of State, as conceived by Plato, the merchant would be yet more degraded in status than he was in actuality at Athens. He must live like cobblers and masons, apart from the aristocracy; he might have a bourgeois marriage and children in his humble hut; he was not to share in the pure, ideal life of the ruling class, who gave up family for self-cultivation. If this perfect State could not be attained, a second form was proposed by Plato, in which a citizen would be punished for carrying out a business deal or becoming an *emporus*, a traveling salesman. Property qualifications would be fixed for all time, so that business men might never rise in influence; bank-deposits, loans at interest and other disreputable practices would be discontinued together with that "despicable cattle-barter" which, throughout the ages, has appeared so incompatible with the pursuit of Pure Truth.

How far the social picture by Plato corresponded to reality is still a matter for argument. But some students like Hasebroek think it was not so very far from the fact—that Plato merely wished to wipe away the increasing commercial taint from the Athenians, but that the framework of his ideal was already in existence, and the separation of the trader from the citizen and his degradation were accepted conditions. Even if this is not the case, Plato shows that, at least in theory, such peoples continued to despise the trader.

How was the trader placed in the commercial communities? Here again, it is difficult to answer because such societies have largely been delivered to obloquy or oblivion. Most of their records have been blotted out completely. What has chiefly survived from the days of their glory has been the condemnation uttered by their victorious enemies. In the eyes of their foes, the trader-societies appeared lacking in spiritual grace, manliness and morals and were, in sum, unfit to command the world. We have little with which to dispute that verdict.

Of the trading cities of Asia Minor and the colonies which the Greeks established in southern Italy and Sicily, it is mostly report of their degeneracy which has survived. Thus the merchant-princes of Sybaris are remembered for their indulgence in good food (the world's first cookbook seems to have appeared there) and their utter laziness. The story was told, by the mocking Greek, Athenaeus, of a Sybarite who rashly went outside the town one day, saw a man actually working, plowing up a field, and, overcome with the shock of seeing such a sweaty creature, rushed to a doctor with his story. The doctor cried, "Just Gods! You saw a man working!" and swooned quite away.

In the mirror of antique writers, the Lydians also appear effete and ridiculous. They were not a Greek people, but Asian, whose chief city, Sardis, was built where a caravan route from inner Asia reached the Mediterranean, and near a river where gold had been panned ever since King Midas bathed in its water. Their King Croesus, the fabulously rich monarch (he was not so rich that he could avoid begging a loan from the banker Sadymatte, who refused his security) is thought to have invented coinage around 560 B.C.

The Ionian Greeks in Asia Minor learned much from the Lydians, and other Asians. They copied the soft Lydian music and as an irate writer about 560 declared, "They learned superfluous display from the Lydians. . . . There they walked in the marketplace with purple robes, pompously stalking about with beautifully dressed hair, reeking with ointments." An early Babbitt-baiter, Heraclitus, said they had grown too fat for sport, and deaf to the call of fame; "most of them lie about, full-fed, in animalic ease."

These Ionians, who traded, unlike the agrarian Athenians and Spartans, gathered the wisdom of the East, which came flowing along the caravan routes. They created a Greek culture from which Athens borrowed with little gratitude. The Ionians had democracy earlier than

other Greeks. They possessed a proverbial lightness and grace in manners and arts, of which the Ionic pillar is the surviving symbol. The
charm of their Aspasia survives in testimony. Perhaps they were the
founders of philosophy itself; the suggestion is offered that they, who
met so many religions in the course of their trading and began to compare them, originated the super-religious, philosophic attitude. Certainly they passed on a great collection of Eastern lore, weights and
measures, the calendar, the alphabet, geometry and astronomy, to other
Greeks who nevertheless despised them profoundly.

Miletus, the city from which Aspasia came to Athens, was a very ancient Ionian center, in which weaving and pottery and other arts had
long been practiced and trade was honorable. It must have been a place
of surpassing loveliness and was probably much more luxurious than
Athens ever became. The magnificent carvings of the marble gate
which stood at the entrance to her business district are preserved in the
Berlin Museum as a mere hint of Ionian splendor. Around the time of
King Croesus, Miletus was the nursery of science, as might have been
expected of a bourgeois town with a rationalistic outlook; its great
merchant, Thales, in his voyaging to Egypt and other shores, brought
back curious lore of navigation and mathematics. He was one of the
Seven Wise Men of antiquity, and, though a merchant, he seems to
have been a statesman, accepted in the ruling group of Miletus.

In this great commercial city, with its traveled merchants, there developed the first great "bourgeois" culture in the sixth century B.C. It
emphasized the cult of the individual, as business men, whether in
Renaissance Florence or the nineteenth century, have ever tended to
do. Thales, the merchant, believed that "Know thyself" was the beginning of wisdom; another Ionian, Heraclitus of Ephesus, proclaimed:
"I have sought myself." These were the antique rugged individualists.
It was, however, through excessive individualism, which prevented
them from forming a cooperative defense system, that the Ionians perished.

The scientific interests of this commercial city may be viewed as a
prelude to later bourgeois-rationalism. Anaximander of Miletus wrote
one of the world's first philosophic books, "Nature," containing in
germ the idea of evolution, and, as time was undoubtedly of monetary
value in this city, he invented the sun-clock. Another Ionian, Anaxag-
oras, taught a primitive version of the atomic theory and urged people
to look on sun-eclipses and the fall of meteors without superstition. He
visited Athens but was banned from that agrarian-mystic center.

Even "Main Street" came from Miletus to the West. The great city-
planner of that city, Hippodamus, visiting the Babylonian towns which
had regular rectangular city blocks and long straight streets intersect-

ing at right angles, transformed Miletus on this scheme as a hygienic measure. He was then invited to carry the system to the great trading city of Rhodes; another trading people, the Etruscans, borrowed it; later, Alexandria was built that way, and had an immense Main Street, or *Mesion Pedion*. So did the caravan cities, such as Ephesus and Palmyra; in the latter, the main street was a kilometer long and lined with 375 pillars on each side, each 17 yards high. This rationalism in city planning, going along with the arts, the medicine, philosophy, science and individualism, was characteristic of the great trading centers. It was a sharp contrast to the crazy-quilt medley of Athens. The trader, whether ancient Miletan or modern American, wants system.

The traders of Rhodes were renowned, like those of Miletus, for love of bombastic oratory, perhaps borrowed from auctions or market chaffering. Cicero studied eloquence there. In keeping with this love for inflated verbiage was the Rhodian thirst for the sensational, the colossal. The vast statue set up at the entrance to the harbor was one of the world wonders and so huge that its fragments, when it was carted away in mediaeval times, loaded seven hundred camels. The wealth to erect such marvels came from slave-dealing largely; Rhodes was one of the chief markets of antiquity until Rome moved that business to Delos. Her merchants developed a maritime law which formed the basis for our own today. And out of her art school, extremely realistic in accordance with bourgeois taste, came the Laocoon statue-group which the rising bourgeoisie in modern times, taught by Lessing, hailed with such delight.

Corinth likewise had its day of glory as a trading center, its magnificence symbolized in the luxuriantly foliated columns known as "Corinthian" and still beloved by the commercial class. Herodotus comments that, in Corinth, of all Greek cities, handiwork was the least despised. Oriental art found a good market there and pottery was manufactured. In the excavated city today the clubs of the old trading corporations stand revealed after the burial of centuries. One such building, presumably belonging to a banking and shipping association, is distinguished for its handsome mosaic floors representing maritime interests. The splendor of Corinth was associated with high prices, so that the ancients remarked: "A trip to Corinth is not for everyone."

There the goddess of love, Aphrodite, was adored; Corinth was the chief seat of that deity in Greece. The trader, whether Phoenician, Babylonian, Corinthian or Etruscan, worshiped the goddess of luck and fecundity in some shape, as Ishtar, Isis, Aphrodite or Fortuna. Nor did his association with such frivolous divinities at all improve his relations with stern agrarians, devoted to grim Jupiter, Mars, Ceres and the grave-browed Minerva.

LADY LUCK

In origin, the trader's goddess was Eastern; Aphrodite was imported to Corinth with other Oriental wares. And it was an Eastern people, the Etruscans, invaders of Italy, who introduced to the West the idea of Chance, supreme ruler of the business man, incorporated in the wilful feminine shape of Fortuna, with her mocking smile and her Wheel, emblem of the business cycle and the Rotarians.

As the leading traffickers of old Italy, the Etruscans were profoundly interested in luck. They had brought dice with them from Lydia and gambled incessantly; they created a pseudo-science of omens, read in lightning and the flight of birds, or in entrails, which they passed on to the Romans, together with the idea of Fortuna as the true director of men's destinies. True, Fortuna was never admitted to Olympus and old-fashioned critics condemned her, but as the Romans turned to trade themselves, they too brought incense to Luck. From Rome her cult spread over the world; she was given other symbols, a spreading sail in her hands and a ball, which became the earth-ball, under her feet. And since then the notion that life is at least partly pure Chance has continued to grow in business societies.

Rome indeed, becoming Christianized, strove to bring the world under her immutable order, her planned divine scheme, and did her best to stamp out the cult of Fortuna. She denounced Luck as well as the profit-seeker who worshiped it, for both endangered her idea of a stable Christendom. But Fortuna came back when trade revived, at the close of the Dark Ages, and, curiously, in Florence, a city where Etruscan blood persisted.

Many things attest a survival of Etruscan skill in business in such sites as Bologna, Milan and Florence, which ever remained different from Rome, a political but never manufacturing city. It is likely that Etruscan blood also lived on, and possibly the Etruscan taste for realism in art; the resemblance between Florentine Renaissance portraits and ancient Etruscan sculptures is too close to seem accidental. One might well think that the enigmatic smile of Fortuna still curved the lips of the Florentine Mona Lisa. At any rate, it was the eminent Florentine, Machiavelli, who insisted that Fortuna had a place in human affairs; and from Florence, home of Fortuna and business individualism, the idea of Luck spread again over the world; soon in German Augsburg, stories were written about Fortunatus, the good-luck youth, and Dutch and German ships were named Fortuna. The Wheel also was retained, for it had been used as a gambling game in the Middle Ages, and, in modern times, was turned into the roulette wheel; thus, at Monte Carlo, where business individualists of the nineteenth century

flung away fortunes, the casinos were really shrines of Etruscan Luck.

From the Etruscans, other elements of the modern heritage are derived. It was they who gave the Romans the block system of city-planning, paved streets, and sewers and aqueducts as well, for plumbing is a characteristic business man's hobby. Other Etruscan contributions were circuses, the purple border on the toga, and the idea of celebrating conquest by a "triumph." Their legal system, the *disciplina etrusca*, formed the basis of Roman law, as their military organization was a model for the Roman. Etruscan cities were governed by clans of merchant-pirates, who were at the same time great landlords, and, like the Carthaginians, worked their estates by gangs of slaves on large-scale business principles; from these oligarchies came the Fasces, the axe-and-bundle symbol, originally Asian, which was adopted by old Rome, and by the modern Mussolini, who, acknowledging his indebtedness, has fostered Etruscology.

These ancient admirers of the Fasces were in the beginning dreaded seafarers, coming probably from the Lydian region, who settled in Italy as conquerors, enslaving the natives and using them in mines and plantations; their cities became centers of pottery-making and metal industry, trading with Carthaginians and Greeks and with Northern barbarians as well. The foremost Twelve Cities were bound together loosely into a Confederacy, somewhat like the later German Hanseatic League of towns; for a time they held most of northern Italy including Rome, and lands over the Alps also. These cities remained independent, however, refusing to centralize powers; so individualistic that they would not even come to one another's assistance when attacked, their lack of unity proved their undoing, and, enormously rich as they were, judging by their tombs, they fell, one by one, before the determined might of the single city, Rome.

Even though crushed by the Romans at last, Etruscan business men tutored their conquerors in business methods. One of the chief army-purveyors, furnishing transport for troops of Julius Caesar, and operator of a wagon system for civilians as well, Ventidius Bassus, was born in an Etruscan region. When he was made consul for his army services, Roman society was horrified by the rise of the vulgar Bassus; but soon a greater man of Etruscan descent, Maecenas, attained far more power. This financier, Maecenas, whose wealth assisted Octavian to become Caesar Augustus, was rewarded by an appointment as governor of all Italy. It was a poetic revenge, for, as once the Etruscan kings of Rome were driven out when the Republic was founded, so at length an Etruscan, who, Horace relates, boasted lineage reaching back to those kings, brought back an emperor to Italy. Maecenas gathered around him poets like Horace who glorified the new régime; possibly, the Etruscans furnished the two supreme examples of very rich men who fostered art with sympathy as well as money, and yet used it for political ends— Maecenas and Lorenzo de' Medici.

At the hands of orthodox historians, the Etruscans have fared ill until very recently. As the culture of the Asian Greeks was minimized in favor of the Athenians, so the contributions of the Etruscans were ignored to enhance Roman pride. Moreover, the Etruscans, like the other trader-peoples, were reputed to be disgracefully gay, wont to go about at night garlanded and reeling with tipsy mirth. They were also bloodthirsty, given to gladiatorial games to which they introduced the simple Romans, who had had no such pleasures for the mob before; and some of their gods were terrifying, like the Carthaginian Moloch; the Etruscan hell reminds one of the gloom of the Calvinist's hell, "paved with the bones of little children." But in evaluating Etruscan as well as other trader-societies, we face the same problem: were they degenerate or were the others raw?

Certainly, to their bucolic neighbors, the trader-societies seemed effete. Prosperous citizens were carried downtown to the office in litters, like Oriental despots, instead of walking briskly as befitted manly members of rural communities. They indulged in rich feeding and then built swimming-pools of marble and gymnasia in which they tried to keep their figures down by exercises instead of martial practice; that they were not always successful, we see from the statue of that plump, jolly Etruscan known to scholars as *obesus etruscus*. Besides, the trader-societies were fond of questionable anecdotes, collected in sales-trips, like the Miletan tales, the first novels; and their pleasure resorts, often in temple groves, were notorious. But, granted all this, were they decadent, that is, from a modern point of view?

The people who scorned them were hardy rustics. The Romans of the early Republic, whose sumptuary laws forbade any silverware on the table save a saltcellar, were disgusted with the Etruscans, whose boards groaned under plate, and with the even more lavish Carthaginians. But that does not prove anything. Nor does the Roman mockery of the Sybarites indicate much, for the Romans had not advanced even to baking bread—they were still living on watery porridge when they sneered at the good cooks of Sybaris. And if the Lydians and Ionians likewise seemed weak to the robust Spartans, they might not to us, for, in our time, any bank clerk may lead a softer life than that of a patrician of old Miletus. The face of the Etruscan *obesus* looks far from feeble. Further, it has been suggested that the remarkable freedom of women in Etruscan towns, as in Miletus and trader-societies generally, led to misinterpretation of their morality on the part of Greek observers. Nowadays, when it is the fashion to offer apology for Imperial

Rome, which, we are told, was not really so vicious after all, it might be possible to make a brief for the comfort-loving bourgeois of the rich cities, who were indeed too fat to fight, but may not have been altogether depraved.

CARTHAGE

More than other commercial cities, Carthage in Africa needs such a defense, for none has been more abused. In this, the chief offshoot of the old Phoenician cities Tyre and Sidon, planted by the Gulf of Tunis, lived merchants who traded from Cornwall to Malabar in pearls, purple dye, ivory, incense, linen, wines and metals. Their powerful fleet swept the Mediterranean and was often allied with that of the sea-roving Etruscans.

Carthage was one of the largest cities of the classic world, with more than 700,000 population. She was also called the richest and had certainly more wealth than Athens in the full height of the Periclean Age. So affluent was she that, despite the cost of campaigns against Rome and the corruption of her government, there was no need to levy taxation directly; even after the smashing defeat of the Second Punic War, she could pay 340,000 thaler indemnity to Rome every year, raising these reparations in the form of a state loan. Tariffs and tolls furnished the municipal revenue.

The business administration of Carthage is her most interesting aspect for, whereas one can only guess at the forms by which traders controlled other societies, the Punic régime was described by Aristotle. The admirable and curious thing which struck him, as a Greek, was the stability of this government; there was neither revolution by the mob nor violence from tyranny. He thought that what kept the people so content was the comfort and well-being provided by a rich commerce and an empire; when times were hard, surplus folk could be sent to the colonies.

Carthage was not precisely an oligarchy, for freemen were able to vote on certain issues. But rich men monopolized the governing jobs and, said Aristotle, were permitted to continue in gainful occupations which Roman senators were supposed to avoid. The bureaucracy was thus dominated by a few chief families—possibly these numbered three hundred. That would seem plausible since, at the height of Rome's wealth, a mere handful of men, two thousand plutocrats, so a Roman declared, were masters of the Empire. At all times, mediaeval or modern as well as classic, a very slight percentage of plutocrats, wavering between 2 and 5 per cent of the population, have stood at the apex of society.

The Carthaginians thought that "officials should be elected with consideration to their wealth, for the poor man could not possibly have leisure to administer an office properly." Officials were not paid, though, believed Aristotle, it would have been more nearly ideal if able men had been given leisure by payment. The Greek student keenly remarked that there were some dangerous drawbacks to this government by the wealthy, which entailed open purchase of office. It was menacing when incapable buyers took military posts. Moreover, "this plan brings riches in higher esteem than ability, and so makes the whole citizenry money-hungry. For whatever the ruling class considers honorable, the majority of the citizens naturally agree to. It is obvious that the buyers of office accustom themselves to making profits in office, since they have had expenses in attaining it."

Carthage was the greatest of the societies ruled over by the antique trader, the richest in money and lands and most advanced in technique. It is undecided whether she had really gone beyond the use of metal bars and coins to token money, using leather, but in any case, by 450 B.C., Carthage possessed a highly perfected financial mechanism while peasant Rome was still in the barter stage, having just introduced a few coins into her rural economy. After Carthage fell in 146 B.C., there was nothing to approach her until the seventeenth century of the Christian Era, when the Dutch sea-cities rose and leagued together. Only Holland could be compared to Carthage as a business man's empire, owning no allegiance, spiritual or temporal, to king or pope.

Naturally, one is curious to know how well these Punic business men ruled, but again, as in the case of the Miletans and Etruscans, it is their evil side which has been preserved for posterity by moralists of the conquering race, who confined their observations to the corruption and sordidness, the proverbial cruelty and treachery of the Punic people. Again, there is no adequate answer to the charges, for almost all that was left of this mightiest city of antiquity, after the Roman conquest, were a few inscriptions and some mournful, weather-beaten stone faces. Carthaginian culture was blotted from view.

Were the Punic people more treacherous than others? Modern historians, and naturally the Germans, sensitive to the war-guilt question, have shown that Rome was more to blame for breach of faith in starting Punic warfare, but afterward laid it unfairly on Carthage. Were the Punic people more cruel than the Romans? They seem indeed to have worshiped hideous and bloody images, and to have flung their first-born infants in the flames of Moloch. Jars containing infants' bones have been found in the foundations of Carthaginian buildings. But it must be remembered that, a generation after Carthage was destroyed, the Romans were still immolating victims by way of state sacrifice; they buried alive two pairs, man and wife, a Gallic and a Greek, as late as 114 B.C.

Were the Carthaginian business men less fit to govern the world than the Romans with whom they fought for sovereignty over the Mediterranean? Were they wrapped in sordid scheming? Their libraries were burned; the verses of their once-famous poets are lost; their science and art are obliterated. We only know that the Greeks seem to have accepted them as apt pupils, if not as peers, and that they intermarried freely with Greek families in Sicily; the bellicose Hannibal had Greek blood. For purer Punic citizens, the charge of unwarlike softness seems undeniable. Even if they could have governed as well as Romans, they could not conquer. They had splendid technical equipment: herds of elephants for army transport, immense walls and forts, marvelous five-decked ships and enormous resources. But they did not like to fight. Out of a swarming population, they could not raise anything resembling the fighting-force that little Rome could assemble. They had no warrior-caste able and large enough to manage campaigns for them, and so had to hire vast numbers of mercenaries, with resultant inefficiency and corruption.

Phoenicians, as a rule, did not fight unless they had to. In Tyre and Sidon, they paid tribute to Oriental monarchs instead of striking for independence. The rich merchants of Carthage did not even wish to attack Rome; they were forced into the clash by the ambitions of the generals Hannibal and Hamilcar, who drew upon the emotions of the plebs to counteract the caution of the rich burghers. Hannibal finally had to make a small revolution to bring to power the people who liked war. The Carthaginian merchant-aristocracy was constantly trying to hold back its military men; it even selected a hundred judges who were supposed to examine the returning generals and establish civilian influence over them. They hanged one military leader for a revolutionary attempt. But in the end, like so many trader-cities in Renaissance Italy, Carthage was at the mercy of condottieri.

THE FALL OF THE ANCIENT TRADER

Carthage and her sister cities, engaged in commerce, were to learn that gold is not a substitute for iron and that wealth cannot always purchase power. These wonderful cities, after developing for many generations, appeared for a time to possess the world. They built mighty navies, filled their treasuries with metal, surrounded themselves with fortifications upon which remarkable military machines were mounted, and hired troops of many nations to man them. They thought their walls impregnable.

Around the sixth century B.C., this trader-might reached a zenith.

Carthage and the Etruscan cities were flourishing, the Lydians were prosperous. About 594 B.C., moreover, even Athens and Rome seemed to offer no threat to commerce. At Athens a merchant, Solon, who had traveled far in pursuit of gain and wisdom, gave the city a timocracy, a government of the richest. This early business man who, with Thales of Miletus, was included among the famous Seven Wise Men, boldly brushed aside barriers of birth and set wealth above aristocracy. He wrote verse to defend his state-planning system. Nevertheless, he was himself brought low and his timocracy overthrown.

The agrarian aristocracy at Rome was similarly broken for a time by the Etruscan King, Tarquin the Proud, who appears to have established a timocracy there too. By his commands, the rich, even if plebeians, were admitted to the highest ruling order and even to army rank. However, proud Tarquin was driven out and men of birth displaced men of money again at Rome. Both Athens and Rome reverted to agrarian-aristocratic ideals.

Two mighty duels at arms decided the fates of the trading versus the agrarian societies. In both passages at arms, the rich commercial cities were decisively defeated by poor peasant societies. The first of these campaigns was against Greece. The Phoenician trader-cities, Tyre and Sidon and Carthage, made the great mistake of siding with the Oriental despots of Persia against little Greece. They agreed to outfit the army and navy of Darius and sent mercenaries to fight along with the Persian hordes. They appear to have followed the invaders as purveyors as well. The Ionian Greeks fell an easy prey to the Persians. Then the concerted attack upon the mainland of Greece and the colonial region of Sicily was made. Together the great fleets of the Carthaginians and Etruscans, allied against the Sicilian Greeks, attacked and were disastrously beaten in the sea fight of Himera. Almost at the same time, the ships of the Persians which the Phoenicians had outfitted were being sunk at Salamis. Thus, in two sea battles in the Mediterranean, almost simultaneously, the mightiest and richest powers went down to humiliation; while Athens and Sparta, the contemners of trade, survived the threat of Eastern autocracy and emerged victorious.

The sea battle of Himera was a decisive one in the history of the ancient business man, for it marked the turning-point of Etruscan power. Thereafter the Roman rustics took advantage of their weakness to wipe out many of their cities and plant soldier-colonies upon the ruins. Then, having disposed of these allies of Carthage, the Romans turned to face that mightiest of trading-cities herself.

In the same year, 146 B.C., the Romans took the two chief merchant-towns of the east and west Mediterranean, Corinth and Carthage, and reduced them both pitilessly to ashes. The Grecian port was burned to the earth. The people of the Punic city were given over to slave-dealers or immolated in flaming temples, while the tall towers, the homes, the public edifices, were destroyed. For seventeen days the ruins smoked, and then, when flames and the axe could do no more, a part of the city was plowed under and salt strewn in the furrows as a sign of condemnation to eternal sterility.

Other remaining cities fell, one by one, before the conquering warrior-landlords of Rome. Alexandria in Egypt was taken; Rhodes was ruined; very much later, the last proud independent survivor, the great caravan-city in the desert, Palmyra, was blasted. Thus the strongholds where the trader had either ruled or risen to great esteem and riches were enchained or ruined. Impoverishment grew in many of these captured centers; there was a great shrinkage of wealth over large areas. Patrician merchants were enslaved, or reduced to bitter struggles for existence. Grass grew in many a marketplace and sheep grazed among the fallen columns of bazaars.

With his wealth, the trader lost prestige. The very memory of his former power was taken from him. History vilified the trader-rulers and exalted Cincinnatus and Cato, the grim tillers and warriors. The trader was not suffered to rise again to political supremacy as long as Rome stood. He was kept subordinated, in a lower status in society, comfortable enough but inglorious. He was absorbed in a tremendous world-embracing social structure, erected and controlled by men of the soil and sword.

In a sense, therefore, the business man has never recovered from the seal of inferiority which was stamped upon him during the Roman conquests. The memorable fights, Himera and Zama, before the destruction of Carthage, were his Waterloos. When the Punic city fell, his pride was lost with it. The plowshare which ripped gashes across the sites of his marketplace and council hall was the symbol of triumphant agrarianism. It is entirely within bounds of possibility that the Battle of Zama ended for all time his chance to rule the earth.

II

ROME AND THE RISE OF FINANCE-CAPITALISM

ROME HAS BEEN conspicuously lacking among Italian cities in business enterprise. She never became a great manufacturing center. Instead, her genius appeared in social and political organization. For two thousand years, she headed mighty supranational structures, first as the pagan capital of a vast empire stretching from Britain to the Black Sea, and then as the heart of Catholic Christendom.

Through twenty centuries, funds poured in upon her, as tribute from the conquered or offerings from the converted. Under the necessity of transmitting such sums across great distances, she resorted to the skill of the money-lender, and enmeshed Europe in a financial, as well as political or spiritual network. Thus, in the course of her conquests over matter and mind, she laid the basis for international finance-capitalism. Without Rome, therefore, commerce might not have taken its present form.

But though Rome has been mother to the modern capitalist, she has been a singularly severe stepmother as well. For, more than any other city, she has scorned trade and sought to bar the trader from advancement to power and salvation. Her warrior-landlords in classic times destroyed the independence of the various trading communities around the Mediterranean. Later on, in the last stages of the Empire, her unruly soldiers carried havoc among the cities, ruining and stripping them so thoroughly that the barbarians, when at last they came down out of the North, found comparatively little left to do.

After the Empire collapsed, the Roman Church took up the task of subduing the profit-maker. She was determined to prevent him from breaking through the ordered system of mediaeval society, by his boundless "avaritia." She maintained a stern disapproval of taking interest on capital, making "money breed money," until the nineteenth century, when Pope Pius VIII, in 1830, at last admitted that money-breeding might be condoned under certain circumstances, and ordered father confessors not to disquiet the interest takers unduly.

From the days of that caustic ancient, Cato the Elder, down past St. Augustine to Pope Pius VIII, therefore, Rome has viewed the ambitions of the business man with a censorious eye. She has been uneasy over the gigantic forces she herself liberated. And indeed it was a strange perversity of fate which compelled that city to foster the finance she condemned, to despise business and yet assist it to transcend local limitations.

In part, the anomalous situation in which the modern business man finds himself today is due to the fact that the early molding of capitalism was performed in the service of Rome. Rome made the capitalist successful and yet, vehemently opposed to the capitalist spirit, thwarted his desire to dominate society. To that "Eternal" City he owes at once his transcendent economic power and his social ignominy and spiritual conflict.

ARISTOCRATS VERSUS PARVENUS

At the outset of her imperial career, when she measured her strength with that of Carthage, Rome was backward in commerce and culture. She had remained, as Britain also did for long, sunk in bucolic simplicity while others shot ahead in wealth and sophistication. Rome's sea-borne commerce was left in the hands of Etruscans, as that of Britain was for many generations monopolized by Hanseatics. Early Rome was as crude in comparison with trading Corinth as Elizabeth's London was in contrast to manufacturing Florence.

Over Rome ruled a caste of warrior-landlords who theoretically were above trade. Practically, they might stoop to anything, but usually it was through the medium of slaves. They kept up the fiction at least of being leisured county gentlemen, engaged only in war and politics. Marketing the yield of their estates was permitted to them, but the only business enterprise deemed respectable was brick-making; in this they were like the Prussian Junkers of a later age, who also condescended to brick-making, a soil-product, as well as to growing sugar-beets and distilling alcohol from potatoes. So, too, the French noblesse made glass.

From this rustic obscurity, Rome, like Britain later, emerged with more martial vigor than the trader-peoples around her in whom commerce had destroyed the taste for camps. Rome and Britain, as rural-aristocratic peoples, beat down the two greatest trader-oligarchies the world has known—Carthage and Holland—and robbed them of sea-dominion.

But the Roman warrior-landlords discovered that empire must be bound together by an economic nexus, and that war is itself the supreme business. To make war the Roman State had to borrow funds from men of capital, trusting to repay them from the booty. Thus, while noble gentlemen conducted campaigns, the usurers in their absence obtained a lien on the Capitol. How insolent these became is shown by Livy. In the Second Punic War, a capitalist consortium advanced ships and cargoes to the State on credit, provided that these goods were insured against risks. They delivered rotten vessels with worthless contents, scuttled them and claimed damages. The Senate held an investigation—in the classic manner—and there was much outcry against corruption, but it all came to nothing. Under the pressure of war, it was necessary to compound with the malefactors.

For all the arms and supplies and even the transport of legions during generations of constant warfare, the Roman State depended largely upon private industry. Only at a late date, in the time of Diocletian, as the Empire was growing old and money economy was tottering, so that cash was becoming scarcer and taxes had to be raised in kind, did the State decide to take over arms manufacture itself and erect state-operated factories for weapons.

Among the names of these munitioneers is that of Piso who, with his father, was engaged in manufacture of arms. Against him Cicero inveighed: "In the Italic War you saw your houses filled with profit when your father had charge of the factories for making arms." Cicero denounced him for making money out of the fraternal strife of the Civil War. But Cicero defended another war-profiteer, Rabirius Posthumus, from the charge of extortion.

But the dependence of the Roman State upon money-lenders and manufacturers was not its only weakness. The disposal of the plunder was left to merchants who followed the armies to buy up the loot of homes and shrines, and the captives. They provided ships to carry it all away and developed an auctioneering system to get rid of valuables, human and material, in wholesale lots. These auctioneers became rich and influential, as indeed they were before the 1840's in the United States until they yielded place before a modern system of agents and jobbers. The father of the poet Horace was one of the ancient auctioneers, an ex-slave who became wealthy enough to educate his son at the best schools in Rome and Athens.

Often enough the traders pushed ahead of the eagles. In Gaul, the traders were in fact so active that it was said no penny could circulate without finding its way into some Roman business man's purse. The wiser of the savage tribes resisted this economic penetration which was the preliminary to conquest. The famous uprising of the Gauls under Vercingetorix was caused by exactions of merchants; when the incensed tribesmen murdered a few traders, Caesar took the pretext for war.

When a war was over, the Roman State was still as much in need of the business man as ever. The collection of reparations could only be managed by financiers; in many cases, the Roman money-lender had to furnish huge sums to the vanquished communities at exorbitant rates, much as the Allies and associates had to lend money to the Germans while they were paying reparations. The moral-philosopher, Seneca, was such a man; he lent the British provincials some 40 million sesterces at so high a rate and pressed his claims so hard, as to be responsible for an uprising of natives on that distant isle in A.D. 60. The elegant friend of Cicero, Atticus, who was content with a mere 48 per cent from distressed municipalities, where he might have exacted 73, was honored with a statue from grateful debtors.

In its works of peace as well as in war, the State required the capitalist. The Roman State was the greatest contract-giver that the antique world produced: it let out contracts for mining and coinage, building roads and aqueducts, and gave these contracts to men of means who owned gangs of slaves. The *societas publicanorum*, the association of publicans, was the antique form of bankers' consortium, which carried out the decrees of the Senate with profit. Shares in these societies were held all over the Empire, and there was a brisk dealing in them at the Forum. Polybius says that there was hardly a rich man in Rome who was not interested in State contracts, and the shares may have been widely distributed in the provinces.

Most coveted of the contracts let out by the State under the Republic was that for collecting taxes. The tax-farmers, "publicans," were permitted to buy the tax-gathering privileges for whole provinces with 10 per cent allowed for costs and profit. They sublet these contracts, until eventually the richest individual in each locality, usually some merchant or landlord, would be compelled to "volunteer" to buy the privilege at a high figure. He had to recoup himself as best he might on his unfortunate fellow-citizens. It was thus a pure "business administration" that enveloped the world, and the natural result was that provinces were so rapidly denuded that aristocratic officials complained there were not enough pickings for them.

One example of such activities was the raising of the indemnity in Asia which the dictator Sulla demanded. He let the contract for $20,000,000 (modern money) to a Roman corporation which collected the sum six times over for itself and was about to repeat the operation when Sulla called a halt. He feared there would be nothing left over for the State another time.

The system of collecting taxes was a constant source of friction between plebeian business men and aristocrats. The latter wanted to supplant it by a bureaucratic administration which they could control and turn to their advantage. The former fiercely defended their precious rights. At last, in the Empire, the bureaucrats won out; but by that time plebeian manipulators had crept into the bureaucracy, especially into the financial department; and besides, the richest harvests had been gleaned.

Obviously, on this and other points, the warrior-landlord and the moneyed plebeian were bound to clash over the spoils of conquest. Each side sought to court the favor of the poor voters by promises. Of course, a line cannot be drawn clearly between the two groups. The noblemen engaged in contracting and munitioneering—a large number must have worked with the publicans. But there remained a cleavage. Noblemen who spent their lives in campaigning and administration were enraged to find that base-born money-lenders engulfed the lion's share of the booty in vanquished lands. The plebeians were equally furious to see that, no matter how rich they became, they were not treated as social equals by men of senatorial rank.

Thus a mighty tussle over war-profits was unavoidable. Wealth and gentility were arrayed against each other for over a century of insurrection and terrorism, after the overthrow of Carthage. With varying turns of fortune, each side enjoyed hours of triumph, but neither could win a definite victory.

CRASSUS, THE BANKER WHO WOULD BE KING

Roman aristocrats, seeing themselves endangered by parvenu munitioneers even before the end of the last Punic War, passed a law barring from high office the *novi homines*, the new men. The moneyed men, excluded from the patriciate, supported the revolutionary movement of the Gracchi. Gaius Gracchus gave them a free hand in tax-gathering among subject peoples and allowed them many coveted social honors.

Around the time of the Gracchi, moneyed men began to consolidate themselves into an order just below the old nobility. They achieved the title of knights, *equites*, with the right to wear golden rings and sit in special circus seats. This knighthood was the most purely commercial on record. Gentle birth was not required of its possessor but a fortune of 400,000 sesterces was indispensable. A knight held his title only for life and lost it even before his death if he failed in business. Whoever went bankrupt had immediately to lay aside his golden ring and the right to be called *clarissimus vir*.

The senatorial order, jealous of the rising knighthood, murdered the last of the Gracchi. The moneyed men transferred their allegiance to the peasant-soldier, Marius, who recompensed them by a blood-bath, a Reign of Terror at Rome. Aristocrats were driven to their death in droves and their estates put up at auction. Business men bought up their effects, a situation duplicated in the French Revolution. The Roman profiteer received from the public a jocose name meaning "he who cashes in."

Remnants of the aristocracy gathered behind the military genius of Sulla, who was able for a time to reestablish the might of the blue-bloods at Rome. He wrought retribution upon the plebeians; sixteen hundred knights who had "cashed in" were wiped out by the sword.

The most ruthless of the revolutionary profiteers was, however, too rich to be touched even by Sulla. Marcus Licinius Crassus, of noble lineage himself, retained the fortune he made by buying up executed noblemen's estates and used it to branch out in business. He speculated in real estate and banking. He bought slaves cheaply, trained them in engineering and resold them at the high prices which good technologists, sound in wind and limb, always fetched in the Roman markets. He started a fire company and sent his chiefs to bargain with persons in distress for the highest possible sums before fire-fighting operations began. It was thus said of Crassus that his money came "from the worst misfortunes of Rome—revolution and fire."

Crassus became the richest man in the Republic, with a fortune approaching $13,000,000 in modern currency (more, in devaluated dollars). The supremely interesting business figure of old Rome, he in many ways suggested other giants of later times, the Fuggers and Rothschilds for instance. Like them, he was proud of remaining simple, even austere, in personal habits. Like them, he manipulated kings with super-royal power. Unique, however, was his aspiration to become king himself. As a Roman, he thirsted for the open emblems of ultimate power.

A taciturn man in the manner of business leaders of all ages, Crassus could not make the eloquent speeches expected of statesmen in Rome. But he found he could win cases in court easily, because the judges were in debt to him. Likewise, though his was not a military mind, he was able to put himself at the head of an army by raising one of his own. As he said, a little pompously, no man ought to call himself rich who cannot feed an army. He even won a victory in the field—against revolting slaves.

Crassus became the co-ruler of Rome with the more soldierly Pompey. He hastened to pull down the aristocratic régime again, and to extend the notorious tax-gathering system, which Sulla had desired to cut down. The publicans, thanks to Crassus, were allowed to fall upon the treasure of the Asians, and before long a newly enriched swarm of plebeian knights replaced those whom Sulla had decapitated.

But Crassus was jealous of Pompey and wished to rule Rome alone. It was not possible for him to win over the affections of the mob, even by his marvelous gifts; the fickle folk would not be bribed. And so the richest man of Rome, unable to buy popularity, stooped to darker methods and began to finance Caesarism—a kind of Fascist revolt—using other persons as decoys.

In the attempts which Crassus made to overthrow the Republic in Rome, one may read a parallel with modern times. It was the wealth of this great speculator and contractor which undermined the popular régime. As Hitler in modern Germany promised to "break interest-slavery" and repress the moneyed men, even while he was accepting funds from the steel-magnate Thyssen, so Catilina (an Etruscan) proceeded, with the secret backing of the banker Crassus; he proposed to annul debts and so rallied around him the idle youth, whose number was swollen by an economic crisis. But Cicero exposed Catilina and he was defeated. (The German Ciceros were asleep.)

Casting about for a better "strong man," Crassus found Julius Caesar, a young politician chiefly remarkable for his ability to incur debts. By bestowing upon this protégé vast sums, to purchase the favor of the masses, a monstrous propaganda activity was launched. Circuses, more splendid than anything ever seen in Rome, with even the cages of the tigers adorned with silver, were offered to the mob. Thus capitalism, personified in Crassus, poured out millions in advertising to make Caesarism palatable.

But the aristocrats were not ready to be crushed without murmur. A wordy quarrel began, each side hurling accusations of corruption and proving its case to the hilt, while the masses listened with delight. Caesar and Cicero, who came over to his side, started to prosecute some of the richest aristocratic officials, such as Verres who plundered Sicily, in order to show up their unfitness to govern. But the Roman Junkers found their staunch defender in Cato the Younger, an agrarian puritan like his grandfather, who denounced the tax-gathering interests in round terms. Cato countered the lavish propaganda of Crassus and Caesar by inveighing against plebeian wealth and luxury, and reverted to the rural simplicity exemplified by his own ancestor, the Censor. He praised the Spartan virtues of the old country gentlemen who had thought the term "a good farmer" the highest praise, and regarded all money-lenders with natural bucolic suspicion, as simple thieves.

Despite the parade of virtues, however, it was the impressive money which won. Crassus and Caesar became co-rulers of Rome. But again there was the difficulty of power shared between two ambitious men. It became clear that only military strength could decide the issue, and each determined to gather it about him. Caesar took his legions to Gaul and led them to plunder among the rich commercial cities, gathering fame and millions. Crassus went to Asia, where even richer spoils awaited the conqueror. The trouble was that Crassus could feed, but could not lead an army. He did not fare so well as Caesar.

In ignominy, Crassus went down. He lost the sacred eagles. Not the fourth man of his legions crawled back to Rome. Old and gray, Crassus committed suicide amid overwhelming disaster. The rejoicing Parthian enemy took his corpse. The bloody head of the overambitious banker, stuck upon a pole, was exhibited in a theater by dancing bacchantes.

AUGUSTAN COMPROMISE

The issue between wealth and feudalism was settled at length by a compromise. Neither blood nor cash won a clear victory, but each shared the power with the other; and both yielded a large sphere to a third force, the power of the sword, which loomed up between them. More and more, the military element became the main prop of the monarchy that took the place of the fallen Republic, and usurped the privileges of civilians.

Theoretically, aristocrats retained control of the Imperial Government, through the Senate. Senators alone might hold high commanding positions in the army and become provincial governors; the Senate ostensibly elected the Emperors. A senator, however, must be a landed gentleman; a moneyed man who broke into their circle must retire from active trading and place a major portion of his means in real estate, a law which boomed Italian land values.

Advancement, to be sure, was made easier for the moneyed men. The numbers of knights was multiplied, taking in provincials. These knights forced their way into the lower bureaucracy and won the lucrative, if less glorious, posts; they supervised the delivery of grain to Rome, naval supplies, the postal service and the financial administration. Their power was extended, but more or less invisibly, and they remained socially inferior.

Some men of plebeian blood rose even to the Imperial Purple, but it was necessarily in the guise of a gentleman free from commercial taint. Augustus himself, the first Emperor, came from a family of small-town bankers. His father and grandfathers had been money-lenders, and some whispered that the founder of the family was a humble sailmaker and that his mother was the daughter of a dealer in African perfumes. He thus represented in his person the interests of finance, and became one of the richest men in the Empire. Financial backing helped him to the throne; behind him stood such men as the notoriously cruel Vedius Pollio, celebrated in legend for feeding slaves to lampreys in his ponds to improve the taste of his fish-courses, and by the more cultivated Etruscan financier, Maecenas.

Augustus, who so obviously embodied the triumph of wealth, was sometimes shown with the attributes of the god Mercury. Mercury, or *Lucri Conservator*, the preserver of wealth, was an old deity of grain-dealers, probably Etruscan in origin, who had become mixed up with Hermes, that dubious divinity of rogues, travelers, messengers and business men, whom the Phoenicians were perhaps the first to worship. The poet Horace not inaptly said that Augustus was the god Mercury come to earth.

Though Augustus was thus of humble origin, he had been made eligible by adoption into the family of Julius Caesar, which traced its lineage back to the goddess Venus. Later emperors of similar low birth had likewise to cleanse themselves of the trading contamination. Vitellius, the notorious glutton, whose hog-jowled portrait is almost a caricature of Roman parvenudom, was the offspring of an ex-slave, a poor cobbler, whose son managed to pull off lucky strokes in real estate and further increased his fortune by marrying the daughter of a rich baker. Their son was able to purchase a knighthood and enter the arcana of state-contracting and finance, whereby he made enough to buy senatorial honors for his four sons and pave the way for his grandson, Vitellius, to mount the throne. The father of another Emperor, Pertinax, was also a business man; he manufactured a coarse woolen stuff, used for slaves' clothing, in Liguria, but his imperial son engaged in business only indirectly, employing slaves as his factors.

Thus, though men of business classes attained the summit of ambition, it could not be said that business, or even money-power, ruled Rome openly. Men who tried to leap from the countinghouse straight up to the Purple were not lucky. In vain Firmus, the wealthy merchant of Alexandria, proclaimed his candidature. Like Crassus, he boasted he could feed an army; in fact, he said he could do it from the proceeds of his paper and glue factories alone. But his hopes, like those of Crassus, were drowned in blood.

In the long duel for dominance, therefore, the pure business man cannot be said to have emerged on top. He captured plains and foothills, but, despite his millions, he remained barred from the last high peaks of power. Those were still reserved for men rich in tradition if not in gold, keen generals as well as bargainers, able to command as well as feed armies.

THE SOCIAL CLIMBERS

The compromise reached in the prosperous period of the Roman Empire, in the first and second centuries, was in many respects like that achieved in the nineteenth century in Victorian Britain. The true gentility had very largely been exterminated or replaced by men with fortunes made in milling and munitions. The survivors had surrendered many scruples, and participated more obviously than before in consortiums and schemes of commerce. But, as the aristocracy became a glittering fiction, plebeians abandoned their old hostility to it and bowed low before their former foes. Senators stooped to pray to Fortuna, and plebeians took up ancestor worship. They revised their family trees and purchased fake ancestral masks to hang in their brand-new marble halls; thus the mere memory of dead aristocrats exercised a compelling fascination over the rising bourgeois.

The same curious blend of vulgarity and formalism was a feature alike of antiquity and Victorianism. In both cases, brash nabobs emerged rapidly from rags to riches and enthusiastically tried to conform to established social conventions. A steady upheaval of social strata was in progress, and yet, so carefully were the outward forms preserved and so little did the institutions change, that nothing seemed to be in motion. Despite all the underground disturbances, there was an air of repose, almost stagnation, hanging over society.

There were other similarities. The Imperial epoch in Roman, as in British history, was one of universalism in commerce and culture. The known world from Wales to China was ransacked for commodities and linked by superior roads; the seas were swept of pirates and the land was freed from old barriers. Peace, stability, order, standardization of law and custom, and considerable economic laissez faire, afforded conditions favorable to commerce on a greater scale than ever before. Investments were so secure that, as Cato remarked of his own, not even Jupiter could touch them.

The expansion of the luxury trades was at any rate immense. It was said that, after the triumph of Augustus, the annual number of ships that sailed for spices and gems to India increased from 20 to 120. The trade in staples, grain, oil, wine, must have enlarged, at least in Italy, after Pompey's sweeping victories over the pirates, when shares leaped up on the Forum Exchange. The *magnarii*, or magnates, the wholesalers who had their agents over the Empire, became more influential. The astrologer, Manlius, who declared that a man born under the zodiacal sign of the Crab was destined to success in wholesaling, described them as men who "sell the goods of the world over the world, connect commerce with unknown lands, and win new riches under new skies."

It is questionable, however, whether the standard of living was rising outside Italy. It is more probable that misery was intensified in the provinces, which were drained of wealth to Rome; the rise in commerce was very largely due to a traffic in luxuries for the enriched conquerors, and did not necessarily indicate greater prosperity on the whole. But, at least, the concentration of wealth in Rome was a portentous fact.

Such swollen tides of gold had not been seen in a single city before. As political capitals have a tendency to do, Rome became the seat of money-might. Power politics produced finance politics. The men of Rome were greater masters of resources than any who had preceded them. Possibly there were fewer business men in the imperial age than before, now that so many cities were mired in poverty and despair; but these few conquerors were richer and more aggressive than their predecessors. Owners of mines, fleets, factories, banks and hosts of slaves, they were the lusty precursors of nineteenth-century imperialists.

Some of their factories outgrew small-shop handicraft proportions and developed division of labor. Such factory production seemed to occur most naturally in bakeries, whose owners became very rich. The Emperor Vitellius was descended from a baker. The most imposing mortuary monument left by an ancient business man is that near the Porta Maggiore in Rome which signalizes in frescoes the achievements of the baker, M. Vergilius Eurysaces, an ex-slave who won freedom and wealth. On this monument, pictures of his production methods show slaves grinding meal and kneading dough under the supervision of toga-clad overseers. The supports on which the building rests are in the form of grain-measures; the roof was once decorated with bread-baskets, and, crowning inspiration of the sentimental confectioner, the remains of his wife were interred in an urn in the shape of a bread-basket.

How far this large-scale production applied in other branches of industry is a matter for conjecture. But it is apparent that commercially made articles of all sorts from city shops were supplanting the home-made products. Lamps, jewels, pottery, tools, the cheapest cloth for slaves and the finest gauze for ladies, were being sent far and wide to market. The manufacture of pins, which Adam Smith took as the classic example of capitalist industry, was well advanced under Roman skill; as fast as Rome could subdue the barbarians, she sold them *fibulae*. At length, after several centuries, the barbarians, particularly in Britain, became themselves sufficiently industrialized to make their own safety-pins, and then began to flood Italy with a still cheaper variety, thus underbidding their teachers.

There were some major publishing houses, like the concern of the brothers Sosii, which reached an estimable size under Augustus. The clothiers attained prominence as well; the well-known monument of the Secundinii family in Igel in the Rhineland, portrays cloth-shops and river transport. And how the clothiers of Rome combined to boost prices is related by Pliny, who complained that they met in the Forum on a certain day of autumn to forecast winter weather: if they thought it would be cold, they agreed to boom the price of cloaks, if warm, they lowered that of cloaks and raised everything else. In other branches there were similar monopolistic arrangements: date and balsam dealers, for instance, had trade agreements limiting production to maintain prices. "Caveat emptor!" (Let the purchaser beware) was the expression of bitter experience.

How nearly this state of things approached modern conditions, it is extremely difficult to say. The utmost caution must be observed in comparing "antique capitalism" with modern. The old Romans had only the vaguest notion of any difference between capital and income. They made one overworked term do for wages, mortgages, price, investment, interest. They lacked a word for Business itself. Their concepts were primitive, and yet it is often astonishing how closely the characters, if not the technique, of these ancients prefigured those of modern times.

The "success-story" hero was as ubiquitous a figure in the early Empire as his counterpart in the nineteenth century, and for the same reason: the steady expansion of empire, the continual "boom," and the constant social upheavals going on in various parts of the world, brought to the fore many types of underdogs who, in a more stabilized period, would have been held down.

Many of these climbers might have stepped from the pages of a modern biography. Cornelius Senecio, for example, worked up from obscurity to riches and the title of *splendidus vir*, but never relaxed his hustling, kept his money working on land and sea, and left no form of enterprise untried. A "Samuel Smiles" type was Sergius Orata, the Neapolitan inventor who created a system of central heating and made rather a good thing out of buying old houses, fitting them up with hypocausts, and renting them at fancy figures.

If there was any difference between the antique and the modern climbers, it was in the relatively greater drama of the former. There the hero often rose, not merely from rags but from gyves. Slaves might become the trusted agents of rich men. Many of them bore confidence-awakening names like Stabilio, Pudens and Celer (the Hustler), which remind one of the virtuous nomenclature chosen by Puritan entrepreneurs in the Anglo-Saxon world. They might buy freedom, win wealth and elbow their way into high places, as did that ex-slave of whom Horace tells, who swaggered down the Via Sacra in an out-size toga, three ells wide and draped in excessive folds. His kind, Horace complained, coolly appropriated the best seats in the circus and used to wear out or "burn up" the roads in carriages drawn by swiftly trotting Gallic ponies.

Who, indeed, should know better than Horace? His own father was an ex-slave who got a respectable fortune, retired and devoted himself to educating Horace as a gentleman. Humbly, the elder Flaccus even took his little son to school as his attendant or *paedagogus*. But the youth turned out a rebel, as business men's sons have a way of doing; he fought with Brutus at Philippi against the forces of dictatorship, and when the monarchists won, they ruined the old man and stripped him of his hard-won estates.

The supreme parvenu of antiquity was of course the fictional figure of Trimalchio, the ex-slave who made good, limned by the novelist Petronius in the reign of Nero. Trimalchio summed up in his person the extravagances of antiquity and remained for all time the matchless caricature of the self-made man; like Falstaff, he is a figure continually being reproduced, yet forever inimitable.

Trimalchio's banquet is an uproarious exhibition of nabobery. Tarts explode perfume; one of the main dishes is "a young boiled heifer with a helmet on her head." The jewels of his wife, Fortunata, are weighed before the guests to show their value in hard money. And in the midst of his dazzled friends lolls Trimalchio himself, the plump magnate, dripping with ointment, swathed in scarlet, loaded with gems, picking his teeth with a silver pin. Beaming, he describes his business successes, breaking anon into song and even dance.

But it is the wistfulness of Trimalchio, his yearning for gentility, which makes him eternally appealing. He would like to prove himself master of the polite art of conversation and introduces such themes as: "Which man has the most difficult profession? I think, either a physician or a banker." Secretly wretched because his ignoble birth prevents him from buying the golden ring of a knight, he wears one of gold studded with iron stars. And in the tomb inscription which he composed for himself, he speaks for all his mute, inglorious fellows in his own and succeeding ages:

HE MIGHT HAVE BEEN A SENATOR, WOULD HE HAVE ACCEPTED. HE RAISED HIMSELF FROM LITTLE OR NOTHING, BUT LEFT BEHIND HIM THIRTY MILLION SESTERCES. YET NEVER HEARD A PHILOSOPHER.

As the old Romans used to say, "Money makes the man." They were not too seriously disturbed by its source. Atticus, who piled up ten millions in all sorts of ventures, some exceedingly shabby, used to say with a sententiousness that appears Victorian: "Little streams make great rivers." He never minded if a few streams were muddy. Indeed the Romans smirked like so many Yankees in the age of Barnum over cheap tales of smart dodges. There was, for instance, the story of how the banker Pythius tricked the simple nobleman Canius into buying a water-front property very dear. He bought a large quantity of fish and hired fishermen to be seen pulling in nets of a heavy catch upon the shore. Canius' eyes bulged. "Quid multa?" he cried. The sum was named, the bargain concluded. Cicero chuckles over what he evidently considers a neat day's work.

More and more, the frank love of money and success grew upon the Romans. Despite their clinging to high theory they shed in practice the last semblance of scorn for vulgar gain. Old and young, remarked the writers, took to carrying wax tablets always under their arms, ready to reckon up profit and loss. They sat in the marketplace, to haggle over investments instead of philosophies. They neglected all deities but Fortuna and prayed "no longer for beauty and health, but solely for profit." Pliny sighed: "Chance is regarded as a god, and hence the existence of God himself becomes doubtful."

In all ages, to be sure, men have hungered for gold, but, in some periods, they have sought it as a means to non-commercial ends, and not for accumulation's sake. They have wanted to nourish a clan of fighting-men, for instance, or have felt it necessary to avow other purposes, such as the attainment of glory. But in the high Roman and Victorian eras, pretense was at a minimum; in both ages, religious convictions were dimming and agrarian prejudices waning, and wealth *per se* was becoming more and more an esteemed goal.

Both the high Romans and the early Victorians, in their money-madness, were ruthless and coldly practical to a startling degree. If a difference be observed between the two, it would be that the Romans would appear more lacking in humanitarianism. As Schmoller declares, the systematic exploitation of human labor and property has never been more shameless and more unrelieved by scruples, than in the high Roman era.

The Victorian hardness of heart has often been attributed to Puritanism and chilling contact with the Machine. All sorts of experiences through many generations, runs the theory, were required to bring the European to the Victorian pitch of concentration upon gain. But the old Romans, without these mechanical or spiritual preparations, were icy of heart and merciless. It could not have been the machine which made them so, since they were anything but technological adepts and had to employ Syrians and Greeks to create their engineering works for them. Yet no modern Taylorization, no Machine Age robotism, has surpassed the "efficiency" of the Roman money-maker, whose methods are revealed in the antique discussions of how to extract the last ounce of profit from slave-labor. He knew how little to feed a slave, how much to drive him so that he might never have a moment to plan revenge, and how early to sell him that he might not become a loss-entry.

ALEXANDRIAN COMMERCIALISM

Almost contemporary appear the ancient money-grubbing and hustling spirit in an old description of the commercial port of Alexandria. This reads like a conventional picture of "business America" as seen by an astonished foreign traveler. Nobody is idle there; everyone in the bustling throngs seems to have some trade, that man being in linen and the other in glass. The very beggars, the lame and blind, are more go-getting than mendicants in other places. Most familiar is the climax: "Their God is Gold."

The city of Alexandria in Egypt, halfway port between East and West, was the greatest manufacturing and trading city of the second century of the Christian Era. She was supreme in commerce, as Rome in finance. In the elegant shops of her Main Street, or *Mesion Pedion*, were assembled the finest wares of the world. Twenty meters broad and lined with pillared arcades for five kilometers, paved with hardest basalt, it was the Fifth Avenue of antiquity.

Some of the luxuries represented there had been brought across the Indian Ocean by seven-sailed vessels and over the desert by camel caravan. To pay for these Eastern goods, the products of the West, wine of Italy, tin of Wales, and amber of Sweden, were gathered in the harbor of Alexandria, watched over by the renowned lighthouse, the marvelous Pharos. The intricacy of this traffic may be illustrated by the exchange of pearls and coral. Pearls were as necessary for the ears of Roman ladies as coral for the rosaries of Buddhist churchmen. To satisfy the former, pearls were shipped from the Persian Gulf, polished in Alexandrian shops, sent by a three weeks' voyage to Puteoli in Italy and thence carried to the shops of the Margaritarii, or pearl-dealers' corporation, in the Roman Forum. The coral, in return, had to be obtained by barter from the shields of barbaric Gallic warriors, and followed the same route back to Alexandria, whence it was dispatched to Ceylon and on to far Tibet.

The energetic merchants of the city were extending trade even beyond the limits of the Roman Empire. Greek sailors, merchants like that Hippalos who discovered the secret of the monsoons in the second century, were as active as Roman soldiers in pushing back boundaries. They coasted to the Ganges and even Canton, seeking the secrets of the silk and pepper routes and braving all sorts of perils to find the Gold Country, China. The rôle of the business man in binding together and expanding empire has been overshadowed in written history by the deeds of military heroes. But what would the Empire built by Roman soldiers have been without the Greek, Syrian and Jewish traders? What were Rome without Alexandria?

The Alexandrian business men were spreaders of civilization, inter-mediaries between hemispheres. They planted colonies in India, repro-ducing the shops, banks, warehouses and temples of their homeland; these were connected by regular post with Alexandria, thus ensuring the circulation of the chatty papyrus letters which are unearthed to-day in Egyptian towns. In the course of this traffic, Alexandrians and other Greeks brought to India the Jewish calendar, Roman law, Baby-lonian astronomy, Greek music and theater and weights and measures. Talented slaves were carried in both directions. India, as Pliny cried, was "brought nearer by lust for gain." She passed on to the West her medicine, legends and textile designs. "Effeminate philosophy and pep-per" came together from the East, as Persius declared, and the trader was the agent for this momentous interchange.

If, therefore, it comes about that Christian and Buddhist saints, in two remote island corners of the world, Ireland and Japan, wear haloes round their heads, it is doubtless due to the spread of the symbol of the sun-ray crown, belonging to the Alexandrian Apollo, in that age of close-knit cultural and commercial connections.

But the trader was responsible for more than the mere spread of symbols and notions over the surface of the earth. He was an accumu-lator and concentrator of knowledge, as well. Alexandria was a focal point of caravan and sea routes, as Miletus had been hundreds of years before. It was the melting-pot of many races, and the result was a cos-mopolitanism of culture, a synthesis of thought, which would only have been possible in a place of such far-sweeping contacts.

A veritable department-store of information was Alexandria. The facts gathered by explorer-traders were collected into treatises like the world geography of Ptolemy. Cosmogonies, universal histories, gen-eral works in broad fields of science, fruitful mergings of philosophies and creeds, were characteristic of Alexandria's wholesale mind. Busi-ness practice was being perfected at the same time through the coun-cils of many men; Rhodian maritime law, Phoenician bookkeeping, Egyptian skill in documentation, Babylonian banking methods, brought by Jewish pupils, were all merged to form a general business practice which was much more complex than that of previous ages.

In this industrial city, where technology was esteemed, training-schools were maintained and science came into its own. The most ad-vanced mechanical contrivances were perfected: washing-machines, gear-wheels, the famous first steam-engine—the steam-driven car of Hiero, which used to roll along the city streets in an annual religious procession. The water-clock was also the inevitable necessity in a town where time was being counted with more care, because it was more valuable than in rural regions. In the medical faculty of the Alexandrian university, dissection was practiced and an anaesthetic developed. Thus Alexandria was groping toward a rationalized, even a mechanized, society. If the city had been free from Roman exactions and interference, she might have gone much further.

Like Paris in the nineteenth century, Alexandria in the second was an arbiter of fashionable taste for the world, as well as the center of luxury trades. She set the styles and sold the goods. Her great garment center, managed largely by Jews, produced embroidered robes of Chinese silk, African cottons and Indian gauzes. She formed the mode in personal adornments, interior decoration, gardening and cookery. She sold the cookbooks, the pepper and spices, the trained cook-slaves, and the richly inlaid dining-tables. She also offered perfumes, incense, medicines from India, ginger, lip-salve, camphor of Sumatra, yak-milk, the melted fat of crocodiles, snow-leopard skins of Tibet, couches adorned with rock-crystal and Malayan tortoiseshell, vases of carnelian, Indian steel swords sheathed in African ivory, and tigers, fed on human flesh, for the circuses of popular and benevolent senators.

The city was a leading labor market as well, where black and white flesh of all kinds, from Spanish dancing-girls to Nubian porters, was available. Ingenious in salesmanship, Alexandria dressed little live children as cupids, and set the fashion of having them at parties to amuse the guests; it then offered babies in wholesale lots. Quaintly enough, the fad of Alexandrian elegants affected the Christian culture which was formed in that city; Christians continued the custom of representing these babies, now turned into cherubs, on their caskets. And so eventually the poor little slaves received their apotheosis in mediaeval religious paintings; often, in the Middle Ages, merchants in ordering pictures of saintly scenes had themselves portrayed kneeling in the foreground, while, from the clouds, the emancipated babies looked down upon the business men.

Comfort and culture were developed in Alexandria with all the more enthusiasm because other outlets for energies were dammed up. Alexandria was taken captive by Rome; it could not direct its own destinies. Barred from high political adventure, the Alexandrians turned to pleasure and distraction. This million-headed city, full of energies and inquiring spirit, its love of music and art and its mocking wit, was frustrated in every pursuit save that of business, pleasure and intellectual experimentation. Since it could not have a public life, it developed a private life.

THE DUEL OF ROME AND ALEXANDRIA

The business man has, throughout history, been the home-builder, the comfort-lover. This is his natural tendency, and of course is greatly increased when he has no need, or no chance, to engage in public activities. Thus the Parisians under the Second Empire, and the Berliners under Wilhelm, who were not permitted to indulge too strenuously in politics, devoted themselves to pleasure; the Londoners under Victoria did the same because they found it unnecessary to interfere with a government so smoothly working in their favor. The Victorians, therefore, for one reason or another, exhibited the same passion for comfort that we find in the Roman Empire.

When a business man is shut out of the king's palace, he seeks to make his own domicile a palace. The Roman *novi homines*, barred so largely from the highest administrative and military positions, made themselves residences that outshone the public buildings they could not occupy. Never before had the houses of the gods been eclipsed by villas of bankers; never before had such emphasis been placed upon domestic magnificence as in this Roman age when rich bourgeois were confined to their homes.

Seneca tells how the rising parvenus bought books in sets to fill the shelves in their new abodes, even though they never peeped inside one of the volumes. They also put statues of the immortal gods in their gardens though they no longer believed in any of them. And they brought art, which had served religion and State, down to domestic decoration.

The effects of such commercial patronage of the arts were increasingly visible. Classic art had remained severely aloof from scenes of manual labor; it served the State and the gods, not the ends of everyday life. Even in the prime of classicism at ancient Athens, however, there had been signs of revolt; in the port-town of Piræus, where the traveling salesmen dwelled, a certain realism developed, and one painter dared to limn scenes of kitchen still-life. The academicians of the times hurled at him the hard word, "Rhyparagraphos," or "dirt-painter," the very term used by Wilhelm II in the nineteenth century to disparage the bourgeois realism of Liebermann. Other commercial cities, like the Etruscan, furthered the growth of realism. The great slave-dealing mart of Rhodes produced the Laocoon group, so shocking to antique sensibilities by its portrayal of human beings in extreme agony—the slave-dealers themselves, presumably, were inured to worse scenes. Alexandria became the heir to Rhodes; she carried on the work by stripping away veil after veil of mysticism and mythology from art.

Manual labor was depicted in wall-paintings, on tombstones. Many business men wished the processes of their industries immortalized on their monuments or in their homes. To be sure, the ancients were still a long way from the grim realism of a Meunier, and they strove to aestheticize work as far as possible. One of the more successful attempts is the series of friezes in the home of a Pompeian banker, L.

Primogenes, showing cupids busily baking bread and waiting on customers in a perfume shop, a sublimation of child labor. In other scenes, the entrepreneur is shown, toga-clad, with the staff of authority, among his workers; he makes the gestures of an Egyptian king, and his foremen and slaves bow obsequiously like subjects. Sometimes an incident of punishment meted out to a faulty slave is introduced to give emphasis to the business man's powers and tell the story of factory discipline. Such portrayals formed the basis of succeeding pictures of industrial life and their motifs survive in modern frescoes.

Mythology was retained, to be sure, by the business man and the artists who served him, for neither dared cast aside all the formal heritage. But faith had fled and the symbols were cold and empty. The high gods were rarely to be persuaded into patronizing factories, in any case. Sometimes Vulcan, the engineer's god, or Juno Saponaria, patron of soap shops, would be introduced to the background. But usually only Fortuna or Mercury, Lady Luck or Lord Lucre, distributed the triumphal wreaths and blessings. These two, accordingly, were worked overtime. Trimalchio, the fictitious parvenu, had himself painted as the spoiled darling of Fortuna; he was a Campanian, from the region around Pompeii; and the real Pompeian bankers, Primogenes and L. Caecilius Jucundus, seem to have shared his tastes and sense of fun, for the former adorned his home with a Mercury proffering a well-filled purse, and the other ordered a sculptured portrait of himself which amusingly illustrates the gulf between the ancient and the modern bourgeois notions of the proprieties.

Long after Pompeii was blotted out, the tradition of the two trader-divinities as geniuses of the bourgeois home was continued. In the Renaissance, Mercury and Fortuna reappeared; the latter spilled cornucopias in the palace of the Fugger, and the former blessed the magnificent chateau of the financier Fouquet, upon which Versailles was modeled. In Victorian times, however, Lady Luck was quietly dropped and though Mercury was still a favorite in proper drawing-rooms, he was portrayed pointing to the skies and not, in the frank classic fashion, offering his host and hostess a sackful of coins.

A well-decorated home does not satisfy the business man; unlike the seigneur, he must also have good piping arrangements. In the Roman Empire, plumbing spread from Antioch to Londinium. The landed gentry resisted this innovation, declaring that cold water scrubs were quite enough; the feudal mind has ever been largely indifferent to hot water and soap. But the bourgeois hobby prevailed, and Frontinus at last could scornfully dismiss the temples of the Greeks as unworthy to be set beside the Roman waterworks. What was a Parthenon compared to running water in the kitchen?

Comfort, however, easily merges into license. And Alexandria, which developed luxurious homes and commanded technicians to create new marvels of heating, lighting and plumbing, became notorious also for extravagant amusements. Her canals were crowded with barges bearing revelers, and lined with inns in whose shelter guests reclined before goblets of Falernian and pasties of flamingo tongues. One of these ruined inns yet bears the defiant bourgeois-pacifistic inscription: "Within these walls sounds only the flute, never the trumpet of war. Here robes, not armor, shine. Here the blood of animals, not men, reddens the earth."

In brief, Alexandria, following the other rich trading communities on record, became unwarlike, effete, "vicious," according to agrarian canons. Like Miletus, Carthage, Corinth and the Etruscan towns, she was filled with bourgeois who loved ease, given to scientific rationalism and cosmopolitan culture. She was correspondingly hated by Rome, the citadel still of the political-military minds, as were her predecessors.

Roman moralists blamed the traders of Alexandria for corrupting the purity of manners in Italy, for tempting Romans to pay out wealth for Eastern luxuries. They saw their own treasures of precious metal, the fruits of conquest, flowing away from them to the East—since the Indians would not accept much besides gold or silver for their gems and spices. This was a gigantic drain on the resources of the Empire; it has been estimated by modern economists that the cost of Eastern luxuries in the Empire, per head of the population, was fully two-thirds of what it was in Europe in Napoleonic times. Many Romans felt that the trader was robbing them of the results of their military and political triumphs, that Alexandria was a parasite which battened on them. On the other hand, the Alexandrians returned the hate. They regarded the Romans as tax-leeches, cheating them of the profits of legitimate commerce. The feeling between the two cities was almost as intense as that between Rome and the previous great commercial metropolis, Carthage.

By malicious repartee, and riots, the Alexandrians attempted to revenge themselves upon the masterful Romans. The Roman answer was force. A Roman army was turned loose by Caracalla in Alexandria; it massacred enormous numbers, practically a younger generation. Later on, in the latter half of the third century (A.D. 273) an Alexandrian business man rose to challenge Rome. Firmus, the wealthy manufacturer and importer of Indian luxuries, raised an army and occupied Alexandria for three months, during which time he called himself Emperor of the Romans and wore the Imperial Purple. He was put down by Aurelian. Nevertheless, the antagonism between feudalism and commercialism, West and East, which had begun when Octavian fought against Cleopatra, went on until both crumbled together with the structure of the Empire. Their mighty duel was resolved by the ruin of both parties.

Each side undermined the other. The Romans became more and more helpless before their own military forces—forces the business man had never been able to control. The armies, becoming Frankenstein monsters on the rampage, looted and destroyed many rich cities. Thus the splendor of Mediterranean civilization was demolished by the wandering armies of Rome before the barbarian hordes swept from their northern European fastnesses to finish its dissolution.

In this havoc-making the trader had also played a part. He had fattened on the loot of Empire himself. He had drained the wealth of the West for "bones and stones" from the East and thereby brought on currency troubles for which there was apparently no remedy. He had tempted the barbarians with trinkets and lured them to march upon the centers of indulgence. He had proved corrupt and inefficient in such local governing as he had enjoyed under Roman supervision. Because he had yielded much to the landed-gentleman ideal, he had tended to draw fortunes away from business to the land, taking wealth out of circulation and energy out of business enterprise. His children, growing up in the country, were often lost to business entirely.

Vainly, as the demoralization proceeded, emperors tried to halt the inflation growing out of debased coinage by fixing prices under the death penalty. They strove to hold merchants to business by law, compelling them to join *collegia*—that is, compulsory "corporations" as Mussolini would call them—and keep up activity under threat of dire penalties. Honors and titles were offered to tempt men to go into business. In the fourth century, a shipper might become a knight; a man who had been a wholesale pig-dealer for five years was dubbed *comites;* but often men took refuge among the barbarians rather than accept the status of ruined though titled pig-dealers. Thus the State had to enter more and more fields of industry, to satisfy its own requirements. Others the Church took over.

CHRISTIANITY AND BUSINESS

In the long agony known as the "Fall" of Rome, Alexandria veered toward Christianity. It was in this world city that Christianity was shaped by Jewish and Christian teachers, mutually influencing each other. It offered a way out of chaos, but ascetic, not economic. It urged the people to forsake Fortuna for the Madonna, turning from Luck to Mercy.

Christianity appealed to the handicraftsmen in the cities. Its appeal was so slight among peasants that the very word "pagan" comes from *paganus,* a country fellow. Among the masses of city slaves and freedmen, among the laborers in the sinking cities of the Near East, in the growing and now permanent crisis, it was otherwise. They were in a state of tumult in many places; strikes were frequent among the linen workers of Tarsus, for instance, and in Alexandria, where workers were famous as a "seditious, vain race of men." These folk had hope only in miracles. With rapture they absorbed the teachings of the Primitive Church, which called private property the creation of man, not God, and urged the sharing of wealth. They hearkened to stories of that divine craftsman, the Carpenter, who had scourged the money-changers from the temple, and taught that it would be no harder for a camel to enter the needle's eye than for a rich man to squeeze into heaven.

Naturally, the emperors made strenuous efforts to suppress doctrines so subversive to a great State. But force could not put an end to the mutterings in workrooms. These went on gathering in volume, surviving proscriptions, and remaining to plague business societies throughout succeeding centuries.

At first, the Church, the refuge of the downtrodden, assumed a severe doctrinary standpoint on property. In the beginning, the Christian brotherhoods held no property of their own, but kept possessions in trust for the poor. The clergy were forbidden to trade; this was settled at the Synod held in A.D. 397 at Carthage, of all places, the ancient seat of Mammon.

The Church tried to override the business man. It could see no valid reason why the middleman who did nothing to improve an article should charge a higher price for it than the maker. This was the view of the artisans themselves, who disliked the man who marketed their work and got better paid for his slight physical efforts than they for their toil. Their Church forbade also the taking of interest on loans. The Fathers of the Church, Cyprian, Irenaeus and the holy Augustine, cited passages from Aristotle and other authorities to support a sweeping condemnation of the middleman and money-lender.

As the power of the Church increased, however, in the first part of the 300's, and Christianity became the official faith of the Roman Empire, it confronted the problem of organization, which resolved itself into the question of finance. It took over the temples and properties of the pagan divinities, and found itself involved in business involuntarily, especially in Egypt, where the temples had long been sites of large-scale enterprises. In Egypt, priests had been bankers and manufacturers; the papyrus leaves adorning the capitals of their temple pillars are memorials of one of their chief monopolies, that of paper-making. The famous Rossetti inscription was a temple-factory contract. Temples had inns, tenement houses for lease, and hospitals; they received tithes and in short did most of the things that the great monasteries in Western Christendom later did.

Not only were Egyptian priests business men in their way, but business men had been eager to obtain lucrative posts in the temples. It was not necessary for them to renounce families or other occupations. One papyrus letter of A.D. 147 reveals the purchase of such a position: "I wish to buy the post of Prophet with the provision that I obtain the right to wave the palm-branch and collect one-fifth of all the income of the temples. I offer . . . a price of 2200 drachmas." These Eastern trader-prophets taught the Christian Church in Egypt how to manage big industrial complexes; they gave the Roman Church much of the technique which enabled it to settle and civilize the wild Northwest of Europe.

Gradually the Church was forced into an unexpected position. It had arisen during the breakdown of capitalism in the antique world, to preach escape from material woes through asceticism; it urged charity as the means of curing the situation. The holy Chrysostom estimated that if all the rich people of Alexandria would bring their gold together, there would be perhaps a million pounds of metal. Since, he thought, there were some fifty thousand souls in dire need in that city, they could all be fed in soup kitchens for this sum for a long time. If the rich would do this, he said, the example would be so splendid that the world would be converted at once.

But charity was not enough in a world so rapidly demoralized. The Church had to keep the economic order functioning, to prevent brigands from taking the last remnants of prosperity, and keep looms going in towns upon which the desert sands were encroaching. It had to teach barbarians how to work as well as pray. And in assuming such functions, the Church went unavoidably into business. Moreover, it had to assimilate the business men who, after Christianity became the compulsory faith, were also in its fold. Most of these men did not propose to surrender their activities; indeed, even at an early date, so mightily did huckstering increase that some Church Fathers declared the agonies of the martyrs were the just punishment of God for backsliding into commercialism.

The story of one converted business man illustrates the percolation of business into the brotherhood. Calixtus, the slave of a chamberlain at the court of the Emperor Commodus, was given a sum of money and told to enlarge it. He started a bank among his fellow-Christians, but it failed. Calixtus feared to face his master and decided to court death by running into a Jewish synagogue, crying on the name of Christ, hop-

ing to be condemned to death for disturbing the peace. But the Roman
magistrate merely sentenced him to the mines, from which he was soon
liberated by the efforts of the Christian mistress of Commodus. He returned to Rome, became Bishop of that city, giving his name to a
group of catacombs.

Crowded with converted business men, and endowed by wealthy
Roman ladies, the Church possessed wealth and mothered business
through the Dark Ages. In its expansion period it had need of the
trader. Hand in hand, missionary and merchant pushed back the frontiers of heathenism in the ninth century, as they have also done in the
New World in the sixteenth century and in Asia in the nineteenth.

Whichever reached Frisia, Saxony or Sweden first, called the other
to follow. One early bishop, on founding a town, quickly wrote to the
nearest large city, inviting Jews to come and settle, since, he said, they
could bring prosperity. Ninth-century Bremen became a center for
pilgrim traffic, and hence a marketplace, as soon as Archbishop Ansgar
had transferred the remains of the holy Willehad from a wooden to a
new stone structure. The merchants of the place had reason to thank
him for writing a little pamphlet describing the wonders of the shrine.

In the new cities, the Church spread peace about the marketplace as
the pagan temples had previously done. Indeed, in very primitive times,
merchants occasionally stored their wares inside cathedrals and held
markets in the aisles. By lavish spending, the princes of the Church encouraged the luxury trades, and called upon merchants to bring incense
and silken vestments, in exchange for products of cloisters and clerical
domains like salt, wine and grain. Plato had complained long ago that
pagan priests fostered commerce by their clamor for incense and purple robes; the magnificence of religion is the opportunity of the trader.
Under these circumstances, the Church began to revise its original attitude toward the private property which it held for the poor. Instead
of continuing to keep it all in its stewardship, the Church, speaking
through a council, divided the property into four parts: a quarter for
the bishops, another for the lesser clergy, a third for cult purposes, and
the rest for the poor. By the time it was found advisable to engulf the
last quarter, a relaxation in dogma seemed inevitable. Then St. Thomas
Aquinas explained that, although communism was undoubtedly the
ideal state for society, it was in actual fact unworkable, owing to the
sinfulness of man.

While the Church receded from its original doctrinaire position, it still
tried to tighten the reins on the business man. It knew that all its carefully
erected hierarchical scheme was endangered by the restless ambition of
this dangerous member of society. Noblemen and serfs might remain
what they were by birth, but not the business man. Insatiable in his

avaritia, he would accept no bounds to his desire for wealth or position. So the Church sought to restrain the striving creature it had helped to nourish. It denied that he had the right to keep all his gains, for a part must go to charity and religion. Persistently, through the ages, the Church claimed a share of all the business man acquired; as incessantly, he struggled to reduce that claim. The fight over income and inheritance was waged, through the quarrels of Jansenist and Jesuit, down to the French Revolution.

The Protestant Reformation was supposed to end this old dilemma by separating the affairs of religion from those of high finance. But the "Reformed" traders and bankers who rejoiced at erecting churches freed from such close connections with business as the Roman, turned out to be themselves the best business men of all. It appears that their form of faith was even more suited than the Roman to provide a flexible psychological basis for modern capitalist mentality. Thus, under any form, Christianity and business were fated to affect each other.

All through the ages, from the dissolution of antique capitalism to the latest crisis of modern capitalism, Christian institutions, whether Catholic, Calvinist or Methodist, have exercised a profound modifying and yet fostering influence upon commerce and the characters of those engaged in it. Christianity, which has ever sought to moderate the profit-seeking of the business man, has assisted him to develop finance and industry. It was the curious destiny of this greatest spiritual force in the Western world to prepare mankind for materialism and mechanization. Yet it has exerted ceaseless pressure on the money-makers to consider the effects of their activities upon society and their own souls. The product of this immensely long development is that anomaly, as the early Fathers would consider him, the Christian business man.

PART TWO

THE PATRICIAN CITY-RULER

III

THE MEDIAEVAL MERCHANT-PATRICIAN

THROUGH THE MANIFOLD DANGERS of a disintegrating world, after the collapse of the Roman system, the business man moved with caution. At every turn, he faced extortion, legal or illegal, from pirates on the high seas, and, on the land, from feudal noblemen lying at ambush in their stone eyries above traffic-lanes. In the northern wildernesses of Europe it was advisable for traveling salesman to go armed to the teeth; nervous men adopted precautions so extreme that one Baltic club, a chamber of commerce, so to speak, of the Dark Ages, voted to exclude from its luncheons any guests carrying swords more than an ell long.

But it would be amiss to waste too great an amount of sympathy upon mediaeval business men as a whole. In the first place, the chaos of Europe was to a considerable extent of their own making and financing. And in the second place, they managed, during the general confusion, to slip into power at innumerable points and establish themselves as patrician trader-rulers, as city-oligarchs, and to enjoy a higher authority, if less wealth, than has been within the reach of business men in more stabilized times.

The merchants of those perilous days must not be pictured exclusively as innocent civilian bystanders, suffering under the tyrannical whims of war-lords and trying bravely to "knit the world together" by ties of commerce in a benighted epoch. On the contrary, many of them were belligerent. In Germany, the Hanse cities were almost incessantly at war to preserve trading posts and monopolies from foreign competitors. The Italians were even more prone to resort to swordplay as a way of settling economic rivalries; in each town, factions of merchants, and particularly of bankers, struggled desperately for the spoils of office; towns strove among themselves, and sometimes a large city would utterly annihilate several market competitors; in short, the principal source of chaos in Italy was of the business man's own creation. Occasionally, for a brief respite, the Church managed to bring a wave of repentance and fraternization over the squabbling mob of money-makers. One of the priestly interventions in the twelfth century brought the merchants of many towns to flagellation orgies in remorse for their fratricidal strife; stripped to the waist, they scourged themselves in solemn processions—but within a few months, were at one another's throats again.

"War, Trade and Piracy," in the Goethean formula, are "Triune, not to be separated." The first two have never been parted and the third has been disengaged only for the rarest moments. Piracy was suppressed during the height of Roman supremacy, and then again in the modern era, in the nineteenth century; but in all other ages, the commercial plunderer has operated, seeking profit at the expense of the more peaceable of his fellow business men. The Phoenicians and Etruscans represented this type, the buccaneering merchant, in antiquity; the Vikings, in the Dark Ages, likewise carried commodities in their dragon-ships, ready to traffic with those too strong to be conquered or fight with the weak. And the robber-merchant became a feature of mediaevalism almost as constant as the robber-baron.

Slave-raiding was a part of his activity, for the trade in slaves went on in Italy up to the end of the Middle Ages. Venice was "the greatest eunuch-factory in Europe," supplying the Byzantine Court with this sort of employee until a late date. Naples was another mart, where Turkish pirates disposed of their victims; the city of Nürnberg vainly tried to redeem one of its merchants who had suffered such a fate there. Besides slave-raiding, the robber merchant also engaged in "hijacking" the cargoes of others, to stock his own ships, or fell upon defenseless coastal towns, particularly in the Near East, where a religious cloak could be given to any kind of rapine practiced upon the Infidel.

One of the earliest forms of modern business association was the *Mahona*, a type of share-holding company formed for privateering exploits, around A.D. 1000, by owners of ships and makers of munitions in Genoa. Subscription books of a Mahona were opened to rich merchant-investors and humble artisans alike, to lay and religious corporations; the booty was divided *pro rata*. Out of these erratic and small-scale aggressions and the Crusades, which were fostered by Genoa and Venice in a desire to make a Holy War out of their struggle for trading-posts, came privileges and loot in the Near East. Had not Venice and Genoa gone mad with jealousy afterward, in struggling over the fruits of victories, the Turks might never have set foot in Europe; for Genoa, seeking revenge on the Venetian shipping-princes who were the trade-allies of the Greeks, helped the Infidel take Constantinople.

Piracy and privateering have enabled many countries—Italy, Holland, Britain, and the American colonies—to form, in their youth, initial accumulations of capital necessary to set up enterprises later on a large scale. After the mediaeval times gave way to modern, in the sixteenth and seventeenth centuries, the Dutch and British laid a basis for their future prosperity by slave-raiding and forays on each other's colonies; the early Merchant Adventurers of London and the Dutch East India Company were only elaborated forms of the old Genoese Mahona. American business men, in a similar fashion, before and during the Revolution, collected by piratical and privateering exploits a large part of the capital which enabled them afterwards to turn to more productive enterprises.

It is a little difficult, therefore, to find sufficient evidence in the past to prove the optimistic-liberal thesis that commerce always and necessarily makes for peace and friendly relations. This thesis, on which the philosopher, Kant, rested his peace hopes, and so commonly accepted today, can only be maintained by dodging those facts which sustain Goethe's thesis instead. War, like piracy, all through the Middle Ages, exercised a developing influence upon business. In equipping the fighting forces during the Hundred Years' War, British merchants acquired a wealth sufficient to buy aristocratic titles; similar outfitting of the Crusaders gave Venice and other Italian cities a long-continued boom; and the financial end of war-making brought out the greatest individual figure of early French business, Jacques Cœur.

Neither can it be argued with sublime confidence that the influence of the business man is bound to increase if the world is "better linked together." For, in the past, he has been most powerful politically during ages of disintegration, such as those preceding and following the Roman Empire.

Over a great and unified society, the business man has never ruled. True, he has attained to colossal fortune, in such mighty structures as the old Roman Empire or in modern nations, but in the main his influence has remained indirect, and has been exerted through politicians or courtiers, or dictators, and in compromise with the desires of other groups, military, agrarian, democratic or aristocratic. He has not been able to impose his wishes and personality upon multitudes, swayed by conflicting interests. Immense as his powers might be, in the background, he has seldom been able, or has seldom dared or wished, to appear openly sovereign over such immense aggregations of men.

In periods of localism, however, when the world has been shattered into fragments, there has been a chance for business men to direct affairs at least in small areas. Seizing a few spots, building up communities at the mouths of rivers or the crossing of traffic-routes, where the dominant interest was obviously commercial and little opposition was to be encountered, the business man has then become, in such miniature states, the patrician, the city father.

Twice has this occurred. The first flowering of commercial cities, in the antique world, we have already reviewed; its commencement may be placed around 1000 B.C. and its full unfoldment nearer 500 B.C.; its decline was gradual, and it was not until three hundred years later that the greatest free antique cities were mowed down by the Roman sword. After Rome fell, the second crop of merchant-managed cities came up around A.D. 1000 and reached a peak of luxury and refinement near A.D. 1500; then this second blooming was cut short by the kings of Europe, arising and forming national armies. Gradually, as before, the business man was again stripped of his authority and independence and suffered submergence in the larger unities of modern nations and empires, as he had once been overwhelmed in the immensity of the Roman Empire. This second decline was also by degrees; the English business men yielded first and most easily, while the French succumbed next. Italians held out very much longer; the afterglow of the Renaissance faded slowly from the skies of Venice. Not until the eighteenth century did the last, and greatest, trader-oligarchy of the world, the Dutch, abdicate. A few freakish German spots held out yet longer: Hamburg, Bremen and Lübeck, the "Free and Hanse Cities," retained remnants of their liberties until the advent of Adolf Hitler, when the last traces of the business-patrician's rule were erased.

THE FORMATION OF MEDIAEVAL PATRICIATES

The mediaeval revival of the business man's authority in urban centers took place near the close of the first millennium after Christ. By that time, the cities of Italy and southern France were recovering their ancient prosperity and, in the northern wildernesses of Europe, new cities were being founded. It is estimated that, between A.D. 900 and 1400, more than two thousand new towns were planted in Germany alone. Slowly, circles of business men began to gather in most of these places: first traders and artisans, then manufacturers and bankers. They seized the reins of government wherever they could and sought to free the cities from the interference of feudal suzerains. The formation of such patriciates, in independent cities, was well advanced in the twelfth and thirteenth centuries.

This process was, of course, far from uniform. The cities had varying degrees of independence. Some were founded by merchants. Yet others had to be taken by violence, and freed from feudal lords by force. Thus the Venetian traders won their freedom from Charlemagne by defeating his navy in a terrible sea battle. In Italian Florence, business men had to take a city already ruled by a feudal nobility. These noble clansmen inhabited scores of thin fortress-towers, twelve or fourteen stories high; counterparts of these curious cliff-dwellings may yet be seen in some parts of Italy, San Gimignano, for instance, where they lend the town a Manhattan sky line. But these nests of the feudality were captured by the rising merchants of Florence in a "reign of terror" in 1282. The insurgents, to whom the Pope was heavily in debt, managed to secure the blessings of the Holy See for their bourgeois rebellion, and they signalized their triumph by an audacious act—in the Florentine Revolution, there fell not one but a hundred and fifty *Bastilles*.

Whereas, in the settled South of Europe, traders had to struggle over towns already built, it was often possible for them to build their own in the northern frontier. Lübeck, for instance, on the Baltic coast, was settled by a consortium of dealers in grain, timber and other commodities of the region, who were looking for a strategic port at the meeting of traffic lanes from Novgorod, Lüneburg and Flanders. This "development scheme" went through in 1158; each realtor received a large block of land and, building his own house on the best corner lot, rented the rest to newcomers. The consortium kept in its hands the booths around the marketplace as well as municipal institutions like baths and bakeries. And of course the city-founders governed. Their descendants, living on the rents, were patricians and senators, and in turn went out to start new towns and rule over them also, until, in the language of Rörig, "it was almost a single group of families that in Lübeck or Riga or Wisby, or in Soest and Münster as well, tied the knots of the political net."

The original realtors of Lübeck did not retain a monopoly of office indefinitely; three generations later, they were forced to move over and make room for a fresh crowd of ambitious merchants, headed by the very rich wholesale grain-dealer Bertram Mornewech. But these newcomers were eager to imitate the property-holders and, in their turn, invested in city real estate—thus, the widow of Mornewech, in 1286, put her heritage, amounting to a million marks in modern money, into various sites and edifices such as the Poorhouse which stands today in the heart of Lübeck. Money seemed safer in land than on the seas; moreover, as time went on, mortgages were increasingly safeguarded by being registered in ground-books, watched over by solicitous city-fathers. Landholding, finally, was respectable; it rendered a merchant eligible for assimilation. The steady income from rents provided leisure for the second generation to enter politics and diplomacy—the statesmen in many German towns were *rentiers*, of business background, like the Roosevelts and Henry Cabot Lodge in our own time. Possibly the third generation might wear the golden circle which designated the Lübeck patrician, and transform the family trade-mark into an armorial bearing.

Real estate speculation was, like piracy and war, one of the chief sources of capital accumulation in the Middle Ages. When cities were being founded and enlarged over all Europe, from 1200 to 1400, ground-rents were steadily climbing; it was possible to make big sums easily by speculations in such developments; each new bridge over the Arno in Florence, for example, led to some new enrichment of the far-sighted or fortunate purchasers of adjacent land-lots. Speculation in steadily rising land values aided the formation of wealth in mediaeval Europe, much as, centuries afterward, it enabled Astor and others to lay the foundations of the earliest fortunes in the New World.

Thanks to the growth of riches, a surge of self-confidence and a thirst for independence swept over the towns of Europe in the thirteenth and fourteenth centuries. In Flanders and Switzerland, the burghers purchased their charters of freedom, or fought for them; in Germany and Italy, the business man managed to crawl to his goal under the clashing swords of rivals, the German Emperors and the Italian Popes, who were striving for the mastery of the Holy Roman Empire. Germans saw that the Emperors were too busy to bother about subjugating municipalities, and were in need of cash for armies, so they bought the right to become "Reich cities," owing allegiance only to the Emperor, but free from any lesser intermediary lords. In Italy, the cities were encouraged by the Popes to revolt against the Emperor and proclaim themselves autonomous.

In the Quattrocento, commercial oligarchies of the most various sorts, more or less independent, were ruling from the Baltic to the Adriatic. Europe presented a marvelous panorama of business administrations. In some cities, the retired *rentier* dominated affairs and made it hard for parvenus to rise directly from trade to office; for instance, the patricians of Augsburg, though but a few steps from bargaining themselves, refused to open the doors of their social club to Jacob Fugger the Rich, the wealthiest man of all Germany in the Renaissance. In other cities, like Ulm and Siena, patricians intermarried with surrounding noble families and became even haughtier, in fact, partly feudalized. In others, however, active men of affairs held the helm. Lübeck was one of these, where it was not necessary to abandon commerce in order to obtain municipal seats; from her councils, all feudal vassals, warriors and priests were excluded. But even among these business-managed towns, there was diversity, for in many places the small merchants raised insistent voices; while in others the wholesalers sternly repressed those beneath them; in Lübeck, the small men did not obtain influence until very late, in the 1600's. Many Italian towns were directed by financiers, notably Florence; municipal destinies in others, as in Venice and Lübeck, were guided by wholesalers and shippers.

The share of labor in these governments was likewise various. Mediaeval gilds of artisans made strenuous efforts to break into politics. At Bruges, in 1359, revolutionists, wearing red hats, stormed the city. In Lübeck, a fleeting "labor government" was set up, but the workers' council was soon ousted and made to do penance in the cathedral; afterwards the victorious patricians made them a speech of clemency which, the chronicler assures us, left no eye dry.

Such revolts were particularly violent in the great manufacturing centers of Flanders. There the business man was indeed hard-pressed, from without and within—from without by the feudal knights and from within by his own workers. Ypres, the rich weaving-city, experienced such an upheaval in the fourteenth century, when a rebellion of artisans frightened the masters of the textile industry. Fearing, as the nervous burghers explained, that "the good people of the city would be in peril of being murdered by night," they forced the workingmen to move outside the walls. But some time later, feudal knights appeared before the walls and annihilated the labor supply of Ypres, after which prosperity fled the spot for a time.

Labor was almost completely crushed in Nürnberg, the greatest handicraft center in all mediaeval Germany. No gild organizations were permitted, except during a single year, 1348–49, by the Nürnberg patricians, who were peculiarly ingrown and renowned for hauteur, in which they more resembled the Venetians than the men of Lübeck. Under their rule, craftsmen had much less influence than in Worms and Strassburg, for instance; they had to accept meekly every regulation laid down to them by the patrician council. Thus, despite the aura of romantic sentiment in which Nürnberg is nowadays viewed, thanks to Wagner's picture of Hans Sachs, the cobbler-poet, the labor situation was indeed anything but idyllic there, long ago; the cobblers, however poetically gifted, were refused the right to have a meeting-place of their own.

The various revolts among the seamen, weavers, metal-workers and other laborers were not all blind struggles for bread. A considerable growth of revolutionary ideas and doctrines has been traced during the 1300's and 1400's. Across England, France, Italy, Flanders and Germany, spread waves of popular criticism and religiously colored communism. Later, the Anabaptists and other sects sought a return to primitive Christianity, and sometimes "renegades" from the bourgeois circles joined them. One such was the Lübeck merchant, Jürgen Wul-

lenwever, who, in the sixteenth century, went over to help the Anabaptists and the common folk, and, after a brief and dramatic radical
career, ended in a horrible death. Popular songs, pamphlets and romances promulgated dangerous notions, contesting the divine right of
kings and the bourgeois right of private property. In Flanders, for example, Van Maerlant exclaimed that if one could only banish those
two words, *mine* and *thine*, "tranquillity, peace would be assured . . .
everything would be in common, nothing in private . . . all along the
ocean as along the Rhine, one would never see homicide again." Others
voiced admiration of the Swiss republican example.

Republicanism, Communism, Pacifism—it was no wonder that the
terrified business men in the cities formed patrician clubs and brotherhoods in self-defense. These mediaeval "Liberty Leagues" were answers to the unrest below. Some of these were the "White Bears,"
"Black Heads," "The Cats" of Constance, and the "Brotherhood of the
Golden Circle," whose members were entitled to wear special insignia
and hang their coats of arms in the society's chapel at Lübeck. The object of such groups, Flemish, Italian, French or German, was to retain
social privileges, like the right to wear high hats or ermine, to dance in
the Rathaus, and to monopolize political advantages in laying taxes and
letting contracts.

Relatively, as examinations of mediaeval tax-lists tend to show, the
rich were probably as rich then as they are today. Property does not
seem to have been distributed with conspicuous equality in the age of
gilds and handicrafts, which appears so romantic nowadays because it
is remote. In Augsburg in 1471, as Sombart points out, over 65 per
cent of the population had no property at all; in parts of the Rhineland, a mere 3 per cent held a third of the urban wealth. At Paris, a
mere 1 per cent paid 27 per cent of the taxes. Such estimates agree with
those of classical antiquity, when 2000 rich men were said to rule
Rome, and they may be paralleled with modern groups, such as the
two hundred bankers said to own France, and the fifty key men reputed to control American business. In truth, the White Bears or the
jealous Cats, or other patrician groups, were but small cliques clinging
to wealth and power in the face of popular discontent inside their cities, and in constant danger of siege from knightly enemies without.

BUSINESS ADMINISTRATIONS

On the whole, the patrician must be said to have exhibited a high
degree of organizing and administrative ability. His reign over the
towns was at least the equal in efficiency of that maintained over the
furrows by feudal lords.

Under patrician rule, the cities developed municipal government; the English towns had elaborate constitutions before a Magna Charta was wrung from a reluctant king for England as a whole. Ideas of budgeting expenditures were common in cities, while monarchs were still royally negligent about the state of their coffers. At first, patricians attempted to rule the towns without accounting to the public any more than feudal lords accounted to their serfs, but it was finally necessary to give the community some notion of what was being done with taxes. No doubt the city-fathers at times juggled accounts, since, as Vanderkindere suggests, it was so easy to mislead simple citizens not acquainted with the Arabic zero and incapable of doing sums in the head. Town councils were prone to nepotism and contract-letting to fellow-members. It is a cynical and weary voice of the 1100's that we hear raised against the rich, asking why they bothered to buy the office of sheriff: "Is it because they seek to do justice? Far from it. It is for the profit they get out of it." But not all cities were always run badly; the complaints against the Lübeck Senate were directed more at its exclusiveness than at its peculations.

The intercity and international ramifications of business also challenged the patricians to build up codes of practice which were widely accepted. The maritime laws of the Middle Ages were developed by the merchants, who owned the ships, not by princes who stayed on land. At such regular markets as the early French fair of Champagne, moreover, where merchants came from many regions, there had to be machinery for the peaceful handling of disputes; Champagne, where Roman tradition and German custom merged in France, laid a basis for modern commercial codes. The cities, constantly quarreling among themselves, had to consider the protection of their members who resided abroad, and therefore built up consulate systems. In short, the generalization may be hazarded that feudalism achieved some international law on the land and in war, whereas mediaeval business created the basis of international law in peace and on the sea.

Business liked to settle disputes by courts, whereas feudal knights, shrinking from a contest of wits, preferred to decide an issue by combat. In fact, knights considered legal action dishonorable. The contrast of minds was clearly illustrated in the case of the Italian cities, which, as early as 1168, were desirous of resorting to arbitration; their efforts were, however, cut short sternly by the German Emperor, Frederick II, to whose chivalric-absolutistic mentality such a pacifistic notion was highly repugnant.

Within their own walls, the cities forbade trial by combat, the knightly way of handling cases, and substituted trial by evidence. Perhaps this meant merely the substitution of the rule of the rich for that of the strong, much of the time; at any rate, the mediaeval poor complained loudly that judges looked the other way "when there was a matter touching their own interest or that of a friend." Still it was a step toward civilization when the masters of society began to use their brains instead of their fists to protect property.

For honor, the knightly code, the business man substituted honesty, which is another matter altogether. The chivalric knight had indeed to support his liege lord, but the restrictions on his native impulses were otherwise few. He could freely rejoice in riotous acts of robbery and violence against anyone else, like that German Junker who estimated that he "had stolen so many horses that if one tied them together heads to tails they would form a line three miles long." The pride of many a "proud old family" was nourished by such exploits. Not so, that of the bourgeois; the conduct of a soap business required a nicer and more extensive set of scruples than the management of a fief.

Upon a widespread sense of honesty in mediaeval Europe, as in old China, depended the very life of commerce. The Hanse League, the Rhenish League, and other institutions, were founded upon good faith in the spoken and written word of merchants. So was the successful exchange of Northern metals for Southern silks which brought wealth to German and Italian trading-groups in the 1340's. The standards of merchants, in regard to living up to obligations, was so much higher than that of contemporary feudal lords, that cities were sometimes called upon to arbitrate between dukes, or act as guarantors to treaties. Thus the cities of Brabant agreed to seize and sell the properties of John I, if he broke an agreement with another prince.

An urban commercial community required more appearance of decorum among its members than was expected of chivalric gentlemen. A knight was supposed, to be sure, to restrain any native impulse he might have to slay female orphans of high rank (his code was not intended to protect humbler orphans). But in Nürnberg, even cursing rendered a man liable to the pillory. Certain puritanic traits were strongly in evidence in pre-puritan times. Records of the old towns are filled with accounts of malefactors set right, with grisly punishments. One may read, for instance, how Willame de Schachtelweghe was marked with a hot iron and banished for seven years for falsifying an official lead seal on inferior dress-goods, or how Tristan Scorboot was condemned to make a pilgrimage from Flanders to Provence for having uttered impertinent words to a bailiff. Flemish cities decreed that men guilty of leading disorderly lives should be ineligible to office—a fiat that, had it been extended to dukes, must have vacated most of the duchies.

The merchant found his every step hedged in by regulations. His bourgeois code enjoined upon him not merely consideration for female orphans of good family, but a certain standard of fair dealing for sailors and apprentices. It was, in many places, illegal for a master entrepreneur to cuff an artisan; in Nürnberg, a *bourgeoise* of the best patrician circle was clapped into jail for attempting to cut off her cook's nose with a carving knife. No doubt, merchants and their wives were often as harsh as circumstances permitted—for the patrician rulers of cities used quite commonly to set the poor outside the city gates to perish, during a siege, while only those persons of substance, who had their own food, were kept inside the walls. But, on the whole, merchants were less brutal toward their dependents than the lords toward their serfs.

While the business governors might be benevolent toward the inhabitants of their towns, and might be cordial in their relations among themselves, they were, however, generally very repressive toward the surrounding peasantry. In a wide radius about their city walls, as far as they could control things, they stamped out village industries which might rival their own; moreover they fixed tariffs for the grain which peasants had to deliver in the city markets, and were cordially hated by the yokelry in return.

A case of this conflict between city and land is afforded by the contest between the Flemish city of Ypres and the village of Poperinghe. Ypres went to law to restrain the latter from imitating her good grades of cloth. The villagers declared that nobody would now buy the coarse stuffs which they formerly made, as living standards were rising, and so they could not help changing their production. The towns of Ghent and Bruges acted as umpires in this dispute; the documents in the case, running to 180 pages, show how mediaeval men, in the thirteenth century, had to strain their minds to find lofty arguments for economic interest.

The villagers of Poperinghe based their contention upon the God-given natural right to work: "The pretensions of Ypres violate natural law, evangelical law and charity, since they tend to prevent Christians from getting their bread freely." To this, the Ypres industrialists replied that "Adam only possessed natural right before the Fall," and he lost it, when he left Paradise. Further, said the men of Ypres, their prosperity was essential to the well-being of the whole land: "The interest of the country is against having many little towns making defective cloth and defrauding foreign merchants." But, nothing daunted, Poperinghe answered:

> The men of Ypres cannot invoke public interest. . . . That resides in the diffusion of industry. Flanders would be more rich if

the little towns like Poperinghe, Dixmude, Furnes, Bergues made as much as Ypres. And even if the cloth-industry of Poperinghe did damage to that of Ypres, that would be no reason to violate the natural liberty. . . . The good of all should be above the good of the few.

Inflexibly, the big men confronted the little men, declaring: "The arguments of Poperinghe are poor cement that will never erect a wall of defense." The villagers stubbornly returned their gaze and announced: "The words of Ypres are seeds falling on a stone." They joined forces with revolting artisans within Ypres.

The only argument to which the industrialists of Ypres, or of other towns, could not resort in such disputes, was loyalty. For business tried to dispense with that feudal principle. The régime of the business governors was founded upon bourgeois honesty, but not upon feudal honor. It held society together by contract, not homage; it substituted the elaborate machinery of the law for the few and simple principles of feudal allegiance.

This was inevitable, since every problem of the business man was so much more complex than that of the agrarian lord. Allegiance settled most issues for the feudal gentlemen: either one was a vassal or a suzerain, paid tribute or received it. The relationship could only be altered by force, or marriage, not by a shrewd bargain or a clever lawyer. But the relationships between business men were much more shifting. Makers of money could climb more subtly, and it could never be so easy to determine their degrees of subordination to one another. In the landed aristocracy, it was possible to bind men together in a mesh of loyalties, from which none escaped; even at the top, the Black Prince still proudly appeared with the motto, "Ich dien"—I serve. But the business man viewed his fellows, not as vassals or superiors, but as consumers or competitors—often both at once. Even if he conquered them, he could not claim loyalty from either, for essentially, his motto was "Ich verdien" —I profit. His loyalty was to a city unit, at best, but was not capable of indefinite extension.

It was, therefore, more difficult for the business man to extend his conquests beyond the city walls, and form large amalgamations of territories. The feudal lord could seize huge dominions and bind them all together with tribute and fealty, leaving the agricultural state unchanged. Whenever a business city enlarged its boundaries, however, it tended to alter the economic life around it. Thus Florence "freed" the serfs in the surrounding regions, but razed rival towns, slew their inhabitants, or branded them with the red lily, and transplanted them to new sites of industry. But it did not build up a hierarchy in industries and commerce; only in modern times, under the trust system, has that been approached.

Feudalism, in short, was a system based upon honor, and administered with brutality. Mediaeval commerce was based upon profit, and operated with honesty watched over by courts. The former made empires. The latter made civilization.

CIVILIZATION IN THE CITIES

European townsmen were turning to the improvement of their cities by paving, rudimentary street lighting, fire prevention and building laws, while the castles were still very largely insanitary stone slums. Burghers were supporting the poor by municipal doles and in charity asylums and were erecting hospitals, while good works in the country were left chiefly to the Church. Frankfurt in mediaeval times was advanced enough to have a city doctor. Nürnberg took the first step toward community health supervision when it hired a man, even if only one, to clean its streets.

On the Continent, in the late 1400's, the merchants of cities were rapidly forging ahead of the lower ranks of the feudal nobility. They outshone all but the highest lords in luxury. The poet Deschamps, in 1383, leaving the city of Brussels with regret, apostrophized it as the capital of good cheer: "Adieu, Brussels . . . fine rooms, Rhine wines, soft beds . . . capon and pheasant . . . gentle company and courteous folk." Unlike a modern bard, Deschamps was too well acquainted with discomfort to cavil at its opposite.

The comfort-hungry German bourgeois, even in mediaeval days, demanded a certain amount of plumbing, and had pipes to bring water from the wells to the kitchens. There were towns baths until the spread of social diseases in the Renaissance made them inadvisable. In fact, the burghers were castigated for their love of ease by popular evangelists, and looked down upon with scorn by the hard-riding and rough-living knighthood—a scorn in which, however, envy of wealth and fear of its subtle power were mingled.

There can be little doubt that the profound gulf between Germany and England in the matter of comfort today is due to the comparatively greater influence of the independent merchant-rulers in the former country in previous ages. In England, where the burghers soon knuckled under to the monarchs, and aristocratic tastes prevailed, the characteristic noble disdain for piping and heating persisted and was accepted. The Hanse Germans might have introduced some alterations had they been permitted to keep their Steelyard in London a few generations longer, until the tile oven was perfected in German towns. But the Hanseatics were ousted before they had a chance to bring England up to Continental standards of bourgeois living.

In Europe, the contrast between the dwellings of the bourgeois and of the minor nobility was astonishing. The noblemen had to spend their means upon strengthening their bastions. The citizens of the towns, trusting to community defenses, could consult their tastes in building habitations. Hence business offices in Germany were cozy nests, paneled in wood, warm with rugs and tapestries, adorned with paintings; one southern German office held a frieze of industrial processes, which has survived; in another building in Lüneburg, once a mediaeval counting-house and now used as headquarters by an automobile firm, the ceiling is carved with a scene depicting Christ driving out the money-changers. On one grand, massive desk of an early business man is still to be seen the delightful inscription: "A new spirit is abroad in the land; it is called 'oil my palm' [an expression for bribing]—if you don't oil my palm, your business will have no good end."

The family apartments, usually under the same roof, in Germany, were equally comfortable. By the 1400's, windows were often filled with rich-hued panes of glass; beds were soft with feathers; a buffet displayed silver dishes and goblets for family festivals; candlesticks, chandeliers and a mirror brightened dark interiors. Before the roaring blaze in the fireplace, or a more modern ornamental oven, stood a long settee cushioned for a doze; here the business man reposed in the long winter season, September to February, when ships were not permitted to sail for distant ports and the roads were impassable.

Of course, the feudal gentry made a great display of fine clothes, but they were hard pressed by the ambitious burghers. Even royalty had occasion to be envious of townsmen, as when a Queen of France expressed her dismay at being outshone at a ball in Madgeburg by wives of business men, wearing toilettes sewn with pearls and emeralds and worth up to $400 (in modern money) apiece. It was also not unusual for high-born dames in local castles to stay home from tournaments because, as they fretfully told their liege lords, they had nothing fit to wear in the company of burgher women.

Merchant circles have ever had the tendency to achieve in fashion the distinction they cannot easily gain through titles, and so it was in the Middle Ages. When the merchant was forbidden to advertise his wares, he was all the more eager to show off his person, majestically draped in fur and golden chains. He was not always subtle in his choice of methods. The rich traders of Thuringia, who wore little bells on their girdles that tinkled at every step, can hardly escape the charge of being a little *loud* in their dress.

Sons of merchants knew no bounds to their extravagance and were undeterred by luxury laws or the railings of preachers. Patrician heirs, whenever they could escape the paternal eye in the countinghouse, liked to stroll about in curious attire, "cow-muzzle" shoes, or that pop-injay costume composed of as many bright-hued pieces "as there are days in a year," a style so fantastic that it is now chiefly remembered as the garb of court fools and jesters, but once represented the effort of young business men to exhibit the "Old Man's" money.

Wives and widows were also glad to be the walking symbols of commercial wealth, their husbands' or their own. As tax-lists in mediaeval Germany show, widows tended to concentrate in their hands the business fortunes—a phenomenon familiar to modern America. There were groups of very rich and often independent burgher women who vied with one another in jewels, high heels and especially high hats. The romantic *hennin*, the towering sharp-pointed headdress of the times, was in reality a charming barometer that rose or fell according to the condition of the family exchequer. Its height indicated private means as much as that of the cathedral spire showed community resources. Rich Lübeck women were notoriously jealous in this regard, and would not let any poor merchant's wife presume to "high hat" them.

On the whole, therefore, the prosperous commercial classes had little reason to envy the lesser nobility in matters of comfort. The German Junkers shivered in draughty stone halls, living with their horses and pigs in filthy familiarity, and nourishing themselves insufficiently upon thin beer and herring-soup, as Ulrich von Hutten complained; while the burghers warmed themselves before their gleaming ovens and dined rather too well. The townsmen of Europe had cash assets, while the nobility was "land-poor." The single city of Florence, in the 1400's, yielded a greater annual revenue to its government than the whole of England, a hundred years later, could scrape up for Queen Elizabeth.

Continental business men had little reason to tremble even before kings. Royalty was then not so majestic as it was later to become, in the 1600's. Even Popes had at times to pawn their tiaras to bankers. The earlier kings of England submitted to galling terms from Italian financiers who thought the credit of the British Crown so shaky that they could consider nothing less than 230 per cent interest. German kings had to borrow silver dishes from usurers to impress their brides. Almost any well-to-do brewer or lumberman on the Continent was better off, among his polished plate and fine linen, than that Irish king of the 1400's, whom an Italian traveler descried among his shoeless courtiers, squatting at dinner, and having as his only "special mark of distinction, a bundle of tender hay beside him upon which to wipe his mouth."

Nor was it merely in liquidity of assets that the business men were ahead of the feudality. Education was more widespread among towns-

men than in the country. While castle dwellers were but slowly progressing in their letters, and still listened to wandering bards, the Italian
and German merchants in the 1400's were collecting fine libraries. Some
Hanse cities, knowing how education paid in business returns, founded
universities; Cologne and Rostock followed the example of Paris, Bologna and Heidelberg. Helping poor students to finish courses was a
favorite form of benefaction among wealthy traders. The cities also
struggled long and bitterly against the Church for the right to form
lay schools. Ypres suffered excommunication in this cause, but persisted; Lübeck, Hamburg and Leipzig were among the first founders
of lay schools in Germany.

 The townsmen's greater knowledge drew into their hands the power
of technology. Business men were undisputed masters of the ocean. As
Sombart has said, with a touch of exaggeration, "No knight has ever
gone to sea." The chivalric gentlemen were too poor to buy ships, too
uninstructed to build them, and too proud to learn. Up to the commencement of modern times, well into the sixteenth century, there
were no considerable royal navies; whenever kings or lords wished to
travel by water or wage sea warfare, they had to rent some vessels from
merchants.

 In the 1400's, the business men of Europe had in their possession a
technological secret which might have enabled them to control the land
as well as the water. That was the art of making cannon and gunpowder, which developed especially in the German cities of that period.
The capitalists of urban communities had the funds for extensive mining and experiments in metal-working; the most skilled artisans were at
their command. They could make better implements of war than the
smiths of the noblemen. And, as the German business men produced
the best cannon and the finest suits of armor, so the Italian cities made
the swords with the keenest cutting edges.

THE ERA OF GREAT OPPORTUNITY

 To sum up, the patrician rulers had immense resources of cash and
education. Their citadels were planted in strategic sites and connected
by far-flung systems of communication and organization. Their technical superiority gave them command of sea and, had they wished, of
land. What might they not have done with this superiority?

 Conceivably, the cities might have remained impregnable; their governors might have sallied forth with muskets and cannon and defeated
the feudal arrays, and battered down the castles along the Rhine and
elsewhere. They might have crushed the forces of feudalism, the then
comparatively weak kings and impoverished nobility. A bourgeois Eu-

rope might have been established in the Quattrocento. Why was this an impossible dream? Why did not the business sovereigns of Europe branch out from the city nucleus and extend their rule over the wider territories beyond their gates? Was it some fatal flaw in the character of business men which prevented them from building and dominating nations as well as cities?

In search of an answer, we are led to look at the three most significant centers of business government in Europe: Lübeck, in northern Germany, head of the Hanseatic League and hence mistress of a trading empire extending from Novgorod to London; Florence, in Italy, whose financial and industrial empire reached from Naples to London; and Venice, which took the Near East as a province. In these three cities, during the Quattrocento, patrician abilities and disabilities were displayed in their fullness. In them, the sovereignty of business men may be examined in utmost detail and watched in its glory and its slow disintegration.

IV

MEDIAEVAL LÜBECK—
A REGULATED COMMERCIAL SOCIETY

THE BALTIC CITY OF LÜBECK, left stranded by receding tides of trade in the 1500's, has preserved her original aspect to a remarkable degree. She still possesses squat-towered gates of reddish brown brick now mellowed to a rare old plum-pudding hue; a group of curiously gabled warehouses along the water-front; patrician homes with carved doorways; an unusual Rathaus and a fine set of tall church spires coated in sea-green copper. These, like so many other architectural relics in Europe, testify to the departure of mediaeval prosperity.

Life presented unending fluctuations to the business man of the Middle Ages, however stagnant it may have been in lonely castles and remote monasteries. Traffic routes were perpetually shifting and leaving fair cities to decay; thus Champagne, in the thirteenth century a meeting-place of Italian and German merchants, was deserted as roads improved and direct communication over the Alps increased. Unforeseen accidents destroyed other towns; at Bruges, for example, sand silted into the canal until big ships could not enter, and trade moved away, leaving warehouses empty and forlorn. Ceaseless changes of style and processes played their part even in the pre-mechanical age. Moreover, a wholesale decimation of customers might unexpectedly occur at any time through plague, famine or war.

Tax-lists reveal swift declines in property and population from time to time, and the production statistics of manufacturing centers disclose the very opposite of stability. At Ypres, for instance, the amount of cloth officially stamped was not the same for two years running; in 1305, it was thirty thousand pieces, but the next year, only fifteen hundred. Thus it was probably even harder to keep investments intact in the Middle Ages than now. The most splendid upsurge of wealth was regularly followed by acute crisis or gradual decay, during which the building trades languished and citizens were forced to patch up their old houses and make them do for generations to come.

The glorious evidences of bygone disasters are scattered over Europe: Bruges, Nürnberg, Dinkelsbühl, Rothenburg, and scores of other places attest the collapse of trade. To a large extent, indeed, the survival of Gothic and Renaissance art is a depression phenomenon. Tourists from "Business America" do well, therefore, to pass reverently among these monuments of the Old World and linger awhile with uncovered heads in the presence of frozen assets so sublime.

Lübeck, however, is more than a "ghost-town," an empty shell like Venice. Better than the former mistress of the Adriatic, the old ruler of the Baltic has happened to preserve her spirit as well as her architecture. As Thomas Mann, the great novelist and scion of a business family of Lübeck, declares in an essay on the town of his birth, there yet stalks down her shadowed lanes an apparition, "spectral, pallid," of the "hysterical Middle Ages . . . one would not be overly surprised if . . . even nowadays there burst out an epidemic of the St. Vitus' Dance or a Children's Crusade."

Mann's detailed novel on the decay of a family of merchant-princes, "Buddenbrooks," brought him the antagonism of Lübeck and a Nobel Prize, much as Sinclair Lewis won world fame by distressing Gopher Prairie and Zenith City. Nor is the life viewed by Mann in Lübeck wholly unlike that perceived by Lewis in the American Main Street; both are marked by narrow provinciality; in both, business men are represented as having scant concern with ideas. Only one character, the last of the *Buddenbrooks*, chances to open a volume of philosophy, which weights the scales in Lübeck's favor; but, to make the balance even again, the women of the *Buddenbrooks*, occupied by culinary works, do not discuss literature even at second hand in a Thanatopsis Club. If the *Buddenbrooks* do not dwell on different intellectual planes from the *Babbitts*, neither can they pretend to a nobler indifference to money, as the sordid marriages into which poor *Toni Buddenbrooks* is forced only too clearly betray.

Yet the *Buddenbrooks* can be distinguished from the *Babbitts*. The difference is largely one of heritage. The life of the Lübeck family is hallowed and given significance by ceremony and tradition; apparel, speech and behavior are determined by the feeling of caste obligation; the sense of family duty and continuity lends meaning to every action, even Toni's sacrifices. The "grand old woman" of the *Buddenbrooks*, the *Frau Consulin*, is supported on her deathbed to the last moment by the almost royal hauteur of the patrician.

This aristocratization of business, while unknown in Zenith City, might be paralleled in America, to some extent, among shipping families of New England or the South, Boston or Charleston. But in Lübeck, where an ingrown caste of wholesalers has retained social supremacy for more than seven hundred years, there are, in Mann's estimation, symptoms of an overripe morbidity, a "nervous eccentricity," which is more Hapsburg than American, and could hardly be duplicated on a younger continent in a mere century or two.

THE TOWN

The best view of Lübeck is obtained today by a traveler approaching from a westerly direction on a late summer evening, when the light, in that latitude, continues bright and serene until nine or ten at night. It is in that enchanted, unnatural glow, that one should catch the first glimpse of Lübeck's cluster of tarnished spires.

The towers of a mediaeval community, like the skyscrapers of an American town today, wrote a business graph of the region upon the sky. This correlation has been shown by Bechtel; he has related the height of cathedrals to the rise of wealth from trading or mining in Nürnberg, Augsburg, Ravensburg and elsewhere. Ulm, for instance, had originally planned a modest tower, but a sudden boom sent it into a magnificent uprush of lateral line. Similarly, the unfinished roofs of other edifices testify, not so much to the dwindling faith as to a shrinking commodity index. And thus, even from a long distance, one may judge the character of Lübeck by her stupendous cones, sheathed in metal, green as the cold northern sky into which they shoot. Narrow, straight, purposeful, devoid of any trifling byplay of ornament, they are the fitting emblems of the doughty Baltic business men who reared them.

Like a ship, revealed by her mast-tops long before her lower bulk rides into view, Lübeck is first discovered by her spires, and for a long time, these dominate the horizon. But at last the grand spectacle unfolds as a whole: all the steep shapes catching the light upon their points and shining together on an eminence above a river. Beneath them lie the remains of an old brick rampart that once confined the city to her hilly island. And then one perceives that, if Lübeck is like a ship, it is a grim man-o'-war.

Cathedral chimes above, cannon below—so a German city had to be prepared to defend as well as symbolize her wealth. She had need for deep moats and bristling ramparts for, in Germany, the nobility was peculiarly aggressive. Knights were more powerful than in Italy, and less restrained by a royal hand than in England or in France. They rendered the roads unsafe by their exploits, catching and squeezing any insufficiently escorted "figsacks" or "peppersacks," as they derisively called the merchants. An indication of their chivalric temper may be found in the titles of address they preferred: a squire wished to be called *vir robustus*, while a knight insisted upon *vir strenuus*. Both scorned the appellations of *viri honorabiles, discreti, circumspecti, probi* or *honesti*, reserved for common traders. Being honest or even honorable was far less of a social asset than being robust and strenuous.

The robust element in Germany was in the majority; less than a quarter of the population, it has been estimated, lived in towns in the Middle Ages. The cities were scattered far apart over a wide expanse of hostile agrarian territory. They were, to repeat the ship-image, like tiny, lonely stone vessels riding at great intervals upon a broad green ocean of field and forest. The pastures rippled right up to their outer defenses, for it was not safe to erect houses or shops outside the walls. Maurauding nobleman nipped the bud of any suburbia. The bourgeois was still the Man-in-a-Burg, the croucher-behind-a-wall. It is a contradiction in terms to call a "suburbanite," as many do now, a "typical bourgeois."

But perhaps because they were so threatened in Germany, the German city-men learned to stand together, lending one another arms and funds to resist sieges, in a fashion quite unknown among the quarreling Italian communes. They had more need of solidarity than ever in the Quattrocento, when knights had returned in numbers from the Crusades, ferocious, impoverished and with appetites whetted by Eastern luxuries. Such knights fell upon the merchants as they had fallen upon the paynim: under the bastions of the rich towns were encamped the tented armies of the war-lords, and before the gates caracoled the plumed and harnessed *viri strenui*. No doubt there were colorful scenes aplenty, fit to delight the imagination of latter-day romanticists, but they were not viewed with a poetic eye by the prosaic dealers in beer, hemp and herring within the gates. These, *viri discreti*, were too busy boiling oil and melting lead.

From 1450 onward, the funds of the German cities were more and more diverted to fortification; and Burgomaster Castorp began to raise the defenses of Lübeck. To be sure, cathedral building continued from 1350 to 1500 in full glory, but, gradually, alarm overmastered pride. To the first hundred years of hope expressed in architecture, succeeded fifty years of fear.

The energies and resources of the German burghers were greatly absorbed in the community enterprises of religion and war; they did not have enough left over to erect splendid individual palaces for themselves, as the richer and more fortunate Italians in the same century were able to do. And hence, as one enters the old core of Lübeck, one finds the homes of the patricians unexpectedly diminutive beside the looming shapes of churches and walls.

After all, though Lübeck looks so mighty and imposing, viewed from afar, it is in fact very small, not more than an armed village. Ordinary towns in the Middle Ages had probably only five thousand inhabitants; Cologne alone of the Hanse League had thirty thousand; no city in England in the 1400's, except London, was as large as the German centers of Lübeck and Nürnberg, with twenty thousand. And their commercial dealings were in keeping with their size: the yearly turnover of goods of such a place as Lübeck could nowadays be brought in two or three trips by a modern steamship.

Small as it was, the town was overcrowded. So narrow was the ring of walls, and so high in consequence the value of ground, that lots were narrow and buildings were set sideways, presenting their ornamented gable-ends to the street. The outward bulge and overhanging façades threw the alleys into a tunnel-like darkness; only here and there, even at high noon, could the sun, like a besieging duke, drop golden shafts of light into the heart of the town. By three o'clock, the sun's trajectory was too flat, and he had to retire from the attack, leaving the booths dim; then the working day, which began at four in the morning, light or no light, was over, and the affluent tradesmen retired to their hotly peppered roasts.

The picturesque chaos of mediaeval cities was thus as much the product of real estate conditions as the haphazard design of modern Manhattan; their little lanes were as congested, relatively, as the greater canyons of today. For lack of space, the home of the merchant was also his warehouse. He unloaded wagons in the courtyard and hoisted his goods with block and tackle to a storage attic; in the rear he stabled his horses among his pigs and fowl. Offices and living quarters were under a single roof—the case too in Hamburg down to the last century. Even the grandest of these homes, despite the distinction of their beautifully carved doorways, are diminutive to modern eyes—the house of the *Buddenbrooks* would not serve today as a gatekeeper's lodge in Newport or Greenwich—and would also have seemed tiny to a Venetian or Florentine of the Quattrocento. There was nothing at Lübeck to compare in any respect with the palaces of the Medici in Italy.

Yet in this little place, this curious, cramped barrow of brick, there grew and was perpetuated a fierce pride, a pride of clan, class and community, which overtops the confidence of far richer and vaster modern aggregations of men. Perhaps, indeed, the very confinement of life to such concentrated quarters developed the talents and social cohesion in Lübeck which are lacking in the greater and more diffused commercial circles of today. Even in modern business, strength has been constantly recruited from small towns and farms.

Lübeck was the head of the Hanse League, made up at one time of ninety cities; under her presidency, from the thirteenth to the seventeenth century, a mighty trading empire was carved out, stubbornly and skillfully defended, and slowly, piecemeal, relinquished. The last Hansetag, or convention of the League, was held in 1699; only then did Lübeck admit her defeat.

Most of the secretarial work of the League devolved upon the men of Lübeck, who were expected to give their time, without pay, not only to the local government but also to the broader activities of the Hanse. These latter were of a diversified character indeed. The League had to make the cities pay their dues; lend arms to members in distress; capture pirates; judge claims in countless suits for damages; compel the King of England to pay for masses to be sung for the souls of merchants flung into the sea by Englishmen; sue the King of France for goods ruined by his troops; manipulate the elections of the kings of Denmark; and thrust an expert hand into the affairs of the emperors of Germany, besides forcing an "open door" on reluctant cities of Italy. Cajoling, decreeing, threatening, boycotting, and often enough leading expansionist warfare—here was work enough for the little group of patricians in the village of Lübeck. It was scarcely a wonder if they lacked the time, as well as the room, to rear themselves wider mansions.

THE HANSE: A BUSINESS BROTHERHOOD

As a rule, the Rathaus in German cities was a single edifice housing both the merchants' exchange and the offices of government. This removed any possible misapprehension about the nature of the ruling class. Hamburg, Bremen and Cologne were thus specific; if Lübeck had two buildings, side by side, for business and administration, it was merely because both had outgrown ordinary bounds.

Much ingenuity was lavished upon the decoration of these seats of patrician power. Hamburg had a painting of the Day of Judgment which showed knights, princes and even Popes being pitchforked into hell, while hard-working grocers and drapers were being raised in bourgeois triumph to the right hand of God. In other towns, the classics were levied upon for suitable themes: the magistrates' chairs were adorned with figures of Cicero, who had once called wholesale operations respectable, and of Seneca, who, being a rich man and a philosopher, once pointed out that riches might be commendable in the hands of a philosopher.

Most of the southern German Rathäuser gained their present form at the end of the Renaissance. And none of the mediaeval edifices, according to Schäfer, "can compare in size and splendor with that of Lübeck." The foundations of her Rathaus go back to the middle of the thirteenth century. Nearly seven hundred years ago it was the seat of a strong merchant administration. In this hall assembled the delegates of scores of cities, together with the ambassadors of foreign potentates, on the solemn occasion of the Hansetag, the greatest of mediaeval business men's conventions.

In the Rathaus the delegates sat with strict regard to precedence, and with much heart-burning. On the right side sat Bremen and Cologne; on the left, very jealous, Hamburg. Ever since Hamburg began to brew better beer than Bremen, reports a chronicler, her pride had increased with her wealth; failing to achieve a place beside Bremen, as she wished, she once played a naughty trick on her neighbor. The delegates of Hamburg sent their horses and servants home and thus could live cheaply during the Hansetag; those from Bremen, keeping their escorts at great expense, used up their money soon and had to go home early. In the absence of the Bremen men, the Hamburg contingent signed the documents in their stead. A fine, hearty mediaeval quarrel was the result.

That sort of squabbling called for all the tact possessed by Lübeck's great burgomaster, Jordan Pleskow, and it tested the patience, skill, and eloquence of such statesmen as Heinrich Castorp. It was no easy matter to keep mediaeval city men, with their local fanaticism, in any sort of order. To hold merchants of such different types and experiences to a long-range program and enforce regulation upon them was an amazing achievement. Among the members of the League were country hamlets and large seaports, Prussian, Wendic, Saxon, Westphalian. Naturally, men from East European Reval would differ from those of Amsterdam. Small towns were loath to aid the larger; delegates from little Saltbommel or Billerbeck, from Roop or Hamm, from Goldingen or Hindelopen, were apt not to appreciate the far-stretching interests of Cologne which might involve them all in expensive negotiations or long foreign wars. The cities of the interior, "over the heath," were as unconcerned by questions of foreign diplomacy as, in our time, are Middle Western American towns; they often refused to aid the seaports—Lüneburg in 1444 denying help to Lübeck on the ground that, being far from the ocean, she had no interest in sea trade. She did not lift her eyes over the heath and enquire where her own salt went beyond the ports.

The main object of the Hanse was the control of the exchange of raw products from the East and North of Europe, such as salted fish and ship-timber, against the manufactured goods of South and West Europe. "Factories," or branch offices, were set up in every zone, from Russia and Norway to Venice, London, Flanders and the Rhine cities. These privileges and monopolies had to be won and kept with a strong hand. Almost perpetual war was the result.

The Slavs and Danes had to be beaten and humbled again and again;

Flanders, Sweden, Scotland, England had to be forced into surrendering their trade into Hanseatic hands. As the Hanse men boasted, they compelled England to sell her wool cheap to them, and buy it back dear, in the shape of Flemish cloth. The Hanse played the same game with England's wool that England, centuries later, played with India's cotton.

But while the Hanse League sought to extend her mighty dominions and appeared insatiable in her ambition, she tried at the same time to repress aggressive individuals in her member-cities. She wanted her people to be aggressive abroad, but humble and cooperative at home. Her ideal was the mighty and jealous community, made up of many little men.

The Hanse tried to crush speculative tendencies among them; in 1417, a solemn conclave laid down the principle that no man should buy grain before it was grown, cloth before it was woven, or herring before they were caught. Advertising was strictly forbidden; the merchants displayed their wares side by side in the great cloth-halls or markets, and it was a punishable offense for any one of them to call out to a customer or praise his wares to the disadvantage of his brethren. The community watched over its members to give them all a fair start; it limited the entry of new men, lest there be too much competition; it regulated city tariffs and prices so that the supply of grain and meat might be steady and cheap for the city-dwellers, however much the peasants might curse and groan.

To uphold the fair name of the Hanse wares, it was necessary to issue business codes, setting forth rules of conduct and standards of value for the scores of member-cities. Naturally, every step in this direction was resisted by local men seeking to preserve the luxuriant growth of mediaeval custom; this town wanted to keep its own shape of wine-tub, while that town objected to turning out a uniform grade of cloth. To bring order out of this chaos was difficult; that business men could perform this feat themselves, without the interposition of a higher impartial power, seems miraculous.

Over the world, the goods of a Hanse merchant were known to be unvaryingly "as represented." They were kept on a very high level of excellence and reliability. It is true that the League dealt largely in wares which could be graded and supervised and controlled in price, such as grain, timber, salt, English wool and Russian furs, wax, honey, beer, hops, bacon and rosaries. Lübeck did a rushing export business of carved wooden prayer beads to Italy; and strangely enough this rosary production was one of the first industries in Europe to attempt standardization. By the 1400's, the making of rosaries was no longer on a handicraft basis; it had gone over to the "putting-out" system; small capitalists supplied funds and materials to poor families who were paid small wages for the work. It is one of the curiosities of economic history that modern industrial capitalism, which destroyed mediaeval religious values, should have thus burst through in the mass production of prayer beads.

Besides the uniformity of goods, Lübeck strove for a standardized coinage. She held her own money to a standard of excellence which was only equaled by the Italian city of Florence, and was never even approached by the debased currencies of contemporary kings or princes. Success, it must be admitted, demanded unrelaxed severity. Counterfeiting was punished as drastically as treason. In the 1400's, one counterfeiter was publicly boiled in oil in the marketplace before the door of Lübeck's Rathaus.

Thus the German as well as the Italian cities in the Middle Ages laid the foundations for the policy of business regulation later known as "mercantilism." The business communities of the mediaeval period practiced self-control over the supply of grain and the value of currencies. In the seventeenth century, when absolutist princes had taken over most of the city-states, they merely continued the established practice, but they controlled business in the interests of wider areas, greater commonwealths and for purposes of higher power. Only when his activities were directed to the good of a national State did the business man begin to object to regulation as unfair in principle. Only then did he begin to shout for "laissez faire" as God's law, forgetting that he himself originated regulation.

THE MEN

The average Hanse man was not a producer but a handler of goods and a small one at that. He did only the amount of business that his tidy little fortune permitted. The community members were not gathered into big corporative bodies, but each man acted for himself; he moved however in concert with the rest, traveling and dwelling abroad in fraternal groups. How petty individual deals could be is shown by Sombart, who ransacked the records of fifteenth-century Lübeck and found only two entries of over 3,000 marks apiece (modern value, 30,000 marks); most of them ranged in value from $10 to $250 (in modern terms).

The difficulties of transport, as well as the limits of their capital, compelled the Hanse men to cling together. It took a remarkable number of men to move a small amount of goods; Sombart estimated that 252 traders, each handling an average of 56 sacks, carried the annual crop of English wool across the Channel. According to the guess of Schulte, the mass of goods moved by many caravans of merchants over the St. Gotthard Pass in the Alps into northern Europe in the course of a year, in mediaeval times, might easily be whisked through in a single night by one or two freight trains today. This meant that the Hanseatic men had to make incessant journeys to fairs, accompanying their springless, creaking carts, heaped with bales of goods. They could not recline in cozy offices, like the Italian banking-princes, and send out directions by letter; they had to take their wares in armed convoys to Great-Novgorod, or in the teeth of a Baltic gale to Wisby, or by caravan along paths cut in the steep faces of Alpine cliffs. And they had to travel besides on all sorts of diplomatic and trade missions. They spent years away from home, undergoing all manner of risk and hardship, doing the work of their cities and of the League, as well as their own.

One of these men, Andreas Ryff, complained with a wry smile that, after going to thirty markets in a year, he had little rest from saddle-burns. Others growled, in letters to their wives, that they had no time to spare from keeping records. This was hardly surprising, considering that their methods of bookkeeping were as befuddled as their modes of travel were cumbersome.

The earliest surviving German business book, the third oldest in Europe, dated 1305, discovered near Nürnberg, was written in Latin; by the 1400's, German was more usual. Such tomes were not labeled with cold formality, "A-Z," but were cozily known as that black book, or "dat rode Bok." They contained diaries, notes of crops, fairs, household expenses, gifts, deals, and the movements of the florin. They held such careless entries as this: "Owed ten gulden by a man since Whitsuntide. I forget his name." Moreover, the sums, it is now known, were often wrong; for even in the 1400's, the Arabic zero was still an importation from Italy not easily used, and the working of simple problems was a feat tasking the most expert accountant.

The Germans of the Middle Ages were probably busier than the most hustling American captains of industry. Certainly, they were in a real sense "business pioneers," for they had "conquered the wilderness" of the Baltic regions, planting cities and defending them against all comers. They had a sense of independence, too, which we are accustomed to think of as American; they had never felt heavily the yoke of the feudal nobility, and were thus exceptionally free and proud among mediaeval business men. It was very commonly observed by their contemporaries that they were "stiff-necked." An English negotiator at Utrecht in 1474 sighed that he would rather deal with "aller Welt Fürsten"—the princes of all the world—than with emissaries of the Hanse Council.

A harsh upbringing helped to prepare them for a life of rigors.

Reared in the monastic discipline of factories abroad, which were really "business barracks," the young apprentices learned obedience and plain living within a democratic group. They were isolated from the backward peoples, the English or Russian, among whom they dwelled, somewhat as British and Americans later dwelt in "foreign settlements" in China. The Germans were forbidden to intermarry with the natives and seldom stooped to social intercourse.

Interesting documents could be presented, if there were space, showing, on the one hand, the rough education of a North German clerk, undergoing the fraternal "hazing" of his fellow-apprentices in a trading post and, on the other, the gay commencement in trade of a young Venetian elegant, a fledgling with a purse full of gold and a retinue of servants, sent by his papa on a galley to try his luck with a speculation in pepper in Egypt.

Hard, haughty, doughty, keen, the men of Lübeck were of a type as different from the Italians as could well be imagined. In Italy the Venetians were individually much richer than the Germans and operated more in families than in commercial groups like the Hanseatic "factories." Since they dealt in such Eastern luxuries as spices and silks and slaves, they were inclined early to speculation. Speculation, frowned upon at Lübeck, was the life of trade in Venice. The merchants of Florence, moreover, were able to climb up to banking and, through the financial system of the Roman Church, attained a power and a treasure far beyond the dreams of the biggest lumberman of North Germany. A single loan by an Italian banking-family to a Pope might easily be larger than the united income of the merchant community of Lübeck in a year.

The German, being poorer, was necessarily more versatile. While the richer Italian could hire condottieri to fight for him, the German had to be his own admiral and general and conduct campaigns by sea and on land. He had to be, by turns, trader, farmer, orator, diplomat, warrior. As the Italian Machiavelli enviously observed, the German burghers were even at that time the best drilled and the most determined to defend their liberties in Europe.

While Lübeck did the work of the League at her own expense, her patricians served it without material reward. They were naturally not selfless idealists; the weal of the community was the condition of their own private fortunes. They were ruthless toward the artisans and the lesser business men; they clung to their monopoly of social, political and economic advantage. But they did not stoop to petty graft; simply and directly, they took all there was to take. And when they went out to a delicate negotiation or dangerous battle, they accepted the challenge of Fate: if they failed, they had to bear the full measure of reproach; if they succeeded, they were rewarded only by the praise and esteem of their fellow-citizens.

The North Germans never felt humbled by the contrast between their own dark little fog-bound town and the more magnificent cities of the South and East. Undazzled by the glories of Venice on her warmer sea and the pillars and gold mosaic of Byzantium, they went on working in the materials of the North that were congenial to them, incorporating their own strength and dignity in brick and copper. They aped nobody; they wasted no time riding around in a gilded barge like the *Bucentaur* of the Venetians, to "wed the sea"; they tackled the Channel blasts without ceremony in stout ships with good plain names like *The Spotted Cow*. And in a downright fashion, long before the codfish-aristocracy of Boston, they acknowledged their origins by putting carved herrings as coats-of-arms on their family pews.

Though they were less polished and educated than the southern Germans or the Italians, they were as profoundly self-sufficient and well satisfied as the English merchants of a later age. Like them, they never deigned to learn a syllable of a silly foreigner's speech; the Germans made the whole world, save Russia, learn their own pithy talk. They were not inclined to waste words. When a Venetian patrician—Foscari, for example—was condemned to death, the Italian chroniclers, Daenell points out, would describe his emotions with Plutarchian eloquence and make a classic tragedy out of his fall; not so the Lübecker. When some statesman of theirs, perhaps as great a leader as Foscari, fell as ignominiously, their chronicler would quietly observe that he was "gehangen," and let it go at that.

The modern business man represents a blend of the two systems. He leads a life much more akin to that of the old Italian, the rich individualist and speculative financier. But in character he is probably more like the old German, taciturn, thrifty, sober, busy, seldom rising to any pitch of enthusiasm, at the most letting himself go in a boisterous fraternization.

COMMUNITY CULTURE

In whatever direction his restless spirit might turn, the North German found his way shaped by the demands of the group, the club, the clan, the crowd, the community. He did not break through the bonds of the community as completely as the richer Italians, and like them create an individualistic culture of his own.

The Germans, weaker as individuals, found their strength in fellowship. They traveled in groups and lived in colonies abroad. At the German House, which the Hanse owned at Venice for instance, they dined in sections, the men from each city at a separate table. Fraternal beyond the wildest dreams of the American Rotarian brothers, the Germans spent a great portion of their lives "at the club." To be sure, there were "ladies' nights," when wool or wax men and their dames would meet to play cards or practice some of the scandalous new dance-steps of the 1400's. Night after night, however, the men gathered alone to sing ballads and pirate songs and consume incredible quantities of assorted beverages. It might take many men to transport a few sacks of wool abroad, but a few men could carry home the contents of many barrels of beer. Occasionally this tippling led to quarrels, despite the strict rule that all pewter cups damaged by collision with skulls must be paid for by wielders of the same.

These merchant-clubs were not unusually picturesque as far as rites went. Perhaps the ordinary costume was fanciful enough. At any rate, the mediaeval German did not envelop wholesaling with any large amount of romantic pretense. At most, in poetic mood, he might name his club an "Arthur's Court." But rituals of initiation and other mummery he left largely to gilds of journeymen and apprentices.

The color of business life was most in evidence at the periodic markets, gay assemblies opened by pompous processions and enlivened by dancing, juggling, exhibits of menageries and exotic wares. The modern circus goes back to such fairs; but the mediaeval merchant made a circus of business, whereas Barnum made a business of circuses.

Nearly everything the German business man did was done in a crowd. Mobs came together to dance, dine, witness shooting-matches among the workers or jousts between patricians. In Nürnberg, at a festrival, a mediaeval statistician counted on a single day, 1300 wagons and 608 carts passing the gates.

This fraternal spirit expressed itself in an odd commingling of club and ecclesiastical architecture. The brotherhood houses imitated the carved, vaulted halls of the Gothic churches; but in return, thinks Vanderkindere, they contributed to church-design the huge common nave in which a community could sit. The churches in North Germany became like mighty merchant halls. Bechtel has elaborated the thesis that the enormous nave developed in Germany was the expression of a rich business community; certainly the Marienkirche at Lübeck coincided with the rise of the wholesale merchant class. However much the two types of architecture inclined toward each other, the club could always be told from the church by its immense, ramified and well-stocked wine-cellars.

Business men often supervised church art; one priceless record reveals to us a group of Würzburg aldermen determining by majority vote that in the next carving by Tilman Riemenschneider, Adam should be portrayed without a beard. Thus carefully did eminent merchants watch over the minutiae of their community edifices. They went further and made a humming export business of sacred paintings and relics. Lübeck supplied the farthest Baltic regions from her own art workshops and by her imports from Flemish and southern German cities; she was the leading distributor of culture as well as of material goods in the North.

Nearly everything the business man touched tended to mass production. He took up music and achieved chorals; the churches of Lübeck rang with this new mass music. He evolved competitions in singing, in which gilds of butchers, leather-workers or bell-casters competed for the prize of Meistersinger. When he turned to poetry, he formed poets' gilds to which no bard of illegitimate birth need apply—for the German business man, even while nominally a Catholic, was already showing signs of incipient Puritanism and wished to certify Pegasus.

Drama has ever been the natural manifestation of the business community. The first theater in mediaeval Paris was, according to Flögel, opened by a chamber of commerce in 1395; it was no more a matter of "art for art's sake" than the Eiffel Tower; it was a speculative venture of a group of merchants hoping to increase traffic to their fairs. The German cities adopted drama a little later. Lübeck produced scores of plays written by leading merchants, who were elected turn and turn about to compose. Some of the playwrights were very bitter against the nobility and one play was called "When King Charles Went A-Stealing." Intercity competitions were frequent; for instance, twenty Flemish cities strove for a prize offered by the Ghent town council for a drama on the subject, "What is the most consolation to the dying?"

When the business man finally got around to literature in Germany, he inevitably produced mass literature, through the printing-press. Lübeck became the center of the Nether-Saxon printing industry in the late 1400's and distributed equipment and books to Scandinavian countries. She supplied cheap ballads and folk-tales; one of the most popular was the German dialect version of "Reynard the Fox," the epic of the French bourgeois who, under the guise of animalic strife, presented his own struggle against law and nobility, personified as Ass and Lion. Such booklets found a wide circulation among the plain people of Europe. To be sure, aristocratic families held out against such commercialism of belles-lettres and refused to have one of those nasty, cheap books in the house; like Ruskin and Morris in modern times, mediaeval aesthetes protested against the mass production which degraded the fine arts. None the less, the business man, seeking profit, pursued his course in the mass production of literature, undeterred by the outcries of the sensitive.

A superb symbolic painting of the *comédie humaine* of the old Hanse town, in which all classes and individuals were bound together in ties of religious and fraternal sentiment, is to be found in a chapel of the Marienkirche in Lübeck. This is a mural depicting the *Totentanz*, or Dance of Death, in commemoration of that strange frenzy which fell upon the cities of Europe during the ravages of the Black Death, when men and women, waiting for the plague to seize them, passed their anxious hours in revelry, sometimes dancing even after they felt the sickness upon them and until they fell to the ground, blackened and swollen in death. Around the walls of the dim little chapel are to be seen a circling throng, made up of all the types and castes that composed the mediaeval citizenry: the bishop with his miter; the smocked artisan; the merchant recognizable by his long furred robe; his wife, wasp-waisted, brocade-gowned. Each has for partner a skeleton; and all, men, women and skeletons, are joined together, living hand to bony hand, in a grim *Reigentanz*, a dancing ring. None among these sad, inscrutably staring figures is seen to smile, yet none shrinks from the measure; proudly, and in company, they accept doom. And as if to emphasize the dominating rôle of the city and community over the life of the individual, there is shown in the background, stretching high above and behind everyone, the pale loveliness of old Lübeck with its broad belt of bulwarks and its slender spires.

This great social fresco of the past invites a comparison with the modern verbal portrait of Lübeck in the novel "Buddenbrooks." In both, there is kindred power and morbid brilliance; in both, there is obsession with the supreme problem of decay. Inevitably, the spectator asks himself: What brought that brotherhood to disintegration? Was it overthrown from without? Or did it contain within itself the germs of its own destruction?

THE WANING OF RELIGIOUS TIES

The North Germans, even in the Middle Ages, were Puritans. Theirs was not a gay and colorful religion. Indeed, says Schulte, the German cities caught their first glimpse of an elaborate religious procession at the Council of Constance, when international financiers met to parley with kings and Popes; the Italian bankers then showed their hosts a gorgeous religious parade through streets adorned with tapestries and blooming flowers. The Germans opened their eyes wide at all this.

The Lübeckers, it is true, had one moment of real religious ecstasy. A bishop sent by the Pope to preach the Crusade against the Infidel in 1464 stirred up a frenzy there. Amid wild rejoicing, two thousand men with 200,000 gulden in their purses left the town for Italy, eager to do their bit in rescuing the Holy Sepulcher. But when they got to Rome, they found the Pope had no ships for them and took no interest in them; indeed, he slightingly observed that he had never "thought that common folk, without princes and lords to rule them, would set forth on travels." So, jeered at by everyone, and with most of their money gone, the Lübeckers struggled home. Their enterprise, which one might call the "Shopkeepers' Crusade," was almost as futile as the more renowned Children's Crusade.

Aside from this moment of exaltation, from which they quickly sobered, the merchants of the Baltic were seldom seriously disturbed by religion. They had perhaps more superstitions than men of today, but fewer illusions in some respects. They might expect more of the next world than we, but they looked for less in this one.

Though they lived in an "age of faith" and signed their ledgers "Jesus Maria, amen," their daily lives were influenced largely by common sense and the price of grain. Their financial operations were not affected by woodcuts, such as the envious artisans loved to look at, depicting horned devils capering around the deathbeds of bargain-driving traders. No doubt they were incapable of such lighthearted irreverence as the American Henry C. Frick, who said to a mediator seeking to reconcile him with Andrew Carnegie: "Tell your friend Carnegie that I will see him in hell, where we are both going." But on the whole, except for fits of St. Vitus' Dance and during storms at sea, the North German business men were not especially concerned with the hereafter.

In the 1100's and 1200's, Church influence was strongest; it was then quite customary for a merchant to order in his testament that that part of his wealth which had been won by usury should be given to the Church to pay for masses sung for his soul. But in the 1300's, though more and more wealth was won by usury, the business man stopped this practice; he left it all to his children, of whom he apparently thought more than of his own soul.

The gradual strengthening of family ties went with the decay of the religious bonds which hallowed the community. The business man found he needed sons and sons-in-law as agents; through dowry contracts he could accumulate capital as skillfully as feudal lords were amalgamating landholdings. As legal forms to hold the family together were being devised and contracts to transmit wealth were being perfected, the bourgeois family received apotheosis in the Holy Family— the favored theme of Church Art. Among the patricians of the Italian town of Siena, the Mary-cult was early developed; from Italy it passed to the French towns in Provence, and the surrounding Provençal knighthood received it from the bourgeois; as it came to Germany, the old chivalric art of the Romanesque gave way to the newer bourgeois art of the Gothic, with its increasingly realistic portrayals of the Mother and Child in a family circle.

Though the business man, in a sense, helped to develop the cult of the Virgin, he did not share in the excesses of sentiment with which the troubadours surrounded it. Karl Marx, it is true, in his "Manifesto," denounces the modern capitalist-bourgeois for callous materialism and declares that "he has torn from the family-relation its pathetic-sentimental veil, and put it on an entirely monetary basis." But even the mediaeval merchant-bourgeois was far from encumbered with romantic notions; he had an eye like a duke's for a dowry.

A pitiful little story is related, by a chronicler, of Ursula Lubbe, a young Danzig woman in the fifteenth century, who wanted to be a nun and was distinguished among her contemporaries by her ability to read. She was compelled to enter three miserable marriages for the sake of property. This true story parallels the plot chosen by Thomas Mann for his novel of nineteenth-century Lübeck. It does not appear that the *Buddenbrooks* had torn away any veils which the Lubbes had previously used.

In fact, the old traveling merchants whose lives are pictured for us in letters and other documents appear to have been as cautious and calculating, as busy and harassed, as modern American merchants who do their work in swivel chairs and airplanes. It is in a recognizably modern tone, for instance, that the mediaeval trader Anton Rem writes in his memoirs: "I have great love and enthusiasm for business, little for women."

Yet the German was capable of a sincere comradeship in marriage. He might weigh his bride's silver accurately, but he offered a fair business partnership which was at least as good as a feudal lord could supply. There is a fine simplicity about the remarks which the aged German merchant Burkhart Zink makes about the happiest of his several marriages: "My wife was dear to me and I was gladly by her . . . and she was amiable and consoled me and said: 'My Burkhart, take care of yourself and don't despair, let us help each other, we will pull through together.' " Similarly effective without eloquence, is the single line appended to an official report by the Hanseatic Burgomaster Vorrath, lying in prison in a distant land: "To be so far from my housewife, that is the heaviest grief to me, that Almighty God knows."

Even before the Cinquecento, the age of Luther and the Protestant Reformation, the German bourgeois had become a secularized, family man, temperate and level-headed; whatever mediaeval religiosity he had possessed was ebbing away. Such is the character revealed, for instance, in the letters exchanged from 1582 to 1598 by Balthasar Paumgartner, traveling for business in Italy, and his "heart's dearest, friendly Magdalena," the wife left behind in Nürnberg. The letters are filled with accounts of weddings, the prices of corn and cloth. Only twice in fifteen years does Paumgartner raise his epistolary voice; once to curse out his brother for a bad business deal, and once to speak pretty sharply to Magdalena when he hears she has given up wine and taken to beer.

Both personalities are blunt, plain, strong, faithful, shrewd. Paumgartner is wrapped up in business and very temperate. When his wife describes merry festivals, he replies: "I am glad there are so many weddings and feasts . . . back home, and I am still gladder, that I cannot attend them, and thus am spared many a harmful drunkenness. Believe me, I am much healthier here."

If nothing distracts Paumgartner from money-getting, he is never dismayed either. Amid the horrors of plague and famine in Italy in 1591, he writes: "It is reckoned that in one year here, one-third of the folk in all Italy has died, and a highly necessary thing too. For were it not for the pest, they must die anyway, as there would not be enough for so many to eat." And Magdalena, touched beyond her wont, pauses in her chronicle of her neighbor's bad cookery and the baptism of somebody's eighteenth child, to answer: "We seem to be sitting in a rose garden here, compared to the famine times you are in. What a miserable life it must be, when the folk so die of hunger. God shield us mercifully from such a plight."

A superb self-portrait of a bright young business man of the same period is presented in the memoirs of Hans Ulrich Krafft. He was just twenty-three when he set out for the Near East for the firm of the Manlichs. Serious, a pious Lutheran, a calm, blond young man, fit to hold his own anywhere, he has drawn a picture of himself to match those portraits his contemporary Holbein was painting of the Hanse merchants.

Wherever he went, he remained amiable, courteous, fond of peace and a good meal, and with a careful eye to values. Amid the barbaric splendors of a Polish wedding, he noted with keen appreciation that the princess' kirtle was made "of a delicate scarlet cloth worth 15 Thaler an ell." When he visited an alchemist in his gloomy den, he paid a well-timed compliment which so pleased the magician that he kissed Hans. With polite interest he studied a ship recently rescued from pirates and still awash with the blood of the beheaded crew. When his firm failed and he was imprisoned for debt in a Turkish jail, he observed with a thoughtful and statistical eye the separate varieties of lice, and appreciated the good manners of his fellow-prisoners.

Like the true traveling salesman, he was always ready for a quip and a wise crack in the inns. He has set down one or two of his best efforts.

Once mine host twitted him, saying, "How does it happen that you Swabian fellows get your fingers into every pie?" Hans says: "I did not think long, but fired right back: 'That's because we Swabians go out into the world to test our powers, whilst other folk like better to sit behind an oven and shoot crickets.'" The inn rang to the rafters with hearty laughter, and the cups clinked on the table. An elderly noble-man shouted to mine host enthusiastically: "He paid you back!" And even in his old age, Hans beams at the recollection.

Certainly Hans had a kind heart; he was moved to tears by the slave market at Aleppo; he was very unhappy to see a Polish nobleman beat-ing a beggar. But he cannot be said to soar. Only once in his recital occurs a moment of feeling: one evening, he admits, he was charmed by the chance song of a girl singing behind a window in Provence. For a moment something stirred in Hans' breast. Caught off his guard, he observed: "To hear her was worth the trouble."

But Hans' marriage was just what might be expected of a prudent, able young business man of his day. When a solid merchant of Ulm, Heinrich Schermer, offered his daughter Susanna, frankly "for the fur-therance of our business relations," the project looked good to Hans. His bride demurred because they would have to leave Ulm for a smaller town, but, says Hans, "after she got used to it, it was all right." There was as little nonsense about Susanna as about her Hans. The couple were presented by My Lord Abbot of Hoheneck with a coin of heavy Rhenish gold with his portrait upon it; Hans had it melted down to have "a strong Toothpick of gold made, and the same is now to be found among my possessions."

Assuredly Hans was lacking in Elizabethan magnificence. His Brit-ish contemporaries were extremely unbourgeois; they had not gone through anything like the long German development and discipline within the commercial community. They were given to an effusive kissing and kneeling which amused and surprised foreigners, and to a remarkable and unbusinesslike eloquence. But Hans had none of the Shakespearean intolerance either. He was a man of the world, not a provincial Elizabethan Englishman. Although he lived while Shake-speare was writing "The Merchant of Venice," Hans was open-minded. He was the grateful guest of a Tripolitan Jew, Meyer Winterbach; though a Lutheran, he attended Catholic services; and, hoping it would not be displeasing to God, he admired many traits in the Mohamme-dans, finding their agreeable nature a pleasing contrast to the "hateful, stiff-necked stubbornness" of so many Christians. Of course Hans had the prejudices of his age, but they were moderated by good sense and practicality. On principle, he was indeed distrustful of Jews; yet he was even more so of Greeks, and utterly so of doctors.

Hans Ulrich Krafft would not have felt at home in the world of *Othello, Hamlet* and *Falstaff*. He belongs rather among ourselves to-day, a pipe in his hand, and his slippers on, reading the *Saturday Evening Post* out loud to Susanna, while she darns.

THE VIRUS OF SOCIAL AMBITION

As the business man became more secularized and family-minded, his thirst for social distinction grew. And this, too, was dangerous to the fraternity ideal, for he wanted to climb above his brothers to a superior class. If possible, he and his wife wanted to stop being business folk at all and become leisured, perhaps even titled, landed gentry.

Ambition was more disastrous to the business community than to other groups. The nobleman might be as eager for new honors as he liked without imperiling the nobility, for he climbed upon the ladder of the feudal hierarchy. Not so the business man; when he had reached the top rung of commercial success he had to shift ladders. He moved into a new world altogether. When he bought land and castles, he and his sons with their wealth were forever lost to the commercial community through which the original profits had come. Thus the cities were constantly losing their best blood and treasure, to be spilled upon the land.

In 1450–70 in the Hanseatic towns was rising a supercaste of lawyers, who considered themselves better than the business men they served, because they wrote Latin. And the merchants took them at their own estimation. They slowly relinquished many of the functions of the State to the lawyers. In 1476 the French King intimated that he would be offended if a mere secretary should come from the Hanse, and he demanded an embassy with a Doctor of Laws at the head.

More and more, too, the patrician caste tended to snobbery in imitation of the landed feudality. The rich parvenu traders struggled to enter the charmed circles of the patricians. The steps in this climb were: a few tactful donations to church and charity; fine dressing; a rich home and lavish entertaining; a coat-of-arms. The last was not so hard for a successful tradesman to procure in the Middle Ages as it is now, when official heraldic experts have become so particular. The coat-of-arms was displayed on windows, ceilings, doors, beds, tombs and dishes. Often the rising merchant put a collection of spears and lances in the parlor, quite as Victorian self-made men bought suits of armor for their brand-new baronial halls—a tactful intimation that one had ancestors just as ferocious as anybody's.

If his moneybags were heavy, the rich man could usually attract a patrician mate for his child. Thus Peter Smilow, a big grain man of ignoble birth in Lübeck, married his daughter in 1386 to a patrician and offered a handsome sum to the Circle Brothers if they would hang his coat-of-arms beside theirs. The Brothers, noting the sum, agreed. One can only imagine the height of Peter Smilow's granddaughter's hat.

But it was not always easy for an uncouth father to keep step with his offspring. Another new-risen grain-dealer of Lübeck, Georg Paulsen, when his child was married to a patrician, had carried before the bridal procession a silver image of Mary Magdalene, the prerogative of the patrician caste. This so incensed the "best families" that they went to law about it and fought seven years in the courts until at last they won judgment against Paulsen.

Moralists of the Middle Ages were fond of dwelling on the unhappy lot of the merchant who marries an "anemic aristocrat" and finds himself out of his element; his wife detests his friends and he, who "looks on horseback as though he were swimming," is despised by hers. This was because the town patricians were self-consciously struggling to be better than their merchant ancestors and to rival the knighthood. They had to hold tournaments in armor. Indeed, some of the finest armor in our museums today was once worn by business men in Nürnberg and other towns at patrician jousts, and never graced a blue-blooded knight at all. It was so well preserved because the patricians seldom clove or even dented one another.

Italian, German and French patricians in the 1400's shared the passion for jousting. This pretense had its ridiculous side which the wits were quick to perceive. As we joke about the fox-hunting soap-boiler, so they teased the tilting salesmen. The Italian Petrarch burlesqued the wretched business man who rides into the fray on a hired nag; some malicious wight puts a thistle under its tail; it bolts home with him; and the injured parvenu is bandaged by a scolding wife. But the funniest parody is the "donkey tournament" ordered depicted in the 1450's by the great French merchant, Jacques Cœur. Perhaps Cœur made fun of the sport because he himself, despite his new-bought patent of nobility, was not received by patricians as well as he wished to be. Any rate, it may be noted that the business man in armor was the butt of jests generations before the knight, in "Don Quixote."

Even when the merchant managed to merge with the patriciate, he was still unhappy. There were heights above him which, poor wretch, he felt he must attain. He accepted the pride of the feudality at face value; he was unable to produce his own scale of values to replace those of the disintegrating community.

Many moralizers of the times reprobated this restless craving. A popular preacher, almost an evangelist, Geiler von Kaisersberg, laments: "In this world, no one wants to remain in the station given him by

God; everyone wants to rise higher." The kitchen-maid must dress like her mistress; the apprentice must wear furs; and "the citizen will be a patrician, the patrician a Freiherr, the Freiherr a count, the count a prince, the prince a duke, the duke a king."

One early broadside discloses the course of the climber. He begins as a hawker of trinkets and is not content till he gets a shop; but then he must have a ship at sea; then social ambition poisons him and his wife; eventually they land in the street again as beggars. The stimulating rôle of women in this social climbing is brought out in Grimm's fairy tale, "The Fisher and His Wife," a characteristic folk-fable of the North German coastal region, which relates the consuming ambition of the wife for titles and honors. She is not satisfied with being king and Pope, but wants to be God; then the couple are hurled back to their original miserable station.

Such thirst for distinctions could be gratified by the rich in the days of Crécy and Agincourt; the Hundred Years' War, in fact, offered a chance to war profiteers and munition makers to rise in the scale of English society. France was not exclusive either; merchants who were making 60 per cent profit out of tax-farming could buy what castles they chose. By comparison, however, the German nobility was more exclusive; it waged feuds with the bourgeois which were really fantastic. Thus Bilgerim von Reischech and his kinsmen of the Hegau nobility were enraged because the tradesman, Hans Besserer of Ravensburg, dared to set his name before his address in a letter like a gentleman. Bilgerim denounced Hans as an impertinent figsack and advised him to remain in beer-halls where he belonged; for years, the noble clansmen harried poor Hans.

Nevertheless, if ducats clinked sweetly enough, titles could be bought even in Germany. One of the Fredericks offered them for sale in almost wholesale lots. True, the route was devious and a supple back was as needful as a ready purse. Thomas Murner scornfully advised the parvenu to send a son to Rome to obtain a Doctorate; to surrender one daughter to a bishop and another to a high priest to obtain their intercession at court; and above all: "what you steal, or can and will cheat from the poor, give that freely, and so you shall be considered better than any milking-cow."

Something was sorely amiss in society, it appears, before America was discovered. As the bitter Geiler cried: "And then there are some who are made noble; rich merchants, shoemakers, tailors, breadbakers and furriers; they all want to be noble, when they have money, *for in our time the nobility has turned into a merchant's gild*."

Ambitious patricians bought villages, hunting-preserves and halls from impoverished nobles. They took care to carve tombstones with shields and helmets and place them in conspicuous positions, like the last of the Muntprats who buried his wife Osanna in the nave of a cathedral. Now and then some strong character withstood this tide, as did sturdy Henggi Humpiss of Ravensburg, who insisted upon being portrayed, not as a knight, but as a simple business man in a long gown and a wool hat, with a moneybag at his side.

Some business fathers discouraged the frivolous tendencies of their offspring and tried to keep the young in trade. The old merchant of Nürnberg, Friedrich Behaim, sent his son to study in an office in France and wrote: "I have sent thee abroad to learn something, to be thrifty, to learn how to make money, and not how to burn it and throw it away." But even in the fifteenth century, it seems, the old folks had been thriftier than the young people were: "I was myself two years abroad and did not waste as much as thou." It was the purchase of two silk waistcoats, or *wammssen,* that especially saddened the father: "Whatever thou seest others have, must thou have too . . . but with these silk wammssen it goes too far. Figsacks should not wear silk wammssen. Somebody might take you for a Count's son." But the boy wrote home to his mother—in mediaeval times, the best point of attack for apologetic sons—explaining that those wammssen were just for the holidays, and anyway, wasn't it better for a boy to look neat than to drink and gamble?

Anxious parents and thundering preachers could not stay the course of ambition. So the mediaeval family tended to pass in "three generations from shirt sleeves to chain mail." Typically, the first generation made money and joined the town council; the son became burgomaster; the third joined the Cats or Bears; the fourth left the home town, disdainful of his friends, to live in a castle and break spears or train hawks. Girls despised housework; Nürnberg nuns, "too delicate in body for any work," were allowed maids by the Pope.

One illustration among many in the 1400's is the story of the Mötteli family of Ravensburg. Hardly three generations kept in business. The first Mötteli rose to fortune in trade; buying land, he left his son, married to a noblewoman, to manage the estate. Old Mötteli and an illegitimate son, Rudolf, kept on with the business in the city. Then the sons of the landed son appeared; one perished in battle; the other, Hans, gave presents and banquets on the account of the firm. Their old uncle, Rudolf, who tried to guide the ne'er-do-well, was furious and tried to get back the money he had paid out for having him instructed in the arts of trade. For years the suit was fought in the law-courts— a typical, fierce, mediaeval feud. But the family was done for. The last Mötteli called himself Ravenstone and led a wandering existence as an aimless expatriate.

The remorseless pace of this process may be followed in Ulm and Constance, where it began early; in Strassburg, where as early as the 1200's merchants coveted the accolade and in 1472 closed high offices to any who were in trade or kept shop (hence the pointed remarks of that city's preacher, Geiler von Kaisersberg). With the help of old tax-lists, Schulte has reconstructed the changing social scene of the old cities and indicated how quickly the patricians, Engelli or Tettikofen, sank out of sight with their fortunes, while the newcomers, Zipp or Schatz, moved into the sun for a brief day before they, too, were ruined or ennobled and in either case lost to the town. Only slowly did Lübeck yield to the prevailing tendency. Nürnberg held out longest of all, until at last even the rugged opponent of the aristocracy, Balthasar Paumgartner, finally bought land.

Thus the social structures of the cities were crumbled before the gates were forced by the absolutist princes. The business man lost self-confidence before he lost his charter of independence. The inner, psychological defeat here preceded material downfall.

SELF-INTEREST VS. COMMUNITY-INTEREST

The tragedy of the Hanseatic League was the eternal tragedy of the business man: the conflict of individual interests against the larger interests of the community. The community, even under the wisest leadership, could not resolve this struggle; at best it could postpone the day of reckoning.

While the rifts within the brotherhood were widening, the enemies of the Hanse cities were rising. Italian financiers stretched their golden snares over France and across the Alps into Germany; by the 1400's they were entangling cities of the Rhine, winning the right to coin money, operate public institutions and farm taxes. Lübeck withstood their subtle power long; she was indeed forced to admit a branch of the Medici banking house to transmit Church money to Rome, but the manager of that office was forbidden to practice usury in the town and was obliged to marry a Lübeck woman as a sign of his willingness to identify himself with the community. None the less, the supremacy of the financier over the trader was growing.

Moreover, various peoples who had tamely accepted the demands of the Hanse now developed industrial initiative of their own. The Dutch entered commerce; the Danes grew menacing. England in the 1460's fought desperately at sea against her Hanseatic teachers. This first Anglo-German sea rivalry was, however, devoid of rhetoric, patriotic or otherwise; the Hanse and England tackled each other frankly as business rivals, with that splendid materialism characteristic of the Middle Ages, when men kept their purses and souls well apart. Neither side, during hostilities or at the peace-table of Utrecht, said a word about ideals.

England began to weave her own wool and, worse yet, to ship it abroad at low prices. A united front among German towns, however, might have staved off ruin awhile; and the statesmen of Lübeck strove with all their might to erect such a breachless barrier around Germany that English goods could not slip through. But the interests of the other members of the League were betrayed by the self-seeking of the port of Hamburg which, for profit's sake, admitted the flood of foreign cloth. Vainly the Hanse tried to plug up the hole in the dyke, for the leaders of the Council knew perfectly well what was happening to their once-mighty empire. But, like the frescoed images in the *Totentanz*, they had to face their doom wide-eyed and helpless.

To be sure, the Hanse went on fighting for trade and against the princes, whose activities were increasing at the same period. With bull-dog tenacity, the Hanse clung to possession, sending forth thousands of foot and horsemen, as well as armadas of big, blunt warships. But the heart of the business man, even the most pugnacious Hanseatic sea trader, was not in warfare.

He really grew more cautious all the time, and shrank from battle. He learned that "war is easy to begin and hard to stop," as a Lübeck leader once said, and agreed with Heinrich Castorp, one of the ablest men of the League, who declared that "a good trade gained is better than a war won."

Certainly some merchants, especially makers of anchors and sails, profited by war; during campaigns, the wharves doubled and many were enriched. But the majority throve best in peace, and even knew it. Their pacific mood was no doubt reinforced by the fact that, if war came, all must bear arms. The patricians went on horseback; the small shopkeepers afoot—none might shirk. They could not thrust the burden upon peasants and workers and a special warrior class was specifically barred from the cities. They were not rich enough to afford hired fighters like the Italians, nor would they shift the onus to a national army like the Frenchmen. Because they had to bear the brunt of trouble, they hesitated to start it even for an alluring object.

A merchant who failed as admiral or general faced trial and possibly execution. Many a defeated amateur at the game of war has stood in that little Rathaus of Lübeck before a jury of his peers. In the 1300's, Johann Wittenborg, cloth-dealer and Burgomaster, lost his head because he conducted a war badly and profiteered, besides, carrying on contraband traffic in private with Flanders although his city and the League had declared a boycott against her.

In 1427, Tidemann Steen was called up for trial. He lost a sea fight and a merchant-fleet of forty-six ships worth a million and a half marks in modern money. He was a herring-trader turned admiral. Not a born Lübecker, he had once been the vassal of a duke and, it seems, had never got over his awe of great folk. When he rode out, flying the red-and-white flag of Lübeck, towering in his high ship above the little Danish vessels, as the chronicler says, like a church above chapels, he saw passing before him a small Danish bark carrying princes, nobles, knights, whose capture would have ended the long war at a single stroke. But Tidemann Steen stayed his hand—he was constitutionally unable to offend a gentleman.

The careful bourgeois who felt that "a good distance is better than a steel shirt," as the saying went, was not likely to make a dangerous match for the feudal lord who fought for the love of action. The business man hesitated to start any campaign that did not promise material rewards; but the lord did not know enough to count the costs of turbulence. So the business man was unable to take the offensive; he usually waited for each siege, as it came, and resisted as best he could.

Pitifully enough, the cities proved utterly unable to control the munitions traffic which was constantly supplying their feudal enemies with weapons. This at least, it would seem, the community might still have achieved in the interests of the majority against the greed of the few. Lübeck statesmen thought so. Being perhaps more impartial because their town was not a considerable maker of munitions, they sought to restrain the members of the League from selling cannon to the war-lords and from providing technologists to instruct them in the secrets of gunpowder-manufacture.

This attempt at a united front proved futile. The early munitioneers would not surrender so profitable a trade. And they were proud of their steady progress. In a church in Amberg there is a tomb, dated 1501, of one of these early industrialists, Martin Mercz, who is beheld standing upon one of his products; his right eye is decked with a plaster, presumably as the result of some unfortunate experiment. Like Mercz, most of the cannon-makers went on cheerfully delivering their goods, regardless of whether they lost thereby their eyesight or their independence.

Lübeck could not hope to persuade Nürnberg, the chief market for armor and outside the League, or Florence in Italy, the best sword-maker, to desist. Other towns, where patricians married feudal gentry, naturally betrayed the secrets of the new technology. And whether, indeed, Lübeck herself managed to restrain her own lively trade in chain shirts with the Nordic nobility is a moot point.

By the end of the Quattrocento, the business man was already beginning to feel the results of his emancipation from the community and his individualism in the matter of munitions. Then the thunder of the heavy artillery of Charles the Bold shook the walls of Dinant, and the burghers of conquered Ghent, wearing ropes around their necks, came creeping to Charles' feet. When it was too late, the dismayed city men of Europe woke up. They feverishly cast more cannon for themselves; they dug enormous moats and threw monstrous walls around their precious towns.

But the thickest ramparts were of no avail against the new explosives. And in the end, there was nothing left for the business man to do but wait, cowering behind his useless heaps of brick and stone, while the engines of death which he had sold to his enemy were trundled up, and, from their bronze mouths, spat back at their maker.

V

MERCHANTS OF VENICE

THE MODERN BUSINESS MAN is the product of a mingling of many cultural strains in Europe and very diverse races and regions have contributed to his development. From the traders of the North have been derived some of his moral concepts, and his practical interpretation of Christianity; the "Protestant capitalist entrepreneur" was made possible by the religious Reformation in Germany. But the appropriate garb for such a figure was perfected in the South of Europe; it was devised in Venice, where merchants in the 1500's were modifying and improving the dress of heathen customers, the Turks.

The forerunner of the "business suit" of today made its earliest dramatic appearance in the Italian *commedia dell' arte* in the closing part of the sixteenth century. It was worn by the comic stock figure of the Venetian merchant *Pantalone*, who gave his name to pantaloons. *Pantalone* represents a survival of the misers in the old Roman comedies, who were too thrifty to throw away a nail-paring. He is a doddering, meddling, suspicious old fellow who does well enough in matters of finance, but remains unlucky in love. This is to some extent the result of his unfortunate lack of fancy in dress; he wears long trousers, a black coat, and an absurd little, stiff top-hat. Naturally, he loses the affections of *Columbine* to his rival *Harlequin*, a fashionable youth emblematic of the class of retired rich who lived in leisure on pensions, estates and investments in Venice, then the greatest center in the world of such *rentiers*. *Harlequin* is not in business. His family has left trade, and his only employment is self-adornment. He wears an extravagant costume composed of multi-colored patches. One might almost imagine that *Harlequin* has some presentiment of the future of men's dress and, aware that whimsy will presently be suppressed, seeks to wear all the hues of the rainbow at once, before it is too late.

Pantalone is undeniably prosaic. And the pantaloon is often called "unromantic" by those who sigh for the age of silver buckles, knee-breeches and powdered heads. But the origins of the mode were colorful enough: *Pantalone*, the merchant of Venice, adopted, in a modified

form, the attire of his best customers, the trousered Turks and Saracens. The pantaloon is thus an emblem of the age-long illicit traffic of
the Venetians with the Infidel; for many centuries they sold slaves and
munitions of war to the heathen potentates of the Near East in exchange for gems and spices. In vain the Popes tried to stop this commerce with the enemies of Christendom; *Pantalone* was superbly oblivious of all threats of hell-fire, and continued his relations with the
pagan, which involved piracy and war. The modern business man's
"sack" suit has thus, properly regarded, its romantic aspect: it is the
dress of an arms-running, city-sacking corsair.

VENETIANS AND THE INFIDEL

The semi-Oriental character and behavior of the Venetians was indicated not only in dress and architecture but also in the status of their
secluded women, lower than elsewhere in Italy. The Venetians were
intermediaries, both for good and ill, between the West and the East.

On the one hand, they brought technique as well as goods from the
Levant. They helped transfer to Europe the capitalistic methods in fi-
nance and industry and the skill in manufacturing objects of luxury,
which had been preserved, after the wreck of the Western half of the
Roman Empire, in the old cities of Alexandria and Constantinople. The
Cathedral of St. Mark in Venice, with its Oriental glitter, is the symbol of such intercourse, housing the bones of a saint brought from
Alexandria, and adorned with the bronze horses of Nero taken from
Constantinople during the Fourth Crusade. The edifice thus proclaims
the triumph of Venice, successor in wealth and commerce to both the
classic ports.

But the Venetians had no eyes for the highest and most precious relics of that classic civilization which had been miraculously kept and
stored in Constantinople. A magnificent heritage of the scientific, historical and artistic wisdom of the ancients, tens of thousands of classical manuscripts, lay in the giant Library of that metropolis; but though
the Venetian merchants traded with the capital of the Greek Empire
for centuries, it seemingly did not occur to them to enter the Library.
Even when they took and sacked Constantinople, they looted everything but the Library. The manuscripts were still there when the
Turks came, two centuries later, and burned them in one swift holo-
caust. Then indeed, other Italian business men, the Florentines, were
grieved and sought to salvage what tantalizing fragments of the classic
culture were left in the world. But still the Venetians remained largely
uninterested, cold amid the ardors of the Renaissance.

Blind as they were to the treasures of the mind which lay at their

front door, so to speak, the imagination of the Venetians was thrilled
by the gaudy ornaments of the Infidel in Asia. In this, Marco Polo, or
as he was jestingly known, "Marco Millions," was a typical representative of his city. Utterly oblivious to the cultural heritage of Constantinople, he was thrilled by the barbaric splendors of the Mongol court
of far-away Kublai Khan. The Venetian love of glitter was to have the
most serious consequences to the peace of Europe.

As spies, allies, arms-deliverers, the Venetians gave aid and encouragement to the three dangerous Asian conquerors, Moslem, Mongol
and Turk, who for seven centuries and more were threatening to deluge Western Europe with their fierce hordes. Thanks in a good measure to this assistance, the Moslems overran the shores of the Mediterranean, the Mongols swept into Hungary and Poland, and, lastly, the
Turks took Constantinople. To hold back the Asian tide, European
chivalry spent its lifeblood. By the tens of thousands, the knights perished at Tours, in the Holy Land, in Spain, Silesia and at Byzantium—
a sacrifice made all the more necessary by the profit-seeking of Venetian business men.

VENICE AND THE SARACENS

The earliest prosperity of the "Serene Republic" on the Adriatic was
secured in supplying the Mohammedans with iron, arms, ship-timber
and naval supplies, besides Christian slaves—women for the harems of
the Infidel and men to serve as galley-slaves or soldiers. To the Caliph
of Cordova, for instance, says Heynen, they sold several thousand
Christians who were used as a bodyguard. This gain-bringing traffic
was actively pushed by the Venetian merchants, who sent embassies to
exhibit wares and press trade-treaties at the courts of heathen potentates in Egypt, Spain, Sicily and elsewhere.

At first, there was little else for the Venetians to offer the more cultivated Saracen pagans. It was some time before Venice got salt in
near-by marshes, or learned the secrets of making glass and fine em-
broideries from Constantinople, and at length became the outlet for
cloth of Florence, which was eagerly bought in the East—at one time,
this cloth export amounted to 16,000 pieces in a year. But even when
their displays grew more various, a major share of the Venetian income was derived through slave-dealing. As Weil says: "The slave-
trade, which brought in a larger and more certain revenue than even
the rich spices and stuffs of the East, was the chief source of the
wealth of Venice."

To seize and stabilize the supply of wood and slaves, the Venetians
were tempted to the first steps in imperial conquest. The wood for

ships came mostly from Dalmatian forests; the slaves, Greek or Russian, if not captured in war, were obtained from Dalmatian pirates. Dalmatia was easily vanquished. In commemoration of the glorious victory, the Venetians instituted their famous festival called "The Espousal of the Sea." On this occasion, the President of the Republic, the Doge, rode forth upon a gilded barge to wed the ocean with a ring, in sign of Venetian rule over the waves. On his way, he passed by the Bishop who blessed him in the pious formula: "Thou shalt purge me with hyssop, O Lord, and I shall be clean."

One annual purge was deemed quite sufficient by the Venetian slave-dealers and arms-deliverers. But Charlemagne and the various Frankish monarchs of the Holy Roman Empire most emphatically disagreed. Watching the advancing forces of the Crescent, which had been repulsed with terrible slaughter by Charles Martel, but continued to harry the European coasts, these monarchs knew their dominion was jeopardized daily by the Venetians. The fleets, the slaves to man them, and the armor of the invading paynim were provided by the merchants of the then crude little town built so strangely on piles over the marshes at the mouth of the Po. Charlemagne determined to wipe out this source of supplies to the Infidel; but his navy was annihilated by the Venetians in a canal ever afterward known as the *Canal of the Orphans*. Not only did the Venetians defeat the mighty monarch, but they wrested from him acknowledgment of their independence, and a treaty admitting them as traders to his broad empire in France and Germany. Presently they began to sell to the Western nobility the wares they obtained from the Infidel.

Where Charlemagne failed, his feebler successors could not control the dangerous traffic of Venice. Threats only elicited some polite expression of regret. Once, indeed, a measure of reform was promised by Doge Candiano IV, who agreed that it was "a grievous pity" for his fellow-citizens to be arming the invader. Before he could put the reform into effect, however, he was assassinated—by laissez fairists, it is presumed.

Quite as shocked as the Frankish monarchs were the Greek rulers of Constantinople, who were nominally suzerains of the region around Venice. Now and then they, too, uttered "terrible threats." But the Venetian navy saved Constantinople from an impending attack by Norman hordes; in return, the traders demanded monopolistic privileges in the Golden Horn. Thereafter they paid no duty there, though all others were charged 10 per cent. In 1071, a Doge of the Serene Republic led home a Greek princess as a bride. She dazzled the simple Venetians with her jewels and amazed them by her strange customs of bathing and eating with a two-pronged fork. They thought her early death was caused by such abnormal habits. But her luxuries whetted their appetite for Eastern adventure. And in time they began to dream of conquering Constantinople and reveling in its treasures.

VENICE, THE MONGOLS AND THE CRUSADES

In the thirteenth century, two kinds of paynim menaced the borders of western Europe: the Mongols and the Saracens. The Venetian friendliness to both was a serious factor in weakening the resistance of European knighthood to the invaders.

At the opening of that century, when Genghis Khan ruled from Korea to Persia, the Mongols were extending their colossal empire westward. Moving into South and Central Russia, they swarmed into Hungary, Poland and Silesia; and at the frightful hecatomb of Liegnitz in 1241, the feudal nobility of East Europe, including the German Knights Templar, was decimated. This Mongol tide, though it eventually receded, left ineffaceable reminders; it Asianized regions of Russia which could never afterward be assimilated into the Western economic-cultural sphere; and it left demoralization in East Europe. But the Mongols did not sweep in wildly and suddenly, like reckless barbarians. No, indeed, they advanced according to careful plan.

At every stage, the Mongol generals informed themselves ahead of time about the state of European courts, and learned what feuds and disorders would be advantageous to their conquests. This valuable knowledge they obtained from Venetian merchants, men like Marco Polo's father. It was thus not without reason that Polo himself was made welcome at the court of Kublai, and became for a time administrator of the Grand Khan. As Hart says, the Mongols

> found the Venetians quite willing to sacrifice the interests of Christian Europe in order to gain an advantage over their great trading rivals, the Genoese. In return for Mongol help in ousting the Genoese trade-centres in the Crimea, the Venetians acted as part of the intelligence service of the Mongols.

While the Mongols were linking vast realms together, the Moslems were also gaining ground in the Near East. For two hundred years, Holy Wars were waged in Palestine to halt their progress; from 1096 to 1291, Western knights in great numbers took the Cross to defend the Holy Land and so check the new flood which might otherwise have poured over Western Europe.

During these two centuries, the Crusaders kept coming to Venice, as well as other port towns, to take ship for the East. In the main the newcomers were rustic gentlemen, stronger in the arm than in the intellect and often inspired by a quite genuine desire to make the world safe for Christianity. Their ingenuous faith and ambition were intensely irritating to the Venetian traders, who had just achieved a satisfactory balance of budgets through trade with the Infidel, and who felt such rampant emotionalism would prove disruptive to business.

Throughout the First, Second and Third Crusades, Venetian business men maintained an unwavering policy of benevolent neutrality. As they had felt no qualms about selling coreligionists into slavery, so they were unstirred by even a passing spasm of religious fervor. They provided both the belligerents with arms and provisions at well-sustained prices. They equipped the chivalric gentlemen from Europe and transported them to the Holy Land; meanwhile they traded heavily with the Saracenic gentlemen of Egypt and Palestine.

This attitude of neutrality toward the belligerents was misunderstood in other parts of Europe. The Greeks dubbed the Venetians "frogs of the marshes," and railed at them as a "depraved, sacrilegious, and miserly folk." The cold-blooded, unemotional concentration upon profit was as highly repugnant to the feudal mind then as, centuries later, the similar businesslike calculations of the bog-dwelling Dutch were to the baroque French. In German folk-lore, for instance, the "merchant of Venice" is a sinister figure who goes about buying the live, beating hearts of men, for which he substitutes stones. According to legend, the Venetian merchants needed the warm hearts of others to keep themselves alive.

Mystery enveloped the Venetian character in the eyes of the European backwoodsmen. Not only did Venice know how to manufacture glass, then almost a black art, but it was also a renowned site of magicians; its people, superstitious as became seafarers and speculators, sought the advice of witches and patronized alchemists. Dabbling in forbidden secrets, the semi-Oriental seclusion of life, and the terrorism of the spy-ridden community under Venetian government, combined to make the lagoon-city an object of suspicion. And in a later period, the Venetian became even more enigmatic than ever, owing to his fondness for wearing a black silk mask.

Time and again these callous bargainers were anathematized by the Holy See. The Republic was laid under papal ban for persisting in its traffic with the Moslem defilers of the Holy Sepulcher. But prospects of future torment held apparently no terrors for merchants of Venice. When Pope Benedict XIII, for instance, forbade unauthorized trade with the Infidel, the Venetians calmly bought up the few letters of authorization which had been issued and passed them from hand to hand, indorsed and sold like ordinary bills of exchange.

One such document was obtained by the rich French merchant of the Quattrocento, Jacques Cœur, and, under its protection, he dealt with the Sultan of Egypt. Denounced for this trade, and accused of delivering arms to the paynim, Cœur was forced to do penance by his King. Thus a Frenchman, and also the German firm of Fugger, which at one time sold arms to the Turks, were also dealers in contraband. But the Venetians were earlier and more active in the business.

As far as outward forms went, the Venetians were indeed strict in religious matters. They were persistent relic-hunters; many of the holy remains in Venice were secured by extraordinary acts of vandalism. But even toward the most sacred objects, the Venetian attitude was tinged with commercial speculation. Thus they accepted the Crown of Thorns, believed to have been the very one pressed on the brows of Christ, as part security on a loan to Baldwin II of Constantinople, who had looted it from a church in that city. The Venetian banking house of Querini held the holy relic for a long time, until it was only too evident that Baldwin would never be able to redeem his Savior's Crown, and then the Querini sold it to the pious King of France, St. Louis, who built the lovely Sainte Chapelle as a repository for it in Paris.

In their continual struggles against the Vatican, the Venetians became increasingly stubborn and impatient of religious restraint. By the end of the 1300's, they had excluded clerics from the Grand Council and from civil employment; even the relatives of churchmen were removed from councils when ecclesiastical affairs were being discussed and were declared ineligible to the post of ambassador to Rome. They refused to permit the Pope to appoint any bishops in territories under their jurisdiction without senatorial permission. Thus Venice, long before England or the German states, separated Church and State for all practical purposes.

The Venetian historian, Daru, says that tolerance in religion was their distinguishing trait and that they allowed Protestants, Armenians, Mohammedans and Jews to have edifices in Venice. "A vigilant police prevented fanatics and innovators from troubling the state. . . . The famous maxim, 'Siamo veneziani, poi christiani' [We are Venetians, and then Christians], was only an energetic formula which merely proved that they wished to place the interests of religion after those of the state."

As Venice had anticipated the Protestant Reformation, so, when that storm broke over Europe, she offered heresy its one secure refuge in Italy. Long after the rebels had been suppressed in Italy, the Venetians encouraged and protected their scholar, the theologian, Paolo Sarpi, of the late Cinquecento, who persisted in researches in natural science, despite the terrors of the Inquisition, and who privately admitted that he was, in fact, a Protestant. The roots of commerce and religious doubt were already grown together in Venice when they were entwined in Florence, Germany and England.

Through friendship with the Infidel, Mongol or Moslem, maintained despite the pleas of monarchs and the threats of Popes, prosperity was assured to Venice. But that Serene Republic did not win real power and wealth through trade alone; her heights of splendor were attained through war. She became magnificent only after she had captured and pillaged the Empire of the Greeks, in defiance of papal interdict. Under the specious pretext of making a Fourth Crusade against the Infidel, she gorged herself on the rich spoil of Christians.

This Fourth Crusade is one of the most instructive episodes in business history. It was a supreme example of imperialist warfare, conducted with little of the usual verbiage, for a clear economic objective; and it was initiated and actually administered by merchants. As such, considering the extraordinary efficiency of its execution, it stands out in startling relief against the dark background of wars bungled by kings and princes.

When the Fourth Crusade was proclaimed in 1204 against the Mohammedan Sultan of Egypt, everyone was surprised to learn that at last Venice had dedicated her heart to the Christian Cause. Had *Pantalone* been converted? Was he then really prepared to take up sword and Cross and sally forth to destroy his best customers? Such altruism seemed astounding. Some suspicions might, however, have been aroused by the vague phraseology of the contract joining Venice to French knights in this enterprise; the astute Doge, Enrico Dandolo, merely agreed "to perform the service of God and of Christianity in whatever place it might be." It is thought, at least by some historians, that Dandolo and the innermost circle of Venetian bankers and shippers may have had ulterior designs from the very beginning.

Many French vassals rushed to embrace the Cross at that time because a Crusader's effects were exempt from confiscation, and they were in difficulties with their king, who accused them of treacherous dealings with the British foe. When they arrived at Venice, however, they were short of money and could not meet the terms set by Dandolo. That eminent statesman had proposed to lead his city's armada, provided with horses, siege engines, grain, wine and other necessaries, "for the love of God" and the sum of 85,000 silver marks—plus one-half the booty in every conquest to be made by sea or on land.

Unable to proceed or go home, the unhappy Frenchmen were detained virtually as prisoners on the Lido for some time. Their Venetian creditors then suggested that the needy warriors could work out their debts by helping subdue the rebellious town of Zara in Dalmatia. The Crusaders from France demurred: when they had placed the holy device of the Cross on breast and back, they had vowed to spare their Christian brethren and turn their blades only on heathen. And the Dalmatians were Christian. Unmoved, the Christian merchants of Venice insisted upon their pounds of flesh.

The Pope, Innocent III, heard of this attempt to sidetrack the Crusade which he had blessed into a punitive expedition against a Christian community. Forthwith he excommunicated the entire force. A number of frightened Frenchmen ran off. But, without turning a hair, the Venetians cajoled and pushed the rest to the siege of Zara, which soon fell. Then the Crusaders, having worked out their debts, were eager to be off at last and meet the Infidel. They wanted to take Egypt. The Venetians were horrified indeed for the Egyptians were excellent customers. Moreover, the Egyptian Sultan sent an embassy to Venice promising favorable tariff regulations in the harbor of Alexandria if they could only contrive to divert the furious Frenchmen.

In this crisis, the aged Dandolo perceived a rare opportunity, if he had not, indeed, envisaged it from the beginning. He proposed an attack upon the Christian Empire, and its capital, Constantinople. This, he explained, would yield more booty, and, if the Crusaders wanted to go on to the Holy Land afterward, they would not lack for funds. Again, some of the feudal gentlemen left Venice in disgust. But the majority of the Crusaders, being nearly penniless, were persuaded to break their vows once more.

Then to the dismay of the Pope and the rest of Europe, the party was conducted by the Venetian Doge, Dandolo, a man over ninety years of age, into the harbor of Constantinople where the Venetians had been favored guests for generations. The "Crusaders" took the splendid city, murdered, burned, destroyed many precious relics and trampled into bloody dust the classic culture of Byzantium. Constantinople was thus ravaged by Christian merchants two centuries before the Turks overran it. If the traders were a little more restrained than the Turks, it was merely because they knew better the value of much that they found.

Though the Venetians were in a minority among the Crusaders, they managed to obtain far more than half the booty of the fallen capital. They made an incalculable number of slaves and secured quantities of gems, stuffs, statues and other loot. In addition they secured trading rights and government offices in the dismembered Greek Empire. They extended their rule over more than a quarter of its area. Assuming purple buskins like an Emperor of ancient Rome, the Doge Dandolo took the title: "Doge of Venice, Lord of one-fourth and one-eighth of the Roman Empire."

Thus, with little inconvenience and almost no cost, the Venetians attained, as Brentano comments, three tremendous objects in one move. First, they got their profit out of the Crusaders after all. Second, they gathered in the booty and territory of the Greeks and fastened themselves at strategic posts. Third, they won valuable monopolies from the grateful Sultan of Egypt. None of the other Holy Wars, directed by fickle and uncommercial knights, by dukes and kings of Europe, was so brief and entirely profitable as this Fourth Crusade in which business men were leaders.

When the fleet came back to the home-lagoons, and the booty was unloaded from *The Pilgrim* and *The Paradise* and other vessels with pious names, the city of Venice was all a-sparkle. No commercial republic had experienced such a victory since Carthage conquered Sicily. Nothing like this fabulous loot was seen in Europe again for three hundred years—until the Spaniards plundered the New World and the British robbed the Spaniards.

Venice then stood at the summit of power. Annually she sent forth the "Caravan of the Levant," a fleet of tall ships convoyed by vessels of war, to procure the luxuries of the East from the ports of her new Empire and from the harbor of Alexandria which was almost a Venetian monopoly. This yearly expedition was an event in mediaeval commerce comparable to the annual passage of Spanish galleons in the sixteenth century, to fetch the gold of Mexico and Peru—indeed the Spanish consciously modeled their armadas upon the Venetian. Like the later treasure-ships, moreover, the Venetian Caravan was ever in danger from pirates, some Saracen but even more Italian.

Gold filled the strong-boxes of the Venetian merchants. Their families donned garments so gorgeous that city-fathers, fearing the new-won wealth might demoralize the rest of the population, passed sumptuary laws forbidding boys under twelve to wear pearl-covered belts and limiting the quantities of gold tissue which patrician ladies might display in public. Worthy of their riches were the palaces built by the parvenus, one of which, the Golden House, or "Casa d'oro," still stands in Venice. Each of the palaces, with its balconies upheld by delicately cut Moorish pillars and walls brilliant with gold-leaf and bright frescoes, was rendered doubly magnificent by having a twin, mirrored in the waters of the canal below.

In the most literal fashion, the Venetians "paraded" their wealth. In constant processions, private and public, to celebrate weddings and funerals, or holidays, the merchant families vied in the splendor of their costumes and festival boats. For such events the aristocratic women escaped the almost haremlike seclusion of their homes and glided about for a few hours exhibiting fortunes in jewels on brows and throats. But higher and more glittering than any private boat rode the Golden Ship, the *Bucentaur* of the Doge, a tremendous *galeazza* sheathed in precious metal.

Only a merchant who could build a Golden House might hope to have his name inscribed in the Golden Book of the patricians; and only those who did appear in this "Libro d'oro" as *nobili*, admitted to the proud title of *patrizio veneto*, could expect to ride, as a Doge, upon the Golden Ship. For the oligarchical system of Venice was erected after the conquest in the East, when the rich families gathered together, closed their ranks and proclaimed a monopoly on the higher public offices.

Venice was thenceforth directed by a small élite. Something over a thousand men and their families, having incomes ranging from 200,000 to 500,000 lire a year, formed the *nobili* in a population of perhaps 190,000. Some of these patricians were rich enough to build and equip an entire *galeazza da commerzia* out of their own pockets; the rest were taxed to build ships in the State Arsenal, which was, incidentally, one of the early examples of large-scale enterprise, conducted with marvelous efficiency and emphasis on speed. Patricians commanded the important ships and derived profits besides from manufactures, revenues from estates on the mainland, gain in financial speculation and tribute from subject provinces.

With a tenacious grip, the Venetian oligarchy maintained itself from the end of the thirteenth century to the close of the eighteenth. Indeed it lasted longer than the Dutch patriciate, and formed a more exclusive political club. Even very rich men were often denied admission, and this was in any case offered at a high price. Giuseppe Persico, for instance, who sold cloth of gold in his shop, the "Crowned Fortuna," paid 100,000 ducats for the patrician title.

The extraordinary longevity of the Venetian aristocracy was in part due to the scheme of inheritance. This was not primogeniture; each son shared in the patrimony and in addition supported himself in public office. Despite this division of the inheritance, the family was kept close together, its members living as a clan and keeping the family wealth as far as possible in one pool. Often an impractical enlargement of the family was prevented by forbidding some sons to marry and packing girls off to convents; for instance, three of the immensely rich Cornaro brothers were refused wives. Sometimes only a single son, the youngest, was permitted to carry on the family. This repression of family life encouraged the keeping of courtesans, brought to Venice in great numbers by slave-dealers who plied their traffic until the seventeenth century opened.

The patrician class at once dazzled the people by pageantry and terrorized them by a spy system which was a byword in Europe. No man dared utter a rebellious word, even in private, for the Council of Ten seemed to hear through walls. Political discussion was so dangerous that Venetians could only discuss remote events with safety. In the eighteenth century, for example, the coffee-house partisans used to hurl abuse at one another in sonnet-sequences, seeking outlet for repressed eloquence in quarreling over the distant Austro-Prussian conflict which did not concern Venice at all. Freedom of speech was not among the luxuries enjoyed by the citizens of the most sumptuous city in Europe, under a business management.

THE FALL OF VENICE

Strict repression of thought and speech, added to an apparently native indifference to matters of the intellect, made Venice relatively backward. Some noblemen, to be sure, went abroad to study; and generally the patricians traveled, in trade or on ambassadorial missions. The reports of the Venetian ambassadors in the courts of Europe offer an abundance of shrewd observation and pithy judgment. But in general the Venetians did not engage in independent research or proclaim their opinions as stridently as citizens in a freer air. And thus the early bloom of scholarship and literature which appeared in other Italian towns could not be paralleled in Venice, or in her rival, Genoa. The touch of the Renaissance reached the lagoon-city very late; painting was an imported interest in Venice and its glory came when commercial might was already waning. The chief contribution of Venice to intellectual activity was the scientific inquiry of Paolo Sarpi, the heretic whom Galileo called "father." And Venice began very early to count the populace in order to assess taxes, thus propagating the notion of public vital statistics. Yet even this idea was probably Byzantine and a heritage of antiquity.

Uncontaminated with ideas as it was, the Venetian patriciate, though it ruled with more-than-royal authority, failed to keep up with the absolutist monarchs of Europe in the eighteenth century, who were experimenting with industrial methods and in agriculture. The proud Venetians remained indifferent to the rising study of political economy, and proved more conservative than kings. "Haughty even at home," the *patrizio veneto* clung to his habitual mask of austerity and prudent reserve except on some festival occasion when he might don a black silk mask instead and mingle with the bibulous crowd. Doubtless the popularity of the masked festival was a reflection of the autocracy of the government: men felt free only in disguise.

As minds stagnated, commercial energies diminished. Sons of rich business men shrank from the perils of the sea, tended to retire from trade and immerse themselves in gambling and other town-pleasures. Or they crossed to the mainland, bought estates and feudal titles, and sank into a more respectable, but equally sterile leisure. In this way, capital and martial valor were lost to the Republic. And as the bravery of her sea fighters faded, a French king scornfully remarked to a Venetian ambassador: "You Venetians are wise in your councils and abound in riches, but so fearful are you of death that you have neither spirit nor manliness in war."

Secure in their tenure, the ingrowing patricians took their power so much for granted that they did not tremble when the third wave of paynim, the wild Turks, rose on their horizon. They had befriended the Mongols and Moslems—why not these? To rouse themselves against the Turks would have meant cooperating with Pisa and Genoa, the Italian rivals for Eastern trade and sea-power whom they hated worse than any Infidel.

With anguish the Popes realized that the bitter rivalry among these Italian cities provided the Turk with his chance. This inter-city animosity had been sharpening constantly. At one time, Venice had even made an out-and-out alliance with the Moslem Sultan, Nasser Mohammed, in return for commercial advantages, excluding Genoa; and the world was treated to the amazing sight of a Christian city fraternizing with the Infidel in order to defeat a Christian business competitor. The Pope excommunicated Venice on this occasion also, but, as usual, without effect.

To one battle in the interminable list of feuds between Venice and Genoa, posterity owes the "Travels of Marco Polo." That active merchant might not have found leisure for writing had he not been captured by the enemy, and amused himself, during years of captivity in a Genoese jail, by composing his memoirs.

During these feuds, the Turk advanced. While the cities were squabbling, tying rival flags to the tails of horses to be dragged in the dust, or burning one another's warehouses, the new invader gained ground. The Venetians offered him treaties, as they had previously done to the Saracens; encouraged also by Genoese, he rushed forward and in 1453, took and sacked Constantinople. And thus, as previously Venice helped the Mongol hordes into East Europe, in order to shatter Genoa, so now the Turk slipped into Europe while the two cities were still raging at each other.

When the Venetians rushed to beg for privileges from the Grand

Turk, however, they discovered to their alarm that this new heathen conqueror was less civilized than others. He was feudal-minded rather than an amiable bargainer. And business did not go on as usual. Instead, the glory of Venice began to shrink. In desperation, she called on the French for help. But that was to invite the French into Italy, with terrible consequences.

The French refused to go home or stay at home. They harried other Italian cities and spread ruin and desolation. After centuries of exhausting strife, the French, under Napoleon, took possession even of Venice. No allies, no friends, could be found by Venice in her awful hour. Then at last the Golden Book was closed. The sea winds ate away the gay colors from the Golden House. The Golden Ship, by the order of Napoleon, was dragged upon the beach and burned, and the precious metal, carefully washed out of the ashes, was carried off as part of the loot to Paris.

But the French, though they proved the conquerors of the Venetians, could not resist the charm of Venetian comedy, and so gave immortality to *Pantaloon*. A French queen, daughter of the Florentine banking house of the Medici, was so fond of the figure that she took it to Paris. French aristocrats laughed heartily at the comic betrousered merchant, and eventually *Pantaloon* became, under the magic of Molière, the central figure of "Le Bourgeois gentilhomme." After a while the French Revolution overthrew the aristocracy; and then, after a brief period of *sans-culottism*, the triumphant middle class at length imposed the garb of *Pantalone*, the bourgeois pantaloon, upon all civilized men. Thus the spirit of Venice was avenged.

SHAKESPEARE'S BUSINESS MAN

It may be a little difficult to imagine the fellow-citizens of Enrico Dandolo, enriched by the spoils of Christian neighbors, staunch assistants to the heathen hordes, and universally execrated as conscienceless despots, in the Shakespearean part of "The Merchant of Venice." Could these hard-bitten imperialists, who set at naught the thunders of the Vatican, and held Our Lord's Crown of Thorns in pawn, possibly have slipped into a trap that a mere *Shylock* could set?

As a matter of fact, when Shakespeare wrote "A Comical History of the Merchant of Venice," in the closing years of the Cinquecento, there were no Jews left in Venice, at least officially. They had been expelled some forty years before and, thanks to the abilities of native Christian merchants, had not been missed.

The humorous part of the "Comical History" is, of course, its revelation, not of life in Venice, but of the commercial backwardness of

Elizabethan England. The Merchant of Venice, *Antonio*, with an insular simplicity, is pictured sending forth "an argosy bound for Tripolis, another to the Indies . . . a third at Mexico, a fourth for England"—and not a bottom insured! Audiences in towns more progressive than London would have rated him at once as a novice who should not have gone into business at all. The British were not accustomed to the notion of ship-insurance; the first example of such practice in England occurs, says Burgon, as late at 1543; the islanders were, as a supercilious foreigner remarked, better pirates than merchants, and hence apt to ignore the safety-factor. But the Italians had been paying insurance, at rates varying between 12 and 15 per cent, on cargoes between Pisa and London, for generations; as early as the 1300's, according to Davidsohn, the Florentines called men who neglected so obvious a precaution fools and misers.

It is not easy for us today to imagine the primitive character of English commerce in comparison with that of Venice. England was so rich in the eloquence of Shakespeare and Marlowe, that we can scarcely realize how poor she was in cash assets. But her glories in that age were still more verbal than visible. Indeed, the very word, "cash," was as yet imperfectly understood in "the City." Like "bankruptcy," it was a strange word recently imported from Italy.

In the sixteenth century, the characters as well as the homes of the English were just commencing to lose their simple military aspect. Erasmus, who had gone to England, observed that the people there were warlike and idle and "not to be roused to any useful occupation even by the hope of gain." They permitted foreigners to control many branches of their industries; and seemed unaware or unashamed that they lacked technical skill and capital resources. German and Italian merchants who came to London were astonished to find crude wooden buildings instead of the carved stone edifices to which their eyes were accustomed.

Only by a sympathetic realization of the backwardness of England, can we understand how Shakespeare came to delineate the Merchant of Venice, *Antonio*, as a pure idealist, an Early Christian in spirit, who gives loans freely without charging a penny of interest on them. Such Fundamentalism may still have flourished in the backwoods of Britain, but it had been long extinguished on the Rialto. The Venetians themselves, and at the very same period, were more correctly picturing themselves under the guise of the covetous *Pantalone*.

Antonio is an other-worldly dreamer; worse, he is a propagandist, who invades business gatherings and in public denounces the money-lender *Shylock* for taking interest. He does not for a moment complain that Shylock demands more than the customary 10 per cent, which any

Christian banker of the Rialto would set as a decent figure; *Antonio* thinks it wrong of *Shylock* to charge anything at all, to make money bear fruit. He would reduce the trade of Venice to a primitive cash basis. As *Shylock* aggrievedly explains:

> *I hate him for he is a Christian,*
> *But more for that in low simplicity*
> *He lends out money gratis and brings down*
> *The rate of usance here in Venice.*
>
> . . . .
>
> *. . . and he rails,*
> *Even there where merchants most do congregate,*
> *On me, my bargains and my well-won thrift,*
> *Which he calls interest. Cursed be my tribe,*
> *If I forgive him!*

It is not surprising that *Antonio* appears to *Shylock*, as he would to us, as a dangerous lunatic, an enemy to Big Business and established society. One can only dimly imagine into what an appalling fury Lorenzo de' Medici would have flown, had anyone dared to invade the lobby of the money-changers in Florence and denounce the Medici for violating canon law. There would have been a corpse in the Arno before dawn, and no vestige of a trial.

Instead of solving his problems by homicide, *Shylock* takes to law. As far as our evidence goes, he is not "grasping"; he is merely defending the right of every man, Jew or Christian, to put his funds to gainwinning use, and therefore merits the approbation of everyone who accepts the most conservative return on any investment. He is speaking, not as a Jew, but as an outraged business man, when there bursts from him the poignant cry:

> *Gaoler, look to him! Tell not me of mercy;*
> *This is the fool that lent out money gratis.*

Was there ever such an idealist as *Antonio* among the upper circles of Italian commerce? The book from which Shakespeare probably took his plot was written in the 1300's by a Florentine, not a Venetian, and was merely a burlesque labeled "of a fool, for fools, by a fool." When we search through the monumental eight volumes of Davidsohn's "History of Florence," we find mention of one Italian, who objected to taking interest on a loan. He was a rustic nobleman, however; that was back in 1302; and finally he did accept 7 per cent from the banking house of Mozzi. But he preferred another name for it; he felt more comfortable when it was called a "gift" tendered "purely out of love and friendship."

In the sixteenth century, a Fugger agent in Italy found a man in Genoa, Lazaro Doria, who exhibited a "pricklesome conscience" that aroused universal wonder. Nevertheless, Doria was a good banker; he took interest to any amount on other people's money and only objected to accepting any on his own capital. As he managed not to call any of the funds in his hands his own, he was not in any danger of starvation. Of such stuff was the most delicate conscience in Cinquecento Italy!

A German of the same period, Sebastian Neidhart, was likewise afflicted with scruples. When a Florentine gambler invited him to join a scheme to corner the money market in Antwerp, Neidhart at first objected that it would be "an ungodly practice." On thinking it over, however, he decided, says Ehrenberg, that he "wanted the highest possible interest and finally himself offered some advice on how to make money still scarcer."

The only genuine conscientious objector was apparently Philip II of Spain. Not that Philip objected to receiving interest; he only hated to pay any. In 1575 he repudiated his debts, saying that he feared to sin against God by handing out interest. Then the Genoese bankers, who had lent him vast sums, rushed to the Pope, also in their debt; and the Pope begged Philip not to worry so much about the welfare of his soul and scripture interpretation but, cheerfully ignoring canon law, to compound with his creditors.

Few practical people, in fact, at that late date, were seriously disturbed by canon law. There were ways of getting around it. In Italy, it had long been punctured; back in the 1300's, the Frescobaldi had charged a king of England no less than 260 per cent. In France and Germany, men's minds had later been quieted by the assurances of Calvin and Luther that a moderate rate of return on capital was necessary and did not endanger the soul. England was, to be sure, far "behind" the Continent; however, even in Shakespeare's day, one of his contemporaries, Thomas Wilson, writing about usury, exclaimed, almost in the words of *Shylock:* "What man is so madde as to deliver his moneye out of his own possession for naughte?" Nobody, it would seem, except *Antonio.*

"Good Queen Bess" was largely responsible for the final removal of the statutory prohibition on interest taking in England. She was urged to do this by the able money-lender, munitioneer and cloth-merchant, Sir Thomas Gresham, who argued that it would enable the British Crown to take up loans among its own citizens, instead of looking abroad to foreigners who were accustomed to asking higher rates. The statutes of usury were invalidated, and 10 per cent was declared the legal rate for any subject, Jew or Christian, to charge, not long before "The Merchant of Venice" was written. The Empire which Shakespeare adorned and Drake enlarged was stabilized on the principles defended by *Shylock*.

THE JEW IN MEDIAEVAL FINANCE

It is hard to say whether *Antonio* or *Shylock* is the more improbable personality. Both are eccentrics, oblivious to material considerations and as such anything but typical of Italian economic life. Only the imagination of an Elizabethan Englishman could picture two such characters together: *Antonio*, the pure Christian who lends his money gratis; *Shylock*, the noble Jew, who prefers revenge to revenue—and set them both in Venice.

What renders *Shylock* so incomprehensible to Christians and Jews is his insistence upon his "pound of flesh" when he might have had cash payment in full. Of course the Christians of the Cinquecento would not have been surprised if *Shylock* had demanded the flesh in case he could not get his dues, for that would have been in harmony with the spirit of the times.

Bodily pledges of honor were commonly called for by Christian creditors of that day. The Querini of Venice compelled Baldwin II of Constantinople to send along his son as hostage as well as to deliver the Crown of Thorns as part security. A good Catholic and energetic lady, the wife of a Visconti of Milan, caught and clapped into irons eleven harmless Florentine travelers to enforce her threats against the Pazzi Brothers' Bank which had neglected for fifteen years to pay her a dividend.

Indignities like that at the hands of Italians, exclusively Christian, had been borne particularly by the English. According to Simmel, the Florentine banking consortiums, which dealt with Edward II and Edward III of England, insisted upon hostages. In 1340, they demanded as security not indeed a pound of the royal flesh, but the whole reverend person of the Archbishop of Canterbury who was then shipped over to the bankers at Brabant without demur.

In 1612, a short time after Shakespeare's play appeared, another case of this kind occurred. London had to offer one of its prominent citizens as a pledge to a banker of Genoa, the illustrious Sir Orazio Pallavicino, a Catholic, a cultivated, humane, dear friend of Queen Elizabeth who knighted him. Pallavicino, eager to defend the country in which he had so heavily invested, outfitted at his own expense a ship to help defeat the Spanish Armada.

In short, *Shylock* had every reason to rely on Christian precedent for his contract exacting a pound of *Antonio's* flesh as well as for demanding interest on his loan. Had he applied to Bologna for legal advice, he might have had the most expert assistance in bolstering up his claim. *Portia*, who defended *Antonio*, was helped by Bologna; and that distinguished school of jurisprudence would not have refused comfort to *Shylock*. Bologna had developed Roman law for the purpose in part of legalizing and sanctifying business corporations; early in the 1500's, she supplied hired lecturers and propagandists to the Germany of Fugger in order that they might help to combat the anti-trust legislation flaring up in southern Germany. Had Bologna failed *Shylock*, he could have turned to Genoa where lawyers were accustomed to million-florin cases; or to Paris whose astute professors had been able to square the operations of Antwerp speculators with the canon law.

When the trial scene opens in Shakespeare's play, the case of *Shylock* is "water-tight"; it cannot be dissolved by "the gentle dew from heaven." If *Shylock* loses the verdict, it is solely because he is *not* a "grasping usurer," eager for his money, but plainly a psychiatric case, a man who forgets profit entirely in his thirst for the highly unbourgeois pleasure of revenge. One may imagine a feudal knight ignoring business interests in his ungovernable wrath; it is difficult to visualize any Cinquecento Venetian, whether Jew or Christian, so chivalric in sentiment. For that reason, when *Antonio* proposes the full discharge of his debt to *Shylock*, and *Shylock*, with romantic insistence, demands the measure of flesh instead, the Jew is condemned as unfit to associate with capitalists.

By one of the curious tricks of the popular mind, *Shylock* has been accepted as a type of hardened mediaeval usurer, though he is certainly the reverse. A similar lack of reflection is responsible for the common notion that the Jews were supreme in European finance in the Middle Ages—that they were crafty wizards who overpowered simple Gentiles. The opposite of this notion is nearer the truth. The Jews were really unable to compete with Christian wizards of finance.

In works not as yet wholly available to the general English-reading public, old concepts of economic history have been overturned by modern French and German scholarship. The newer researchers, who have opened the dusty archives of cities and the files of old merchant papers, have proved conclusively that the dominant figures in international finance, from the thirteenth to the seventeenth centuries, were Christians. In the light of these historical studies the rôle of the Jews is seen as subordinate. If they attracted folk-animosity more than the Christians, this was due, it now seems, to their being humbler and closer to the plain people, making them easier targets. Yet this is not the whole truth for the plain people, in Italy, England, and particularly in Germany, raged also at the Christian monopolists and often rose against them—a phase of business history hitherto lightly passed over by conventional studies of economic progress.

Even in the Dark Ages, when Jewish influence was strongest, it was far from complete. Probably, some Jewish families carried over wealth and capitalist technique from the dissolving Roman Empire into the feudal world, and were able to outwit many rough war-lords who knew nothing of arithmetic and could only add by force and divide with a hatchet. In Spain, the Jews were able to master industries and maintain their sway for a long time, for the Spanish nobility was unusually un-tutored and belligerent. But Spain was the one sphere of undisputed triumph for the mediaeval Jews. Elsewhere, they were less successful; they never did win a prominent position in North Germany, among the Hanseatics; nor were they ever able to compete with the natives in Italian Florence. More than in Germany or Italy, which were relatively advanced economically, the Jews found foothold in France and England, realms slower to develop money-economy. But even in France and England, by the 1200's, they were being pushed to the wall by Italian bankers.

The supposed might of Jewish usurers shrinks to a comparatively puny size in the cold light of modern scholarship, now that the actual records have been dragged forth and studied. It now becomes evident that Florentines, rather than Jews, taught Europe the advanced methods of finance-capitalism. And the Florentines needed no instruction in the arts of gouging and gaining from Orientals.

The ancestors of the Florentines, the ancient Etruscans, were in business while the forebears of the Jews were largely engaged in tilling fields and vineyards in Palestine. So unpropitious was the climate of mediaeval Florence to strangers that, as Renard points out, her early annals contain the name of but a single Jew, and he baptized. Only for one brief moment do Jews appear to have been admitted to that city; they were expressly invited by Lorenzo the Magnificent himself, who hoped, explains De Reumont, that the Jews would lend *at a much lower rate than Christians*, and so relieve the poor. Of course, they were only supposed to take over the small loan business among the lower classes, matters too insignificant for Lorenzo himself. In those days, the Medi-cean balls adorned palaces—they had not yet become symbols of pawn-shops. After a short while, the Jews were excluded from Florence, with permission to take their profits along.

The reason for Florentine superiority was an access to two sources of capital denied to mediaeval Jews: industry and church finance. Ac-cumulating funds far beyond the reach of the most "grasping" mere-usurer, they attained a power and arrogance which were unmatched in

Europe. With such advantages, they easily ousted the Jews from France in the 1200's. By the century when Shakespeare wrote "The Merchant of Venice," France, under a Medicean Queen, was wholly a prey to Italian leeches. In the 1200's, also, Florentines had extended their influence across the Channel and dominated England.

The figure of the money-lender, *Isaac*, in Walter Scott's "Ivanhoe," is deeply graven on the popular mind, while no novelist has so powerfully portrayed the Italian financiers who were bleeding the English people in that period. Whenever Jews were squeezed by the English kings, this was in fact usually to pay debts contracted to some Italian banking consortium. As the Della Scala and Dal Borgo families of Florence, all good Catholics, lent the British Crown half a million gold lire in 1256, they demanded as security a lien on most of the royal income, including not only revenues from the King's forests, but also the tax on Jews. They took 60 per cent interest in view of the risks involved in lending to so unstable an institution as the British Throne. And poor Henry III, who had to pay this and other debts to Christian lenders, amounting to 19,000,000 gold lire in all, or 250,000 pounds sterling, was forced to bleed the Jews of London. He assembled them and declared: "By the Head of Christ, it is fearful to think of the debts I have contracted." To be just to that harassed monarch, it is only fair to observe that he squeezed the prelates of the English churches as ruthlessly as he drained the Jews—but all the movable wealth in England could not satisfy Florentine avarice.

Jews were expelled from England in 1290 and were unable to return until, generations later, Cromwell invited them back to help finance a war for trade; but the Italians were not shaken from that country until the Protestant Reformation. Of course some Jews survived the edicts but they were relegated to the background. They could only carry on in a small way or in local regions. Far outshone by the rich creditors of the British Crown, by men like Pallavicino or Gresham, they were reduced to annoying local merchants such as, for instance, Shakespeare's father. Thus "The Merchant of Venice" is a symptom of the Stratford-on-Avon, lower-bourgeois mentality, making it the more probable that Shakespeare really wrote it, and not Bacon, Lord Verulam, who moved in more sophisticated circles.

At the close of the Cinquecento, as Shakespeare's comedy was composed, Jews were everywhere being supplanted by competent Gentile financiers. A wave of expulsions had driven them from many of the principal ports and marts of Europe: they had to leave Cologne in 1425; Augsburg in 1439; Nürnberg in 1498 and Ulm in the next year; Spain and Sicily in 1492, Naples in 1540; Genoa and Venice in 1550. And, throughout that century, the leading financiers were exclusively Christians. Jacob Fugger was a theological student and friend of the Jesuits. Gresham was a Protestant, as well he might be, since his father was perhaps the largest single profiteer from the confiscation of church property under Henry VIII. In the company of the Capponi, Grimaldi, Paumgartner, Welser, Höchstetter, Imhof, Tucher, Kleberg, Chigi, Ducci and the firm of Haug, Langnauer and Company, all Christian creditors of Christian kings, not a single Jewish magnate of remotely comparable importance has been found.

To be quite accurate, one Jewish name is revealed in the detailed and painstaking survey of high finance in the Cinquecento, made by the German scholar, Ehrenberg. After he had studied the major deals of a hundred years, Ehrenberg did finally discover, far down on the lists of money-lenders, vastly overshadowed by the mighty Christian bankers, a solitary Jew who actually lent a considerable sum to Nürnberg. But on nearer inspection, it turned out that this old money-lender was merely acting as the agent—for an abbot.

The Nürnberg transaction, which was so unique in including a Jewish name, was the flotation of a loan for constructing the enormous ramparts yet visible around that city. The funds were provided by a Christian consortium headed by the pious mayor, Endres Imhof, which charged the city 12 per cent and, to make a profit, borrowed the money from others at a much lower rate. Most of it was procured from Christians. But a very minor share was obtained from the above-mentioned character, the "modest Jew Joseph of the Golden Swan," as he was styled, who owned none of it himself, but was merely showing a local prelate how to invest his surplus advantageously.

In short, "The Merchant of Venice" was written at the close of a long period of development in Europe, during which the canon law prohibiting usury had been broken down by Catholic interpretation, or by defiance, and by Protestants; so Christians had superseded Jews with a clear conscience. The play must therefore be regarded as a quaint relic, and not as a picture of contemporary business on the Continent; it is indicative mainly of English backwardness.

Hence discussion of Jewish participation in European finance may be passed over until a later period. Jews really remained insignificant in high finance from the Cinquecento to the nineteenth century, the era of the Rothschilds. For the full story of the development of capitalism it is necessary to turn to that remarkable town of Florence, in which the movement to break down religious restrictions upon business was most aggressively furthered, by Christian manipulators of startling abilities. Florence, and not the Jew, was the instructor of the rustic denizens of Northern Europe. She taught them the rudiments of finance-capitalism—through their skins.

Florence was thus the third city-republic of the Middle Ages to contribute vital features to the business man's system. For if he derived his morals from the Germans, and got his pants from the Venetians, he received an important share of his methods and ideas from the old seat of the goddess Fortuna on the river Arno.

VI

FLORENCE: TURBULENT CITY OF INDIVIDUALISM

WHILE THE RÔLE of the Jews in the evolution of modern capitalism has received exaggerated emphasis in the popular mind, including that of Professor Sombart, the prodigious share of the Italians in forming business practices and concepts has been correspondingly underestimated. In England and America, for a variety of reasons, misconceptions about Italy are particularly abundant; the Anglo-Saxon tends to view Italy through a roseate haze, as the home of a passionate and impractical people, devoted to art and religion rather than to profit-making. Yet in the past, Italy was in fact the scene of pagan revolt against clerical restraints on trade; at an extremely early date, it produced capitalistic methods of industrial and financial exploitation and some business dictatorships which exhibited many of the characteristics of present-day Fascism.

The sweet illusion respecting the nature of the old Italian commercial life which was implanted in the British mind by William Shakespeare, was still further strengthened in the nineteenth century by other writers like George Eliot and especially by John Ruskin, the great social critic who conjured up the most magical visions of mediaeval Italian society, out of his own imagination and without benefit of research. Ruskin was the son of a conservative wine-merchant whose journeys in wine-growing regions brought the impressionable youth to Italy; there Ruskin found in Italian relics of art a message of social salvation for England, then undergoing the most shocking early phases of the Industrial Revolution. Inspired by the matchless beauty of Florence and Venice, Ruskin returned to look at the North of England, blackened and defiled by soot and slag; much to the chagrin of his parent, he attacked the machine as the destroyer of human dignity and denounced the then sacred doctrine of laissez faire as a mere pretext for untrammeled greed.

Many Victorians accepted Ruskin's vision of Italy for the same reasons. Another recalcitrant son of a business man, William Morris, escaped the paternal brokerage office and devoted himself to spreading the gospel of the gilds and handicrafts. The aesthetes known as "Pre-Raphaelites," who followed the leadership of Ruskin and Morris, helped to nourish the legend of a pure and lofty old Italy, a kind of lost Garden of Eden, in which venders and makers of goods had dwelt peacefully together as happy gild-brothers, united in "honest Christian faith and vital craftsmanship," unspoiled by vulgarities of commercial mass-production.

These enthusiastic "mediaevalists" urged England to hush her wheels and give heed to her soul. Preaching regeneration through observing the sublime example set in the "Age of Giotto," they did have a decided influence in deflecting the course of English capitalism. They aroused consumers to demand some aesthetic values in the products of the machine. And they focused attention on the worst evils of industrialism so stridently that many Englishmen, when they read about the spiritual serenity of the old Italians, felt abashed at their own earthy greed. But compelling and useful as this wonderful myth appeared, it was without documentary foundation.

At the time Ruskin began to study art in Italy in the 1830's, little was known of economic history in Europe. The origins of the machine, of competitive individualism, of scientific rationalism, of factory organization, had not yet been traced back by French and German scholars to mediaeval days. The dust of centuries still lay thick upon the yellowed documents in the archives of the old towns. What a herculean task had yet to be performed in deciphering and evaluating these manuscripts, may be judged from the fact that a single business house in Italy, that of Francesco Datini, who died in 1410, left records filling 97 yards of shelf, and besides, a correspondence of 140,000 letters.

Without such material at his disposal to reconstruct the actual background of early Italian life, Ruskin had to rely mainly on the evidence of his eyes. Gazing upon the portraits of Italian merchants, he was delighted with their "healthy serenity" of mien, and announced "I see no hypocrisy in their countenances." He inferred that "a deep and constant tone of individual religion" had lent "a peculiar dignity to the conduct even of their commercial transactions." In his "Ariadne Florentina," Ruskin declared that the innocent Italians had repudiated, "with universal contempt and malediction," the nefarious practice of receiving interest until the fifteenth century, and had left usury to Jews. For this assertion, Ruskin adduced no proof except Shakespeare's "Merchant of Venice." And he advanced none at all for his claim that it was the wicked Germans of Augsburg who at length corrupted this paradise of simplicity.

Art, argued Ruskin, can only spring from a "good society"; Florence and Venice were more beautiful than Manchester or Liverpool; hence they must have been more virtuous. How could Venice, "fair city of graceful arcades and gleaming walls," appear like a white "vestal from the sea," if she had not known "a depth of devotion, in which lay all her strength"? Whence came the radiance in the paintings of the Florentine Giotto, if it was not the reflection of a nobler social scheme?

In Ruskin's youth, his countrymen supposed, some with pride and a few with contrition, that they had invented the machine. They would have scouted as ridiculous the idea that Englishmen had ever been forced to learn, from a parcel of foreigners, how to make money. Least of all, would they have believed that their old tutors had been Germans and Italians. Both Germany and Italy had fallen into such poverty and apathy by the 1830's, that they no longer seemed capable of ever having invented anything rational or profitable.

Germany at that period had reverted to bucolic simplicity. A casual visitor there would not have guessed that, in the 1400's, she had been famous as a "land of machines" and miraculous contrivances. Nor would anyone have supposed that, in just a few decades, by the 1870's, she could suddenly regain her old ingenuity and, at one bound, overleap England again in technological skill.

Similarly unimpressive at that day was Italy, exhausted by Napoleonic exactions. Her people, wrapped in rags and dwelling amid ruins, seemed lazy and superstitious to the British. It was natural to suppose, as Ruskin did, that their ancestors must have been even more childlike and oblivious to material advantages. It was easy to set up a fictitious ideal society in that sunlit scenery.

Ruskin did not realize, when he fled to Italy from the filth and noise of England's "Black Triangle," that he was not escaping industrialism, but was actually making a pilgrimage to its cradle. The sources of the evils he most deplored at home lay in those two mellow towns which exerted the strongest fascination over him, Venice and Florence. Venice was founded, like Liverpool, upon the slave-trade. Florence, in the age of Giotto, was already a mediaeval Manchester, bringing raw materials from afar, making them up by highly complex processes, and distributing them throughout Europe more cheaply than the craftsmen of other places could afford to do. Led by a malicious Fate, therefore, Ruskin, burning with desire for a society built on social justice and aesthetic rapture, fixed his ideal society in the very country, the exact cities, and even the precise period, in which capitalism unfolded its early buds.

CITY OF FORTUNE

Florence and Venice were in fact the two most irreligious cities in mediaeval Italy. Their relations with clerical Rome, however, were far from similar. While Venice carefully retained the forms of faith, her government was constantly clashing with the Holy See. Florence, on the contrary, was usually on the side of Rome officially, for she was the chief banker of the Popes and supported them against the claims of the German Emperors. But privately the Florentines were extremely pagan and boasted their kinship with the classic past; more than any other men of Italy, they assisted in the revival, or Renaissance, of the Greek and Roman culture.

Both Florence and Venice had ties with pre-Christian antiquity and the Infidel Turk. Venice restored to Europe much of the business lore which had been preserved in Constantinople and Alexandria from Roman times. Florence also had relations with these sites of classic culture. The monks and nuns who came from Alexandria to Florence in the thirteenth century and set up spinning and weaving establishments belonged to an Eastern sect, the Humiliati, which maintained that ascetics should support themselves by business and not by begging. This view of business as compatible with spirituality, so characteristically Alexandrian, easily took root by the Arno. Florentine connections with Constantinople were established much later, but they were profitable ties, for after the Grand Turk took that city in 1453 the Florentines obtained formal trading privileges in the Golden Horn. The Turk feared Venice and Genoa, suspecting that they had designs upon his territories as well as his markets, and welcomed the Florentines by preference. At once jealous Venice thought of fighting Florence, but the wily Florentine, Cosimo de' Medici, skillfully drained Venetian banks of their gold and thus withdrew the sinews of war from the rival.

Despite the papal bans upon such unholy intercourse, the two cities struggled for the trade of the Infidel. Florence had marketed her cloth abundantly through Venetian merchants in the Near East until at last she established direct connections with the Turks. Neither city for a moment intended to abandon this illicit traffic. Venice dealt with the Infidel without apology. But Florence justified her actions by appealing to pagan philosophy; it was hardly an accident, as Doren points out, that Cosimo de' Medici was founding his Platonic Academy to foster the spirit of the heathen thinkers, while he was extending the hand of friendship to the Turk.

Moreover, Florentine rebellion against Rome had traditional roots. Florence lies in that region of Italy called Tuscany after the race of powerful Etruscan merchants, foes of the Romans, who lived there in very ancient times. Though the Etruscans finally surrendered to the Roman sword, they never succumbed to Roman agrarian views, but continued to struggle against Roman dominance with the subtle methods of finance, until at last the masterful financier, Maecenas, who, as

Horace declares, boasted his descent from Etruscan monarchs, managed to place Octavian on the throne as the first Emperor of the Roman world. Maecenas, the power behind this throne, reaped rich harvests in Egyptian real estate and, becoming Prefect of all Italy, was a virtual ruler of the Italian people.

Resistance to Rome continued under another guise in the last years of the Empire, when Christianity was spreading from the Roman center. Roman Christianity was agrarian rather than commercial; its hierarchical order was founded upon agriculture as the most stable basis for society. Furthermore the Roman Church declared that the world was ruled by Divine Plan and not by chance and competition. St. Augustine denounced the Etruscan deity, Fortuna, as a dangerous creature whose whims destroyed social order, and he warned her devotees, the ambitious merchants, against attempting to hurt the heavenly scheme by adherence to her cult. Naturally this conception of life was coldly received by the Etruscans; Schillman states that the market-town of Florence was particularly loath to tear down pagan statues. One of the last places in Italy to accept Christianity, it held out until after the new faith was official. Though dethroned formally, the goddess Fortuna, the beloved, continued to dwell in the hearts, if not on the altars, of her commercial followers.

The Tuscans may have been subdued for a few centuries after the so-called "Fall" of Rome in 410. This Fall was of course not a sudden cataclysm appearing out of nowhere, but was rather a gradual impoverishment of the world, as cash disappeared—probably eastward—and trade was replaced by barter. For a while this left the Florentines with little scope for their talents, but by 753, at any rate, their marketplace had won back a measure of privileges and importance; and by the year 1000 it was apparent that the Tuscans were confirmed individualists who could not be integrated into a rural scheme. They were beginning again to draw the Roman metropolis into their debt, and were starting afresh on a renewed campaign against Rome which was to end, not with a Maecenas as Italian Prefect, but with a Medici as wearer of the papal tiara.

The sky-line of Tuscan towns, around the year 1000, was dominated not by church spires but by the skyscraper offices of rival business families, who took occasional pot-shots at their competitors through lofty loopholes. In Pisa, it is said, there were a thousand of these stone towers, some ten or fifteen stories high, in which merchants had shops as well as homes. Florence had scores of such edifices and her rich men were known as "delle torre," towered men. How other towns must have looked, is illustrated by the unique survival today of San Gimignano, that queer little mediaeval Manhattan. And indeed, in old Tuscany and in modern America, skyscraper building was the sign of a similar social phenomenon—intense competition among embattled interests. It was the outward evidence of resistance to feudal regimentation and state planning.

The towered men of Florence were, as a matter of fact, profiteering on the increasing distress of agrarians around them. Money-economy was slowly reviving, toward the year 1000, and many landed men fell into debt and misery because they could not raise cash even on the broadest acres. From such a land-poor nobility, even a very little coin might procure big estates. And the Florentines had ready cash in abundance, not only because they were traders and, in a small way, makers of goods, but also because kings and priests then began to send their funds to Florence for safe keeping and enlargement. Few chances for investment were at hand, and the Florentines acquired renown as holders and lenders of funds. Thus the city was soon known as the "fontana dell' oro," the fountain of gold.

The money-changers of many-towered Tuscany extended their holdings through the North of Italy and into the South of France, where they acquired châteaux and noble titles by purchase, and substituted their sons as lords and prelates in place of the old incumbents. Their power grew at home until, by the opening of the fourteenth century, the Trecento, the environs of Florence had been largely absorbed by bourgeois. This process met some resistance, to be sure, from chivalric debtors, many of whom were Germans and who appealed to the suzerain of Tuscany, the German Emperor, for protection against the loan sharks. To combat them, the Florentine moneyed men turned to the opposing party of the Popes, called the Guelfs, in distinction to the Emperor's men, the Ghibellines. No doubt it was a little ironical for the usurers of Florence to seek succor from the Church which forbade usury, but by so doing, they freed themselves from the jurisdiction of the imperial courts and could, proclaiming their independence, possess themselves of their debtors' goods.

Their rapacity won the contempt of the poet, Dante, who believed in the imperial cause and was banned from Florence during one of the triumphs of the money-lending party. He had all the more reason to bear them a grudge because the father of his Divine Lady, Beatrice, whom he makes his guide through Paradise, was a banker, Portinari. Portinari did not propose to have his daughter marry a mere poet but gave her instead to a substantial banker like himself, an aged man with a grown son, the latter being one of the more notorious financiers and skinflints of the city. With an understandable animosity, Dante places the usurers in his "Inferno," not among the merely avaricious, but deeper down, among those guilty of crimes of violence; that was because they resorted to such shocking means to seize the persons and chattels of their victims. One of the men described by Dante belonged to a family which so despoiled an entire community as to cause a folk-uprising.

Needless to say, these are all good Christians whom Dante descries cowering on the burning sands of Maleboge, each with a moneybag around his neck stamped with the arms of his firm. By these coats-of-arms, they can be identified as prominent usurers of well-known families. In order of their appearance in Canto VII, they are: the Gianfigliazzi, the Ubbriachi, the de' Scovegni; Vitaliano Vitaliani of Padua; and Messer Giovanni de' Bicci of Florence, whose family was allied with the Medici.

Through the eyes their grief was bursting forth; on this side, on that, they with their hands kept warding off, sometimes the flames, sometimes the burning soil.

Not otherwise the dogs in summer do, now with snout, now with paw, when they are bitten by fleas, or flies . . .

After I had set my eyes upon the visages of several on whom the dolorous fire falls, I knew not any of them; but I observed

That from the neck of each there hung a pouch, which had a certain colour and a certain impress . . .

As I came among them looking, on a yellow purse I saw azure, that had the semblance and gesture of a lion.

Then, my look continuing its course, I saw another of them, red as blood, display a goose more white than butter.

And one who, with a sow azure and pregnant, had his argent sacklet, stamped, said to me: "What art thou doing in this pit?

Get thee gone; and as thou art alive, know that my neighbour Vitaliano shall sit here at my left side.

With these Florentines am I, a Paduan; many times they din my ears, shouting: 'Let the sovereign cavalier come,

Who will bring the pouch with the three goats!' " Then he writhed his mouth, and thrust his tongue out, like an ox that licks his nose.

Though the men consigned to Hell by Dante were professional money-changers, it was not their gild which in fact wielded the supreme financial power in Florence. The chief families of the city were not primarily and openly bankers, but ostensibly merchants; in the course of merchandising, however, they lent on a far larger scale than the mere money-changers, and to more distant customers, and yet escaped the odium which fell upon those dealing frankly in coins. These merchants, importers of raw materials and exporters of finished products, were grouped in the Arte di Calimala, the big gild deriving its name from a lane in which its gorgeous shops were set up—a lane formerly the abode of courtesans and hence called the Evil Street. It was the mercantile brethren of the Evil Street, and not the simple usurers on Dante's burning sands, who are regarded by modern scholars as the true financial talents of Florence.

Closely allied with the exporters were the manufacturers, enrolled in the wool gild. The distinction was not always clear between them, for the latter could hold shares in the firms of the former and participate in their ventures. Money-getting was not narrowed down as yet and divided among specialists. An illustration of the diversification of interests then prevailing is afforded by the Scali family. They engaged in the wool trade of England and lent money to the British Crown; they had large interests in France and bought the right to farm taxes in Paris, Toulouse, Narbonne and Bordeaux; they held the right to coin money at Naples; they formed a consortium which collected taxes in the city of Florence and paid for the privilege by supplying grain to the annual value of 400,000 gold florins. The coat-of-arms of this versatile family bore the ideal device of a self-made man: a ladder.

The Acciaiuoli were of humble origin, but members of their widely distributed clan attained brilliant distinctions in France and became dukes of Athens and Thebes. They dealt in hides, wool, cloth, and the excellent products of the weapon-factories of Florence. They also farmed taxes in many communities and held mortgages on distant regions. On the other hand, the Bardi were originally noblemen who turned to trading; as rich bankers, they lent millions of florins of their own capital and funds of depositors to potentates; as merchants, they provisioned Neapolitan armies, and dealt in spices and cheese.

Comparatively late on the scene were the plebeian Medici, whose power was not shown until late in the 1300's, when many of the oldest firms had fallen. Part of the secret of the Medicean strength was an even wider diversification and distribution of *rischio* than that practiced by their predecessors. As manufacturers, they ran silk and wool plants. As traders, they had extensive connections; the Bruges office, for example, shipped Oriental spices, almonds, sugar and cloth to the London office in exchange for wool and hides. The head of the Medici had the books of all branches sent him for yearly inspection and in the late 1400's these included 24 from France, 37 from Naples and 50 from Turkey. As bankers, they were involved in foreign diplomacy; thus the Medici forced a branch office upon Milan by supporting a tyrant, Sforza, who protected them while they induced courtiers and clerics to buy shares in their bank.

Of course all these men took what amounted to interest on their money. But it was not given so bad a name. The return on investments or loans was termed often a "gift"; or a man might "buy" a jewel or a horse at an enormous price, not described as a loan. Or, when lending 100 florins, a banker might write down 200 florins on the books to cover interest. Such practices, however, were not suffered to escape the eyes of the Church, for in the Middle Ages, the cloistered monks were often far from cloudy mystics. Many of the confessors were fully the equal of the confessed, and could dispute about the most subtle transactions, pointing their argument by learned references to the horse-trade. Yet there was one Florentine trick which had them all puzzled, the so-called *baratto*.

The *baratto* was an exchange of wares which merchants sometimes found easier than shipments of money. For instance, a man might buy cloth at 30 shillings an ell for cash, or at 35 shillings if payment was deferred. Choosing the latter, he would pay two-fifths in wool, which again cost more if the time-factor entered. Now was this, or was it not, interest-taking? Little money changed hands. No percentages were mentioned. Many a theologian in Florence must have wished that he had only simple questions to consider such as vexed the monks of Paris—like the number of angels able to stand on a pin-point.

Theoretically, the fathers of the Church remained adamant against the practice of making money bear fruit. Not even the holy Antoninus, friend of the Medici and Bishop of Florence, who came nearest to excusing the operations of the financiers, could exonerate them all. The Church condemned business men to render, on their deathbeds, that part of their wealth which had been won by usury. Often, as Davidsohn found, dying merchants did comply with this demand in order to win burial in holy ground (Portinari, father of Beatrice, did so). They were not responsible if their heirs refused to obey their last will and testament. And the Church could not insist so effectively, after the religious offices around Florence were filled with relatives of the leading moneyed families.

Whatever it was called, interest at very high rates was taken and given from the 1100's down to the 1500's, during the period considered by Ruskin as far too pure for such exactions. The Peruzzi and Frescobaldi were known to demand as high as 266 per cent on bad risks like the English. The rate appears to have fallen as money economy spread and cash grew more plentiful; before 1210 it was regularly 50-60 per cent, while in 1420 attempts were made by the government, though in vain, to establish 20 per cent as a maximum, at least on loans to the poor. The current Florentine proverb contained truth as well as jest: "25 per cent is nothing at all; 50 per cent will pass the time away; 100 per cent is interesting."

THE COMING OF THE MACHINE

As the estates around Florence were absorbed by money-lenders and neighboring towns were captured and despoiled by military force, the character of rural life was altered to a degree unexampled elsewhere in the Middle Ages. Serfs were "emancipated" and flocked to town as labor proletariat. In the villages a "putting-out system" of spinning was established. Traveling agents from the city brought raw materials to the village homes and paid the workers, mostly women, for their labor. To increase the speed and quality of the work, leaders of the great Florentine wool gild urged the Church to cooperate. On their insistence, says Renard, the village priests read pastoral letters thrice a year to their flocks, threatening any unsubmissive spinners with exclusion from Communion. Only upon payment of a large sum could a guilty woman reenter the fold. This, as Davidsohn remarks, furnished revenue to many priests, but a number of others, like Fra Giordano da Rinalto, thundered against the abuses of the system.

The wide-eyed yokelry of the Trecento, accordingly, were awed by the gilded frescoes of the Giotto-esque saints, and frightened by threats of anathema from the pulpit in case they should neglect their wheels. They were already in a state not unlike that prevailing in Europe many generations later, on the eve of the Industrial Revolution. Their "emancipation" was similar to that preceding high capitalism in nineteenth-century Germany; the putting-out system was close to that spread in the North of England on the eve of the invention of the Power-Machine.

The Machine had indeed made its appearance in Florence in the 1300's, though of course it lacked the impetus of steam to make the revolution complete. Even the water-driven or hand-operated mechanical contrivances of mediaeval Florence, however, had broken into the old security of the small handicraft method of production.

This machinery was introduced by the big merchants of the chief gilds who had capital and initiative, enabling them to transcend the established narrow routine. Such accumulation of capital was possible partly because Florentine merchants did not deal primarily in low-cost goods like the Hanseatics, but instead in the highest grades of weapons and textiles, which brought large profits. By 1300 they were making and selling fine imitations of Chinese silk brocades. To obtain the raw materials for such manufactures, they had to look far away and gather considerable amounts of capital; the ramifications of the cloth industry required bringing raw silk from the Far East, wool from Spain and England and alum from Turkey. The quantities so handled were by no means negligible: in one year, 607,155 pounds of oil were used in the cloth-works, and 400,000 pounds of alum for processing. So costly was the latter that the manufacturers thought it worth while to engage a duke and six thousand mercenaries to ruin the town of Volterra which dared to break a lease of a Florentine company on an alum-mine.

Big entrepreneurs, accordingly, managed the production and distribution of Florentine wares. In 1338, they turned out some 100,000 pieces of cloth worth, in the modern equivalent, perhaps three million dollars; this was the estimate of Villani, the old chronicler and himself a business man. In the effort to speed up industry, and make profits out of industries requiring so heavy an outlay, many sorts of machines were introduced in the Trecento, for grinding wheat or cleaning wool. The silk industry had perhaps the most advanced types, often very complex, like that silk-mill, run by water-power at Bologna, which in 1341, did "the work of 4,000 spinning women," as the old contract with the municipality specifies.

While the spirit of innovation was widespread in the North of Italy, Florence was the center. At the opening of that century, a preacher declared: "Any day, a new art may arise. . . . The end of invention is not yet in sight. It is hardly twenty years since eyeglasses were invented. . . . I saw the man who made them first and spoke with him." This Florentine alertness was needed to keep ahead in certain markets, as in England. Florence could bring wool from England, make it into cloth and ship it back through Hanseatic Germans or Genoese, and yet undersell the weavers of that island. But Florence could only undercut the Britons by careful planning of industry, just as Britain, centuries later, underbid the poor craftsmen of India with her technology.

Steadily the improvements in Florentine plants advanced, until by 1407, wool passed through at least thirty hands, no person performing more than one task. In large carding and washing and other establishments, wage-earners were employed, summoned and released by the ringing of a bell; they were paid a tariff fixed by the masters and were relentlessly watched and speeded up by foremen. Such laborers formed a floating population comprising tens of thousands, much like that of a modern industrial town. Some were employed but a small part of the year; they were in danger of lockouts and often were dismissed at a day's notice, for feudal obligations ceased at the gates of Florence. To lower the wage-rate, laborers were drawn from the manufacturing centers of Flanders or Germany, and were segregated to ensure docility. All such non-gild workers were forbidden to combine, even in religious groups, except by express permission. Politically they were without rights. Often they were paid in kind or in depreciated money; and if rebellious, they could be sentenced to the jail or the lash by judges who were at the same time their employers.

Even within the gilds, class lines were rigorously drawn. The lesser craftsmen in them were better organized than the "proletariat" indeed, but nevertheless were under a rigid hierarchy. In the wool gild, for instance, high offices were monopolized by the richest members. The regulations admitted to leadership only men who did not have to work with their own hands, and who produced large amounts of cloth from plants operated by the labor of others—true employers. But the number of such men declined; if 300 textile plants were going at the opening of the 1300's, these had been cut down to 200 by 1339, and the owners of these fewer but larger plants laid down the law to 30,000 workers. In reality, the leaders of the wool gild were fewer than 200, for there was an inner ring among them. Against their decrees, said Machiavelli, there was no appeal, when smaller men felt "they were not sufficiently paid for their work or were oppressed by their masters."

Such gilds were states within the State. The city government could not interfere with them to regulate prices or wages. At times it did indeed struggle, though in vain, against their monopolistic practices. Measures were fruitlessly passed to check price-raising rings, and sometimes offenders were threatened with the scaffold. But, while a few petty butchers paid for extortion with their heads, there is no record, says Davidsohn, that a great merchant or manufacturer suffered the extreme penalty for much larger frauds. On the whole, he thinks: "the might of the small mediaeval city-state was as little able to cope with the task of hindering the formation of trusts, as that of modern monarchies."

The régime of the Trecento gildsmen was one of laissez faire, no whit less coldly calculated than that of Ruskin's England. They were the most ruthless exploiters in Europe at that time, showing their power even more openly than their contemporaries in Cologne or Bruges. One of the leading students of old Florence, Doren, has framed the indictment:

> There is hardly any period in world-history, in which the natural superiority of capital over the property-less and the capitalless handicrafts has appeared more heedless, less bound by moral and legal restrictions, than in the flowering-period of the Florentine cloth-industry.

Had England, therefore, chosen to follow the prescriptions of Ruskin and Morris in the nineteenth century, and tried to reproduce the social life of old Florence in order to create similar beauty, she would have had first of all to close trades unions, let factories run at night as well as by day, and censor such talks to workingmen as Ruskin delighted to give, since the Medici were frankly opposed to the higher education of labor. Had England accepted Ruskin's premise that economic status determines art, she could not have had a Giotto and a Botticelli at the same time. The two painters belonged to very different periods economically; Giotto painted at the height of Florentine prosperity, while Botticelli drew his "Spring" in the late autumn of his city's industry. To attain a Botticelli, England would have had to go into a bankruptcy and let some financier like Rothschild play the part of a Medici by engrossing the entire state income. But of course this is idle fantasy; modern skeptics, aware of the rôle played by other than economic factors in the making of art, doubt whether the result, even of such sacrifices, would have been the making of a Botticelli out of an Aubrey Beardsley.

FINANCE—IMPERIALISM AND THE CRUSADES

This industrial and social transformation, going on within and around the city of Florence, coincided with the extension of Florentine financial power over Europe, and the struggle within Florence itself of the bourgeoisie against the nobility. In this latter class-strife, the Church played a decisive part, because it and the bourgeoisie were bound together by financial and political interests.

It was not frivolous extravagance that threw the earlier Popes into the arms of the Florentine money-lenders, but the grim necessity for raising funds to defeat the forces of feudal disintegration and chaos; the Church had to contest the claims of feudal lords who sought to break down the Christian community of Europe. Rome was thus striving against the noblemen's party, as much as the Florentine bankers. Priests and bankers, whether they wished or not, were forced to lend one another mutual encouragement.

Very early, the Popes became enmeshed in the Florentine financial network. Imprisoned Pope John had to obtain ransom from Giovanni de' Medici, who sent the money through the German importing firm of Rommel & Company. How large some of these debts were may be judged from the fact that Boniface VII borrowed more than $100,000 (in modern terms) from one Florentine firm, and a quarter of a million from another. Renard tells us that Pope Urban IV raised a loan from the Bardi and Frescobaldi for which he had to give all his own jewels and silver vases as security, and in addition strip the Roman churches of ornaments. Even so, he could not satisfy the Tuscan bankers. Bitterly he asked them whether, perhaps, they "expected him to perform a miracle?"

The cooperation of Church and Business was sealed during the Crusades. The Holy Wars against the Infidel in the East, blessed by the Popes, offered opportunities for Florence as well as Venice to carve out a commercial empire. The two Italian cities were expanding their power simultaneously, in the 1200's; while the Venetians were taking Constantinople and the Eastern markets, the Florentines were stretching their financial influence westward instead, over France and England. Then, when the Venetians were consolidating their gains and setting up an oligarchy over the city, the Florentines, also flushed with wealth and success, were completing the formation of their own plutocracy.

The conquests of the Florentines, however, were more subtle than those of Venice or the other Italians. They invaded France as collectors of contributions to the Crusades. Their Christianity, it happened, enabled them to supplant the Jews as money-lenders, for only Christians could well have gathered funds for a Holy War. France, where money-economy was not so widespread as in Italy, was a prey to usurers of various sorts who took advantage of her land-poor noblesse. She expelled the Jews, but Italians came in as ostensibly honest Christian merchants, and practiced a secret usury more baneful than the open lending of the Jews. The French king put many of these Italians in jail. But when the Florentines at last came in under the protection of the Church on so sacred a mission, the State was powerless to molest them.

Too numerous to list were the Florentine families who swarmed over France, buying up the privileges of the towns and absorbing the revenues of the lords. Nothing could stop them. The formidable walls of old Carcassonne, which overawe the tourist today, made no impression whatever on the agents of the Peruzzi firm. A shower of molten lead from the battlements might keep out a knightly invader, but there was no way to bar entry to the Peruzzi who, in 1336, according to Meltzing, gathered up the municipal income there.

Two of the more notorious adventurers of the period were the brothers Franzesi, popularly called Biche and Mouche. Their sister was the first wife of the rich banker, Simone de' Bardi, who later won the hand, in second marriage, of Dante's adored Beatrice. The brothers were immortalized in the satirical verse of the "Decamerone" by Boccaccio, who was himself the son of a Parisian agent of the firm of Bardi and must have known their story at first hand.

Biche and Mouche were the most famous gamblers, swindlers and all-around rogues of Trecento Florence. Nobody was considered worse save only their nephew, the stepson of Dante's Beatrice, who was perhaps the most hated tax-gatherer in France; the French populace rejoiced when he was condemned for a terrible crime. The brothers and the nephew for a long time held France in a comprehensive grasp. Brother Biche, provisioner to the king, squeezed the Paris merchants and speculated in salt and grain. Brother Mouche, as royal treasurer, was also a munitions deliverer. Between them they set up a grand "racketeer" system of expensive "protection" over most of France. They lured the French courtiers into debt so hopelessly that, on one occasion, Brother Mouche was able to prevent the Duke of Brabant from going to war by threatening to take back all the duke's best clothes.

Mouche and Biche bought châteaux in France and became feudal lords. No doubt it irked many a proud French vassal to stoop before the two Italian racketeers, but there was no help for it. They represented the country abroad in utmost splendor; Mouche was ambassador to the Pope in Rome, and once he went with sumpter-mules laden with coin to purchase the neutrality of a German state. The Franzesi also kept in touch with affairs in their home-city of Florence, and were participants in that strife between the papal and imperial parties which resulted in the exile of Dante.

For their loyalty to the papal cause, Mouche and Biche were made papal bankers, and pardoned previous transgressions by the Holy See. But they were trusted and tempted too far. They took in custody the entire papal treasure. That is the end of the story, for the treasure immediately disappeared from the ken of man, and so did Biche and Mouche.

Another Florentine family, much more respectable, though allied with the Franzesi, namely the Bardi, played a powerful rôle in the Hundred Years' War between France and England. They helped both sides. Their cash provided arms for the noble gentlemen who fought at Crécy and at Agincourt, in either party. This attitude of benevolent toleration on the part of the Bardi was not very well understood by the French, who, unsophisticated and chivalric in temper, were not able to appreciate the broad outlook of an international financier. In fact, the French king in a rage once laid hands on some of the Bardi men.

All wars were alike to the Bardi, so far as there was profit for them and their beloved Florence. While England and France were tussling for a century, they and other Italians seized the favorable opportunity to enchain both combatants. An early chance to enslave the Britons came in 1255 when Pope Alexander IV offered the throne of Naples to the King of England, Henry III, for his son. The throne was already occupied, it is true. But the English king was urged to join in a war to remove the occupant, who had been so friendly with the Infidel that the Pope feared for his safety. The Pope offered to bless the enterprise as a Holy War. The expenses were to be raised in England through Church tithes—collected by Florentine bankers.

The Florentines were too wise to suppose that they could raise much cash in the dreamy vales of merry old England. They took wool, instead, to recoup themselves for the large sums lent to the Holy War. The French were charging a high price for their wool, and the Florentines wanted to beat them down. Soon the bankers loaned to the English abbeys and took the sheep as well as the wool for security. Before long, the bankers took the pastures too.

Many Italian firms joined in the great shearing of England. The Frescobaldi, for instance, advanced a few thousand pounds and won the right to collect dues at English and Irish ports. They also supplied wines at fancy prices to the inordinately thirsty English Court. But the chief exploiters remained the Bardi and Peruzzi. The latter, in return for helping Henry III with running expenses, asked 120 per cent interest and charged 60 per cent more when he was not prompt. They took a lien on the state income and set two merchants as guards to supervise his household accounts.

About two generations before the saintly Giotto lived, therefore, the English forefathers of Ruskin and Morris and the Pre-Raphaelites were struggling in the grip of Florentine finance-imperialism. Unlike the painters, the early bankers of Italy were not "Primitives," and their net was so well woven that the English king and his barons writhed in vain in its folds. Unhappy Henry protested that he did not want the Neapolitan throne after all, but the Pope threatened him with excommunication if he backed out. At length Edward III, with a royal gesture, repudiated every penny of his debts and cast some of the agents into the Tower. Then the proud firms of the Bardi and Peruzzi failed and in their collapse shook Florence. Tremors were felt through the courts and markets of Europe.

Merely the bankruptcy of England, of course, would not in itself have been sufficient to shake so great a house as the Bardi. Their embarrassment was really caused by a variety and accumulation of troubles. Florence happened to be quarreling with Naples at the time and the Neapolitans started a run on the Bardi Bank. The loss of several hundred thousand florins lent to the British Crown was indeed a contributory factor, but far from the sole one. And even in their ruin, the Bardi were able to pay their shareholders 46 per cent.

Thereafter the burden of financing England was taken up by other Italians. The Medici, eager to compete with the English weaving industry, which was assuming larger proportions, moved some of their textile plants to that country, much as, in modern times, the English erected mills in China in the hope of retaining the Oriental market.

Until 1490 the wool of England continued to go in great quantities to Florence; but finally the English took their export trade into their own hands. Then Florence was shaken for a second time, and a crisis more grave than the first occurred. Thus, one of the prime reasons for the collapse of that "ideal" society adored by Ruskin was the effective resistance of the English to Florentine exploitation.

The Florentine bankers had hoped to use Englishmen to conquer Naples for them. When this proved impossible, they gladly helped the new French Pope, Urban IV, to bring a party of Frenchmen across Italy for the purpose. To be sure, this was introducing a horde of alien soldiers in a land already torn by German invasions, but the prospect of winning a free hand in Naples was too alluring. Moreover, in return for lending 148,000 livres to the Pope to pay for the expedition, they gathered in treasures of Rome for security. In addition, declares Renard, they were granted the right to sell into slavery the captured Saracen allies of the defeated monarch.

Winning the coveted foothold in Naples, the Florentines continued for many a day to drain that kingdom. They coined money and collected taxes; they provisioned the troops and armed them with weapons of Florentine make. They kept a monopoly on important commodities such as armor, silks, wax, pearls, oil and grain; at one time, when they were about to ship away thousands of tons of grain from Naples, the famished populace demonstrated in the harbor and menaced the Florentine shippers, but without effect. Indeed, there was no way for the natives to defend themselves, since the Florentines had acquired extraterritorial jurisdiction lest any proud Peruzzi suffer indignities at the hands of a native judge. By taking over the royal income and many functions, they reduced the king to a mere scepter-waving puppet. In fact, says Meltzing, he sometimes did not even have a scepter to wave, or a crown to wear, for these were on occasion pawned to the Acciaiuoli family in Florence.

Following the Crusades therefore, the Florentines could count blessings as manifold as those of the Venetians. They had gathered in the statues and jewels of Rome as security and established an authority there which could not be shaken off; they had subdued the French and British; they held mortgages on almost everything in Naples. Nor was this all. As one of the conditions of their support of the Popes, they obtained papal sanction for the little bourgeois revolution which they executed in Florence in 1282.

Blessed by the Holy See, the leading business families of Florence carried out a small armed revolt to set up a reformed government, and effectively excluded from office those stubborn spirits among the feudal noblemen who had not, like the Bardi, gone in for trafficking in hides and cheeses. The rule over the city was entrusted to the priors—or *signori*, as they were later called—who might indeed be noble or plebeian, but in either case must be engaged in some sort of business and enrolled in a commercial gild. This completed the amazing triumph of the Florentine bourgeoisie; it was now in power at home as well as in most of the Christian world.

AGE OF GIOTTO: SOCIAL TRANSFORMATION

"In the thirteenth century," wrote Ruskin, "men wake as if they heard an alarum through the whole vault of heaven, and true human life begins again, and the cradle of this life is the Val d'Arno." At the close of this century, and the opening of the Trecento, the exquisite Giotto, adored master of the English Pre-Raphaelites, was maturing. The year 1300, when Dante is supposed to have had his vision of Hell and Heaven, was taken by Ruskin as the perfect moment in which to contemplate Florentine art and life.

By 1300, the various revolutions, financial, industrial, social and political, were approaching a culminating point. Davidsohn sets 1310 as the time when Florence absorbed most of the terrain around her by war or foreclosure; by the same year the independent craftsmen were thoroughly under the yoke of capitalist manufacturers. By 1282, the merchant-bankers had exploited most of Europe and seated themselves in the saddle at Florence. It is not surprising that art, as well, underwent momentous changes in the life-span of Giotto (1276–1336).

Giotto's career as well as his art illustrate the new age. He was himself a small capitalist. Belonging to the wool gild, he was one of those business men responsible for destroying the handicraft order which Ruskin adored. Presumably he was not a manager of a plant, but he rented looms to poor artisans unable to scrape together the rather large sums needed to buy the new machinery. Giotto charged them exorbitant rates. With reluctance, the scholarly Davidsohn admits: "Master Giotto, painter of divine Madonnas . . . took one hundred and twenty per cent of the worth of the loom as rent, while others, less immortal, contented themselves with fifty per cent."

Thus acquainted with Florentine industry from the inside, Giotto had apparently few delusions about his fellow-citizens. At least, says Renard, he painted a remarkable social fresco for a near-by town, Arezzo, which had suffered much from the claims of Florentines. This fresco has disappeared, but we know from records that it depicted Florence in the guise of a highway robber, snatching the moneybags and even the clothes, from a shivering old man, personifying the community of Arezzo.

Giotto, who could on occasion satirize his fellow-capitalists so merrily, while himself charging poor workingmen more than most, gave expression through his divine brush to the tastes of the rising commercial classes. He and his contemporaries were imparting a warmer touch to the old, stiff Byzantine art; their Madonnas had lovelier and more human faces. Such a trend toward realism met the desires of the Florentine merchants, who, being all-too human themselves, could not worship saints too coldly aloof from mankind. Those severe, angular seraphs who glimmered in the ikons of the Early Christian Church, would have had no compassion upon an erring money-lender.

For the Bardi and Peruzzi, the creditors of England, Giotto painted memorial chapels in the Church of Santa Croce. The former ordered scenes from the life of St. Francis and symbolic figures of Poverty, Chastity and Obedience. At the same time, other rich families were eagerly employing their wealth in church building and decoration. One of these wealthy patrons, minor but typical, was Lamberto Velluti. He was one of the Peruzzi agents who invaded Carcassonne. A moneychanger, banker, dealer in horses and cloth, he had many adventures in Europe and Morocco; at the age of seventy-one, still full of energy, he came home. A hale and hearty old man, Velluti spent his last years supervising the erection of many churches, "by preference upon the lovely hills overlooking the city, from which he returned with liberated soul and boundless appetite" after tours of inspection, as he confessed in the memoirs which he also found time to write.

A fever of building spread among the successful gilds, which, now that they had engrossed the municipal offices, were lavish in adorning the captured community. They built a government palace, a chamber of commerce and beautified the Or San Michele, an edifice thriftily employed as a church below and a warehouse above. Various gilds, lesser and greater, united in the latter enterprise. Bricklayers, apothecaries, butchers and judges contributed statues; the armament manufacturers ordered a St. George by Donatello; the money-changers presented a St. Matthew, perhaps, it may be hazarded, because his Gospel was more favorable to usury than that according to St. Luke.

The Baptistery was given bronze doors, cast by Andrea Pisano, in 1336 depicting human advance in the arts and sciences since the first humble tasks of Adam and Eve. Such dignity could have been accorded to mere work only in a great commercial town like Florence, where business circles, no longer accepting the static social order which was the ideal of cleric and aristocrat, wished to have their infants imbued, at the very baptismal font, with the bourgeois ideal of progress.

For a long time, the gild-brethren exhibited their power in splendid rituals and colorful pageants. Once a year the corporations paraded through streets of shops hung with their most precious wares. The inn-keepers followed a banner with the symbol of a red horse; the cloth-merchants had a woolly lamb upon an azure field; the bankers were preceded by a crimson flag sprinkled with golden coins; the stonework-ers had a red flag with a hammer and sickle on it, but, unlike the mod-ern Soviet emblem, it held also a saw and a chisel. Each gild provided in addition a cart surmounted by a monstrous garlanded tower, many-storied as a wedding-cake, dragged along by teams of oxen. These carts were symbolic floats; when, in a later age, the financial interests had won predominance over the manufacturing, the new era was rep-resented, appropriately if not subtly, by a wagon bearing a huge, golden statue of Midas.

The supreme effort of the mercantile community was the mighty Cathedral. At first all the gilds contributed to its enlargement; in turn, the importers, druggists or dry-goods dealers supervised the construc-tion work. Committees formed among 450 traders met to pass upon designs and apportion funds. Inside the immense building, statues of the leading business men of Florence were set up, by the hundreds. These wax portrait-images, often life-size, clothed in garments of the richest materials, sometimes set on horseback, formed a veritable Ma-dame Tussaud exhibition. An immense host of them were still to be seen down to Napoleonic times.

The dome of this edifice, as critics have remarked, is slightly at odds with the rest of the structure. This is owing to a shift in arrangements, whereby the wool gild took over the entire work, paying for every-thing. The wool-merchants raised as high as 51,500 gold lire a year for the purpose. But they were a different group from the small retailers who had voted before on designs. Economically and artistically, they were expansionist. Looking abroad for foreign markets, they voted for a merchant fleet to win them an Eastern outlet for cloth. And, as Doren points out, they voted approval of the dome-design in the very year that, flushed with imperialist pride, they acquired the harbor of Livorno.

But the era of these gild and community expressions in architecture lasted less than a hundred years. Before the 1300's were fairly over, the diminished enthusiasm of the business man for spending his wealth on such projects was evident. The trend was then toward individual mag-nificence—private palaces, personal portraits. So reluctant did the rich merchants become to contribute to the Cathedral that the building was left unfinished; the malicious public said that the Medici would not give anything to an edifice which did not bear their six balls.

Presently, the millionaires of Florence were spending their fortunes on villas in the country. Instead of continuing to enjoy the big fraternal rallies of the gild-brothers, they moved to the suburbs, where they kept fit by pottering about the garden. Incidentally, they escaped urban taxes as well as boredom. No longer so willing to pay for public frescoes, they wished to adorn their own homes instead; and perhaps some of the bombast observable in a later period in Italian art is traceable to the fact that painters, once trained to express a community in heroic breadth of style, were confined and forced to bend their powers to the depiction of a single family and the adornment of private domiciles.

Incurable individualists, after all, were the rich men of Florence. They had not been satisfied with a mastery of municipal offices and the gilds. They turned against one another in furious rivalry. Of their dangerous pride and thirst for display, Machiavelli observed: "The city might have lived in peace, had the Great contented themselves with appearing modestly, and in keeping with bourgeois conditions. But they did the opposite: for as private men, they scorned their comrades and as magistrates they wanted to be lords. No day passed without some evidence of their overweening pride. This displeased the Folk, which complained, instead of one tyrant, it had a thousand."

The spirit of turbulent individualism began to rise ominously within a generation after the triumph of the gilds. By 1313, the Peruzzi began to separate personal expenses from the accounts of their business firm, and their example was followed by others; this was an attempt of the more capable members to eliminate less businesslike relatives from control. At the same time, insurgents were rebelling against the fetters of the community; the pagan culture which blew from the East in the 1400's, with fleeing Greek scholars from ruined Constantinople, encouraged self-development and skepticism.

In this Florence was leading the rest of Europe, where a somewhat similar development was going on. Big merchants were assuming functions and honors setting them apart from lesser craftsmen and small shopkeepers. Men of heavy purses insisted that they alone were important enough to carry the palanquin of the King of France. In London, the richest demanded the right to elect the Lord Mayor. A separation of business into great and petty spheres was going on. And of course the despised smaller men, and the yet more oppressed workers, were increasingly self-conscious.

The last quarter of the Trecento has been compared to the years 1848-51, because it was marked by a series of revolutionary upheavals in many parts of Europe, directed against the rising authority of the big merchants and manufacturers. Lucca, Siena and Florence experienced brief "labor governments"; elsewhere, the embattled dyers, or "blue nails," of Flanders, and the Maillotins of Paris, were challenging the assumptions of the "haute commerce." Thus the individualism of the rich, manifested in display and factional fights, was answered by the unrest of the poor.

As the individualism was more distinguished in Florence than elsewhere, so the unrest was particularly acute. Because this was so large a manufacturing center and the proletarization of labor was advanced, a deeper gulf lay between the capitalistic and the toiling classes. Workers in Florence were more detached from the soil, and hence more at the mercy of employers. The intensity of industry also increased, tasks being performed even at night by artificial light; such innovations were bitterly received by men accustomed to the leisurely mediaeval way of doing things.

In the promotion of class hostility at Florence, teachings of agitators played a part. Many wandering monks in Europe were spreading subversive doctrines among the poor, such as Jean de la Roque Taillade, who once narrowly escaped death for his activities, and who went about crying: "I am sent to punish this century and avenge humanity!" But of them all, none was so amazing and beloved a figure as "French John" from Assisi, a town not far away from Florence, and in the Florentine grip.

French John was a bourgeois renegade; his father, a rich merchant dealing in wool from France, had destined him for the same pursuit, and taught him French—hence his nickname of "Francesco," often borne by Italian business men in that line of trade. Giovanni Bernadone, commonly called Giovanni Francesco, or French John, was discontented with business and the stuffy circles of Assisi, and went forth to preach the gospel of poverty. Wandering through the industrial districts of southern France and northern Italy, he preached the inflammable dogma that Christ had never possessed private property. The influence of "St. Francis of Assisi," as he became known afterward, persisted in Florence. Perhaps Franciscan Christian Communism was not so welcome to the artisans in the gilds, but the lowest, least secure ranks of laborers were inspired by its precepts, and it had a vital share in Florentine upheavals.

The distinction between rich and poor in Florence was recognized with the hearty frankness characteristic of the mediaeval mind. The upper classes were called the fat people, or *popolo grasso;* while the poor were known as the small or lean folk, the *popolo minuto.* Some attempts were made to disguise this rivalry by reviving names of Guelf and Ghibelline, or Blacks and Whites, but, in the eyes of the Florentine Machiavelli, such fancy titles could not obscure political rivalries of the Fat and the Thin, or the yet more desperate strife of the Fat among themselves.

The quarrels among the Fat were what really endangered the peace of Florence. These were conducted with a remarkable virulence. In other leading trading-cities of Europe, patricians generally managed to come to some sort of accord, despite plots and upheavals of various sorts. The rich families of the German cities formed interlocking directorates, so to speak, through marriage-alliances; so, too, the Venetian oligarchy maintained itself through the buffetings of centuries. Even more ingenious was the manner in which continuity of power was preserved at Genoa through the Bank of St. George.

At Genoa, the Bank of St. George was, in fact, the State, and it survived the internecine feuds of families. It had acquired this position originally by offering a loan to the City for the conduct of a trade war, in return for privileges of collecting much of the municipal income. Gradually it assumed many of the functions of the State, as well as keeping the revenues; any party which came uppermost had to swear loyalty to the Bank. Such stability was greatly envied by the Florentine Machiavelli, who wistfully observed:

> It is certainly a rare example, such as never occurred in the many actual and imagined republics of the philosophers. . . . For that institution in Genoa alone preserves the old, honorable customs. If it happens, as is inevitable in time, that the entire city falls into the hands of St. George, such a republic would certainly be even stranger than the Venetian.

Unhappy Florence had no such convenient institution to assure a steady focus of power. Her rich families would not agree among themselves, while her common people were unusually tumultuous. Under these conditions, it was natural that the social struggle should take exciting shapes. Every sort of rule was tried: rule by gilds; rule by workers; theocratic rule, under the monk Savonarola; tyranny, under the Duke of Athens; and Fascism, if so up-to-date a name may be given to the régime of the Medicean family which introduced "strong men" supported by popular acclaim. Restlessly, the Florentines kept altering their government until the sixteenth century.

At least, there was hardly a moment of "stagnation." Everlasting conspiracy, clash in public square, dagger play in the dark lanes at night, and more subtle hidden tussles of financial rivals, marked the course of Florentine life. The conflict was continuously illuminated by the orations of the great bishops of the city, by the vituperative poetry of Dante, the mellow remonstrances of the humanists, and the biting criticism of men and methods, which Machiavelli dedicated to his patron, the banker Rucellai.

RED LILY AND RED CROSS: CIVIL WAR

The proud families who had achieved the "bourgeois revolution" of 1282 and overthrown the nobility, had but a brief time to rejoice, and deck themselves with ornaments, before the convulsion of a financial crisis shook the city. The Peruzzi, the Macci, the Mozzi failed for enormous sums; in 1326, the Scali tumbled with 400,000 gold florins of debts outstanding and two hundred creditors, including the King of France, clamored for settlement. The Frescobaldi fell and were exiled in disgrace. The turn came of the magnificent Bardi, who had 5,550,000 gold florins outstanding of which the better part was irrecoverable; they joined the Frescobaldi in exile.

Fretting in their retreats, the Frescobaldi and Bardi plotted to raise up a "strong man" in Florence, who would permit them to return. Other business families as well, says Machiavelli, such as the Peruzzi and Acciaiuoli, "oppressed by debts," wished "to shift their burdens from their necks at the expense of others, and through the servitude of the fatherland to free themselves from the servitude in which their creditors held them."

While the crisis was deep in Florence and unemployed filled the streets, the chosen dictator of the bankrupts made his appearance. The Duke of Athens was an adventurer, half French and half Levantine, who won the acclaim of the folk and was named "Conservator" of the City. Under his brief reign the first experiment of a Fascist sort was tried. The Fasces, symbol of Fascism, it will be recalled, was originally Etruscan; and the modern dictator, Mussolini, has acknowledged his indebtedness to the ancient oligarch for his insignia. Naturally, one should not insist heavily upon race or region, for the blood of Romans streamed in Florentine veins and many of the aristocrats were Germans. But at least the analogy is entertaining, the more so as the first Fascist experiment in Florence was so ignominious a failure.

The bankers' puppet was not willing to be a weak tool of his backers. He needed popular support as well. So he hanged several members of the most prominent commercial circles for what seemed trifling peccadillos. For instance, he dealt death to a member of the Bardi firm for the slight offense of strangling a workingman. He punished another well-known citizen for raping a common laborer's daughter. He even condemned a Medici to the ultimate penalty for making illicit profits in munitions. Needless to say, as Machiavelli reported, "These judgments frightened the burghers of the middle class and only pleased the nobles and the mob, the latter because it lies in its nature to rejoice over evil."

The Duke went from bad to worse. He taxed the rich to support men at arms, and thereby "annoyed the great." Making democratic gestures, to "flatter the folk," he permitted the most oppressed artisans, among them the dyers, to escape from the big gilds, and form their own organizations. Since the rulers of the big gilds had had power to punish lesser members by chopping off their hands if they failed to deliver goods at the contracted date, the artisans were understandably anxious to remove themselves from such jurisdiction. The newly created organizations, with fresh flags, were invited to parade in a great May Day fête in 1343 before the Duke, who told the people that "through him Florence would be freed of parties . . . and so would gain, not lose, freedom."

Spectacles like this made the wealthy burghers conclude that Fascism had been a mistake. They beheld "laws destroyed, honest life ruined." And so they drew together in plots, "the nobles, the leading popular families, the manufacturers." Big families such as the Bardi, Frescobaldi, Scali, Strozzi, Altoviti, Rucellai, Albizzi, Pazzi, Acciaiuoli and Medici, forgot their feuds and formed a conspiracy against the Duke which was headed by Messer Agnolo of the Acciaiuoli family, Bishop of Florence. With long knives drawn, the resolute capitalists sought out the tyrant. He fled to the Government Palace, where they besieged him. Through a ruse, he escaped.

Ten months this reign had lasted, before the business families proceeded to erase its effects, dissolving the dyers' organization and seizing offices again. But business was not so easily brought back to "normalcy." A famine was upon the land. Then Messer Andrea of the banking firm of Strozzi decided to take advantage of the grain shortage to make himself tyrant. Buying up a great quantity of grain, he sold it at his residence at cut-rate prices; as the people streamed to his dwelling, Messer Andrea appeared on horseback and summoned them to revolt. About 4,000 customers, estimated Machiavelli, followed this ambitious banker toward the Government Palace, but few of them actually reached the public square. They felt Messer Andrea had not demonstrated his qualifications for leadership as convincingly as his benevolence.

The whole city was in an uproar. Plundering mobs besieged the house of the Pazzi; the Frescobaldi defended one bridge and the Bardi another. The crowd took and sacked many dwellings "with such fury, that the cruelest enemy of the Florentine name could have been ashamed of such wild destruction." But at the height of the insurrection, which as yet lacked aim, appeared the Medici and Capponi, with arms in their hands, urging the people to raid and demolish the homes of older and better established competitors. This action was typical of these two houses; thenceforth there was always a Medici or a Capponi to stir up the folk against prominent older bankers, while these parvenus promoted their own fortunes.

Fattening upon civil dissensions, and gathering prestige as leaders of the people, the Medici were ready to guide the revolution of 1378. A large assembly of citizens had hoped to prevent such a crisis by putting through a reform program. As they said in their petition, religion and honor had reached the vanishing point, "Bad men are praised as clever and good men are laughed at as simpletons. . . . Youth is idle, the aged are licentious." But when Salvestro de' Medici was elected as one of the officers to achieve reforms, he laid down the honor with a stirring oration in which he declared the malice of the mighty prevented him from assisting the people. The restless laborers of the city rose in arms, with Salvestro at the head.

The insurgents were recruited especially among wool-combers, who had long been trying to organize labor not only in Florence but in other cities and combine local groups. The employers had resisted their activities, and decapitated one such organizer. Violence seemed the only way out, as an impassioned labor leader proclaimed. For his own part, he declared, he would prefer "quiet poverty to precarious gain," but since "the city is full of hate against us . . . to gain forgiveness, we must commit new sins, increase our robbery and incendiarism and get new allies. For where many sin, no one will be punished." He invited his companions to look at the rich people of Florence:

> Look at the activities of the men, and you will see that all those who attain great riches and power have reached them through treachery or force . . . they call what they have won by the honorable name of profit, to make us forget the sorry way they won it. . . . The loyal servant remains the loyal servant, the honest folk remain poor folk, and only the disloyal and brazen shake off their servitude; only the dishonest and rapacious shed their rags.

Laborers need not fear to unite, continued the orator:

> Those who oppose us are disunited and rich; their discord will help us to victory; and their riches, once in our possession, will assure our triumph. Do not be frightened by the age and respectability of the families. Men have all the same origin. . . . Nature has made them all in the same shape. Take off our clothes and you would see us all equal; let us wear their robes, and without doubt we would seem respectable and they common. Let not conscience trouble us, for whoever, like us, must fear hunger and prison, ought not and cannot trouble himself about Hell.

A barefoot fellow, one Michele di Lando, led the wool-combers when they seized the Palace. A brief reign of labor was experienced. Interest rates were reduced for the poor; combers and dyers got back their organizations. Still, Machiavelli goes on to report, Michele made the populace furious by giving many favors to business men, particularly Salvestro de' Medici, to whom he assigned the rent of the shops on the Ponte Vecchio. Not only the people saw the Medicean threat, however, but the other rival industrialists and merchants as well became terrified. They closed their factories. They secured the cooperation of near-by landlords in cutting the city's grain and food supply. And, by many a subtle ruse, they undermined confidence in the new government.

As Renard tells the merry tale, the cloth manufacturer Sacchetti was seized by the revolutionary committee and ordered to open his plant at once and produce 3,000 florins' worth of goods without delay. Cordially, even enthusiastically, Sacchetti cried: "Too little! We must produce 6,000 florins' worth!" And winking, "Come, let us seal the bargain with a little drink!" Leading the unsuspecting committee to his excellent cellar, and encouraging the brethren to drink his health, Sacchetti slipped out through a side door and was seen no more in Florence until bourgeois order was restored.

The unhappy plight of the revolutionists was complicated by schism in their own ranks. Skilled handicraftsmen, conservative and organized, could not agree on action with the more violent and undisciplined proletariat of the industrial plants who were often inflamed with Franciscan Christian-Communism. Moreover, spies and tools of the ousted property owners fomented such discords. And so the revolutionary banner, representing an angel with a flaming sword, waved over a parlous situation.

At last the revolution was put down in hand-to-hand fighting through the tortuous lanes of the city. In that desperate engagement, the bankers and manufacturers were not in the front-line positions. Their surrogates were muscular armorers from the munitions plants and the hotel-keepers, brawny hosts of inns who had been bemoaning the total absence of traveling salesmen. When the industrialists triumphed, Michele di Lando was exiled. The old banner of the Commune, with the emblem of a red lily, was again unfolded, while the People's Party, with its flag showing a red cross on a white ground, withdrew to collect its forces. The Medici managed to escape blame, and continued to be identified with the red cross element, but they were thenceforth more chary of seeking public office.

Working with more caution than before, the Medici advanced their fortunes through ingenious schemes instead of bloody revolts. Giovanni d'Averardo de' Medici, for instance, put over a graduated income tax, which he turned against rival families. And it was through indirect management of taxation that his yet greater son, Cosimo, finally achieved the ruin of the chief enemies of his clan.

MEDICEAN METHODS

Business competition was increasing in intensity with every generation in Florence. Tariff walls were raised against her manufacturers by other Italian towns; the French and English were determined to make their own cloth. So the business men were forced to ever more desperate expedients; they conducted savage raids on Pisa and Siena and other places and, after a long trade war, divided up the North of Italy with Venice. Moreover, turning expansionist, they built a fleet and tried to acquire Eastern customers. But they did not want to pay for this imperialism; the new financial burdens were skillfully laid on the Lean People.

The extent to which capitalists of the 1300's could go in dodging taxes is illustrated by a popular treatise written then by a merchant, Morelli. Giving youth advice on rising in business, Morelli declares that perpetual grumbling and lying about taxes is needful:

> When you are in business, never cease to complain of taxes, saying that you should pay much less, pointing out your heavy losses, the poor harvest and the bad times. Don't be afraid of lying, since you do no wrong to anybody thus; it is necessary to lie just enough to acquire a reputation for the truth.

Morelli was not content with urging his pupils to say that they could not pay taxes. He added:

> Do not pay. Rise against the Commune. If you have ready money, place it in such a manner that nobody knows it belongs to you. Put it in wool, where money rests a long time, and then sell your wool against notes on Venice or Genoa, and record the order of payment itself as a total loss.

This sage advice about a tax-strike must have been well followed, for during that era the most persistent efforts of the People's Party to get the books of firms opened for state inspection proved unavailing. Proposals were made to invite notaries from other cities, who could not be prejudiced. This was declined. Not until early in the next century did Giovanni de' Medici, in that party, manage to lay heavier

taxes on the rich than any they had yet borne. Radicals insisted that
the millionaires ought to pay back taxes too; on their part, the rich
protested that they had given so much time to the State, that they had
neglected their businesses, and so it was not fair to penalize them; but,
according to Machiavelli, the rich quickly received this answer: "If
you have gained less, you will have less to pay under a graduated income tax, so you have no cause to grumble." And finally Giovanni
soothed both sides with the assertion: "It does not help to rake up the
past. Let us look to the future."

When Giovanni died in 1429, he enjoined the same policy upon his
son, Cosimo. In his last testament, Giovanni wrote: "I leave you in
possession of the great wealth which my own good fortune has bestowed upon me, and which your good mother and my own hard work
have enabled me to preserve. I leave you with a larger business than any
other in the Tuscan land." To keep this intact he admonished his son,
"Be charitable to the poor" and belong to the popular party, but "Speak
not as though giving advice . . . not puffed up with pride at receiving
many votes. . . . Avoid litigation. . . . Be careful not to attract public
attention."

This soft-shoe method was assiduously pursued by Cosimo, who was
in many respects the giant of the Medici. Cosimo was no crude revolutionary, no vulgar flaunter of wealth. He was careful to avoid such
ostentation as his rivals displayed; he appeared always as the plain friend
of the people and, when he could, dressed like a peasant. He shrank
from the limelight, explaining: "I have not led the life of a villain, but
of an honest and good merchant. Even if I have not always been fault-
less, I have always tried to merit the love of good men, because my actions were good. . . . I always declined to be nominated an official,
which is often prejudicial to the body and hurtful to the soul." Unlike
other vain Florentines, he understood the true value of modesty.

Cosimo established himself through financial agility as master of the
city. Jailed by his foes, he bribed his way out, smiling at the naïveté of
his jailer who accepted a mere thousand florins when Cosimo would
have given him ten thousand. Exiled, he did not mope like Dante, but
moved his headquarters to Venice. There, living in patrician style, he
conducted financial operations against his competitors at home. He began to drain the gold of Florence and succeeded in bringing about a
crisis which he sharpened by shutting down the Medici textile plants,
thereby throwing crowds of workers on the streets. As the confusion
spread, his fellow-citizens entreated Cosimo to come home—they felt
lost without him.

Once repatriated, he set about removing his enemies by exile, auction
or, in extreme cases, the dagger. It was observed that he was very

thorough. Tentatively a party colleague approached him on this point, inquiring whether, perhaps, the best families were not dying off a little *too* rapidly? And would there not presently ensue a positive dearth of respectable names in the upper circles? But Cosimo, with his delightful smile, recommended patience: given a few yards of scarlet cloth, he remarked, at any time he could create any number of imposing burghers and fill all vacancies.

For a space he operated behind a violent townsman, the vain and dazzling banker Luca Pitti. Later, when Pitti seemed to be getting out of hand, Cosimo, still with his charming ease, admonished him: "You strive toward the indefinite; I toward the definite. You plant your ladder in the air: I place mine on the earth so that I may not climb up so high as to fall. It seems to me but just and natural that I should desire the honor and reputation of my house to surpass yours. Let us therefore do like two big dogs which sniff one at the other when they meet, and then, both showing teeth, separate and go their ways; you to attend to your concerns, I to look after mine." Pitti showed his teeth, however, once too often and paid the price of exile, leaving his palace, today the Pitti Museum, as a cyclopean monument to the folly of crossing Florence's leading banker.

On the whole it was an indirect power that Cosimo de' Medici wielded. Apparently he detested the formal and official, shrank from titles and dressy clothes. He seemed to prefer pruning in his vineyard to sharing in the pomp of Florence. From first to last, a professed friend of the people and champion of democracy, Cosimo remained a private citizen of simple habits and judicious temper, always in the background, often indeed in a dark corner. In his retreat, he studied the art of manipulating elections and popular moods.

The tactful Cosimo himself suggested the splendid title, "Princes of Liberty" for the chief politicians, without aspiring to wear it himself, being quite content with control over elections. The only thing he liked better than being unsung was being unseen. Ordinary affairs he left to the "Princes of Liberty"—except one minor detail: the supervision of municipal finances. This he attended to himself, and distributed with cunning the burdens of the graduated income tax devised by his father; so it frequently happened that before a Prince of Liberty could bat an eye, some prominent citizen of mistaken views on important matters found himself outside the gate without a shirt to his back.

Ever gracious to poets and scholars, Cosimo was the ideal host as well as a loyal business partner and a staunch upholder of the Republic. As a family man, he was exemplary and provided for all his relatives with tender care, even securing a comfortable church benefice for his illegitimate son by a slave-girl. In short, there appeared to be nothing about him that anybody could take amiss, except the way he managed the fiscus in Florence—his rôle, so to speak, as single-taxer.

Cosimo's profile is worthy of study. The line of the protruding, implacably set mouth should be carved in basalt; marble is too soft a material for it. Irony and pride are written along the nostrils. The mass of wrinkles on brow and lid would close any other eyes but his. It is an impressive face; and one well understands how the tall, handsome Medici, whose will and vision must have been apparent at a glance, should have gained the respect of the greatly diminished number of his fellow-citizens.

The inner strength of the man, who labored and studied to the last hours of his seventy-seven years, whose soul "was as humble as any man's, and yet great and exalted," lay perhaps in the double consolation that the Christian religion and ancient philosophy afforded. He gave great sums to monasteries and often retired to meditate in a rude cell. Yet, while he was at peace within the Church, he studied the classics for twelve years with that noble scholar, Marsilio Ficino, who wrote: "Certainly I owe much to Plato, but must confess that I owe no less to Cosimo. Inasmuch as Plato once showed me the idea of courage, Cosimo showed it me every day."

The heroic quality of all the Medici was made manifest in their deaths. That of Cosimo was Olympian in serenity. In his garden he sat reviewing his gathered experiences of three-quarters of a century; when his wife asked him why he was so silent, he replied, "You take fifteen days to make ready when we move to the country; I am preparing for a longer journey." And the result of his cogitations was assuredly satisfying; a last note he sent to Ficino is the enviably tranquil farewell of a contented ancient:

Yesterday I came to the villa of Careggi, not to cultivate my fields but my soul. Come to us, Marsilio, as soon as possible. Bring with thee our Plato's book *De Summo Bono*. This, I suppose, you have already translated from the Greek language into Latin as you promised. I desire nothing so much as to know the best road to happiness. Farewell and do not come without the Orphean lyre.

IL MAGNIFICO

"It is ill living for the rich in Florence unless they rule the state," wrote the grandson of Cosimo, the Magnificent Lorenzo, in his "Ricordi," or "Memoirs." He explains that, if he did not propose to be assassinated as well as ruined, there was nothing for him to do but take up his grandfather's work and continue the family's domination of the city by means of election control and taxation. Lorenzo desired posterity to know, however, that he assumed the burden solely for his personal advantage and not for mere ambition or yearning to display his power. He was acting according to the purest self-interest—"solely for the safety of our friends and possessions."

Under Lorenzo, superb pageantry was offered to the public as glorious propaganda and beguilement, since it was upon the favor of the public that the Medici had based their splendor. And while the unparalleled processions and the speed of Medicean building were making Florence the most sumptuous of cities, Lorenzo led her energies outward to imperialism. Expansion was increasingly necessary, for Lorenzo and his family had ruined so many citizens and engrossed so much of the government's income for their private use that only foreign adventure promised new resources.

A characteristic example of the search for new wealth was the struggle to monopolize alum needed in the manufacture of cloth. Little of this ingredient existed in Europe. An alum-mine in Italy had been leased to a Florentine company; but the Commune of Volterra voided this lease. The Company appealed to patriotism; and men of Florence, under Lorenzo, who was said to be a silent partner in the concern, destroyed Volterra. Since the only other alum deposits were thought to be in the Turkish dominion, the men of Florence presumed that they had a monopoly of the European supply. But new mines were discovered in the Papal States. At once the Medici addressed a message to the Pope, in 1466, offering to advance the capital for the development of these mines, adding: "There can be no doubt that our conduct will be to the satisfaction and interest of our Holy Father." In order to form an alum-ring for all Christendom, they persuaded their new partner, the Pope, to excommunicate any person henceforth importing alum from the heathen Turk.

While his rule was bent to the advantage of his "friends and possessions," Lorenzo ventured his person abroad with a bravery displayed in our times chiefly in South America. On one occasion when Florence was menaced by deadly enemies, Lorenzo went directly into the nest of wasps, determined to win them over or accept assassination. Being the richest man in Florence, he ought to be the boldest, he explained to the community: "Having a greater position and larger stake in our city, not only than I deserve but probably than any citizen in our days, I am more bound than any other man to give up all to my country, even my life."

The documents relating to Lorenzo the Magnificent reveal him in moods of affection and gaiety: as the most charming of companions;

in terrible rages, crying out that he would to God he could go away for six months to some place where he would never hear of Italian affairs. Whatever his mood, he is uncannily frank—free from the veils of verbiage which Calvinism, Nationalism and other isms later cast over the minds of business men. In several letters, he offers advice to his little son, just made Cardinal, the youngest ever to attain that office; he urges the child to establish a reputation for honesty as the surest means of attracting attention in the Eternal City. Rome, he says, has "always been the ruin of Italy, because being ignorant and not knowing how to govern, the priests put the whole world in peril. If His Majesty [of Naples] puts an end to the Barons, he will then teach the Pope how to read."

True, said Lorenzo to his fourteen-year-old son, the Cardinal, the advantage of God and the Church must be paramount, but "while doing this it will not be difficult for you to aid the city and our house." He urged Giovanni to "Keep steadfastly to your above-mentioned duty of setting the interests of the Church above everything else." Yet, he continued, with good sense and management, "I think it is likely a way will be found to save, as the proverb says, the goat and the cabbages."

To the Pope himself, Lorenzo was equally open. He had lent Innocent VIII hundreds of thousands of florins. As security, the Pope pawned his jewels; then silver; then the cattle-tolls of Rome, a castle, the stipends of priests. Lorenzo married his daughter to an illegitimate son of the Pope (who afterward murdered the girl), and insisted on provisions for the pair. Reminding His Sanctity that all men are mortal, he urged speed, concluding with engaging candor, that the young married couple were "praying that God grant Your Holiness a long life in order that their affairs may be adjusted." Who could bear a grudge against a man so open and above-board? It was no wonder that Lorenzo had hundreds of enemies, but few critics.

Sustained by the full, serene philosophy of the Renaissance, Lorenzo weathered a thousand storms without growing bitter. Fortified by the old Roman stoicism which he admired, he faced everything as it came. The business manager of the Pazzi Bank intrigued against his Roman branch; not content with this, the Pazzi plotted with the aid of Pope Sixtus IV to remove the Medici by murder. Two priests during High Mass in the Cathedral of Florence fell upon the Medici, and Lorenzo's own brother sank at his side with a dozen wounds. But his personal grief did not cloud his keenness of view. With perfect presence of mind, Lorenzo took advantage of the disorder in the city to withdraw 200,-000 gold florins from the civic treasury, which he needed to cover the default of his Bruges branch.

Well might such a man consider himself the equal of the Romans. And he did. In a poetic drama, performed in public with his son in the star rôle, he puts into the mouths of two Emperors, Constantine the Great and Julian the Apostate, lines on the cases and duties of statecraft which suggest his own rich experience. Julian, the pagan renegade, played by Lorenzo's son, pleaded for the classic philosophy which the Medici had done so much to revive, and for a noble conception of the ruler as a trustee of wealth.

As trustees of wealth, however, the Medici had wrecked the city. Even while they were fostering the classic culture and philosophy, with its emphasis upon the beauties of personal development, the Medici were assiduously ridding themselves of all personalities likely to challenge their rule. They killed or ruined potential rivals around them, until the private funds of Florence sank to a low ebb, and there were no longer enough rich and able men to conduct either economic or political affairs with sufficient firmness. The Renaissance culture of turbulent individualism had left, so to speak, but a single individual in triumph, Lorenzo himself.

The results of this stewardship were soon evident. Not only were the people poorer, but the municipality went bankrupt. Lorenzo, growing more careless, dipped too deeply in the treasury. City bonds fell when the interest was reduced from 5 to 1½ per cent in the effort to save the situation. Finally, while other markets were failing, came the blow of the English, who cut off the wool-trade. Again Florence wallowed in crisis, and, amid the spreading gloom, arose the monk Savonarola, foe of big business.

With grim resolution, Savonarola refused the last sacrament to the dying Lorenzo. And after the death of the once Magnificent, Savonarola endeavored to undo the work of the Medici and to lead Florence, after three hundred years of money-madness, to repentance and reform. He set up a religious State with strict laws against usury. In his compelling presence, and especially as municipal bonds continued to fall, the people of that once-gay city were convinced of the vanity of mortal things. In a revivalist hysteria, they threw their gewgaws to the flames in the public square. Only one visitor to the scene, a cold-blooded merchant of Venice, remained dry-eyed and unimpressed. He offered to buy up the whole lot of cast-away finery for a good round sum, but was repulsed.

Alarmed by this revivalism, the Pope condemned the theocratical experiment and excommunicated the audacious monk. The business element in the city, much as it dreaded the Medici, feared the monk more. And so the old family was soon restored to its former position, and Savonarola, archenemy of the money-changers, was brought to the stake and burned in the public square. He has not been made a saint.

The commercial prestige of Florence was irreparably shattered. But a certain fresh release for her energy was provided, for a time, when the Medici, becoming ducal and allying themselves with the Crown of France, opened that country yet further than before to career-seeking Florentines of every description. Then, in the 1500's, the Medici, though they never regained their old financial empire, exerted a profound cultural influence over the rest of Europe. Through the two Medicean queens in Paris as well as under a Medicean Pope at Rome, there was transplanted to other regions that culture of the Renaissance, that philosophy of turbulent individualism, which had already reached its full and deadly flower in Florence.

VII

THE TRIUMPH OF FORTUNA

THE INTERACTIONS OF BUSINESS AND CULTURE, one upon the other, form one of the least explored phases of history. For such a study, no city would appear better fitted than Florence, so richly dowered with both economic and spiritual vitality. In Florence, great fluid wealth gave sustenance to art; art and philosophy nourished the ambitions of business men; business and culture, or as Riezler would say, Interest and Idea, unfolded in continuous interplay.

The variety of economic activities in Florence set her apart from other cities. Rouen and Ypres were manufacturing towns; Venice, Genoa and Lübeck were primarily trading centers. But Florence produced, sold and lent. Machine-capitalism and finance-capitalism, a combination unequaled elsewhere in Europe, flourished together in Florence; and as she sheltered men competent in many kinds of business enterprise, so she mothered an amazing throng of various talents in painting, architecture, sculpture, poetry, music, science, and history. Not only did she have geniuses in many fields, but, in Leonardo da Vinci, the "universal genius," she possessed the most versatile man of the Renaissance and perhaps of history. Only the last reaches of the intellect failed to be represented in Florence. High abstract thinking did not absorb these essentially practical, plastically gifted people. Even Leonardo's scientific speculations were for useful ends; Galileo, the astronomer, viewed the universe pictorially. The Florentines had rare abilities for image-building and a warm love of form and life, but they were not metaphysicians.

Whether the culture of Florence was so rich because her wealth provided an adequate basis, or whether she possessed wealth because her children were so exceptional, cannot of course be determined. At least it is apparent that the environment was immensely stimulating. Every few years the design of government altered, often violently and radically. What other merchant-city could display such political versatility, ranging from theocracy and military tyranny to a labor government and to the despotism now of manufacturing, then of finance? Such political upheavals kept the minds of the Florentines from stagnation. In this electric atmosphere, in this city of geniuses set in sublime natural surroundings, under a warm sun, occurred that marvelous burst of human energy and spirit—the Renaissance.

The culture of the Renaissance, so largely a Florentine creation, was inextricably bound to the capitalism which thrived there. Much of the art of the age was a handmaid of wealth, serving the pride of the rich. Much of the theology and scholarship was a reflection of the individual Florentine's striving to free himself from all restrictions whether of clan, community or religion. Yet the thought of the Renaissance showed an anticapitalistic as well as a capitalistic trend: many sons of business men, notably Boccaccio and Alberti, turned to classic art and poetry in an effort to escape from their own scene and find a contrast to the evils of the gold-crazed city of Florence. Out of this city, accordingly, flowed two streams of activity and thought—one leading to modern capitalistic competition; the other to the modern aesthetic and humanistic revolt against untrammeled capitalism. To Florence may be traced the movements which, developing as parallels, produced eventually a Manchester and a Ruskin. Both tendencies reached America, the land named after Amerigo, scion of the famous Florentine business house of the Vespucci.

BUSINESS AND THE CHURCH

The interaction of business and culture in this city was fundamentally determined by the relation of the Church toward business. The basic attitude of the mediaeval Church in this matter is illustrated in a story told by the monk, Humbertus de Romanis. A man, he said, went into a cloister and was astonished to behold every nook and cranny full of devils! He went into a marketplace, and lo! there he saw but one devil and he high up on a pillar! Why was this? Because it took a crowd of evil spirits to corrupt the monks, while a single devil sufficed in the trading quarter where every man was one himself.

The Church desired a stable world order. In the plan for a universal Christian brotherhood, the nobles and serfs, content to stay in their God-appointed stations, presented no dangers. Only the business man appeared menacing to the plan, for he was insatiable for possessions, unresting, boundless in *avaritia*, disruptive to the grand religious social scheme because he crept out of his sphere and climbed into the nobleman's rank where he behaved with ostentation. His parvenu display lured gentlemen into debt and ruin. Then the simple folk became discontented with their social assignment for they grudged magnificence to the plebeian *arrivé*, as they would not to an established lord.

The contest between Church and Business was less severe in Germany than in Italy, on the whole. German traders were genuinely afraid of their desperate nobility and less alarmed by Church interference. This was decidedly different from the Italian situation where the nobility soon ceased to vex the business man while his quarrel with the Church went on incessantly. It is true that Germany was the first country to break away from the Christian fellowship of the Roman Church, but the Reformation movement should not be interpreted as a big business man's movement against the Church. On the contrary the main economic background of Lutheranism was the protest of the common people and the small merchants in Middle Germany against the powerful papal bankers, such as the Fuggers, who were accused of draining German gold to Rome. The Fuggers and a few other families were at the same time boosting prices and destroying opportunities for their small competitors by building monopolistic rings. Thus the Reformation in Germany represented, in part, an attempt by the lower order of retailers and consumers to cleanse the Church from its alliance with big business. In the ensuing conflicts, the Fuggers fought for the Roman Church and against Reform.

Most of the Germans, in the North particularly, were middlemen without large capitalistic dealings and they were not seriously reproached by the Church. Only the Southern Germans, like the Fuggers, and at a late period, went into large-scale finance. But the Italians, and particularly the Tuscans, the Florentines, were financiers preeminently. As money-lenders, receivers of interest, they were outcasts, theoretically, who should be denied the sacraments and refused burial in holy ground. Thus the Church was forced into the difficult position of being compelled to denounce, in theory, the business men who were nearest to her and upon whom she most heavily relied for financial aid. In this equivocal position she did what she could: accepting loans from the Tuscans and yet refusing to relax her canon law condemning their mode of living.

With this subtle enemy, Italians had to reckon. While Germans were arming themselves with cannon to resist feudal chivalry by force, Italians were resorting to diplomacy, argument and guile as weapons to be used against their more refined foes, the theologians. In the course of this mighty struggle of wits in Italy, the foundations were laid upon which all modern discussions of business ethics were erected. The Northern Protestants, Luther and Calvin, and the English Puritans merely continued the process of breaking down canon law which had begun in Florence generations before the Reformation, under the pressure of Italian business men.

One of the outstanding opponents of business operations in Italy was

St. Francis of Assisi, who insisted on the sanctity of poverty and who went so far as to deny that Christ had possessed private property, a position so extreme that the Vatican was troubled, for it presaged a revival of Primitive Christianity. This religious problem the officials of the Church faced by incorporating the Order of St. Francis; while allowing the brethren to remain poor, it gave them the use of handsome palaces and thus institutionalized what had been altogether too informal a body. Some of the disciples of Francis, in an effort to be true to their master and refuse such ostentation, suffered death at the stake.

The defense of the temperate orthodox position was undertaken by the Dominicans. The Franciscans upheld cleanliness as well as communism, both of which were revolutionary doctrines in the Middle Ages. The Dominicans were conservative all along the line; they stood up for private property and they repudiated baths. Ingeniously, they employed art in popular argument. Brentano declares that they ordered painters to depict Christ taking money from a purse. More, they had a picture painted which showed Him with one hand nailed to the Cross and the other putting coins into a purse at His girdle. Could the case for private property be more graphically stated?

Franciscan communism was of course extremely disturbing to the industrialists of Florence as to the Dominicans; but, after the labor government of 1378–82 was put down, the menace was over. Business, as well as the Church, had withstood the attack. It was now time to accept Francis as a patron saint of respectability. In their monastery at Florence, many of the poor monks of the Franciscan Order wished to remain in the simplicity befitting their vows; but some of the rich merchant families had joined their number and Schillman says that these youths wanted to build a gorgeous church, the very sort of thing that Francis had denounced. They had their way. In 1442 the Santa Croce was erected—the largest church ever dedicated to a mendicant brotherhood.

By this date, doctrinal confusion had come. Some Franciscans had changed their original attitude so far that they were now actually championing the right of the Florentine State to charge interest on its loans; and the Dominicans, still conservative, attacked this political innovation. Evidently the merchants of Florence, with their political affiliations, were glad to favor brethren so progressive as the Franciscans. Cosimo de' Medici gave them a monastery, and reserved a cell in it for his private meditations. It was adorned by Fra Angelico with scenes from the Saint's life.

The surrender of Francis to the Church, when he permitted the incorporation of his Order by the Pope, was a theme chosen by two great business families in Florence for paintings. The Bardi commissioned

Giotto to depict the scene for their family chapel. The supreme portrayal of the surrender was painted by Ghirlandajo for the family chapel of the banker Sassetti in the Santa Trinita. This fresco shows the Saint kneeling before the Pope; in the background is the Florentine Piazza; in the foreground are the gigantic figures of the Sassetti family —which Warburg has identified—with a Medici included just to show their wide business connections. The fascinatingly ugly Lorenzo de' Medici, with his luminous eyes and wild black hair, carrying his head like a king, is summoning, with a royal gesture, his little sons to his side. This portrait makes very clear the compelling mixture of the charming, the imperious, and the demoniac in Lorenzo.

Beside Lorenzo stands the elder Sassetti, white-haired, shrewd-eyed. Both he and Lorenzo are Renaissance types. But the younger Sassetti is a modern; he has a jutting chin and beak, a bald head, low brow and thick neck; he appears not unkind nor undignified, but excessively well seasoned. With a sack suit substituted for his long robe and set down in a modern stock exchange, he would, one feels, learn within three weeks, every trick that had been invented since 1485, and within four weeks, have a corner on the market.

Only after some minutes' contemplation of this picture does one notice, kneeling in the darkened background, the ethereal Francis, at whom no one is looking but the Pope; and the Pope sits on the side of the bankers. Yet the full appreciation of this fresco is not complete until one has recalled a fact which Warburg fails to mention. It was an earlier Sassetti, Tommaso, who took two papal tiaras as security on a loan from John XXIII and handed them over to Giovanni Medici; the Medici held yet another tiara in pawn, and when the Pope, wishing to wear it at an important Council, desired to have it back, the Medici only let it go after every measure had been employed by the Pope, including threats of excommunication. Thus a Sassetti and a Medici, whose ancestors had held in pawn the highest symbol of Rome's authority, dominated the chief Italian painting showing the submission to Rome of the last great mediaeval communistic preacher.

One might perhaps think that this would be about all a Renaissance business man could do for the memory of St. Francis; but the imagination of the Italians was fertile. Not merely was Francis of Assisi, a merchant's son who had rebelled against the whole code of business, now turned into a patron saint of the richest Florentine bankers; not only was an enormous church erected for brethren on whom he had enjoined the strictest poverty; not only was he painted in the act of surrender between a background of the Florentine business district and a foreground portraying the city's chief capitalists; the crown of the whole matter was unquestionably the munificence of Cosimo de' Medici toward Assisi. Cosimo had grasped the birthplace of the Saint, Assisi, as security on a loan to a Pope; and, with a gesture of benevolence which many critics are accustomed to regarding as purely American, he gave the town, according to Heyck, a brand-new paved street and a first-class system of waterworks.

It was another Saint, this time a Florentine, the charming, gentle, charitable and laborious Archbishop Antoninus, who finally made business respectable within the Roman Church, by personal example and through his epochal work, the "Summa Theologica." He is not so well known to posterity as Savonarola, the dark-browed depression phenomenon, the prophet of doom, who attacked business at a time of economic crisis, when even Florentines were discouraged and ready to renounce the world. Antoninus lived at a prosperity peak, and was correspondingly a sweeter character.

In his lifetime, Antoninus was beloved by his fellow-citizens. The wool-merchants aided him by supporting his Foundling Hospital, still one of the tourist sights of Florence, with its swaddled *bambini*, done in majolica, by Luca della Robbia. Cosimo de' Medici admired him intensely. The affection and reverence which Antoninus inspired remained his through life and won him a sainthood; while Savonarola, after the crisis was over, was burned at the stake.

The views of the saint would not appear sufficiently conservative for most fashionable pulpits today. Though he was more conciliatory than other Church Fathers toward business, he was still full of mediaeval doctrinaire notions. Thus he attacked the whole problem of advertising, which was coming up in the Quattrocento. Advertising which explains the real merits of an article is useful, he decided; that consisting only of *verba adulatoria*, words that flatter the consumer, is theologically reprehensible.

Antoninus, though conceding much, would not yield all. He retained the view that a merchant's activities must be subordinated to the commonweal. He insisted that the distribution of wealth is as important to consider as its production. But John Ruskin, in nineteenth-century England, preaching the same thing, called old Florence the paradise in which distribution had been achieved; Antoninus, actually in that old Florence, knew that he desired what should be, not what was, or what had ever been, in Italy.

Well did he know his contemporaries; he was as worldly-wise as his great friend Cosimo. In a chapter, "De variis fraudibus," and elsewhere, as Ilgner shows, he indicates his familiarity with the tricks of every trade, from jerry-building, or paying workers in kind instead of cash, to monopolistic rings and speculations on the Exchange. If he makes concessions to a class of men capable of such varied frauds, it is not through ignorance. However, he fully realized that shouting at the business man would not reform him. So he aspired to work through business, rather than against it, for the welfare of the poor. As Machiavelli wished to employ the shady tricks and the slippery minds of the Renaissance politicians, if need be, for the glorious end, peace in Italy, so Antoninus wanted to use the wealth of industrialists and bankers to help the unfortunate. Both men were commonly misunderstood by posterity. Machiavelli is remembered as the apologist for every deviltry, while his dream of peace is ignored. Antoninus' plea for social justice was lost to sight while his concessions to business remained vivid.

For that day, these were radical enough. He allowed monopolies, save in foodstuffs. He agreed that credit is necessary and that the State must raise loans and pay interest, though he thought that 5 per cent was more nearly just than 15. He admitted that capital must make profit; that a business man is entitled to the returns he makes by his brains, if not by his hands. He decided that a "just price" is a social necessity, but that there may be devious ways of arriving at it: rarity may be considered of value in an article; in some cases more than a just price is permissible. In short, by the time a merchant had taken into account all the factors mentioned by the Father, he could have a fair certainty of slipping past the pearly gates.

Antoninus even accepted the practice of taking a loan with a promise to pay back in a month at the current rate of exchange in Florence. True, the keen-eyed saint had observed that this generally turned out to the money-lender's profit, but he let that pass. What he could not approve was borrowing a sum with a promise to pay back at whatever the current rate of exchange might be in the future in Genoa or Venice. That was pure gambling, he thought, only to be expiated in the fires of Purgatory.

Having made such sweeping concessions, Antoninus demanded something in return. He thought the miserably poor could not be expected to be moral. So he advocated a wage for workingmen which would provide decent home life; he asked help for the aged and the diseased; he wanted a regulated and not merely haphazard charity. He desired kindly nurses and doctors, humane as well as philanthropic treatment. The position later adopted by Puritans, that aid should be tendered only to the "deserving" poor, was flatly opposed by Antoninus. He was, moreover, aware that the State must direct such a scheme and regulate business to some extent; and he reminded the business man to be modest, for God had not created private property in the Beginning.

Step by step, theologians gave way before the rise of Italian capitalism. And this slow retreat was symbolized in art. In one of the early church paintings of Florence, a usurer was depicted being struck by heavenly fire as he approached the Communion. But as time went on, the bankers of Florence were admitted by artists to hallowed places in Christian scenes. The Medici and their associates ordered various paintings which incorporated their portraits in holy surroundings. We may examine for ourselves a group of portraits of banking and trading agents of the Medici at Bruges, with their wives, in the foreground of Hans Memling's great picture of the Resurrection, now in Danzig. Here the business men with their families are shown among those huddled souls who are arising from their graves, at the word of the Archangel, to enter upon everlasting bliss. The head of the Bruges office-force is represented here, unclad, eyes uplifted, kneeling on one plate of a pair of scales—being tried in the balance and not found wanting.

The money-lender and merchant who thus confidently ordered himself, with his relatives and friends, portrayed among the blessed on the Last Day, has been identified by Warburg as a Portinari. This discovery need hardly surprise us, in view of the fact that it was a daughter of the Portinari whom Dante had described as so thoroughly at home in heaven. The history of the painting is full of curious incidents. It was part of a cargo of a richly laden ship belonging to the Medici, which was captured by Baltic pirates and taken to Danzig, where it was turned over as a dividend to the pirate company. The loss of the cargo by the Medici, Meltzing thinks, was one of the principal factors in the near-bankruptcy of the Bruges branch of the family enterprise, managed by Portinari. Utter ruin was averted, however, by Lorenzo il Magnifico who dipped into the municipal treasury.

The Medici had themselves immortalized like their agents. Cosimo de' Medici commissioned Benozzo Gozzoli to portray his entire family, gorgeously attired, on horseback, with sumpter mules laden with treasure, in the train of the Three Kings, going to lay tokens of their regal wealth at the feet of the Holy Child.

Another and more famous painting, by Botticelli, depicts the scene of homage itself. The whole Medici family is grouped in the foreground, with Cosimo doing the honors for them all. He is kneeling, in a magnificent costume, his head gravely inclined before the lovely, meek Mother. But the rest of his family are paying scant attention to the ceremony; the handsome Giuliano, in fact, the Beau Brummel of Florence, has turned his back on the proceedings and is striking a pose which exhibits his elegant dress and admirable figure to the highest advantage.

The Florentine financier's conquest of the Roman Church went even farther than this. He not only wrung doctrinal concessions and sanctification through art, but at last, so far did Church and Finance merge, that two Medici sat in the very chair of Peter: Leo X, the Pope against whom Luther loosed the Reformation, and Clemens VII, the illegitimate offspring left by the murdered Giuliano who, before his untimely end, had been associated with his father Cosimo in the wool-business and banking. Leo used his high office to procure the ducal rank for his family in Tuscany. Thus, when the Reformers assailed the lavish display and demoralization in the Church in the sixteenth century, they were, in fact, denouncing the business men's influence in Rome. The corruption of Rome was at its greatest height when an Italian Medici wore the tiara, and the German Fugger helped to drain his own country of gold at the behest of the Florentine.

One might suppose that the completeness of this conquest would have satisfied the Florentine financiers, even the Medici. They had humbled the proud theologians; they had used religious pretexts as the cloak for commercial exploits; they had won admission to heaven, at least through art; they had grasped the tiara. But it was with the Medici as with the poor fisherman's wife in the old German fairy tale. They could not be satisfied with being duke, or Pope. They wanted to be God. In the seventeenth century, they had a ceiling in their palace in Florence frescoed with their apotheosis: here they were deities of light, being received with divine honors by the Olympians.

Why had the Florentine business man, when things were going so pleasantly and he was finding accommodation within the Church, turned pagan? Lorenzo de' Medici, it will be recalled, supported the brilliant skeptic, Pico della Mirandola, in his quarrel with the Church of Rome, the institution through which the Medici had won their immense wealth. Fundamentally, there could be no accord between business men, demanding untrammeled freedom for profit-making, and Christian priests, who sought, however feebly at times, to uphold order and union, faith and charity, compromise and restraint, in distraught Europe.

THE BUSINESS MAN AS PATRON OF PAGAN CULTURE

The business man has managed to escape, in interpretations of history, his due share of responsibility for the cultural and political upheavals of the Renaissance and Reformation in Europe. The honors have gone to scholars and poets, to the Humanists who denounced the sins of aristocrats and clergy, revived the culture of antiquity, and promoted liberal, individualistic, and rationalistic modes of thought. The blame for the misdeeds of that period, on the other hand, has been apportioned to the lesser orders of monks, who failed to live up to their vows. But the business man, who had undermined the whole fabric of Christian mediaeval society, by his operations, slipped quietly from the pages of the record. Unreproached and unpraised, in fact hardly observed, he pocketed the profits of the wars of religion. And, under the clouds of combat, he changed his base. The Medici and the Fuggers, like the Bardi and the Acciaiuoli before them, like the Corsini, the Frescobaldi and the Capponi after them, gracefully disappeared into the aristocracy.

Though so little attention was paid to the business men, actually they played a fundamental part in the development of Italian culture. The first great cathedral in Tuscany, for example, the model for generations to come, was reared by Pisan merchants, in the first flush of a triumphant trade war; they adorned it with marble and porphyry brought back from commercial voyages to the Levant. The earliest poets in Tuscany sang in praise of the band of Pisan trader-warriors who returned to the city after wresting a favorable commercial treaty from the Emir of Tunis. The earliest important monuments betraying the French Gothic influence in Italy were the villas of bankers in Siena, who symbolized their commercial relations with France on the façades of their homes, and are thought to have acquired their Madonna-worship from the romantic citizenry of Provence.

In its earlier phases, the Renaissance is almost completely identified with Florence, the greatest commercial city. It did not start in Naples, ruled by a landed aristocracy too proud to intermarry with a family that stooped even to sell wine from its vineyards. It did not begin in Rome, whose principal families were too conventional for profit-making more regularized than banditry. Nor was its origin in Venice, where the patriciate remained so extremely exclusive, even in trade. Sea-traders, as Seveking suggests, are naturally inclined to conservatism.

In Florence, however, where the business man was working out his liberation from the bondage of family, clan, community, and Church, the freedom of the individual was the social ideal. Scholars, lawyers, and artists, celebrated and explained and justified the emergence of the individual out of the mass—a thing the business man was attaining in practice as well as theory.

The lawyers in Florence were called upon to let out the seams of jurisprudence to fit the lusty growth of commercial practice. It was necessary in that city to make Roman law, as well as canon law, keep pace with the expanding needs of capitalism. Fine and hair-splitting arguments were evolved by the keen minds of Italian doctors of law, as well as by theologians, able to define the members of a business company as one person, *una persona*. The business corporations of Florence became personified while the glorification of personality went on.

Out of the legal groups of Florence, closely allied by marriage to the mercantile, and attached to them by a common purpose, came some of the leaders of the cultural movement: Petrarch, the great initiator of the Renaissance, and Machiavelli, who wrote its epilogue. Petrarch thought that the business man would be improved by a dose of classical education; Machiavelli, having seen that tried, recommended the cold douche of poverty.

While the business corporation was achieving a personality, and the business man was loosening the ties of community, the sculptor began to detach his figures from the background; instead of the customary bas-reliefs, he now created images "in the round" and in the open. The first sculptured busts, however, according to one theory at least, were those effigies of bankrupts and disgraced salesmen who were thus exposed to public infamy in Florence. So the painter likewise turned more and more to portraiture alone. Noblemen and kings, in the opinion of Heyck, are more conscious of family and position than of their individualities. It is the merchant who wishes to preserve his own peculiar lineaments; self-made, he cherishes his creation. The earliest important painted portraits in Italy, as in Germany, were of business men. One of Giovanni de' Medici was epoch-making and the Medici continued, as parvenus, to patronize portraiture particularly.

As the power of the business man grew in Italy, in Germany, and in Flanders, the same result was evident: the fading away of mysticism. The business man was on the side of those seeking to control the forces of nature, rather than to pay them a mystic's reverence. He was immersed in activity and in the present; if he thought of the future, it was largely in connection with the probable rate of exchange in Genoa. He was engaged in the organization of monopolies and mercenary armies; in shipbuilding and fortification; in the rationalization of taxes and tariffs. He was pushing inventors forward; he was fostering the application of reason and scientific method to social problems as he experienced them.

The business men of Florence had no use for alchemists and magicians; as bankers, able to charge 260 per cent, they perhaps felt it unnecessary to resort to the black arts. We do not find Cosimo or Lorenzo entertaining at their tables any long-bearded caldron-stirrers and pestle-pounders. They left superstitious practices to simple-minded kings, such as the French monarchs in debt to the Medici, who could think of no other way to repay the bankers than to try to make money out of lead.

The business men were not expecting magical solutions of their immediate problems. They were looking for realistic solutions. Step by step, they urged on mechanical and chemical invention. Sombart has described the interrelation of business and science, each aiding the other toward the final triumph of the steam-engine and the Machine Age. Thus he shows the invention of artillery bringing about mass-armies;

mass-armies in turn providing the earliest large-scale opportunities for merchants to ship grain and make standardized textiles for clothing; the demand for great grain deliveries encouraging a more rational and capitalistic agriculture. To win metal for the cannon in such armies, the Fuggers had to invest more and more in mining; to mold cannon, which the warriors wished to see in ever-larger format, bigger furnaces had to be built; the casting of the cannon-bores taught men to make the first big metal pipes; then they were ready to produce cylinders for the steam-engine.

Art reflected this process of development. Inevitably, as the merchant loomed larger in painting, the halo shrank. And backgrounds changed; jewels, furniture, clothes shone out in profuse detail to please the newly rich bourgeois. With uncanny prescience, artists developed perspective in that half-century before Columbus, when merchants were reaching out farther and farther for fame, adventure, gold.

The spiritual quality of art cleared away like a haze toward high noon. More and more sharply, as the dream faded, life was revealed. Peasants were now seen in the tavern, and merchants in their booths offering cloth and gems. Instead of the romantic chivalric figures of knights and ladies in flowery meads, appeared the long-gowned captain of industry in his packing-room, instructing porters, or money-changers with glittering cold eyes and fingers crooked in a perpetual grasp. These are no longer the thin, radiant, identical faces of the early Romanesque art; these are expressions, gross or sly, bluff or arrogant, full of earthly experience, belonging to men who, when St. George was mentioned, thought of an excellent Italian bank, and not of a dragon-slayer.

Scholars were as ready as artists to reassure the business man about his new-won individuality. Poggio da Bracciolini pointed out, much to the delight of the Medici, who were sensitive about their plebeian origins, that the old Romans had considered talent superior to blue blood. Poets aided. Thus Petrarch, the Florentine singer, surpassed even the Florentine bankers in arrogant ambition; he conducted himself with studied insolence in aristocratic circles; he suggested to the Pope of Rome and the King of Naples that there was only one man in the world, himself, worthy to be Poet Laureate. He got them both to press crowns of laurel on his brow and at Rome he insisted upon having *three* crowns to wear, one above the other.

No business man in history's pages has been so arrogant as Petrarch. Even the Magnificent Lorenzo was always very courteous to royalty, no matter how much it was in his debt; he was not unduly puffed up when the King of France called him cousin and removed his hat in the presence of Medicean agents. But poetic license was the final flower of bourgeois license. The wool-men of Florence had removed aristocrats from power in that city before Petrarch was born; they had reduced Italian nobility to a state of enfeebled insignificance in which it could safely be ridiculed by men of letters.

The business men provided the material basis for the new cultural expression. Three generations of the Medici alone spent on endowments, buildings and taxes for upkeep a sum which in the modern equivalent would be $10,000,000. The palaces and chapels which marked the development of the Renaissance bore the arms of these families and of lesser clans: the chains of the Alberti and the castle of the Bardi, the lion of the Rucellai and the fish of the Ricci, the busy bees, lambs, peacocks and scissors of other firms. The work which proclaimed the arrival of the Renaissance was the Church of Santa Croce, for which the Pazzi helped to pay.

Merchants took over for their own ends, if at all, the mythological themes which the scholars and artists offered them. The sumptuous Palazzo Chigi, later the Foreign Office in Rome, was erected by a Tuscan financier, Agostino Chigi, who moved to that city and acquired financial power there. He bought social distinction by lending 400,000 ducats to Pope Julius II, obtaining in return adoption into the Pope's family, the della Rovere, and permission to use their insignia. Once in the Pope's family, it was natural for Chigi to invite Julius and fourteen cardinals to attend the baptism of one of his illegitimate children by a famous courtesan. On this occasion, Chigi served parrots' tongues and other classic dishes on platters of gold designed by Raphael, and, after the feast, ordered the dishes to be thrown into the Tiber. This gesture was carelessly impressive, but some skeptics in Rome insisted that he carefully fished them all out again next day.

The Palazzo Chigi was draped with gold and crimson cloth and adorned by a fresco showing the life and achievements of Alexander the Great. It was so filled with precious works of art that the Spanish ambassador, the story goes, invited there to dine one day, spat in the butler's face because, as he apologized, he could see no other vacant spot.

The first great libraries in Italy were those of the Pazzi, the Sassetti and the Strozzi, and the one collected by Boccaccio, a merchant's son, which was afterwards enlarged by a retired trader, Niccoli, and finally housed by Cosimo de' Medici. The first Italian drama was produced by an intimate of Lorenzo's household; under Medicean influence, the earliest operas were composed in Florence, including a "Eurydice," presented with pomp at the marriage of the banker's daughter, Maria de' Medici, with the King of France. Maria carried the Florentine tradition to France; she protected the Florentine composer Lully, the great initiator in concert and operatic forms, who, with true Florentine business acumen, first procured a monopoly in France, and had a law passed prohibiting any other orchestra from having as many instruments as his own.

In the molding of the Tuscan popular tongue into a literary vehicle, fit to stand beside Latin, business men had also a hand. Merchants used the Tuscan in their documents before the poets made an aesthetic instrument of it; the first record in this vulgar tongue seems to be the register of a Florentine banker in 1211; this was some time before Dante Alighieri, related as some think to the Parisian agent of a banking house, employed it in the "Divine Comedy." The banker, Lorenzo, was especially active in pushing on that development and wrote in the vernacular himself. The earliest academy that discussed the reformation of the Tuscan tongue was held in the Villa Paradiso of the renowned merchant Alberti.

Another important rôle of the business man was that of middleman for various cultural groups. At his table or in his garden, he brought together the mathematician and the architect; he enabled the sculptor to catch themes from the scholar, and the poet to get inspiration from the painter. The academies which united the various enthusiasts of the Renaissance were held in the homes of merchants: in the Villa Paradiso of the Alberti, for example. The Platonic Academy met in the villa of the Medici, and its successor in the palace of the banker Bernardo Rucellai, where Machiavelli read from his "Art of War." The most attractive picture of such assemblies was drawn of the first one, where the host was Antonio degli Alberti, merchant and amateur poet. Here churchmen, mathematicians and traders, physicians and statesmen, lawyers, rich and witty ladies, composers, young and old, learned and merely eager, met in garden parties. To suit the varied tastes of such an assembly, Voigt tells us, mass was first heard; there followed music, dancing, ball games and refreshments of finest wines; then came talks on Ovid, Livy, Dante, Homer, Petrarch, with occasional tales in the manner of the "Decamerone" for comic relief.

As important, if less colorful, were the library scenes in the palace of Niccolo de' Niccoli. Niccolo retired from business late in life with a modest fortune; he then took pleasure in giving banquets at which simple food was served, in the choicest antique vessels, to innumerable scholars whom he drew into his plans for recovering ancient manuscripts. His library became a news agency devoted to gathering and spreading reports concerning a vanished classic world. Through his friends, he inquired after chests of books from Byzantium and manuscripts in Lübeck monasteries. He advised, copied, edited; he collected gems, coins, statues and maps, the latter of service to explorers. The merry, sarcastic little man was fond of describing himself as a "spider in a web"—his web covering most of Europe.

Of course the business man as a patron, as manager of a cultural stock exchange, so to speak, often abused his power. The great Leonardo cried: "The Medici have made me and broken me!" And Michelangelo was bitterly humiliated when a late, degenerate member of that family could find no fitter employment for his titanic powers than the carving of a snow-man in the dooryard.

Even so, it should be remembered that, in those days, the patron sometimes underwent risks like the patronized. In the Renaissance, fostering the fine arts was not the sport of weaklings. Academic freedom meant something: it meant that members of one academy felt free to assault audiences assembling to hear a talk in a rival institution; it meant that a professor assumed the right to vilify the family of his colleagues and to cast more doubts upon the legitimacy of their offspring than of their footnotes. In this sort of atmosphere, it took courage, as well as a gold-filled purse, to be a trustee.

Lorenzo the Magnificent, with his iron nerve, was ideally fitted for the place. A man like that, who never batted an eye when his partisans hung an archbishop in full regalia by the neck until he was dead from the window of the government palace, was not the one to shrink from an academy committee meeting. When he ousted Francesco Filelfo from his lectureship at Florence, that venomous scholar promptly hired an assassin to murder members of the Medici family. The plan did not succeed, and Lorenzo bore him no grudge, having the fullest sympathy for the spirit of revenge. Indeed he at last recalled and reinstated Filelfo in full honors, an example of broad-mindedness which, in a trustee, is surely worthy of record.

The patron of the Renaissance, however, found more direct uses for art and learning than his modern counterpart. Sumptuous gifts were a part of diplomacy; for high politico-commercial ends, Lorenzo used to lend the services of painters and sculptors to potentates whom he wished to please. He sometimes sought to curry favor with enemies or solemnize treaties by benefactions; thus, after he had waged a war of ruthless extermination against Pisa, the hapless commercial rival of Florence, he founded a university amid the ruins of that town, to conciliate such of the population as had managed to survive.

Display was a part of economic competition in those times. The successful business men of Florence vied with one another in the extravagance of their robes and jewels, the splendor of their homes and gardens, the expensiveness of their weddings and funerals. This peacock rivalry was not the mere expression of vanity; many of the richest men really hated to wear cumbersome satin gowns and go through all the fittings with the dressmakers. Cosimo de' Medici was only too happy to dress like a peasant when he could. Others, like Sassetti, had few traces of natural beauty which they could have wished to enhance. One should not believe all that one reads in the costume books to the effect that "the men of the Renaissance wore their hair floating to their shoulders." Some of the most prominent bankers of Florence had not a hair to float.

But it was necessary for even the busiest man to display his credit upon his person. He could not leave to his wife, in modern fashion, the advertisement of his commercial solidity. Gossips on the Exchange were only too ready to pass rumors of approaching bankruptcy, if a broker happened to come to dinner in too simple a frock or an out-moded hat. The continual parading of wealth was thus a part of the everlasting struggle of Florentine families for business prestige. The danger-point was reached when prestige came to mean more to many than business. Hence a large part of old letters is taken up by discussing what other men wore. We find, for instance, one business associate writing to another and criticizing the appearance of a third in what, in a woman, would be regarded as a "catty" manner: "John came to the party in a dress of gold brocade with black velvet trimmings, open at the throat to show an eagle done in pearls. It made a good show, though it was not very expensive, but rather what you could call pretty."

The firm of Benci, when it wished to ally itself with that of the rich Palla Strozzi, gave a dazzling exhibition of its wealth. Young Benci appeared before the balcony of Strozzi's daughter, with his friends, all of them dressed in the most sumptuous costumes, dripping jeweled chains; they were attended by thirty pages bearing torches, and presented a symbolic float illustrating "The Triumph of Love." This was followed by jousting and the distribution of sweetmeats to the populace. But Strozzi remained unmoved by this spectacle and turned over his daughter to a firm he considered yet more solid.

The competitive spirit among these gorgeous, jealous men of Florence was responsible for much nourishing of the arts. Whereas business men nowadays compete in greater modesty and obscurity, those of the Renaissance did not fear the reproaches of the "mob" when they exhibited their riches. Indeed Lorenzo il Magnifico, who brought display to its greatest perfection in Florence, gave magnificent spectacles to the people which apparently delighted them immensely; he knew how to amuse them by pageantry, while he held them in his dictatorial grasp. It was therefore for the ends of statecraft that he appeared at a tournament in a costume worth more than 80,000 ducats, with a pearl-embroidered scarf and a jeweled aigrette in his black velvet cap. His commercial relations with France were symbolized by the three lilies on his shield, and the great Medici diamond, Il Libro, that blazed in the center, impressed the spectators as much as any yearly statement of his solvency.

BUSINESS MEN AS PARTICIPANTS

The rôle of the business man in the cultural movement of the Renaissance went beyond that of patron and sympathetic promoter. He was more than a passive nucleus, a merely benevolent giver. A number of business men engaged directly in humanistic pursuits. Thus the first great historical work in the Italian language was written by a merchant, Giovanni Villani; his intellectual work, it must be confessed, however, interfered with his business and he was, for a time, imprisoned in the debtors' tower in Florence, the Stinché. The brothers, Luigi and Luca Pulci, wrote the first long romantic epics, the "Ciriffo" and "Morgante"; and with them, as with Villani, art seems to have hampered profit-making, for one died in the Stinché, and Luigi, the younger and wittier, and the better poet, had to be helped by loans from Lorenzo.

Gianozzo Manetti had a banking and business career before he retired to devote himself to literature and scholarship and to write the history of his native city, Florence. He had served this city so faithfully and honestly as a tax-gatherer that the community had presented him with a silver helmet. But Manetti's income was wiped out by Cosimo de' Medici, who taxed the tax-gatherer out of everything he had. Fleeing to Naples, he recouped his fortunes by a stroke so brilliant that one is at a loss whether to admire him more as a man of letters or of commerce. He delivered so eloquent an oration in Latin before King Alfonso, so the story runs, that, although a fly settled on the royal nose during the peroration, the monarch did not even lift a finger to drive it away. From the enchanted Alfonso, Manetti then procured a monopoly in cloth importation for his son, which caused much searching of hearts among the other Florentines who lost out heavily.

Some niches should be reserved in business history too for those Italian traders and bankers who aided in the discovery of new worlds, in the East, the West and the past. More than a hundred years after the Venetian merchant Marco Polo described Asia, and about sixty years before the wool-merchant's son of Genoa, Columbus, discovered the Western hemisphere, another Italian, this time from Ancona, was engaged in exploring a third, and buried world, that of pagan antiquity. Though the credit of reviving the culture of Greece and Rome in the fourteenth, fifteenth and sixteenth centuries is chiefly given to scholars and artists, some measure of remembrance should also go to the bustling, jolly, vain, good-hearted, self-made Ciriaco de' Pizzicolli da Ancona, father of the tourist tribe, forerunner of the modern merchant-archaeologists—and the first modern man to take serious notice of the Acropolis.

It has been characteristic of business men that they love to dig up fragments of the past and preserve them, while they are revolutionizing the life around them. Henry Ford collects old buggies, which his own business activities have rendered valueless; and many modern merchants, like Schliemann who excavated Troy, applied great funds to archaeology, even while their new capitalistic methods have drawn a deeper gulf than ever between themselves and the past. So in the Renaissance, while Italian bankers and manufacturers were destroying the fabric of mediaeval society, they were becoming eager antiquarians. The banker Rucellai pointed out to his contemporaries that stones, like parchments, might speak of the vanished age; Ciriaco also urged his friends not to sit dreaming of past glories in cloisters, but to go out and dig up the past.

Ciriaco used his commercial voyages to Egypt, Greece and Asia Minor to collect inscriptions from monuments and tombs. While the scholars of the age were searching for manuscripts and comparing texts, Ciriaco, the practical hustler, was measuring ancient walls and harbors, mines and bridges. All his traveling salesmen were instructed by him to collect inscriptions as well as sales-orders. He himself went everywhere. From Alexandria he visited the Pyramids; in Rome, with the business man's natural interest in plumbing, he inspected the classical waterworks. And in the course of one momentous voyage, he accidentally came upon the Parthenon. On an April day in 1437, he stood with tears in his eyes before that temple, more eloquent than any manuscript of the past, still unmarred by man or time.

Nor was Ciriaco devoid of interest in books. On a sales trip to Adrianople he found a Hesiod; elsewhere a Plutarch, a Plato, a Herodotus. He managed to learn enough Latin to read the "Aeneid," and Greek sufficient for Homer. But he was never remotely a "high-brow." He was a tremendously practical pusher. He liked best that part of the past which could be exhumed and drawn; he wanted to weigh, measure, collect, in short, *do* something. Not content with reading about Cleopatra, he proposed an archaeological expedition into inner Egypt; when he saw that people in Rome were burning marble monuments to make cheap gypsum, he went straight to the Pope to protest. When he found a ruin in a desert, he pleaded with the Turkish governor for its preservation.

Garrulous, bright, unbaffled, Ciriaco was forever trying to hustle the Renaissance. As he foresaw the catastrophe to civilization that would result from a Turkish conquest of Constantinople, he hurried from one Italian court to another, preaching a united front against the Turk to save civilization. Had he been successful, two hundred thousand volumes might have been spared from devouring flames. The proposal of this busy trader, had it been listened to, would have done more to preserve the civilization of antiquity than all the subsequent dusty labor of scholars.

Full of shining enthusiasm and foggy ignorance, Ciriaco dashed about Italy, stirring up humanists in their retreats, urging professors to rally around, suggesting worthwhile activities to kings and tyrants. A literal-minded, simple fellow, Ciriaco also took very seriously the absurd notion that a new land might lie out in the Western waters, as yet beyond human ken; he believed in Ultima Thule. At least, so he argued, one never would know it did not exist unless one had looked for it. He even besought that cynical financier Cosimo to finance a searching-party. Cosimo, like the literati in Florence, chuckled heartily. Nothing was done about it for two generations. Cosimo and Ciriaco were both dead before Columbus found the new land across the Atlantic. Then, however, Florence held a celebration in honor of the occasion, and lighted honorary torches before the house of Amerigo Vespucci, whose family's firm was connected with the well-known house of Berardi in Seville, and who provided a name for Ultima Thule.

Ciriaco was a citizen of Ancona, but his great friends were in Florence. His letters were eagerly received by the merchant Niccolo de' Niccoli, whose library had become a clearing-house for European scholarship. Ciriaco's purchases of ancient relics were aided by the liberal credit opened for him in every foreign branch of the Levant by that untitled prince of Italian bankers, Cosimo de' Medici. He was always welcomed at the gatherings of enthusiasts in Florentine villas.

It is true that Ciriaco's more learned and sedentary friends found him a good deal of a pest at times, and said so to one another. He boasted of his own poems; he talked as tirelessly as he traveled; in the disputations at the dinners of such cultivated bankers as Palla Strozzi and Cosimo de' Medici, he often waded out beyond his depth. He wished his friends to call him Orpheus, awakener of the dead. Perhaps that name was more symbolic than they knew—for as happened to Orpheus, most of the precious details that Ciriaco had rescued from the underworld slipped back to it again when the three huge volumes of his travel-notes were suffered to disappear by careless heirs.

Some memorial of Ciriaco's activities remains in the modern popularity of the statuettes of the Winged Mercury. According to Voigt, it was he who, instinctively seizing upon this ancient god of the traders, collected images of Mercury and prayed to him during storms at sea. Florentine friends even called him, teasingly, "Our Mercury." Perhaps to Ciriaco we owe the fact that Victorian drawing-rooms in England and America were so plentifully supplied with statues of the little winged god of duplicity.

Perhaps, also, for Ciriaco's sake, some little mercy might be shown by supercilious aesthetes today toward the guided flocks of retired brokers and packers who stand, Baedeker in hand, helpless before the monuments of antiquity. As might rudely be asked, who rediscovered the Parthenon anyway? Not a poet, a professor, an artist, a dreamer, but a business man in his off hours.

THE REBIRTH OF FORTUNA

While Ciriaco rediscovered the ancient trader's deity, Mercury, the other patron saint of classic business, Fortuna, was likewise being restored to popularity. It would be difficult to single out any business man as individually responsible for this; but perhaps the great banker Bernardo Rucellai had as much of a hand in it as anyone, for he was patron of Machiavelli, generally taken as the writer who brought back the concept of Fortuna.

The Rucellai family was old and illustrious; its fortunes were laid in the 1260's in Florence by a monopoly of the violet dye process. It produced many men of talent who combined war and politics with the cloth-trade and financial speculation. Giovanni Rucellai (1403–81) had entered the bank of the rich, cultured, but fatally ambitious Palla Strozzi. He married Strozzi's daughter with a ceremony remarkable for its display even in ostentatious Florence; it was preceded by eight days of feasting in the bride's home and followed by another week of rejoicing in the palace of the Rucellai. But at the strategically correct moment, Rucellai moved out of his father-in-law's camp and without a backward look, joined the implacable enemy of Strozzi, Cosimo de' Medici.

Now Rucellai's palmy days began. At Cosimo's suggestion, he took public office; he spread his business afar and opened a branch at Constantinople. With immensely increasing riches, he covered the face of Santa Maria Novella with black-and-white marble and employed Alberti to design a classic palace which is still his memorial. The crowning event of his life was the marriage of his son Bernardo with the daughter of a Medici, Nannina. Then he felt, and said, that he had "stepped into the ship of Fortune" of the Medici. He ordered a picture, described by Warburg as the depiction of a Fortuna-ship, with a richly dressed Nannina at the helm; the young bridegroom stands, naked, at the mast, holding a sail to catch the favoring breeze. This tasteful composition bears the motto: *Lasciate Portare alla Fortuna Sperando alfin dauer Buona Ventura*. The Medici, incidentally, were from very old times accustomed to sign their business ledgers, not with a "Jesus Maria, amen," like the pious Germans, but with a thanks to "God and Good Fortune."

Old Rucellai was right in his estimate of his son; the young man knew how to trim his sails. The wedding had been a sensation; Alberti himself had designed the pavilion covered with garlands and illuminated by a thousand candles; the joy had continued three days and nights and cost 3,686 gold florins, as the Florentines all learned, for they loved to know the prices of art works and festivals down to the last scudi. The happy bridegroom, now in the government, initiated an ostensible fiscal reform netting his brother-in-law, Lorenzo de' Medici, in fact, some 50,000 scudi.

But soon the storm blew. It was not long after the marriage that the bride Nannina began to write to her mother: "Whoso wants to do as he pleases should not be born a woman." It was clear that she was not steering the ship. When the appropriate moment came, Bernardo deserted his bride's family, as his father had left his mother's. He welcomed Savonarola when the depression came to Florence, when the Medici were driven out; enthusiastically, he endorsed the theocratic and anticapitalistic régime of the monk, and he was widely acclaimed as a lover of liberty and religion. He joined the monk's government. But the instant he realized that the breezes had shifted, he caught a diplomatic illness which incapacitated him from further office-holding for some time—at least until after the implacable Savonarola had gone to the stake.

The Rucellai may therefore be taken as "merchants of fortune," full of agility and intuition, and hence splendid types of the Renaissance. Bernardo was aware of this dependence upon the willful goddess, Fortuna, and sought the aid of literati to clarify his mind. As Cosimo de' Medici wrote to the scholar Marsilio Ficino to inquire of him the way to happiness, so Rucellai addressed himself to the same authority and posed the question: "Can human reason and practical wisdom do anything against the accidents of fate, of Fortuna?" The noble reply advised Rucellai to avoid too unequal a struggle, and to make terms with the guileful deity.

Was it Bernardo who put the problem before Machiavelli, or the writer who stimulated the business man to think about Fortuna and Success? Bernardo was a man of taste and discrimination; he took time from finance and politics to serve the city as ambassador; he wrote books on war and one on classic Rome deemed by Erasmus worthy of a Sallust. In his salon were read the maxims of the idealist Machiavelli arguing that, since double dealing was the way of life, it should at least be used in the cause of union and peace in Italy.

In his two books dedicated to bankers, though later read more thoroughly by kings, Machiavelli sums up the characteristics of the successful men of the Renaissance. The ideal is a man who, like a centaur, is half animal, half human. He must remember that his contemporaries are more inspired by greed than by any disinterested motives: "A man sooner forgets the death of his father than the loss of his property." As to the careers of the rich and great, Machiavelli judiciously decides: "I hold it for an evident truth, that men seldom rise from a lower class into a higher without force or deceit. . . . I also believe that force alone has never been enough; deceit alone, however, one finds has sufficed."

It was Machiavelli who described life as the conflict between Fortuna and Virtù within the iron ring of necessity. He felt that Fortuna ruled over human affairs, and that against many of her decisions there was no appeal; but by force of character and prudence, by *virtù*, he believed that man might at least regulate matters so that Fortuna "would not show, at every rising of the sun, what she can do."

This concept of a world dominated by Chance and Competition, accepted so naturally today, was the supreme ideological achievement of the Renaissance from the business man's point of view. Renaissance thought not only encouraged him to stand alone as an individual, but removed all divine authority from above him, save only Chance.

How far the lingering tradition of the ancient Etruscan goddess was a factor in this revival in Florence, is of course impossible to say. But, according to Bezold's study of the "Fortleben der antiken Götter im Mittelalter," it was Venus and Fortuna who survived best in the folk-memory, after the pagan deities were overthrown by Christianity. Venus, however, was anathematized as a witch, the helpmeet of Satan, who waylaid pilgrims in her Venusberg. It was more difficult to find a suitable place for Fortuna; vainly the Church Fathers thundered against her, and denied Lady Luck a niche in their order and harmonious universe, designed by an All-Wise Father, who let no sparrow fall to earth without notice. The common people would not forget one who had been the most adored deity of the later period of the Roman Empire.

Fortuna even made her way into the Christian churches; her image, with bandaged eyes and a wheel at her side, was placed there as the symbol of the uncertainty of things temporal. Her wheel, emblem of mutation, was lifted on high and transformed into those glorious rose windows, in the shape of spoked wheels, at Rheims and Chartres. But this wheel was put to more frivolous uses; on church festivals in some

parts of Europe, people played a game of chance with it—forerunner
of modern roulette, the beloved toy of high capitalism. Apparently this
love of chance-games persisted, especially among the financially talented men of northern Italy; for in 1271, we find a certain Nicholas
of the Barterers, as he was called, a merchant, who came to Venice
and, by his engineering skill, raised up in the Piazza two enormous
pillars brought as booty from a sea expedition. In return, he demanded
the right to open gambling tables between the pillars. This incensed
the city-fathers of Venice so much that, although they had to agree,
they in turn hanged condemned criminals there. Ruskin thinks that
this latter action proves the sublime purity of Venetian morals. It may,
but it also indicates the survival of the gambling instinct among other
Italians, who, in the most ancient times, had been dice-lovers, students
of omens, speculators, worshipers of Fortune.

Florence, the last city to surrender her pagan gods, if Schillman is
right, may perhaps never have forgotten Fortuna entirely. At any rate,
in the last years of the 1200's, we find the problem of her behavior
discussed by Dante, the great mediaeval poet of Florence. It was perhaps no wonder that the citizens of Florence were agitated on the
point, for the bourgeois revolution had but recently taken place, with
all its dramatic reversals of men's lives and fortunes. Many must have
wondered whether this was mere accident, Fortune's whim. But Dante,
profoundly religious, believed that Fortuna was the minister chosen by
God to "change the vain possessions" of this world and bring the
avaricious to defeat. Though he himself suffered exile in one of the
swift political overturns of Florence, he maintained that Fortuna was
the angel of the Lord; she was not the Devil's, like Venus, but God's
own agent. She is described in the Seventh Canto of the "Inferno." When
Virgil takes Dante to see the torments of those souls damned for
avarice, he says:

"But thou, my Son, mayest see the brief mockery of the goods that are
    committed unto Fortuna, for which the human kind contend with
    one another.
For all the gold that is beneath the moon, or ever was, could not give
    rest to a single one of these weary souls."
"Master," I said to him, "now tell me also: this Fortuna, of which thou
    hintest to me; what is she, that has the good things of the world
    thus within her clutches?"
And he to me: "O ye foolish creatures, how great is the ignorance that
    falls upon ye! . . . He whose wisdom is transcendent over all . . .
    ordained a general minister and guide,
To change betimes the vain possessions, from people to people, and

from one kindred to another, beyond the hindrance of human
wisdom . . .
Your knowledge cannot understand her: she provides, judges, and
maintains her kingdom, as the other Gods do theirs.
Her permutations have no truce; necessity makes her be swift. . . .
This is she, who is so much reviled, even by those who ought to
praise her. . . . But she is in bliss, and hears it not: with the other
Primal Creatures joyful, she wheels her sphere, and tastes her
blessedness."

A century and more after Dante, the paganization of thought was
so far advanced that Fortuna was celebrated in Florence, as a ruler,
not a minister. Lorenzo il Magnifico, according to Andral, ordered a
great tapestry woven to represent the Triumph of Fortuna. Bernardo
Rucellai, his brother-in-law, discussed her power with Machiavelli
and Ficino.

From Florence, where she had regained her old altars, Fortuna traveled to the North of Europe; she went wherever the financial network
of the Florentine bankers could carry her, to South Germany and
Holland. Hans Fugger, Lill states, had her image frescoed many times
on the ceiling of his castle at Kirchheim, with hourglass and trumpet,
bearing a world-globe, or scooping coins out of a heavy sack. From
the Fuggers' native town of Augsburg spread the popular folk-tale of
Fortunatus, the youth beloved by Luck. German merchants bore her
fame to Britain, where Holbein, in London, Woltmann says, painted
her Wheel for the Hanse House, though Britain, and America later,
never really took her to their hearts.

In her progress, through Europe, however, she underwent a strange
transformation. Doren points out that her new worshipers, in the sixteenth century, in the Age of Exploration, unbound her eyes; they let
the bandage roll behind her like a sail to symbolize the winds that
were driving the ships of the explorers and sending back the heavy
galleons of the Silver Fleet. They put in her hands a brimming jeweled
goblet or an overflowing cornucopia to represent the increasing rich-
ness of the earth. They took away her wheel which had revolved on a
stationary axis, such as suited the narrow mediaeval mind, and set her
feet upon an ever *forward*-revolving globe. The globe, as one writer
on military affairs of that time said, was appropriate to Fortuna; for it
was the round cannon-ball which was putting so much uncertainty
into war and leaving even the cleverest generals at the mercy of Fortuna's whims.

We meet Fortuna at her zenith, in Dürer's great engraving, open-
eyed, gift-bringing, swept by a favorable wind on a swift sphere

above the cities of men—a perfect divinity for merchants who were conquistadores, eager to exploit the treasures of new empires, discovered by divine accident.

As speculation and riches constantly grew in Europe, while the precious metals of the New World poured in and capitalism yielded high dividends, men threw caution to the winds and adored Fortuna as a Luck-bringer solely, forgetting that in ancient times, she had been the Doom-Fulfiller as well. They thought only of her better side. Intoxicated as they were by the discovery of fresh lands, new machines, new methods, Fortuna seemed to be opening vistas of endless bliss. Soon after the voyage of Columbus into the unknown, a tournament was held at Bologna in which two knights fought as supporters of Fortuna on the one hand and of Wisdom, Sapientia, on the other—divinities personified by local belles on floats. To the immense joy of the populace, he who wore the colors of the Luck-goddess overthrew the cavalier of Foresight. What wonder that, at a moment when Columbus had discovered a new world by reckless daring, the Bolognese should rejoice at the downfall of prudence and hail happy chance?

In the rosy flush of the first extravagant boom-period of Europe, 1551–57, it was easy to ignore the fleeting character of Fortuna's favor. Not until a century later, after the long-drawn-out misery which followed, had taught mankind a lesson in the variability of business success, do we find a picture of Fortuna in a sharp contrast to that by Dürer. This new picture is the work of Rembrandt, whom Neumann invites us to remember in this connection, as having lost every penny of his fortune on the Amsterdam Stock Market by gambling in East India Company shares. Rembrandt limns the goddess standing on a ship with its sails already unfurled; her back is turned to the land, while deserted on the shore, a defeated warrior with withered laurels, spreads his arms to her in vain entreaty.

How the fickle Fortuna might behave toward traders is illustrated by the experience of Glückstadt, Luck-City, founded by the Danes near the mouth of the Elbe in the seventeenth century. The mercantilist Danes thought they could crush Hamburg, farther up the river, and monopolize all the commerce of the coast and of the Elbe. Their plan was well framed; the town was laid out according to a remarkably beautiful and practical design. All that Sapientia could do for a town was done; and in addition, it was dedicated to Fortuna; her image appeared on the coins and over the Rathaus door. Nevertheless all prudence and all respect for luck failed to bring the desired riches. Though Hamburg was more remote and was, besides, an inconvenient mediaeval mess, the merchants persistently clung to it through force of habit. So the Luck-City stagnated and today is an almost ghostly village. The kings of Denmark learned, to their cost, that calculations alone cannot win business wealth and that Fortuna's favor may not be caught merely by invocation.

Sobered by many disasters, Europeans at length began to question again the place of Chance in the affairs of men. For a time, however, the Puritans saved the day by declaring that the world was run by God's will, mysteriously manifested. Their conception of Providence was peculiarly acceptable to business men, because it seemed to afford plenty of leeway for competition and chance and yet offered the consoling reflection that whatever happened was willed by a logical, masculine divinity. Encouraged by this Calvinist view, the Puritan capitalist entrepreneur embarked upon his remarkable career.

In the nineteenth century, however, belief in Providence began to wane, as scientific skepticism made its way. A substitute was found in Nature's Law, laissez faire. Nature worked through competition, it was averred, in apparently arbitrary ways, but always toward a higher goal. Chance thus was reinterpreted as the agent of Progress. For a time this was satisfactory also, since it was assumed that, to some extent, the business man could control Chance by *virtù*, by rationalization of his methods, the speeding up of his processes, efficiency and economy. Only recently has another crisis of faith in Fortuna arisen. Disenchanted by economic disorders, skeptics begin to doubt the inevitability of Progress so conceived and revalue the past; they assert that freedom, the great bourgeois slogan, leads to anarchy; that freedom, of press, of trade, of individual development, is not enough to bring the perfect economic balance. The swing back to the idea of planning, whether religious, Socialistic, Fascistic or Liberal, has begun. Even business men are a little frightened by being left alone with hard, blind, cold Fortuna, and are dubious of their own *virtù*. The Rotarians, though taking the wheel as a symbol, put ratchets on it, to show it is geared to a social machine. Others, more Fascist, have shown signs of turning to the Machiavellian ideal of the dictatorship. And so the old concepts of Divine Plan versus Fortuna, which agitated the Middle Ages, reappear again in modern times under fresh guises, as Planned Economy versus Competitive Individualism.

ART AS ESCAPE FROM BUSINESS

The movements of the Renaissance furthered, on the whole, the development of capitalism: they freed the individual; they restored the idea of competition and chance to the world. But there were anti-capitalistic trends as well and in these several sons of business men were leaders. Boccaccio and Alberti were rebels against the ways and world of their fathers, through which, at the same time, they derived a comfortable income. Ruskin and Morris followed a similar course in nineteenth-century England.

Boccaccio, who influenced conceptions of the Poet as Genius, was the son of a Parisian agent of the banking firm of Bardi. Forced into a countinghouse for a time, the youth satirized bankers in his ribald "Decamerone." When the father died, Boccaccio retired from the practical struggle and spent a green old age in a country villa, as a plump, merry scholar, universally beloved. He had only one regret, that he had misspent so many years in business that he could never be a poet himself. He tried, however, to point the good way to others.

A more fortunate son of a greater banker, Leon Battista Alberti, was permitted to exchange the ledger for the law when his lack of fitness for business was only too evident. But even the law proved too hard on his health; at Bologna he fell into such a dolorous languor that doctors feared for his life. Allowed to return to Florence and do what he liked, he instantly recovered and became a fencer, mountain-climber, sculptor, painter, architect, scientist and writer, a man of such energy as to astonish even the dynamic and versatile Leonardo. Maintaining a severe distance from commerce, he wrote an excellent treatise on economy. Remaining a bachelor, he composed a splendid treatise on matrimony. Supported by a comfortable patrimony, he proclaimed mankind's duty to spurn profit-making. He urged the Architect and Artist to rise above the artisan and become a Scholar, despising cash and living only for the laurel wreaths of fame.

Thus the doctrine of individualism worked both ways. It supported the business man in his strivings for emancipation. It also encouraged the artists and scholars to develop their personalities and look down upon the business man as a mere moneygrubber. Florence, which Sombart has called the "Bethlehem of the Capitalist spirit," cradled the two sworn enemies of that spirit as well—the Poet and the Artist.

Boccaccio and Alberti, and many another wistful renegade from the paternal office, turned back to the classic past in search of inspiration for a nobler life. Scorning what they felt was the crass commercialism of the society about them, they could find nothing perfect this side of pagan, republican Rome—about twelve hundred years before they were born. The parallel between Boccaccio and Alberti, on the one hand, and Ruskin and Morris, on the other, becomes even more complete. The Victorians looked back with yearning to Pre-Raphaelite Florence; the Pre-Raphaelites themselves shuddered at the conditions in Florence, and thought that what she needed most was a few persons, call them poets or artists or by any other name, who cared nothing about money.

The prescription of such men as Boccaccio and Alberti was tried. Business men of Florence seized upon culture with an unexampled gusto, a boundless appetite. They gave to art and learning the most enthusiastic support. But after the glory of the Renaissance had unfolded, another Florentine, Machiavelli, looked upon it with a jaded eye. He decided that the only perfect society was a poor one.

In a book which Machiavelli sent to the Medici, he proposed one of the profoundest questions ever put to a business man: "Which are more dangerous to a state—persons who wish to profit, or persons who fear to lose?" His answer was: "Revolutions are usually made by those who already possess," by the rich, wishing to keep what they have. The only way, he thought, to prevent tumult and tyranny was to keep the community perpetually poor, and continually at war. Though he brought forward the idea of Fortuna as the regulator of human life, he thought that strong laws, imposed by dictators, if in no other way, would have to bring order into the anarchy of Italy. Thus Machiavelli recommended, in fact, the undoing of the Renaissance; he beheld his country, torn by competitive individualism, by the strife of the rich and the greedy; he longed for a strong hand, even were it a Borgia's, to bring order out of anarchy. Thus the individualism of the Renaissance ended in the cry for Fascism, as reaction. Machiavelli, however, was more read than understood. Indeed, a king of France happened to be carrying a copy of his book advising princes how to avoid assassination, on the very day of his death—by an assassin.

It is difficult to decide whether it really paid the Renaissance business man to be kind to artists and scholars. Humanism, which appeared to be the tool of the business man, turned out to be a boomerang. In the beginning, by recognition of talent, it encouraged the baseborn merchant; at last, by emphasizing intellectual talent, it excluded him again from the highest circles.

The results of philanthropy are always beyond calculation. Did not Cosimo de' Medici endow and build the cloister that sheltered finally the implacable enemy of his family, Savonarola? Did he not bestow upon it the very bell that summoned hysterical crowds to hear denunciations of the Medicean régime?

The Humanism of the Renaissance turned out to be very much like Cosimo's beautiful, cupid-covered bell that clamored for his foes. Scholars and artists, as they climbed above the business man, turned to princes for admiration and support, and away from the bourgeois who had helped them up the social ladder. They fixed upon the business man a worse stigma than that set by the mediaeval Church or the feudal nobility—that of ignorance. As that virulent man of letters Erasmus of Rotterdam maintained, the world was becoming divided into many classes, among which that of the merchants was the filthiest. The suave friend of Erasmus, Sir Thomas More, though an intimate of the cultivated Italian banker, Spinola, shut out financiers from his lucreless Utopia, thus setting a style for succeeding dream-worlds from which business men have been regularly eliminated. Even in the sixteenth century the trader and banker already found arrayed against them the scholar, poet, and artist, whom they had patronized. The libraries and universities they had founded nourished their detractors. And so the Renaissance, which provided science, individualism and belief in Fortune as the background for modern capitalism, also produced the inevitable antithesis.

VIII

THE DIFFUSION OF ITALIAN FINANCE
AND CULTURE IN EUROPE UP TO
THE BOOM 1551–1557

THE SPREAD of Italian culture was coincident with that of Italian finance, during the century 1450–1550. Wherever the commercial connections of the Italians reached, their individualist art and philosophy, their classic columns and cupids, Fortuna and Mercury, were also borne. The old mediaeval community-crafts society of Northern Europe, as it broke down, was replaced by the new scheme, capitalistic and classic. Thus, the Italian financiers managed to recapture by loans and art, drama and music, most of the territories which old pagan Rome had once seized by brute force and lost. Indeed the second empire of Italy, though built upon intangible and invisible assets, was as audaciously fashioned as the first.

Of course, it cannot be pretended that diffusion of culture was entirely a one-sided process. Throughout the Gothic period, as well as the Renaissance, the mutual exchange of ideas and goods had been pursued along the principal trade-routes of Europe. French Provence had given Madonna-worship and Gothic style to Italy through the merchants of Siena. Germans had helped plan and build some of the most remarkable Italian Gothic buildings. Through Venice and other towns in touch with the Near East had come fruitful Asian influences to the North and West. In the Renaissance, Italy again was the receiver as well as the giver. From Flanders, through the Medicean business relations, came stirring artistic impulses; the highly realistic paintings of the Flemish artists ordered by Italian business agents, like Portinari and Arnolfini, were of profound importance in the development of Italian art. Germany for many centuries provided mechanical skill; even in the last part of the thirteenth century, Italians marveled at her ingenuity, and of course, in the fifteenth, they accepted printing and gunpowder, as well as the finest armor and many industrial processes, from beyond the Alps.

This cultural interaction is symbolized by the beautiful fountain in the center of the marketplace in Nürnberg, the focus of technical progress in the 1500's. In this fountain the water jets from the muzzles of bronze artillery pieces; on each weapon sits a laughing baby, drinking, fiddling or aiming a bow—by that time an obsolescent weapon, at least in warfare. In this allegory of cupid and cannon, Northern and Southern Europe, the past and the future, are brought together. The cannon represents the inventive genius of Germany, which produced the printing-press to further the religious Reformation and the firearm to ensure the deadliness of religious warfare. The little amoretti represent the classic revival in Italy, which encouraged the merchants and manufacturers of the rest of Europe to assert themselves in the demand for individual liberty. The cannon typifies an age when war absorbed more and more of the wealth of the financier and the energies of the manufacturer; the careless cupids stand for the period when Art turned from the adornment of churches to the decoration first of merchant-homes and then the glorification of the warrior. Art then sank from the rôle of preacher and prophet to that of a gilded Eros perched above the mouth of a modern gun.

GENOA AND SPAIN

Italian bankers and artists conquered Spain comparatively late. This was the one European country in which the Jews had held a virtual monopoly of trade and finance until the end of the fifteenth century. The Spanish Gentiles were and remained the least gifted of Europeans for business and when the Jews were broken and exiled in 1492, to the immense economic misfortune of Spain, Genoese and Florentine money-lenders slipped rapidly over the border and proceeded to strip and ruin Spain with the thoroughness of an invading Roman army. With the creditors, painters and sculptors of Tuscany also poured into the amalgamated territory.

Spanish art in the Renaissance represented the blending of many strains. Through Spanish exploration, trade was opening with India, and many bizarre and monstrous forms in Spain reflected this intercourse. The trade with Flanders resulted in the domestication of fabulous heraldic fauna amid the native Moorish vegetable tracery. And when Italian classicist art followed the bankers to Spain, it formed, so to speak, a holding company, merging the Moorish, Flemish, Indian, native Gothic and Romanesque assets, and resulting in a combination as marvelously extravagant as a South Sea Bubble.

Genoa, even more than Florence, stamped herself on Spain. But Genoa faced a grim rival in the South German firm of Fugger; for the latter, who had grown rich through their Italian contacts, also laid claim to Spain. For a century and a half, the Italian and German Christian financiers struggled over the heritage of the Jews in that unhappy land. Though the duel ended with the bankruptcy of the Germans, the triumph of Genoa was short-lived, and presently both the rivals were exhausted like Spain, their prey.

Since this financial warfare between Genoa, the home of Ansaldo Grimaldi, and Augsburg, the town of the Fuggers, was more decisive in the affairs of Europe than the mere dynastic quarrels of impoverished rulers, it may be well to trace some of the steps in the drama.

Both the Genoese and the Fuggers, as well as other South German houses, dreamed of a business man's empire in the East. When the Portuguese Vasco da Gama discovered the route to India, these two merchant powers seized upon the trade and erected a monopoly of the spice distribution throughout Europe. Then, after a Genoese had discovered America, the fellow-citizens of Christopher Columbus disputed with the Fuggers over the Spanish Empire and the division of the New World spoils.

The explorers could hardly have left their harbors without the backing of business men, who supplied funds to Spain and Portugal. A Genoese son of a merchant discovered America; and afterward most of the trips of explorers to the New World meant a fresh loan at some Genoese firm and an increase in the Spanish debt; the proceeds of conquest were therefore earmarked before they arrived. The galleons of the Silver Fleet, laden with ingots of American metals, were awaited with eagerness by Italian bankers, who had mortgages on the cargoes and left hardly a fleck of precious dust sticking to Spanish fingers.

The South Germans, however, wished to send out their own explorers, instead of absorbing indirectly the profits of discoveries made by others. The firm of Jacob Fugger, together with the Welser, Höchstetter and other German firms, and some of the Genoese, combined to exploit the route to India discovered by Vasco da Gama. They outfitted a fleet in 1515 at a cost of 66,000 ducats, and sent it forth to evict the Arabs from their Asian monopoly and collect pepper. The Portuguese military men, however, managed to prevent the merchants from establishing a trading foothold; they kept all titles and claims in their own hands. Thus the merchants had to accept the titular supremacy of Portugal. But it was only a shadow-victory won by the king, for the spices of Portugal, like the silver of Spain, were mortgaged before they were docked, and taken over by Genoese and Germans. Portugal, nominally ruler of an empire, went bankrupt almost a century before the firm of Fugger, which engulfed the riches of that empire.

The chief conquistador among the Renaissance merchants was probably the visionary Bartholmä, a younger member of the firm of Welser. His portrait shows him as bluff and big, with a square-cut beard, outthrust jaw and dilated eyes, looking more like a sea-captain than a captain of industry. But he wanted to be both. When he took over the firm, he changed its previous policy of caution in dealing with crowned heads and perilous ventures. Bartholmä scorned the soft, tame life of his fathers, spent in sacking spices, cornering sugar, boosting prices, and gathering in dividends from a conservative, steady traffic in Negroes. He longed for adventure. Buying a title in 1532, he became a frequenter as well as a creditor of courts. Military ambitions went to his head. In return for loans, he obtained vague claims to imperial tracts in the jungles of Venezuela. He strained the resources of his firm to send three hundred colonists overseas and an expedition to search for gold. The Spaniards used his wealth and organizing ability, but found ways to separate him from the fruits of his adventures.

No doubt Welser was impractical, yet business men of a later and soberer time have followed in his very footsteps. Thus the German banker David Hansemann, at the opening of the twentieth century, involved his bank's resources in an ill-fated Venezuela railroad venture and besought the German Government to intervene in the affairs of the New World. At that time, as Alfred Vagts recounts, the parallel was drawn between Hansemann and Welser; a newspaper, urging governmental interference, pointed out the fact that German Landsknechte had once tramped in Venezuelan wildernesses.

For a long time, Germans and Genoese shared the riches of Spain and helped to determine her policies. At one period, four Genoese bankers as treasurers held the entire expenditure of Spain in their power; Genoese transmitted the gigantic sums from Spain to Italy and the Netherlands that supported the enormous bureaucracy and far-flung military forces of the Spanish Empire. A conception of what this involved may be gained from the fact that a single Genoese, Ottavio Centurioni, transferred in one deal the sum of 10,000,000 scudi from Spain to the Netherlands.

Some of the Genoese, Ansaldo Grimaldi for instance, in character and achievements resembled the Fuggers, their rivals. They built splendid palaces, as the Fuggers did; Grimaldi, like Jacob Fugger the Rich, was famous both for the boldness with which he admonished kings and for the modesty which he reserved for addressing his fellowcitizens. The later Grimaldi, like the last Fugger, turned aristocratic; Agostino finally acquired the principality of Salerno together with a title; he built so vast a palace at Genoa that he was popularly called, not merely Prince but *il monarca*. From the Grimaldi descended a line of Spanish dukes; the Fuggers survive today as princes and counts.

The centers of this financial power, Augsburg and Genoa, were ruled by banking plutocracies. In Augsburg, the disproportion between the rich and the poor was astonishing; it was an early Newport, a small town full of millionaires. In 1467, a mere 39 men had fortunes totaling 260,000 gulden; by 1540, there were 278 citizens with a wealth of about 10,000,000 gold gulden. And these moneyed magnates lived in a town of little more than 18,000 persons.

In Genoa, as the city's historian Spinola relates, "after the year 1528 the greatest part of the wealth of the city was concentrated in the hands of the *nobili vecchi*." The old nobility, "who had formerly been engaged in goods-trading, now went over to the exchange of credit and contracts with princes, especially with the Spanish court. They thus made extraordinary profits, but grew more and more alienated from the life and customs of their fellow-citizens, built royal palaces, bought domains, and even entire territories, especially in the Kingdom of Naples, and lived with such pomp that it far surpassed the ordinary wont of citizens." Some of these homes, faced with black and yellow marble, still form the ornament of Genoa; they had wide and stately staircases and were frescoed inside and out with the Labors of Hercules and the Recreations of Jupiter.

It is certainly curious that social revolutions took place in both cities in exactly the same year, 1547. In Genoa, as in Augsburg, the populace and the artisans formed a front against the oldest business men and drew support from some of the younger parvenus. In Genoa, the "new nobility" was very embittered by the taunts of the old nobility which considered itself removed from the taint of shopkeeping. In Augsburg, a gild-leader and labor organizer, one Schwartz, procured his own election as burgomaster repeatedly. Then he grew overbold, broke his own sumptuary laws and, by dressing in gorgeous silks, affronted the patricians with his splendor. Finally he had executed two patricians who were charged merely with uttering deprecatory remarks about him. Before the year was out, the patricians invoked the German Emperor's aid and seized Schwartz, who was hanged, dressed in his best robes of office.

The old nobility of Genoa asserted itself in the same year against the insurgents. Moreover, it invoked the aid of the same German Emperor. It is perhaps odd to find the bankers of two cities, who were such jealous rivals, calling in the identical Emperor to assure their political positions. But, as Ehrenberg says, the Emperor was in debt to both the Genoese and the Augsburgers, and could do no less than support those by whose wealth he conducted his wars.

Until the middle of the seventeenth century, Italian and German bankers clung to Spain; they could not let go, indeed, without being ruined. For a time the Fuggers seemed transcendent; eventually, like the monarch they supported, Charles V, they had spread their dominion too wide and could not defend it all. Their credit, extended to most of Europe, was shaken by widespread bankruptcies, and they failed toward 1650 for eight million gulden. The Genoese, to whom the Fuggers owed money, received depreciated Spanish state paper in lieu of payment, and pushed these over on their creditors, including their own fellow-citizens in Genoa. However, they only kept afloat a little while longer by such subterfuges. From the wreck which involved both Augsburg and Genoa, only the richest and most foresighted bankers, who had invested in landed estates, saved a part of their fortunes.

The influence of Genoese gold upon Europe had far-reaching consequences. These Italian financiers upheld the vast imperialistic designs of Philip II of Spain, that ruined Spain and Flanders and threatened England with conquest. The British, awakened to their peril largely by the great merchant, Sir Thomas Gresham, adviser of the three sovereign children of Henry the Eighth, accepted Gresham's economic as well as military proposals for defense. Gresham knew that armaments alone could not defeat Spain; Genoese gold must be matched by British cash. To gain the sinews of war, Gresham managed to transfer English commerce from Antwerp to Hamburg; through that German port, he began to pour English wares into Germany and the Continent. Vainly the frantic North Germans, the Hanseatics, who saw their danger-hour approaching, held conferences, proposed boycotts, sent a princely orator to the Reichstag with two or three "tons" of gold for bribes. They issued pamphlets begging help to exclude British cloth: "If we sleep, others will be awake and will wake us up too late." They said that the English, given an inch, always took a yard; that they would enslave the Continent, and take bread from the mouths of weavers and sheep-growers; that the next generation would see the beggary of German cities.

Unheeded by the Emperor Charles V, the dismal warnings of the Hanseatic merchants were borne out by events. Northern Germany was impoverished through the loss of her trading monopoly; South Germany lost the markets for her textiles to a large extent and was further injured by the bankruptcies of the Fuggers. In her distress, Germany could not prevent the alien British, Dutch and Swedes from seizing her rivers and sealing up their mouths, nor the war-lords of Europe from trampling over her lands. A colossal prey, like modern China, due to the disruption of her economic life, Germany was delivered over to a highly Chinese confusion under such *tuchuns* as Wallenstein, and marauding foreign bands.

Even worse results flowed from the intolerable jealousy which Genoa felt toward other Italian cities. Genoese rivalry with Venice permitted the Turks to take Constantinople. Genoese hatred of Florence, as Ehrenberg points out, caused the devastation of Rome and the general chaos into which Italy finally dissolved.

The Genoese financial powers wavered continually between the two contending dynasties, the Valois and the Hapsburgs, for the throne of the Holy Roman Empire. In general the Florentines and the Nürnbergers supported the French Valois; the Fuggers were loyal adherents of the Hapsburgs. By changing fronts the Genoese prevented a clear decision between the two. First, through hostility to Florence, they financed the French king's invasion of Italy and his capture and looting of Florence. Then, convinced that the Hapsburgs were a better gamble after all, since they could hand over huge real estate tracts in the Kingdom of Naples to banking consortiums, a Genoese banking group helped the German Emperor, in turn, to invade Italy—yes, and even to take the city of Genoa itself.

Ansaldo Grimaldi appears to have been engaged in this latter speculation. Grimaldi was very much like Cosimo de' Medici and Jacob Fugger in general type; indeed all three Renaissance merchants may well be characterized by the words which a Genoese chronicler employs for Grimaldi: "A man of friendly and merry aspect, short of words, proud, distinguished, very rich, thrifty in his ways, in shrewdness the equal of anybody . . . he was very bold toward the King, but without being overbearing; his chief wish was to be rather than to appear great."

His compatriots found something very suspicious about the sudden growth in Grimaldi's towering fortunes, after 1512, in which year the Germans stripped and looted Genoa. They whispered that Grimaldi had not merely favored, perhaps urged, the onrush of the alien conqueror, but had bought up the booty from the German troops and disposed of it at considerable profit, thus enriching himself by the ruin of his fellow-townsmen. So bitter was the criticism that Grimaldi attempted to conciliate popular opinion by presenting the city with 4,000 shares in St. George's Bank, the sum to be used for charitable purposes. A statue was erected to him, and no more was said about the matter.

It was also the Genoese bankers who brought the Spanish, their debtors, into Italy and supported their imperialism with loans. Thus the Genoese played a most portentous rôle in the sixteenth and seventeenth centuries. It may briefly be summed up as follows: a Genoese merchant's son found America, though a Florentine merchant's son furnished a name for it. By helping to destroy the Fuggers, the Genoese impoverished Southern Germany. By supporting the vast schemes of the Spanish king and aiding him to send his Armada against England, they exhausted the last resources of Spain, awoke England to commercial as well as military energy, and ruined North Germany indirectly. Finally they brought hideous devastation upon Italy, and even on their own home town. Thus, one is tempted to say, they discovered the New World, and wore out the Old.

FLORENCE AND FRANCE

If France today seems a land of classic culture, close-linked to her Italian "sister," this is unquestionably a matter of gold even more than of blood. As a matter of fact, the effects of Roman conquest were forgotten in the Dark Ages, and the infusion of Roman blood was, as modern historians believe, negligible. A certain amount of cultural as well as commercial interchange went on through the Middle Ages between southern French cities of Provence, and those of northern Italy, but it was France which was the donor of Gothic taste to Italy, and not the reverse. Northern France was feudal, military, Gothic, in manners uncouth, and illiterate, until near the sixteenth century. She pursued a path which led her as far away from any "classic tradition" as Germany. But Germany was spared the second conquest of the Italians, in the Renaissance; the Fuggers saved her the second time, as Hermann and the other wild fighters saved her the first time. France, on the other hand, was recaptured as easily by Florentine finance as she had once been by Caesar's arms; and it was the second transplantation of classic culture which gave France her present aspect.

The first noteworthy attempt to bring back to France the classic art which was being revived in Italy was, it is true, that of the French merchant Jacques Cœur in the middle of the fifteenth century. Cœur had ramified commercial and financial relations with Italy, as an exporter of goods, including arms, to the Near East; and in return he was inspired by Italian sojourns to build the first imposing Renaissance monument on French soil, a private palace. He had bought twenty fiefs of feudal lordlings, but none of them was modern enough for Cœur. So he built two palaces, one in the Renaissance style. In Bruges, his home was elaborately carved with figures of spinners, since he was a textile-man, and of servants; he himself is represented holding a stonemason's hammer in the left hand and presenting his wife a bouquet with the other. The mottoes chosen by Cœur were, first, a perfect business man's reflection: "Dire, Faire, Taire" (Order, Do, Be Silent); and then a play on his own name, "A Cœur vaillant rien impossible," (Nothing is impossible to the brave heart).

A generation after Cœur lived, French armies at the invitation of

Italian bankers roamed ruthlessly over large parts of Italy, even entering Florence. They were charmed by the conquered people; and swarms of Italian adventurers followed them home, while Italian financiers offered to lend them enchantingly large sums in return for tax-gathering privileges in France and liens on municipal and royal incomes. It was not long before two Florentine queens of the Medicean House ruled over France; their mastery, and that of their agile countrymen, lasted a hundred years—from 1533, when Catherine de' Medici married Henri II, to 1640, when Maria de' Medici fled from the hostile nation to an asylum in Cologne.

During that hundred years, history seemed to repeat itself. As the Etruscans, bowing to Roman arms, had entangled the Romans in their financial nets, so, two thousand years later, though conquered by French arms, they revenged themselves by swallowing up the revenues of France. The great *partisans*, as they were called, financiers who lent the Crown money in return for the right to farm taxes, in reality carried on the antique tradition of the "publicans," the old tax-gatherers who sucked the blood of Rome's captured provinces. Neither Germany nor England was a prey to partisans, as France was under the financial ministry of the Italian cardinal, Mazarin.

Since the financial affairs of France were largely in the hands of Catholic priests and Florentine money-lenders, the power of the Catholics was great enough to cast down the Huguenots. Protestantism swept over a great part of Germany, although the Fuggers, good Catholics and agents of the Roman Church, managed to save a large section of South Germany for Catholicism. In France, however, the Italian Catholic money-power was transcendent; and many Italian bankers and their sons engaged in stamping out a heresy so dangerous to their financial empire as well as their faith. In trampling on the opposition, they did irreparable injury to France.

The Florentine bankers sought to destroy their rivals, the thrifty, bustling, exceedingly able group of Protestant entrepreneurs and artisans. Catherine de' Medici, the Florentine queen, organized against the Huguenots the hideous Massacre of St. Bartholomew; a banker and tax-gatherer of the famous Florentine family of the Rucellai, who was at the same time an agent for the Italian branch of the Medici and a French diplomat, was financial counselor for the queen and procured aid from Florence and Rome for the projected butchery; two of the chief figures in the Massacre, one the ruthless Duke of Retz, were of the notorious banking family of Florence, the Gondi. An Italian of an old banking family, the Tosinghi, was slaying side by side with the Gondi, and it was he who despoiled the body of the murdered Admiral Coligny. The funds for the Catholic side were to a large extent provided by that famous rogue and tax-farmer, Sebastiano Zametto, a careerist in the bank of the Capponi; he was said to have given trunkfuls of money to help put down the Protestants. In the usual purely political histories, very little has been written to clarify the rôle of finance and commerce in the Religious Reformation. Surely however it is significant to observe Florentine bankers, as financiers of the Church, crushing Protestantism in France, while the Fuggers in Germany were doing the same thing, and also later assisting the Jesuits to bring on the Counter-Reformation.

Alien financiers in France thus destroyed the very bud of French business genius; on the other hand they brought technical skill in the luxury trades; they taught diplomacy and appreciation of art to the French; they gave them theater, opera, concerts, art collections; indeed, even the much acclaimed French art of "amour" was perfected by the Italian financiers. Catherine de' Medici, when she came to the French throne, carried with her a superb family collection of art objects; since there was no suitable edifice to house them in France, which had no museums at that time, she built the Tuileries.

The building of the Tuileries was supervised by members of a great Florentine banking house, the Gondi, who had moved to Lyons. The Gondi bought titles and places: one became Bishop of Paris; another was the Duke of Retz, Grand Chamberlain, Ambassador, Marshal, and massacrer; yet another was Bishop of France, Cardinal, patron of poets and orators. The Gondi held salons; they were patrons of the arts; they were high in favor with their crowned countrywomen. Sparkling with decorations and titles, they were, however, hated by the French people. The biting satirist, L'Estoile, singled them out for his especial detestation. Only in his times, said L'Estoile, could one "see an ass of Milan as chancellor; a banker as marshal; a peasant as knight; that is the fruit produced by the seeds of Florence." Of Giambattista Gondi he said: "By his manners one would take him for a pork-merchant rather than a gentleman."

Another favorite of the queen was Ludovico Diaceto, who had fled Florence on account of a murder. Supposed to be an adept with poison and dagger, he was a special secret agent of the queen. He had come, comparatively poor, to Lyons, made a fortune on the Exchange there, and opened a branch of his bank in Paris. He was a munificent patron of arts and letters, assisting, among others, the poet Ronsard; his salon was held in a gorgeous palace, upon the decoration of which alone he had spent 150,000 écus. He became a count and married a duke's daughter; winning the favor of the queen, he secured extraordinary privileges. He could keep the tax-farming rights on a province even though the population rose in open revolt against his exactions. Unfortunately for Diaceto, in 1584 an inconvenient commission was appointed to investigate the doings of Italian financiers, and he judged the moment opportune to disappear from the eyes and subpoenas of commissioners and historians.

The Strozzi family of Florence, to whom reference has been made, hated by the Italian branch of the Medici, moved to France and did very well. Giambattista Filippo Strozzi had married into the Medici family and was trying to heal the feud; he conducted Catherine to France; but later he was strangled by design of the Medici in Florence. His son, Piero Strozzi, a banker, gathered loans from the Florentines which he let the French have for 23 per cent. He bought the baton of Marshal of France. And as a warrior, as well as money-lender, he carried the private family quarrels of Florence forward into international spheres. It is a very complicated picture presented to us when a Strozzi, hereditary foe of the Medici, as a French general, with troops paid for by Florentine loans which he had raised, defends Siena in the French interests, for a French queen, by birth a Florentine Medici, *against* a Florentine Medicean duke.

Of Maria de' Medici a French writer said: "At last we were sent from the banks of the Arno a Queen to whom pictures had become a necessary luxury, and who began to make the love of painting obligatory in courtiers." She also brought the Italian theater to France, with *Pantalone*, the comic merchant of Venice who later, in the hands of Molière, became the *bourgeois gentilhomme*.

The mercantile and the cultural transplantations of the two queens were simultaneous. Their love of luxury brought across the Alps the manufacturing of silk, faïence, furniture, embroidery, while they introduced, at the same time, science, the pastoral, the burlesque, opera, ballet, and the academy. It was an Italian marquise, de Rambouillet, who helped Frenchwomen to be "blue stockings"; in the salon of this woman of a commercial race, "for the first time, aristocrats and bourgeois met on equal terms" in France. Deliberately she set out to improve the French, whom she found barbaric, and their language which was so ungrammatical.

Moreover, the Italian Minister in France, Mazarin, was the collector of paintings and statuary on a gigantic scale; and used the power of his high office to obtain additions from all quarters. He taught Louis XIV that a rich man had to collect art; to be both a Maecenas and a Medici. This information Louis imparted to the French noblesse.

To say nothing of the other adventurers, the contribution of the bankers alone to French culture is enormous. Scores of business houses might be described, most of them carrying on the Italian tradition of generosity to the arts and patronage of letters. Thus the Martelli had a silk and wool trade in France and were a cultivated group, producing poets as well as warriors and merchants. The bankers of Provence, the Buonaccorsi, helped bring Benvenuto Cellini, the sculptor, to France. Army provisioners, the Spini, used their war-profits for cultural ends. The Galilei, parents of the famous astronomer, were Italians living in France for business reasons. The Rucellai, patrons of Machiavelli in Florence, went to France with learned favorites in their entourage. Sebastiano Zametto, a salt-tax farmer, purchased the title of Baron de Billy, and a superb mansion in Paris, the Maison de Zamet, where the king, Henri IV, was happy to come to dine, repose, and receive his mistresses as well as loans of immense size, amid surroundings of artistic luxury.

The Guadagni, a family originally sent into exile from Florence by Cosimo de' Medici, were particularly noted patrons. Tomaso I, very rich and generous, was a builder of churches and hospitals in France; Tomaso II achieved the title of Il Magnifico, as Master of the Court under Catherine de' Medici; he took many titles, built splendid palaces for himself, protected printers, poets, savants, and in return was celebrated in epigrams, both Latin and French. One of his sons, a count of Verdun, was a soldier and Protestant-killer; another was a scholar and studied under the Humanists. Thus with such versatility the Guadagni family brought weal and woe to France, slaying her business men, but cultivating her nobility, the former perhaps more thoroughly than the latter.

From Florence the great banker Bernardo Salviati moved to Lyons, and a succession of proud Salviati won honors. His daughter Cassandra was immortalized as a beauty in the verse of Ronsard; his grandson was a Cardinal and diplomat; a son was Cardinal, Knight of Malta, banker and state financier; other Salviati were palace-builders and French ambassadors. Indeed Lyons became known as French Tuscany, and over it another Italian family, the Capponi, reigned until the last years of the sixteenth century; they intermarried with the family of Tomaso il Magnifico and won French titles; they patronized Torquato Tasso and other literati.

Among the business men, too numerous to be listed here in full, who helped to mold French civilization were: the Nazi; the Panciatichi, bankers of Lyons with a palace in Florence as well, active in the Bartholomew Massacre; the Bartoli, bankers and warriors; the Mannelli, bankers of Lyons and literary patrons; the famous family of the Pazzi of Florence, one member of whom in France was a banker and translator of Aristotle. The Del Bene were distinguished in the literary as well as the political and economic history of France; their founder was a Lyons banker; sons were in the army, court, church, and royal finance; they were tax-gatherers and diplomats, poets and historians. There were also the Bini, the Dei, Antinori, Ginori, Martini, Ridolfi, Sertini, Infangati, Uguccioni, Marucelli, Bettoni, Tedaldi, Ducci, Mellini, Buondelmonte, Nobili, Lottini, but the curious reader is referred to the works of Picot and Dumesnil for further details.

Wherever these Italian business men settled in France, classic pillar and *putti* appeared as well as the discount-note. With one hand, they spread light amid the rural darkness which enveloped the fierce, rude French nobility; with the other, they fastened upon the French people the grip of ruthless exactions. The despoliations of Diaceto roused a province to revolt; and those of Particelli d'Émeri, in the opinion of Renard, were very largely responsible for the terrible national uprising of the *Fronde*, inspired by popular hostility toward the aliens.

As a natural expression of the Italian dominance, there crowded on the façades of houses in Tours, Poitiers, Angers, and Orléans, the classic motifs of the conch, the scroll, the laurel wreath. Everywhere the old-fashioned native gargoyle vanished in favor of the caryatid, the muscular giant groaning under the weight of carved balconies in the Renaissance manner. This caryatid became the very emblem of the French population, staggering under the burden of Italian bankers. For generations there seemed no hope of shaking them off. The overthrow of the Florentines, under the queen called "Medea" instead of Medici by her subjects, seemed as vain a dream as Victor Hugo's famous nightmare in Frankfurt-am-Main, in which he envisioned "the awakening, unchaining and revenge of the caryatides."

The French struggled against this domination by force of arms (the Huguenot revolt), by the strikes and terrorism of the Fronde, by epigrams and satires (L'Estoile), and by protests which led to investigating commissions. In 1575, the height of Florentine power, L'Estoile wrote a fiery denunciation of Sardini, Gondi. and Diaceto, reading:

> *Justice is in the hands of Biraga,*
> *Arms in the hands of Gonzaga,*
> *The Strozzi and also the Peron;*
> *The Italian does everything here.*
> *You French people, leave France then*
> *And seek shelter elsewhere,*
> *And if you still care*
> *For the country where you were born,*
> *Seize lance and take cuirass,*
> *Chase out these poltroons . . .*
> *Crush the vermin*
> *That Florence has produced here.*

On the doors of the Royal Palace in 1578 a rhymed placard was nailed, addressed to "Messire Poltroon Scorpion Sardini, *sarredenier*, and his accomplices, the Messires of Italy." This was an affront to Scipione Sardini, a negotiator of foreign loans, a provisioner and raiser of armies, and a tax-farmer. The Italians in France replied by a placard explaining their actions, trying "to justify so many seigneurs, gentlemen and men of honor of Italy, who are residing in this Kingdom for good and praiseworthy reasons. Some are here to recover what they have lent for the urgent affairs of the King. . . . Others have married here. . . . Some are attending to international commerce." And anyway, the proclamation concluded, there were just as many French rogues as Italian: "It is notorious that there are in France more Frelucs, Jules, Andras, Chastillions, Spifames, Vaschers, Escaloppiers, Hurraults, Cleres, Gourques, Marteaux, Grandrus, de Brais, Hennequins, than there are Sardini, Diaceti, Del Bene, Martelli, Gondi and Rucellai."

What finally ended the Italian occupation was sheer exhaustion. Swollen with wealth, the Italians turned to buying titles and lands; they became land-poor feudal gentlemen, or wasted their estates in gambling. Forsaking trade and finance, the sources of their strength, they left the bourgeois class. At last, in the seventeenth century, they were largely replaced by native French talent. But the French financiers were trained in the Italian school, and they merely continued the methods and culture of their tutors. In France, from the age of the Florentines down to recent times, bankers close to the State have exercised commanding power, over politics and society.

Far too much emphasis is popularly placed on the Sun-King, Louis XIV, as the individual who set a cultural stamp on France. In fact, as will be shown later, he was influenced in his youth by the German banker Jabach, owner of the finest art collection in Paris, filled with treasures bought at auction, when the effects of Charles I of England were, like that unhappy monarch, brought to the block. Mazarin, the rich and deft Italian financier, further inspired the Grand Monarch; Fouquet, the most elegant French banker and tax-farmer on record, set him the model for Versailles; and the wool-merchant who became his minister, Colbert, forced him to wear fine clothes and buy artworks in order to stimulate French luxury industries. Then from the time of Louis onward, bourgeois women took a hand in determining French taste; the art of the rococo was in large measure the creation of Madame de Pompadour, wife of a Parisian banker and mistress of Louis XV. In the succeeding reign, the luxury of the Paris financiers far outshone that of the nobility. Marie Antoinette acquired her frivolous tastes during secret sorties into the masked balls of Parisian bourgeois.

Not entirely incongruous, therefore, was the craze of the new-rich American millionaires of the "Gilded Age," after the Civil War, for châteaux and salons decorated in the French styles. In fact, they were but following fashions set originally to a large extent by Florentine and French financiers. Perhaps it was somewhat inappropriate for a modern business man to choose baroque furniture, because in the age of Louis XIV the shadow of the king was mighty enough to dwarf the bankers; but there is no real reason why any beef-baron or tin-plate czar should not indulge to the limit in the period of Louis XVI, with rococo gilt chairs, pink damask and mirrors in profusion, since such dainty objects were created especially to suit the tastes of men like the Crozat brothers, patrons of Watteau, the financier Paris de Montmartel, close friend of La Pompadour, and the rich banker Sam Bernard.

FLORENCE AND THE BIG BOOM IN FRANCE

Florentine bankers supported the claims of the French dynasty of the Valois to the throne of the Holy Roman and German Empire. Had they been successful in their strenuous efforts to put a Valois over Europe, the fate of that Continent might have been vastly different. Florence might have Italianized Europe as well as France; Medicean influence might have dominated and transformed lands from the Baltic to the Straits of Gibraltar; and Medicean compatriots might have had a world to devour.

Of course, the relation of the Florentines to the Valois was not one of idyllic affection. France was the only resource open to the Florentines, who had lost England and the Netherlands; in France, they found one of the last economically underdeveloped and capitalistically unexploited fields. They had to keep their final foothold beyond the Alps, the city of Lyons; and the French kings threatened them with exclusion from its Exchange if they did not bring together loans and indemnities and even open the gates of Florence to French troops. The Tuscans, therefore, moved by hate and dread, revenged themselves by gathering up all they could in France, and they proposed to win back their former vast economic empire by setting up a Valois. However the Hapsburg, who also pretended to the throne, finally thwarted the scheme.

Endeavoring to raise money to help the Valois in their imperial designs, the Florentines bore to French soil popular loans—a device never before tried out on a great scale in a monarchy, though familiar enough in Italian cities. By this instrument the king's previous debts were consolidated and a new loan for a fresh war was raised at the same time, the whole sum involved in this measure reaching perhaps two and two-thirds million crowns. The French king, swayed by his advisers, opened his big public subscription loan in 1553, at a rate of 18 per cent, to all his subjects, high and low, and to strangers of every clime and degree. The result was a tremendous boom, such as Florence had already experienced but Europe had not yet known on so tremendous a scale.

"Everybody ran as though to a fire." Women pawned their ornaments to buy war loans; widows exchanged their safe investments at low rates for the new "grand parti"; servants brought savings. Rich merchants, Swiss, Italian, German, Flemish, raced to invest before it was too late; even in far-away Turkey, some pashas and traders heard about it and rushed funds to Lyons. Everybody who paid up at the Office of the General Receiver there obtained a "king's letter," beautifully sealed and inscribed on the very best parchment. So that even churchmen could participate and nobody's conscience could possibly be disturbed by taking 18 per cent, interest was to be distributed by an officer cheerfully entitled "Dispenser of Free Gifts."

The boom kept up, despite the revelations of rotten national finance at the death of the king, Henry II, who left forty-four million livres of debts. The French Estates proposed to have an investigating committee go thoroughly into the facts; but proud nobles, especially the Duc de Guise, who had enriched themselves at state expense and dreaded a show-down, had the motion quashed. Thus the downward push of the "bears" was ineffective and the bulls had their way; "le grand parti" was selling at 99, and the new king was still able to borrow, just before the crash. He promised a financial reform, to please the people, and on the strength of that assurance took up 500,000 crowns more from German merchants at 16 per cent, remarking privately, as he did so, to the Venetian ambassador: "To tell the truth I am myself astonished at such lavish giving in such a situation." Three months after he had solemnly declared that he would keep faith with the public, in 1577, he stopped payment of both interest and capital and plunged France into bankruptcy.

This was a frightful lesson for France as well as for a large part of Europe. But hardly two centuries elapsed before France again fell victim to an erratic alien genius, this time from Scotland. John Law organized a marvelous state bank, started a boom of unprecedented size, which drew in the wealth of all classes, only to collapse suddenly, leaving the *ancien régime* bankrupt and ripe for its fall. Twice, therefore, were the supposedly logical, cautious, thrifty French people brought to the heights of hysteria, and then to the depths of disaster, by scheming financiers from foreign lands.

ITALY AND THE ANTWERP BOOM

The fine Italian hand was also displayed in the great boom which was dexterously blown on the Antwerp Bourse, simultaneously with that on the Lyons Exchange in France. The notion of an Exchange was Italian to begin with. Italians had been accustomed from early times to hold money markets and play at risky games in them; and whenever they planted posts or colonies in northern Europe, they held regular meetings for the exchange of letters of credit. Thus they had brought the art and technique of speculation to the more backward regions of the Continent. But they had never, even in Italy, had such a free field for operation as sixteenth-century Antwerp presented, where the market met every day instead of at seasons only, and where the great quantities and standardized quality of the world's wares, pouring into her port, made it possible to hold a goods-market, as well as a money market, of unprecedented size.

The traffic of Antwerp surpassed all previous notions. Every week 1,000 freight-wagons with wares from France and Germany entered the gates; more than 10,000 peasant carts brought provisions from the countryside; and every day came and went 500 pleasure vehicles and 200 passenger wagons. Postal messengers hurried to and fro, in a service paid for and organized by merchants, so that the most distant royal wedding or war might react as soon as possible upon the money market.

The goods concentrated at Antwerp were of amazing variety and quantity. Perhaps never again will so great a proportion of the universal trade pass through a single harbor, or such an immense part of the world's credit-operations be transacted on a single exchange. Certainly, since Alexandrian times, there had not been seen in the Old World so many products assembled from so many ports, dealt with in such amounts by companies so powerful and men of such international orientation.

Antwerp was the copper and spice mart of Europe, a depot of the English Adventurers, the Hanseatic traders, the South German and Italian bankers. Loans were floated here for the governments of England, Germany, Portugal, the Netherlands, and, under cover, France. Here were traded the laces of Mechlin and Valenciennes; tapestries of Brussels made after Italian designs; jewels, glass and clocks; Flemish sculpture produced *en gros* for Spain or Greenland; leatherware, pewter, iron of Namur and munitions of Liége; Spanish cochineal and paints for the palettes of the "colorist" schools. England stood in relation to Antwerp as old Rome had stood to Alexandria; she sent coarse products like canvas, tin, lead, sheep and rabbit skins, to exchange for manufactured and refined articles—cloth of gold, sugar and spices, furniture and mirrors, armor and breviaries.

Irresistibly, indeed, Antwerp invites comparison with classic Alexandria, being the first modern city to approach the cosmopolitan character of that old Egyptian port. Florence and Lübeck prohibited foreigners from slipping through their gates and snatching trade from their citizens. On the contrary, the Flemish city welcomed every nationality, trade and religion, as she did every commodity and loan.

On the river Schelde rode blunt beflagged ships that had just made a trip of a few days or a week from the English or French coasts, from Norway, Denmark, or Spain; of months, from India. Though a rival city, young Amsterdam, felt proud to exhibit 500 ships at a time with cargoes of grain and herring, at Antwerp almost as many often came in on a single tide and sometimes 2,500 ships might be seen riding together at anchor and blurring the horizon with their spars.

All the European costumes mingled on the streets of Antwerp and all tongues were heard there. It was common for men and women to speak six or seven languages and the balls and banquets of the city were as cosmopolitan as the Bourse. Indeed the chief business was not carried on by the natives who acted mainly as brokers and hotel-keepers; it was managed by the alien: English, German, Portuguese, Spanish, Dutch, Italian. Antwerp was a port-city—an excrescence on Flanders as modern Shanghai is on China.

Promises of freedom to all comers, such as no mediaeval city had dreamed of making, were given by Antwerp. "In the city of Antwerp, all men are free and cannot be enslaved." A slave setting foot there was automatically emancipated. Within his own house, a citizen was safe from arrest. The citizenship of Antwerp as of Switzerland was often sought by cautious merchants anxious to find security for their fortunes.

Every religion was represented by the merchants. The Italians, Spanish, Portuguese and many South Germans were Catholics. The French Huguenots turned their houses into headquarters for Calvinists. The English brought their national Church and the Germans their Lutheranism; hand-workers ran to communistic Anabaptism. Refugees from terror-swept lands augmented the crowds; some 6,000 of the "Reformed" were numbered in 1565. Notable among the Calvinists was Gilles Hoofmann, a wealthy merchant who, through his daughter Anne, sent Puritanism across the Channel into the family of the Lord Protector and maker of the bourgeois Revolution, Oliver Cromwell.

Mercenaries, willing to fight for any cause, came to Antwerp for hire. Artists eager to study new modes arrived; after 1540, especially, they were wandering birds flocking in foreign colonies. Artisans, driven by war and turbulence from land to land, carrying their trades with them, introduced the arts of making cloth, bells, spurs, leather, silk, Venetian glass and pottery to Antwerp. If trade and capital had become expatriate in this century, so had art, war and religion.

Over the door of the Antwerp Exchange was written in 1531: "For the service of merchants of all nations and languages." Within that ornamental quadrangle assembled every day 5,000 men whose diversity of speech and garments bore witness to the inscription. On festive occasions, to be sure, the merchants came in procession, each in his own national group, the Germans preceded by a brass band the gigantic instruments of which in the museum still astonish tourists. But once within the magic walls, fatherlands were forgotten; talent and not race was the determining factor.

The racial medley in the Exchange was mirrored by the cultural medley in the great art-selling gallery which was housed in the second story of the Exchange. The relation of finance and art, all under the same roof, could hardly be more strikingly symbolized.

In the various cities of Europe at that time, the commercial soil usually affected the growth and character of culture. Thus Danzig, which sent grain to Amsterdam, received Dutch architecture in return. Cologne, at the crossroads of France, Germany and the Netherlands, produced a great colorist school reflecting the glories of all three. Venice was decked in the glittering ornaments of her Eastern customers. Nürnberg, commercially connected with Venice and Antwerp, lent her great artist Dürer to both cities; in Venice he painted for the German House where the merchants lived, and he came to Antwerp under the patronage of a Portuguese merchant. Dürer, widely traveled and receptive to the most various tendencies of his age, adopted for his scutcheon a symbol, with a play on his own name, an Open Door. It might well have stood on Antwerp's civic shield, for Antwerp, as the center of universal traffic, held her gates open to universal culture.

Antwerp's first great painter, Quentin Matsys, united the streams of Italian and Flemish influences. In his art, Southern classicism met Northern fable and genre-spirit; serenity conflicted with sarcasm; he painted both madonnas and money-changers. The Italian and Flemish business connections bore wonderful fruition in the arts; tapestries of Flanders were executed after designs by Raphael, while Italian merchants ordered their portraits painted by Flemish artists. Thus Northern craftsmen were inspired by Italian Renaissance spirit, while Italy received Northern realism.

A noteworthy example of international affiliations in Antwerp was the great geography school of Gerard Mercator, which correlated Portuguese and Spanish discoveries with the science of German astronomers and the technique of Venetian map-makers. In Antwerp, too, Erasmus met Holbein; there Holbein took ship for London, when England, after shaking off Italian sculptors together with Italian bankers and the Roman Church, turned to German and Flemish finance and art.

Antwerp was in fact an exchanger of ideas as well as of wares and shares. As a printing center, she distributed books and engravings; her edition of Vitruvius carried the standardized models of that architectural schoolbook over all northern Europe. She provisioned Europe, as someone has said, with marble, artists, statues and patterns. She outfitted the minds as well as the homes of Europe's rising and aspiring burgher-class.

Art was made a paying industry in Antwerp, catering to a large consuming class. Out of Antwerp went "lives of saints by the mile," on tapestries, as Pirenne says. There went sculptures too, according to Michel, to fill North France, up the Rhine and to Sweden, even to Greenland, and down to Spain. It was an art "easy and abundant and of semi-industrial production," made in ateliers the patented trademarks of which are easier to distinguish than the individual artists. These products were of a type appealing to the bourgeois consumer: polychrome, realistic, often bordering upon caricature, rich in costumes with plenty of accessories.

It is also highly characteristic of Antwerp that her final, greatest painter, the sublime Rubens, should also have been the most remarkable business genius among artists. His organization of studio production, the warehouse in which supplies of ready-made canvases were stored, the excellent personnel management which kept the best talents of the day employed without jealousies and strife, the swift tempo which enabled him to turn out thirty-five vast canvases for the Louvre within a year would do credit to any business man. Was it in the blood? His grandfather, before him, was a capable dealer in spices.

Antwerp, finally, achieved the perfect bourgeois architecture. That too was logical and to be expected. Where North and South met in finance and business, appeared the proper blend of Renaissance playfulness with Northern comfort; here the use of bands of stone to tie together expanses of brick, was discovered, a mode which was transmitted to England and Scandinavia. From Antwerp went out those editions of Palladio which were copied by architects everywhere.

It was an age of home-building by rich business men. The Genoese were putting up their palaces; in Vienna, the houses were said to be as vast below as above the ground, because of their wine-cellars; of Nürnberg it was remarked that a king of Scotland would wish in vain to live as superbly as a middle-class citizen of that town. The palaces of the business men, notably of Leonardo Spina in Lyons, Diaceto and

Girolamo Gondi in Paris, and the Hirschvogel in Nürnberg, were being erected with lavish ornamentation. The gorgeous Villa Farnesina of the Tuscan banker Chigi was perhaps the supreme edifice of all, on account of the fabulous collections of art it contained. The gayest residences, however, were those just between Italy and Germany, such as the Haus zum Tanz in Basel, the walls of which were decorated outside by Holbein with figures of rollicking flower-crowned peasants dancing, with cupids and peacocks—and high up, just as though the artist had forgotten it, a paint-pot.

Antwerp, if it did not break records for splendor, acquired at least a variety of homes: the fine hôtels of the Fuggers; the many-towered, moated castle of Grobbendonck where Gasper Schetz welcomed Thomas Gresham; the "Golden Rose" of the Welsers; the beautiful estate of Hoboken on which Gaspar Ducci entertained royally; the Great Goose and Little Goose in which the rich Gilles Hoofmann lived and stored his goods. Most ornate, perhaps, was the much admired Hôtel de Moelenere, built in 1549, belonging to the merchant and financier Guillaume de Moelenere. It has a great flagged courtyard with a carved balcony; the windows are enclosed in a mass of carving, the tiny, painted panes being swallowed up in a riot of satyrs and garlands; and the whole overhanging structure is supported on brackets that are a strange, typically Antwerpian mixture of Southern caryatid and Northern gargoyle.

In Antwerp, the South and North formed the most comfortable medley consistent with classic taste. These odd houses, strangely mixed in style, with little chimneys smoking above Renaissance balconies, and great fireplaces in the form of Doric temples, were the beginnings of modern mansions. Kings sighed in vain for such luxury as they contained, with their tessellated pavements and paneled walls, candelabra and mirrors, wonderful tile ovens, cages of parrots and nightingales, beds hung with red and green silks, stores of silver plate, warm rugs, bright glass, fine linen. The Antwerp bourgeois set the standards for aristocratic imitators.

It was from Antwerp that a decisive influence went out to England. England's art and culture had been, like those of other lands, closely related to her commercial situation. As long as the Italian bankers and the Church of Rome dominated, so did Italian culture; but the group of Italian painters and sculptors around the financier Orazio Pallavicino represented about the last of this influence. When the bankers and their followers were chased away and England's chief business was with the Germans and Flemish in Antwerp, the shift was noticeable in her art; she welcomed Holbein, introduced to Europe largely by the German Hanseatics. Later Antwerp architecture took England by storm.

THE ANTWERP BOOM

In this great world-city, international finance was slowly formed along modern lines. For the first time, princes and governments came to have regular access to the purses of the public; this privilege had been enjoyed on a small scale in Florence before; now, in Lyons and in Antwerp, it became regularized. Before this, states had had to deal with merchant firms; now they could call for public subscriptions. This practice had its dangerous side for, in those days, European states, with the exception of England, were run with less order and good sense than the humblest business house. While states were being admitted to the Antwerp Bourse, a new public was created; for the first time, large numbers of non-business men, of inexpert outsiders, even more liable to hysteria and stampede than seasoned merchants, were introduced to speculative grounds. In Antwerp, for the first time in Europe, governmental wolves and citizen sheep were brought together.

The result was a new phenomenon: a public opinion registered in quotations. Mediaeval hopes and fears had been worked out in crusades or epidemics of the St. Vitus Dance, but now they vented themselves on the Antwerp Bourse. This became the pulse of Europe, and, all too soon, indicated fever.

In the new Bourse, mediaeval caution vanished. One could no longer investigate each man and each transaction with care. It became the habit for merchants to trust anyone called *ditta di borsa:* that is, in good standing on the Bourse. All the more blindly did the non-mercantile elements give allegiance to such men. Thus merchants misled the public, and the public of ignorant buyers, in return, became a menace to the merchants.

The market-price was no longer, at Antwerp, fixed by a few experienced traders. It tended to be fixed by opinions built in distant lands, by rumors, by the political and economic trends of the whole world—by reports on Peruvian mines, Javanese crops, a Hungarian royal wedding, the Turkish War. In a city so cosmopolitan, so well connected by postal service, the contagion of popular opinion, swayed by innumerable hopes and fears, was almost irresistible. All but the hardiest veterans were caught at times. And, as Ehrenberg sagaciously notes, this new and modern market opinion was *not* built on a better knowledge of the facts than had been the case at mediaeval fairs. Being a mirror of larger circumference, reflecting more factors, it gave a more fascinating, but no more reliable picture, than that of mediaeval men.

It was an Italian, Gaspar Ducci, to whom Ehrenberg gives the honor of being the shrewdest manipulator of the Antwerp Exchange and the greatest tutor of this assembly of brilliant talents. Broker and speculator, he was one of the first modern types of agent; instead of dealing in concrete articles like a mediaeval trader, he lived like a spider in his own aerial contrivance spun from invisible assets. He had a corner on alum and a grip on the Netherlands tolls-system; he floated loans and boomed valueless papers by tricks which he invented; he was a banker, a leader of financial syndicates and a broker, and in these capacities he managed large transactions for merchants or princes. In one single deal, 259,200 gulden were involved. In addition, he was the inventor of the most scandalous abuses on the Antwerp Bourse.

Ducci has been called by Ehrenberg a man of startling modernity, and so he was. But he was only a transition type after all, uniting twentieth-century ingenuity in abstract thinking with a Renaissance temper. He won his profits like a modern stock-pirate but spent them in Quattrocento luxury and violence. According to Gérard, Ducci lived in ducal splendor on his Hoboken estate, where he entertained Flemish nobility and the Emperor Charles. Because he had enemies among his colleagues on the Exchange, who could not appreciate his new technique and often denounced the most interesting innovations, Ducci found it necessary to keep a band of twenty hired bravos to beat up, maim, and even slay the more stubborn conservatives.

Though the first of the great modern speculators, Ducci was misunderstood and ill appreciated, and he felt it deeply. So he employed men to attack Gilbert van Schoenbeke, the brewer and architect, before the very doors of the Exchange. Vainly the courts summoned Ducci to account for this misconduct; he only laughed and would not go. Only after a long time did his foes obtain the dissolution of Ducci's company on the ground that it was a monopoly. Eventually Ducci himself was removed by assassins in the service of a foe.

What Ducci floated upon the Exchange were, like himself, products of a transition age. Among these were obligations of the Brussels Court guaranteed only by the private fortune of a prominent official; when the crash came, it was found that only a fraction of the letters issued was covered by cash. There were also shares on business firms which were not anonymous, but inscribed with the owners' names, given as payment for goods instead of cash, to be handed over as security or sold at a discount. Also appeared the obligations of the governments of Spain, Portugal, the city of Antwerp, and England. The annual turnover of the Exchange was reckoned by a contemporary at 40,-000,000 ducats.

The scramble for such papers was as keen at Antwerp as at Lyons— while the boom lasted. Millions of ducats were inscribed, entrusted to such men as Ducci, but only that part lent to Antwerp and England was secure. All the rest of the investments were lost in 1557, with the bankruptcy of Spain and her Netherlands, followed by that of Portugal in 1560, and finally the wreck of France. To show for 20,000,000 ducats sunk in those countries, nothing was left but parchments from which all magic had evaporated. The parchments were hopefully preserved nevertheless. They still fill trunks, it seems, in the attics of old patrician houses in Europe.

THE INTERNATIONALISM OF FINANCE

Gaspar Ducci, the dashing Italian speculator, was ostensibly the representative of the German Kaiser and the Brussels Government at Antwerp. Under cover, he was in league with the Florentine crowd in Lyons and managed to slip out very large sums to them and the French enemy, which he collected from German financiers in Brussels, the foe of France. In this work he was assisted by two Germans, Alexius Grimel and Hieronymus Seiler.

Such behavior was not rare in the sixteenth century, however. The chief advisers in business matters of the states, save in England alone, included alien merchants. Thus the Florentine Piero Spino was a royal agent of the Valois; the affairs of Charles V were in the hands of an astute and ruthless Spaniard, Francesco Erasso, manipulator of a Spanish game against the German merchants who supported that Hapsburg monarch. Again, an agent of the Spanish interests was a Flemish merchant, Gaspar Schetz, charming as a host, amateur poet, and patron of the arts, and equally versatile in his loyalties; he not only made his fine house at Antwerp the headquarters of the Briton, Sir Thomas Gresham, implacable foe of Spain, but also sold information of Spanish doings to the British.

The remarkable internationalism of the Antwerp munitions market was evidenced especially in the matter of British purchases. Presumably the Netherlands was under Spain, then preparing to challenge and destroy Britain. But Sir Thomas Gresham found it possible to equip England with gunpowder and other necessaries, to hold off the Spanish, with the aid of Antwerp in the Netherlands. In this enterprise he had the assistance of Alexander Bonvisi, a cultured Genoese financier, friend of Sir Thomas More. Bonvisi, though a Genoese, did not mind helping to supply the British with "3,500 Hackequebutts; 1,000 Pistoletts; 500 Pondera de Macches; 100,000 Pondera Petre Salse; 3,000 Corselettes; 2,000 Mourreyens," reported by Burgon in one deal in 1558. It is true that the Genoese bankers were largely behind the schemes of the Spanish, but there was at least this one Genoese, Bonvisi, to take the other side.

Of course, when Gresham bought contraband arms and saltpeter at

Antwerp, with funds raised from all nationalities and with the help of
Flemish and Genoese, under the very noses of the Spanish, he had to
proceed with some secrecy. He had to defy the death penalty and
operate, as he informed Queen Elizabeth, through "men corroptyd
with monneyes." He had to refer in his letters to gunpowder as velvet;
and he had to hide pike-heads and morions in bags of pepper. But it
was all undertaken in the spirit of Elizabethan adventure.

Nothing is, in fact, more revelatory of the internationalism of business in Renaissance Europe than the manner in which the British
equipped themselves with the arms, which they could not possibly
have made themselves, for raising their military might above those who
supplied them. In 1511, Henry VIII paid Luigi and Alessandro de
Fava, Italian brothers, £200 for arquebuses; in the same year, his
agent, Sir Richard Jermingham, was scouring Germany and Italy for
arms and reported a good purchase in German armor for 5,000 foot
soldiers, which he concluded in Milan; a doge of Venice took part in
another deal. Thus armor was made in Nürnberg or Augsburg, sold
perhaps in Venice or Milan, and smuggled out of Antwerp, ostensibly
on the Spanish side, with the aid of agents of Spain, and paid for by
money raised from all regions. When England finally decided to build
her own munition plants, she was gladly assisted in the task by imported French, Brabant, German and Italian entrepreneurs bringing
capital and workers.

Another example of the bewildering conditions in that century was
the behavior of a military member of the great German merchant house
of Fugger. When Philip II of Spain, the chief debtor of the Fugger,
took Antwerp, this officer, Anton Fugger, was in the Spanish army;
he looted and sacked his own cousin's warehouse.

These German merchants of Nürnberg who helped the French, these
Italian bankers who brought Spanish and French troops upon Italy,
these Spanish subjects who assisted Britain to defeat Spain, were not to
be regarded as "betrayers" of a country. With the exception of England, there were no countries to betray at the time—or at least able to
claim the loyalties of business men. Merchants had hitherto known
only the narrow confines of petty city-patriotism and even in that case
a partial allegiance only. They had not fallen under the broader limitations of national patriotism. Jacob Fugger, it is true, was stubbornly
loyal to a dynasty, that of the Hapsburgs, but he was unaware of a
duty to consider a Germany in the large; he merely thought of his city
and his king. Gresham, the Englishman, is the one great figure of the
age who appears nationalistic; in his case, since England was London,
and London was England, and all his business interests, as royal purveyor of munitions, for example, lay in line with those of the Crown, it

was exceptionally easy for him to proceed steadily toward a well-defined goal.

The sixteenth century was, on the whole, an age of cosmopolitan relationships in culture and finance which might well occasion envy among modern internationalists. Though we pride ourselves nowadays upon our rapid transportation and communication, these technical advantages are to a large extent nullified by our racial and national prejudices. It is of course true that our bankers and munitioneers tend to disregard frontiers; during the Great War, for example, the Allied forces received barbed wire supplied from Germany and returned nickel in exchange, through Switzerland. Yet this impartiality is anything but modern, as many critics suppose.

Neither is it due to the "internationalism of Jewish finance," as various writers, including Sombart, have maintained. Sombart strives to make a case by producing examples of Jewish army provisioners in the 1600's who equipped forces of many lands with grain and provisions. As a matter of fact, as other scholars have shown, internationalism goes far behind the modern age and "Jewish influence." It is national loyalty which is really the new phenomenon.

In classic times, for example, Roman merchants traded with the Punic foe. In the Middle Ages, Lübeck and other cities sold cannon to their feudal enemies; Jacques Cœur and the Venetians equipped the Infidel against the Christian Crusader. The Florentine Bardi financed the English and French against each other, thereby prolonging what might have been a brief spat into a Hundred Years' War. The city of Suhl in the seventeenth century sent its cannon to Spain, France, Switzerland, Venice, Cracow, Vilna, Prussia and other parts and ports.

Perhaps the most notoriously "objective" people were the Dutch of the seventeenth century. Oliver Cromwell who, despite a strain of Netherlands ancestry, considered himself pure British, thundered forth in Parliament against the Dutch: "They have professed a principle which, thanks be to God, we never knew. They will sell arms to their enemies, and lend their ships to their enemies. They will do so."

There was good ground for this accusation. Dutch merchants sold grain for the troops of Louis XIV of France, when that monarch found himself seriously embarrassed for want of provisions; he might not have been able to invade Holland without Dutch help. Then there was the case of the Amsterdam merchant Beylant accused, in 1638, of hurting the Dutch cause by selling powder to the enemy; he did not deny the fact, but argued that, as a free trader, he was opposed to interference with the normal course of business by merely military considerations. And, anyway, said Beylant, if there was a profit to be had, he would sail right through Hell to get it, even if it scorched his sails.

Impartiality is, therefore, not a specific achievement of modern times. Business men of the Gentile persuasion, in all ages, have disregarded localism. As the holy Ambrosius once said, long ago, with a sigh: *"Ubi jus belli, ibi jus usurae."* But it was in the city of Antwerp, in the middle of the Cinquecento, that the most serene objectivity was attained by cannon-makers and money-lenders. In that free and alien port, men felt as far removed from the ties of home, as the Jews in the *Diaspora*.

THE REDISCOVERY OF TIME

For such adventures, minutes were reckoned as precious. The merchant needed more elaborate and ingenious clocks to capture minutes —and even seconds—which had become so valuable, since every one of them ticked off interest on his loans.

Ancient Alexandria had invented the water-clock and striven to make the most of time, but this knowledge was suffered to pass away during the Middle Ages. The mediaeval Europeans, though they cut up their lands into the most confusingly minute parcels, had an almost unbroken concept of Time. While they began to sweep aside local barriers, they now began to carve the hours into their last trivial seconds. They unified territories, but divided Time.

More and more time-tolling belfries of Europe were raised, as the business men grew busier. Florence in the Quattrocento had paid great attention to regular bell-ringing for her factories; and in Flanders, big industrial centers like Ypres and Ghent summoned their workers by punctual clangor and placed on their high towers three symbols, of religion, defense and industry: a madonna, a bronze dragon and a bell. Now such simple methods would no longer suffice.

Though the pocket-watch was invented at Nürnberg, Antwerp led in the manufacture and sale of these new timepieces. Industry in that city was carefully regulated by a *Werkclock* and an *Avondclock*, by which all workers were supposed to act. Vagabondage, the waste of time, was punished with appalling severity. And as a symbol of the new age, the huge golden circle of a timepiece was set high on the stone fretwork of Our Lady's Cathedral, covering up several old Gothic windows.

Naturally, however, the more accurately he counted time, the less the business man had of it. Old Jacob Fugger the Rich, besought to take a rest on his deathbed, muttered, "I must get my gains while I can," and went on scheming and fighting to his last hours. He could not take off a few days, like Cosimo de' Medici, to prepare his soul by reading the classics for the long dark journey. Anton Rem, unlike

Lorenzo il Magnifico, could not find a place for women in his schedule. Lazarus Tucher was so occupied entertaining business acquaintances that he did not dine at home ten times a year. Balthasar Paumgartner was so busy that he forgot to get his little son a birthday present.

In a world growing daily richer, with gold flooding in from Peru and silks from China, only the supply of Time was dwindling. Backward peoples, aborigines, peasants and princes might continue to have a sufficient amount on hand for holiday-making; but the progressive bourgeois quickened his steps and grew more and more earnest and long-faced; his eye was hypnotized by the hands of his clock, apparently speeding faster as the timepieces grew smaller. He lent a willing ear to scientists who told him that the sun, moon and stars led just as punctual a life as he, and that the universe was merely a vast mechanism which had once been wound up and would go on, as he would, until it ran down.

Thus Antwerp sold clocks and shares to the profit-seekers of Europe, and impressed the business men of the Cinquecento with the value of every minute. Too many simple profit-makers, however, during the great Antwerp Boom of 1551–57, in their eagerness to turn time into money, chose the wrong time.

IX

THE MIGHT OF MILLIONAIRES IN THE AGE OF THE FUGGERS

THE MODERN ERA is generally supposed to have opened about 1500; around that time, the feudal and Catholic order of western Europe was shaken by a remarkable variety of happenings: the discovery of America and the sea-route to the wealth of India, the invention of gunpowder and printing, and the separation of the Protestant Northern countries from the Catholic South. The first half of that "modern" century was a period of unprecedented triumph for the business man; the second brought him for a time to the depths of affliction and humiliation.

Up to the 1550's, when the big bubbles were blown on the stockmarkets of Lyons and Antwerp, the European merchants and moneylenders rode high. Amazing opportunities gave them riches which enabled them to manipulate kings and commandeer artists. But after the break in the money-markets followed a period of terrible misfortunes; nearly all the principal houses of the Continent were shaken and collapsed one after the other; pillaging armies began to eat up the last remnants of prosperity and to destroy the independence of the business oligarchs; Lyons and Antwerp were sacked as well as bankrupted. From this fearful ordeal, only the Dutch merchants, secure among their bogs and dunes, and the English, equally remote in their island, emerged with profit and power.

The story of the first hundred years of modern life is, accordingly, one of the *hybris* of the Christian business man of Europe. He had boundless ambition for wealth; he exhibited his magnificence in unabashed pomp. But he had a fatal inability to transmute his gold into power for his own purposes; his head was turned by contact with princes; and he let the precious moments of his chance for omnipotence slip by. When the resources of the Italians, French and Germans were exhausted, the Dutch and English, as business men comparatively poor and insignificant in the sixteenth century, rose in turn to wealth and importance.

THE OPPORTUNITIES

In the modern era, cities grew huge again, as they had been in antiquity. Including Paris, London and Antwerp there were now perhaps a baker's dozen in the 100,000 class. But their leadership was not to be measured by numbers or size alone. Unlike the mediaeval towns, which could be fed from the environs, these enlarging centers had to be supplied by wholesale importers with provisions from afar. Even in the fifteenth century, Florence and Flanders had had to feed their industrial populations by large-scale imports; but now there were more cities and they were reaching out wider for foodstuffs. Thus Europe returned to the classic economy marked by all-devouring cities such as Carthage, Rome and Alexandria that called forth a great organization of business including transportation, backed by considerable capital.

The consuming groups in the new cities of the sixteenth century were increasingly luxurious. Venice was the seat of patrician rentiers. Rome was a magnet drawing absentee landlords, churchmen and pilgrims by the hundred thousands. Paris and London had court circles. Antwerp attracted business men of all nations. Whether bourgeois, courtiers, or prelates formed the leading consumer group, all developed expensive tastes and habits. Their furniture, jewels and plate might still be made by skilled handicraftsmen but many of their demands, especially for silks, could only be met by a more capitalistic technique. So the silk-machines of Italy and Italian workers were brought over to Lyons and Paris. And the acquisitive spirit spread from the big cities to the small towns and even to the countryside; in Germany and Flanders the peddlers of Nürnberg and Scotland tempted the richer peasantry with the commodities they carried to their doors. The swaggering *soldateska* of the innumerable wars with their picturesque female camp followers also served as the mirror of fashions, especially in the latter half of the century. And what a boon they were to cloth manufacturers may be inferred from the fact that a pair of modishly slashed breeches for men might require one hundred yards of material. Sumptuary laws were weakening and even poor women were ready to forgo bread to buy plumes—a state of mind highly satisfactory to business interests.

New colonies as well as great cities opened markets for the entrepreneur. Cargoes of wine and other luxuries were shipped to the Spanish settlers in the New World. The traffic in African slaves for the colonies paid ten per cent to the firm of Welser, but this was a small profit owing to the perishable nature of the goods. To ensnare the hapless Africans, tremendous numbers of knives and other metal wares for barter were made in German craft centers. And from the colonial plantations came back sugar and spices in such quantities that they could not be handled by mediaeval methods. Only a grand consortium could buy up the year's crop, dispose of the commodities and withstand the sharp fluctuations in prices.

As they grew in size and perfected their mechanical equipment, the armies and navies of the various countries provided a still more important stimulus for capitalism. Navies were getting bigger and more costly every year; it might take £9,000 to build an Elizabethan warship and hordes of private contractors were enriched by warship construction and furnishing. The Invincible Armada of Spain, designed to overwhelm the British fleet, was a large-scale commercial as well as political enterprise. Genoese bankers provided handsome sums necessary to equip its ships and men with the quantities of things they needed, as for instance: 2,431 cannon and 123,790 shot; 7,000 arquebuses; 10,000 pikes and 1,000 muskets. The provisioning, clothing, and even the raising of troops had profitable aspects, for the traffic in white men paid as well as in black men. Hamburg was one of the cities where men were "enlisted," that is sold, and Conrad Pfenning, an agent who dealt in soldiers for England, admitted that the men were "treated more like heads of cattle than like Christians."

Munition-makers had their hands full outfitting the swelling ranks of combatants. Bigger and better factories were built, of a more and more modern type for a swifter and swifter tempo. Like silk-spinning, armor-making had been a complex business in Trecento Florence; the division of processes had been intricate and the maker of greaves, for example, had nothing to do with the maker of neckpieces. Yet the manufacture of muskets called for more technique and standardization than that of armor; the casting of cannon, a more elaborate affair, was far beyond the resources of the old-fashioned petty craftsman. If Ghent's *Mad Margaret* had excited the awe of mediaeval Flanders and Ulm's *Little Katey*, 700 pounds in weight, established a Quattrocento record, both were pygmies in comparison with the seven monstrous cannon cast by Corneille Wagevens in 1543 at Antwerp. One of these was a 5,000 pound *Saturn* fifteen feet long; another was a 3,000 pound *Jupiter*.

NÜRNBERG, CENTER OF MUSIC AND MUNITIONS

A chief complaint of our age, standardization, may be traced back to that city now patronizingly called "Quaint Old Nürnberg" by tourists. There, about 1540, one Hartmann invented a method of calibrating fire-arms, after which there was no halting the forward-striding mechanical development. Before the century was out, the mass-production of standardized articles had gone so far that a manufacturer of Augsburg was able to offer an enemy of Augsburg, the Duke of Bavaria, 900 muskets "all planned to take one type of ball."

In the Germanisches Museum in Nürnberg, samples of the early steel armament manufactures may be seen: impressive displays of the pikes and spears, provided by the merchants of Nürnberg in lots of three and 5,000, beside steel hats and gauntlets of assorted sizes. The ateliers of that city developed a specialty of sets of armor molded to fit the limbs of individual warriors, custom-made from toe to visor; these suits could be turned out in quantities on a rush order. Within three months, the city once exported 400 such suits.

Even the armor of the period bore the stamp of mechanical progress. These products of the early steel garment trade, produced with prodigious skill and distributed throughout Europe *en gros*, are in fact perfect illustrations of that purposefulness which Gropius, Corbusier, Frank Lloyd Wright and the Russians have just been demanding of modern Machine Age art. Each helmet shape is as flawless as that of the most modern prow or fender. The breastplates are free from meretricious ornament and meaningless flares; they rely for beauty solely on bolts and hinges, neatly overlapping plates and marvelously modeled joints, on rhythmic line and high-lights.

There is of course a bit of fantasy on the shields accompanying the suits, just as there is on radiator-caps today, but that was also purely for advertising purposes and was executed in a broad, effective poster-style. The Nürnberg suits of armor, pleasing by the "inevitability of design," were superb results of business acumen, like the motor-cars or plumbing-fixtures on which we pride ourselves in the twentieth century. Indeed, in modern times, perhaps only the flying-machine may compare with that old armor, for it too has the fascination of a beautiful contraption in which to defy and meet death.

Nürnberg merchants, being the chief exporters of sculpture in wood, stone and bronze, also took care of that last emergency of the consumer. One atelier had a practical monopoly on the supply of cast-bronze mortuary monuments in Germany and Southern and Eastern Europe, as far as Innsbruck and Moscow. Thus, with the expert eyes the Nürnberg business men gauged the market of their times and provided the European with what he chiefly clamored for: armor and a tomb.

Even in Germany, the greatest "land of machines" in Europe at that period, Nürnberg held the first place for mechanical ingenuity. Since it made the best musical instruments, the music-trade was centered there like the book-trade at Frankfurt. In this city the pocket-watch was invented, the first globe was made for a geographer, and compasses were turned out in quantity for conquistadores. The Machine Age was presaged by the inventions of Hans Lobsinger, a contemporary of Hans Sachs, who invented a water-power mill to grind powder—so simple that a little boy could operate it. His saw-mill could cut 100 boards a day; another of his devices could saw marble; and three of his diamond-cutters were run by one horse. He was full of good ideas for improving the printing-press and cannon, as were the Danner Brothers, also of Nürnberg, who specialized on screw-devices capable of raising the heaviest guns, breaking down fortifications, or speeding up the multiplication of picture-books.

By a curious stroke of fate, a Nürnberg business company made the invention which set England far along on the path toward her Industrial Revolution. It happened in this way. The firm of Haug, Langnauer and Company was invited to manage English mining. Faced with the depletion of the English forests, its engineers solved the fuel-problem by devising a method of using sea-coal, instead of wood, in the preparation of iron. Thus the ingenuity of the Germans, assisting British cannon-making, enabled Britain to develop her great resources of mineral wealth, and pace Germany in commercial development for the clash of nations later.

THE MINING BOOM

The mining of metals to make armor and cannon produced capitalistic phenomena in Germany during the Cinquecento. War created the major demand for copper, tin and iron. Armies and navies were the chief consumers of iron and Sombart has shown how closely the production of that commodity corresponded with the amounts used in cannon and balls. The need for metals was enormously increased as time went on and very large transactions took place; in 1496, for instance, the Venetians bought 80,000 pounds of copper for cannon from a German firm—for those times a huge figure.

Within the mining regions, through this spurring on of demand, striking transformations, a revolution both social and economic, took place. The uprush of "boom towns" in the Tyrol has often been compared to that in nineteenth-century California. Villages grew magically to cities. The earliest mining movement was in the hands of priests and princes, or small private operators like Martin Luther's father, all without great capital. But this "Forty-Niner" stage did not last long. Shafts had to be sunk more deeply, water-power machinery was installed and better refineries were built, while the transportation to distant regions was arranged. Thus the mines fell into the hands of rich monopolistic merchants.

In mediaeval times mining was controlled by the gilds which often owned shafts and paid tribute in metals to a feudal lord who owned the subsoil rights. In this case the miner was part artisan, part vassal. The gilds had their own flags and treasuries, strict rules about hours of labor, oaths of allegiance, the treatment of workers and apprenticeship. This type of mixed-gild labor-union or knappschaft, kept on for some time but was not immortal. Its days were clearly numbered when mines passed into the possession of wealthy absentee owners. Many of these new owners never knew the mining fields personally; they simply met their agents occasionally, at such events as the great annual congress of mining entrepreneurs at the Leipzig Fair, where questions of management were talked over and books were balanced.

Naturally the merchant-owners who acquired control of the mines complained of the short working day—eight hours only—and the slow work of the gildsmen; while the gildsmen on their side claimed that they were cheated when they had to exchange their ores for foodstuffs. Serious strikes of miners occurred and conferences on the matter were arranged by princes with referees on hand. In 1496, for example, to settle a dispute, it was agreed to execute ten leaders of the miners and three of the company officials. In Tyrol, toward 1500, the striking miners joined the radical peasant movement. Nevertheless rebellion and violence were of little avail against the inexorable movement of capitalism. By 1500 the change from the gild ownership system to a wage system was general; in some places, by 1518, the miners' unions were no longer allowed to assemble without permission of the employers' officials. That the great Fugger family denied their men the right to choose even their own beliefs is evident in a letter from their Augsburg headquarters, dated 1569, and addressed to the agents at their mines:

> In Schwaz [in Tyrol] it appears the miners intend to rebel for religious reasons. . . . That will incite the other poor wretches. But that is easy to prevent, by discharging the officials, or making it plain to them that they must follow the custom of the country and shut their jaws. The others must pray or work, whether they will or no, and therefore will be easy to keep well-bridled.

SPECULATION

As the control of the mines passed into the power of absentees, speculation superseded caution. A "wild-cat" period ensued and so numerous were the swindlers, with worthless mining stocks to sell in southern Germany, that a number of cities in the 1500's passed legislation on the point.

Besides these heralds of the modern era, mighty monopolists appeared among the Germans, and planned gigantic schemes to corner

the world supply of metals or spices, as coolly as Spanish conquistadores were taking possession of oceans and continents. The Höchstetter
attempted to corner quicksilver, a scheme which only succeeded, at a
much later period, in the hands of the Rothschilds. Conrad Rott made
another failure, in pepper; Anton Fugger lost half a million gulden in
1550 in an effort to monopolize the Bohemian and Saxon tin supply for
Middle and East Europe. One of the rare triumphs was the copper-
corner achieved by Jacob Fugger, Gossembrot, Paumgartner and
Herwart.

Economic speculation became rife when the horizons of men were
widening. The bourgeois helped to outfit the explorers and exploit
their discoveries. Caught by their contagious enthusiasm, the bourgeois
even dreamed of an Eldorado to be found at home, through investing
in shares on the Lyons and Antwerp Exchanges. He supposed that
fabulous gains might be picked up without working for them, and
without even the discomforts of an ocean voyage; and so he took the
"royal letters" in return for his money, in the same spirit of jubilant
adventure as conquistadores received their charters to kingdoms as yet
undiscovered and unexplored.

The great public of merchants, nobles, artisans, servants, widows and
orphans, who invested in royal loans, were not troubled if all their
money went to finance warfare; they were as ready as Balboa or
Pizarro to wade through blood for profit. And the wealth poured into
the state coffers by these open subscriptions actually did go into warfare. Armies and navies were becoming steadily more gigantic and
costly. Yet campaigning was an expense out of all proportion, as a
rule, to the object to be attained. Spain, for instance, spent three million
gold crowns a year to subjugate the Netherlands, for a time, despite
the fact that this exceeded what that captured land could produce in
revenues. Wars on the whole no longer paid. Nevertheless the money
of the business world went out to support warfare on a vast scale.
Three years out of every four in that century were filled with major
military operations.

From the standpoint of economy this meant that gambling in war
ate up a tremendous part of the wealth which Europe had stored up
in her business cities. When Spain, France, Portugal and the Netherlands went bankrupt in 1557–60, the losses of business men on loans
to the monarchs of these states was about 200 million marks, in modern
value. But this sum was, in the estimates of Ehrenberg, only a small
part of the total treasure which all the states gathered from many
sources and expended upon warfare. There was another aspect to the
case: the entire production of precious metals, in the New World as in
the Old, was worth but 115 million marks between 1521 and 1560. The

discrepancy between the two figures of losses and metal-production indicated, Ehrenberg supposes, that not only did all the fruits of exploration and mining go into war, but, in addition, a large part of the accumulated profits from trading in silks, spices and other wares. The greatest part of European business profits were therefore "flung into a fiery furnace," in the vain hope of augmenting them yet more.

If we also consider that the precious metals from the New World were not clear profit to the bankers who outfitted the explorers and the Silver Fleet, and if we reckon up the costs of exploration and conquest largely borne by business men and subtract them from the gain of the New World, it is easy to see that the discovery of America was an expensive mistake for mere business enterprise. It would have been better in the long run for the practical business men of old Europe if they had let Eldorado alone.

The pearls and spices, the gold and silver of the East and the West were not used to enrich the Continent, but to impoverish it. In fact, the business man financed all sides in innumerable quarrels running along more or less simultaneously: the Catholics against the Lutherans and Calvinists; Valois against Hapsburg; English against Spanish; Spanish against Flemish; Hanseatics against the English; Portugal against the Arabs. He enabled the French to ally themselves with the Turks and assisted the Germans to attack the Turks. In all these conflicts, it is true, religious and racial passions ran high and political animosities were conspicuous; but the economic rivalries were equally intense, if less noted in written history. Like the shadow-counterpart of the grim physical combats, there went on in the background a desperate though bloodless tussle between the merchants and lenders of all nations, fighting with loans and monopolies and inflicting gaping wounds upon each other's purses.

THE RICHES OF THE FUGGER

The weightiest economic factor in the European situation was the House of Fugger. The capital of the Fugger firm surpassed that of the Medici; under Anton it was five times that of the Florentine house and the total wealth of the family was probably very much more. Including its estates, the family fortune has been estimated at six million gulden in 1546. The sources of this wealth were multifarious; indeed a description of them reads like a résumé of economic history.

Jacob Fugger, for instance, had the right to coin money like a king. He held a quasi-monopoly on the metals which provided most of Europe with currency. Thus he controlled the silver of Tyrol and Carinthia; he lent the capital and organized the mines and refineries;

he managed the transportation of the products over bad roads and through wild, bandit-infested territories, to the chief mints, acquiring from this affair alone a profit of 200,000 gulden a year. And to this he added a close grip on the entire Hungarian production of silver and copper, which he managed in conjunction with Italian capitalists and the engineering-pioneer, Johann Thurzo. Together he and Thurzo erected new, water-driven machinery perfected by the latter; they sold the metals to Venice, Nürnberg, Danzig, Antwerp, Poland, Prussia and Russia, and between 1495 and 1510 each of the two partners received 500,583 gold gulden, a value in modern terms equal to twenty million marks.

Then Fugger anticipated the Rothschilds in acquiring control of the quicksilver mines of Spain, ancient and profitable works which had been a source of wealth to Romans. Whoever managed these mines, and had a mortgage on the incomes of the three knightly orders, had a grip on the chief sources of income of the Spanish State. Up to 1634, these were almost always in the possession of the Fugger.

Mining was only a part of the Fugger enterprise. The family kept up a regular traffic in wares of many sorts. They were among the leading spice-importers from Portugal to the rest of Europe, and it was a poor year when they did not make 20 per cent. They brought cotton from Venice to their cloth-factories in southern Germany, organized on so large and extensive a plan as to ruin many competitors; they also controlled the distribution of the products, sending 9,000 pieces a year to Spain alone. In addition, as side-lines, the Fuggers handled silks, jewels and other luxury articles for the courts of Europe. For years they made a profit of 54½ per cent on their capital.

Metal-monopoly and the production and sale of commodities formed merely the first layer of the wonderful pyramid of the Fugger concern. Upon this foundation they erected their banking-system. Their facilities were used by merchants, traveling students, and even by miners, to send savings to families in distant regions. An example of what the Fugger Bank could do in the way of advancing and transmitting funds is given by Opitz: Maximilian I, about to declare war on Venice, was promised the great sum of 170,000 ducats from his allies, the Pope, Spain and France; nobody could manage the shipping of such amounts from far corners to Augsburg except Fugger, who had it paid out to the Emperor, within six weeks, down to the last coin. Perhaps, to get a true perspective on this deal, it would be well to recall that the yearly income of a rich count was in that day but 4,000 gulden (a gulden is slightly more than a ducat). It would have taken all the annual resources of a large proportion of the German nobility to accomplish that which Fugger individually achieved so easily.

Hence it was natural for the contemporaries of Fugger, for a Martin Luther, to regard the Fugger Bank with awe. This famous story is told by Luther, fulminating against Fugger's connections with the Church:

Once a Bishop of Brixen died in Rome, and when he was dead, no money was found by him, except a little piece of paper a finger in length, that was stuck in his sleeve. When Pope Julius sent that soon to the Fugger factor and asked him if he knew the writing, the latter said: 'Yes, it is the debt which Fugger and Company owe to the Cardinal and totals three times a hundred thousand gulden.' The Pope asked: 'When could you send the money?' The servant of the Fugger replied: 'At any hour.' Then the Pope turned to the Cardinals of France and England and asked: 'Could your Kings also deliver three tons of gold in an hour?' They said: 'No.' Then he said: 'But that is what a citizen of Augsburg can do.'

As a matter of fact, it was only 200,000 gold gulden which the Company owed the Bishop of Brixen, but they did pay it very promptly. Fugger enabled the Pope to inaugurate and support the Swiss Guards. He not only dealt with the Popes and cardinals; he also had a hand in the election of both. Originally, Jacob Fugger had intended to be a prelate himself, and other members of his family, especially Marcus Fugger, were high in the Church, loaded with offices and stipends. Bernhard von Adelmann, a high official in the Cathedral of Augsburg, once said that Fugger declared he would make his candidate Bishop in Augsburg, "since he had Pope and Emperor in his purse." The enemy of Fugger, the knight and Humanist scholar, Hutten, called him "rex denariorum," the money-king, and said: "Now nobody has a good stipend in Germany, unless he has served in Rome, or won it by donations, or bought it for gold through the Fuggers."

As Jacob Fugger successfully barred Italian financiers from the profits gained by managing the papal financial system in northern and eastern Europe, so he permitted no rival to compete with him in lending to the Hapsburgs; he squeezed out those Genoese who attempted to edge in. His loyalty to the Hapsburgs, Schulte thinks, was partly, at any rate, due to the fact that he owed to them his monopolistic position in Austrian mining; through them, moreover, his firm managed to get the upper hand over Spanish national incomes and mines in pawn for his loans. Through Emperors and Popes, the Fugger ruled the money-markets of Germany, Hungary, Poland, Sweden and Italy, and could at least dispute for mastery in the Swiss, French and Spanish markets.

At the height of the Fugger power, an enormous organization was under the control of the Augsburg center and the dictatorship of the leading Fuggers, Jacob and Anton. In other lands seventeen branches were in operation, managed by agents sufficiently talented to keep foreign courts well bribed and thoroughly intimidated. With these was united a capable bureaucracy, such as kings sighed for in vain, to superintend shipping, mining, factory production, banking, road transportation and a news service without a parallel. The fortune of the family included, besides cash and firm-assets, great agricultural estates, castles, a treasure of precious plate, collections of rare objects of art and jewels.

BUSINESS DICTATORSHIPS

The heads of the Fugger firm exercised a dictatorship over their business which, Strieder says, is not to be encountered a second time in economic history. Jacob Fugger the Rich, the wealthiest man of the century, *il Duce* of commerce, directed alone his multifarious projects. Only members of the Fugger family were admitted to the firm, and even these could not withdraw their shares at will or interfere with the chosen leader. The capital of the firm might not be divided: not a dish, a picture, a rug, of the common household treasure, could be disposed of at will. Jacob Fugger not only made kings, but was one; in his last testament, he left everything, like a monarch, to the single selected inheritor of his vast estate.

The business man, among the South Germans and Italians, in this age generally enjoyed an autocratic power such as he had never had before and may very likely never experience again. As yet he was not hampered either by the stockholders' assembly meeting under him, or by an absolute monarchy above him. The Church's effort to restrict usury could be ignored more completely than in mediaeval times. Moreover, the feudal nobility, common foe of traders, was suffering in the transformation of the armies due to the introduction of cannon and muskets and hence was less of an obstacle. Renaissance culture placed its emphasis upon individualism, *virtù* and Fortuna. Its very art consecrated the individual and tended to give the great sixteenth-century magnate a self-confidence so overweening that it was not matched again until the nineteenth-century exploiters, supported by the sacred doctrine of laissez faire, came upon the historic stage. The two periods have much in common.

In the sixteenth as in the nineteenth there were continents to be explored and seized, and nations to be formed. The great masters of merchandizing and finance stood forth as powerful autocrats: Jacob Fugger, Hans Kleberg, Thomas Gresham, Bartholmä Welser, Endres Imhof, Lazarus Tucher, Gaspar Ducci, Ansaldo Grimaldi, to name but a few—these were forerunners of Harriman, Carnegie, Siemens, Hansemann. The men of the Middle Ages had been in the shadow of the Church and the Aristocracy; the men of the seventeenth to nineteenth centuries were dwarfed by absolute princes, the impersonal chartered companies, and Calvin's God. But in the nineteenth they emerged again from the darkness into the light.

The earlier business men were closely linked with the condottieri and conquistadores, their contemporaries in the fighting world. In a sense, the condottieri were themselves entrepreneurs who raised capital, hired armies and conducted warfare as a profit-seeking venture. Business men employed the condottieri, or provided the funds to keep them going. And the conquistadores, who annexed the territories of Asia and America, were also frequently outfitted by bankers' loans; the fruits of their discoveries might go to the coffers of the Grimaldi and Fugger and Welser. In short, business, in the sixteenth century, was all-pervasive; the strong State had not yet stepped between business men and warriors, setting limits for them both, and assuming the weighty rôle of umpire.

The high-handedness of the Cinquecento business man was an inheritance from the Middle Ages. Though the mediaeval form of family-association had been broadened to the point of receiving deposits from outside, the depositors had no special guarantees, and were denied a voice in the conduct of affairs. Such investors had no redress and could exert no pressure. An abstraction like the State or the Stock-Company had not yet come between the managerial despots and the investors. The investors, if they experienced a bankruptcy, could only bewail their losses and cry, as did an anguished loser of Augsburg in 1512, quoted by Schmoller: "The managers of the Companies who make out the balance-sheets get richer than those who are not in the secrets; it is to be believed that there exist no greater thieves than the directors in several Companies."

Such complaints were of long standing in Italy. As far back as 1295 the Frescobaldi in Florence, so Davidsohn informs us, told Edward I of England, when they lent him 2½ million gold lire (modern value), that they would never dream of letting their depositors know what risks their money ran. Now in the sixteenth century, the system spread to Germany and other lands as well. The English formed only an apparent exception; without the long-accumulated wealth and experience of the Germans and Italians, they had to cling together in companies. So did the Japanese in modern times when they made their debut into commercial life. However, the English companies were not corporations issuing stock to the general public; they were rather cartels of individual operators; thus the Company of Merchant Adventurers, to which Gresham belonged, was really a union of cloth-exporters, each acting independently but all agreeing to follow certain rules and accept the supervision of a board of governors.

Individual initiative, accordingly, had full sway; it had burst the mediaeval bondage of community, and not been caught in the restraints of the share-issuing corporation. And what tyrants there were in the world of business in the sixteenth century may be illustrated by the description which a chronicler of Augsburg gave of the firm of Höchstetter, the remorseless German monopolists:

> To Ambrosius Höchstetter the princes, counts, nobles, citizens, peasants, men-servants and maid-servants brought what funds they had, and he paid them five per cent. Many field-hands who did not have more than five gulden, gave them to his Company, thinking the money in good care. For a while, he is said to have paid out interest on a million gulden. . . . He has been a good Christian and entirely against the Lutherans. But with his practices he has often oppressed the poor men, not only in articles of world commerce, but in petty wares, [like wine, grain, timber, which he sold] entirely at his pleasure.

This firm was brought low at last by the failure of its attempt at a world-wide quicksilver monopoly. New sources of supply were inopportunely found.

THE POLITICAL POWER OF BUSINESS MEN

Before the might and magnificence of such absolute business men, mere royalty made a very poor showing in the sixteenth century. Kings had not yet dared to pretend to anything like the power of a Höchstetter or a Grimaldi. They had to accept the dictated terms of financiers, as meekly as the investors.

No king of Europe had such a news-gathering system as Fugger and Gresham perfected. No king dared to lay taxation without restraint or representation upon his restive towns and nobles; if he had tried it, he could not have collected the taxes without a competent bureaucracy and, in those times, the only good bureaucrats were those watched by the shrewd eye of Fugger. Since state incomes were so slender and varied from year to year, there could be no state planning; royal treasurers could only make vaguely hopeful guesses at the probable condition of exchequers. There was no more budgetary order in Europe then than there is in China today.

Kings were thus often under the most embarrassing and pitiful obligations to merchants. For example the Emperor Ferdinand III was unable to leave Augsburg after a Reichstag, because the unpaid artisans laid chains around his stable and even seized the bridle of his horse. The merchants of that city were not willing to lend him any ready cash; he was lucky to be relieved by the Cologne merchants, who paid the fellows off and enabled the annoyed monarch to gallop away to an urgent war.

The Höchstetter won the heart of Emperor Maximilian by lending him some pocket-money once, while he languished in jail, held captive by the irate citizens of Bruges. The elder Schetz, the extremely able speculator of Antwerp, charmed Emperor Charles V by paying the wages of sailors to transport that monarch from England across the Channel to a scene of war. Without the kindliness of Schetz, Charles might have waved himself to exhaustion from the cliffs of Albion before he found a single seaman innocent enough to trust the head of the Holy Roman Empire.

So striking was the superiority of bankers to princes, and so obvious even to the common people, that a pretty folk-myth was circulated about a rich banker who generously destroyed an I.O.U. of a king. However, the same story is told about many of the great bankers and is declared false in every case by historians. Anton Fugger, for instance, is supposed to have cast such a document of Charles V into a fire of cinnamon-logs in his home; Gaspar Schetz is said to have touched a similar document of the same monarch to a candle at Antwerp. Of at least two English bankers such a tale is told. The fable is arresting in that it demonstrates how unbusinesslike the common people still were and also how hard it was to invent anything romantic about bankers, since the same story had to cover them all.

In cold actuality, bankers were apt to be rather severe and reproachful to royal debtors. Ansaldo Grimaldi, the Genoese, was famed for his boldness to kings. Hans Kleberg wrote to the King of France that, if payment were not forthcoming, he, Hans, would appeal to some personages more influential than the king and stir up great trouble for France. And the supreme examples of merchant hauteur are provided by Jacob Fugger the Rich, in Germany, and Thomas Gresham, in England.

FUGGER AND THE HAPSBURGS

Jacob Fugger the Rich had not only an imposing fortune, but a shrewd mind and a dignified presence as well. He struck more awe into his contemporaries than his butterfly monarch, the gallant Maximilian I. The splendor with which Fugger surrounded himself quite eclipsed the show made by Max, but Fugger often obliged his king by lending him some of his household treasures in emergencies. Thus, at the Vienna Congress, when the marriages of Maximilian's grand-children to those of the Hungarian King Ladislaw were being arranged, Fugger was by all odds the most stately figure present. He was putting up the necessary dowries. He lent the gold and silver dishes and all the tableware from his own private house at Augsburg to help Max give grand banquets. He also lent, but did not give, Max and his entire Court sufficient jewels with which to shine before their guests. And then he distributed the gifts. With a magnificently arrayed escort, Fugger arrived at the Congress; calm, suave, gracious of mien if chary of words, Fugger handed out trinkets to such princes and dukes as seemed to him likely to be useful in the future—here a golden ring with a costly gem, there a necklace set with pearls, or a fine damask gown. In all, declares Strieder, Fugger spent 10,000 Rhenish gulden on such trifles alone.

A contemporary chronicler describes Max as being, in most ways, the pathetic opposite of Fugger: "He was pious, and not very intelligent, and was always poor . . . He continually wanted to conduct wars and yet had no money. At times, when he intended to ride to battle, his servants were so poor that they (together with the Kaiser) could not pay their way out of the inns." So suspicious of their king, in fact, were the merchants of Augsburg that they, as councillors of that city, refused to allow Maximilian to buy a house in town; much as they enjoyed his visits, they felt there would be a disadvantage in having so needy a monarch for a permanent resident in a place governed by millionaires.

On more than one occasion, the visionary Max was put in his place by Fugger. Once, for example, he seriously thought of making himself Pope of Rome, and thus solve the age-long conflicts of Crown and Tiara by setting both on his own head. But he had to approach a money-lender first, and Jacob Fugger quite coldly and firmly put his foot down on the proposition.

Curiously, and ominously, the rich business men of Augsburg, whom one might expect to find despising such a man as Max, were ready on the contrary to fawn at his feet. Though he was poor and incompetent, he had for them a romantic air, charm and gallantry. To the snobbish middle-class of Germany, his personality made an appeal which it could not have made to the cold, stiff aristocracy of Spain. The merchants loved to see Max parade in armor, though it was by that time becoming rather old-fashioned; they gladly paid the steel-tailors of this "last of the knights." In return, Max was happier in that city than anywhere else. He joined the burghers in their festivals; he attended the funerals of prominent citizens and spoke a few well-chosen words; he cheerfully forgave quips at his expense and played the master of ceremonies at municipal balls. He bade the debutantes dance before him and, through the good offices of a cardinal, on one occasion he persuaded their mothers to appear with unveiled heads in his presence. Such pastimes caused the King of France to sneer at him as "Burgomaster of Augsburg"—since France was not to have a bourgeois royalty until Louis-Philippe, the Umbrella King, came to the throne in the nineteenth century. Max, the dancing mayor of Augsburg, was frantically admired by the bourgeois women, and perhaps this feeling on their part helped him to dip into their husbands' pockets.

The Augsburg merchants, Fugger among them, had economic and social ambitions which bound them to the Hapsburgs. And so they engineered the election of a Hapsburg to the throne of the Holy Roman Empire in 1519, as Charles V. The raising of funds for bribes to the Electors has been called by Ehrenberg the biggest business deal of the century.

The election was a great trial of strength for the chief money-powers of Europe. The French Valois drew upon Italian gold; the Hapsburg contenders were backed by a consortium of the Welser, Fugger and others. Each side bestowed gifts upon the various Electoral Princes, only one of whom refused such bribes. Most of these princes, such as the Electors of Mainz and Trier, were easily satisfied with a reasonable sum. But one single Elector held out to the uttermost, the poor Joachim of Brandenburg, who wanted treasure to water his Prussian sands. To please this beggar-prince, the bankers of Europe stretched their resources to the limit. In a dramatic climax, the Valois promised him a French princess with a royal dowry, to be raised by the Southern bankers. Joachim wavered. Then Fugger promised him a Hapsburg princess with 300,000 gulden of good Rhenish gold—and he fell.

The destinies of Europe were decided by the Fugger wealth. Had the Valois won, France and Germany might possibly have been united, saving much trouble for succeeding generations; it may be that the peace-making efforts of our time will be exhausted in vain to undo the work of Jacob Fugger. But, had the Valois won, the Italian financiers might have prevailed also; Florentine queens might have sat upon the throne of all Europe, and let in their countrymen to seize the mines and tolls of the Continent. Such speculation is, of course, futile; the unification of Europe under Florentine finance was blocked by German power as successfully as the attempts of the Roman Empire and of the Italian adventurer, Napoleon, to bring that land-mass under one head were foiled. Italians mastered the whole of Europe only in the spirit, through the Roman Church, and through the art and culture of the Renaissance.

After his election, the policies of Charles V were made in close co-operation with the countinghouse of Augsburg; wherever the Haps-burgs expanded by war or diplomacy, they needed Fugger loans. Only by such support could they push back the dukes of Bavaria from Tyrol; crush revolts in Flanders; struggle with Charles VIII and Fran-cis I of France, and against Venice, or the Turks. Before any important move, the Fuggers were consulted. And, as the Rothschilds helped to defeat Napoleon by transmitting English subsidies over the Pyrenees into Spain, so the Fuggers brought English subsidies within reach of the condottieri and the diplomats of the Hapsburgs wherever they might be needed most.

When the new Emperor, Charles V, proved fractious and ungrate-ful, Fugger wrote him a letter in 1523, in which he mentioned the handsome sums the election had cost and demanded a speedy repay-ment. With the utmost frankness he reproved the monarch whom he had set upon the throne and pointed out to him the feebleness of royal pretensions without cash backing:

> It is evident and clear as day, that Your Majesty could not have secured the Roman Crown without me, and I can show documents to prove it with the signatures of all Your Majesty's agents. In this I have not pursued selfish interests. Had I drawn back from the Austrian House and chosen to further France, I should have at-tained large estates and gold, which were offered to me. What a disadvantage this would have been to Your Majesty and the House of Austria, may easily be judged by Your Majesty on due and reasonable reflection.
>
> Accordingly, I humbly request Your Majesty graciously to recollect my loyal and humble services which have been advanced to the welfare of Your Majesty, and to command that my out-standing sum of money together with the interest for the same be returned and paid out to me without any further delay.

KLEBERG AND THE VALOIS

The contest between the Valois and the Hapsburgs was not ended by the election. It was fought out in the field for many a year. Though Fugger and many other Germans aided their Emperor, the financial backing of the two parties was not wholly on national lines; some German men, particularly Hans Kleberg, went over to the French. Hans was a most enigmatic character. Was he guilty of hideous crimes,

as his fellow-citizens of Nürnberg whispered, or was he "le bon Alle-
mand," the good German, as the French called him? One may look
long at his portrait by Albrecht Dürer, the Nürnberg artist, without
deciding. Extraordinary qualities, whether for good or evil, seem
divined and expressed in the high, bulging forehead, the large, staring,
luminous eyes, and the extreme nervous tensity of nostrils and mouth.
Certainly, Kleberg was inordinately ambitious, brilliant and vain; and
he may have aroused envy in the narrow Nürnberg patriciate.

Despite the fact that he was an upstart, a plebeian, he tried to push
his way into exclusive circles of the town. Worse yet, he was the first big
man of Nürnberg to devote himself wholly and frankly to money-
lending. The patricians of that city were merchants and manufacturers
chiefly. Certainly they also lent large sums and dealt usuriously, but Kleberg was the first high financier in their midst. They were full of venom
against him as a plebeian and usurer; they started rumors that he had
poisoned his wife, the daughter of the Humanist scholar and jurist,
Willibald Pirckheimer, friend and adviser of the great business men of
his day.

Kleberg fled to France and worked hand-in-glove with the Florentine financiers in Lyons. He bought his way into the French nobility
and took possession of the confiscated châteaux of an unlucky warrior, the Constable of Bourbon. The parvenu who thus supplanted the
fallen hero in his estates, had a scutcheon painted with a triple-pointed
golden mountain on a blood-red field and the smug device, "Wisdom is
better than the arms of war." His wisdom dictated a safe retirement
from the firing-line, as a banker providing large loans to assist the
Valois. His mountain of gold thus rose only too directly from the
sanguine-hued battlegrounds of Europe.

Nevertheless Kleberg was too shrewd to adventure his own money
in the service of the French king. He became "valet de chambre du roi
de France," but, as no man is a hero to his valet, Kleberg suspected
the weakness of the French Crown. Instead of backing France with his
fortune, he inveigled the patricians of Nürnberg into the French game,
enticing them with hope of enormous gains.

The Nürnberg merchants had long maintained connections with
Italy and France. Their city lay between Venice and the Netherlands.
Many of its best citizens were Italians, the Odeschalchi, for example,
who came in from Milan; an Odeschalchi became Pope Innocent XI
and retained his love of Germany. One of the richest men in Germany
was Bartholomäus Viatis, once a poor Italian apprentice from Venice,
who had come to Nürnberg, married his master's widow and risen to
the post of City Counsellor. Viatis had fifteen children and disinherited
those unfit for his trade in leather, linen, ostrich feathers and notions;

he built a great house, filled with Italian treasures, in which he entertained Venetian nobles and ambassadors. On his monument are the words, "I have fought a good fight."

Such Nürnberg merchants as the Behaims, Francki and Fetzer were familiar with the South. Paul Praum formed a remarkable art-collection in Nürnberg which he enriched with treasures discovered in Italy. The architecture of the city reflected these contacts. True, the heart of the city remained Gothic, for its main business was manufacturing for German markets; but a certain touch of French and Italian influence brushed the façades of many homes, as it pervaded the lives of many citizens. The Tucher family, dealing in cloth with France, built a home in French style; the Hirschvogel advertised their Italianate relations with a fine mansion in the pure Renaissance manner, complete with marble pillars and helmeted cupids.

A large number of the wealthy merchants and manufacturers of Nürnberg were inclined toward the Valois side by their natural interests, as Fugger was drawn to the Hapsburgs by his. And, even though they had such reason to hate and fear Kleberg, whom they had driven from their midst, they could not resist the temptation of enormous returns on their investments. They lost everything, of course, in the bankruptcy of France; Kleberg had the delicious revenge of telling the pleading patricians of his home town that he could do nothing for them. He kept his own money, however, and died in the arms of the Church, leaving a large sum to a charitable institution in Lyons. The grateful citizens of that Italianized city erected a statue showing him clad in the armor of a Roman Emperor, holding a lance in one hand and in the other a well-filled purse.

GRESHAM AND THE TUDORS

In Queen Elizabeth's day, there was no necessity for conspiracies of munitions-makers; manufacturers did not have to propagandize, to work through high naval officials, or play upon the public feelings. Everything could be very simply and expeditiously settled, by a single brief note, such as that which Thomas Gresham wrote to the Queen's Minister on March 21, 1562, explaining: (1) that a big navy would be a good thing for probable emergencies; (2) that more modern armaments were desirable; (3) that he, Gresham, could provide them. The queen, said he

is armyd with all kinds of armewr, and munission; whyche ys not a little spoken of here amonges all nacyones; and what a moment they make of it, I will leave for moleasting you therewith, because *I* was the doer thereof. And so, Sir, considering this dangerous world that ys like to be, I wold I were of that credit with the Queene's Majestie, and I were abill to perswade her Highness to make provisione for some xm li worthe of salte peter; by the reason there ys no weppon so estemyd as the gun is.

In the refreshing atmosphere of Gloriana's reign, this little document could do the work which nowadays requires a thousand pamphlets, editorials and speeches. For the Queen's Majesty was so impressed with the picture of the "dangerous world that ys like to be," that she commissioned Gresham, the great purveyor of "munission," to furnish Britain with generous quantities of cuirasses, pistols, muskets and the best German powder. With such a start in naval competition, the British were ready when the Spanish at last sent their Invincible Armada, outfitted with the help of the Genoese bankers, against the English coasts.

Gresham united in his single person functions which we today distribute over a variety of agencies: the Associated Press; the Diplomatic and Consular Service; the Secret Service; the Board of Estimates. He was spy, ambassador, consul and councillor. He advised the Government upon its Navy, and outfitted it. He served in delicate negotiations at foreign courts; he was a news-gatherer, having in his pay any number of spies upon the Spanish, and had his regular letter-carriers, who kept England informed, better than most states, of European events. As a private citizen, he raised money for the Crown, going security for the sums himself and transmitting it quietly to his rulers; this was necessary, for naturally nobody on the Continent would have lent any large sum to a ruler of England in those days without the written guarantee of some prominent business man of unquestioned integrity like Gresham.

Gresham was Royal Agent, like his father before him. He was also a successful trader, enrolled in the Company of Merchant Adventurers; in one of their biennial shipments of 50,000 pieces of cloth to Antwerp, he participated to the extent of 4,500 pieces. Thus he could act as liaison officer between the mercantile and the royal interests. This frank alignment of business and politics, so much closer in the Elizabethan Age than in our own, made for swift and effective action. It was surprising what one energetic queen and one able munitions-purveyor could do, when they were not being perpetually interfered with by investigating commissions. Moreover, it made for great intellectual honesty, if not for clear separation of private and public purse.

For instance, Gresham could urge the queen to aid the Protestant cause in Europe in order to lift the British pound. It was not necessary for him to plead patriotic or religious motives, as Cromwell had to do a hundred years later when a Parliament had to be persuaded. Cromwell had to urge war on the ground that it would be agreeable to God who had intended to let the British instead of the wicked Papists have the North Sea trade. But Gresham in 1562 merely wrote that the defeat of the Huguenots in France "hathe made such an alteracione of credit as this penn cannot write you." Two weeks later, with yet more concern, he expressed anxiety about the fate of the British pound: "Here ys soche great dowtes cast upon our Estate, as the creadyte of the Queen's Majestie and all the whole nacyon ys at a stay; and glad ys that man that maye be quit of an Englishman's bill."

Gresham was a stout Protestant. His father, Richard, Tawney says, had been Lord Mayor of London and Royal Agent to King Henry VIII and was the largest single profiteer in the Reformation from the confiscation of Church lands. Thomas, the son, was heir to the lands, the cloth-business and the office of Royal Agent and won one of the greatest fortunes of the age in these three capacities.

The Greshams helped determine England's commercial policies for four reigns. They attained an overweening importance which would not have been possible in Germany, France or Italy at that time. The Fuggers, Grimaldi and the other magnates of the Continent were far richer than Gresham, but too many aristocratic prejudices hedged around the kings. The bankers might oppose some measures and advocate others, but they were not listened to so closely as the Greshams in England. This was partly because the old nobility of Britain was largely exterminated in the Wars of the Roses; only twenty-nine families survived into the Tudor Age, and Henry VIII and his three children created 146 peerages for the benefit of rising commoners. The new English nobility was infiltrated with commercial blood and still more with commercial ideas as the old aristocracy on the Continent was not. Hence it is not surprising to find Thomas Gresham, himself a new-made knight, telling the descendants of "plain Mr. Owen Tudor," and, on the maternal side, of the merchant Bulleyn, just how he expected them to behave.

Edward VI was but a child when Gresham was called in 1551 "to know my oppynyone what way wythe the leaste charge his majestie might grow out of debt." And Gresham told his majesty that there was but one way that would be "honnorable and profitable"—namely, to pay the debts. If the king's Catholic sister, Mary, thought she could dispense with the stiff-necked Protestant, she soon saw that nobody else could provide the "pollitycke handeling" needful to raise loans at Antwerp; so she sent for Gresham and he kindly agreed to do as much for her as he had done for her brother:

When I took this servis in hande, the King's Majestie's credit on the other syde was small; and yet, after his deathe, he was in such credit both with strangers and his own marchaunts . . . whereby his enymyes began to fear him; for the commodities of his realme, and power among Prynsis, was not known before.

Toward the successor, Queen Elizabeth, he was less querulous and more pedagogic, for with her acceptance of Italian culture, she was readier to understand State reason. He explained Gresham's Law to her with unwearied patience. He laid down certain fundamental principles which made England the only financially sound nation left in Europe by the end of the century. He kept up the credit of the Crown by breaking down the statutes of usury and teaching British merchants to lend to their rulers; he insisted that the Crown also keep faith with its subjects, as European royalty could not and would not do. The five rules which Gresham laid down to Queen Elizabeth were as important to English development as Magna Charta:

An it please your Majestie to restore this your realme into such estate as heretofore it hath bene,—First, your hyghnes hath none other wayes, butt, when time and opertunyty serveth, to bringe your base money into fine, of xi ounces fine. And so, gowlde.

Secondly, nott to restore the (Hanseatic) Still-yards to their usorped privelidge.

Thirdly, to grant as few licences as you can.

Fourthly, to come in as small debt as you can beyond seas.

Fifthly, to keep your credit; and specially with your owne merchants; for it is they who must stand by you, at all events in your necessity.

By his own skill and the cooperation of Schetz, the agent of his Spanish enemy, Gresham upheld the credit of the Crown in Antwerp. He advanced the rate there from 16 to 22 Flemish shillings to the pound, for instance, and paid off some Crown debts very favorably, even though his fellow-merchants foamed with rage, even though his own uncle was furious: "he and I was at great words, lyke to fall out; but ere we departyd, we drank eche to other."

Raising loans, chiefly from Lazarus Tucher, the expert negotiator of the great Nürnberg house (still doing business to this day), Gresham had to smuggle the bullion as well as arms out of Antwerp disguised in bales of merchandise. Because Antwerp was in the hands of the Spanish enemy, it took cunning to raise money and buy ammunitions there for the British. Yet he succeeded and at the same time kept urging armaments upon his native land, pressing fresh supplies of "brymstone" and bow staves upon the queen, and above all gunpowder; for "be you right assewrd, it will be only *that* thing she shall lacke, if warres should chance."

It was a fortunate thing for Britain that her own national interests coincided with the private advancement of so powerful a man. She was luckier than other European states in this respect. But Gresham, as a merchant, profited from driving out the Hanseatics and the raising of Crown loans; as an arms supplier, he gained by the creation of a fleet able to defeat the Armada. He had only to pursue his own advantage to achieve, incidentally, the solidification of the British Empire. On the Continent, such perfect harmony was not to be found.

It was Gresham who broke the fortunes of the city of Antwerp by transferring British cloth-dealings from that port up to Hamburg. Lübeck, head of the Hanseatic League, was well aware of the nature of the blow when the first English ships went up the North Sea to deliver their cargoes into the open port of Hamburg; Spain also knew what a mighty loss it meant to her great harbor of Antwerp. The voyage instigated by the Englishman was as momentous as that of Vasco da Gama; it created an empire even more lasting.

Not only did Gresham defeat the Hanseatics, driving them out of England and ruining their monopoly at home; not only did he seriously threaten Spanish prosperity and prepare the English, through a Spanish stock-exchange, to defend themselves against the Armada; he also saw to it that "warres" came. He was particularly active in fomenting the troubles between England and Spain.

What brought about the unhealable breach between England and Spain was perhaps the seizure of Spanish treasure-ships by the English, immediately answered by Alva's seizure of English merchants; this was followed by the sequestration in England of the goods of Spanish resident merchants. In all this reprisal against commerce, Gresham was to the fore, advising, urging the retention of the Spanish treasure, proposing the seizure of the enemy merchants and the stoppage of payments on all debts to the Spanish. Thus the great merchant and munitioneer of England, Gresham, at last caused the great "warres" for which he had so long and zealously prepared.

FUGGER AND GRESHAM, THE MEN

Fugger and Gresham were, superficially, poles apart. Gresham wore a sober suit with a small, neat ruff; Fugger, more ostentatious, quite let himself go in the matter of millinery. Gresham was dry, harsh, penurious, didactic; he quibbled over every penny of his traveling allowance, although he was one of the richest men in England; and if he patronized letters it was through the person of George Fox, the martyr-historian. Fugger was a Catholic and a Maecenas who enjoyed a revel and a fresco in relaxation from his immense labors. The two men were as different as the two scutcheons they chose for themselves when they bought their way into the nobility: Fugger, when he got himself the title of Count, selected lilies for his emblem; Gresham, created a knight, bore a grasshopper rampant on his shield.

These men, however, had in common an immense capacity for work. Both were loyal. In an age of blatant corruption, when mediaeval fealty was dead and modern patriotism unborn, they were unusual in their resistance to bribery and temptation. Fugger never swerved in his loyalty to the Hapsburgs; nor did Gresham swerve from the interests of the Tudors. Both were characterized by a monstrous coolness and self-esteem. In the midst of disastrous wars and dynastic quarrels, they preserved their fortunes and their equanimity. Cautious and determined, they watched the interplay of politics, trade and finance, and judged when and how to interfere. They remained undazzled by the outward show of Elizabethan courtiers or the pretensions of the heirs to the Holy Roman Empire, and never fell victim either to ambition or the mere speculative urge. Both Gresham and Fugger remained aloof, impervious, supported in the just awareness of inner worth.

How highly Gresham estimated himself is apparent from his self-praise in letters. He is forever reminding Queen Bess that he has got her "not a little spoken of here amonges all nacyones," and boasting how he has mastered the Exchange and put fear into the hearts of speculators, so that they would not dare to play with the pound: "I have so plagued the strangers, that from hens forth they will beware how to meddyll with the exchange for London; and as for our own merchants, I have put them in such a fere that they dare not meddill."

The poise of Anton and Jacob Fugger was also extraordinary. Playing games for the highest stakes, they never went in too deeply. Anton was indeed a little nervous sometimes; but Jacob Fugger never lost a sound night's sleep, or a gulden in his gambles. The portrait of Jacob by the elder Holbein shows him as the quiet, shrewd, cool citizen. He was a good host, a perfect statesman, irreproachable in his morals as in his religious faith and patriotic loyalty, and, without vanity, profoundly conscious of his own worth. Composing his own epitaph for the pompous, cupid-laden chapel of Augsburg, since he had to be his own public relations counselor, he wrote:

To the best, greatest God! Jacob Fugger of Augsburg, the ornament of his class and people, imperial councillor under Maximilian

I and Charles V, who was behind no one in the attainment of extraordinary wealth, in generosity, purity of morals and greatness of soul, is, as he was not comparable with anyone in his lifetime, even after death not to be counted among the mortals.

The Fuggers and Gresham were regarded with bewilderment and awe by their contemporaries, to whom there seemed something monstrous about millionaires; the world was not yet accustomed to the idea of wealth overriding barriers of caste. Legends were told about how Fugger astonished the Pope and the Emperor; in England, a favorite story ran the rounds about Gresham's great house in which Queen Elizabeth honored him by an extended visit. The queen, so it was said, made a suggestion for a wall in one part of the estate; overnight an army of masons was set to work and the wall was ready on the morrow when the astounded courtiers arose. One wit exclaimed: "This man can change a building as easily as build a 'change!" This was an allusion to the permanent house which Gresham gave the London Stock Exchange. A play written in 1606 by Thomas Heywood, called: "If you know not me, you know nobody; or the troubles of Queen Elizabeth," features the dedicating of this new edifice. The Queen has graced the occasion by her presence; Gresham, following the example of Cleopatra, dissolves a fabulous pearl in a goblet and drains it to her health, saying:

> *Here 15 hundred pounds at one clap goes!*
> *Instead of sugar, Gresham drinks the pearl*
> *Unto his queen and mistress: pledge it lords!*

But there was a limit to the grandeur even of the millionaire. Jacob Fugger the Rich, one of the most magnificent and powerful business men of history, had outmaneuvered the greatest financiers of his day; he was the friend of kings, embraced by the Pope, universally regarded with fear and awe, even by his boldest enemy, Martin Luther. But there was one thing this mighty man could not do: he could not get the Augsburg patricians to regard him as an equal. Jacob, after all, despite his new-bought title of Count and his castles and scutcheons, was still the son of a self-made man, the grandson of a village weaver.

This was the smarting wound in Jacob's self-esteem. He begged most humbly to be allowed to build a new *Weinstube* for the social gatherings of the best families of Augsburg, would they only permit him to hang his freshly painted shield beside theirs. But they snubbed him and declined the offer. And thus Jacob the Rich, who had conditioned the destinies of Europe for a generation and even helped to start the

Reformation by exciting popular animosity in Germany, who had enthroned and admonished kings and amassed such wealth as had not been
seen in so concentrated a form since the days of the Caesars—Jacob
Fugger never really did succeed, to the day of his death, in crashing
the social gate in his home town.

FUGGER AS A BENEFACTOR

Both men died without direct heirs, leaving a part of their fortunes
to charitable and public-spirited enterprise. Gresham gave a large sum
to found a college in London; and he is remembered by a statue today
before the London Stock Exchange which he once gave a shelter. Fugger founded the most remarkable social experiment of his age: the
Fuggerei, a beautiful garden city which is still perfectly preserved at
Augsburg and used for workers' dwellings.

Whoever walks through the wide, sunny lanes of this "unit," complete with fountain and chapel, notes the simple, practical, ample
houses, mellow in color and finely proportioned, and reflects upon the
rise of such a novelty as this amid the filthy chaos of mediaeval cities,
must come to a fuller appreciation of Fugger himself. This man had
outgrown the mediaeval world. His *Fuggerei* as it stands today, with
hardly any alteration except the introduction of modern plumbing, is
a model village fulfilling the specifications of city planners, and indeed
serving as an inspiration in modern times. Over the entrance was set
an inscription which breathes the proud consciousness of family power
and the acknowledgment of the social obligation of wealth:

> Ulrich, George and Jacob Fugger of Augsburg, brothers, firmly
> convinced that they were born to the best good of the city and that
> they owe their immense fortune above all to the All-Highest and
> Almighty God, out of piety and as an example of especial generos-
> ity, have given, presented and dedicated 106 dwellings complete to
> such of their fellow-citizens as are upright but impoverished.

Fugger wished to go farther than this. At one time he offered a plan
to the city whereby a great sum would be set aside by him, from the
interest on which could be bought free bread for the poor of Augsburg
forever. But the city-fathers, busy in the grain-trade, could not agree
to a scheme which might imperil their profits. Consequently the bulk
of Fugger's fortune went into more conventional lines—the patronage
of art in the approved Renaissance manner.

The South Germans and Flemish in that era continued the traditions
of the Italians as patrons. All three were temperamentally fitted to trans-

act business and yet enjoy leisured life hugely—a capacity which became rarer among business men until, in our age, it is found chiefly among the Chinese, a few French financiers, a Greek munitioneer like Sir Basil Zaharoff, and some European Jews.

The chief merchant-patrons even in the sixteenth century were still the Italians, men like the agreeable financier Orazio Pallavicino, one of the leading importers of Renaissance culture to Elizabethan England, or the Bonvisi of Lucca who could charm the exquisite Sir Thomas More, and yet later join Gresham in supplying morions, hauberks and salpetre to the Queen's Navy. At Rome, the splendor of the late-Renaissance was paid for by a Medicean Pope and the enormously rich bankers, Bindo Altoviti and Agostino Chigi. The latter, for instance, gave the money to Raphael for frescoes; his famous hetaira, Imperia, provided the inspiration, and Castiglione contributed the concept. Genoese bankers also bought paintings with a lavish hand.

This grand manner the Flemish were to some extent taking over. At Antwerp, Gaspar Schetz was a poet and friend of the painters' gild as well as a great speculator. The Spanish merchant Jean Brandon protected Dürer. Art collections were formed by Corneille van der Geest, Pierre Stevens, Diego Douarte. The Fuggers assumed the same rôle in South Germany.

A curious parallel might be drawn between the patronage of Jacques Cœur and Jacob Fugger, for the buildings favored by them marked an art revolution in France and Germany respectively. As the château of Cœur indicated the first important break with the French native Gothic, so the Chapel of St. Anne, reared in 1512 by Jacob Fugger at Augsburg, was the first noteworthy monument of the same trend towards the Renaissance on German soil.

The connection of art with finance is also strikingly illustrated by the difference in architecture between Nürnberg and Augsburg. The former, founded upon industry and merchandising, was conservative; it went on with the Gothic, with few exceptions such as the Renaissance palace of the Hirschvogel, who, however, were financiers. But Augsburg, as Woltmann observes, is mostly Renaissance; there is hardly anything of the mediaeval left about it: the great palaces of the patricians with their broad-spanned arcades and tremendous painted wall-spaces, the gild-houses of the weavers, bakers and butchers—all are as "modern" as the industry and finance that Augsburg introduced.

The Fuggers represented economically a complete divorce from the mediaeval and Gothic past. They were giants of cloth-manufacturing and mining, the first capitalistically organized industries on a modern scale; they were the sponsors of modern financial speculation in Germany. As their spice-ships and banking-system connected the known world, so they were cosmopolitans. With their caravans over the snow-covered Alps, visible in the distance at Augsburg, came the Italian Renaissance into Germany.

Augsburg was the successor of Florence. In many ways the German city was fairer and finer than the Italian. Life, as Æneas Sylvius found it, was jollier and safer at Augsburg; the absence of party feuds and tyrannical families made for a great enjoyment of property and personal liberty. It was, as has been said before, a village of millionaires; but these great men, for all their jealousies and petty vindictiveness, employed no assassins against one another. The city became very charming indeed; the patrician houses were not frowning and turreted and grim like those along the Arno. Instead they were painted with the gayest imaginable scenes in the most splendid colors, so that the whole town was filled with images, and to turn a corner was like turning a page in a picture-book. To the bright colors was added the plash of many fountains, dedicated to Hercules, to Augustus, after whom the city was named, and to Mercury, God of Trade.

Out of Augsburg came the first German painter who is pure Renaissance, Holbein the Younger. He broke from the artistic past as Fugger, his patron, was detached from the economic trammels of the mediaeval times. Holbein's father painted many of the merchants of the city; in the Basilica of St. Paul there is a fresco of the best citizens of the town, gathered to listen to the preaching of the Saint, and devoutly attentive —except one, who is asleep.

Men in the circle around the Fuggers helped along the Renaissance. Dr. Conrad Peutinger, for instance, the lawyer who aided the Fuggers to resist the trust-busting campaign in the early sixteenth century, was the first to collect and write about Roman relics in the vicinity of Augusta Vindelicorum, as Augsburg was known to the Romans. Raimund Fugger had an Italian garden and the first great collection of Italian antiques on German ground. The chief art-patron of the family, however, was Hans.

Hans was, like Lorenzo, representative of the somewhat effeminate younger generation, in whom the gifts for business was slowly fading and the aristocratization process had begun. He was educated strictly in business, but also trained at a university, in courts, and by travel. He wore a pointed beard in the patrician fashion, and had himself carved on his tomb in full armor, with a sword and a pair of iron gloves by his side. Thus he represented the type just between business and full assimilation into the nobility which, as experience shows, is best fitted for the rôle of Maecenas.

This Fugger had one undisputed merit: he was the first of all German collectors to house his treasures worthily. For this purpose, he had his rooms frescoed by imported artists; these rooms were unique in Germany in their time, decorated with landscapes, tritons and satyrs, and the busts of Roman Emperors. Everywhere were shown the golden lilies of the Fugger scutcheon and the strange little Moorish girl crowned with a bishop's mitre who formed part of the coat-of-arms.

Hans collected Greek manuscripts, battle pictures, coins, clocks, guns and crucifixes, with the utmost impartiality. He was particularly proud of having a complete collection of 234 portraits of the various Popes, as a testimony to the papal banking relations of the Fuggers. As to his tastes, opinions differ. He certainly was not a Lorenzo, for one cannot imagine the great Italian writing as Hans did in 1567 about antiques. Ordering through his bankers, the Olgiati at Rome, and a German trader at Venice, Otto, some first-rate antique goods, he stated his needs: "Would very much like to have 2 or 3 pieces more of the same size as the Venus, she is 2⅛ Augsburg yards high . . . to decorate a salon. It makes no difference, if it is a Remus, Hercules, Apollo, Mercury, or any other nice bit." His agents found a Juno and Jupiter of guaranteed provenance, and just the right height, but with damaged noses. Hans was still too much the bourgeois amateur to accept them. He replied: "What is missing on them, that is to say, that the noses must be reconstructed and also the diadem on the Juno is broken. . . . Those are great faults, dear David, especially as the noses are in that condition, that would be a great nuisance."

Though Hans was not so crude as Nathan Rothschild in the nineteenth century, who treated a great painter like a carpenter, Hans still undeniably preferred an artist to keep good artisan hours; he liked a painter to finish in eight days what another would take a month over; he liked best an Italian who was "loyal, pious, hard-working . . . and absolutely never asks a holiday or to go out walking."

The crudities of the early stages of business patronage might, however, have been removed and a culture built in South Germany to parallel that of Florence. But the period of prosperity was too short. These patrons, like those of Antwerp, lost their fortunes too early, instead of preserving and developing them through generations like many Florentines. And after them, came no more of the great patrons in the Lorenzo grand manner.

In contrast to such old patrons, the British and Dutch had single-track minds with no taste for frivolity; neither created a culture so many-sided, and dominated by the business man, as that of Italy. The French were too subservient to the monarchy to exhibit a bourgeois independence in artistic matters.

The chief effect of the Fugger patronage was, therefore, to influence the taste of the German nobility. Hans was a friend of Duke William of Bavaria. It was Hans who excited the envy of the Duke; and then agreed to act as negotiator, ordering paints and painters, books and professors, choir-singers, diamonds and ermines, to enable dukes to catch up with the Augsburg patricians. More important still, Hans lent the Duke tens of thousands of florins (which were never repaid). As a result, George Lill maintains, the Munich we know took form; the Michaelskirche, "most powerful creation of the German Renaissance," and the rich artistic movement around the Wittelsbach Court, owe their original inspiration to a Fugger. Thus in Germany, as in Italy, merchants taught the nobility how to live.

X

THE FALL OF THE ITALIAN AND GERMAN OLIGARCHS

AT NO TIME, perhaps, has purely commercial wealth been displayed with so little rivalry from aristocratic wealth as in the late Renaissance. As yet, the courts had not concentrated national pomp and luxury as they were soon to do; no Versailles existed as a pattern of imitation for Europeans. Only dignitaries of the Church celebrated power at that period with a sumptuousness that could overshadow the outbursts of the new-made millionaires.

This was of course not without elements of danger to business; in the absence of royal models, which in a way have sanctified the parade of wealth, the populace viewed with malicious envy many of the manifestations of moneyed pride. The marble eagle of the Hirschvogel looked like a bird of prey to them; the men and women in magnificent attire who took the best pews in the churches were resented by the poor, who thought the blatant orgy of spending was at their expense. This has not been felt so much about kings, for the people considered kingly splendor to be, in a way, their own splendor.

Yet millionaires had first to show the way to kings, and explain to those monarchs, as yet fresh from feudal penury, how to enjoy themselves. Credit for this pace-setting has hardly been given them, however, for the popular mind, dazzled by the pageantry of the Sun-King or the Merry Monarch, has not enquired into the source of the regal concepts; in many ways, these royal spendthrifts learned from business men what comfort might be, and by what various means wealth and power might be advertised.

In housing, for instance, the patricians of Genoa, Florence, Augsburg, Basel, Antwerp, pointed the way for the palaces of the kings. Versailles itself was modeled after a financier's private home, the Château de Vaux of Fouquet. Up to the 1680's, Fouquet was the most resplendent man in France, far outshining the young king, Louis XIV. The grandson of a merchant of Nantes, he had become a royal financier and banker and had brought into his chains the court, the State and the merchants of Paris. He was, as a French historian said, "a veritable bourgeois patrician, so rare with us, for this class of the nation had always had petty instincts and petty tastes"; in France he carried on the Italian "grand seigneur" tradition of banking and spending. "Venice or Florence would have been a setting more appropriate for this sumptuous and incomparable dissipator."

The notion of building Versailles was instilled into the king's mind when he visited his great banker. Fouquet entertained him with a fête, at which the dinner alone, for 6,000 guests, cost 120,000 livres; there was a lottery with jewels and horses as prizes. The throngs admired his 500 dozen silver and gold plates, his domed hall with antique statues, his ceilings painted by Lebrun and walls hung with tapestries; his labyrinths, grottoes and the fountains which La Fontaine hymned. The banker had taste as well as wealth: he gave annual pensions of four millions to artists, savants, men of letters, who remained true to their Maecenas even in his misfortunes. Corneille, Mme. de Sévigné, Mlle. de Scudéry and others sang his praises and tried to intercede for him when he was imprisoned. The jealous king, however, threw Fouquet into jail, where, after nineteen years of captivity, he died; it was claimed that Fouquet was the mysterious *Man in the Iron Mask*. The monarch built Versailles to show the people that he had taken the sovereignty of France from the bankers.

In fine living, as well as housing, business men had much to exhibit that kings could well copy. Emperor Rudolf II was entertained all summer long by Hans Fugger and was so enchanted that Fugger had to furnish a large sum to get him to go away. It was no wonder, for what king of that age lived as Fugger did? Every day came delicacies for the Fugger table from the most remote regions: in season, he had carp, crabs, caviar, oysters, artichokes and truffles, olives from Bologna, pheasants from Venice, asparagus of Brion, and pomegranates out of Antwerp. The clothing of the family was assembled with equal care: white shoes from Cologne; gloves and ivory combs from Venice; silk stockings from Spain; diamonds and ostrich feathers from Antwerp. For the house and garden were brought rugs of the Levant and African leopardskins, peacocks and canaries, Indian sunflower seeds and tulip bulbs of the Near East. Out of Spain he ordered honey, wine, rubies and Peruvian jewels; his horses came from Vienna; his dogs were Turkish and Hungarian.

If Hans Fugger was perhaps the most elaborate individual *bon vivant*, the greatest class of spenders as a whole was probably in Antwerp. The Venetian ambassador, Guicciardini, sighed when he came there. In this gayest of cosmopolitan centers, he beheld even the displays of his commercial homeland surpassed. A very "diamond in the ring of the world," he considered it to be. He said:

> Though this folk has its mind chiefly on trading profits, yet it puts much money into houses and estates and every kind of ornament, so that the city from day to day spreads out marvelously and is enriched in appearance. And although usually the common people and a few wise men keep to the old practices of a thrifty life, one finds in general great display here, perhaps indeed more than is proper. Men and women of every age make much ado about clothing to show off their position and fortunes, always in the newest and most magnificent fashion, but not seldom far more costly than decency and morals bid. Also one sees continually marriage festivals, banquets and dances, and everywhere one hears merry song and music, in a word, in every nook and corner one sees the richness, the power, the pomp and the magnificence of this city.

The sixteenth century was opened by a bankers' holiday without a parallel. The occasion was the celebration of the new Pope, Leo X of the House of Medici; it was a moment when the business and the religious power of Italy were at their height and closest unity, and in the last hours of the zenith. The most gorgeous decorations in honor of the Pontifex were put up in the bankers' quarters in Rome but the Medici, naturally, were called upon to rejoice most, and their exhibition consisted of "six balls," with real wine flowing from them all day long. All the Florentine bankers erected triumphal arches adorned with pictures of their patron saints. And of course the Fuggers felt they should not be found wanting; so their factor, Johannes Zink, provided an enormous arch beautified with tapestries and a great painting of the arts and sciences presided over by Fortuna. However, the most splendid display was that of Agostino Chigi, the richest banker of Rome; before his house on Bank Street he had an arch erected, with Mercury, the God of Gold, floating above the standards of the Medici and the Chigi; the virtues and vices were depicted in frescoes round about; and in one of the niches with their living statues, a nymph recited verses in honor of the Pope.

In the procession the bankers also took part. In fact, Florentine business men, prominent among whom were Francesco Borgarini, Bindo Altoviti and Bernardo Bini, headed it. Next came the Germans; only then followed the nobles, trailed by a dozen asses laden with gold and silver plate; after that the foreign ambassadors; and eventually the prelates. Among 250 mitred churchmen on horseback, and cardinals, came the Pope on a great white Turkish horse decked to the earth in taffeta.

Behind him rode an official equipped with two great baskets of papal coins which he flung to the scrambling crowd.

German merchants brought some of this glory of the Renaissance into England. By far the most sumptuous thing ever seen in London was the spectacle provided by the Hanse merchants in honor of the wedding of Henry VIII with Anne of Cleves. For this festivity, business men commissioned Holbein to design them a Parnassus on wheels —one of the first important signs that the Renaissance had reached Britain, and also an advertisement for the Rhine wines which Cologne sold in London. On this Parnassus, Apollo and the Nine Muses were grouped about the Sacred Spring; down the sides of the heavenly mountain flowed the choicest Rhine wine, from morning until evening. The citizens of London, vastly impressed by this combination of classic culture and bibulous advertisement, stood before it all day, fairly drinking it in.

But Antwerp, the greatest commercial city of Europe, outdid all others in festivity. To the merchants of that town, expense was no object. When the Archduke, later Charles V, came to visit them in 1515, the city accorded him a "joyeuse entrée"; it was his aim to borrow £166,000 of the bankers, but they received him with such joy that one might have thought him a valued depositor. Their great celebration came of course at the height of prosperity in Antwerp and this was the most splendid commercial festival of Europe, far surpassing the previous bank holiday in Rome. Whereas Leo X had been proud of spending 100,000 ducats on his procession, the citizens of Antwerp gave as many pounds for their "Landjuweel," a folk-festival representing the triumph of art, science and industry, supported by trade. Fourteen cities sent their best poets to compete with the *Violieren* of Antwerp; for three weeks the competitions went on between them, followed by two weeks of matches between village poets. For a solid month, business was at a standstill in this greatest port of Europe and the city gave itself up to feasting, dancing, pageantry, and to welcoming the processions from other cities. Each participating city sent its poets, accompanied by patricians and burghers in their grandest attire. From the lace-city, Mechlin, came bards who called themselves "The Peacocks," in a party of three hundred riders, wearing red garments and gold crowns, leading seven chariots with allegorical figures; two by two they rode into Antwerp, a pair carrying torches alternating with a pair carrying flowers. From Brussels, the tapestry-city, came a thousand men clad in antique helmets, white waistcoats, white gloves and crimson robes, with four-score ornamental floats.

Impressed with this unparalleled spectacle, epitome of the boom-spirit, the Englishman, Arthur Clough, wrote home: "I would to God that some of our noblemen, who think the world is made of porridge, could have seen this; then they would realize that there are men of another manner than they." The grand manner that is nowadays thought aristocratic was at that time still unblushingly commercial. Hence if modern millionaires exhibit their wealth in the building of cinema theaters, châteaux, skyscrapers, in expensive balls and receptions, they are not so much copying aristocratic manners, as reclaiming their own.

Even in behavior, business men made a considerable contribution to the seigneurial tradition. For Castiglione, whose book, "The Courtier," had so profound an influence as a textbook of etiquette and personal development for the courts of Europe, wrote it in the form of a dialogue, and one of the persons in it was a Medici. The Medici, by the end of the sixteenth century were as glad to agree with a Castiglione that blue blood was important, as they had earlier been happy to support Bracciolini in the contention that talent was better than birth. They had themselves become aristocrats. A large and steadily increasing number of rich men throughout Europe were at that time entering the nobility, and proving, very naturally, greater sticklers for etiquette than the old rough-and-ready feudal gentry had been.

Titles were easy to procure from corrupt and needy courts. Gaspar Schetz at Antwerp produced a line of dukes; so did the Genoese Grimaldi. Hans Paumgartner and Bartholmä Welser were ennobled; so was Kleberg in France. The Fugger obtained the title of count, two castles pawned for loans unpaid by the Emperor, and a scutcheon which was as original as could be: it contained lilies, a white horn, and a little Negress wearing a bishop's mitre. In England, Orazio Pallavicino was knighted by Queen Elizabeth; Thomas Gresham, dubbed in 1559, then changed his residence from Lombard Street to a new mansion outside London, for, in England, to "keep shop" or even live near one's office after receiving a knighthood was disgraceful. Sir Baptist Hickes, later Viscount Camden, a mercer under James I, was, according to Burgon, one of the first citizens who kept shop after receiving a title, and for this he was remonstrated with by London aldermen.

In England the nobility was especially hospitable to the influx of traders. Such merging was hardly noticeable in northern Germany, for the reason perhaps that there were few men wealthy enough to buy their way into the German nobility during the devastations caused by the Wars of Religion. But in England, where the Tudors, themselves with shopkeeping ancestry, had made a fairly clean sweep of the old families, it was not too difficult. Thus in 1592, a conduct-book for budding tradesmen was published by Richard Johnson, entitled: "The nine worthies of London, Explayning . . . the memorable attempts of magnanimous minds. Pleasant for Gentlemen, not unseemly for Magistrates, and most profitable for Prentices." In this work, Clio is led among the Elysian fields by Fame, and interviews nine worthies on their achievements; these are all business men who began poor, made good, and reached the height of a title: Sir William Walworth, fishmonger; Sir Henry Pitchard, wine-merchant; Sir Wm. Sevenoak, grocer; Sir Thomas White, merchant-tailor; Sir John Bonham, mercer; Sir Christopher Croker, vintner; Sir John Hawkwood, merchant-tailor; Sir Hugh Calverly, silk-weaver; Sir Henry Malevert, grocer. The gaping prentices who bought the book must have been dazzled indeed by the spectacle of so many lordly grocers and ennobled tailors.

THE IDEA OF THE TRIUMPH

In his full flush of prosperity, the business man produced a great symbol: the Triumph. We are accustomed nowadays to think that the allegorical representation of triumph was aristocratic. In fact, long before the Sun-King ordered himself painted in triumphant attitudes, business men had developed the art of self-glorification to a high point. They advertised themselves in the Cinquecento instead of their products, until most of the great nations of Europe and nearly all the leading banking houses had gone bankrupt and so there was almost no occasion left to celebrate. Only then did business relinquish the Triumph to monarchs.

The idea of the Triumph itself, of an honorary procession with allegorical figures, was, it appears, originally the product of a commercial race, the Etruscans. The Romans took from them the triumph, together with Fortuna and the Fasces. After the long lapse of the Dark Ages, the memory of the Roman triumphs was revived by that Etruscan city of Florence. Eventually the Florentine poet Petrarch described so eloquently the Roman triumphal processions that Lorenzo de' Medici, seizing upon the idea, ordered tapestries of the Triumph of Fame and the Triumph of Love. Finally in 1491, in the latter days of Florentine commercial glory, he held a superb festival representing the triumph of the Roman General, Paulus Aemilius, as nearly as possible according to the antique description given by Plutarch.

This ancient method of celebrating success, like the concept of Fortuna, caught the imagination of other commercial cities. Then throughout Europe appeared a wave of pictorial representations of business success. The German merchants, in the Fondaco de' Tedeschi at Venice, employed Titian to adorn their house and commissioned Dürer in 1506 to paint for their chapel his famous *Rosenkranz* Madonna showing the members of the German colony kneeling about the Virgin, while flying cherubim distribute chaplets to crown them all. The German merchants in London, who formed the most prosperous group there for so long and the one most in touch with Continental culture, commissioned Holbein to paint their portraits, showing them in their offices, opening letters. For their banquet hall they got from him a "Triumph of Wealth," now unhappily lost, which was said to have been worthy of Raphael. As we know from a surviving design, however, it showed an old, bald, bent Plutus, God of Riches, seated upon money-bags in a triumphal car. Behind him rode Midas, Croesus and Tantalus. Before him rushed Fortuna, scattering coins to the winds. His charioteer was Reason who, despite the cries of "Faster!" gripped short and firm the reins: Will and Knowledge. Ahead, two frantic pairs of horses, called Usury and Contract, Avarice and Imposture, were subdued by the goddesses Equality, Justice, Liberality and Good Faith. All about hastened a varied throng, the famous greedy men of history, Queen Dido's husband, the venal poets and generals of antiquity, and Pythias, of that ancient commercial people the Lydians, who was offered a plateful of gold by his wife to still his appetite.

In this interesting sketch the artist remembered to add a flying Nemesis, pursuing the wealthy. And the motto, in view of the imminent downfall of the Hanse and the surrender of the old hall to Queen Bess, who chased the Germans out of England, is full of melancholic presagement: "Gold is the father of joy and the son of sorrow; who lacks it grieves, and who has it trembles."

Such was the style in which the Hanse wholesalers, like the Florentine bankers, chose to celebrate their triumphs in the last hours of prosperity, just before the death-knell was rung. So did the Fuggers. In 1580, as the firm was slowly going down grade, Hans Fugger ordered a "Triumph of the Four World Quarters," with a self-assurance which would have done credit to a Bourbon or a Hapsburg. Hans had a big castle to fill with works of art; he had ordered in rapid succession pictures of the Triumphs of Earth, Air, Water and Fire; the Five Senses; the Tower of Babel; sea-gods, shepherds, the Seven Virtues; allegories of Trade, Agriculture, Music and Science. His best idea however was undoubtedly a representation of the entire earth, laid under tribute to the House of Fugger.

In these pictures Asia rides in a camel-drawn wagon surrounded by gift-bearing Orientals; Africa on a float pulled by elephants and accompanied by Negroes bearing spices, an allusion to the Fugger monopoly. Europe is brought in by white steeds and characterized by a waterworks system. Germania, Italia, Hispania, Gallia, the chief debtors of Jacob the Rich, are painted in symbolic forms. Finally America appears, drawn by lions; Peru and Brazil accompany her, as well as a shackled pair of unlucky native wretches. Of the four pictures, two displeased Hans, who insisted that they had been painted in too great a hurry, though they are the most highly rated today. Hans liked best the American scene which is nowadays adjudged the worst.

Antwerp merchants brought the triumph concept a few stages farther along. In 1585 they decorated the city for the entry of Alexander Farnese, and on this occasion the various "nations" of merchants, Spanish, Portuguese, Italian, contributed money and ideas. They built a model of the Coliseum and filled it with symbolic representations of the Arts and Industries; there was a procession with floats, attended by amazons, nymphs and buffoons, ending in a public illumination of the great square, where amazing artificial birds flew about by the light of blazing pitch-barrels. For this fête, a gigantic engraving was ordered from Jean Neudorfer of Nürnberg, which depicts the wealth of Antwerp as a flowing fountain, around which hang the shields of all the commercial cities of Europe. A panorama of the harbor fills the background. Symbolic personages busy themselves in the foreground: Mercury, balancing on his scales Debit and Credit; Fortuna with a smoking urn, emblem of her elusiveness; Occasion, the winged goddess, with a forelock to be seized ere she soars away; as well as Discretion, Integrity and Linguistic Talent.

The best Triumph of wealth was probably the immense one of 1635, planned by Antwerp to impress the Spanish Infante Ferdinand into giving her commercial privileges. For this display, Antwerp set up a series of triumphal arches, after Rubens and the best Flemish artists had made the designs, which cost the prominent merchants 78,000 florins. From the sketches, preserved to this day, it is clear what the business man really could do when he wished to publicize his wealth, and had no inhibitions. One of these arches, symbolizing the Commerce of Antwerp, was laden with shipmasts, cornucopias and dolphins, with an Industria and a Mercury. An Arch of Money showed Fortuna with a ship, a lamb with a golden fleece, rivergods, miners and smiths, and bore the motto, "Labor Omnia Vincit"—the whole affair draped and festooned and fairly dripping with garlands of gold coins.

The result of this demonstration, it is painful to add, was the precise contrary to the expectations of the merchant community. The jealousy of the neighboring port of Amsterdam was aroused and the Infante Ferdinand was persuaded to keep the harbor of Antwerp closed to trade. Thus the unparalleled display led all too directly to ruin.

Just as Antwerp thus adorned herself, before her sacrifice, so much of the glory of commercial cities in general came during their decline. The great golden Rathaus of Augsburg was erected after the hey-day of prosperity was over. That splendid hall, with its portrayals of triumphing Emperors and its gleaming expanses of gold, was built to receive the German rulers whose bad faith had already reduced Augsburg to a mere village, as Hans Fugger complained. It was a golden monument to their own folly, set up by the Augsburg millionaires. So, too, was Antwerp's Rathaus an emblem signifying the last hours of such wealth. Both edifices are great examples of Renaissance architecture, left stranded like shells on a beach, by the receding tides of trade.

All over Southern Europe, business demanded pictures of its triumph when this period of actual triumphs was drawing to a close. The Indian summer of the Renaissance oligarch's independence was marked by a high and rich autumnal color. It was the age of the German, Flemish and Venetian colorists. The angels ordered by the patricians of Nürnberg, in the last years of that city's industrial height, were robed, winged and haloed in gold; indeed, that was almost the last glitter of this precious metal left in Germany, as the Thirty Years' War drew on. And, of course, the supreme painting of Venice was finished in a time almost of after-glow; decay had set in along the lagoons when Tintoretto, Veronese and Titian painted there; they were the multi-colored clouds that gather around a setting sun.

When it was sure of itself, commerce could outdo kings. Such self-assertion was illustrated by the Triumph of Venice, ordered from Veronese for the City Hall. This allegorical painting remains the answer to those who claim that only royalty, not commerce, can commandeer great art. In Veronese's picture, Venice is impersonated by a plump and begemmed beauty, round-faced and snub-nosed, dressed in the most splendid silks cut in the fashion of the times. She does not disguise the fact that she is heartily pleased by the tributes of Fame, Virtue, Justice, Peace, War and Art, who are bringing her laurels. Her dazzling smile and sparkling eyes mark her appetite for honor; she leans back laughing to receive her reward from heaven. On a somewhat inadequate cloud, this gorgeously voracious creature is wafted upward to the empyrean where various heavenly beings loop the loop, while one, in a spectacular nose-dive, offers a crown to the Queen City of the Adriatic.

Only in a city where business men were untroubled in their consciences could this allegory have been produced. Veronese's Venice does not worry about the sinfulness of big business, the slave-trade, the illegitimate arms-traffic, or the acceptance of unearned increment. Modern business, on the contrary, even in the recently fresco-mad America, is too timorous to continue the grand line of European Triumphs of Wealth. Much as some of our captains of industry might secretly like to have their home towns personified by corn-fed damsels, blond as wheat, covered with diamonds and ermine, to erect triumphal arches festooned with golden coins, or represent their customers as chained slaves bearing tribute to their firms, they lack the nerve to commission such projects. In our commercial towns, great business interests are represented by stern-visaged sportswomen, angular of form and pedantic of gesture, dressed after an outmoded fashion in cheesecloth, who received the homage of Sardanapalus, Julius Caesar, the Boy Scouts and the Spirit of International Good Will, without the cordial smile that hospitality would seem to dictate.

The trouble with public art of our times is not that business has supplanted royalty as a patron, but that business even in boom-time no longer has that late-Renaissance self-assurance. Even if we had a Veronese in our midst, he would get no orders from the nervous, faltering and insecure rich men of modern times in Europe or America, who wear the garb of the Venetian *Pantaloon*, but have not inherited his cheek.

THE MEDICI AS INTERMEDIARIES BETWEEN BUSINESS AND ROYALTY

Meanwhile, however, the business man struggled with royalty, and in the contest each took from the other. For example, the Florentine Medici family passed through many stages, from parvenu plebeians, to powerful individualists towering above the local nobility, and at last into the aristocracy itself. In so doing, it carried into royal circles many of the commercial ideas, with which it had been associated, including the concept of the Triumph. It was the ennobled financier's offspring, Maria de' Medici, who brought the notion to France. Following the Medicean example, later French kings had themselves painted on horseback too, in triumphs of their own, and encouraged other kings and princelings to do likewise. But mere monarchs never really equaled that Triumph which Maria ordered for herself from the atelier of Rubens. She wished to make up, by a fictitious canvas glory, for the humiliations she had actually endured in life, from her royal husband's amours and the mutinies of her son. For her victory she chose the topics herself. It was a delicate task to please her, without enraging the son, who was not on speaking terms with his mother. It was hard to glorify the hated House of Medici without offending France; and it was a strain to envelop the portly form of an overdressed dowager, and the heavy, pouched, sensual face with the little, cruel mouth. But in those days, artists were artists. So instead of grumbling about the difficulties of truckling to bankers, or the humiliation of advertising the Medicean red balls, Rubens, gathering up his brushes, exclaimed: "No topic has ever got the better of me!" And set to work.

Courageously, he depicted Maria receiving her education from the gods and her beauty from the graces. He painted the astonishment of the French king on beholding her portrait borne toward him through the skies by Amor and Hymen, in the contemplation of which His

Majesty quite forgets the city which he and his army had been busy burning in the background. Warming to his theme, Rubens called up the divinities of the deep to guide the bridal ship, with the scutcheon of the Medici, into Marseilles. With masterly ingenuity he got over the childbirth scene and went on to symbolic representations of good government. For these he erected cathedrals and palaces; he populated the skies with angels and the pavements with cupids; he flung bundles of light rays against the shields and morions of soldiers; he introduced the eagle of Jupiter and the peacocks of Juno to the fox of Wisdom; he flung the spotlight now on Florence in her lion-chariot and now on the burly amazon, La France, with her petticoats tucked up for action and her arms akimbo. Even in the gusto of creative frenzy, Rubens forgot nothing; he always remembered to include the little yapping pet dog of the queen.

As canvas after canvas was filled, it seemed that nothing more could be possible to the invention of man. Maria was seen riding to war, guiding the Ship of State, arrayed in ermine and holding the scales of justice. But in the final scene, "Time Brings Truth to Light," Rubens gathered his powers for one final thrust. With inexhaustible verve he portrayed a grizzled Time-God hoisting into the air the superb bulk of a blonde Flemish Truth, who is pointing, as well she might, at the rolling clouds whereon Maria receives at last her due: her rebellious son, in a blaze of silver armor, bends toward her and tenders a little testimonial of affection—a burning heart enclosed within a wreath. As Rubens himself said of the series: "Had I only been allowed to choose the topics myself, I could have made the whole thing still more tactful."

Thus, out of commerce, came the impetus for the splendor of Absolute Monarchies. In turn, then, kings began to order tapestries depicting themselves amid chained elephants and sacrificial bulls, accompanied by Diana, Apollo, Moses, Music and Pomona. The great public, oddly enough, accepted such self-glorification as more appropriate to kings than to the millionaires from whom they borrowed the whole idea. A triumph of autocrats or generals, Monarchy or Mars, was popular, but not one of Wealth.

FOLK HOSTILITY TO WEALTH

In proportion to the flaunting of his gains, hostility toward the business man grew during the sixteenth century. The most diverse elements of the population found in that opposition a common front. Classes otherwise irreconcilable were joined together by their animosity: peasants and their natural foes, the impoverished nobles; small shopkeepers and artisans; skeptical satirists and devout preachers both of Catholic and Protestant creeds. The cobbler-poet, Hans Sachs, agreed with the cosmopolitan scholar, Erasmus.

This may have been because prices were steadily rising; they went up so much that a sum of money sufficient to buy a whole costume in one generation would only purchase a pair of shoes in the next. The phenomenon is supposed, by modern students, to have been due to the continual influx of precious metals from Peru and the increased European mining; it was comparable to that tremendous boost in the prices of land and pigs and other commodities which, it has been discovered, followed the conquests of Alexander the Great in the Near East, when his armies poured the treasures of the Eastern kings upon the Mediterranean commerce. But the common people, needless to say, in the sixteenth century, unanimously laid the blame on the business man, whose unscrupulous monopolies were thought to cause the whole distress. Upon Ambrosius Höchstetter German hatred largely centered; yet the crowd also turned on Fugger, as in modern times it turns a congressional investigation upon individual trust-builders or speculators as scapegoats.

Small shopkeepers, manufacturers and importers felt a grievance greater than that even of consumers. Cloth-producers complained that the large-scale Fugger methods were cutting into their businesses. Everywhere small men were ousted by the big, in mining, sugar and spice importation, grain and textile traffic. The expanding, international intercourse of the Cinquecento pressed the mediaeval, petty type of trader to the wall. He also harbored grievances against the financiers. At Lyons, about 1551–56, the French traders in goods wrote lively remonstrances against Italian bankers, accusing them of sucking up all the gold and removing it from the country, to the damage of business in general.

Perhaps it is a little strange to find impoverished noblemen allying themselves openly with small shopkeepers in the German Reichstag. But the minor nobility sympathized with the minor business men. The poor and uneducated sons of the lesser nobles found themselves pushed out of high places in Church and state by the progeny of rich merchants. Thus that chief mouthpiece of the knighthood during the Reformation, Ulrich von Hutten, bore a bitter resentment toward Fugger, partly on religious and partly on economic grounds.

Peasants, though the intransigent enemies of the nobles, were of their opinion when it came to accusing the monopolists. Not only were they hit by the rising prices of manufactured commodities. They were also hit by other exactions of the cities. As the great cities grew, they spread their power over the surrounding countryside to assure a steady supply of grain and, with such inadequate transportation, only cruel measures and forced sales could save a city of 100,000 souls from starvation. Those on the land suffered to keep those in town alive.

English farming folk likewise abhorred the business men who, coming out from London and settling down as "esquires," turned the farmers out to starve and let the "sheep eat out the men." In their eagerness to produce the profitable wool, the squires drove Englishmen from the furrow, creating a houseless, landless proletariat until, in the late 1700's, almost nothing was lacking for industrialism but the steam.

German peasants were even more embittered than the English because, during the peasants' wars, the cities had joined the nobles in putting down the wretched rural revolters. The city burghers, however, met their own doom when the nobles, in the service of princes, turned to destroying the freedom of the towns.

Such complaints filled the age. In Rome, a mob pounded on the gates of the Strozzi bankers, who held the monopoly for grain-provision and were thought responsible for producing a scarcity. In Spain, the Cortes wailed incessantly about the Genoese bankers and the flow of gold to Antwerp; the second bankruptcy of Philip II in 1575 endeared him to the hearts of his humbler subjects, pleased that alien bankers were getting their just deserts.

An interesting case of "technological unemployment" in Antwerp, also a phenomenon of the times, is mentioned by Gérard. In 1554, Gilbert van Schoonbeke established new breweries, and invented a great machine to pump water into them. This sealed the doom of the small brewers who had trouble in getting their water supply. The crowd went hunting Schoonbeke and howled before his house. Blood was shed, and the inventor-entrepreneur fled by night to Hungary.

In Germany the anti-plutocratic movement was well and consciously organized because Germany had been a paradise for the petty bourgeois, compared with the rest of Europe. In every German Reichstag since the opening of the century, the trust-busters and foes of the chainstore, or rather branch-office, system launched their agitation. At the Reichstag in Worms in 1521, a proposal was made to disband the great companies and shut down the monopolists. Nürnberg and Ulm wanted to restrict firms to a capital of only 50,000 florins, and permit only three branch offices.

The great trial of strength was held in 1523. The foes of the big business men proposed to call them upon the carpet before the *Reichskammergericht*. They intended to investigate Fugger especially. When the invitation to the trial reached him, the grey-haired old Jacob Fugger was sitting in his famous Golden Writing Room. Without delay, he penned a note to Duke George of Saxony and to

Charles V. The trial was put off indefinitely. As Jacob said to Duke George, with Renaissance frankness: "Many are my enemies. They say, I am rich. And I *am* rich, by God's grace and no harm to anyone."

Of course, this movement could have but one outcome. The great firms kept their monopolies. How could it be otherwise? It was true that Charles V had been elected as Emperor of Germany on a platform containing a plank opposing trusts; but, since Jacob Fugger managed the bribery of the Electors and insisted upon some sort of return for the outlay, the monarch, however embarrassed he felt, had no choice in the matter.

In the light of modern times, the elaborate tissue of defense is interesting to review. A long and learned brief laid before the Reichstag declared that the merchants were not the only monopolists; the princes, who gave the privileges away in the first place, should also be investigated. Naturally this suggestion touched a tender spot in the upper ranks. The university groups, as well, must have been impressed by the lectures of Dr. Eck—whom Dr. Martin Luther called Dreck—the learned opponent of Luther on economic and religious matters. Eck's traveling expenses were paid by the firm of Fugger. Antagonists with conscientious scruples were met by the humanist scholar and jurist, Dr. Conrad Peutinger, whom the Fugger engaged to prepare their legal case before the Reichstag. Peutinger, as Strieder states, was the defender of absolute freedom of trade, genuine laissez faire; he explained the necessity of private-capitalistic monopolies and cartels as a part of that freedom. In complete opposition to Luther, he laid down the principle: "Every merchant may sell his wares as dear as he can and wishes. Thereby he does not sin against common law."

Companies were on the defensive in England too, but not until the turn of the century. It was not until 1601 that the Secretary of the Merchant Adventurers, John Wheeler, felt it obligatory to write a pamphlet entitled: "A Treatise of Commerce, wherein are shewed the commodities arising by a well-ordered and ruled trade, such as that of the Society of Merchant Adventurers is proved to be, written principallie for the better information of those, who doubt of the necessariness of the said Societie in the State of the Realme of England."

A precedent for coming generations in other lands was set by the early German anti-monopoly movement. Indeed, its echoes ring to this very hour for, around 1905, a German Ambassador, Speck von Sternberg, urged a study of the German anti-monopoly movement upon the great American trust-buster, Theodore Roosevelt. In his study of "Germany and America in World Politics," Alfred Vagts brings out the fact that von Sternberg told the President that the arguments and laws of the 1500's in Germany would be pertinent for his purposes.

TRUST-BUSTING AND RELIGIOUS REFORM

Behind the glitter of the Renaissance pageantry, accordingly, was a dark, seething background of hatred and envy. Popular animosity toward monopolists, bankers and speculators naturally played into the movement to reform the Roman Church. Economic and religious trends flowed together.

The connection is shown in such art works as those of Quentin Matsys, who lived in Antwerp, the most gorgeous city of Europe, and yet drew grotesques more diabolic than the cartoons of a Diego Rivera in our twentieth-century society. Matsys painted the richly dressed burghers, jesting in the candlelight, while, in the dim shadows above them, an uncanny visage sneered. He delineated the Christian usurers, their faces showing bloated lust, unclean cupidity; he depicted the wife of the money-changer, turning from her prayer-book to watch with fascinated eyes the coins slipping through her husband's fingers. Another Flemish artist, Marinus van Romerswael, in 1538 produced a painting of St. Matthew which, Brising remarks, was a reflection of the rising wrath against tax-collectors. Here the Saint is portrayed in his employment as a publican, a Roman tax-gatherer; Christ appears before him to convert him, gesturing to Matthew to renounce his profession. In 1575, Jan Sanders painted Christ chasing the money-changers from the temple; by that time, they were being ruined in Antwerp by their own folly, if not by a higher power.

The feeling which underlay such portrayals was expressed by the religious reformers of the age. Both Luther and Calvin were opponents of big business as much as of the Church, at least in the beginning; indeed, they viewed the two problems as parts of the same thing. Lesser evangelists also cried out upon the subject of monopolists; Geiler von Kaisersberg, for instance, preached in the very citadel of the Fuggers, at Augsburg, and denounced the Christian usurers whom he compared very unfavorably with the Jews. He advised the extermination of monopolists, as of wolves, without mercy.

If there was no Reformation in Italy, it may have been because men had seen so much of commercial as well as monkish corruption that they were skeptical of reforming either. Savonarola had failed to purge Florence, in his brief theocratic experiment. The only prescription left was the doleful one of Machiavelli who thought that poverty alone could produce a stern and virtuous race of burghers to equal the early Romans. While the Italians were too well acquainted with the difficulties of restraining bankers and merchants to undertake a great crusade, the French and Germans were still naïve enough to try. In these capitalistically less-experienced lands, a Calvin could propose the subjection of the business man to an autocratic government of deacons. And a Luther likewise arose to suggest more modestly that every man's conscience would lead him to virtue.

Calvin's bold experiment in controlling business is one of the most famous attempts of the kind. It lasted far longer than Savonarola's, although, like the earlier experiment it ended in failure. In Geneva, under Calvin, for a number of years, everything was regulated in minute detail by a body of clergy and laymen, the Consistory, with power to supervise matters moral and commercial. They ordered markets, prices, rents and rates; they forbade the opening of new banks and put heretics to death. Any luxury in clothes that might make new banks necessary was repressed. They proposed to excommunicate drunkards, dancers and usurers. Geneva was to be the "most perfect school of Christ that ever was on earth since the days of the Apostles."

But even the will of men grim enough to burn to death 150 heretics inside 60 years was not sufficient to stop usury. No usurer was put to the ultimate punishment, although, as Tawney says, a mere child was beheaded for striking its parents. The difficulties in the way of condemning malpractices in business were illustrated when Theodore Beza, Calvin's successor, had to cry out in 1574 against members of the holy Council itself who had speculated in wheat.

Not only did Calvinism fail to repress business enterprise, but it became, ironically or dialectically enough, the very promoter of capitalism. The most able business men of France embraced the creed with enthusiasm; and when they suffered exile, they carried it with them to England and Germany. Calvinism seemed to nourish the virtues of thrift, sobriety, and single-mindedness, which made for business success. Moreover, Calvin, though eager to restrain big business, was glad to assist moderate business; though he wished to forbid excessive rates, unproductive loans and the mulcting of the poor, he stopped short of the early Christian attitude of uncompromising hostility to interest-taking. Indeed, since his father had been the financial agent of a bishop, this realistic attitude was not surprising; in a famous tract, Calvin justified the acceptance of a moderate rate as being in harmony with the good life. This doctrine met with warm approval in many quarters. Though Weber denies that it produced a rush of business men to Calvinism, it certainly inspired some converts. Tawney quotes a British pamphleteer as saying: "It took with the brethren like polygamy with the Turks."

Parallel to the story of Calvinism, ran that of Lutheranism. Luther, like Calvin, was the foe of exorbitant profits; yet he, too, was willing to meet the business man half-way, in the hope that, by compromise, it would be possible to regulate his actions. And the result was, in Germany as in Switzerland, where Calvin actually tried his scheme, and France, where he made his chief converts, that the concessions were appreciated while the condemnations were ineffective. Thus Protestantism, though it started out to reform business, ended by producing the Puritan entrepreneur, ideally fitted to form modern capitalism.

LUTHER AND BIG BUSINESS

Luther was more conservative than Calvin. The son of a man who owned a small ore-refinery, Luther inherited the lower-middleclass economic point of view. He had a horror of the money-lender, like the mining magnate Fugger, who enslaved men of his father's class. He thought it very unfair of a lender to force a producer to pay the same rate of interest year after year, what with the pests and bad harvests, when God made the years so uneven. Nevertheless he had no desire to abolish interest altogether, like the early Christian Fathers. He thought that four to six per cent was consistent with salvation and agreed that widows and orphans especially might live on rents and investments. This ideal was widely accepted by popular opinion and, as a tractarian declared, made "divers zealous ministers wish to pass for orphans of the first rank."

Luther trusted in an appeal to the business man's conscience. In a powerful pamphlet, "On Trade and Usury," he issued one of the most sweeping indictments of business known to history. This treatise ignored Jews entirely; it was directed exclusively at men of the purest Saxon and Anglo-Saxon stock and of the deepest piety—at the Danes, the English, and the inhabitants of Lüneburg and Augsburg. Luther said that the folk of that supremely Nordic-Christian region, Holstein, were so vicious that it would not be surprising to see them chew up one another. Not content with lending at ten per cent, they forced the unhappy debtor to take the sum in over-valued stocks of goods. "Ei," cried Luther, "these are not highway robbers, but house-robbers and stable-robbers . . . They are not men, but wolves and unreasonable beasts that do not believe there is a God." In fact, surveying the European situation, Luther exclaimed: "I wonder that, with such immeasurable usury, the world still stands!"

This document was written in 1524, at the very height of the anti-trust movement in Germany. Luther also preached in Augsburg, in the camp of the enemy, the Fugger firm. He analyzed the evils of society and proposed a cure. In his condemnation, Luther attacked the very roots of the society taking form as our own. His proposed remedies would send us all back to the plow.

Luther despised a merchant who, instead of traveling about over land and sea, preferred to sit at home in a "rich trade-city" and sell, for a high price, goods which he did not even have in his warehouse but proceeded to buy for less than he received as a salesman. Such "fynantzer" were admired by some folk as "great, clever men," but Luther gave them a good early German name—"gorgel stecher," cut-throats. Dealing in futures, he thought, is "a trick very plainly against God's word, against reason and all righteousness, out of sheer un-checked rapacity." Those who go further and take advantage of a scarcity to sell dearer he called "public thieves, robbers and usurers." He raged at merchants engaged in transferring German money to Rome for the Church, to Portugal for spices, to England for wool, or to Calcutta for silk—all for goods "that only serve show and no useful purpose, and suck the gold out of land and folk, and would not be allowed if we had a government." Thus Luther revived the ancient complaint of the Greeks and Romans condemning the merchant for bearing their good metal away to the East for luxuries.

Against cartels, Luther fumed: "This trick, I hear, the English mer-chants work most glaringly and often . . . See now, what greed can and dares do!" Against monopolists his wrath was boundless: "They raise or lower the price at their pleasure and suppress and destroy all small merchants, just as the carp devours the small fish, just as though they were lords over all God's creatures and free from all laws of faith and love . . . Is it any wonder they are become kings and we beggars?"

If the world were perfect, according to Luther, there would be only barter and no man would dare to sell as dear as he chose. Middlemen would be eliminated. But if the world remained imperfect, at least every merchant should content himself with a bare living and no thought of excessive profit; everybody should pay cash for all goods; nobody should go security on another's loan. Finally, those who lent money should share the risks of the borrower; those who invest should make sure exactly in what they put their money and never "play blind man's buff." And of course, the great trusts and monopolies must go: "If the great Companies remain, Right and Honesty must go under. If Right and Honesty are to stay, the Companies must go. The bed is too narrow, sayeth Isaiah; one must fall out." And again: "Let no one ask how he may, with a good conscience, join in these companies. There is no advice but: stay out!"

LUTHER AND THE FUGGERS

Luther was to the Fuggers what Savonarola, a few years before, had been to the Medici: a grim monkish enemy. In an open letter to the Medicean Pope, Luther absolved Leo of blame for the corruption in the Church. It was the Fuggers whom he denounced. He wished to separate finance and religion from what he considered their unholy alliance. He particularly objected to the tendency to make a large-scale business out of the sale of offices and papal documents remitting sins. He blamed the preacher Tetzel for traveling about with these documents, selling them to the people. But still more he blamed the Fuggers, whose agent accompanied Tetzel, collected the money and transmitted it, minus a handsome commission, to Rome.

This apparent draining of gold to Rome was a real foundation of the Protestant complaint in Germany. So it was also in England, where the shipment of a large sum of money out of that country by Italian bankers to pay for Cardinal Wolsey's hat was one of the prime causes of popular indignation before the Reformation swept out both Church and bankers. But in the case of Germany, the popular complaint was not grounded entirely upon facts. As some scholars, notably Schulte, have pointed out, it was not Rome alone which sought to raise money from the sale of remissions of sins, but German business men likewise; and the aims of many of these sales were really sincerely charitable and meritorious.

The Pope wanted to raise money because, being a Florentine, he was an expansionist. It was his intention to enlarge, by force, the boundaries of the Papal States and, at the same time, to symbolize his papal-imperialist enlargement by erecting a vast dome on top of St. Peter's. Just as the Florentine wool-merchants had built their mighty Dome by the Arno, while they seized new markets in the East, so the Medici in Rome intended to expand aesthetically as well as literally. But while the Pope called for great funds, and used the Fuggers as his agents, the clamor for funds was quite as loud in German cities; the business patricians of the various towns in South Germany also were caught by the building boom. They wished to put up a hospital for the poor and for infants in Strassburg, for example; cathedrals in Cracow, Augsburg and Trier; and to erect or repair other edifices in Constance, Ingolstadt, Bamberg, Nürnberg; and the mining-town of Annaberg in Saxony, with its mushroom growth, now wished to have a Gothic cathedral like old towns. All these bourgeois councillors hoped to raise money by obtaining the aid of the Church. The Church would sell remissions of sins; the business men would manage the affair and take a percentage of the proceeds. As a matter of fact, what was done was on a footing with what takes place today in community drives and appeals for charitable and aesthetic causes. And the older practice at least resulted in a glory of late Gothic art over Germany. Nevertheless it was, undeniably, poor business; such a large part of each transaction went into "overhead," the painting of gorgeous documents upon sheepskin, the processions with choristers and candles and banners, that there was never much left for the original "cause." Poor business management, in the end, was heavily responsible for the religious Reformation in Germany.

Once started, the Reformation might have been effected as thoroughly in Germany as in England, had not the tremendous power of the Catholic Fugger, allied with the Church, stood in the way. There was no such English business interest to stop the English Reformation. But Anton Fugger financed the Catholic Hapsburgs, and, since there were few Protestant bankers willing or able to supply troops for the cause of Reform, the integral victory of German Protestantism was doomed in the directors' sanctum before it was tried in the field.

One Protestant business man, to be sure, was willing to stake his fortune for his faith. Jacob Herbrot, a self-made man who rose in cloth-manufacture to banking and became Mayor of Augsburg, did try to place his office and his wealth at the service of the Lutherans in the Schmalkaldic War. However, his plebeian origin and his faith were both an offense to the Catholic patricians of that city; with the Fuggers as allies, they started a run on Herbrot's bank. Vainly the Emperor tried to raise credit to save him for, though an opponent of Herbrot's cause, the Emperor was heavily in debt to Herbrot. But no one would lend a ducat to the Emperor; thus Herbrot failed for 766,029 florins and died in a debtors' jail. A greater victory was thereby won without blood for the Catholic cause than many a pious general obtained in campaigning.

Besides stirring up opposition that favored the Reformation and then resisting its spread, the Fuggers helped to bring on the "Counter-Reformation" of the Jesuits bent on restoring the power of the Church in Germany. Hans Fugger built the Jesuits a college in Augsburg and richly endowed it. The close connection of the fortunes and faith of the firm may be illustrated in a story recited by Lill: "As in 1582, the glad news came that the King of Spain intended to pay up his gigantic debts to the Fugger," Hans "ordered in his first moment of joy a silver robe for the celebration of mass, to be made in Florence, which he wanted to give out of gratitude to the newly built Jesuit college. Was the order carried out, when the report was proved false?"

The rôle of the financier, or, as Luther called him, the "fynantzer," in the religious movements of Europe has been insufficiently studied. But at least an interesting parallel may be drawn between the Fugger who helped to prevent a clear victory of Lutheranism in Germany and the various Italian bankers, such as Diaceto and the Gondi, who kept Calvinism from a triumph in France. England's easier lot was partly due to a less complex financial situation.

THE GREAT CRASH

While the business men were still riding high, filled with colossal ambitions, the Emperors, to whom they had lent huge sums, were growing nervous. It is said that one of the reasons why Charles V abdicated suddenly and went into a monastery was his horror before the mounting piles of his debts. His son, Philip II, heir to the Spanish part of the Empire, observed that he could not pay his father's debts even if he had peace and a good administration. Since he had neither, his plight was even more hopeless. Feverishly he pawned mines and domains, mortgaged the silver fleets before they sailed, confiscated his subjects' property. In his desperation, he consulted theologians about the canon law, and enquired whether paying interest were not a sin. Going bankrupt in 1557, upon their advice, he found that he had eight million ducats of debts and three million ducats of running expenses; but, to meet them, only one and one-third millions in assets. Yet the blind business men went on lending to him until Spain was bankrupt a second time.

Portugal fared no better. Having flung away millions in loans upon a Turkish war and the upkeep of courts, there was nothing left to do but declare that the king's conscience forbade him to pay usurers, and let Nürnberg, Antwerp, Augsburg and Genoa suffer. So the two proud empires, built upon discovery and conquest, passed mournfully into bankruptcy, and the European investing public faced ruin. The sequel to the magnificent adventures of the conquistadores was pitiable indeed.

France and the Spanish Netherlands became bankrupt likewise. Hardly anything was left for repayment of the enormous sums which the business men had poured into these countries. Almost universal tragedy overtook European business toward the close of the sixteenth century. As the scholar Ehrenberg has been at such pains to show, nearly all the chief firms in Europe ended in disaster, brought on by their over-optimism during the glow of the Age of Discovery. The rich Manlichs, who owned a shipping line to the Levant and employed Hans Ulrich Krafft, to whose memoirs we have previously alluded, were wrecked by imposing too much faith in princes. So were the Neidharts; the Welser lost not only the Venezuela jungles which they had explored but 182,199 florins in French royal letters and loans to Spain and the Netherlands. By 1580, those of the Welser clan who could do so, sold out and retired; by 1614, the firm collapsed and the last members ended wretchedly in irons. Even the great Fuggers, though they steered a skillful course, failed toward the middle of the seventeenth century; they could not get out of Spain even after her second bankruptcy in 1575 had disclosed some thirty-seven millions of ducats in debts on the royal books, and almost trivial assets. Hoping and lending, bribing courtiers and indeed the king's confessor, the Fuggers clung to the wreck, until they at last went under themselves for eight million gulden. Nothing remained but a title and a few farms which Jacob Fugger the Rich, in the preceding century, had bought because, while they only yielded three per cent income, he felt safer with a plow in the background.

There were only half-a-dozen really big firms, according to Ehrenberg, which came through with success, and they had all been guided by skeptical men proof against popular hysteria. These men, oddly enough, were all Nürnbergers. The wisest heads in the firm of Anton Haug and Hans Langnauer knew when to stay out; they passed out of that company while it was still making forty-seven per cent a year on silks, cotton, copper, silver and English wool. The rest of the partners hung on, however, buying royal letters of Portugal and Spain, and putting a fortune into mines. By 1561, they found themselves with frozen assets or total losses.

Old Endres Imhof, who had sat in the council-chamber of Nürnberg fifty-six years, knew too much of politics to trust the big boom in Antwerp or Lyons. As long as he could he restrained the younger members of his house; when he saw they were bent on folly, he withdrew his own capital and retired in person. His firm emerged from the general crash shaken but alive. The memorial left by the Imhof family in Nürnberg is the marvelous tabernacle made by Adam Krafft in the Sanct Lorenz Church—a miniature skyscraper, encrusted with figures of legend and story, soaring upward with delicacy and daring. In its day, it caused a great sensation among the monument-fancying business men.

One shining example of a perspicacious business man in that century was furnished by the Tucher family, also of Nürnberg. The Tucher family outlasted even the Fugger in commerce; it is still doing business in the old city—one of the most venerable concerns afloat on earth. This unique firm owes its remarkable preservation to the healthy distrust of kings and investors exhibited by Lienhard, Anton and Lazarus Tucher during the first modern boom.

Anton, the highly respectable Burgomaster of Nürnberg, owning a great wholesale business with branch offices in Antwerp and Lyons, resisted the infectious enthusiasm of both Exchanges. He kept to his fixed principle of refusing to lend a penny to a crowned head. In 1561, Lienhard wrote to his distant cousin, Lazarus:

> The hard wars have now lasted many years, and the great potentates in many countries have taken up great sums of money

at high interest rates . . . Everybody wanted to get rich . . . took what he could buy . . . and did not think in what difficulties he would fall if the princes did not keep their promises, and it is at last evident, that faith will no longer be kept among the great powers.

Lazarus, living in Antwerp where he helped Thomas Gresham, was one of the most seasoned manipulators of his time. Admitting he had lost 40,000 ducats to the King of Portugal, he replied that he was unusually lucky:

> There are times when one, especially I who am an old courtier, cannot avoid serving the Great; only two days ago, I was compelled to yield to repeated urgent insistence and lend 1500 florins to my gracious Lord, the Prince of Orange, for his marriage . . . Nowadays I demand neither too much nor too little interest, in order to facilitate the repayment of my capital. For my efforts are all now aimed at one goal, to pry myself loose from all potentates and lords and so to invest my wealth that I can get it at my pleasure, as the hard times at present demand, and my own age and the weakness of my body. I now think more than ever of achieving peaceful days for the rest of my life, and therefore spend the summers in my house Gallifort, where I am seldom without excellent company. (Ehrenberg)

Lazarus pulled out in time. He and the little band of shrewd and hard-headed merchants of Nürnberg were the sole survivors of the catastrophe. The century, which had opened with such joy, experienced hideous reverses. The Wars of Religion engulfed the Continent and could not be extinguished for a hundred years. Warfare now turned into a Chinese anarchy. Starving armies, without funds, turned to pillage like bandits and lived as they could off the land. Even kings and queens, pawning their plate and jewels, began to beg, bully and coerce merchants. Merchants became hunted creatures, fleeing from city to city. The two chief money-markets, Antwerp and Lyons, were laid waste.

Thus the Cinquecento, opening with the Triumph idea and the glorification of Fortuna, closed on a note of profound tragedy. It seems obvious enough that the cause of this tragedy was not the malevolence of Hebrew usurers, but the bad faith of Christian kings coupled with the overweening ambition and pride of the Christian money-lenders. Christian merchants aided Christian kings to break the Church law against usury; they put their wealth out at interest in royal loans. The Spanish and Portuguese kings, when they could not repay a penny, turned Church law against their creditors and made religious scruples the excuse for bankruptcy. The greatest Christian business men of Europe were then not only beggared but disgraced as usurers. Yet it was in 1596–98 that Shakespeare wrote "The Merchant of Venice"—an attack on the Jews.

Surely the *hybris* of the Christian money-lender was more typical of the age than that of a Jew. Much more characteristic, it would seem, was the true story of Heinrich Wolf of Nürnberg, who lent his monarch, Maximilian I, a handsome sum of money which was of course not repaid. Seeking to save this sum, he threw good money after bad, and lent until his fortune was all gone. As he went bankrupt, the heart of Max felt a slight twinge of remorse; to make some amends to his creditor, Max raised Wolf's son Balthasar to the nobility and made him a court councillor. But this only turned the knife in the wound, for the son, become a lord, grew proud and was ashamed of his plebeian and ruined father. Scorned by his own flesh and blood, stripped of his fortunes by a faithless king, Wolf knew the bitterness of a *Lear* or a *Shylock* and died of a broken heart.

With the Continent delivered over to the *Four Horsemen of the Apocalypse*, whose ravages were pictured by Dürer, there was an end to the European merchant power in the old centers of Europe. But the oligarch had one more chance. A fresh race of successful business rulers arose in the bogs of Holland.

XI

THE DUTCH BUSINESS EMPIRE

UP TO THE SEVENTEENTH CENTURY, the trader was often able to rule cities, more or less independently of superior control, and to direct far-flung federations of towns. Alexandria, Lübeck, Florence, Antwerp, and Augsburg were evidence enough of his governmental abilities. But in the seventeenth century came his first chance to run an entire country. At last, in Holland—to give the briefer name to the United Provinces of the Netherlands—he was absolute and undisputed master over a whole folk.

Necessity compelled this self-assertion. He had to beat off the claims of Catholic Spain, at no matter what cost of blood and coin, because the Dutch, the folk most completely absorbed in commercial to the exclusion of other activities, could not wring the slightest sympathy from the Spanish, who were in that age the people with the very least understanding or talent for trade. The Spanish State was absolutist and insolvent; it was the worst imaginable debtor; it was delivered up to a clergy with mediaeval notions of restricting trade and men, and to an aristocracy of the most extreme type, entirely devoid of comprehension for any "useful" activity. Even had there been no Luther or Calvin, commercial liberalism and aristocratic absolutism would have been unable to harmonize.

And there were other very cogent reasons for the rebellion of the Dutch business men against Spain. The chief insurgents at Amsterdam, by far the richest and most important city in the revolting provinces, were after all the mildest of men and the most concerned economically in keeping peace with Spain. They were a body of Protestant grain-dealers who were all closely related by marriage, lived together in the same quarter of town, and professed the same creed which happened to be that of the men of the Baltic North from whom they bought their supplies. These insurgents were the wealthiest block of tax-payers in Amsterdam, says Elias, and their best customer was Spain. Hence they did not rush madly off to attack the "wicked" Papists, who were after all the chief purchasers of their grain-cargoes. Instead they waited—until a despotic Catholic parvenu merchant, one Hendrik Dirckszoon, called the "grooten Monarcha," who had seized the government of the city in a thoroughly Medicean manner and thought to rid himself of the richest families in the city, banished them on the excellent pretext of religious difference. It was this mishap that finally convinced amiable Protestant wholesalers that they must sacrifice fortunes and necks in the holy cause of faith and freedom.

Mynheer Dirckszoon was an extraordinary person. He seized the reins of government in 1535 on the ground that the excesses of Anabaptist workingmen required a firm hand and ruthlessly suppressed this menace to religion and capitalism. That he was a fanatic Catholic and put Lutherans as well as Anabaptists to death, even having the seventy-year-old Baerdesen flogged and jailed, was doubtless difficult for the Protestant grain-dealers to endure. But that he grasped and monopolized the offices at Amsterdam was intolerable. The great Monarcha was a burgomaster no less than fourteen times; his son Dirck once; his son-in-law three times; his sister's husband twelve times and her son twice; his cousin Bam five times; one of the intermarried clan of the Occos, relatives of the rich merchant and factor of the Danish king, Popius Occo, four times; and a cousin of the closely allied Buick family, no less than seventeen times. This situation could not be suffered. So Protestant grain-dealers, aided by a good many Catholics, strove to oust the tyrant. For their temerity he sent them into exile but thereby created deadly enemies for himself and for Spain.

Who does not know the melodramatic story of what the fugitive traders did? During their years of banishment, they kept up the conflict with Spain out of funds they had carried with them in their flight. Some, taking up arms, joined the semi-piratical crews which cleared the ocean highways of Spanish ships. Who can forget the tales told by the American historian, Motley, of these wild bands, sneeringly called "beggars" by the enemy, who proudly adopted the title of "Oude Wader-Geuzen" (Old Sea-Beggars) and, wearing over their armor the tattered chasubles from some looted church, boarded and sank the tall galleons of Alva? Who needs to be reminded of the fight off Bergen op Zoom, in which the Dutchman showed just how far he could go when thoroughly aroused? In that epic conflict, the Zeelanders were carried to such heights of blind fury that they actually flung Spaniards overboard without even stopping to strip the gold chains from their victims' necks!

This was certainly the heroic age of the Dutch trader, marked by a grim strength and Puritan simplicity that later generations could only envy. He knew danger and exile as well as profit and loss. His thirst for gain was ennobled by the highest motives of religion and patriotism, the latter fortunately running parallel with, and seldom counter to, the former.

Yet one must be cautious about exaggerating the blind ferocity of those rebel Protestant grain-dealers. The battle of Bergen op Zoom was admittedly unique, and the Zeelanders were known to be much more given to war and privateering than other Dutch; a rage so blind as to overlook the glitter of gold was uncommon. The merchant generally confined his activities to cash transactions; ardently patriotic and Protestant as was the prominent Amsterdam family of the Nuts, it is unrecorded if Lubbert Lubbertszoon Nut ever, in a fit of pure choler, threw a gold chain into the sea, even though it were attached to the neck of a Papist. Few of the exiled traders, while they one and all adopted the name of "Sea-Beggars," were to be found swarming, cutlass in hand, as Motley might say, over the decks of the foe; most of them merely paid a lot of hungry Dutch and Germans to do their swarming for them. Moreover, they relented very far toward Catholics in general and Spain in particular, as soon as they had reached the nearest goal: the spoils of office at Amsterdam.

They retook the city in 1578. It was their turn to send into exile the great Monarcha, now grey-haired but still doughty and derisive. He went out between two bristling rows of spears; and with him departed the Bams and Occos, while, in the excitement, a lot of old Buicks were scrapped too. But with this accomplished, the war-fury of the Sea-Beggars began to cool.

The triumphant traders were not bigots; they did not open up such a reign of terror as "Bloody Mary" launched in contemporary England; their tolerance was as calculated as had been Dirckszoon's fanaticism. They were very generous to Catholics, many of whom had opposed the Monarcha; the new government was a coalition in which a full third was of King Philip's faith. And they all got along quite amicably together under the new motto, "deal gently" or "zagetiljck handeln." The war with Spain was not prosecuted with such vigor as before; and at last, by 1609, the twelve-year truce with the enemy was signed. There were indeed weighty reasons for the Sea-Beggars and still more for their sons to spare the "wicked" Papists, who were still the best customers for Baltic grain. The silver supply from Spanish mines was needed for currency; merchants were tired of paying half their incomes in war-taxes; and the directors of the East India Company had already attained what they wanted: a free hand in the Indian waters hitherto monopolized by Portugal and Spain.

The Sea-Beggars, as they continued to be called, rested upon their laurels; they began to form, paradoxically as it sounds, a Beggar-Aristocracy. They had founded the East India Company, the Amsterdam Bank and the Amsterdam Exchange, three great institutions that lasted for two centuries. Pioneers had opened up in every quarter of the world new fields for exploitation. The Beggars, and still more their sons, began to retire from active life, from business as from war; they built fine palaces and commenced to look up their genealogies. The settling-back process was soon far advanced. The ruling class desired only peace and the status quo.

No ruling class at Amsterdam, however, got a chance to maintain a status quo very long. The dynasties of business men were more un-stable than those of kings. No sooner had one group of traders, satiated with the proceeds of a war well won, settled back in supine repletion, to live on rents and grow fat in peace—than there arose a fresh body of lean and hungry seekers for more trouble and fresh openings. And so, after the Beggars calmed down and their ardor against the national foe had been dampened, they were rudely put out of office by a group of men in whom both economic ambition and religious conviction now burned brighter: the Calvinists.

The Calvinist régime of eleven years (1611–22) at Amsterdam was entirely different from the Geneva experiment in the early 1500's. Cal-vin had determined at Geneva to build a Utopian state in which the business man should be subdued; Calvinist traders at Amsterdam seized the government only to further mighty business projects. Calvin at Geneva had intended to forbid usury and monopoly and reduce the business man to social harmlessness; the group around Reynier Pauw, the staunch Calvinist at Amsterdam, was bent on forming a new and immense monopoly, a great trading company which could wrest from Spain and Portugal the colonies of America, as the East India Company had taken the colonies of the Orient.

The Sea-Beggars could not be made to take an interest in the project. Though they remained as inimical to the national enemy as before, they knew that a fresh war with the Papists might endanger the opera-tion of the East India Company, already so well established, and of which they monopolized the directorial positions. The Calvinists were not only aroused by religious fervor to attack Catholic Spain; they had the most solid economic reasons for wishing to fight her afresh and, in the pamphlet literature of the period, it was the latter they chiefly adduced.

The relative weight of the two motives, religious and economic, it is very difficult to judge in men of a period so remote. Reynier Pauw was the very pattern of the Calvinist business man; he might have been brought forward by Max Weber as an instance of the Puritan influence in the formation of the capitalist mentality. Violent and hot-tempered, convinced of his holy calling as defender of the faith, nar-row and upright and simple in his mode of living, he was a grim and respected figure. Perhaps Calvinism played the greater part in the formation of this man's character, according to the Weber thesis; it may have been responsible for his single-minded pursuit of his one aim, shutting out the distractions of art and pleasure to the better concentration upon wealth-gathering; no doubt his leadership was strengthened by the amazing self-assurance of one who knew himself the Elect of God and responsible to no earthly power for his conscience or his salvation.

For Pauw there existed no conflict between religion and business; both were furthered by the same means. He forced through the war with Spain and helped bring to the block the grey head of the peace-advocate, Van Oldenbarneveldt; he put through the Assembly of the States-General a law forming a West Indies Company, and he and his friends sat in the high seats thereof. Of the seven directors appointed to administer that Company from Amsterdam, all were close to the Calvinist leaders: three were relatives of Pauw himself, who also secured for his nephew the command of the Company's fleet sent to Brazil. The other four posts were shared by a nephew and son-in-law of the Calvinist Witsen and relatives of Cromhout and Oetgens, two other ringleaders. True, religion was by no means forgotten: a strict Calvinist régime was put through at Amsterdam. But religious matters did not engross the entire attention of the men in power, who seem to have had plenty of time to speculate with State money in the Company's shares.

Merely as a religious group, the Calvinists could not have held Amsterdam; they had the narrowest majority in the government and some of their members were pure opportunists "converted" with suspicious haste. In fact their rule was upheld by other men who also sought the spoils of the West Indies. Unquestionably, Reynier Pauw was the most sincere Calvinist of the entire body; yet even he was not so fanatic as to refuse to sell enormous quantities of butter and cheese to the Romanist enemy, during the very war he had himself stirred up against Spain. His chief ally, Gerrit Jacob Witsen, son of a self-made grain-and-herring trader, was devout but unsteady; Witsen deserted Pauw to join a group of real-estate conspirators, and thus broke up the Calvinist régime. And there can exist no doubt whatever about the nature of the two other leading Calvinists, the backsliding brothers-in-law, Barthold Cromhout, who had made a fortune in overseas plantations, and Frans Hendrickszoon Oetgens, a rich grain importer. These turned to the new creed in the intention of securing high posts in the West Indies Company and are characterized by the sober historian Elias as "shameless freebooters" to whom "everything had its price, even their own conscience."

Oetgens and Cromhout were perfectly willing to wreck the party of their adopted creed when a new scheme to make money turned up; with some other Calvinists they bought up a good deal of waste land which they tried to force Amsterdam to purchase and turn into streets and canals, in a gigantic building and improvement plan. The one upright Calvinist was Reynier Pauw, who had to call in men of the other religious dogma, sons of the Sea-Beggars he had long fought, in order to thwart, or, to use the good Dutch phrase, "dwarsboomen" the scheme. Then he was betrayed by his close ally, Gerrit Witsen, who had shared in the West Indian spoils and had let his son be made burgomaster by Pauw; Witsen went over to the real-estate speculators just in time to get his son in on that deal too. So the great Calvinist experiment at Amsterdam came to an ignominious end. The following of Pauw "slonk" together, as the Dutch say; the big deal was put over and Oetgens and Cromhout saw their lands purchased by the State. Nothing was left to Pauw but to resign and devote himself to his rapidly growing business in butter and cheese with the enemy whom he had so energetically bought, Spain.

In this curious story, there seems little to confirm any sweeping thesis basing the development of the capitalist mentality upon Calvinism. And indeed the Netherlands offer many contradictions to that popular and in many ways well-supported theory. In Amsterdam, the helm of State was in the hands of so-called "libertarians," men of tolerant views and Lutheran persuasion generally; and only for one brief stretch of eleven years was it held by a narrow margin by Calvinists. Comparing one régime with another, it is hard to believe that the Calvinists had a better eye to the main chance than libertarian business men before and after them.

Moreover, Calvinism did not always tend to spur the business man on to yet more desperate pursuit of profit, as a Weberite would contend. Some of the most placid and retired Dutch, with the least trace of initiative, were the very jealously Calvinist ruling classes of Delft. These Calvinists, as Eisler shows, were about the least "hustling" of all Dutch traders; very early they retired from the brewing industry to live upon investments in the East India Company; they kept down industrial development, and did not even finance the famous Delft faïence venture which was in the hands of foreign émigrés; they vetoed the proposals for enlargement and improvement of Delft as harbor and commercial center. They are the sleepy and dreaming citizens portrayed in the sunny interiors of Vermeer, always looking at themselves in mirrors, reading a billet doux, languidly lifted a wine-glass or laying aside a lute. They are people as far apart from the money-grubbing, success-worshiping "Puritan capitalist" of the Weber description as

can be. On the other hand, some of the most enterprising and successful founders of industries in the Netherlands were—French Roman
Catholics.

Among the Calvinists of the second generation even at Amsterdam,
an insidious tendency to settle back from activity and indulge in
worldly pleasures was observable. The sons of Reynier Pauw, their
heads turned by the wealth of the old oligarch, bought landed estates
and adopted the title of "Ridder," grew pompous and luxurious and
were quite as eager for peace with the Catholics as had been the old
Sea-Beggars when their appetites, too, had been appeased. A son of
Reynier Pauw aided the great Andries Bicker in the immensely difficult task of securing the Peace of Münster in 1648, which gave Holland the first breathing-space she had had in eighty years, with the exception of the twelve-year truce.

There was now no cause left, save that of religious difference of
opinion, to incite the Dutch merchants against Spain; and they determined to have peace. Andries Bicker, as Burgomaster at Amsterdam,
forced the bellicose Stadtholder at The Hague, Prince Frederik Hendrik,
who as an aristocrat was a professional war-maker, to sign the Treaty.
Such martial elements as remained among the merchants were silenced.
The old Calvinist Oetgens allowed his consent to peace to be purchased, for Bicker compelled the city of Amsterdam to buy up a lot
of his remaining real estate at a fancy figure; thus Oetgens became a
pacifist, as he had become a Calvinist, at a high price. And at last the
merchants were able to conduct the actual peace negotiations: the
trader Jan Reynst was sent to Paris and Adriaen Pauw, son of the old
Reynier Pauw, was sent to Spain, his father's long-fought foe; the merchant Gerard Schaep was also eventually sent to London to deal with
the English Puritans, the rising mercantile class of England, who had
"murdered" Charles I. This latter move of Bicker's was a sore blow to
the Stadtholder who felt sympathy for the Stuarts and kinship with the
Cavaliers.

Peace with Spain was kept only by the most strenuous efforts of the
resolute Bicker. Most of the merchants of his city supported him, it is
true, but the Prince clamored for war. The son of Oetgens, who had
adopted the title of Van Waverens, retained a martial tradition; and
Bicker's close friend, Jan Geelvinck, a versatile man formerly burgomaster, merchant and pirate with equal success, turned against Bicker
at last. The old buccaneer found the strain of peace too great.

The Prince accused Bicker of treacherously selling ammunition to
the enemy, charges which Bicker never thought for a moment of denying, but which he maintained were insufficient to cause him to relinquish his high office. Finally the Prince sent an army against Amster-

dam; but the Bicker family was waiting for it and Cornelis Bicker drew up the drawbridge and set cannon on the walls. The army retired in confusion, and the merchants won the first round.

Then the Prince, outraged at these traders who continued to spite and "dwarsboomen" him at every point, issued a solemn ultimatum to Amsterdam that the whole Bicker clan must go. The city was in uproar; the Bickers armed to resist. Nevertheless economic interest at last prevailed; the panic that spread on the Stock Exchange was too dangerous, for the losses in trade amounted within a very few days to ten million guilders. Faced with this situation, the merchants of the city gave in; the Bickers retired to France, embittered men, "remplis de vent et de vengeance," where they remained until, not long afterward, the Prince suddenly died. Then, just two days after the bells had tolled at Amsterdam, the Bickers were back in triumph. They, or rather their relatives by blood or marriage, among the latter the gentle and learned Jan de Witt, continued to steer the ship of State in the interest of peace for many a year.

By such steps the Dutch business man rose to the heights of independence, wealth and world dominion. At the middle of the century, in the era of Andries Bicker, he stood at the zenith. This was his supreme hour: when the colonies were won, the foes were humbled, the loot of past warfare and present trading monopolies was accumulating and forming great funds of capital to be invested in industry, recklessly expended in speculation, or perhaps laid out in splendid country estates and portraits by Rembrandt. And peace crowned all. After the Peace of Münster, in 1648, however, a decline set in, at first imperceptible, by the 60's and 70's apparent, and by 1713 sealed. New groups arose at Amsterdam, convinced that fresh wars would regain the fleeting prosperity. A war-party murdered the peace-advocating Jan de Witt; the Valckenier clique, a motley group composed of a whale-oil seller, a dealer with Russia and one with France, and a gunpowder-maker who was later indicted for misuse of office, seized the government. With Medicean strategy, they ruined what was left of the Bicker clan by outrageous taxation. Eventually they forced Holland into fatal hostilities with England, a struggle "for the fairest mistress of the world, trade."

All through this hundred years, the Dutch business man was uncontested sovereign within his own borders. He was the greatest, as he was the last, of the oligarchs who—Greek, Italian or German—for so many centuries demonstrated that they knew how to rule as well as trade. Amsterdam was the proudest and the last of the cities which, like Alexandria, Lübeck or Venice, had aspired to sea-empire; her citizens laughed aloud at Rome, "content with the spoils of but a single world."

CLAN-POLITICS

Modern capitalists are wont to preen themselves upon the diversified nature of their operations, but after all those of the Dutch oligarch were more manifold still: he brought government as well as business under his interlocking directorate. Such a man as Bicker would put even a Ford to blush, for *his* activities covered the globe, and *his* horizontal trust covered not only trade and the State, but Church and army as well.

The four Bicker boys with their father divided among them the trade of the world: the eldest son, Burgomaster Andries, took the Russian fur monopoly and managed it so well that the other merchants of Amsterdam complained to the States-General that no pelts but his could appear on the market; the youngest son, Cornelis, took the American sphere and won two large fortunes; the second son had the Baltic regions; the third accepted South Europe and the Levant, besides a flourishing ship-building business; while the father, a master-hand in the East India Company, took on any projects between the White Sea and Peru that were left over. Automatically, as things stood in Holland, such a combination of economic interests obtained political power equally great at Amsterdam: the brothers, with some relatives, apportioned the available civic posts as easily as they carved up seas and continents. The eldest naturally became burgomaster and a manager of the East India Company; the youngest led the Church and the West India Company; a son-in-law of Andries, as captain-major, commanded the municipal garrison; a nephew led the Baltic convoy-fleet; relatives held strategic posts in other cities besides. As a contemporary pamphleteer cried, "the Bickers are everything!"

The case of Bicker was merely a striking illustration of the general rule. A successful Dutch merchant expected to make a corner on State revenues as naturally as on the sugar or tobacco markets; he reserved for himself and his numerous relatives not only burgomaster seats and leading posts in the semi-State trading companies, but also all the good jobs in schools, postoffices, churches, the militia, and all expeditions, by sea or on land, for purposes of war, trade or piracy. In each city of the Netherlands the ornamental as well as lucrative stations were monopolized by a small clique or "kring" of the richest families, which, having won wealth in brewing or soap-boiling, took all the rest as "emoluments thereto appertaining." The only quarrel was, not between merchant and non-merchant, but between patrician and parvenu; all too soon, the sons became patrician and the grandsons degenerated, and another crop of new-rich stormed the city afresh.

It was so at Amsterdam as in other places, except that the spoils naturally were more attractive. Each of its governments was formed by some leading man "cum suis," as was said, meaning with all his available male relations. Thus, within one space of twelve years, out of seventeen newcomers to burgomaster seats, nine were sons or sons-in-law (schoonzoons) of men already in office, and all the rest were nephews or cousins. Thus clan succeeded clan: now it was the Occos and Bams and Buicks; then the Hoofts, the Booms, the Bas, the Cats and Cants and Nuts; or the Bickers brothers; or the heirs of the merchant Dirck Corver who for two generations cornered the municipal payrolls. And so it went on. In the eighteenth century, the connection between City Hall and Exchange only tightened: between 1752 and 1795, Elias reports, nearly a third of Amsterdam's burgomasters were active in business, while almost every one of the rest had relatives in high points of the trading world, the chief banks and importing firms. All through the city's history, business controlled politics; and whoever mastered Amsterdam, cast the decisive vote in the Dutch national deliberations.

As time passed, things got worse at Amsterdam instead of better. Throughout the seventeenth century, the trader-oligarchs at least divided the loot among able-bodied relations; but in the eighteenth century, while Holland sank to a "rentier" State with less and less of an active rôle in business and politics, corruption became so flagrant that even infants were so dowered. The newborn son of Burgomaster Jan Six in 1730 was presented with a double postmastership at 11,000 florins a year. And perhaps the classic instance is given by Burgomaster Willem Munter who, in 1748, formed a government at Amsterdam with two sons, a son-in-law, four brothers-in-law, two nephews and a cousin; he got for a son-in-law the office of naval treasurer and appointed his three baby grandsons to rich postmasterships—two of the boys were four years old and little Gerard just one year of age. For other sons and grandsons there were posts in the East India Company; and one child of three and a half years was made captain in the Amsterdam garrison.

There was never anything quite like it; Baasch says that this was an unparalleled spectacle of private persons reaping national resources for their family uses. The Protestant Dutch traders were as given to nepotism as so many Renaissance Popes; they were as clan- and family-minded as mediaeval Italians and Germans or as modern Jews and Chinese business men. Moreover, they had much more scope for their affections. Thus when the doughty Calvinist, Reynier Pauw, became burgomaster, he had his nephew made tax-gatherer, while he himself and a brother-in-law took the monopoly of supplying gunpowder for the State. Burgomaster Huydecooper made his brother-in-law leader of a West Indian expedition and Burgomaster Gerrit Witsen appointed his uncle as Governor General of the East Indies. And besides such posts, to other zoons and schoonzoons, went fat contracts to collect taxes, build ships, lead convoy expeditions, supply cheese or ammunition to colonies, garrisons or the navy. Nor should one forget the tips on the Exchange, for the group in power in government could nominate the heads of the Companies and both together control the fate of shares.

The Dutch trader had, therefore, not only a much larger territory under his thumb than any of his predecessors in previous centuries and countries. He also had one far more completely in his control. He did not have to reckon with an aristocracy, whereas the haughtiest of mediaeval Germans had perpetually before their eyes the neighboring warlords, either as menace or model, and even a Jacob Fugger was snubbed by patricians of Augsburg. The Dutchman had shaken off clerical dominion, whereas the Italians of the Renaissance waged ceaseless conflicts with the power of the Church. And finally, he had no king, whereas a Gresham or a Fugger, though he might use a monarch as a pawn, had to work behind a throne.

All the ancient and hereditary orders that for so many ages had pretended superiority to merchants were in seventeenth-century Holland absent or abolished. There was a petty court at The Hague, but it had no power to set even a social tone, and the foreign policies of the Netherlands were determined not there, as a rule, but in the City Hall of Amsterdam which was, in the language of Elias, just "a branch office of the Exchange."

There happened to have been very little blue blood in this poor, infertile, new-rich "land of united bogs." This lack had to be filled by merchants themselves. Some bought a piece of property and called themselves Esquire or "Heer van Zuidpoldsbroek" or some such thing; many got long family trees and hung coats-of-arms over their pews; "from shop-sign to shield is but a step" as a wit observed. Others bought titles abroad for cold cash, long before Americans like the Astors indulged in that luxury. Thus in 1616, Dirck Bas was knighted by a prince of Muscovy and Laurens Reael in 1626 by Charles I of England; Willem Backer got a title from a doge of Venice and one of the Cats another from France; the Puritan oligarch, Reynier Pauw, achieved letters of nobility from both France and England. But all this did as little to alter the bourgeois character of Dutch society as marriages of lumber kings' daughters to foreign counts have altered America. Money counted— not blue blood. Whoever lost his fortune, lost his claim to govern. Once bankrupt, a man's list of probable grandfathers, acquired with whatever pains and expense, could never restore him to the burgomaster's cushion.

As the merchants substituted for aristocracy, so they took the places of the clergy, ousted with Spanish dominion. Calmly the Dutch turned cloisters, as at Delft, into factories of cloth or faïence; they stripped cathedrals of holy images and replaced these by mortuary monuments, more or less pompous—of themselves. And the relatives of the richest merchants of each city held the religious offices, as a brother of Burgomaster Bicker ran the Church at Amsterdam. Under such a business administration, the main concern was a tolerance beneficial to trade. Every man's religion was held his own concern; Catholics were tolerated by Calvinists, and both joined Libertarians in trade and politics. Holland escaped that terrible vehemence in matters of religion which was, in that century, sending out to exile the very best merchant classes of both France and England—the Huguenots and the Puritans. The Dutch were unique in their tolerance, not merely of the Jews, but of one another.

Thus firmly in the saddle, unchallenged by king, duke or monk, the Dutch oligarch did not need to work behind the scenes. The Dutchman attained his ends without subterfuge or an assassin's dagger. The Dutch trader was more obvious in his methods and his power than the greatest of modern capitalists would dare to appear. He was, in fact, *the* "grand old man" of business.

THE DUTCH OLIGARCH

Only against his background can the Dutch oligarch be judged. He was more than a mere contemporary of the Stuarts and Bourbons—he was their peer. He was an absolute monarch, as unchallenged in his domains as they—an autocrat among autocrats. He, too, made not the slightest pretense of democracy: he allowed neither labor, the peasants nor his stockholders a voice in the direction of affairs. Ruthlessly as he eliminated kings, nobles and a too dominating clergy from his domains, he was ready to stamp out the slightest signs of independence in furrow or factory. His aims at world dominion were as sweeping as those of any monarch of his day. He wanted the Polar Circle and Africa, the monopoly of Baltic grain and Russian fur, the carrying-trade of France, England, and half Germany; he intended to extract the last penny of profit from Brazil and Japan and from both banks of the Hudson River; he proposed to fish in British waters and poach in Portuguese territories, to hold most of India and much of both Americas and humble the Sultan of Morocco; while from the Amsterdam Bank he dictated the currency values of the world.

Though entitled to all the cargo of the ship of State, an oligarch must shoulder all responsibility for the ship's steady course; in case of disaster there is no chance for him to steal away unobserved from the sinking wreck. He must accept greater risks than men who grasp at lesser prizes. And the admirable thing about the Dutchman was the aplomb with which responsibility and risks were both assumed. Neither apology nor cant accompanied his plundering nor were his mistakes put on other shoulders. With iron nerve and a steady hand he kept the helm of the Dutch State; for more than a century the world lay at his feet and when at last, in the eighteenth century, he stepped aside it was not because he had grown weak and undecided, but merely because, like Napoleon, he had "taken in too much territory."

About this rock-like man, this Absolute Trader, there was a majesty, similar to that which enveloped the most sultanic and unmoral King-by-Divine-Right. Certainly the director of an Eastern trade colony was a despotic ruler over defeated natives and slaves, could be merciless and brutal, was often a boor and a bore, and sometimes an out-and-out pirate like Burgomaster Geelvinck. Nevertheless, as Elias says of Bicker, he was "a freebooter but a man all-of-one-piece." He was capable of fraud and violence, but not of sham, fake and palaver.

Unquestionably, a Bicker and a Pauw were lacking in the charms and graces of their throned contemporaries, a Louis or a Charles. Although a Dutch burgomaster was entitled to the appellation of Magnificus, none was ever Il Magnifico in the Renaissance sense of cultural leadership. Indeed, the Dutch trader was much more likely to be called, during altercations in the City Hall with his brother-administrators, by such resonant terms as "claphoutcooper" or "onweetende plymstrijcker." For none of his characters can the Dutch historian Elias find any honeyed words. Most of the traders were, in his opinion, *koppig*, *barsch*, *oploopend*, *stug-hooghartig*, when not positively to be denounced as sly, tricky, "cynical and greedy" buccaneers. At best—well, the *very* best seems to be "ehrlijck en rondborstig"—honest and round-bosomed.

The sheer massive strength of such men was their imposing quality. A Jan Corver, a Reynier Cant, an Adriaen Pauw, an Andries Bicker, were quite powerful enough to dispense with the glittering accessories of royalty. They could do without a flashing crowd of courtiers; they sought no flattery and gave none. They could manage with the dark, plain, Puritan costume instead of the silks and laces of the Sun-King and the Merry Monarch; the mere outline of their prow-like noses and grim jaws was sufficiently respect-inspiring. They could even get along without a theory of divine sanction unless Calvinism, which hallowed trade as God's work and elevated the merchant to the position of God's Elect, was the merchant's counterpart to Stuart Absolutism.

And just as the absolute kings impressed the portrait-painters more than any later constitutional monarchs, so the Dutch business man was glorified by artists more than his successors, however much more cultured, ethical or respectable the newer generations might be. This stubborn, blunt, homely man without either fear or shame, who dared to *be* the State, to pocket its resources and direct its destinies, was granted an apotheosis in art, at the hands of Rembrandt and his fellows, such as none of the crowned absolutists of the age, for all their ostentation, could achieve.

Both the Dutch business man and the absolute monarch, to continue the parallel, were types doomed to perish: an Andries Bicker, as much as a King James of England, was the final flower of a species now extinct. In the succeeding, the eighteenth, century, democracy broke into business as into government. The mobs of Paris demanding universal rights in the French Revolution were paralleled by restless stockholders insisting upon a vote in the great trading corporations. The stockholders' meeting was a phenomenon corresponding to parliamentary representation. However, the Dutch business man, faced with doom, proved that he knew how to resign as well as reign. He did not wait to have his head cut off, like Charles I or Louis XVI. On the contrary, as the French Revolutionary forces approached Amsterdam, the Dutch oligarchs decided to forestall conquest and plundering by proclaiming a Republic. Thus they signed the end to their long rule and, without fuss or popular demonstration, abdicated as successfully as they had governed.

THE BUSINESS CONCEPT OF EMPIRE

Though in innate strength and outward power the Dutchman was the full peer of crowned monarchs, yet he differed from them profoundly in many respects. In outlook, aims and methods, the commercial and the royal autocrats were very far apart. Most divergent were their conceptions of empire.

An agricultural aristocracy could think only in terms of more and more land. The Dutchman on the other hand did not seek to extend his landed estate; he was willing to let kings carve up the Continent, for he knew, as the poet laureate of the Dutch bourgeoisie, Joost van den Vondel, phrased it, the world's *goods*, so long as Bicker's flag overshadows the mighty ocean, would sleep in Holland's bosom:

Zoo wijt als Bickers vlagh den grooten Oceaen
Beschaduwde en doorsnee met rijck gelade schepen,
Die's weerelts gouden oegst in Hollants boezem slepen.

The Spanish, French and English monarchs were busily marking off the unknown as well as the known reaches of both Americas and were furiously quarreling over imaginary lines drawn across unexplored space. Not so the Dutchman; he was not going to fight about any non-interest-bearing, unimproved real estate that quite possibly might fail to exist. While the kings of Europe were thinking of boundaries, he kept his eye on the balance-sheet, and, leaving the French and English undisturbed in the possession of their colonies, he only insisted upon monopolizing the carrying-trade to and from those colonies.

Such a man was not likely to be led by romantic enthusiasm into making unprofitable gestures. We do not hear of any Dutchman wading out into the Pacific Ocean like Balboa, with drawn sword and flag, taking possession of the uncharted seas in the name of his God and Country. Certainly it was not because the Dutchman was so modest as to consider the Pacific Ocean too large a property to claim; but, as he could not represent it on the credit-sheet to a directors' meeting, he preferred to leave the Ocean to Balboa and Balboa's king, while quietly spearing all the whales in it for himself.

In short the Dutchman sought real, rather than illusory, conquests. He had gathered some colonies, but he was readily content with economic exploitation where political subjugation would cost too much. He did not insist upon calling a country his own if he could grasp its foreign trade. He would not plant his flag upon a shore if he could make twenty-six per cent on every cargo that approached or left that shore. This was commonsense, but did not produce good legends or romantic poetry.

It was an economic empire that the Dutch business man sought: one of those kingdoms, vast, unseen and undeclared, that are none the less as imposing a creation of man as any dominions welded together by monarchs and military genius. Such invisible realms cost as much in brains, sweat and blood as actual territorial empires; yet, because they have not been dazzling to the average eye, they have been generally overlooked in favor of the achievements of an Alexander or a Napoleon. Economic empires must be dearly bought and skillfully administered. Thus the Alexandrian Greeks held the trade of the ancient world, though Rome was nominally master; so Lübeck as head of the Hanseatic League dominated Northern Europe more effectively than an emperor; so Florence, entangling kings in debt, held many nations in a financial servitude more oppressive than the political. Amsterdam but added a new economic empire to an already imposing list, though hers was of a greater scope than any before; it covered the world and endured more than a century. The period from 1602 to 1713 is generally taken as the time of Amsterdam's commercial supremacy.

All these cities, including Amsterdam, owed their extraordinary positions to the same fact: the economic backwardness in most of Europe.

Indeed it was not until the eighteenth century that the business man had to turn farther away and seek the extensive exploitation of more and more capitalistically undeveloped regions in South America, China, India and Africa. Up to that time, he had free play on the Continent of Europe, among his neighbors. Thus Alexandria played upon the simplicity of Romans fresh from the furrows; the Hanseatics, upon the rusticity of England; the Florentines, upon the innocence in money-matters of the Cinquecento French. The Dutch at last were aided by the inexperience in ship-building and navigation of the French and English, as well as by the chaos created by disastrous "wars of religion" which set back economic development in so much of Europe.

The Dutch did not owe their supremacy to a financial wizardry such as the Italians displayed; nor to a superiority in manufacture which the ancient Greeks possessed; nor to a monopoly in ores, fuel and technical skill like that of the Victorian English. As the Englishman, Defoe, in 1728, put it, the Dutch had "neither Corn, Hemp, Tar, Timber, Lead, Iron, Arms, Ammunition, woollen Manufacture, or Fish of their own Growth." Such industries as flourished in Holland, notably the preparation of sugar, tobacco and the clay pipes in which to smoke it, whale-oil, soap, paper, pottery, gunpowder and brandy, were not beyond imitation by other folk. In fact, too, all the more refined and complex processes of the textile industry had been transplanted by fleeing refugees from Catholic lands, by those thousands of rich and able merchants who, to avoid repression in France or Flanders, rushed with capital and skill to an asylum in Holland. All that had been transplanted so rapidly could vanish again—once the Dutch lost control of the seas. That was their secret: they were not promoters, technologists and financiers, so much as universal middlemen, "waggoners of the waves," with a touch of the conquistador, the patroon and the pirate.

Defoe clearly recognized the peculiarity of Holland's position. Producing very little of her own, she yet amassed enormous wealth by dealing in the products of every other nation. "The Dutch," he said, "must be understood to be as they really are, the *Carryers of the World*, the middle Persons in Trade, the Factors and Brokers of Europe: That, as is said above, they *buy* to *sell* again, *take* in to *send* out; and the greatest Part of their vast Commerce consists in being supply'd from all Parts of the World, that they may supply all the World again: Thus they supply some Nations with Corn, others with Ships, or Naval Stores for Ships; others with Arms and Ammunition of all kinds; such as Powder, Shot, Shells, Lead, Iron, Copper, Cannon, Mortars, etc. others with Fish, others with woollen Manufactures. *and the like.*"

During the early part of the seventeenth century, hardly anything could be moved anywhere without a Dutchman's help. The bulk of Holland's ships were taken up by the necessities of life: grain, wood, salt, fish. But they carried luxuries as well: the wines of Spain, the furs of Russia, the pottery of Japan, and the textiles of India. They furnished the distant colonies of America with gunpowder and slaves, and returned home with tobacco, sugar and other raw materials. Their outposts were on the island of Nagasaki in Japan, in Java and Borneo, in Manhattan and Bombay. They alone could transport the curiosities of the farthest Orient to the last nooks of the Baltic. As an English pamphleteer in 1625 apostrophized Holland:

> Like the Arabian bird thy nest to build,
> With nimble wings thou flyest for Indian sweets,
> And incense which the Labaan forrests yield. . . .
> (Which thy foes hope shall serve thy funerall rites.)

Such enterprise was possible only because the Dutch, even as late as the middle of that century, owned three-quarters of the bigger sea-going ships of Europe. For the whole of Europe there were then perhaps 20,000 vessels of a respectable size and of these the Netherlands possessed 16,000. A great country like France had, all in all, about 500 ships, and of these the majority were tiny tubs in no way comparable to the majestic, high-pooped "koopvaarder" of the East India Company. This close grip on sea-commerce was maintained by the Dutch monopoly on both ship-building and control of the raw material sources for that industry. The art of constructing vessels was still largely a matter of rule-of-thumb, of guess-work, and the citizens of Zaandam guessed better than anyone else. Dutch ships were much less likely to turn turtle on being launched, or to fill up like a sieve and sink on their maiden voyage, than the so often wretchedly built tubs of other dockyards. Since the Dutch controlled the sources of supply, the timber, hemp and tar, for example; and since the capital was furnished for industrial enterprises more plentifully and at a lower rate of interest in Holland than elsewhere, the Dutch could have ships at a third what they cost the English.

The result was that the neighbors of Holland not only left their carrying trade in large measure to her, but depended on her for their navies. Thus the French had to purchase through Holland the stores with which to build the very fleet they intended to set fighting Dutch supremacy; so a king of Spain had to buy, fully equipped, a war-fleet from Burgomaster Bicker, during his war against Holland. The Bicker family were mighty in this branch of industry, the key to all the others. A brother of Andries, Doctor Jan Bicker, had a large ship-carpentering works on an island outside Amsterdam, long known as "het Bickers-eiland." He lived beside the plant in a formidably walled and fortified mansion, combined with a great warehouse, protected by a three-storied gateway, and bearing his coat-of-arms on the gable. Here he ruled in patriarchal style and supervised from his window the rapid rise of a forest of masts.

There was no corner of earth in which the Dutch trader was not a familiar figure. In countless early prints of Holland and Japan, his appearance is recorded: a big, hearty man in a millstone ruff, balloon knickerbockers and ten-gallon boots, frequently with a three-foot pipe in his mouth, very often with a monstrous musket in his hand, always wholly at his ease. In every situation, however strange, he preserves his unequalled composure. So he sits like a great cheerful bear in the home of a Japanese samurai, drinking and endeavoring to hold the alarmed daughters of the house on his knee. Anon he is sailing on a high-castled ship along the African coast among canoes full of yelling savages, or trafficking under the trees with American Indians. Sometimes he is condescending toward heathen royalty, shaking hands for instance with the befeathered King of Candy.

The Dutch trader, to be sure, more often claimed trading-rights than territories but of these he insisted on a well-nigh universal set. He demanded the right of entry to the Baltic regions for his eastward shipments of salt, wine, pepper, rice, indigo, sugar, cloth and a million pounds yearly of tobacco, and for his westward cargoes of grain, furs and lumber; though he acquired this East-borne trade only at the cost of incessant quarreling and fighting with the Swedes and Danes. He obtained a stranglehold on the lower Rhine traffic, blocking up the great artery of Germany and controlling the German exports of wood, grain and metals, as well as the imports of drugs, and spices. He burst into the Mediterranean under the very nose of Spain, despite the Moorish pirates, and captured the Levant markets. He struggled with Venice for the mastery of the Adriatic. He opened Japan before Perry. He skirted the coasts of Australia and occupied Java. He cut out the French from the trade in their own West African and Canadian colonies, and kept the greater part of the trade with France herself. He robbed Portugal even of colonies in the New World and shut their markets to everyone else. He stole the Indian traffic in spices and cottons from the Spanish and defended it against the British and French. He had a monopoly on the exchange of guns for furs with Russia. He not only monopolized the carrying business with England and England's colonies, but also fought for the right to fish for herring and whales in their adjacent waters. Manhattan he bought from the Indians for a little brandy; then divided it into building lots and set it up in business. To repeat the words of the English balladist: "Are they by Force unable to Invade? No matter: they'll undo the world by Trade."

Eventually Holland's neighbors began to perceive that their purely feudal-agrarian ideas of what constituted an empire sorely needed revision. The French banker's son, Colbert, who virtually dictated to the French commercial world, patterned himself as far as possible on the Dutch example and sought Dutch advice. He was bitterly jealous because the Dutch had in their hands almost the whole sea-trade with France; they brought there in 1646, for example, more than 21 million livres' worth of herring, cheese and butter, candles, metals, spices and sugar, jewels, feathers and drugs, books and pictures, whale-oil, fine cloth, masts and planks for ships, metal for armament. And they took away from France but 15 million livres' worth of such simple things as she had to sell: wine, grain, linen, honey and wax and salt, leaving an adverse balance that set all French mercantilists to wringing their hands. To repel this economic invasion, France under Colbert started to enlarge her own navy and erect tariff walls. The outcome was her military death-struggle with Holland.

As for the English the sight of the immense prosperity and the overweening pretensions of the small Dutch country of "united Bogs," this poor, barren land with a population of between one and two million souls only, was likewise an exasperation and a model. An immense pamphlet literature arose proclaiming England's future to lie upon the high seas, in the imitation and defeat of the Dutch. By 1623 the English king, claiming the seas about his island as his exclusive private property, had put up a "No Trespassing" sign for Dutch ships. And by 1651 the Navigation Act forced the carrying of colonial goods in English bottoms. At last, as in the case of France, there was no way out but war. In such a contest there could be no other issue than an armed combat. An English pamphleteer in 1623 stated the case clearly: "It seems there is some inevitable destiny; that these differences should be therein decided."

The wars between Holland and England were urged by merchants on both sides. The Earl of Clarendon, quoted by Tawney, declared that the English-Dutch conflict of 1665–67 was brought on principally by the Royal African Company, and was a "bare-faced war" for commerce: "The merchants took much delight to enlarge themselves upon this argument, and shortly after to discourse 'of the infinite benefit that would accrue from a bare-faced war against the Dutch, how easily they might be subdued and the trade carried by the English.' " On the Dutch side, the animus was equally obvious; behind warfare with England, Elias maintains, lay rivalry between the Amsterdam Exchange and the London Exchange for the mastery of world trade. The outfitting of an armada of 150 warships to participate in the first war, and the expedition of a flotilla under De Ruyter to the African coast that opened the second war were both the work, not of the Hague court, but of the ruling clique which governed the Amsterdam Exchange.

Even invisible empires must be cemented with blood. Amsterdam had to fight as constantly for her economic monopolies as though she had claimed actual territories from her neighbors. While the Dutchman was still an humble member of the Hanse League, he had learned from his great tutor, Lübeck, how to fight as well as trade. And he turned first on his teacher; in the sixteenth century, Dutch ships wore broomsticks at their mastheads—a sign that they meant to sweep the seas clear of the Hanse ships. No sooner had they won their commercial independence, than they fought, turn by turn, Spanish, French, English, Danes and Swedes, not to mention Turks and other heathen peoples.

It is a fashion among modern "free traders" to argue that the exchange of goods on a non-tariff basis will serve only to cement national friendships by bringing the world into relations of mutual dependence. The eighteenth-century philosopher Kant was one of the first to dream that a world more closely knit by trade would enjoy universal peace. However that may be in the future, unquestionably in the past the business man continuously felt within his breast a "categorical imperative" to battle.

The business man has not in fact been a meek man of peace, endeavoring to carry on his occupations humbly amid the clash of feudal lords. He has been as grim and dogged a fighter as any professional warrior. While he was a ruler of German or Italian cities or of the Netherlands, he was as steadily in a state of armed conflict or of preparation for military adventures, as the most bellicose feudal aristocrat. War has been the business man's major preoccupation in political history. The chief difference between the Dutch oligarch and Napoleon was that the Dutch oligarch, while equally ready to exhaust his country's wealth in his pursuit of world-dominion, spared her sons' lives somewhat better; he could hire alien blood to spill. In the words of an early perspicacious Englishman, "he that hath coyne shall have strangers to fight for him . . ."

And where there was not the clash of steel, there was economic struggle, "a politique secret warre," often as terrible in its consequences. Indeed the final French invasion of Holland in 1672 was but the culmination of many years of tariff-warfare; it was the armed answer to Holland's last high protective barrier, the barrier in turn but a reprisal for a similar wall of Colbert's making. The whole century was consumed with such maneuvers—with Navigation Acts, the English declaration of sovereignty on the high seas countering the Dutch claim to "freedom of the seas," which were to be opened to all, but especially to the Dutch. The economic hostilities of the age were described with a beautiful clarity by an Englishman, John Hagthorne, Gent., as early as 1625: "The glory and sovereignty at sea hath at this day three competitors, the English, Dutch and Spanish Nations, between whom, though there were no open hostilities, yet there is a politique secret warre, by striving to undermyne and beate each other, out of their trades; which may not improperly be called a warre, for the deprivation and cutting off the trades of a Kingdom, may be to some Prince more losse, if his revenues depend thereon, than the killing of armies."

In view of his perpetual state of defense or attack, whether his weapons were edicts or muskets, it is impossible to consider the Dutch trader solely from the business angle. War was a regular part of his business; as owner of the State, he was involved in the whole war issue more directly than business men in other states, then and since, ostensibly controlled at least by monarchs or democracies. The Dutchman, as burgomaster, voted for or against war; his brothers were the admirals who led the expeditions; and he himself at least during the first part of the period, had to see the war through, for his own trading-ships were expected to be men-o'-war.

Each trader had to look on a possible sea-battle as part of the year's activities. The East India Company was intended as a fighting no less than a trading corporation; its purpose, like that of the West India Company, was to weaken Spain as much as to collect dividends. The Eastern corporation had its own armed convoy system; the great East India House at Amsterdam was arsenal as well as warehouse and office. This East India House was a tremendous plant: its cellars fairly burst with spices; its great halls were decorated with the weapons and armor of conquered savage folk and the art-works of Japan and China; it contained shops and offices and quarters for the troops; in the spacious courtyard the soldiers lined up for their pay or passed in review before embarkation for the colonies; in the rear was a slaughter-house where a thousand oxen a year were killed and salted down as food for the crews and soldiers. Some of the Company's big ships carried 400 to 500 warriors; and their high castles were abristle with cannon.

Not only were the great Companies martial. Every shipper had to arm his vessels or send them under escort, ready for sudden attack, since most of the long sea-struggles of Holland were carried on by just such ships. In the war with Spain, there were few big naval encounters;

the Spanish were defeated only after innumerable sea-duels between pairs or small parties of merchant-koopvaarders. And so it was in other, later wars; indeed, part of the Dutch success was due to their development of the frigate, a new type of lower and longer ship, swift and stable, suited to cargo-carrying or conflict according to need, uniting commercial and martial aspects.

Many prominent Dutch merchants were not merely prepared to take part in war; they diligently sought their prey on the high seas. Equipped with letters of marque authorizing the seizure of enemy ships, there left Dutch harbors in 1606, in one single month, no less than 130 vessels. These mercantile, legalized, patriotic pirates seized Spanish, English, French, Danes and Hamburgers; often they took neutrals, robbed and tortured them and sold them to the Barbary sea-rovers as slaves. In return, naturally, they were preyed upon; thus the trading fleet going to Archangel was captured by the Spanish in 1643; within eight years, 1626–34, the Dutch lost 400 hulls, large and small, and within three of those years the financial loss was estimated at twelve million gulden.

It was extremely difficult to draw a line between legitimate commerce—combined with a laudable and patriotic bellicosity—and sheer piracy. Some of the merchants, going too far in the pursuit of profit, were looked upon as "disreputatious"; among such was Burgomaster Geelvinck. Others, however, won laurels of which an admiral might be proud; among these were the two brother merchants, Adriaen and Cornelis Lampsins, flourishing shippers of Flushing. Within three years in the 1630's they had captured seventeen great Spanish ships and set free a score of Dutch vessels which had been captured by the enemy. So splendid were the exploits of these business brothers, turned informal naval experts, that the Dutch insurance rates fell from ten to three per cent.

So certain were the Dutch traders of their martial talents that they were determined to keep a thumb on all naval operations. Merchant directors managed the convoy fleets owned by the several cities. And the business men, particularly of Amsterdam, wanted to control the fighting navy; they would not surrender it to admirals, bureaucrats and the Stadtholder at The Hague. But the perpetual aim of the Stadtholder was to wrest the navy from merchant control and manage it himself. The merchants of Holland wished to decide the ever-present issue, "Does war or peace pay better? And whom?" solely on its economic aspects, whereas a body of professional fighters, out of leash, might of course indulge in hostilities merely to keep themselves fit. The Dutch trader wished to conduct wars himself, and had every right to do so, since it was he who started them.

BUSINESS IN WAR

If the Dutch business man found it necessary to carry on warfare as incessantly as the aristocrats, he had nevertheless a very different attitude toward the exercise of arms. He could not forget, like simple feudal lords, everything but blind rage and determination to beat the enemy down with every weapon; he knew that the most "wicked" Papist was, after all, a customer. Thus he could not pay homage to the ideal of "la guerre absolue," created by the professional soldiers, the absolute and unmitigated state of warfare; for the Dutchman could not bear to separate his military from his commercial activities. He would not pursue just one of these at a time.

Reynier Pauw, as we have seen, sold butter and cheese to the Spaniards, though he stirred up war against them. Lodewijck de Geer, the "Dutch Krupp," in the Thirty Years' War built an immense munitions plant in Sweden, which not only had the result of stopping Holland's armament exports to that country but also provided weapons which the Swedish, in their quarrels with the Dutch over the entry to the Baltic, could turn against de Geer's fatherland. Andries Bicker went farther; with his friends, Abraham Boom and Burgomaster Geelvinck, he fitted up and sold a war-navy, complete to the last cannon and powder-keg, to the King of Spain. And then Bicker formed a consortium which brought over some twelve million florins in silver to the southern Netherlands to pay the Spanish troops then engaged in fighting Bicker's own country—and this while Bicker was still Burgomaster of Amsterdam! The deed was too much for the Stadtholder, Prince Frederik Hendrik, who had a chivalric soul and all the disinterested bellicosity of a feudal aristocrat; he wanted Bicker put out of office for such treachery. Bicker cheerfully explained that, if the Dutch didn't do it, the Danes or somebody else would.

Nor was it the aristocratic Prince alone who considered the conduct of merchants dishonorable; the very populace of Amsterdam was incensed, at times, against the profit-at-any-price policy of the big business men. During the alliance of Holland with England against France, it was agreed that the best method of crushing the foe was to keep up a strict economic blockade. But the Dutch had great sums invested in France and they were not willing to close the money-routes that led through France to Spain. They had also a good many things to sell the enemy and some raw materials they needed to buy from her. They would not cut this trade all off and prosecute a blockade with sufficient vigor to please the British, who were not only very martial but who had no large stake in French trade or investments abroad to blur their chivalric attitude. When it saw with what perfect openness Dutch merchants were loading their ships to trade with the enemy, the mob of Amsterdam was moved to riot. The poor people and the aristocrats were alike disinterested and shocked. They believed in the *guerre absolue.*

The neighbors of Holland, still economically backward, still living in a haze of mediaeval ideals and sentiments, could not understand the cold, realistic, blunt, modern Dutch business man at all. One choleric English writer in 1672 wrote: "An Hollander: this is the name of a people that esteem nothing sacred but their own profit; and live under no obligations of honour, honesty, or religion, but interest." Another, later, toward 1703, recorded with surprise that it seemed to be among the Dutch "a maxim not to exasperate their enemies by bloody battles." Instead of raging heedlessly forward "in hopes of conquest," they thought "rather to secure what they have and expect an advantageous peace." A Frenchman said that there was no land in the world where so many kinds of open egotism, local and national, private and municipal, prevailed, as in the Netherlands. And the Dutch did little to contradict such critics; it was a Dutchman who declared that his ship of state steered "with Profit for a Compass and Greed for North Star."

The Dutchman threw up no smokescreen of resplendent verbiage, such as obscured the actions and dimmed the motives of men in other countries. He was content to be seen by his neighbors, as by his artists, in all his homeliness. He did not consider war in itself a glorious career, nor did he thirst for military honor. He fought only for profits and very flatly said so. He considered economic motives a full and sufficient justification for war or for any other extreme measure and did not deem it necessary to bring forward any other or more exalted reasoning. Though he waged war in support of vast imperial designs as continuously as the Bourbons, he waged it in a profoundly different temper.

The French noblemen on the contrary were enamored of the art and discipline of war; fighting was to them a ballet of death. A French marshal, inviting the Sun-King, Louis XIV, to give the signal for battle, said: "Sire, the guests are gathered, the violins are in readiness, the beautiful Masques are waiting before the door—an it please Your Majesty, we may now begin the Ballet." This was just the sort of thing no business man, and certainly no Dutchman, would think of saying; to him war was not a mummery; he did not hide his economic motives behind a splendid masque; he opened war in cold-blooded deliberation, not to the intoxicating music of violins. And when the negotiations for peace between Holland and Louis XIV were in progress at Nimwegen, the Dutch clamored for an immediate end to hostilities. Vainly the Stadtholder urged them to hold out for glory and honor against the

Sun-King's pretensions. They replied that "it was not reasonable to expect from them to beggar themselves."

Like the French, the English could not weigh profit and loss with Dutch equanimity. They felt that the "honourable horror of War" should have some other excuse than a balance-sheet. One English writer proved the war against Holland "to be just, honourable and necessary," on the grounds that the honour of his King had been injured by the "rude and barbarous" expressions used by the Dutch: "How much more ought we to resent it where the dignity and honour of our prince (upon whose reputation abroad and at home, not only the national renown, and general commerce, but the welfare and being of each man is suspended) is concerned. . . . It is no vain, or empty design, for a prince to preserve that credit and renown which appertain unto his quality." Further he sought to stir up a Holy War against the Dutch who, he maintained, were not really Christians: "I should injure Christendom to reckon the United Netherlands a part thereof; such are their practices, that it is a crime in them to profess that religion."

Into this chivalric atmosphere, the Dutch brought their new point of view. The French and English were but carrying on a very ancient tradition, which the classic Polybius observed to be in force at Rome: "The true reason for war is always concealed and the most plausible one put forward." Now, however, Dutch pamphlet literature reversed time-honored practice and put forward only true reasons: those affecting the pocket rather than the head. Thus the Dutch merchant, Willem Usselincx, urging his countrymen to make war on Spain, produced the cogent argument that, whereas in peace-time only the single city of Amsterdam gained in trade, during hostilities the trade of Holland as a whole would increase.

XII

THE SUNSET OF THE OLIGARCH

THE DUTCH TRADER obtained this unparalleled position of dominance, paradoxically, at a time when nearly everywhere else in Europe, merchants were losing ground; the power they had possessed in the Cinquecento was being rapidly swept away, and commercial interests were being thrust into the background by emerging "absolute monarchs" who claimed a divine right to govern alone. In impoverished Italy there now ruled, instead of Medicean bankers, a horde of petty dukes and princes. In Germany likewise, the heritage of mediaeval urban independence was disappearing as ambitious princes stripped the cities of their privileges; the grasping rulers of Brandenburg and other growing territories were divesting the business man of his rights as rapidly as the Thirty Years' War was wiping out his business.

In France things were as bad from the point of view of the independent trader. The Sun-King, Louis XIV, and his trade-dictator, Minister Colbert, were imposing on their subjects a rigid strait-jacket of regulations covering every detail of trade and manufacture. They interfered in the processes of industry and also in the creeds of the industrialists; they oppressed the French Huguenots, the most capable merchants of France, and sent them into exile, thereby depopulating rich cities and lopping off flourishing branches of commerce and industry. And if the French merchant, who grumbled even as he grovelled, chose to make protest, he had to take a long and devious route to Versailles, a corrupt trail that led through the gates of courtiers and the back-parlors of the king's mistresses.

It was impossible for a Frenchman to imagine a government like that of the Dutch, no more formal or ornamental than a chamber of commerce—quite as impossible as for a Dutchman to fancy himself doing business in a boudoir. The two folk were divided by an impassable gulf of ideals. At the very opposite end of the human scale from the bustling butter-and-egg men of Batavia were the French noblemen, contemporaries of *D'Artagnan* and the *Three Musketeers* and akin to these heroes of Dumas' romance in their spendthrift attitude toward sordid

cash and their thirst for blood and glory. Particularly in the first half
of the Sun-King's reign (at the height of Dutch prosperity and during
the reign of Andries Bicker at Amsterdam), was built up in France the
ideal of the perfect courtier, hedged in from the bourgeois world by
elaborate ceremonial. The French were still living in a fantasy-realm,
shedding tears over the knightly adventures of *Lancelot* and *Tristan;*
they had not yet begun to read "Don Quixote" even in translation and
laugh at the figure of the baroque knight. So contemptuous of the
Dutch business men were the French aristocrats that their Sun-King
actually refused in 1669 to enter into negotiations for peace through
Jan de Witt, declaring: "It is not appropriate for merchants, who are
themselves usurpers, to decide in a sovereign manner over the interests
of the two greatest monarchies of Christendom."

If not quite so extreme as the French in their denunciation, the English of that day were still very far from becoming "a nation of shopkeepers" either. To the swaggering Stuart cavaliers the Dutch seemed
a set of stupid fellows who took the blubber-market more seriously
than religion or even love. And though the "roundheads," the shorn-
polled Puritans of the merchant-class, were more like their colleagues
in Holland, they were as yet under-dogs, still struggling partly under
the banners of religion, against the monopolies and trade-restrictions
of the Stuarts, who claimed the same absolute sovereignty as their
French cousins. It was King James I who said: "The merchants think
the whole Commonwealth is ordained to keep them up." This remark,
which in England appeared a royal sneer, would have seemed to a
Dutchman the most obvious of platitudes. "For what else, pray, is a
Commonwealth ordained?" he would have asked.

One could hardly expect such neighbors to admire the bourgeois
Dutch. They assailed the trader of Holland for money-grubbing commercialism, lack of conversation and aesthetic comprehension. His
women were imperious and cold, his children spoilt brats, the flapper
daughters intolerably free, the merchant himself too busy to philander
with ladies, and deaf to the call of religion. In short, supercilious foreign critics were raising the same outcries against bourgeois society,
while it was still in the bud, that their kind later raised, in the nineteenth and twentieth centuries, when it was in flower. Critical frosts
however had, apparently, no power to kill capitalism even when it was
a tender new plant. There is an extraordinary similarity in all these
complaints. Hermann Levy has pointed out that, a full century and a
half before the so-called Industrial Revolution, Dutch bourgeois society
was condemned for the very same aesthetic shortcomings which, long
afterward, Matthew Arnold and Ruskin found in their own Britain.
One might add that these complaints are still raised today in as loud

a voice as ever against America, and in particular against New York, that daughter-colony of Old Holland. So far Nieuw Amsterdam on the Hudson has but inherited, along with so much Dutch blood, the enmities incurred by Old Amsterdam on the Amstel.

One of the complaints against the American business man—his Puritanism—has perhaps the longest ancestry; it came to America by way of Venice and Amsterdam, through England and Germany. Already in the seventeenth century, the Catholic French, according to Murris, had laid the money-worship of the Dutch at the door of Calvin, apparently ignoring the rather evident fact that Calvin was a Frenchman. An Italian, as early as 1618, says Baasch, even more surprisingly, was horrified by the monstrous "avidità e avarizia" of the Dutch and likewise blamed Calvin. Thus commercialism and religion were connected by observers in the early stages of capitalism, centuries before the Puritan origin of the capitalist mentality was expounded by the English Matthew Arnold and elaborated by the German Max Weber.

The Dutch business man's family relations were criticized as thoroughly as the American's were to be condemned three hundred years or so later. The Dutchman, the English and French agreed, was too preoccupied to remember his wife. Said the scornful English gentleman, Sir William Temple: "Through the general inclination of every man to business" in Holland, merchants had not even the leisure to keep a mistress. Partly for this reason, the "neglected" wives of the Dutchmen were rated as cold and tyrannical. They were often in business on their own and how masterful they could be, we may judge by Rembrandt's portrait of a rich business woman, Elisabeth Bas, who ran the best hotel in Amsterdam; she had a very Gibraltar of a face. The French found the Dutchman bossed by his wife. Quaint as it seemed, in Holland at that time it was actually illegal to beat a woman. What could one expect?

It seemed too that the children of the Dutch business man were badly brought up. They were not in awe of their fathers. The French, Murris observed, were shocked to discover a total lack of corporal punishment in schools. Young women were especially free-mannered, saucy minxes. In short, the Dutch merchant could control neither his wife nor his offspring. He let them all run wild at least as far as wildness was possible in such a trim garden as Holland, while he stuck to his money-making.

The French could hardly bring themselves to take the Netherlands seriously even as a State. "They are rather a company of merchants than a political power," wrote a contemporary of the Sun-King. Having made such a cult of leisure, the French complained of Dutch "hustle" and, preposterous as it may sound to us today, derided unholy mechanization. Montesquieu, watching everybody in Amsterdam, even women and infants, fetching and carrying, rolling sacks and bales, declared the Dutch reminded him of the ants changed by Jupiter to men in order to people some Ægean isle. And Madame du Bocage, who in 1750 visited the village of Zaandam, where great windmills prepared oil, mustard, paper, lumber and gunpowder, was startled into a strangely modern epigram. Those giant winged towers which seem to us the very symbol of Dutch tranquillity, appalled the seventeenth-century Frenchwoman just as giant American dynamos now shock Europeans. "Ici les machines agissent comme des hommes et les hommes comme des machines!" she cried. Her exclamation might come from any present-day travel-book on America and Fordism.

A few hum-drum virtues appropriate to bourgeois life were recognized. A shirt-sleeved democratic simplicity was smilingly admired. The Dutch were amiable to servants; they were thrifty; they were temperate in religion if by no means in alcohol. They were clean, though even this spotlessness was originally economically motivated: it was found that microbes spoilt cheeses. They were honest; in fact Sir William Temple called them the most upright merchants of the entire world—not, he hastened to add, because of their more tender conscience, but out of sheer necessity, since world trade rests upon a common honesty as war upon a common discipline.

As seen by Sir William Temple, the business man of Amsterdam was calm, level-headed, tolerant, amiable. Profit meant more to him than honor; common sense more than wit and spirit; good-humor was his most desired quality. His chief notion of diversion was going out solemnly, arrayed in "plus-forty-eights" to play golf or "kolf," on the ice. But seventeenth-century Englishmen were not attracted by such dull fellows as these; a merely amiable, honest merchant would be tedious company to a fantastical, hot-tempered "blood" and wit, patron of Restoration drama and courtier of King James. "Out of such a nation" as Holland, concluded Sir William, "can come neither good conversation nor great statesmanship."

The cultural limitations of the Dutch were painful to courtiers of the Bourbons and favorites of the Stuarts. Traveling philosophers turned up their noses, even while they enjoyed comforts and toleration in the Dutch asylum for harried exiles. Descartes, who had to spend the years 1629-40 there, grumbled, "Every man thinks only of himself and of his business interests, and whoever has nothing to do with business and trade, may enjoy freedom but is completely disregarded." Others were found, both within and without Holland, to declare of Amsterdam that, "in the city of Mercury, wisdom is silent"; or, more bluntly, "in the harbor of Circe, men live like swine."

The typical attitude of Holland's neighbors, an attitude mingled of envy, awe and disgust, was expressed in a penny broadsheet of 1667, in which an English balladmonger described those "Hogen Mogen Frogs" (hochvermögend-powerful, high and mighty)—the obscure and rude denizens of noisome swamps who had so suddenly swelled to the magnitude of "Gogs and Gog Magogs," and worried the citizens of more cultivated parts:

> Low Country Provinces, united Bogs,
> Once distrest States, now Hogen Mogen Frogs,
> Royal and Noble Int'rest gone, command;
> Grown formidable both at Sea and Land;
> Who but a Century of years before
> Dabbled in Fishing, despicably poor,
> In seamless Vessels, Troughs, cut out of Logs,
> Catch'd Whiting Mops; now Gogs and Gog Magogs,
> In stately Pines new Constellations raise,
> Ploughing up Billow two and thirty ways;
> Through boiling Brine, through Cakes of crushed Ice,
> For Gold and Silver, Ivory, Oyl, and Spice
> What Straights, Gulphs, trading ways, spare they to pierce,
> By water to take in the Universe?
> Are they with Force not able to invade?
> No matter; they'll undo the world by Trade. . . .

The conclusion to this tirade was inevitable: "A new Sun is rising in the West"—England! That was always in the minds of both the English and the French onlookers. Given a chance, they felt, they could do ever so much better than the Dutch. *They* could preserve wit, love, art, religion, aristocratic manners and good conversation, the dignity of princes and the loveliness of womanhood—at the same time beating out the Dutch in matters of commerce and navigation.

Most cheerfully did a London pamphleteer, John Hagthorne, Gent., in 1625, urge his fellow-citizens to outdo the Dutch at their own game, in "England's Exchequer. . . . Wherein by the way, is likewise set downe the great Commodities and Victories the Portingalls, Spaniards, Dutch and others, have gotten by Navigation and Plantations, in the West-Indies and elsewhere. Written as an encouragement to our English Nation to affect the like." After painting a glorious picture of Holland's wealth, in whose "nest the goods of each Pole meet," he sends forth a trumpet-call to Englishmen. Not indeed, to become dull, tiresome, thrifty merchants like the Dutch, but to rise up and rob them of all their plantations and the seas. It is, he says, "the nature and condition of the English considered, who had rather fight once a weeke, to live at ease by the sweate of others, than to sweate thrice a weeke to live well by the labour of themselves which make me wish them store of such employment as best suits their conditions."

With a simple sea-rover gusto the English set out on their path to commercial glory. They thought to rob the Dutch of their colonies by outmatching their sails upon the oceans—but they had not the slightest intention of becoming sober, thrifty, prosaic producers of useful wares. Indeed, even as late as 1728, just before the first puffs of steam heralded the Industrial Revolution, which would soon compel the English "to sweate thrice a weeke to live well by the labour of themselves," Daniel Defoe was still gloating over the contrast between the Dutch and the English temperaments. The Dutch "Way of Living is sparing, their Excesses few and mean, and their Ostentation or Gayety is very low priz'd," he writes; on the other hand "in *England*, the . . . Way of Living, [is] large, luxurious, vain and expensive, even to a Profusion, the Temper of the People gay, ostentatious, vicious, and full of Excesses; even criminally so in some Things, and too much increasing in them all."

Though both the French and English, in the seventeenth century, were sure they could beat the Dutch at their own game, they supposed they could achieve this end without yielding an iota of their charm, gusto and fantasticality. The French did not foresee that, before they could become a great capitalist power, they would have to guillotine their aristocracy and exchange their gorgeous raiment for the drab, standardized garb of the *roturier*. The English did not imagine themselves working in Lancashire spinning mills and living in drab suburbs, held down by the moral precepts of the Victorian Age and turned into just such quiet, amiable, domestic fellows as the Dutch they so despised; nor could they look into the future and see themselves being damned by Ruskin and Arnold for the very faults that Sir William Temple pointed out in the Netherlands.

THE ABSENCE OF IDEOLOGY

An almost complete absence of heart-stirring slogans and imposing abstractions, in the whole range of Dutch economic literature, has been noted by Laspeyres. Solely and coldly in the light of profit and loss, the Dutch carried on their discussion of their major problems: how to keep the navy and the monopoly companies at once powerful and free from corruption; their colonial management; slavery; beer versus brandy; warfare. The efforts of the pamphlet-writers were designed, Laspeyres says, "to proclaim the interests of a small party to be the interests of all." There was never the slightest pretense that the interests of any were spiritual.

All the economic writing, with rare exceptions, was done by interested parties urging specific action on concrete issues; the authors were not professorial theorists. A typical example was Willem Usselincx who, urging war against Spain, produced as his most effective argument, and the one most likely to influence his hearers, the contention that the best ordinary business adventures paid only ten per cent per annum, mortgages yielded four to six and deposits five to six, while agriculture returned but a paltry three per cent—whereas the monopolistic East India Company had paid twenty-four per cent. And so, of course, it would be worth while to fight Spain for the purpose of launching a new corporation, the West India Company, of which he, Usselincx, proposed to be a principal director.

Holland produced no such figure as the French military engineer, Vauban, who urged the Sun-King to patronize industry and allow the aristocracy to engage in it, in order that the feudal clans, the best fighters and the most loyal upholders of the State, might not suffer poverty and die out. Such an argument was unthinkable in Holland, where there was no such class of feudal clansmen as Vauban represented. The truth is the Dutch business man sought just the opposite goal: instead of urging the State to foster trade in order to nourish fighters, he intended to nourish fighters merely to foster trade.

A great body of so-called "mercantilists" in France and England urged upon their respective governments all sorts of diverse experiments, agricultural, manufacturing and military, each and all on the ground that these would increase the glory and riches of the king and the welfare and strength of the State. But these were mere "projectors," men without power themselves, appealing for aid in their projects through kings and an aristocracy, and using the arguments most likely to engage noble ears. On the contrary the Dutch merchants, being the State, needed only to discuss what would benefit themselves. This they did with a total lack of metaphysics and with inimitable aplomb. Sometimes, it is true, a Dutch war-party found that bribery and economic logic were insufficient and resorted to violence; in such disorder occurred the deaths of Holland's two great and noble advocates of peace, Van Oldenbarneveldt and Doctor Jan de Witt. Yet this mishap was rare. In general, in Holland, political murder was as scarce as eloquence.

The apparent exceptions to the rule are seen, on a closer examination of the facts presented by Laspeyres and Elias, to be none. Thus that much-vaunted slogan, "the freedom of the seas," that famous doctrine, laid down by the learned jurist, Hugo Grotius, which deeply influenced international law development, was not, after all, an example of abstract thinking about the loftier things of life. It was propaganda on the highest imaginable level put forward at the request of a big merchant company and intended to sway opinion, not in Holland, but abroad, in Spain and England, where people were more sensitive to high-sounding phraseology.

The Dutch East India Company had to prove its right to poach in English and Spanish Indian waters. It commissioned the brilliant twenty-five-year-old jurist of Delft, Grotius, to present its case for alien consumption. And Grotius, in "Mare Librum," did prove to the consternation especially of the British, always easily affected by moral argument, that monopoly was wicked; that the Portuguese and Spanish had no title to the oceans or their trade in India, and certainly not by grace of the Pope, by right of which they could exclude the Dutchmen. This superb brief against monopolistic practice was floated by the East India Company, soon to become the greatest monopoly in the world. Subsequently it found the doctrine of Grotius a bit embarrassing until Barbeyrac "re-interpreted" it to mean that the Dutch Company had the right to exclude all non-Dutchmen from India. According to Brentano, the doctrine even embarrassed Grotius himself in later life; for when he served the cause of France and hence of State monopolistic practice, he quashed the efforts of a relative to defend the "Mare Librum" against an English attack; Grotius thought it was better to leave well enough alone.

The Dutch did not need such a device for home audiences. They would have been perfectly satisfied had Grotius called the oceans, not free, but simply Dutch. Similarly, they practiced free trade without enveloping it in a doctrinaire cloak. They broke down the monopolies of the great companies in favor of the smaller merchants, but without evolving such a classic as Adam Smith's "Wealth of Nations"; they did as they pleased, not bothering to call it laissez faire.

Thus the youngest of the Bicker brothers, Cornelis, reversed his practices without the slightest necessity for a doctrinary somersault. He put all his fortune in the West India Company and became a chief director, or *Bewindhebber*. He rose to immense wealth with the Company, after the memorable year 1628 when the Admiral Piet Heyn captured the Spanish silver fleet and a fifty per cent dividend was declared, due at least as much to piracy as to business. However, Cornelis was a far-sighted man; he sold out promptly at great advantage. Then he went to work through his elder brother, Burgomaster Andries, who had the government of Amsterdam under his thumb, against the Company in which he had been so prominent. The Bicker clan put through a law ending the West India Company's monopoly of trade with America. Despite the wails of the Company's defenders, who protested that the republic would be ruined and Spain delighted, the trade was opened to private citizens. And Bicker, by fitting out his own ships and competing with the Company he formerly directed, made a splendid harvest. Though Cornelis Bicker became overnight an antagonist of monopoly, he used rough-and-ready tactics instead of polished formulas; though head of the Church at Amsterdam, he did not allude to religion; he was nearer to the Old Adam than to Adam Smith.

This is not to say that even the Englishman's opinions were absolutely theoretical. Adam Smith was denied a desired post in the English East India Company; had he not been shut out of this great monopolistic concern, it is doubtful whether the "Wealth of Nations," attacking monopoly, would have been written, or published at least. Curiously, the two great monopolistic companies of the world gave impetus to free trade: the Dutch, by hiring Grotius to write the brief for them; the English by antagonizing Smith.

FREEDOM FROM CONFLICTS

The Dutch business man was unique in his utter frankness. He achieved a monumental bluntness that has probably never been equalled before or since. An anecdote that illustrates the point concerns Anthony van Waverens, the son of the old Calvinist companion of Pauw, and Oetgens the real-estate speculator. It had been the perpetual endeavor of the Bicker party to keep Anthony out of the burgomaster seat; when he tried it for the last time, being then in his seventy-third year, his enemies charged him with peculations in State funds and barred him again. Anthony never for a moment sought to deny the charge. Though much irritated at the inopportune moment chosen by his opponents, he merely shook his grizzled head and murmured: "Now that is the second time I have been so thwarted."

Grim old Dirckszoon, the Catholic Monarcha, defeated yet unbroken, going out with an ironic smile to exile between rows of spears; Andries Bicker, refusing to apologize to the Prince Stadtholder for selling guns to Spain and fighting to the very last hours of his career for power; Waverens, shaking his head in sad surprise but not a bit repentant—these are the incomparable types produced in Holland by an oligarchy!

Because he said so little to justify his actions, the Dutch business man was frequently indicted for taciturnity. He had no gift of conversation, all his neighbors scornfully declared. But perhaps this silence was due, less to racial peculiarity, than to his supreme power. What, after all, need he say? He did not have to cajole La Pompadour or her sisterhood, like a Frenchman, to get through a project for a royally privileged factory; he did not have to beg for patronage at a courtier's door, as did pre-Cromwellian Englishmen; he never had to discuss canon law with a monk opposed to usury. If he got rich, he never tried to imitate the etiquette and deportment of an effeminate aristocracy, for the most he aspired to was a fine house, a big garden, a title and a custom-made family tree. He did not have to lobby among legislators, for he or his brother-in-law *were* the legislators. He never tried to lead or mislead peasants or workers by fine rhetoric, for he made no accounting to shareholders and consoled no widows and orphans. He seldom so much as replied to accusations of piracy or misuse of State funds. Having none of the political and religious problems which vexed his neighbors, being moderate in his personal habits, finding no use for ideology, the demand upon the Dutchman's conversational powers was minimal. His mouth served principally as the terminus for an abnormally long pipe-stem.

When a Dutch merchant had made his pile, whether abroad in the colonies or at home in velvets or brandy, he could retire to his tulip-garden and rest in speechless tranquillity for the remainder of his days. His ears would not be assaulted by the roar of a striking mob, or his conscience attacked by a preacher; nor would his wife drag him to a lecture in an endeavor to uplift his cultural level. There were in Holland no such terrible peasant-revolts as the French Jacquerie, or revolutions of red-capped artisans as in mediaeval Flanders; there arose no Martin Luther to assail usury, no Cicero to condemn the practice of monopolists, no Savonarola or Calvin to attempt a utopian anti-business régime. Not even the son of a merchant, like a Boccaccio or a Ruskin, turned from business to glorify the aesthetic life. In fact, the questioning spirit which everywhere else accompanied business enterprise was strangely absent in Holland.

In that he was not seriously menaced by democratic upheavals, the seventeenth-century Dutchman was better off than modern capitalists as well as mediaeval merchants. There was not only no power, royal, clerical or aristocratic, above him to dictate to him; there was no one below this fortunate man able to make serious trouble for him. And he did not have many of the problems of capitalism, for, while it was then unfolding in Holland, it had not yet betrayed its dangerous potentialities. Capitalism appeared in trading corporations and in shipping concerns, but was less evident in manufacture. Some factories, especially silk-mills, became so capitalistic as to attract wide attention among foreigners; toward the end of the century Haarlem was definitely a factory-town and in 1672 at Leyden occurred a serious strike. Generally, however, the laboring population was small and, kept down by a severe police, was never suffered to get out of hand; the chief agitation was among the wretchedly underpaid and underfed sailors, very largely foreign-born, who formed an easily managed proletariat of the sea. Their workhouses, the ships of the seventeenth century, far exceeded in horrible conditions the factories of the nineteenth century.

In the pleasant land of Holland, windmills were as yet the only signs of the beginning mechanization of industry. The true, and appalling, evils perpetrated by the Dutch capitalists were very far away—in the colonies, on the West Indian and Javanese plantations, in the slave-capturing and slave-driving trades. And the Dutch stockholders, kept content by the regularity of East India Company dividends, averaging eighteen per cent over a period of 198 years, were not disposed to look half a world away for muckraking sensations. If nothing in twentieth-century Chicago could surpass the agonies endured by the toiling wretches in the real and terrible "Jungle" of the Brazilian and Surinam colonies, no Upton Sinclair drove home the point in letters.

Certainly there was poverty and misery in Holland. Even during the "Golden Age," the early part of the seventeenth century, the poor suffered from crises in industry. The discrepancy between the patricians and the lowly was painted by Rembrandt who portrayed the former in their jewels and then, cast out by "society," went to live in the ghetto and placed the latter on canvas in their rags. Still discrepancy did not constitute a real problem for the Dutch oligarch: he did not dread, as mediaeval German burghers did, the artisan revolts and interludes of "labor government." He did not have to gull the populace by festivals like the Medici; or to feed it, like the Romans. Only after 1672, in the declining years of Dutch trade, did it become necessary to organize a public system of poor relief in Holland; up to that time, the business man had been able to tide his capital nicely over every crisis to the next upturn, and let the poor take care of themselves. He had not believed in doles.

Extremely fortunate was the Dutch merchant in the fact that no foe sprang out of the furrow. His day was almost the only historical period in which the ancient enemies, urban trade and agriculture, enjoyed a sort of truce. For once was stilled the perpetual strife, that had burned in the ancient Roman Empire, in Renaissance Germany and Italy, as it does today in modern France, England, Germany and America.

The Dutch business man had a remarkable grip on the land. As half the population lived in cities by 1623, this was not surprising. The price of land was so high that agriculture would only pay if run scientifically; how to do this, the business man of Holland realized before his fellows in other countries. He spread new ideas through the peasantry, or preempted land himself, organized farms on a big basis, often with migratory labor from Germany, and produced high-grade, standardized products such as butter, cheese, fancy vegetables and flowers which could command urban sales and a wide export market. And it was he, Baasch says, who built those famous dykes of Holland: these were not peasant enterprises, but the schemes of weathy capitalists with money to invest in land improvements; among them was a rich French émigré.

The mellow serenity of Dutch landscape painting corresponded faithfully to the social torpor of the countryside. The fat cows, depicted by Paul Potter, indicate the invasion of business efficiency into agriculture. So do the giant windmills that dominate so many rural scenes. Towering above the dunes in old pictures, the windmills were the symbol of the trader's triumph over feudal stagnation. It was for good reason that the last feudal knight, *Don Quixote*, tilted against a windmill.

In this problem-less land—this capitalist utopia on earth—where so few menaces to property or even to conscience arose, the well-known Dutch "placidity" easily developed. The Victorian English, at the height of the industrialist's triumph, also achieved a wonderful poise and leisure, but in England there were always too many grievous social problems to permit the development of that utter resigned stillness of Holland. The ex-beer-brewing families of Delft invested their fortunes in the East India Company and, thereafter, generation upon generation, did nothing. Max Eisler has drawn the uncanny parallel between their steady shrinking from all forms of commercial activity and the ever-increasing inwardness of Delft's paintings, culminating in those of Vermeer.

Year by year, the rentiers of Delft withdrew from life. First they found landscapes too breezy and, withdrawing indoors, ordered church interiors; these soon seemed too expensive and they took to cozy home interiors. Vermeer painted the happy investors, surrounded by their bright, brittle treasures of glass and porcelain, in unvarying sunshine. They lounge in a replete fashion at table; they stare at their own reflections in a mirror, or at their pearls; sometimes they frankly and soundly sleep. And in these paintings, year by year, *the walls are seen coming closer and closer*. Year by year the world of the Delft brewers and their families grew narrower and narrower, though it remained eternally sunny; year by year, the bright, blank, warm walls encroached upon them, shutting them ever more inevitably in upon themselves.

The long, bright trance of Dutch prosperity was not broken by rude questionings. There were no penetrating discussions of business ethics or the causes of prosperity up to the Peace of Münster in 1648, for up to that time "industry bloomed and learning was mute." Only years afterward, when a blight fell upon the land, did Dutch authors rouse themselves to make inquiry into the causes and cure of depression. As long as things went well, Laspeyres, who made a careful examination of Dutch economic literature, thinks there was a lack of any critical discussion of business. It was not attacked as such: a few youths wrote university dissertations on the attitude of the classic authors toward trade, but came unanimously to the conclusion that Cicero and other ancient critics had been wrong in their judgments.

Holland had no class of "intelligenzia" opposed to business. A certain number of Dutch were indeed anxious to introduce some cultural interests into business circles; one statesman of a rich merchant family, Drosde Hooft, famous as one of the Sea-Beggars, who was said to have read Tacitus fifty-four times to improve his style, presided over a kind of salon at which his guests, some of the most exclusive patricians of Amsterdam, were supposed never to breathe a word about business. Yet one hears of no other salon in which remarks on the fluctuations in India shares or the butter market were so sternly barred.

One rather notable attack upon business was made, it is true, by the philosopher Caspar Barläus. A group of Amsterdam citizens, eager to have their city known for something besides wealth and the Bank and Exchange, founded in 1631 the Amsterdamer Athenæum. This was opened by Barläus with an address upon the "mercator sapiens," or "the useful connection of Trade and Philosophy." He was eager to prove to his audience that the arts might find some room in a commercial center and invited the townsmen, as subjects of the God of Wealth, Plutus, to make room for Apollo and Minerva. But then, quite untactfully, he launched into a discourse upon the attitude of Cicero toward monopolies and his condemnation of the same. Coming at the time of the Calvinist real-estate grabbing scandals, the discourse touched his hearers on a tender spot; they were convinced he was making "references to allusions." A storm blew over the Athenæum and many wellfed subjects of Plutus wondered whether Apollo and Minerva were going to prove very well-behaved guests.

Barläus was the exception. Though a Spinoza might grumble at the Philistines and declare that the five universities of Holland did more to narrow than improve the mind, he was a foreigner, after all, and he belonged rather to the post-prosperity period. In the bloom time, learning, like agriculture, offered no peril to business. Indeed the professors in one city formed a trust and were accused of being themselves too effective as business men: "Through this their monopoly they put across learning at the highest possible price to their students."

Of course there were very many attacks upon specific evils in business—nepotism and graft in the companies, speculation in shares. The great East India Company was charged with misdeeds. Enemies declared that it kept offices within a clique of families; that its contractors profited on the outfitting of unnecessary ships; that its directors created artificial scarcities and then dumped upon the market; that they gambled in shares, holding back dividends until widows and orphans had sold at low prices, then bought these up and boosted the value of the shares by suddenly "cutting a melon." Finally, it was charged, the Company made no reckonings, on the specious ground that these must be kept secret from Spain. But in the face of all these accusations the Company, undismayed, issued only a small and laconic brochure which said in effect: "Indeed? Dissolve us and try to do better."

Criticism of the great trading companies was indeed loud in Holland, especially after the 1630's. However, this agitation was of a very different character from the early German folk-movement against monopolies in the 1500's, for example. Then the Germans had clamored for suppression; a bewildered common people who believed themselves mulcted by the Fugger or Höchstetter had turned on these men as foes. In Holland, on the contrary, few voices were raised in favor of abolishing the companies, corrupt and inefficient as they were generally conceded to have become within a very few years after their foundation. The Dutch critical movement was rather that of private traders who wanted a share in the profits, and obtained it; they claimed that the companies, once excellent as engines of conquest, failed in the work of peaceful colonization; the result was merely a relaxing of monopoly bands and the opening of trade in all articles, save slaves and ammunition, to private competition. It was not a revolutionary folk-movement like the Cinquecento German; nor was it, like the eighteenth century English laissez faire movement, thorough-going and backed by dogmatic theories.

The anti-speculation movement was similarly feeble. A law was passed by the States-General forbidding the speculation in East India Company shares, but, as the lawgivers in that solemn assembly were themselves the chief speculators, getting inside information from their relatives who were the directors of the Company, not much attention was paid to the enforcement of the law, and it was recognized as simply a graceful gesture. Though the speculation grew steadily worse, though many proposals were made in the 1650's to limit it by taxing all sham-sales, nothing much was done until the next century.

The classic illustration of the speculative mania in Holland was in tulip-bulbs. The curious story has often been told, of how these Eastern flowers, acclimatized in Europe, commanded higher and higher prices until, from 1634–38, a feverish gambling delirium possessed Holland. At first everybody won; "flower-exchanges" were set up in corner pubs and shops; rare tulip-bulbs were as much sought, says Wirth, as railroad shares in the bubble of 1844. Many people speculated on the delivery of a certain kind of tulip; when it happened that there were only two of that kind on the market, at an enormous price, they had to sell oxen, horses, houses and lands to pay the difference. People never saw the tulips; they were gambled in without buyer or seller ever touching them. In one city in 1637, to benefit an orphanage, 120 bulbs were sold at a total of 90,000 florins by public auction; in another city, in a year or two, ten million gulden was the turnover for bulbs. One flower called "Admiral Liefken," cost 4400 florins for 400 *As*. Almost a record was established by "Semper Augustus," of which 200 *As* cost 5500 florins.

All the phenomena later associated with Mexican mines, Western land-banks, railroads, South Sea monopoly companies, were here associated with flowers. The delirium ran the same course: there were amazing spectacles of sudden wealth reaped by beggars; the inevitable overturn; the equally disastrous panic; the ruining of countless speculators; and the pitiful efforts of the flower-mongers to restore public confidence in their wares by making speeches to the public, assuring it that the intrinsic value of tulip-bulbs was just as high as it ever had been.

GROWTH OF DUTCH CAPITALISM

Already, entrepreneurs of a modern stamp appeared sparsely against this background, men who could organize large-scale plants, and capitalists who furnished funds and materials to small manufacturers. Thus the money-lenders of Amsterdam kept in tow the smaller producers of oil, soap, beer and cloth in a number of other cities. Nevertheless, the weaving was still done more in weavers' homes than in factories; the bulk of Dutch capital was in shipping, trading and distant plantations. The investor was a better-perfected type than the capitalist-producer.

Though the Dutch business men had created two epoch-making institutions, the Bank and the Exchange of Amsterdam, both of these were slow in developing to a modern technique. The Bank did not engage in lending to industries: it was used for ordinary transfers of funds, and for aid in the changing of coins, the confusion in European currency being of the most shocking character. From this Bank at Amsterdam, however, and others at Leyden and Haarlem, came a form of paper-money, the *recepis*, a receipt for deposited coins and a promise to pay in six months the same variety of coins plus a small percentage. These promises to pay circulated as money.

As for the Exchange, opened in a new building in 1611, it was designed at first for transactions in wares: iron and tin, copper and quicksilver; cotton, wool, whale-oil and fish; Eastern dyes, spices, drugs, American tobacco and sugar, Mediterranean rice, oil and wine. Some of the dealing in such goods was of a speculative nature; especially was this the case with whale-oil and pepper, owing to the seasonal and variable production; but such operations were forbidden by law to grain-dealers. As a financial center, the Amsterdam Exchange was very slow in developing; it did not begin where the old Exchange at Antwerp in Flanders had left off; it took two generations before fleeing emigrants (not Jews, says Ehrenberg) from Flanders introduced to the simpler Dutch the subtlety of the older financial world and transplanted the elaborate technique evolved elsewhere, during preceding centuries.

During the early heroic period of Holland, under the rule of the Sea-Beggars, the conquistadores and world-rovers, Dutch finance knew few complications. The only shares on the Exchange, for quite a time, were those of the East India Company; and these were buoyed up by public enthusiasm for the war-successes of this semi-governmental institution to 140 and even 200 per cent; until 1608, the last years of the Sea-Beggar rule, there was no bear-work done at Amsterdam. It was a bull market; the "liefhebber," or the lovers' party, had everything its own way. From 1608 on "counterminers," the bears, appeared and made the first artificial depressions.

The first counterminers to trouble and complicate the simplicity at Amsterdam were the subtle men of Flanders: Le Maire, Moucheron and others, who had been mighty in the East India Company but who, disagreeing with the Dutch members, withdrew, sold big blocks of shares, spread disconcerting rumors about the corruption and mismanagement of the Company, about which they had every reason to know a great deal intimately, and finally, Ehrenberg states, actually intrigued with the French king, Henri IV, for the formation of a rival company to beat the Dutch concern. These men, so indifferently patriotic toward their adopted land, were the original "counterminers" at Amsterdam.

While the Exchange then became an arena for the bulls and bears, their number was limited and the prizes were few. About twenty men controlled the market, raised or lowered the prices of shares at will, for a long period. The market became a free field for large numbers only toward the latter half of the century. Industry then began to seek the market for its funds; State loans were floated: Spain borrowed many millions of florins from its former deadly foe, in the 60's and 70's; England, for all her enmity to Holland, was glad to seek money there to bolster up her finances; Brandenburg and Sweden had also floated loans at Amsterdam before the century was out. By 1672 the modern system of credit-making in wartime had been launched; Holland, in desperate straits owing to the French invasion, paid her allies in obligations instead of cash. By the 80's Amsterdam had become an international money-lender, and could, as war-loan center, exert influence over diplomacy at home and abroad; it was the first true financial pulse of nations.

It took the Dutch sixty or seventy years to acquire the complexities of financial technique, and to gamble in more than pepper, flowers and a few company-shares. By the 80's, however, they had reached that stadium; and one of the members of the Spanish Jewish colony at Amsterdam, Joseph de la Vega, who was said to have won and lost five fortunes on the Exchange, and thereupon turned philosopher, wrote a remarkable description of the Exchange and the men who frequented it. This treatise, published in 1688 was called by the apt title: "Confusion de confusiones, dialogos curiosos entre un Philosopho agudo, un Mercador discreto y un Accionista erudito. . . ." Ehrenberg has analyzed this strange document which reveals at once naïveté and yet kinship with contemporary life.

The battle of the bulls and bears was by that time in full swing. Both the lovers and the counterminers had their "cabalas," their rings and consortiums, to control the course of the Exchange, and to boost or depress the market by wild rumors of splendid harvests or disastrous defeats. It was easy to spread rumors in such a small place, it appears, for it could be done by merely leaving a letter with false information openly lying about, or by loudly whispering in a friend's ear. Or if a big capitalist began to unload Dutch State-obligations, the rumor would be broadcast that he had private information of approaching disaster, and presently all the sheep would follow. Thus the enemies of the West India Company spread "infernal" reports with damaging results to Calvinist "lovers."

Peculiarly interesting was the fact that the boosters were closely connected with patriotism; the counterminers or "Misantropos de las Acciones" were viewed as mischievous and unpatriotic. This reminds one of the saying of the elder Morgan to his son: "Never be a bear on your country!" Loyalty could be urged on the ground that the East and West India Companies were semi-governmental; whoever believed in them, believed in the future of Holland; to sell the Companies short was to sell Holland short. The patriotic "lovers" would never, Vega says, admit the slightest damaging evidence: an earthquake was to them but a gentle dance, an Egyptian darkness but a twilight and lightning only a harmless fireworks display. But the sinister counterminers saw terror everywhere: every mouse was to them an elephant and every tavern-brawl a revolution; they went about proclaiming the collapse of the world.

How was the would-be investor to choose between the delirious boosting of the lovers and the melancholy croaking of the Misantropos? Vega says one may to some extent follow the general trends; but a time always comes when there is really nothing to do but to shut the eyes and take a chance. And he describes the business man taking chances. One is on the way to the Exchange, undecided, wrestling in his own mind, wondering which of his thoughts is a true guide; suddenly, without cogent reason, save that a cloud or a funeral procession has crossed his field of vision, he rushes to the arena, crying: "I will sell everything at any price!" Another comes in, trying to appear as casual and unprejudiced as possible; he goes through a dumb show of indecision: he chews his finger-nails, closes his eyes, makes four steps and holds four monologues with himself, makes passes at his forehead and holds his cheek as though he had the toothache; then, in a moment, without apparent cause, he flings himself into the center of the crowd, and making wild gestures with one hand to attract attention, while with the other executing a superstitious motion to avoid sorcery, he begins to buy shares as though they were so much cream cheese.

Vega did not think much logic and reason ruled in the financial world. Perhaps the loss of his fifth fortune weighed heavily on his mind. He failed to find the guiding principle of reason in the Amsterdam Exchange which a great contemporary philosopher of that city, Spinoza, discovered in the universe at large. Vega could see only the madness and the uncertainty. "Inexplicable agonia! Incomparable solicitud!" The poor wretches seized by the gambling fever could not rest from their torments: when they ate, shares were their meals; when they studied, shares were their books; when they slept, shares were their dreams; when they died, shares were the subjects of their last anxieties. Though the financial world has since grown so infinitely vaster and subtler, though the fortunes made and lost on modern exchanges are in figures that would escape comprehension for a seventeenth-century man, yet there are strong points of contact between the earlier "gente de especulacion" and those of today. As Ehrenberg points out, the advice of the melancholy Vega should not be despised or disregarded now: never give advice to anyone about buying or selling. Take every gain without hesitation and feel no pangs of regret if the price continues to soar. Do not hold shares too long; one must not marry them. Remember that the gains made in gambling are but witches' gifts, but fairy diamonds that vanish like the morning dew, like the tears of Aurora—"lagrimas de la Aurora, ya lagrimas."

DUTCH PAINTING

About this taciturn trader, so frank in his pursuit of gain and so stodgy in his enjoyment of success, arose a civilization based upon commonsense and rationality. As such it was a prefiguration—an early working model—of the social environment created a century or so later by English shopkeepers and industrialists, who very consciously adopted many Dutch thought-patterns. It was unadulteratedly bourgeois and the greatest possible contrast with that growing up in more southern and aristocratic climes.

The prosperous and problem-less land of Holland, which the visiting Voltaire found on that account a "lethargic hell," was spared the crises and upheavals that were expressed in other regions by a more tumultuous and passionate art. Not in Holland arose the organ-music, through which spoke the German folk-soul, wrung by the horrors of the Thirty Years' War and consoled by religion; not in Holland arose Grand Opera, supported by the dazzling courts at the expense of beggared populaces; nor an extravagant sculpture like that of France, Italy and South Germany, with its lurid mingling of the macabre and the sentimental—gilded skeletons alternating with what Sitwell calls the "bloated babies" of the baroque. Such fancy stopped at the borderlines of the realm ruled over by the level-headed, matter-of-fact Dutch business man; he was incapable of appreciating the emotional bulge of the baroque or the aspiring point of the gothic. The farthest he would go towards curvature was the admission of some conch-shells and dolphins' tails—souvenirs of his shipping enterprises. Otherwise, only a quantity-production, Taylorized classicism, could suit his controlled, and perhaps submerged, soul.

He played his rôle as a patron of culture and the arts, but it was in a spirit very different from that of the Fugger and the Medici. The old merchant-princes were gone, with their patriarchal-aristocratic way of living, their splendid gestures and their air of grandezza. Now that the scepter of commercial supremacy had passed from the Italians and Flemish and South Germans, the last chance was lost for the continuation of the old-fashioned combination of culture with business; an immense cultural promise departed when the commercial center of gravity shifted northward from Flanders and Augsburg. Perhaps the only men who have carried on the venerable aesthetic tradition have been the Chinese and Japanese business men—nowadays so looked down upon for lack of hustle by Nordic go-getters. They might have fitted in with the leisured Medici and Fugger—with their lavish giving of gifts and banquets; their transaction of affairs in tea-houses to the accompaniment of wine and the music of geisha or sing-song girls; their accumulation of art treasures to adorn ancestral estates and serve family and clan prestige.

It was now to a wholly new type of merchant—to the Protestant, northern business man with no nonsense about him—that the future of European culture was entrusted. But if he was not naturally a patron of the arts, it was not because he was Protestant, and still less because he was in the wholesale and shipping business. True, there has always been something about finance that inclines the sympathies to luxurious dilettantism; bankers have always been born collectors. But the North Germans, the English and the Dutch had never had the centuries-long cultural development of the South. Even in mediaeval, Catholic times, North Germany had been severe, plain, antithetical to Italy; she had not begun to hold beautiful church festivals spontaneously. And if Lübeck had always been puritan in habit, long before puritanism, so her once poor and humble pupil, Holland, had no preparation for the great rôle among nations she was to play; her people, fishers and sailors, were unready for the use of the enormous wealth gained through suddenly-won empire. A merchant like Reynier Pauw, the great Calvinist butter-and-cheese man, would probably have been no Lorenzo il Magnifico, even if Luther and Calvin had never been born; he was predestined to Predestinarianism.

Amsterdam was American in the tempo of her rise; unlike Florence, mellowed through the centuries before the Renaissance, she was a newcomer to power. She and most of her merchants might have adopted the motto chosen by a successful trader-adventurer, Van Linschoten: "Il faut soufrir pour parvenir." Suddenly, this small town had succeeded to the shipping monopoly of Lübeck and the financial power of Florence; but she was unfitted to carry on the classic culture that had come down to her from Alexandria through a chain of commercial cities, handed on by Florence to Augsburg and Antwerp.

True, Amsterdam felt a certain duty in this regard. Very self-consciously, a Bicker paid tribute to a Medici in 1638, when a famous water-festival was given in honor of a visiting French Medicean princess. Then the patricians felt that it would not be enough to appear in their plumes and jewels on beflagged barges, laid poop by poop along the waterfront. Some claims to culture must be made. So the East India Company opened its museum collections of Eastern art. Classic allusions must be shown at home on the Amstel as well as the Arno. A triumphal arch was flung across the Pig Market; Mercury made a speech; and a sturdy, helmeted Dutchwoman in the guise of Minerva carried the Medicean balls. But all this was distinctly an effort; in general, the Dutch business men had no need to amuse the *polloi* with circuses, or to feed it with bread.

It was a late member of the Medicean house who appreciated Rembrandt when he was misunderstood by the rich business circles of Holland and, cast out by the patrician society for which he had formerly painted, dwelt in a garret in Amsterdam's Ghetto. The Dutch merchants felt there was quite enough Stygian darkness in real life—as for example, enveloping the account-books of the East India Company—and they did not want it in art. They could not see why Rembrandt cast so ambiguous and flickering a light about their faces, or drew so impervious a curtain of shadow across their backgrounds. Princes and gods stood in the full light of noon. Why should the fierce light that beats about a throne be unbecoming to a Batavian butter-man? And the orthodox Vondel, who expressed popular sentiments, remarked: "Who loves life, can do without shadows and, as a child of light, need not seek out spiderwebs and twilit hiding-holes." It was a late Cosimo of the Florentine branch of the Medici who came to visit the "spider" Rembrandt, understanding the art of veiling truth.

Yet, even in this all too-temperate zone of Holland, under the patronage of men like Bicker who, though crafty and firm as the first Cosimo, never felt the need of slipping away from a directors' meeting to preside over a platonic academy—under all these discouraging circumstances—supreme contributions to European culture could be made. The Dutchman had not enough community spirit to develop a Gothic art, like the German merchants; nor could he, like the Florentines, promote the revival of an ancient art that had been buried under his feet. He was almost wholly without group spirit or cultural background; he was an individualist and a parvenu. Nevertheless his contemporaries, the haughty French and English, were mistaken in thinking he could do nothing.

The very fact that he was so free of gild and other traditions, aristocratic prejudices, religious mysticism, established forms of behavior, and that he believed only in "freedom of the seas" and "freedom of trade" even to the damage of the community in wartime—all this pioneer naïveté—was exactly what enabled him to produce a *modern* civilization in Holland. A rebirth of a past world was impossible there; but the birth of a new life took place. Commercial Florence had the honor of sheltering the Renaissance; it was a Naissance that gave Amsterdam a place in cultural history.

In Holland men had made a deep break with the past in art as in economic life. As investors, as speculators or entrepreneurs, they were individualistic, bourgeois, capitalist. They led a different kind of private life—and architecture was adapted to their requirements. They had no time to waste on alchemists, as did the needy and fantastic French and other men; but they were interested in practical sciences, in geography and navigation, optics, and medicine. They looked very different from any previous ruling class—and artists viewed them in a wholly new, an entirely modern way.

To the periods of boom-prosperity and decline, correspond many of the cultural phenomena of Dutch life. Through the first half of the seventeenth century, and on past the Bicker régime well into the 60's, while prosperity and carefree expenditure were common, the originality of Dutch architecture and the warmth of Dutch palettes bore witness to the wealth of several generations of successful merchants who retired to build homes and order their portraits painted. Then, towards the end of the century, as economic decline set in, appeared an economic literature that questioned the causes of prosperity and set-backs, considered the fitness of the Dutch people to colonize and trade, and compared them with other nations. Coincidentally appeared a philosophy—Spinoza's—that sought a way out in Reason for despairing mankind. At the same time, the artists, afflicted by the general gloom (and not only spiritually, for Rembrandt lost his fortune in East India shares), began to emphasize in landscapes, as economists in life, the gathering shadows. The business man in his earliest heroic period needed only an architect to carry out his plans; in his full tide of prosperity he gladly submitted to glorification by the artist; but his decline was "sicklied o'er with the pale cast of thought," as economists and philosophers sought to explain away his failures and artists re-echoed his melancholy in those ever more and more subdued tones of brown which have given them the name of "the sepia school" or, more disparagingly, "the prune-sauce school." After East India Company shares fell from 160 per cent, he really could not expect painters to represent him in a red sash; they would not paint him standing in the clear light of noon when the sun of prosperity was behind a cloud.

Architecture is perhaps of all the fine arts the one most obviously under the control of the patron. And the merchant oligarchs of Amsterdam kept a remarkably close grip on the building activities of their city. Over a long period of years, up to 1621, the fathers in the Rathaus empowered the architect Hendrik de Keyzer to act as style-dictator; under close cooperation of merchants, burgomasters and architects, was created a wonderfully harmonious and unified city-picture by the Amstel. Everything came under the central authority for approval: not merely churches, city gates, towers and private dwellings, but also shops, offices, marketplaces, and the warehouses of wholesalers. Then, after 1621, business men and architects outstripped governmental control: the Calvinist real-estate speculators, under the reign of Reynier Pauw, determined to glorify Amsterdam and benefit their own purses by building harbors and canals and "developments." Vainly old moralists like Drosde Hooft protested that architectural beauty, purchased by corrupt realtor deals, was too high at the price. Such Catonian croakers as Hooft, who came of a Sea-Beggar family which had already made its pile and retired to read up in the classics, and who felt that the new generation of business men were far more corrupt than his own had been—such were unheeded. The architect and the realtor boomed Amsterdam.

Mere ostentation, however, was not sought by the Dutch business man. He did not advertise his power; he built no palace for a Rathaus, but an edifice which was merely a private burgher-dwelling greatly magnified, and hence eminently suited to house a governmental body which was nothing more nor less than a business man's club. He was quite content with this. Though he might have said "L'état c'est moi" as proudly as his contemporary Louis XIV, he never in fact needed to state so plain a truth; he had no recalcitrant feudal nobility around him that must ever and again be impressed. Though the Dutch trader appropriated the national resources, coolly as a Bourbon, he did not have to employ the major part of them in building palaces to entertain a dangerous lot of loafing aristocrats. The pomp of the Bourbons was largely called out in the effort to keep the feudal lords and ladies quiet and amused. The bourgeois simplicity of the Dutch merchant-princes was not merely a matter of taste but of happy fortune. *They* did not need to build fortress-palazzi like the Medici to retire into in case of an uproar; they were not afraid of assassination from unethical competitors or from mob uprisings. They could build their houses as simply and openly as they liked. And so, apparently more modest than the Medici or Bourbons, but in reality far more presuming, they spent the loot of the nation upon their own private dwellings. They produced, instead of a Versailles—a modern home.

Really the work of the Dutch trader was the modern home later improved and adapted by the English and Americans. This was the first shell created for man "as a free and individual being," Hermann declares. The shell was not a fortress in the Florentine manner with cautiously placed loop holes; it had the biggest and highest windows ever seen, so enormous and plentiful that the whole house looked transparent—a glass abode for men whose purses and consciences were equally assured. Unlike the palaces of France and South Germany, the Dutch home was very modest, and found almost its only ornamentation in carved doorways. And, instead of forming an integral part of a community group, like the homes of the Northern German mediaeval merchants, it frequently stood apart, by itself—as the trader stood apart from the gild in Holland. The country homes of Hoogevecht, Quderhoek, Ter Meer and Van Zeyst, are square, simple, bourgeois block-houses, with scant decoration; but they are surrounded by amazing numbers of statues and trees, present in wholesale quantities and arranged in the neatest of rows—a form of gardening especially adapted to the dry-goods wholesalers.

Though the Dutch trader was an individualist, he was devoid of individual whimsy; he had detached himself from the mass in his business dealings, but he yielded to the mass judgment in aesthetic matters. With chill correctitude, the rich Sea-Beggars, after their fortunes were made in the East India Company, set up homes along the Heerengracht at Amsterdam: rows of classic columns, rows of chimney-pots, rows of porticoed doorways. Nowhere to be seen was a bit of freakish fantasy, a mermaid or a unicorn on a gable-end, in which the German merchants, so bound down in action by the gild regulations, found aesthetic recompense. So, too, the Exchange, opened in 1611, allowed not a trace of exuberant foliation to break the repetitive monotony of plain columns and windows—a conveyor-belt classicism. That was the ideal of the Dutch trader, an ideal which has since been maintained by American banks: a cold, pure, classic balance, which should be striven for in account-books and must, in any case, be achieved by the façade.

True, the Dutch business man was not insensible to whimsy, but he did not produce it himself: he imported it at considerable expense from the Far East and made it into an article of capitalistic industry with a world-wide market. Toward the 1660's, an attempt was made in Delft to imitate the curious conceits of Japanese potters, introduced to Europe by the East India Company and in high favor at Delft, especially among the rich retired investors in that Company. But this attempt was very old-fashioned at the outset, made by workmen under mediaeval gild-regulations, in a small atelier; and it was initiated, not by Dutchmen, and certainly not by the somnolent rentiers of Delft, but by an Englishman, a Frenchman and a Fleming. For a while the Delft faïence was very exclusive and expensive; then, as it became a vogue, capitalists took over the production and made one of the earliest modern industries out of it. The entrepreneur supplied funds and opened the markets of all Europe; but to do this he had to cut prices to very low levels, and sell a dozen of the great blue plates for 50 sous; hence he had to lower the wages of the artists to mere pittances. Then he had to take their freedom of imagination away; to compete with Sweden, Germany and England, he had to produce more and more cheap, popular, rococco patterns; he degraded and levelized Delft faïence, and in so doing, he ruined himself, for the Delftware became a cheap article easy of imitation, and by 1800 England had proved she could do that sort of thing better. After that, Delft was defeated in the game of making folk-whimsy a wholesale article. Thus early, before the Industrial Revolu-

tion, at Delft, the battle between capitalists and artists was being fought
—with both losing.

The business man and the artist represented antipodes, as both knew.
This fact had been glossed over during the Renaissance, while it was
still possible to paint the Medici in heroic poses against monumental
backgrounds and while, at least on festival days, the merchants still
capered in parti-colored clothes behind the chariot of Midas. But more
and more the rift between the two stood revealed. As the bourgeois
rose to his position of dominance in Holland, he discarded church and
gild festivals, such as had given color to the life of Florence and the
earlier Netherlands; he dropped legends and folk-customs, dramatic
gestures and the trappings of the aristocratic-clerical past. Thus, for
example, the rich governing class at Delft forbade the excesses of popular gayety in the yearly fairs. Long before the Industrial Revolution,
the bourgeois world was growing drab and dull, and the business man
himself presented a harder problem to his depictor.

The artists, who in Italy, France, Spain or England were then busy
immortalizing monarchs on order, had all the decoration of courts to
aid them. They could paint the Infante on prancing steeds; Louis had
his vast wig and crimson coat and was followed by an army with banners; Charles had his laces, his curls and pet dogs. A far more difficult
task confronted the Dutch painters, assigned the work of symbolizing
the power of the merchant-oligarch. By what signs should the purely
inner majesty of this sober bourgeois ruler be made manifest?

Rembrandt laid darkness about the shoulders of the Dutchman, and
lo, it became him better than an ermine mantle! He lent a somber mystery to his unpretentious sitters by enveloping them in gloom. At first,
he employed such lighting effects with melodramatic flourish: he
painted the Dutch bourgeois in his capacity as militiaman, with sash
and saber, by the flare of torches, in "The Night Watch." But gradually
Rembrandt began to realize that such tricks and costumery were not
necessary to emphasize the imposing weight of the Dutchman; he could
disdain both in his superb "Cloth-Gild," produced in 1662, toward the
closing years of Holland's "Golden Age" of commercial supremacy.
This is a painting as effortlessly impressive as the Dutch business man
himself.

In this depiction of a directors' meeting, a group of merchants are
seen sitting or standing about a plain conference table, on which rests
merely a book of records. The background is negligable and even the
shadows are not in the least melodramatic. The men are not especially
clever or interesting in appearance; they are not caught in a moment
of emotional stress and they make no deeply significant gestures. Yet,
marvelously enough, without the aid of decoration, whether of room

or costume, without emotion and gesture, without startling characters, or even the mystery of peculiar lighting, Rembrandt gave these men presence. They have heroic format; they breathe a repose and a strength that transcends superficial ornament. What monarch has attained to this last height of regal dignity?

This picture, which represents a directors' meeting with a higher art than other painters have summoned for the gatherings of kings and generals, was the last word, if not in portraiture, certainly in portraiture of the business man. Since that date, art has had nothing further to say about him. She has turned to sketching his bridges and factories, his employees in mines or docks, but about himself she has apparently been unable to utter a syllable more. The Dutch trader was thus not only the last merchant to command the State. He was the last to impress the artist.

Even he could not do this indefinitely. For about fifty years, Dutch painting stood in its full bloom. During this period the artist accomplished the extraordinary feat of making the business man's world as interesting aesthetically as that of kings and Olympians. But to do this he had to cast aside all antique canons of the Beautiful; he had to envelop Ugliness, destined more and more to prevail, in his scheme. This he accomplished by disregarding the objects before him and concentrating on the light that fell upon them. The mystery of Light, then being explored scientifically by the optical experimenters of Holland, was still so great that the artist could absorb himself in that; and for many years he did not care whether rays so holy and fascinating fell upon Venus or an "old woman cutting her finger-nails," upon a monarch or a merchant.

But this could not last. For a time the light in Dutch pictures was rich and full; it fell upon jewels and cloth of gold. During the tulip-boom and the peaceful era of the Bicker reign, the young Rembrandt, who painted several scores of Amsterdam patricians between 1630–40, let the flood pour upon magnificent textiles and precious gems, such as formed some of the chief export-articles of Amsterdam. During the economic crises of the 60's and the social unrest of the 70's, it was noticeable that the light grew feebler and greyer, and it fell less and less often upon damask and diamonds. The older, ruined Rembrandt devoted himself to the study of cavernous gloom, scenes of death and conspiracy at midnight; his successors in Holland and their imitators in England and North Europe generally ceased to discover new sensations in the objects before them, or in the light that shone upon these, and they sank into a banal monotony of brown and grey. Their palettes were limited to the hues of muddy coffee, dune sand and prune-sauce.

True, one isolated patch of color remained in Northern Europe:

Delft. In that quiet backwater, where investors long lived in peace upon their rents, untouched by the storms that shook Amsterdam, painters still managed to look with joy on the sun; here, until the 80's, the tide of noon was let in by Vermeer to glance on the tile floors, the pearl necklaces and starched ruffs of the retired brewers. Thus one remarkable bright spot stood on the map; but though the sun still shone over Delft, it was upon a stagnant pool.

The Dutch could only view their ocean, now carrying the ships of their victorious rivals, with sadness; even in seascapes, it was covered with menacing clouds. And the drab landscapes were dominated by the robots of the eighteenth century, the wind-mills with their mechanical arms, seeming to say: "Ici les hommes agissent comme des machines." The trees turned autumnal brown; in brown shadows stood the cows, the houses, the grass on the dunes. In the most literal manner, the Dutch painters *fore-shadowed* the Industrial Revolution and the monotony of the modern world.

The long night that fell over bourgeois Europe was not lifted until Turner painted a Venetian dawn and Ruskin, his prophet, hailed him as the bearer of color and light back to the sooty, gloomy Victorian world. Turner was the first painter in England after the Industrial Revolution who had seen a dawn, and men were blinded by it. The coloration of Turner was the most vivid in northern Europe after Vermeer died at Delft. Anybody who happened to be devoted to collecting evidences for the Marxist theory of the ideological superstructure might work out a neat connection between booze and brightness in art; he might show how the light that had vanished with the retired beer-brewers of Delft was hailed again by the retired wine-merchant's son, Ruskin. The rest of us must just consider it a jolly coincidence.

PART THREE

THE MONOPOLIST

XIII

FROM OLIGARCH TO BOURGEOIS GENTILHOMME

FOR OVER SIX HUNDRED YEARS the succession of business oligarchies may be traced without a gap. In the time between the 1100's and
the late 1700's there was indeed a constant rise and fall of cities and their
masters, but no break in the line; no sooner had one town decayed,
than a fresh group of traders appeared to snatch the scepter of commercial dominion as it fell. And each of these patriciates seemed more
formidable than the last; apparently the business-ruler was enlarging
his skill, wealth and scope of operations constantly through the Dark
Ages, into the pageantry of the Renaissance and the happy surfeit of
Old Holland. But then, just as he attained the fullest emancipation
from feudal trammels and an aesthetic apotheosis, his story comes at
once to a climax and an end.

There were no successors worthy of the "burgher-crown" of the
Bickers, the greatest as well as the last of the trader-oligarchs. About
the same time that Amsterdam surrendered before the Napoleonic
revolutionary waves emanating from France, the Venetian nobili were
likewise overwhelmed in the same tide. A while before, the Medicean
family had died out in Tuscany. Vestiges of patrician rule survived, it
is true, in some corners much longer; some "free cities" retained independence in Germany until the modern Empire was formed, and a few
of these, like Lübeck, clung to airs and titles up to 1937, when Hitler
abolished them. But such freakish examples do not alter the fact that
the business man no longer counted as a governor. This thread of his
history had snapped short.

The steps in the fall of the burgomaster are, however, not altogether
clear. Much more effort has been expended by the bards and historians upon explaining the collapse of the feudal baron, which occurred at about the same time, through the same weapons. Well known,
even to weariness, is the story of the barons' struggle against the
encroachments of the Crowns. But the fate of the burgomaster has
been more obscure. He much resembled the baron, his worst foe, in

quarrelsome individualism; he, too, desperately clung to some petty slice of territory, and fought jealously with his fellows and against the gathering might of kings. Yet the drama in his downfall went unperceived; literary men were very slow in coming to an appreciation of theatrical elements in business.

Don Quixote symbolizes the dying feudal chivalry, with its ludicrous-pathetic failure to grasp the real situation. But surely there were walking caricatures among the business contemporaries of *Don Quixote* who deserved a Cervantes of their own and never found one. Full many a pompous merchant-mayor of Europe, enveloped in bright velvets, continued to waddle solemnly under a canopy to a gargantuan banquet in the city hall, long after he had been shorn of his power, and retained nothing of his former estate save his gold chains—and his quondam thirst.

There was pathos also in the process by which the business man, as he yielded his sovereignty, sank to the status of a docile subject or citizen in a broad, integrated and bureaucratic modern State. Inevitably this involved a heavy loss in outward grandeur and inner self-satisfaction. From the level of a proud patrician city-father, holding the insignia of authority, he descended to the pose of an ingratiating seeker of Court favor, with a crooked back and bowed knee, signing himself "Respectfully" and "Your obedient servant." He who had set dukes at naught, when he was secure behind his bastions, was helpless without his walls as a poor snail without a shell; he fawned upon noble personages and based his fortune on a ducal smile. He who had formerly provided beggarly monarchs with pocket-money, now had to attend, hat in hand, upon the pleasure of minor ministers, or the lackeys of mistresses of ministers.

Il Magnifico was dead, and his successor was the *Bourgeois Gentilhomme*. But though the latter had less pride than his predecessor in the city-stage of economy, he of course found enormous material recompense in the golden harvests reaped from the new national States which were being formed in Europe during the seventeenth, eighteenth and nineteenth centuries. These States amalgamated into large social units the myriad local areas of which the feudal world had been composed; petty toll-lines were swept away and small spheres traversed by new roads and canals; coinages, measures, prices and processes were standardized and uniform codes worked out for workshops and market-places of wide regions. New consuming groups were formed as national armies and navies grew in size, demanding ever larger quantities of goods, delivered with increasing speed; the luxury-trades were stimulated as aristocrats were drawn around the courts, where their vanity was purposely played upon by sovereigns, in order to divert into fashionable emulation the passions which had formerly found vent in bloody jousting. Upon the parading of fops and favorites, the tailors flourished.

But these gains for business were not made automatically and unconsciously. The strong States of the seventeenth century, under rulers who proclaimed themselves divinely appointed delegates of God on earth, Absolute in powers, were most willful and witting in their applications of planning and stimuli to industry and trade. Along the lines laid down by advocates of a State-planned economy, the Mercantilists, States prepared to subdue and regiment the old-fashioned, town-minded merchants and manufacturers at the sword's point. Royal whim suppressed some industries, while royal largesse fostered others lavishly. The State borrowed huge funds from bankers, who took heavy profits from the transactions, and generously handed them over to monopolists for the extension of business. Eagerly the State sought colonies and organized them for purposes of commerce. It even captured and trained the poor, in barracks and workshops, to make a disciplined working population for industry; the abundant holidays of the mediaeval times were pruned away, and the lazy, frolicsome European, at least north of the Alps, was gradually reduced to a serious, assiduous toiler. And so it was not long before this centralization of authority in the political sphere was reflected in a corresponding enlargement and consolidation in the economic world. Absolutism was paralleled at length by its form of Capitalism.

Capitalism must therefore be regarded as something other than the simple outcome of the business man's thirst for profit-taking. It is doubtful how far it was the work of the business man at all, and how far it was the consequence of the overthrow and suppression of the trader by the military might of the Absolute State. It may be viewed from one angle as an achievement of the State won in spite of the individualist, local-minded oligarch—as, in sum, a byproduct of "government interference in business."

THE STRUGGLE OF OLIGARCHY AND ABSOLUTISM

The formation of these States in Europe was strenuously resisted by many business leaders in the seventeenth century, to whom any sort of widespread regimentation was extremely repugnant. The business oligarchs had always been essentially city-centered. Body and soul they were bound up with some small urban nucleus, no matter how wide their interests stretched. This was true of those magnificent imperialists, the Venetians, whose patriotism was ever bounded by their own Piazza. It was characteristic of the Florentines who, while embracing half Europe in their schemes, yet refused to countenance "foreign airs" at home; one prominent merchant among them, it is said, tried to interlard his speech with German phrases, but was snubbed so coldly that he died of a broken heart. Even the Dutchmen were filled with similar provincial and urban jealousies, for Holland remained an aggregation of towns and provinces always at odds with one another and restrained from fratricidal strife only by the predominance of mighty Amsterdam.

To be sure, the business oligarch did his share in breaking down the walls of the feudal world and disrupting its many compartments. He was binding many lands with lines of trade and negotiation and mingling their cultures. But he lacked either the wish or the brutal will to power to weld together politically the units which he was so busily fastening with financial or mental ties. At best he produced in his own time only loosely-jointed federations of cities like the Hanseatic or Rhenish, in which each town stoutly maintained its individuality; or, like the Medici, he juggled many units in a skillful game of "balance of powers." But this was only combination or manipulation, and not true consolidation. Either he did not see the possibilities inherent in expansion, or he felt it would not pay in the long run.

Sensible men with an eye to the balance-sheet might well shrink from an attempt to make a modern nation, which would include within its borders so many hopelessly inharmonious interests, agrarian as well as commercial, and would require so vast an overhead for running expenses. No doubt Holland was too sober and calculating to thirst for broad extensions of power over the land; this madness she left to Baroque France and Prussia, who had not learned to weigh accounts. And thus the Dutch, though so much more "modern" in dress and behavior than any of their contemporaries, were not ready to create a State, and hence prepare the preconditions of modern capitalism. They developed machines, indeed, but machine-industry itself was to appear instead among their strutting and impractical neighbors, the French and British, so absurdly overdressed and exaggerated in gesture, so filled with vaporous notions of loyalty to caste and Crown, and so entirely ignorant that they had as yet no fear of power.

Ironically, therefore, those very peoples of the Baroque who most scorned the trader were in reality shaping the world for capitalism, by their reckless concentration of wealth and might. One might draw a parallel: the Fascists of modern Italy and Germany, despite their anachronistic preaching of Teutonic or Antique "Mythos," have rushed into yet vaster centralization of industry in the Totalitarian State than their democratic neighbors. So also the earlier Baroque French, Prussians and British, affirming their feudal sentiments, wrought in reality a more socialized society. Business peoples draw back from such power-ventures.

The strong State was most easily created in regions like Sweden and Brandenburg-Prussia, which had ever lacked great cities, or in agrarian Russia and unbusinesslike Spain. It grew up readily enough in lands like France and England, in which burgomasters had never been extremely rich and powerful. But no such structure could be imposed at once upon any part of Italy or non-Prussian Germany where embattled oligarchs still remained, entrenched behind moats and armed to the teeth, ready to resist collectivism to the last gasp.

So bitter was the struggle in Italy and Germany that a national unification could not be achieved until recent times; not before the latter half of the nineteenth century was it possible to form a Germany and an Italy as modern nations. Up to then, largely owing to the fierce self-defense of business men, both lands remained in a welter of localism. True, Absolutism was established in principle during the seventeenth century there also, but only in miniature form. Local tyrants or petty princelings managed to bring together a few towns and acres, and set up toy courts, but no larger consolidation was possible.

As they grew poorer, the Italian city-men only redoubled their local squabbles, instead of seeking relief through combination. Their Eastern traffic was lessened by the new sea-routes to the Indies, and their banking operations were cut down when the Reformation diminished the flow of gold to Rome. But, far from uniting to salvage the remnants of prosperity, the towns fought more venomously than ever over each scrap. Unable to afford condottieri as freely as before in these battles, they invited foreigners to assist them, luring them by hope of booty. Successive invaders recouped themselves by looting the last reservoirs of Italian capital, even the Church *monts de piété*, final refuge of investors.

Matters might not have been so serious in Italy had there been a genuine knighthood left to protect it. But that country had become over-civilized and urbanized; many of the cities had systematically exterminated their nobili, or, like Genoa, compelled rustic gentlemen to take shares in trading-corporations, enter the grocery business, and buy corner lots in town. When they acquired municipal securities and a taste for city excitement, the most hardened agrarians grew mellow; and so there was no longer in Italy, as in France and Germany, a ferocious landed caste to repel invasion and indeed to force business men to collaborate through fear of chivalric reprisals. The Absolutism which grew up in Italy was hence a peculiar one, which spread from within the towns themselves.

As the hired military leaders of the Italian towns took possession of the city governments, turning themselves into tyrants and then into aristocratic despots, they surrounded themselves with artificially-created courtier castes, and gave themselves airs of sovereignty. But few were able to extend their domains beyond the old confines of the original city-state, and none could embrace all Italy. And this curiously petty, urban Absolutism in Italy was not of a sort to foster business growth and stimulate capitalistic trends; instead its principal achievement was to "freeze chaos." In this the Church assisted.

Equally unfortunate, though for different reasons, were the German oligarchs. They were indeed compelled to band together for protection against the feudal gentry, and they did not tear one another asunder in the Italian fashion. But they could not form any reasonable alliance with the German Emperors, and persuade them into making a sound bargain with commerce, as the Crowns of England and France were ready to do. The German Emperors remained too scornful of trade, too filled with wild dreams of foreign conquest, to realize the chances at home which lay in utilizing the good will of the business cities. And so in Germany the two forces of chivalry and commerce were left alone without a strong umpire, to fight it out to the death, and a long agony they made of it.

In Germany the new little States were not formed from within the cities as in Italy—instead, the towns were captured by neighboring princes. But so violent was the resistance of the business individualists that no prince could bring them all into his fold; indeed some fifty towns out of originally triple that number managed to remain free from the yoke into the eighteenth century. And the rest yielded very slowly. Few princes could capture *two* important towns. Most had to be content with enchaining a single metropolis, and even this was seldom to be achieved by a sudden siege. Most of the cities surrendered their rights piecemeal, through endless boycott and litigation, over many decades. In the majority of cases, it was not gunpowder but poverty which broke the spirit of the oligarch.

As trade-routes changed, life in the old towns stagnated; and the Thirty Years' War not only destroyed craftsmanship, capital and initiative, but sealed up the Germans within an economic tomb. Since the mouths of the principal rivers fell into the hands of Swedes, Spanish, Dutch or French, it was impossible for German merchants to join the race for colonies and world commerce. At last they had so little manufacture left that, as a bitter jester said, their principal export was sand. Shippers of Bremen had nothing to bring for exchange to the French port of Nantes, and so carried a ballast of sand, which was dumped out, forming little hills in the harbor which became known as "Les produits de l'Allemagne."

Even where the towns remained nominally free, the trade had shrunk so far that traders were usually excluded from the administration. Frankfurt, Bremen, Lübeck and Hamburg still admitted business men to their councils, but only the latter city was wealthy enough to count seriously. In most of the towns, the patrician castes hardened, withdrew from business, lived by monopoly of city posts, and absorbed as much as possible of the municipal revenues. In Nürnberg, for instance, patricians forced the municipality to provide free dowries and travel abroad for their children; merchants were compelled to pay forty per cent of their incomes in taxes and besides were denied civic jobs and hustled off the sidewalks. Only the haughty patricians could wear feather and sword. Naturally, where merchants had sunk to so low an estate, and their persons and property lay at the mercy of courts, they did not thrive.

In the cities which submitted to the princes, they became even poorer than in those which remained free. This was so obvious that a traveling Puritan business man of England, Slingsby Bethel, who visited them in the seventeenth century, observed that it had been a costly mistake for German princes not to maintain "the free Towns in their just rights and liberties":

> For I dare undertake to foretell, that those Princes which do promise to themselves great advantage in the subduing of their Neighbor Republicks, shall find more loss by the decay of Trade . . . than they will profit by becoming Masters of them, for nothing makes countries rich but Trade, and nothing increaseth Trade but Freedom; as *Stade, Magdeburg*, and *Munster* . . . do sufficiently evince, those Cities, as well as the Countries wherein they lie, being now miserably poor to what they formerly were under liberty; and I have been credibly informed, that the Duke of *Brunswick*, from a sense he hath of the decay of Trade in his Country, since his reducement of the City of Brunswick, doth already repent his taking of it.

And so it appeared that the very strength of the German was to prove his undoing. He resisted so obstinately that he exhausted himself in the process. When he yielded, he had been bled of capital and ambition and was as unproductive as an Indian in slavery. In his bondage, he forgot his old political adroitness and his former pride. He had failed to make his peace with the State while there was yet time, and having given nothing, could exact nothing. And thus he, like the Italian, failed to derive the ultimate benefits of princely centralization. And both these types of business men, who had been so mighty and creative in freedom, turned out to be most humble and spiritless under Absolutism, and even beyond it.

BARGAINING IN ENGLAND AND FRANCE

The extreme opposite of the Italian and German situation was represented by those agrarian countries like Sweden, Austria, Brandenburg-Prussia and Russia, where business and hence business resistance were minimal and Absolutism was left without a dangerous opponent. In Prussia and Russia, indeed, with their lack of urban tradition, business has never become really independent, even in modern times, and so the newest Fascism and Communism there may be viewed as a mere continuation of the royal and bureaucratic authoritarianism of the Baroque period.

Between the two extremes of Russia and Italy, there were two countries of compromise, England and France. In both, of course, there had been centers like the towns of old Provence and the ports of Britain, which held the makings of patriciates. But none of these had ever formed a federation to match the Hanseatic, a trading-monopoly as wide as the Venetian, or a financial empire like the Florentine. None could seriously dispute the sway of kings.

Certainly, London and Paris were capitals in ceaseless rebellion against regal tyranny. Each city fostered in time a revolution through which a kingly Absolutist was brought to the executioner—Charles I was as much a victim of London determination as Louis XVI of Paris fury. But the two cities, however commercially dominated, were not hostile to the idea of centralization, only to its abuses. They throve upon the concentration of authority, and would never oppose the State in principle.

The lesser communities of France were speedily drawn into dependence upon the French monarchs who early began to sell their municipal offices to the highest bidders. Rogues, if they had the price, might win the highest posts; in the scramble for the spoils of office, mounting from the middle of the fourteenth century, French burghers lost probity and dignity, and were unable to achieve respectable business administrations. Moreover, their attention was very soon diverted from manufacture to the looting of the royal treasury; in this, the Italian adventurers showed the way to native talent, and a very rich group of financiers, tax-farmers and monopolists formed, which heartily favored centralization of royal powers. Finally, as the uncouth feudality of France grew ever more menacing, the burghers in the towns became weary of defending themselves and asked nothing better than to let the Crown protect them with a national army. In the fifteenth century, under the leadership of Jacques Cœur, the local militia were neglected and with a sigh of relief the business man surrendered his sword to the king.

Poorer and fewer than the French were the English towns, and still less able to resist the advance of kings. The port of Bristol may serve as example; it held sea-merchants of some stature like Sir Robert Thorne, who were not slow in enterprise; once, indeed, a group of Bristol merchants, distraught during a depression, begged the canny Italian, John Cabot, for advice, and when he proposed to turn away from the saturated markets of the Old World and seek fresh fields in the western Eldorado, they gladly financed his voyage to Newfoundland. But how far such men were from being oligarchs on the Italian or German model is shown by the case of a great shipper and fishing-master, one of the mayors of Bristol, Sir William Canynge, who found it impossible to escape the exactions of Edward IV except by fleeing to holy orders. He died, not as a defiant oligarch, but as Dean of Westbury.

Never having known the heights and sweets of independent splendor, the French and English business man had never developed cultures of their own and social patterns for their behavior. Hence they were willing to follow those set by royalty. Comparatively poor and lacking in technical skill, they were only too glad to accept cash and advice from the governmental authorities. And so they bowed their necks to the chains of autocracy and soon learned how to gild, and even break, their fetters.

It was their good fortune that, about the same time they submitted, the aristocracies of either land were also brought under the yoke. Both the English and French sword-bearing castes had rubbed each other down considerably during the Hundred Years' War, and thereafter underwent profuse blood-letting in civil carnage. By Tudor times the English nobility was sadly drained of prominent names, and it was necessary for Henry VIII and his successors to create a new nobility, largely recruited from men of commerce, to replace that destroyed in the Wars of the Roses. The French aristocracy was indeed less weakened, despite its combats, but it remained poorer than the English because it was denied entrance to commercial activities even for younger sons; this in turn made it more subject to the temptation of marrying financiers' daughters, and so, in time, it became almost as thoroughly renewed from below as that in England.

Despite this general similarity in the fates of English and French business men, their positions were not exactly alike. The Frenchman was on the whole more dependent upon the State, more humiliated by the aristocratic pretensions. The former was more favored by circumstances, and though his Puritan revolution did not establish a permanent business government, it won many advantages for him. Absorbed in a more democratic society, however, the Englishman became as dependent upon public opinion as the Frenchman upon the State.

In both countries through perpetual process of compromise and bargaining, it proved possible to establish some sort of harmony and equilibrium between noble warriors and plebeian profit-makers, with the Crowns holding the balance even. And thus these two States alone managed to attain a unity decorated with aristocratic magnificence and enriched by commercial progress, and to become strong as well as prosperous.

KINGS AS COPYISTS OF THE OLIGARCHS

About 1660, to set a date arbitrarily, the triumph of the States in Europe was assured. Holland, to be sure, remained a puzzling exception, a little realm of fog and bog reserved for traders. But almost everywhere else, the principle of authoritarianism had been accepted, whether on a large scale as in France, or in miniature, as in the duchies of Italy. The world presented a spectacle of governments riding rough-shod over business men.

By that period, the attempt of Puritan and other merchants to set up a Republic in England had failed; the Stuarts were restored, and the Merry Monarch was busily winning back the favor of the populace to the Crown. Across the Channel the supreme example of Absolutism, Louis XIV, the Sun-King, had crushed the revolt of the Fronde and was now ruling without a parliament or other check on his powers. Over the Rhine, as the Thirty Years' War had ended, the German lands were divided into a multitude of little States, in each of which some local ruler determined the creed and code of his subjects; parliamentary institutions failed and the Hanseatic League dissolved. And in the Orient, to make the universal picture more complete, a powerful Shogunate had been established in Japan; there merchants had been deprived of the right to bear swords, and by the Seclusion Act of 1643, autarchy was established, cutting off the island from the main stream of foreign commerce.

Intoxicated by these successes, the new race of rulers made a perpetual fiesta of their lives; to celebrate their just-won battles the superb art of the Baroque was unfolded in the 1660's, with all its extravagant worship of power and victory, its protuberant symbolic figures raising pæans to laureled and helmeted conquerors who were shown, now riding on chargers across the contorted shapes of captives, and now enthroned amid a litter of trophies, eagles and urns, receiving the tribute of suppliants. All across Europe were built the throne-rooms,

theaters and orangeries of the new masters, from Vienna and Versailles to Dresden, Kassel and Potsdam, far-away Russian Peterhof and
the corners of Poland and Hungary. In these palaces nothing was
neglected that could be done by miracles of glass and water-jets,
frescoes, gilt paint and pink marble, to illustrate the exuberance of
fresh-found might. And at the same time in Japan, as well, the Shoguns
had begun to rear their heavily carved memorials of red and yellow
lacquer at Nikko, and in the South were building out over lakes their
pleasure-pavilions, in which the paper walls were powdered with
precious dust, forming, when caught by sunlight, long vistas of trans-
lucent gold or silver as a background for crimson robes of state. In
all these abodes, Eastern or Western, now moved a tribe of courtiers
sublimely "above trade."

Yet this majesty, built upon the abasement of the business classes,
was heavily indebted to business men for its methods and ideas, as well
as for its culture. The grandeur of kings was founded upon the previous luxury of business-rulers in the Renaissance. Financiers like the
Fugger and Medici, Spinola or Fouquet, had been the tutors of the
Hapsburgs, Stuarts, Valois and Bourbons in aesthetic matters; they
taught the kings how to stage a "triumph," what sort of homes to build
and in what attitudes to have themselves painted. The fine art of propa-
gandizing power, so essential to the monarchies, was based upon lessons
taught by the Italian city-patriciates. Even in Japan, to draw one more
parallel, the rich merchants of an earlier age, who built gold-lined residences and hired Chinese servitors, were the teachers in taste of the
Shoguns who humiliated them.

If the new States were culturally heavily indebted to the formerly
independent cities, they also derived ideas from the same source. They
did not pluck the notions of Mercantilism from the air; rather they
absorbed the heritage of experience and skill which had been accumulating so long in the old urban centers. The cities had ever been
better managed than the fiefs, and if a State required an efficient
bureaucracy, it had to find it among townsmen. The first mediaeval
State in Europe to develop such a model system, the Kingdom of
Naples in the twelfth century, did so under the direction of an Italian,
Giorgio Magio, representing olive-oil and other interests, who was
the Colbert of Roger II. The idea of taking a census and gathering
statistics as a basis of taxation and planning, so fundamental to modern
governments, had been elaborated in Venice and Florence. These two
cities, likewise, offered the chief patterns of consular and diplomatic
services; the latter taught the arts of diplomacy to the French, who in
turn educated the rest of Europe in finesse.

Again, the States copied the amazing network of postal service, news-gathering and espionage which had been constructed by such rich Renaissance merchants as Fugger and Gresham. Currencies had been managed by Lübeck and Florence for many generations before any European monarch brought his monetary affairs upon so sound a basis. Public loans were invented and floated by Florence before national governments resorted to the device. The Bank of England, forming the firm core of the English State, so closely resembled the Bank of St. George, which absorbed and dominated the city-state of Genoa, that many scholars fancy it to have been a direct imitation of the older Italian institution. Thus the financial framework which gives stability to modern States was in large part an adaptation of that which strengthened governments in the independent cities previously.

Royal navies had inevitably to be planned along the lines of Venetian, Dutch or Hanseatic fleets, since there was no knightly navy in existence to be copied, for feudal gentlemen were notoriously reluctant to face water in any form. The big royal armadas sent by Spain and Portugal to bring home the precious freight of gold and silver from South America, because private ships sailing singly would have offered too great a temptation to pirates, were consciously patterned upon the large convoyed fleet, the Caravan of the Levant, sent out every year by the city of Venice to bring home the silks and spices of the Near East.

Even the new armies of the States were planned upon the model of the excellent municipal forces, and particularly those of burgher-Holland, rather than upon the ineffectual arrays of feudal knighthood. The modern transportation of fighting masses was developed by Nürnberg with her wagon-trains. Holland showed the way to business-methods in armies, efficiency in mass-drill, under foremen-officers, with excellent standardized equipment. And therefore it was business men who prepared a basis for the national armies of France and Prussia, even though these were led by elegant cavaliers who, in full panoply of war, with steel breastplates half hidden in lace and curls, presented a spectacle which seemed the antithesis of commercialism. And even the professed aims, as well as the methods of warfare of the Absolute Monarchies resembled those of their business predecessors. The new kings fought for colonies, markets, routes as the trader-oligarchs had done; and the wars of the eighteenth century became a cut-throat competition between royal entrepreneurs which repeated, on a colossal scale, the spiteful quarrels of Venice versus Genoa, or of Pisa versus Florence.

But not only the ways and means of gaining, perpetuating and advertising power were adapted from city-experience; the whole notion of planned economy, which characterized the Age of Absolutism, with its Mercantilist philosophy, was an outgrowth of previous town-policies. The mediaeval and Renaissance cities, guided by business burgomasters, had likewise passed sumptuary laws to regulate display and keep caste apart from caste; they had all tried to assure a steady food supply by fixing prices for grain delivery, or arranging long-distance transportation of foodstuffs, to be paid for by taxes and public loans. Municipal governments had struggled with problems of competition, and balance of trade. They had tried to restrain trust-formations, regulate wages and wares, prices and profits; they had surrounded themselves with tariff walls and restricted immigration. Many of the ideas which are commonly considered most characteristic of the Mercantilists were in fact prefigured in the cities; in Venice, as Heckscher has pointed out, from the year 1328 onward, it was forbidden to foreign merchants to bring into the city wares of greater worth than they took away; and England's attempt to preserve a favorable balance of trade by a similar "Statute of Employment" in 1390 is thought to have been cut along the Venetian pattern.

The very notion of governmental regulation of business is thus seen to stem originally from business men themselves, much as they later chose to denounce it, whenever it ran counter to their interests, as tyrannical and contrary to the laws of Nature and Reason. In fact, all the independent cities under merchant-patrician rule were miniature examples of planned economy; all were managed for what was conceived to be the community advantage; none for a moment left the course of commerce to regulate itself. It was the long and varied experience of these city-patriciates in protectionism, trust-busting, imperialism and the formulation of industrial codes which furnished the background for the vaster attempts of modern nations to design the economy of million-headed populations.

SOVEREIGNS IN BUSINESS

In a sense, the new States only overthrew the business-oligarch, in order to bring his ideas to fuller expansion. Nay, more, the States themselves went into business.

All the European rulers desired wealth to dazzle one another. The Japanese Shoguns were quite unique in officially choosing poverty and limitation in size for their State; realizing that the longer-lived government would be the one founded upon stable agriculture, avoiding as far as possible the dangerous fluctuations and expansion of business, the Japanese announced their decision not only to force the merchants to their knees, but to keep them down by throttling commercial life to a bare minimum. The Europeans were not attracted by this scheme of poverty, much as they, too, realized the dangers of wealth to the strong authoritarian State. Perhaps the Prussians most nearly approached the Japanese formula in repudiating business ideals; they refused to ennoble even wealthy merchants, and preserved a calculating hostility to bankers; yet even the Prussians admitted the necessity of fostering some industries. Quite clearly was the choice put to Henry IV of France, when the merchant Laffémas was plucking at one sleeve, begging him to encourage trade, while at the other elbow stood grave Sully, the warrior-aristocrat, warning him that rich traders were risky citizens; the humane Henry leaned toward the money-bags. And as France went, so also went other Europeans, some with reluctance and others with zeal; the doctrine was generally accepted that the strong State must be rich and that business men must be prodded and assisted, even though carefully watched.

Could the State promote commerce, and yet prevent the parvenus from growing ambitious and rebellious? Could Western statesmen achieve what the wisest sages of the Far East had declared impossible? This was, in sum, the aim of Western planning. To this end the keenest flights of "State Reason" were directed. With this in view, the various European States went into business. They laid claim to soil and subsoil resources and assumed control of mining operations; they entered all sorts of monopolistic enterprises from the building of navies to the production of painted fans. Plunging into speculative ventures, kings and dukes began to set up tapestry-works, engage in banking and slave-dealing, and thereby discovered for themselves the tribulations of commercial life.

Soon Europe was as full of kings in business as it had formerly been of millionaires manipulating kings. Instead of a Jacob Fugger shaping the policies of the Hapsburgs in his countinghouse, there was presented a still more entertaining spectacle of a Bourbon monarch presiding, if with rather ill grace, over a shareholders' assembly of the French East India Company. Where once merchants had ruled their city-states in the interests of business, there now appeared sovereigns who sought to control and turn business to the interest of the State.

The leading "go-getter" among the crowned heads of Europe was Louis XIV, who opened factories, "modeled" his own dress-goods and used his royal position to advertise his wares throughout the Continent. Other rulers copied his super-salesmanship as eagerly as his garden statuary and waistcoat-patterns. Business became fashionable. Directors' meetings were held beneath the crystal chandeliers of palace boudoirs. Royal brows were wrinkled over reports. Lovely mistresses proffered suggestions for new styles.

Among the numberless imitators of Louis, the most talented hustler was unquestionably Frederick the Great of Prussia, who tried to introduce Bourbon business methods to Potsdam. Declaring that "all foreign states and almost the entire world is busied with manufacture," he strove to industrialize his kingdom as well as militarize it, and was as proud of a sale from his silk-machines as of a victory by his machine-like army. This commercialization of royalty infected even the potentates of two-by-four principalities, each of whom felt it incumbent upon him to keep up a miniature Gobelins-works as well as a toy army, though the one was generally as useless as the other, for the shareholders outnumbered consumers in the former as officers outnumbered privates in the other. To the very frontier of European civilization the mercantilist ardor spread until it caught Peter the Great of Russia, who forthwith came to Holland and undertook to learn ship-building from the keel to the mast. The get-rich-quick fever became epidemic among kinglets as far away as the Congo, who cruised about in canoes looking for black folk to sell to the foreign slave-traders, with a view to maintaining a favorable trade-balance and insuring a steady supply of rum and cutlasses.

Though the English Stuarts were willing enough to open a royal factory and grant monopolies, they were not so ready as the Prussian, Russian and French rulers to capitalize their positions. Apparently they had no taste for demonstrating home-made dress-goods and pressing them upon reluctant courtiers. In vain their subjects urged them to "Buy British." In 1663 Samuel Fortrey wrote: "If only His Majesty would be pleased to commend to his people by his own example, the esteem and value he hath of his commodities . . . it seems to be more honourable for a king of England, rather to become a pattern to his own people, than to conform to the humours and fancies of other nations. . . . This alone, without further trouble, would be at least ten hundred thousand pounds a year to the advantage of his people." When the Stuarts failed the business men, they were driven from the throne. Then a Dutch king, William III, who knew how to curry favor in a land of shopkeepers, was imported; and from William's day, the commercialization of English royalty steadily proceeded until the Prince of Wales in the reign of George V became frankly the national traveling salesman and gloried in the rôle.

Among such blue-blooded manufacturers, the Medici in Tuscany continued to occupy a peculiar place. They were of course business men who had become ducal, and not vice versa; purchasing a title and adopting a crest of industrious bees, they filled their duchy with aristocrats by ennobling all available rich men and inviting foreigners to reside there. Nevertheless they clung to trade until well into the seventeenth century. The Medicean bank continued to operate branches, with politico-financial aims, in various places and the Medicean monopoly on industries and trades grew more and more oppressive and ruinous to Florentine economic life, as the family strove to squeeze out funds for its aristocratic ambitions. Though the Medici supported a notable porcelain-works, such enterprises were more than balanced by the tremendous burdens of taxation they imposed on the State and the frightful terrorism by which they kept themselves in power. A grave mistake was also made by refusing to harbor a multitude of French Huguenot refugees who might have brought a fresh commercial bloom to the city as such exiles did to Prussia, Holland and England.

As autocrats, the Medici proved rather blinder than genuine royalty which went into business. They failed both in commerce and in the attempt to get themselves accepted as peers by other sovereigns. Yet they were constantly observed with interest by Mercantilist writers of the age, who, urging their States to promote commerce, pointed to the Italian methods. Englishmen, advising a similar establishment for London, kept calling attention to the Medicean example of banking and public finance. And when it was proposed to bring over a Florentine bride for an English prince and vehement outcries were raised against the baseness of the Medicean blood, Sir Walter Raleigh defended the Italian house with warmth:

> The Kings of France are twice come out of the Florentine . . . [The Medici] are very ancient, and ancient in virtue and fame. It is true, that long ago they were merchants, and so was Solomon too . . . the kings in old time . . . traded with nature and with the earth. . . . All the gentry and nobility in Europe trade their grass, and corn, and cattle, their vines and other fruits. . . . The King of Spain is now the greatest merchant. The King of Portugal was . . .

EXPERIMENTS IN STATE MANAGEMENT

In varying degrees, the States of Europe had become laboratories in which all sorts of curious and edifying experiments in controlling social and economic development were being performed. The theories of dogmatic "experts" were tested regardless of expense or hurt feelings, under the full pressure of autocracy. Businesses were stunted or fostered by arbitrary decrees; industries were transplanted or uprooted; working habits and consumption habits were altered; immense shifts and dislocations were undertaken light-heartedly. It is no wonder, therefore, that the Baroque, more than other periods, appears fertile in amusing parallels with present experience.

Whatever modern critics have to say about the ineptitude of State-control of business enterprise, for instance, is poignantly illustrated by the failure of the English Government to conduct its Bible-printing monopoly to the consumers' satisfaction. In producing the notorious "Unrighteous Bible," containing the howler, "the *un*righteous shall inherit the earth," it left a lasting memorial to a gross mismanagement of a public utility. So, too, the absurdities of paternalism were embodied in the hated "Kaffee-Schnüffler" of Prussian Frederick, those official agents who prowled with nostrils a-quiver for a fragrant trace of the illicit coffee-bean in homes and shops.

As was natural, governmental theorists often went very far astray in their choice of industries to protect. Thus Bavarian dukes permitted a fine old native linen manufacture to decay while they spent fortunes trying to force up a printed-cotton industry which was doomed in a land so far from ports where raw cotton could flow in cheaply. Quite to the contrary, the French went astray in suppressing the same printed-cottons, done in the Indian manner, because they were competing with the products of the royally favored silk-looms. It is said that the campaign to crush the cotton-industry cost the lives of 16,000 men in riots and hangings, not to mention the victims condemned to the galleys or those who fled the country. Tremendous sums were expended upon spying and policing. But the outcome was an incalculable loss to France; her merchants and artisans stole away to foreign lands and there built up enormously profitable businesses; the industrial greatness of England in the eighteenth and nineteenth centuries was built upon the developed cotton-craft of French exiles.

A similar miscalculation was made by the Prussian Frederick II in imitating the French silks. Uninterested in the native cloth-industry, he devoted tireless energy and great sums to promoting sericulture in his chilly domains, where it was necessary to compel heavy-handed Prussian peasants to tend the delicate worms, which they loathed; machines and foremen were imported from Lyons and Amsterdam and orphans were collected in wholesale lots to spin; finally the subjects had to be coerced into purchasing the resultant high-priced and inferior goods. The most insistent State protection and aid could not bring this industry to the perfection enjoyed in sunnier regions, and it perished as soon as royal solicitude was withdrawn.

Frederick was even more in error in refusing to consider his markets as seriously as his production methods. He did everything possible to prevent the rise of the bourgeois to aristocratic standing, refusing to let them purchase noble estates or marry titles. In so doing, he choked off the best consumers for his silks. But he was not alone in this astigmatism. Most of the princely entrepreneurs thought of dealing in luxury-articles for a strictly limited circle of buyers; their factories were planned to produce the most elegant and costly objects, tall mirrors and gilt chairs, ribbons and ormolu clocks. The more expensive the article, they fancied, the more profit there would be; but for their consuming public they had chiefly one another's courts, containing merely the tiny caste of the high-born, and each ruler was jealously seeking to monopolize his own local market. Thus the kings of Europe were, in effect, trying to make a living by selling one another porcelain snuff-boxes—"taking in one another's washing."

The notion of a constantly enlarging market was foreign to thinkers of the Mercantilist period; they did not foresee future expansion either through a growing population or one rising in standards of living. In their view, the stream of European commerce was constant in volume, and though each nation tried to take a greater share of that stream for itself, it occurred to few, except possibly the English, that consumption might be stimulated as readily as production. The English formed an exception, for very early they began to see that snobbery and social climbing made more customers for fine clothes and coaches; the remarks of Mandeville on "private vices publick benefits" were expanded by succeeding writers on economic topics, throughout the seventeenth century, and it was generally agreed that the spread of luxury was the source of new opportunity and power for England's men of trade. On the Continent, however, ambitious bourgeois were still repressed and intimidated by rulers who would not adopt a theory savoring of revolution.

The Swedish and some German princes, wishing to heighten the prosperity of their capital cities, did not encourage the middle classes to develop new tastes; instead, they solemnly set about choking off the trade of lesser towns in their realms, in the fond hope that the capitals would gain it all instead. In France the lesser bourgeois were forbidden even slight innovations in dress-goods and styles. Though the Court changed its fashions seven times a week, it was feared that if a multitude followed suit, there would be hopeless confusion in the industrial codes, as well as dangerous erasure of class-distinctions. Thus Louis XIV prohibited anyone in his realm outside of the Court from wearing the new cloth-covered buttons; the bourgeois must be content with buttons of metal or horn. But bourgeois men lusted after cloth-covered buttons, and bribed tailors to sew them on secretly. All offenders caught were severely punished. Vainly La Reynie, the Police Chief, ventured a mild protest to the king. His Majesty, frowning portentously, declared that he would be "obeyed on that point as in everything else."

Under these circumstances, the French royal factories and those modeled after them in Moscow, Spain, Bavaria, Denmark and else-where could not be viewed purely from a monetary standpoint; their returns were in pride rather than profit. And the war-industries, which were even more tenderly cherished by the States, were still less likely to pay, for, though many of the wars of the age were declared to have solid economic goals, all of them cost huge sums out of all proportion to any immediate financial return. The "planned economy" of the States was thus clearly unbalanced; production was planned, but the problems of consumption were not worked out.

Despite lamentable failures, however, the ventures of the State in business were at least successful from the national standpoint. The French Crown was virtually bankrupt when Louis XIV died, but France as a whole was wealthier. The State had given its means to supervising and boosting industries, and though the Crown had not profited ultimately, it had certainly permitted numberless individuals to line their pockets heavily. Those who held contracts, managed plants and companies, loaned funds to the State, and directed the upswing, found plenty of chances to accumulate fortunes. State experimentation provided greater amounts of capital than any private concern could have found at that stage of French development; governmental pressure produced larger workshops, better organization and higher skill than could have been brought forth by the competition of petty private manufacturers.

The same thing was observable elsewhere. England's monarchs first turned their people from a pathetic dependence upon foreign traders to independent manufacture of woolen cloth. Royal pressure was needed to effect this change from passive endurance of exploitation to aggressive pursuit of profit in England. So, too, the silk-enterprise of Frederick the Great, however injudicious, was the first lesson in larger industry offered to the agrarian Prussians; it introduced capital and foreign instruction to the village of Berlin and other places. Generally, therefore, the effect of governmental interference with business was the stimulation and growth of industry. The State may not have cleared cash profits from its sallies into business, but it immeasurably assisted that very figure whom it had intended to keep in thralldom—the business man.

BUSINESS STOOPS TO CONQUER

There have been three periods of State control over the business man: the Antique, the Absolutist and our own. Of the three, certainly the second employed the most high-flown language, claiming divine rights for its kings and asserting the unqualified supremacy of "State Reason."

But it does not follow that, in practice, the big business man was more helpless then than now.

Absolutist codes often proclaimed startlingly severe penalties, and manufacturers might be pilloried or exiled with arbitrary suddenness; often also the codes descended to ludicrously petty details. But the machinery for carrying out the State's purposes was still inadequate, in a time of crude communications and imperfect technique. Much of the direction of the French governmental program had to be left in the hands of business men, since there were not enough bureaucrats with the slightest knowledge of commerce; these directors often did not separate public duties from private speculations. And always of course, in France, the bankers upon whom the State drew for financing its program remained outside the scheme; whereas England had begun to study the problem of making bankers serve the ends of the State, and in Prussia, bureaucrats themselves were the State bankers.

Vainly the frantic bureaucrats of France piled up their regulations; the codes became so intricate at last that not even officials could understand them, much less the illiterate artisans expected to apply their regulations. The interpretation of rulings was left to officials who might differ among themselves so widely that the manufacturer who complied with one decision might be ruined by that of a second. Inevitably the administration of such codes proceeded amid increasing bitterness and bewilderment, with the concomitant of corruption. Through bribery and intrigue, the bigger business men broke through the meshes of the system, escaped taxes, evaded laws, pocketed subsidies without even declaration of intention to make a return on them. In short, the loopholes for the important business man were then much greater than in a modern State.

In England the actual supervision of the rich was slighter than in France. Lacking the elaborate industries of the French, their bureaucratic machinery was far smaller. The mighty monopolists were virtually independent, obtaining vast sweeps of foreign territories and rights to trade but making little accounting. The directors of the East India and Hudson's Bay Companies were potentates abroad, owning only bare allegiance to the Crown. Here, as in other countries, the small business man had perhaps a more restricted sphere than his counterpart today; but the mighty magnate enjoyed an open access to State coffers which is now impossible.

The strongest of the Baroque States could not establish anything like the surveillance of modern Fascist Italy and Germany or Communist Russia over entire populations; so open were the frontiers of France, for instance, that the Huguenots could slip out with large quantities of capital and tools, to found new branches of trade abroad, a thing denied to Jewish or any other business men under Germany's modern currency control. As Heckscher has suggested, the omnipotence of modern Neo-Absolutism is far beyond the dreams of the older Absolutism.

But the earlier Absolutism had a crushing effect in the psychological sphere. Kings humiliated the bourgeois and forced him to conform to aristocratic molds, even though they left him certain avenues to power and riches. Today, on the contrary, Fascism has reduced the business man's liberty of movement far more, but has given him in compensation for his loss, the consolation of patriotism and racial pride. The older monopolist had to bend the knee and bow the head, in return for his privileges; he had to render himself eligible in manners, to insinuate himself as far as possible into the courtier caste. Around all the courts of Europe, accordingly, formed a business fringe.

Among these hangers-on of the courts were royally privileged merchants who controlled tobacco or cotton; there were industrialists who operated mines and shipyards, contractors who supplied materials for palaces and canals and outfitted the armies and navies; tax-gatherers and bankers formed another group, and apart from these stood the exploiters of colonial tracts. Somewhat different from ordinary monopolists, and forming a new type of business man, was the *projector*, the *homme d'avis*, who offered his magnificent schemes to the State in return for a reward for his inventive genius.

The projector was a transition figure, midway between the mediaeval alchemist who annnounced he could make gold out of lead, and the more modern speculator and inventor, the stock-jobber of the eighteenth century, who proposed to make gold out of bubbles. This halfway man, the projector, was not a dabbler in science, like the former, nor in the still blacker arts of finance, like the latter. He simply offered plans, sometimes practical, often of a highly visionary character, which he whispered into the ears of the noblemen and especially of the court-ladies, whose weakness for "projects" was notorious, in the hope that he would find a patron to take him to the king.

Among the earliest projectors to perceive the possibilities of exploiting the newly strengthened States were Italian adventurers. Some of these were evidently men of sense, with reasonable advice to proffer. One Benevento of Florence made a lucrative venture of salt-making in Spain, while about the same time, a Venetian suggested to Queen Elizabeth a plan for a labor-saving device in the cloth-industry. The latter was turned down, however, because the English Government at that time was perplexed with the unemployment problem and wished to save anything but labor. Other States, according to Sombart, were equally cold to labor-saving improvements in machinery; even the efficiency-loving French statesman, Colbert, rejected such *instrumenta* with horror. And therefore the projectors were turned away from the fields of mechanical improvements; they had better luck with less substantial visions for getting rich quick.

Molière has depicted a projector in his "Fâcheux." He is a "whisperer, one of those people who have nothing and always come to promise you so much." The France of Molière's day was swarming with such ready talkers, glib of tongue and wild of eye, with all the irresistible arguments and ingratiating politeness of a modern bond salesman, but still lacking anything tangible to promote. The further step was taken in England, toward the close of the seventeenth century, when the patent-system was introduced. An agile promoter could then secure a patent on some device, form a company and sell stock to the gullible public, and then decamp overnight. Insensibly, the technique of stock-jobbing improved until the master-promoter, John Law, the Scotch financial wizard, appeared. John Law, bringing perfected English skill to France, the land which had been most enamored of visions, found there the perfect theater for his famous bank bubble.

These monopolists and projectors, hunters of governmental places and favors, were somewhat different from the simpler types of parvenus in previous times. True, the eternal temptation of the rich merchant all through mediaeval times had been the aping of knightly ways; nevertheless, he was restrained by civic pride and responsibility. Moreover, the imitation of feudal ways had been a financial loss, and was undertaken purely out of vanity. Now, however, imitation of the aristocracy had become immensely profitable to those who sought privileges; and there was no longer a civic pride to limit the business man's abasement. All that was left was the consciousness that, being a practical man, he was intrinsically better than the frivolous noblemen before whom he bent the leg.

In this way, the aristocratization of business proceeded as a counterpart of the commercialization of royalty. The business man, seeking his avenues of power, became more subtle in his manipulations of men and more veiled in his phraseology. The middle classes, from high to low, were filled with the spirit of emulation; lesser business men longed to follow the leaders; simple bourgeois grew stiff and courtly, as they and their womenfolk put on airs of gentility and studied the minuet, which was but elegant practice in back-crooking, set to music.

With the loss of position, went a corresponding diminution in manifestations of power. True, the very successful monopolists and financiers were quite as gorgeous as the courtiers, and in some cases far outshone the high nobility by the splendor of their châteaux and apparel. But they no longer held supreme political office, and had less need of the arts as advertisement. Art became more and more an escape instead to the bourgeois. Now that he ceased to be a city-dictator, ablaze with ornament, indicating his power by the cost of his festivals, he turned to make-believe. Drama offered him a consoling world of illusion. In Hamburg, Paris, Charleston or Osaka, the theater became the obsession of the eighteenth-century business man. More and more, he supported the arts at second-hand; he became the purchaser of books rather than the friend of the literati; he bought pictures but less often dictated the themes. Indeed, he would not have dared to commission painters to depict him on horseback in triumph, or floating toward Olympus, now that royalty had usurped such concepts; he had perforce to content himself with pretty decorations of shepherdesses or genre scenes in kitchens and inns. In short, he had become the reader, the spectator, the man-in-the-audience, and no longer the chief performer.

Even the mightiest of the monopolists took shelter within the forms of the aristocracy, and became indistinguishable, if possible, from the oldest nobles. The lesser bourgeois followed as far as they dared, but in many places in Germany and France more than in England, they knew that too great a parade of wealth would mean being pressed for more taxes or a prison sentence for transgressing sumptuary laws. So, from high to low, the business man retreated, temporized, and left the foot-lights to the nobles and warriors, the "feathered gallants and tavern roarers." Those who look back upon the age have difficulty in seeing any business men at all, so skillfully have they concealed themselves. They are unknown, or in disguise. But there was an exception—the Puritan.

THE PURITAN INDIVIDUALIST

Dark of dress and dour of mien, animated by an overweening pride in his own judgment, the Puritan man of business stood out in striking contrast to the servile crowd of his contemporaries. He alone refused to follow the fashions and amusements of the aristocracies. He alone would not admit the divine right of kings or priests to interfere with the forms of his worship, or acknowledge any authority higher than his own conscience. It was therefore his mission to keep alive the older individualism of the Renaissance all through the period of Absolutism, and so form a link between the mighty magnates of the 1500's and the modern entrepreneurs of the 1900's.

In effect, the Puritan was a hang-over from the Renaissance. He was an anachronism in the age of strong States, representing a creed which had taken shape in the early 1500's, while the Fuggers and other Renais-sance monopolists were at the height of their audacity and powers. John Calvin, its founder, was steeped in the liberal Humanist philosophy of the Renaissance, which had developed in the commercial cities of Italy; his broad views on the ethics of usury had been foreshadowed by the apologists of business in those cities long before. And not only was Calvin the heir to Italian culture; he was also a realistic student of contemporary business life, and a friend and counselor of business men. At Paris he lived with the rich merchant, Etienne de la Forge; his celebrated letters, including the one of 1545, which interpreted Scripture with considerable latitude for capitalists, were written in answer to troubled investors who had approached him with their souls' perplexities. Calvin was in fact proud of his acquaintance with business methods and law (he had specialized in the law of mortgages) and advised other ministers of the Gospel to do likewise, that they might counsel traders to better advantage.

But Calvin had put a religious seal upon the individualism of his age. The culture of the Italians had been pagan in its emphasis. Calvin had given business a new religious sanctification and a new ethos. Therein lay his great importance. Through him, individualism was given a fresh chance for survival, despite the crushing weight of Absolutism. Even after the independence of the cities was gone, and the freedom of the business man was but a memory, Calvinistic individualism survived. The business man could no longer trumpet his egotism in the frank manner of the pagan Renaissance; but he could still insist that what he chose to do was the Lord's will and he was in immediate communication with the Lord. He could demand the right to elect his own ministers, though other self-government was taken from him; he could follow his conscience, if not his anarchic desires. And so Calvinism perpetuated the tradition of business independence under the guise of religious dissent, and prevented a too complete submission of business to the State.

How far was Calvinism a cause and how far was it a cloak of business resistance to Absolutism? Did the adoption of so stern a creed, preaching inflexible self-reliance, tend to further political independence among business men, or did the recalcitrant business men willingly become converts to a creed which suited their tastes? There is much evidence on both sides, and the answer depends largely upon what weight one is disposed to give Idea and Interest in human affairs—whether one believes men more affected by concepts or chances. The two outstanding advocates on either side were Max Weber and Lujo Brentano, representing Idea and Interest respectively; both were sons of business families, whose ideas were influenced by divergent economic backgrounds.

Weber was on either side descended from Puritan artisans and business men who had fled from persecution to the haven of Berlin. From his devout mother he learned that the foundations of commercial success lay in practicing the virtues pleasing to God, thrift, sobriety, incessant toil. Unlike the Lutheran or Catholic God, the Calvinist deity would not be content with prayer and repentance, but exacted work from His Elect. Carnal pleasures, distracting from work, must be shunned. Success in work, which might be shown on the credit side of the ledger, was visible evidence of Divine approval. Seeing how steadily the precepts of the Calvinist faith led in the direction of bourgeois virtues and hence, it seemed to him, of business aptitude, Weber concluded that Calvinism had been the most important factor in forming the modern capitalist mentality.

True, the earlier Puritans were not all perfect examples of Calvinist virtues. In the seventeenth century, the Dutch Calvinists were anything but blue-nosed enemies of good cheer; their heavy meals, with wine and song, were far from ascetic. On the whole the French Huguenots were gayer than the English Puritans; they were fond of music, and the theater which the English put on a level with bear-baiting. In exile, many of the French blossomed into quite surprising extravagances, and their communities in Charleston and Hamburg were noted for fashion and amusements. In England, moreover, the Calvinists often found Court favor and enjoyed fat monopolies, comporting themselves in a manner scarcely different from that of the cynical freebooters of orthodox persuasion. But it must be said that the Puritan, whatever his behavior, represented theoretically an individualism which was highly dangerous to the Absolutist State; he challenged the principles of authority upon which "State Reason" rested. Religion and economic interest together led him into revolutionary protest against authoritarianism.

Was religion the garment of righteousness chosen to disguise the thirst for profit? Brentano, the opponent of Weber, came from an old and rich business family of South Germany, with Italian connections and of Catholic belief. This different setting disposed Brentano to flout the hypothesis of Calvinist influence, and spurn the notion that Italians or Catholics in general had been deficient in business acumen or the ability to concentrate upon money-getting; if they failed to rival the English and Dutch, he argued, it was not because they lacked Puritan repressions, but because of climatic, geographical and political factors. Bourgeois virtues, he contended, were not the main factors in forming the successful capitalist; he was animated by greed for power and riches, and this greed had ever been rooted in human nature, needing but little impulse from John Calvin. Calvinism he assumed to have been a happily discovered ideological set-up for the British. Perhaps Brentano dismissed the importance of ideology too lightly, just as Weber too quickly passed over the long development toward the emancipation of business in Italy. Even a cloak must be taken seriously, especially in a democratic country like Britain, where clothes may make the man, and little can be done without some appropriate argument. Could freedom for business from Absolutism have been won there without the Puritan slogans of Cromwell?

Neither concept seems wide enough to embrace the confusing immensity of the facts. And neither sufficiently explains the evolution of capitalism. For regardless of whether the capitalist was a creature of his virtues or of his greed, it is dubious how far the capitalist made capitalism and how far the reverse was true. As has just been said, the strong State pushed business in the direction of large-scale production; rulers of Europe forced an ever-greater concentration of industry in part to provide for their growing armies and in part to furnish the luxuries for their courtesans, who set the fashionable pace for the rich—Sombart, referring to the rôle of the courtesan in the fostering of industry, has called capitalism the "child of illegitimate love." Thus modern methods were in part the product of instincts more primordial than those admitted by either Weber or Brentano—capitalism in this light may be viewed as the offspring of war and love, Mars and Venus.

But perhaps the Puritan was temperamentally best fitted to bring up this curiously parented infant. Possibly the Protestants, who severed their connections with the Catholic Church because they hated its corrupt connections with high finance, were forced, by their very Protestantism, to become better financiers than ever the Catholics had been. Possibly also the grimmest of all the Protestants, the Calvinists, with their disapproval of royal authority and of carnal pleasures, were formed by their very Calvinism into the best possible caterers to the needs of the State and the appetites of the idle rich, becoming the ideal purveyors of cannon for the king's fleets and silk stockings for his mistresses. It is possible, and at any rate it would be a pity to exclude altogether what is the only hilarious theory in the entire depressing range of the "dismal science" of economics.

XIV

BOURGEOIS AND PURITAN IN FRANCE

DURING THE SECOND PHASE of the business man's history, that in which his adjustment to a national design was being made, the most interesting theater of events was France. Here large-scale capitalist manufacture appeared, in the *grande industrie* of Colbert; here also the great types of the Conformist and the Nonconformist business man, the Bourgeois and the Puritan, were evolved, the one furnishing the manners and the other the ethos of the modern man. Here the noblest and most persuasive slogans originated, including the sublime Laissez Faire, Nature's Law and the Rights of Man; and here, finally, the modern costume, as well as methods, character and concepts, of the modern business man were perfected.

It may seem a little strange that all this should have taken place in France, but, in fact, there appears to have been a division of labor among the peoples, by which the French undertook the ideological preparation for capitalism, and the Anglo-Saxons did the manual work. France gave the English and Americans their religious sanction for trade, in Puritanism, and their "scientific" arguments for individualism, as well, through the revolutionary clamor for laissez faire. France held up the highest models of manufacture for imitation, and provided them even with her dearest blood, that of the exiled French Huguenots, to ensure the smooth transplantation of French achievements on foreign soil. This was of immeasurable advantage to the Anglo-Saxons; it saved them the bother of thinking, and enabled them to attend strictly to business.

But it was not so happy for France that the apportionment of tasks left her the verbal glories without the material profits. She sowed where others reaped. Though the supreme types of Puritans came of French blood, Puritanism was at last wiped away from French soil. Though the buds of capitalism were watered in France, the flower bloomed only when the plants had been uprooted and set down in other lands. Though the superb argumentative defense of rugged individualism and untrammeled freedom for commerce was made by Frenchmen, the

French were not able to become, themselves, either individualists or really free; they remained clubby, conservative and dependent upon the State. Thus the endeavors of the French business men wear a tragic air, on the whole.

Tragedy, in fact, filled the life-stories of the greatest men, natives or immigrants, who arose from business or near it in France, and strove to harness the State to the desires of Business—Jacques Cœur, Laffémas, Colbert, Law, Necker, Ouvrard. This was an extraordinary series of giants who struggled through the centuries against the State; each seemed for a time about to succeed in his tremendous attempt, but all of them, except Laffémas, died in despair amid the wreck of their designs; four of the six, Cœur, Law, Necker and Ouvrard, perished ignominiously in exile. The French State was too strong to be tamed easily for business purposes.

In part this failure may be attributed to geographical situation. France lay between Holland, the paradise of plump traders, and Spain, the most unbusinesslike country in Europe. She coveted the triumphs of both, and sought to be as haughty as Spain and rich as Holland; her troops were ceaselessly hurled both south and north for conquest. But the Southern ideal of hidalgo pride and the Northern ideal of bourgeois profit were incompatible; and unhappily, France's aristocracy and Crown looked in one direction, her middle classes in the other.

Influenced in manners and outlook by hidalgos, the French noblemen were, next to the Spanish, the proudest and idlest in Europe. They refused to work, even in the pinch of poverty, and were even reluctant to marry money earned in commercial enterprise; but they developed luxurious tastes which could only be satisfied by the rarest products of the utmost industrial skill. Unwilling to live economically on their estates, like the Prussians, they demanded splendors far beyond the purchasing powers of mere agriculture; they could only be supported by enormous State favors. But though fed by the State so largely, the French aristocrats would not perform any useful function, save the military, for the society which maintained them. They would not invest in trading companies like the British or enter bureaucracies like the Prussians. Disdainful of toil, insistent upon a continuous parade of fashions and an unlimited indulgence in gambling, eager for war at any cost, they were a most dangerous element for business men to oppose.

Possibly the French business men might have subdued even these adversaries, had they been united among themselves. They were, however, undone by their very talents. The old Italians had tutored them in finance and industry, while their Dutch and English neighbors gave them lessons in merchandizing; for a time, the French business men represented the very cream of European business abilities. But this manysidedness was their undoing; manufacturers and merchants could not agree, and both hated the bankers worse than noblemen. The bankers clung to the Crown which gave and ensured wealth, and would not have joined a revolt against it. Thus there could be no such clear alignment of forces as in Holland and England, where merchants were so definitely predominant and leagued together by common interests.

Moreover, the relation of Crown and Commerce in France was not one of simple antagonism. Each was peculiarly dependent upon the other. French business, more than any other, grew rich upon government privileges; while the French State, in turn, was peculiarly dependent upon the will of bankers and the profits of industry. Locked in this unbreakable grip, each felt itself the aggrieved victim of the other. And both the rivals were inordinately strong: for two centuries, until the fall of Napoleon, the French State was the greatest, most absolute, in Europe; while at the same time, French industry attained a size and perfection unapproached by other countries.

Across the complex lines of interest in France the religious question cast a baffling and obscuring shadow. It hid the economic issues. To be sure, the best business men were in the Protestant camp, but the leaders were noblemen, whose furious feuds and general intolerance and ferocity helped to prevent any reasonable compromise with the Catholic Crown. Minds were confused and economic antagonisms were terribly sharpened by this struggle of the creeds, and the end could only be the destruction of French Protestantism, and with it the best hope of France for business supremacy over the rest of Europe.

Out of this peculiar background may be explained both the periods of stability which other nations envied France, and those occasional orgies of frenzied bloodshed which shocked the rest of the world. So long as the tug-of-war between the almost equally mighty contestants, Commerce and Crown, gave neither the advantage, there might result an appearance of calm, of standstill, of perfectly balanced elements and forces. But sooner or later the taut rope would break, and a mad scramble begin; such moments, when decision was sought by the knife, were the Massacre of St. Bartholomew, in 1572, when the Puritans were cut down, and the Reign of Terror, just a little more than two centuries later, when it was the turn of the aristocrats and clergy for decimation and exile.

The intensity of this centuries-long duel, the intransigeance of both parties, led to a higher development of ideas in France than elsewhere; scheming and planning were necessary, and an absorption in the problems of manipulating and exploiting, or overthrowing, governments, which made the French business man unique among his fellows. He could never sink into the happy wordless torpor of the Dutchman;

words, words and more words were his weapons. Nor could he arrange everything behind the scenes by affable gentlemen's agreements, like the Briton; he needed a peculiar brand of oratory, a legalistic line of argument, which ultimately formed the Gallic character. And in this conflict, throughout the generations, it was inevitable that types should be more sharply defined in France than elsewhere: one was either a conformist, a submissive and ingratiating *bourgeois*, doing his best to ape the ways of the aristocrats, and be respectable, or one was the severe Nonconformist, the grim Puritan, who is usually depicted in portraits with a skull by his side, emblem of a stern faith enduring unto the death. In France, a business man had to choose which he would become; only in England, where both concepts were eventually transplanted, was it possible for him to become an "occasional nonconformist," a *puritan bourgeois*, insisting on his individualism whenever it suited him, but cheerfully merging into society the rest of the time.

THE BEGINNING OF THE DUEL

At the commencement of this battle between Commerce and the Crown, we find the former assisting the latter to eminence, in fact, creating the power of its future foe. That extraordinary late-mediaeval figure, Jacques Cœur, as we have already seen, laid the foundations for a national army in France, on which the great powers of the French State were based securely at an early time. Under his persuasions, the various cities agreed to help the king raise a large force, which would be more efficient than their civil militias; thanks to this, the king could put down the warring nobility at home as well as repulse the English invaders. Cœur's manipulations of the currency, by simple falsification, raised funds to purchase munitions for Jeanne Darc and her captains at the siege of Orleans. Cœur's money provided artillery, "the largest number of huge bombards, great cannon, *veuglaires*, serpentines, mortars . . . that ever the memory of man had seen in possession of a Christian King." Thanks to the Maid and his munitioneer, the weak puppet, Charles VII, was elevated high above his subjects and enemies, a position which he could never have won himself.

But the downfall of Cœur was one of the most spectacular collapses of mediaeval times. Popular hostility against this enormously rich man had mounted. The poor whispered that he shod his horses with silver; small business men were furious at the three-score assistants of Cœur who had also made huge profits, and engrossed trade from lesser fellows; the old families eyed with equal jealousy this upstart who purchased a patent of nobility and drew the aristocrats into his debt. Cœur became the hated symbol of big business in Old France, nor did he attempt to wipe away this bad impression by publicity. Taciturn in the conventional manner of millionaires, his favorite motto was "Bouche close. Neutre. Entendre Dire. Faire. Taire" (Mouth shut. Neutral. Hear what is said. Do. Keep still).

At first imprisoned for cheapening the king's money, Cœur was later faced by more serious charges—illicit arms-traffic with the Infidel. On June 5, 1453, he was forced to kneel, bare-headed, with a candle in his hands, repenting that "he had wickedly sent armor and arms and caused them to be presented to the Sultan, enemy of the Christian faith and of the King." Then he was charged with poisoning the king's mistress, stripped of his fortune, and flung into jail. He escaped from the dungeon, by friendly aid, only to die soon after in exile.

Though this first effort of business to aid the Crown had ended with so dismal a misadventure, the French middle classes continued to trust their kings. They could not fight the marauding petty nobility in person, and wished to uphold the king for the sake of peace, imagining that they could keep him on their side by freely opening their purses. A hundred and fifty years after Cœur, appeared that eccentric Puritan merchant, Barthélemy Laffémas, who in 1596 proposed a New Deal to the Merry Monarch, Henry IV.

Laffémas was one of those occasional self-made men in the world of business who, by startling commonsense and sheer energy, outdistance the learned pedants of their day. He wrote a prodigious number of works, effusive and incoherent, including some moral admonitions, in execrable stumbling verse, of which he was enormously proud. He had not troubled himself to look into the solemn theories of his times, and ransack Latin authors; he was a man of action, feverishly busy scheming and pushing, penning his pamphlets and poems, urging a total reorganization and reorientation of French economic life. Far from being abashed by his lack of methodic knowledge, he boasted about it in his prefaces, saying, "This author has never been in schools, and the little he knows he has learned while trafficking in merchandise, furnishing silver to the King" of Navarre.

This quaint, proud character, as he is presented to us by Hauser, laid before his King, who had become master of France, an ambitious scheme for rejuvenating commerce. His plan involved the national unification of weights and measures; the free circulation of goods within the realm, unhampered by local tolls; the creation of a series of industrial and commercial codes to be written by a body of government supervisors cooperating with chambers of commerce to be set up in the cities, and to be enforced by bureaucrats and merchants acting together to supervise wages, prices, goods and the conduct of labor. Laffémas proposed a harbor police system and the erection of labor camps for the unemployed. He urged the suppression of great bankers for the good of the State, and government regulation of the interest rate. He wanted to see industry stimulated by high tariffs and the prohibition of certain foreign commodities, even on pain of death. He sought to have new French companies organized and subsidized to flood the land with native-made luxury-wares. In short, his National Recovery Act was comprehensive and about three centuries ahead of his contemporaries. So astounded was Royal Henry upon having it read to him that he swore: "Ventre-Saint-Gris! If my tailor takes to writing books, very soon, I suppose, my ministers will be cobbling my boots."

Against the tailor's bold scheme, the agrarian-noble, Minister Sully, argued with passionate conviction. He foresaw the embourgeoisement of the French State, were merchants admitted to such a rôle. Whereas Laffémas had promised to make France rich by industry, Sully retorted that a rich France would be corrupt and effete. Laffémas argued that the courtiers' silk robes ought to be made at home; Sully answered that they ought to wear wool. Were silks and velvets made at home, declared Sully, this would

> only throw your people into luxury, idleness and excessive expenditure, which have always been the principal causes of the fall of kingdoms and republics, and the destruction of the loyal, valiant, and hard-working soldiers, of which Your Majesty has far more need than of all these Court mannequins, and townsmen dressed up in gold and purple, men of justice, police and finance, secretaries and bourgeois who now live more luxuriously than any.

Thus the French King was faced by the alternative which, two centuries later, was to confront a Prussian monarch, when a proposal was made to establish a State bank, and Minister von Altenstein, like Sully, argued for poverty and genteel militarism. Both the old French and the later Prussian Minister knew that to let business men put a foot in the door was to lose the door; poverty was the price of nobility, the price that Spain paid for her hidalgos and Japan for her samurai. The Prussian King was willing to pay that price—not so the Merry Henry. He was not the man to put all France into patched rags and deprive his courtiers and his mistresses of their fine feathers.

The result was a compromise between Laffémas and Sully. Since France could not be standardized overnight, and since the great importing and banking firms of Lyons were resolutely opposed to the manufacturing center of Tours, which supported Laffémas, a large part of the plan was quashed. But Henry did set up big factories, donating 670,000 livres for some dozen establishments, the rest of the capital being provided by associations of merchants. The King graciously ennobled some of the entrepreneurs, such as Cadeau, Soyer and Hindret the stocking-maker; to the beneficiaries belong the Protestants, Olivier de Serres, who had a stake in silk-raising, and Laffémas himself. In 1602 Laffémas was made comptroller general of commerce, and continued his flood of writing; his son Isaac a little later wrote one of the earliest compendious histories of business.

To this rapidly enriched bourgeoisie, as the old noble, Sully, had foreseen, the administration of the State was more and more a prey. In 1604 the King issued the notorious decree, La Paulette, which permitted the holder of a government post to hand his office down to his son, in return for a price. As holders of such offices were usually tax-exempt, this meant that any rich merchant could buy administrative position, often with a title attached, and tax-exemption, and pass this sinecure to his children—this was by far the most alluring opportunity to preserve and transmit capital offered to any European business men at the time. Security-loving French have been pioneers of the insurance business, which later took the place of this State-insurance.

To be sure, office-buying with its attendant corruption was far older in France; but making the offices hereditary vastly increased the prices which men were willing to pay. Whoever bought one at so high a value had to recoup himself by gouging the taxpayers still harder; and as the wealthy purchased tax-exemption most easily, the groups of tax-yielders grew ever smaller, a most unfortunate set of circumstances. Delighted by the increase in revenues, the State then created more and more useless offices to fling among the frenzied purchasers, and so, by the middle of the century, Minister Colbert found that there were 45,-780 offices in the justice and finance departments alone of which, he estimated cautiously, at least 40,000 were superfluous.

The holders of such posts formed a titled bourgeoisie, intermarried, possessors of châteaux and salons and great power. This group, derived and constantly renewed from business wealth, formed the administrative aristocracy of France, the noblesse de la robe, only lower than the true, haughty noblesse of the sword. Both aristocracies became a handicap on business enterprise, perhaps the former even more than the latter. As Charles Normand says:

There was in France—and it is justice to say it—a class more improvident, more egotistic, more routinière and more blameworthy than the nobility; that was the bastard aristocracy . . . the high bourgeoisie, a class narrow in spirit, avid of gain, grasping for places and honors, holding privileges in fief, as forgetful of its origins as it was jealous of those whose birth placed them above it.

Thus the business classes, even while they seemed to be winning tremendous advantages over the Crown, were creating dissensions within their own camp. Merchants who could buy their way into the Government could not afford to oppose the State too completely. Indeed, it was the French middle classes who begged the French king to declare himself Absolute. As Oncken has made clear, this first pronouncement of the Royal Absolutism was not the result of overweening pride on the part of the monarch; it was at the urgent bidding of the Third Estate, the bourgeoisie, in 1614, that he agreed to proclaim his might at the meeting of the Estate General, demanding a teachers' oath incidentally:

> The King is sovereign in his State, he has the Crown from God alone and therefore there is no might on earth, whether spiritual or temporal, which has any claim over his empire. . . . All subjects, of whatever quality they be, must hold this law as holy and true, as springing from the word of God. . . . This law shall be signed by all officials, by all teachers . . . doctors and preachers are compelled to teach this law.

Too much pity, therefore, need not be poured upon the business men under Absolutism in France. They were not suddenly struck down by an almighty monarch; rather they made him strong that he might subsidize their enterprises, defend them against their noble enemies and secure them in enjoyment of wealth, as rentiers. They hoped by supporting him to guarantee their possession of landed estates as well; for by 1596 merchants had been buying out titles and lands from the best families, worn out in civil war, to such an extent that noblemen demanded a law to stop the practice. In the Assembly of that year, the noblemen declared that, were this thirst of the roturiers to "monsieuriser" their sons unchecked, the blue blood of France will be soon debased. Clinging to the Crown assured their grip upon such properties, as well as entry into the administration. For well-chosen reasons, accordingly, the earlier French business men erected their strong State and created that condition of affairs which their descendants were to deplore and denounce with such fury as monstrous, unnatural and unscientific.

RELIGION AND BUSINESS IN CIVIL WAR

Possibly the compromise achieved in the time of the Protestant Laffémas, under Henry, who was a Protestant in origin, might have been maintained indefinitely, had it not been for local, racial and religious differences, which tore apart the French middle classes, and prevented any hope of solidarity.

Certain business towns were in most respects stubbornly opposed to others. Thus Lyons, importer of silks, where the flood of Italian Renaissance taste had entered France, was naturally cosmopolitan, and Italianate; it did not desire an all-French autarchy, and her merchant-rulers were not so often Calvinist as the artisans. It was otherwise in the ports of Dieppe, La Rochelle and Bordeaux, where the provisioners of the royal ships lived—these munition-purveyors were strongly Calvinist, and La Rochelle, in particular, the great trading-port, almost completely bourgeois, was the stronghold of Calvinism in France until it was reduced after an heroic siege. Bordeaux was also to a large extent Calvinist, and it was, moreover, subject to Northern influences. Unlike Italian Lyons, it was in constant communication with England, Flanders and Holland, the consumers of Bordeaux wines; numbers of these foreigners lived in the city, and their influence was felt politically.

Bordeaux was the door to English revolutionary ideas into France, as Lyons was the door to Italian culture. Not only did visiting merchants from Bordeaux become inspired by English freedom, but many exiled Protestants from Bordeaux fled to London, made fortunes there, furthered the Puritan Revolution of Cromwell, and wrote home to their envious relatives about this triumph. Bordeaux even wished to secede from France in the mid-seventeenth century, and set up an independent republic. And later on, it continued to strive for an English constitutional monarchy, and was a center of agitation as the period of the French Revolution drew nigh. Republican and revolutionary Bordeaux and munitioneering La Rochelle were nests of Protestant rebellion, and to these must be added another focus, the Protestant bankers of Paris.

Bankers found it somewhat easier to dwell within the folds of the Calvinists than in that of the French orthodox Church, which never inclined to so lenient a view of interest-taking or of commercial practice generally as the mellowed Mother Church of Italy. And they also viewed with animosity the Italian Catholic bankers who clustered around the Italian queens and stripped the royal treasury, leaving so much less for native sons to collect. This alignment of racial and religious with economic antagonisms was so obvious that it could be perceived even by the simple, if gallant captain, Blaise de Monluc. That implacable foe of the Huguenots noted in his *Memoirs* that, in the 1560's "the majority of those who mingled in finance were of that religion," the Protestant, a fact which he explained by the inborn tendency of business men "to love novelties."

Certainly, the economic background of the French religious strife may be traced with some degree of clarity; the Catholic banking families who played a major part in the Massacre of St. Bartholomew, and the Protestants who coveted their government alliances, were both sincerely convinced of heavenly favor in their separate causes. But behind the Wars of Religion was no mere simple story of economic conflicts; weighty as the material interest was, it was far from being the whole. On the Protestant side were not only bankers, shippers of wine and provisioners of the navy, but also profoundly religious noblemen, whose warlike gusto and unquenchable spirit of vendetta prohibited compromise. Vainly the Italian queen, Catherine de' Medici, sought to conciliate the parties; she was not a religious fanatic—what Medici could be?—but the plotting of the Protestant noblemen threatened her family's life and power; though she would undoubtedly have permitted the Protestants to share in spoils of government, she could not permit feudal localism to survive. And so, in the Massacre, blood-letting was found the only answer.

Though the Massacre drove out hundreds of rich Protestant business men, who came to Amsterdam and London with capital and tools, the end of the struggle in France did not come until a hundred years later, when the Edict of Nantes was revoked in 1685, and Protestantism was at last extirpated. In that intervening hundred years the Protestant business men maintained a precarious foothold, climbing into the government offices, ousting the Italian bankers from financial control of the nation, and developing French industry. Meanwhile, they strove against royal tyranny.

For a little while, in the mid-seventeenth century, it looked as though France might follow the example of England. While English merchants were sweeping to victory under Puritan slogans, led by Cromwell, a somewhat similar struggle was going on across the Channel. The Fronde, the terrible civil conflict of 1648–54, raged during the years that a Puritan Commonwealth was being established in England. To some extent the two movements were related; through Bordeaux, as we have seen, came an impetus to revolution and Cromwell at one time thought of intervening. The focal point was, however, Paris.

The starting-point of the Fronde was a commercial quarrel, the resistance of manufacturers to a special levy of 700,000 livres. Shutting down their factories, they told their workers that the levy had impoverished them to the point of bankruptcy. Labor took up the cudgels for its employers. Rioting mobs and barricaded streets gave Paris a foretaste of revolution, over a hundred years before the great conflagration of 1789. In various ways, the Fronde was a practice bout for that future match between bourgeois and the Crown. A revolutionary parliament was called which set up a cry for liberty, democracy and light taxes. Business demanded that the royal system of supervisors should be abolished; the Government must take its hands off.

But no such gathering of forces was possible in France as happened in England. The rich royal merchants, subsidized with State funds, were not inclined to make common cause with these lesser manufacturers of Paris; religious and local divergences cut athwart class lines. The Fronde, taken up and sustained by the nobility, degenerated into an aimless, sporadic, fratricidal strife and was finally crushed.

BUSINESS UNDER STATE TUTELAGE

When this ill-timed and unplanned revolt was stamped out, the French middle classes found themselves enslaved to the mighty State which they had helped to create. Louis XIV, the Sun-King, thenceforth to his death reigned without a parliament or an opposition to his royal whim. The State, now consolidated, could drill and regiment the business elements. Certain towns drooped under the burden; Bordeaux became almost prostrated, and, as her merchants continued to smuggle in forbidden pamphlets from Amsterdam, the "Gazettes de Holland," they had to be watched by special police. But Lyons flourished, under the sun of royal favor.

Thus it happened that the French remained for a century longer than the British under the strict pedagogy of Absolutism, with results upon their character and business which have not yet been effaced. To this very day, the emphasis upon luxury-trades, catering to the moneyed few, instead of mass-production for popular markets, has remained. So, too, the tendency of French bourgeois to retire upon government *rentes* as soon as possible is a heritage of that aristocratic régime. The power of finance, bound with the State, over industry, is yet another result of Absolutism. As a people, the French acquired habits of industry under this discipline, and were shaped into skilled and obedient workers long before swashbuckling English had ceased to discuss, purely in the realm of theory, the benefits which might be derived from commerce.

As an outcome of these distinct fates, the development of the French business man took a turn opposite to the Briton's. The French people were tamed and trained; then, only, did they feel the stirrings of revolutionary resentment. The British, on the contrary, got their revolution out of the way, and then settled back in bourgeois contentment. The semi-piratical islanders were just turning into a "nation of shopkeepers," as Napoleon called them, at a time when the prosy industrial French, under Napoleon's leadership, were becoming the conquerors of Europe.

This prosiness of the French was more the result of their political misfortunes than their Gallic nature, for, in the pre-capitalist age, they were not in any way different from other Europeans in their general aversion to work. Europeans were in the main very much like South Sea Islanders today, willing only to work under the lash of necessity. Old France was quite as "merry" as Old England; nearly a third of the year was taken up in holidays, spent in festivals and drunken sprees. The common people stoutly resisted entering factories and, in many cases, had to be driven there and restrained in barracks, lest they run away, as was also the case in nineteenth-century Japan. The exceptional Puritans alone exhibited true assiduity and temperance.

The man chiefly responsible for this national metamorphosis, for the embourgeoisement of France, was the almost-Absolute Minister of the Absolute King. Colbert, coordinator and dictator of France, governed for more than twenty years, from 1661 to his death in 1683, holding in that time the departments of administration, finance, the navy, commerce and agriculture—all indeed, save war. Master of the country, he set about remodeling it along business principles. He was the great *bourgeois gentilhomme*, indeed the supreme *bourgeois Duce*.

Minister Colbert was indeed not strictly a business man, though he incidentally made a fortune in business enterprises; but he had been trained in business methods by his cloth-dealing father, and his banker-uncle in Paris. Moreover, he remained thoroughly *roturier*, despite his dazzling ascent. As the king bluntly said, he kept "the manners of a bourgeois" at Court; and the courtiers would never receive him as their equal, no matter how rich or powerful he became, and though he had three dukes as sons-in-law. The trouble with M. Colbert was mainly his passionate addiction to work; he worked fifteen hours a day for twenty-two years and made everyone around him do likewise. Though he became titled, he never relaxed in seigneurial ease; rather, he tried to impose factory rules on his serfs, making them toil in forges and a cloth-mill under the lash, if they objected to the modern industrial servitude which he superimposed on their feudal bondage.

His ambition was to make all France as industrious as her Minister. A teetotaller himself, he tried to reduce drinking among workers. He lopped off their holidays ruthlessly, since business came ever before religion in his mind. He viewed the Huguenots with a favorable eye, so long as they were useful; though he was ready to put any superfluous heretic, a nobleman, to death, he was ever disposed to protect a merchant or even an artisan of a wrong creed. When pipe-manufacturers of La Rochelle objected to a Dutch Protestant competitor on the score of his religion, Colbert told them to be quiet, for "we have certainly no cleverer man in this branch in the kingdom." He also strove to protect Jews, at least those "of value to commerce," in the periodic excesses of royal zeal.

In short, Colbert was himself the flawless example of a "Bourgeois Gentilhomme," that type which was caricatured on the stage of Molière during his lifetime. Whether or not he recognized himself in the comedy figure of *M. Jourdain*, there is no doubt that he enjoyed it heartily; indeed, he seems to have suggested one of its scenes to the author, the one in which the *Gentilhomme* studies dancing. The adventures of the parvenu in the realms of high society were, of course, the dramatic reflection of the steadily rising commercial wealth and ambitions under Colbert's administration. Colbert thus helped to create, and to caricature, the French bourgeois.

But he was not satisfied with mere comic delineation of the parvenu; Colbert wanted more and more young men to aspire to the heights attained by *M. Jourdain*. He urged another author, Jacques Savary, a merchant who had joined his administration, to write "Le Parfait Négoçiant," which tells poor youth how to become *bourgeois gentilshommes*. This work, written in 1675, lays down rules for aspiring apprentices; it encourages them to hope that, by thrift and sobriety, they will "assuredly found a good family."

The ideal young business hero, as painted by Savary, must be robust, cheerful and folksy, since "most of the world prefers to do business with a good-looking and agreeable man," and his tongue should be well hung, "subtle and quick at replying by arguments." Above all, he must be wholly devoted to business. Away with Latin and the humanities! The days of the magnificent Lorenzo are over! Savary had an extremely low opinion of a college education (on which Huguenots were prone to insist) as a preparation for business:

> Experience teaches us that the children sent by their mothers and fathers to college to study Latin, Grammar, Rhetoric and Philosophy, up to the age of sixteen or eighteen, are never fit for commercial pursuits, and that out of thirty such, there will not be four glad to give themselves over to this profession . . . Philosophy gives them too good an opinion of themselves . . . making them thereby insupportable to everybody, so that one has all the difficulty in the world in reducing them to order.

Most business men, said Savary, arise from lowly beginnings, and succeed through eschewing vice and folly, cultivating obedience and humility. They are good-humored, modest in apparel and filled "with love and fear of God, without which God will never bless their work." Upon such bright, worthy young men, as Savary would agree with the modern Andrew Carnegie, millionaires are eagerly waiting to bestow their daughters. God-fearing apprentices

> win the good graces of their Masters, who, seeing them clever, sometimes take them into partnership, and give them their daughters in marriage, generally having more regard for their virtue and capacity than to the goods which they might have.

But virtue, Savary thought, like Schwab today, must be supplemented by salesmanship. Some suppleness of back and tongue are needed to render oneself

> agreeable to those who are customers . . . in gentleness of words . . . representing with honesty that the stuffs are fine and good . . . If, after having employed all adroitness and reason to persuade them, they leave without buying, it is necessary, instead of flying into a rage and scolding them, to . . . say with a gentle and smiling voice, that he regrets having been unable to sell to them.

Apparently, the Old French were as impatient with intractable customers as the Old English of Defoe's day. But they learned self-control earlier; English travelers, of the eighteenth century, when Defoe was still urging politeness in the shop as a novelty, were much impressed by the fine manners of shop-people in France, and by the custom of employing personable young ladies behind counters.

In Savary's work, though written by a Catholic at the behest of a Catholic, may be found most of those traits supposed to be peculiarly Puritan. It contains most of the leading ideas, as well as the homely optimism, of later writers, from Benjamin Franklin to Andrew Carnegie and Schwab. But it differs in one important respect: this seventeenth-century guide to business did not absolutely guarantee results. Let the merchant be virtuous, honest, agreeable, and he ought to win riches. But there is a lingering doubt. At any rate, he will have a good conscience, and this, thinks Savary, insofar the Catholic, is better than riches. Business had not become completely secularized.

FIRST SHOOTS OF CAPITALISM

In Savary, in Molière, and in the figure of Colbert himself, the successful French bourgeois was mirrored. Under the administration of the all-powerful Minister, the commercialization of France took on forms recognizably modern. Colbert's first move was to loosen the grip of the tax-gatherers and financiers, who diverted into their coffers the funds which, he thought, should water business enterprise. He brought low the superbly insolent Fouquet, owner of a fabulously sumptuous château famed throughout France; this he achieved by whispering to the young King that he might have a palace even more splendid than Fouquet's, that he might become rich and powerful himself if he could cast down the bankers and elevate the industrialists. Through such machinations, Fouquet was brought to trial and cast into a donjon where he died, after nineteen years of captivity.

The next step was to extend police power over the whole of France. Colbert reformed the entire State apparatus, unified the provinces by constructing roads and tearing down many toll-barriers. Around the newly achieved unity of the nation he erected high tariff walls. Under his régime, the French State was able to control economic life as it had not been done since Roman days. This omnipotent State could stamp out local industries and replace them with centralized manufactures of another type. For instance, to rival Italy's laces, Colbert imported Italian and Flemish women workers to teach peasant girls their arts; other peasants were forbidden to make any of the types so monopolized by the State. Those who were forced into the factories against their will revolted, and so did those who were suddenly deprived of their accustomed occupations. But such resistance was in vain.

Inevitably the results of State management of economy were centralization and concentration. Industry was placed at fewer spots and in larger plants. Thus arose the first significant group of industries run with considerable capital and on an impressive scale, often uniting many processes under a single roof. *La grande industrie,* as it was called to distinguish it from the petty crafts of an older time in France, was still without steam-power; it was not radically different from the highest organized efforts in Renaissance Florence. But it was a national industry, serving a national market.

In these factories labor was forced into the routine which has since become expected and habitual. A sharper control was exercised over workers than had been possible in small plants. Not only were they often confined in barracks, but the factory was run like a drill-yard, with corporal punishment meted out for singing or talking. In a cloth-of-gold factory at St. Maur, in the 1600's, where hundreds of workers were employed, not a whisper could interrupt the long day; the pay was from twelve to thirty sous. Nothing resembling a labor union was allowed. Supervision was extended over outside hours as well. Whether these conditions were more severe than the old, under the small-shop system, is a moot point, but the most recent students are inclined to believe that workers, on the whole, had fared better under mediaeval methods.

Undoubtedly, the spread of *grande industrie* increased the wealth of the nation as a whole. All through the *ancien régime* down to the Revolution, the fortunes of the bourgeois enlarged, their splendors grew, and some of this wealth trickled down below. The education and standards of living of the "menu peuple" tended to increase. However, while the coming of capitalism raised the level of life, it also produced periodic crises of a perilous character. Life was better at some times, for some people, but it was also more unstable for most people.

The contrast between booms and crashes was very violent in France, perhaps more so than in England; though in both countries depressions occurred every decade or so throughout the seventeenth and eighteenth centuries; in the view of Martin, there was a more wholesale dismissal of workers in bad years in France, whereas in England the better banking facilities in the latter century at least enabled manufacturers to keep their plants running in hard times. It is possible therefore that French workers suffered more intensely from the repeated panics. As a contemporary wrote of them: "In good times they feed and clothe themselves like bourgeois; in bad times . . . they must starve."

The herding together of labor in such enlarged factories naturally increased the temptation to combine for revolt, despite draconian laws. Angrily the great Calvinist manufacturer, Van Robais, sent a message to Colbert complaining that his striking workers seem to "believe that industry is created solely for the purpose of supporting them and they do not reflect that industry is not made for them in the least, but that they are made for industry."

By the eighteenth century, accordingly, the phenomena of modern capitalism were observable in France. Yet big business had not "made itself"; it had been forced into hot-house growth, under the State; the part of business lay in supporting that State, working through it. Very reluctantly in most cases, did bourgeois part with the funds demanded by Colbert to found his royal companies to trade with the Baltic, the Levant, China, Hudson Bay or Guinea. They were much more eager to share in the favors showered by the State upon the fortunate, which might include loans, tax-exemption, free land and buildings, forced labor, and even noble titles.

Within the terms of Colbert's office, the number of royal manufactures rose from 68 to 113. On the textile industry alone the State had spent ten million livres; millions more were lavished on manufacturing glass, tapestries, mosaics or lace and promoting war-industries and naval construction. The seats of French industry then chosen were almost the same as today; they were wealthier than ever before, and yet subject to more dreadful unrest as well. Within Rouen, for example, as cloth-production was speeded up, far more wealth was exhibited than in mediaeval times; in the 1700's one Legendre of that town had a fortune estimated at six millions, far beyond anything Rouen could show in former ages. But Rouen (home of the ancestors of the Du Ponts) was racked by crises worse than before: in 1757, so many workers were abruptly dismissed that, within a few months, 10,000 joined the army, in those days a desperate act.

The good and evil of the mounting capitalism were both demonstrated at Lyons. This city received special consideration from Colbert because it was generous in loans to the State. Its good-will was remunerated by the grant of many monopolies which ruined other competing cities. All the raw silk of France, for instance, had first to go through Lyons; only Lyons could manufacture black silk stockings, and so on. Nevertheless, despite the demolition of rivals, Lyons was regularly hard hit. A bad harvest, a fall in the silk market, the sudden wearing of mourning by the Court, could wreck its business at any time. Crises in 1766, 1771 and 1788 stopped thousands of looms and filled the city with parading workers who cried for relief. During an especially grave disturbance in 1744, revolutionaries under the sign of the White Cross mishandled merchants and pillaged homes and shops, until royal troops restored order and sent the ringleaders to the galleys. The Revolution might easily have started in Lyons instead of Paris.

By this centralization of industry, achieved quite as much despite the will of business men as with it, Colbert had planned to strengthen and enrich the Absolute State. Actually, however, he created many new danger-zones; he brought unrest to a sharper focus, by producing an ever keener antagonism between capital and labor, and more serious recurrences of depression. At the bottom of society he created a militant and often desperate proletariat in the cities, ready to shout for the hangman to begin his work; higher up he formed a new class of capitalists, growing in riches, terrified by crises, forever seeking fresh aid from the State and, becoming militant also, threatening the foundations of the Government. Thus a force was nourished which could menace the authority of the Crown.

THE STRUGGLE WITH THE KING

The shadows of that coming struggle were already cast over the last part of Colbert's régime. Colbert had fostered big business, but he could not carry out his projected commercialization of everything in

France, even the court and king. Had he obtained his dream, Colbert would have put everything, even luxury and war, upon a business basis. But in this he ran counter to the dearest prejudices of the Grand Monarch, who intended to enjoy both fashion and fighting, like a true seigneur, for their own sakes.

Vainly Colbert conducted his sly little campaigns in education, deluging Louis with documents and long letters explaining that war, in the seventeenth century, had come to depend upon financial and industrial factors as much as upon martial valor. Trading-companies, he argued, were as useful as armies, and new manufactures were reserve corps. "Your Majesty . . . has undertaken a money-war against all the States of Europe," said Colbert. Not all the strategy of noble generals would win, without wealth, against a trading-nation like Holland, "the mightiest Republic that has existed since the Roman." Dutchmen could only be beaten by matching Dutch wealth with French, which must therefore be created and fostered.

The King, like all feudal gentlemen, was land-minded, and thought of war in terms of territorial grabbing and cavalry charges. The bourgeois Colbert could not bring him to take an interest in the Navy, as a means of defeating the great sea-trading countries, Holland and England. Colbert insisted that there were only two ways for a nation to enrich itself, "either by the discovery of a new, hitherto unknown kind of trade"—and that, Colbert fancied, was quite unlikely—or by "diminishing the number of vessels of other nations." Not on land, but on the ocean, could France defeat her rivals. War therefore he viewed as inseparable from business. Industry must be encouraged to provide the sinews of war; war must be waged primarily to preserve commerce. This meant incessant combat, to Colbert as to Louis, "a constant battle between all the nations of Europe to decide which among them is to grasp the greater share for itself" of commerce. But this, to Louis, meant taking all the enjoyment out of combat. Louis was bent on acquiring more land, not upon naval rivalries. One might as well have tried to expound a treatise on war-profiteering to *d'Artagnan* and his fellow-musketeers, as convince the Sun-King that war must be regarded commercially.

Nor would the King view his pleasures from the standpoint of profit. Most of the large industries set up by Colbert were to make articles of luxury; if France was to sell them abroad, to obtain the steady flow of gold which mercantilists thought necessary, she must become arbiter of fashion. She must set the modes, as well as supply them; it was as important for her to develop cultured taste as to acquire habits of industry; she must become educated as well as busy. To promote foreign trade, Colbert urged language study; in the interests of technological progress, he opened the Academy of Sciences; he sought in every way to broaden the cultural interests of the middle classes.

Purely from the business point of view, Colbert throught it necessary to encourage, indeed to create, a French art. With industry in mind, he started to rebuild the Louvre as a museum and school giving lectures on art to consumers as well as producers of products. Not an aesthete himself, since his training took place in a bank and without benefit of the humanities, he suffered his taste to be molded by the Italian financier, Mazarin, and later by the German banker, Jabach, both foreigners who introduced the fine art of collecting to Paris. This tutelage was reflected when Colbert urged his King to acquire pictures and statues that would be serviceable in shaping French popular tastes. Under Colbert's guidance, Louis enlarged his collection from 200 to 2,500 pictures. But how little the King appreciated these treasures or their purpose, is indicated by the fact that the collection was allowed to run down, and much of it fell to ruin by sheer neglect after the Minister died.

In this way, Colbert set a precedent, as Neymarck points out: "Our contemporaries think they have imagined industrial art; before them Colbert did better, he created artistic industry." To foster design for commercial ends, he sent artisans to study in Rome. Bourgeois to the core, however, he endeavored to regulate their inspiration with the precision of a factory foreman. All artists were to rise at five in the morning exactly, be in bed at ten, and deliver a masterpiece to the Minister every three months. So also he hired literary men to produce panegyrics of the State to order.

All this Louis was willing to suffer, but he drew back when his bustling Minister begged him to dwell in the Louvre, in this glorified museum-school-lecture hall. Colbert argued that it would be a splendid way to promote sales, by conducting the pageantry of the Court amid the bourgeoisie of Paris, where consumer demand could be stimulated to fantastic heights. All the rising parvenus, together with foreign visitors, would be impressed by the splendor of the Sun-King as supreme demonstrator of French dress-goods.

In this vast politico-economic program, Colbert had the support of business men, who were keenly aware of the value of the King as a pace-setter for their wares. In most decided terms, the manufacturers of Languedoc petitioned the King to heed this request:

If it would please the King, in favor of the manufacturers of the realm, to dress himself each year in two sorts of stuffs, for example heavy cloth in winter and in spring, during three or four months, in some pretty lighter stuff such as is made at Reims, at Amiens, in Poitou, at Mans, etc., the lords and other persons of the court could not fail to imitate His Majesty. Paris and the rest of the realm would do likewise. And one may say that we should set the fashion indubitably for all the neighboring states, a thing which would produce an incredible movement of commerce and an extraordinary consumption of all these lighter stuffs.

Unhappily for the grand plan of the merchants and their Minister, the King turned recalcitrant at this point. He often insisted upon wearing fancy waistcoat-materials made by his enemies, the Dutch, quite regardless of the advertising-effect. And he absolutely refused to live in an industrial art school, surrounded by *bourgeois gentilshommes*. He desired no nearer contact with parvenus than could be derived from Molière's comedies.

Coldly brushing aside the entreaties of the broken-hearted Colbert, the King moved out to the aloof distance of Versailles, there to erect his chill, formal palace and dwell in splendid isolation from the bourgeois world. The Sun-King wanted no traders around him, even if they were his best customers. Nobody might hunt with him who could not trace his lineage back to, and including, the year 1400.

Some French noblemen agreed in a measure with the merchants and with Colbert; Vauban, a minor noble, thought that some compromise would help the aristocracy itself. As a much-traveled man, he had observed how the English landed gentry prospered through connection with trade; he would like to see the law of France, which still barred even the small nobility from trade, emended. If the country gentry of France could make money, it would marry and increase, producing more loyal soldiers for the State. But the King would not listen either to Vauban, who wanted the aristocrats to come down to trade, or to Colbert, who wished traders to come to Court. He allowed both men to die unthanked, broken-hearted in old age.

A ROYAL BUSINESS FLOP

As time advanced, the King grew weary of the enterprises launched by Minister Colbert. At first he was gracious enough to show his countenance at soap, silk and furniture factories. Meekly he had said to Colbert: "I will go to the factories of Abbeville and Beauvais and will speak as I believe I should and as you advise me." He had announced: "Out of the love His Majesty bears his people, he has consented to take, from the few hours left for his pleasure, yet two hours more every fortnight for a meeting of the chamber of commerce." And when Colbert persuaded him to head the board of directors of the new French East India Company, it was no doubt an amusing little adventure for the King, like sheep-raising later for Marie Antoinette.

So the palace was opened for the assembly of directors; the ballots were unfolded privately in the King's chamber, so that he could juggle the returns as he liked. In fact, the King was more willing to receive the shareholders, than the latter were to come; they suspected some new trick to open their purses. Colbert had to drag the tradesmen to the palace, and put on the screws to obtain the capital for his enterprise.

In playing his part, the King thought simply of colonial glory quite unsullied by returns on investments. Hence instead of rushing the fleet to India to buy cotton-goods, he sent an armada in charge of an aged ex-alchemist to found an empire in the jungles of Madagascar. Their worst fears realized, the shareholders protested against this crazy attempt to rule "a great savage island" and demanded that the Company proceed to "open branch offices and establish commerce" at once. Promising to turn over a new leaf, the King then invited the disgruntled shareholders to a grand meeting at the Tuileries, which was held on December 15, 1668. This must have been the most impressive shareholders' meeting in recorded history. What a pageant! What a fancy-dress party! It is odd that American millionaires, so fond of holding costume balls in the French "period" settings, should have missed the opportunity to issue invitations for a Louis-Quatorze Stockholders' Assembly, which would be so appropriate.

At this function, the superb figure of the Sun-King was surrounded by princes, lords of the Court, councillors and officers of Parliament, in their most gorgeous raiment. Nor to be outdone, the shareholders wore their best wigs and waistcoats. Minister Colbert read the report, announcing that the King was giving up his idea of vainglorious conquests and would now get down to brass tacks and subscribe four million livres for a fresh deal. Next His Majesty spoke, but briefly and irritably, making no royal pledges, and expressing lordly displeasure, in fact, at all his guests who had not yet paid in full on their subscriptions. Too many in that glittering throng, apparently, were holding out on their Sovereign.

Sure enough, the royal upswing failed to materialize. Ships returned to France with unsalable cargoes. Or they never came back. Or they could not even get started: the *Elephant* foundered on her maiden voyage out, the *Orient* capsized in the harbor. English privateers snapped up others. Dutch employees betrayed their French masters. Missionaries bickered with the military element; both snubbed the merchants; all got into rows with the natives. By 1675 there was no trade, no empire, and nothing in the treasury but bills amounting to millions. The

King, urged by Colbert, decided to pass the thing off in a regal manner.

Yet another meeting was held at the Tuileries, on May 8, 1675. But this was a sorry performance; bedizened courtiers were absent. Even the royal chair at the head of the long, green-velvet-covered table was vacant: the King could not bear to hear his own report. Minister Colbert himself lacked the nerve to appear in person, and sent a deputy who shamefacedly read a report which, while admitting that exaggerated optimism was out of place, pretended that there were encouraging elements in the situation. After all not every sou was lost—perhaps a ship or a fort would realize a tidy sum if anybody could be induced to buy it. No doubt many a shareholder's heart was ready to burst beneath his canary-colored waistcoat while this report was being read, but a shareholder in an Absolute State, with a king at the head of his company, had no recourse when his losses were written off in the grand style. He could not even write to the newspapers about it.

Such experience naturally confirmed Louis in his prejudices against vulgar trade. After that he wanted no more shareholders around the Tuileries. He grew more and more tired of lectures and advice, of chambers of commerce and visits to factories. He was bored with tolerance and prudence and bourgeois virtues—bored, enfin, with Colbert himself. In 1683, stricken to the heart, the old Colbert died. At his last hour, the King repented his harshness toward his Minister and dispatched a letter which Colbert, on his death-bed, waved away. Turning his face to the wall, he murmured: "I do not wish to hear talk of the King—I make myself ready for the King of Kings."

THE EXILE OF THE HUGUENOTS

After the bourgeois gentleman, Colbert, was dead, the King still had thirty-two years of life, free from lectures on the budget, in which he could impose his aristocratic will. In this span, he undid the work of Colbert as far as he could, jailing or beggaring the most active agents and prominent merchants who had assisted the Minister, leaving the collections of the Louvre to decay, and re-affirming the exclusive character of French noblesse. Under the influence of the zealous Madame de Maintenon, who had always disapproved of the Colbertian calculations, the King expelled the Huguenots, this time finally.

The revocation of the Edict of Nantes, two years after the death of Colbert, swiftly and drastically cut athwart French commercial development. The earlier heresy-hunts had expelled many noblemen as well as bourgeois; this time, however, the Puritans involved were overwhelmingly business men, the best in France. To be sure, the sweep was not altogether clean: some of the greatest, such as the industrialist,

Van Robais, and the financier, Sam Bernard, continued to flourish; and according to Rosenstock, the city of Paris was so opposed to the religious fanaticism of the King that it sheltered a hundred thousand refugees from Government persecution. Still, the provinces were cleared in a wholesale fashion, and those who did remain had lost the most precious qualities which Calvinism fosters—namely, initiative and independence.

The havoc was terrifying to watch, even to Catholic noblemen, to Vauban, for instance, who saw the sinews of war rapidly vanishing, and felt that no victories in the field could compensate for this economic destruction. The ports of France, where the navy-furnishers had lived, were decimated. The inland centers of industry were stricken as though by a hideous plague. Out of 18,000 looms in Lyons, but 4,000 were left humming; a few capitalists of that place took with them 600,000 crowns to Holland and England. Sedan was impoverished overnight; most of Metz moved to Prussian Brandenburg. In one city, Mézières, but 8 shops were left open out of 109; in Angoumois, but 16 out of 60 paper mills continued to operate. At Tours, only 4,000 workers retained employment out of an original 40,000; but 54 tanneries out of an original 400 continued to function, and just 70 silk mills of 700. More than 50,000 families went into exile, taking with them industrial knowledge, tools, and very great sums of money. When the Government, too late aware of its losses, tried to prevent capital export, it only laid so many restrictions on trade that its national balance suffered. And it was soon too late to recover either men or funds; within two years the fury of destruction had burned itself out.

Colbert had built up an early capitalism in France. Now the King, in his blind wrath, scattered the seeds of capitalism over the rest of Europe. Perhaps it would have been generations before England could have caught up with the fine technique of the French royal industries; certainly it would have been long before Prussia learned the lesson; but now, within a very brief time, Louis had literally imposed teachers of business on his worst rivals. Irretrievably, France had lost the chance to lead Europe in manufacturing; she soon fell ten or fifteen years behind England in mechanical invention and development after that. With her best naval munitioneers gone, she also gave up a large part of her interest in sea-adventures. Moreover, her State, as revenues from industries sank, fell again into the hands of the money-lenders from whom Colbert had striven to rescue it. Even from the point of view of the purely martial aristocrats, the effect was deplorable, for France was weakened for warfare, while Holland and England, thanks to Huguenot aid and officers, prospered exceedingly.

Wherever the fleeing Huguenot business families went, they brought

a remarkable refreshment to commerce. Amsterdam offered them freedom from taxes for three years, and opened all trades to them; they
brought so much money with them that the rate of interest sank to
half what it had been. Bringing every branch of the silk trade, hat-
making, even gardening, not to speak of advanced medicine and mathematics, the improvement which they produced was visible within a
very brief time. Three years after the expulsion, by 1688, they were
able to help Dutch William III, a Calvinist, to the throne of England.
They gave him money, and Huguenot ex-officers formed and led some
of his most valuable troops. Thus they had an even more favorable position in England than ever.

England, at the time of the expulsion, had been buying 200,000 livres'
worth of French fancy dress-goods; three years later this amount was
so far reduced that she could prohibit the importation of taffetas. Soon
she could dispense with some five million pounds' worth of sail-cloth
annually. The Huguenots opened twenty churches in London, and established banks; passing to the North, they spread into Calvinist Scotland, especially Edinburgh; they entered Dublin and Cork; in the North
of England, where there had been few trades before, they set up their
weaving establishments, and laid the basis for the future industrial development of the entire Manchester region. A Huguenot descendant,
Lewis Paul, is said to have outlined as early as 1738 a machine for spinning by rollers which was revived by Arkwright. This immigration
was of the most decisive influence upon the development of England.
Not only did it bring several million pounds of fresh capital to a country then poor in fluid resources; not only did it implant the first finer
industries which had been seen in England, which had been very backward in technique; not only did the French financiers build up the
Bank of England, the mainstay of the Crown; but the able naval provisioners of France also assisted in the rounding out of the British
Navy, while French military experts rejuvenated the land forces. And
finally, through England, the Huguenots won a foothold in the American colonies.

Huguenot enterprise had long coveted a share in developments overseas in the right places. In 1666 two French-Canadian Huguenots
opened up the fur trade around Hudson Bay, but, finding no support
from their home government at Paris, they turned to London, where
they received assistance. Charles II formed the Hudson's Bay Company in 1670, which a few years later was paying 50 per cent dividends, and by 1690 handed out 75 per cent. The English Government
also let them into the West Indies, where they established commercial
firms; and Alexander Hamilton, born in the West Indies of a Huguenot mother, perhaps inherited the French financial genius. Thus

Huguenot exiles contributed to the establishment of both financial systems, the British through Houblon, and the Americans through Hamilton, and also De Saussure, director of the Mint under Washington—later to be carried further by another Frenchman, not a Huguenot though from the rebellious city of Bordeaux, Stephen Girard, the first "colossal" millionaire in America.

Though so few in number, the Huguenots played a highly important share in early American business life. Merchants like Peter Faneuil, whose Hall acquired Revolutionary fame, clustered around Boston; they had a colony in New York, from which the Jays sprang. But their most important seat was Charleston, where they rapidly became so wealthy in the loan and mortgage business that the phrase, "as rich as a Huguenot" was transferred from the Old to the New World. These families took a great share in the Revolutionary movement, lending money, shouldering diplomatic tasks with great ability, and providing some of the best soldiers.

Charleston, with its parade of fashion among merchants, the Manigaults and d'Harriettes, the Hugers and the Laurens family, was paralleled in the eighteenth century by Hamburg, where Huguenot traders like the Godeffroys, Vidal and Boué were the most resplendent in Germany. In Charleston and in Hamburg, these Puritan exiles showed themselves extremely fond of good cheer, and were famous for their wines and costumes, their mansions and coaches and particularly for their keen love of the theater. Occasionally, one of them recollected Puritanism with some remorse, like the gay wife of Francis Brasseur, merchant of Charleston, who had created a sensation with her gold shoes and lace kerchiefs; stricken with grief on hearing a sermon, she committed suicide. But this was a very rare occurrence among the French Puritans, who seldom succumbed to revivalism.

Thus everywhere, from Italy up to Denmark, from Berlin to London, Hamburg, New York and Charleston, the ideas and methods of the French business men spread. Perhaps the Huguenots formed only a tenth of the population of France at the time of their expulsion, but it was the most vital tenth commercially; and this extraordinary dissemination of a nation's best business talents was to have a profound influence upon the business man's history in other countries. Indeed, before he died, Louis XIV himself felt the effects of it; his Government was practically bankrupt, before he handed it to his heir, and his imperial projects had been checked by the growing might of England, maintained by the stream of bullion provided through the abilities of the Huguenot banker, Houblon, who took extreme personal pleasure in his revenge.

XV

PURITANISM, BUSINESS AND REVO-LUTION IN ENGLAND

ALL THROUGH THE CENTURIES of commercial rise and decline in the cities of Germany and Italy, the Englishman had remained comparatively untouched, in his island isolation, by Continental business developments. Even when his close political rival, France, was making strenuous efforts to monopolize the markets of Europe, he did not stir himself to compete. Others prepared the stage for modern capitalism, while its chief actor lay dozing in the wings.

Until well into the seventeenth century, the English were more backward economically and more feudal mentally, though not socially, than other European peoples, the Spanish excepted. Before the second and largest invasion of the Huguenots, the English had lacked the skill for the finer branches of industry, and had no ambition to acquire it; they could indeed make a plain, honest wool cloth which sold very widely, and a fairly satisfactory type of plain pin, but that was about all of their achievements in manufacturing. Their sonnets remained considerably better than their soap. And even English Puritans seemed less hustling than those of other lands; instead of goods, John Milton produced only a vast Miltonic moan about the vindictiveness of Satan, author of work, who had forced Adam and Eve to sweat for their livings. "Paradise Lost," however, marked an epoch; it presaged the passing of the careless, rural times in which England had been a garden, if not altogether a blissful one.

How did the transformation come about? What changed the English country-dwellers into a "nation of shopkeepers" and then into the foremost industrial nation? They were never dragged to the factory-gate by a ministerial hand so strong as that of autocratic Colbert in France; the alteration, it would seem, was more spontaneous, from within. And it came so rapidly as to astound the rest of Europe. Before they really knew what was happening in that island, the English, so little urban or urbane, began to create modern urban society; and Northern Englishmen, among the least industrious of Europeans up to the verge of the nineteenth century, were the only experimentalists ready to make the Industrial Revolution. Naturally, this mystery has been attractive to historians, but the religious theory commonly offered to clear it up is as paradoxical as the facts it purports to explain: this is the theory, commonly associated with Weber, that the peculiar predatory ruthlessness of the early British capitalist was the product of his exceptional piety.

Though attached to the name of Weber, this idea is in essence much older; even in the sixteenth century, a Venetian ambassador had noted the connection between Protestantism and good business turn-over. And the contemporaries of the Puritans, puzzled themselves by the mighty and strange metamorphosis of England, were not slow in coming to the same notion. Three English merchants of the seventeenth century, Bethel, North and Child, speculated upon the cause of England's commercial growth.

The firmest adherent of the religious theory, as one might expect, was the Puritan man of business, Slingsby Bethel, who set down his observations in 1680. In all his travels, he remarked, he had never observed a Protestant beggar. His own faith, he felt, was somehow linked to profits:

> There is a kind of Natural Unaptness in the Popish Religion to business, whereas, on the contrary, amongst the Reformed, the greater their zeal, the greater is their inclination to Trade and Industry, as holding Idleness unlawful . . . [Bethel considered the advance of England to be due to Protestantism,] there being no Popish Country in the World, but were they Protestants, would be more than of double consideration to what they now are, as those that are so now, are so much more rich, great, and formidable, than when they were under Popish Darkness, which proceeds from an unaptness to business, begot in men of that Religion, by the slavery they are in to the Church, and the encouragement given by it to Idleness . . .
>
> As in *Spain* and *Italy* no one City can boast of any great Trade driven by their Natives, the greatest part of their Commerce being carried on by Protestant Strangers, *Amsterdam* alone having more Trade than all the Sea-Towns of *Italy* and *Spain* . . . In Germany, even in those Cities where they are Papists, without toleration to any other, there the Reformed may be said to carry all the Trade, as at Colne; in other Towns where they are *Lutherans*, with a publick tolerance to Papists, which is denied to *Calvinists*, there the Reformed carry the Trade clearly from both Lutherans and *Papists* . . . In other places, where the Cities are half Papists, half

Lutherans . . . there the latter have the Trade, as at Augsburgh. In France, the Reformed, for their number, are the greatest Traders.

The idea that bourgeois virtues make for eminence in business is of course older than Bethel; it could be traced backwards many generations, and ahead through Savary, Defoe, Samuel Smiles, Benjamin Franklin and Matthew Arnold to Weber. But there has always been another side to public opinion. Some persons have maintained that thirst for power and wealth is more important to success than the practice of the virtues and tend to minimize the effect of religion; among these in the seventeenth century, was Sir Dudley North, contemporary of Bethel, a great and cynical merchant of the Restoration Period. Certainly he had watched the Puritans, but when he summed up his rich observations upon men and affairs, in 1691, he emphasized power-hunger as a mainspring of action: "The main spur to Trade, or rather to industry and ingenuity, is the exorbitant appetite of men, which they will take pains to gratify, and so be disposed to work, when nothing else will incline them to it."

North was a very unscrupulous and dangerous man himself, but, since he was vastly more successful in business enterprise than the Puritan, Bethel, his words carry perhaps more weight in gold. Richer, however, than either of these was the outstanding English monopolist, Sir Josiah Child, who ran the East India Company, and held the English Government in his pocket for a time. Child thought that there was some truth in both views; that the exorbitant appetite of men was indeed a spur, but that some connection existed between commerce and religion: "Trade never thrives in any country that is not protestant." Especially in England, it is necessary to "admit that our reformation to the protestant religion were one principal cause at first of our advance in trade and navigation." Yet, he went on, it was no longer possible to separate cause and effect, in a country where ideals and economic factors had been so perfectly blended:

> It is now manifest, that the increase of our trade and navigation is a great means, under God, to secure and preserve our protestant religion; foreign trade produceth riches, riches power, power preserves trade and religion; they mutually work one upon another and for the preservation of the other.

PURITANISM AND PIRACY

Upon appetite or creed, as Bethel or North would express it, or upon a felicitous combination of both, as Sir Josiah would prefer to believe, the commercial greatness of England was founded. At least in the early stages, the former must have been the more important element. Her initial start in commerce came, not through the practice of thrift, sobriety and assiduity, and the other bourgeois virtues, which Puritanism is supposed to foster, but upon precisely opposite qualities. Her merchants amassed riches and markets because, better than any others, they knew how to combine piracy with a trading-voyage, turning aside at any point to lay waste the towns of helpless Spaniards, and burn, rape and torture without mercy or qualm. One may go so far as to claim that it was the fortunate absence of bourgeois virtues which enabled the English to win a head start over other nations in the race for business empire and capital-accumulation; they seized the territories first, and learned to supply them afterward.

At the time when English merchant adventurers began to cut a considerable figure, in the age of Elizabeth, the world was in fearful chaos. Turkish hordes menaced the East of Europe; within Europe the rising new States were engaged in deadly strife, and each was torn by civil dissension; even outside the waters of Europe "there was no peace beyond the line." In this fierce struggle for survival which filled the sixteenth century, the soft ultra-urban were pushed to the wall by the healthily barbarous. It was an unhappy epoch for the long-civilized burghers of Italy and Germany, who found the old order of mediaeval handicrafts falling about their ears, and yet were powerless to make another. Temperamentally as well as geographically, they were unfitted to take advantage of the new situation. Citizens of Nürnberg, for instance, went on in their routine way, nicely calculating profits to the tenth of a penny, and happy with 6 per cent; not for a moment did they realize that if they sailed out as pirates, like Drake and Hawkins, they might realize 1,600 per cent at a swoop. And even if they had, they were now unused to sword and saddle, as Machiavelli complained; grown flabby from centuries of sitting in countinghouses and clubs, they manufactured but could not wield weapons.

But the English, in that juncture, fresh from the furrows, were unspoiled by formal concepts of foreign exchange and capital assessment. They alone rejoiced in the carnage, setting up their Shakespearean shout of joy amid "alarums and trumpets." They were very much like the Dutch at the same period, as far as fighting vitality went, but considerably less affected by the business calculations which the Dutch acquired from their neighbors up the Rhine. At that time, the minds of Englishmen worked in feudal patterns, even though their society was no longer feudal. That is to say, they demanded wealth in tangible form. Little aware of the intricacies of liens and notes, they sought their gains on the hoof, and in the ingot.

Unashamed of what North would call his "exorbitant appetite," Sir Walter Raleigh, a leading monopolist of wine and tin, and on that account one of the best-hated men in England by the populace, lustfully described the opportunities awaiting his adventurers in South America, a virgin country "yet . . . never sacked, the graves not opened for gold . . . nor the images pulled down out of the temples." As yet untinged by Calvinism, Raleigh did not feel it necessary to envelop his appetite in a mantle of Biblical quotations, as the later Cromwell did, when he projected his Irish land-seizure or a Baltic trade-war. Cromwell felt he must justify expansion by calling it the will of God; Raleigh, when proposing to capture the Spanish plate fleet, countered the objection of Sir Francis Bacon that it might appear piracy, with a loud: "Tush, did you ever hear of men being pirates for millions?"

It was this search for wealth in its most obvious forms that led to British preeminence in one of the oldest and most primitive forms of commerce, the slave-trade. The pioneer in this branch in Elizabeth's Age was John Hawkins, who began voyaging to the Canary Islands with Negroes to exchange for sugar and hides. His best ship was a big one bought from the Germans, called the *Jesus*, admirably fitted in all but name for his purposes. On this vessel he held his crew to the observance of three rules: "Serve God daily; love one another; preserve your victuals."

His slave-voyages began with forcible capture of the Negroes, who, as one of Hawkins' men described it in a diary, used to flee at their approach, "leaping and turning their tailes, that it was most strange to see and gave us great pleasure to behold them." Once the cargo was obtained by force, it was necessary to dispose of it also by violence, beating down "consumer resistance." At one spot in the West Indies, Hawkins had to land a hundred men with pikes to persuade the Spanish to buy his cargo at his own price. At another, Rio de la Hache, the citizens pretended their inability to pay cash, but yielded when Hawkins threatened them with a hot English "breakfast of javelins and arrows." Hawkins thus concluded the sale and left, but, a little later, decided to return to Rio and clean up the town. Putting the inhabitants to the sword, plundering all valuables that could be crammed into his hulks, he sailed home to the thunderous applause of his countrymen—and a knighthood.

Hawkins was not a Calvinist, but a good Anglican. Yet he employed a phrase often considered typically Calvinist, talking of himself as one of "God's Elect"; once, when becalmed with a cargo of Negroes, he was relieved when "Almighty God, which never suffereth his elect to perish, sent us the ordinary breeze." Nor does he seem to have needed Calvinist indoctrination to give him an attitude of pride in his work;

he was sufficiently proud of it to choose as his scutcheon, when he was knighted, "a demi-Moor, in his proper colour, bound and captive." His portrait hardly shows a timid man; the velvet beret is cocked over a hard and healthy face, set with eyes sharp and shifty as a weasel's; his hand fingers his sword-hilt. He does not look especially like a man who needs a lesson in self-reliance from a Frenchman.

Nevertheless, Puritanism exercised a certain influence over this trade. The Puritan Revolution helped merchants to widen the circles of royal monopolists; as Brentano shows, the rebels in that movement were particularly anxious to free the slave-trade from government limitation; it was not, however, until after the second or Glorious Revolution, in 1688, with its slogans of freedom and equality, that the monopoly was finally overthrown and the slave-trade opened to English subjects to the fullest extent.

During succeeding generations, as the slave-trade became one of England's leading sources of prosperity, there was indeed observable an infiltration of the "bourgeois virtues." As competitors increased, and the overhead grew larger, more calculation was in order; the business shifted from the control of feudal-bellicose men like Hawkins to the more "business-like" merchants of Liverpool.

In the region about Liverpool there was much Puritanism, later merging into Methodism. Possibly, it may be argued, the Puritan temperament triumphed here; it was because these Liverpool men were so thrifty, figuring their expenses to the last shilling, that they beat the more reckless Portuguese and other Catholic competitors in this field. By 1751, whatever the cause, Liverpool was rising in the traffic, having 87 ships with a capacity of 25,000 captives; eleven years later, she had 878 slavers taking 303,737 slaves to the Indies, valued at no less than £15,186,850. Out of this wealth was accumulated the capital which was later poured into the perfection of the steam-machines of Manchester; thus it might be urged that Puritan virtues produced a large measure of the capital for the Industrial Revolution. The exclusion of Nonconformists from politics until 1828, kept their energies in trade and greatly promoted British railroading.

Still, the slave-trade was one which always involved risk as well as bookkeeping. It called for the best qualities of the sea-pirate as well as the Puritan-Bourgeois; only the English had this well-balanced mixture of traits, enabling them to wrest the lion's share of the trade away from Spanish, Dutch and French and hold it until it was legally abolished, even continuing the smuggling until far into the nineteenth century. Hijackers were everywhere to be expected and Liverpool men had to be ready to defend themselves and to hijack in return. One Liverpool firm in 1762 instructed Captain Ambrose Lace what to do "should you be fortunate enough to take any vesell or vesells from the Enemy." Such letters of instruction are interesting illustrations of the blend of the military and bourgeois: on the one hand, captains are urged to exercise great thrift: "Pray mind to be very choice in your slaves. Buy no Distempered or old Ones." But at the same time, they are told to keep a weather eye out for prizes. The ideal captain was expected to be a cross between John Hawkins and Samuel Smiles.

Thus, Thos. Langland and Company, giving Captain Caesar Lawson his sailing orders, insisted on due caution in buying sound mahogany and bargaining sharply for

> prime Negroes, ivory and Palm Oil. By Law this vessel is allowed to carry 400 Negroes, and we request that they may all be males if possible to get them, at any rate buy as few females as in your power, because we look to a Spanish market for the disposal of your cargo, where Females are a very tedious sale.

When Caesar had laid in yarns, wood, water and so on, he was to proceed "with a press of sail for Barbadoes." But, said the firm, it would be a pity to let a stray ship alone: "We have taken out Letters of Marque against the French and Batavian Republic, and if you are so fortunate as to fall in with and capture any of their vessels send the same direct to this Port." In case "of your capturing a Guineaman with Slaves on board, send her to the address of Messrs. Bogle, Jopp & Co. of Kingston, Jamaica." But—"do not molest any neutral ship, as it would involve us in an expensive lawsuit."

Captain Lawson, as Dow relates, was worthy of his trust. In his ship, the *Enterprise,* he managed to detain a Spanish brig with slaves and much loot, and recapture the *John* of Liverpool, for which his firm got salvage money. On the islands he sold: 194 men, 32 "men boys," 66 boys, 42 women, 36 "women girls" and 42 girls. Only 19 died on his hands and one girl, being subject to fits, could not be disposed of at a profit. When he returned to Liverpool, the firm found that the net profits of elephants' teeth, logwood, sugar, men boys, and so on, amounted to the tidy sum of £24,430. It was one of the best paying forms of commerce and England, through the eighteenth century, absorbed its chief profits, carrying 60,000 slaves annually out of a world total of 97,000.

Out of the Liverpool commerce ultimately came that supreme embodiment of the Victorian bourgeois gentleman, William Ewart Gladstone. His father was one of the richest grain-merchants in the city and owner of slave-worked plantations in the West Indies, and a devout builder of churches. In his youth, before he turned Liberal, William

Gladstone was the perfect representative of his city's interests and character; so pious that he made the frivolous sons of Southern gentry ashamed of themselves, he defended slavery, the great economic basis of Liverpool, by excerpts from the Bible.

In the slave-trade of England, accordingly, business and religion were indeed intertwined. From the pure old pirate, Hawkins, sure of God's favoring breezes, down to the towering figure of Gladstone, the line may be traced. But which element was predominant? Contemplating this happy combination, one must agree with Josiah Child that "they mutually work one upon another and for the preservation of the other."

THE MONOPOLISTS

The slave-trade was a clear indication of the economic backwardness of England; another was the persistence of privateering and a natural inclination to violence on the high seas on the part of merchants. Speculative companies were formed for capturing prizes, like the Providence Island Company, which founded and colonized the most famous pirates' den in the West Indies, long a menace to "the Galeons and their King's yearly and mighty treasure." The most respectable merchants gladly invested in ventures which regularly netted 35 per cent, and might on occasion bring in 8,000 per cent. Was it an accident that one of the greatest of these organizers of piratical expeditions was a Calvinist, Lord Rich?

Where the English could not so directly conquer wealth, they assumed the feudal rôle of the robber baron, who holds the key to trade lanes and exacts tribute from the traffic. For a long time they sought new routes, not as outlets for their manufactures so much as to obtain tribute; they held the ocean-avenue to the spice-islands for a long time before it occurred to them to start business upon the mainland. They went over only when the Dutch drove them from their island nook; reluctantly and under necessity, they went to trade with India, instead of living upon those who traded there.

These trading companies, as they were first organized, won their high dividends not by underbidding competitors in world markets for industrial products, but by exacting tithes as monopolists. Not only was the slave-trade a rich monopoly for which England fought long and fiercely with France, but other sources of wealth were found by the companies in looting the Indian Empire, pillaging the Spanish Empire, gaining exclusive entry into Russia by inviting the Czar to become a shareholder. And incidentally, of course, the companies extorted from both ends, from their countrymen as well as from foreigners.

One of the worst sinners among these bodies of merchant adventurers was the Russia Company, "a strong and shameful monopoly," as the public called it, which boosted the price of cordage and other supplies to the British Navy by 150 per cent, and cheated investors, who sought redress in vain from the law. By 1605 the popular indignation against these "bloodsuckers of the commonwealth"—the phrase was coined in Elizabeth's day, if not before—culminated in a parliamentary investigation, at which a blazing speech was made against the whole system of the English companies:

> All men are born heritable as to their land, as also to the free exercise of their industry. . . . It is against the natural right and liberty of the subjects of England to restrain it into the hands of some few; for, although there may be some 5,000 or 6,000 persons, counting children and apprentices, free of the several companies of the merchants, in the whole; yet apparent it is, that the governors of the companies, by their monopolising orders, have so handled the matter, as that the mass of the whole trade of the realm is in the hands of some 200 persons at the most, the rest serving for a show and reaping small benefit.

The speaker, Sir Edwin Sandys, should have known the subject intimately, for later he turned out to be a big monopolist himself, as treasurer of the Virginia Company, which had a corner on tobacco. Allowing for exaggerations of phrase, it was true, as Sandys said, that the few big, rich monopolists held in their grasp the overseas trade of England and lived by extortion and not by production. And this remained so until well into the eighteenth century, when as Scott's informing work shows, though joint-stock companies were formed, it was still for non-productive enterprises. Very few were formed to make anything, whether armaments or coaches; the overwhelming majority, even in the opening of the 1700's, were for overseas trade or speculation. There were indeed banking, and fire-fighting companies; waterworks associations, forever quarreling and fighting for the right to make the streets of England insecure by tearing up and laying down leaky wooden pipes; and postal companies which conducted forays against one another, stealing sacks of mail, breaking postmen's heads and bribing their way to monopolistic contracts. Some equally belligerent street-lighting companies appeared also. The rest were schemes of unsavory reputation, though with beautiful names: the Noble and Honest Society at the *Sign of the Vine*, vied for favor with the Undoubted Profitable Society at the *Sign of the Ship*, or the Unquestionable Society at the *White Lion*. But all that time, the higher orders of manufacturing were either lacking, or largely in the hands of foreign immigrants, who were, it is true, to a great extent Puritans.

Yet this very absence of polite virtues and eager industry were of the utmost advantage to England's progress. A more speedy adoption of Continental technique might have done grave injury. As things stood, England could be a great military power, engaging in rash campaigns without fear of losing customers or upsetting any delicate mechanisms at home. Moreover, it allowed the diversion of her energies to enterprises which might be immediately non-productive, like the discovery, settling and securing of a vast empire. More fortunate than soberer lands, England first won her markets and then proceeded to glut them with Manchester cottons. Had industry flourished at this time, merchants might have invested their funds in it, instead of holding them gladly for exploration and colonization. This ready reservoir of merchant capital made possible the backing of discoverers like Cabot, sent by sea-traders of Bristol, or Frobisher, backed by the Russia Company. The East India Company could finance men like Henry Middleton to scout for new routes, buy pepper and incidentally pick up Portuguese treasure-ships. Merchants colonized as well as explored, and settled the New World. The Plymouth, the Mosquito Islands, the Massachusetts Bay and the Caribbees Companies were all private associations; it is claimed that for an outlay of £25,000, English merchants acquired most of New England by 1624.

Possibly also, the lack of industrial tradition extending from a mediaeval background was helpful to England's flights of invention. She was not hampered by the accretions of the centuries; just as American aloofness from European contacts has made for rapid technological change, so it was with England. She produced a Manchester, and a Birmingham, precisely because she had no Florence and no Nürnberg.

A third happy outcome of England's backwardness was the development of her political genius. English merchants could hardly have attained the enormous political power they won in the seventeenth century had they been timid bourgeois producers of goods, owners of factories, under the supervision of bureaucrats. Only because their wealth lay overseas, or on the seas, could they escape governmental inspection and control; only because they were pirates, not humdrum manufacturers, were the aristocrats willing to respect them and cooperate with them. If the English gentry stooped to business it was not because of a broader and more amiable view of trade than the French; it was because the English business, which at that time so largely consisted in war and robbery, was fitter for a gentleman to engage in than French business, which mainly involved the vulgar production of useful articles.

On the Continent, a business man was a meek calculator in a counting-house; in England he might be a combination of Sven Hedin and Admiral Peary, Nelson and Blackbeard, with the powers of an ambassador, general, commodore and often of a potentate. Save the Dutch alone, there were no Europeans able, like the British, to govern territories vaster than those of monarchs, and derive the major share of their revenues from hijacking cargoes on the Main, a frank piracy in which no duke need hesitate for a moment to join. And it was that cooperation which ensured the success of the Puritan Revolution.

BUSINESS AND THE PURITAN REVOLUTION

Religion was a potent factor in that remarkable rebellion of business men against the would-be Absolute King, Charles I. And yet it is extremely difficult to disentangle the emotional from the economic in the politics of mid-seventeenth-century England. Undoubtedly the flocking of a great many French Huguenot weavers into the North of England, around Manchester, may have helped to fasten Calvinism upon the region; but this was a dark hinterland, devoid of splendid cities, naturally hostile to the luxuries of the South, and favorable to a Puritan character. How far the gloomy Calvinism of Manchester business men disposed them to the cause of Cromwell is, however, difficult to say.

One case may be cited as suggestive, that of Worsley of Platt. Worsley's family had risen in Manchester from haberdashery to a trade in yarn; his father was a petty entrepreneur who made enough money to buy an estate and add "of Platt" to his name. The son, a step removed from trade, but still Puritan, went into the Cromwellian army, empowered as Major-General to run the Manchester region. Ruthlessly he pressed out funds from the families of the "malignant party"—very likely, those who had frowned on parvenus like himself—and ferociously he put down frivolity and fun. One cannot say how far the case of Platt is typical, until more thorough studies are made of other Puritans in that countryside, to see whether they were likewise new-rich haberdashers with a grudge against county gentry.

Puritanism was of course not confined to the North; it spread in the South as well, making converts among the lower ranks of tradesmen. In the words of a pamphleteer:

> Presbyterian hopes . . . are chiefly in the Common People . . . to take and amuse vulgar and low Capacities . . . 'tis the Mean Man they look after . . . or Fat and Wealthy Traders, their best and surest prize; where they flock and abound, as in London or other Cities, Teachers catch 'em as Fowlers do Plovers.

By fat traders was meant tradesmen, shopkeepers, and not whole-salers, who alone in those days were dignified by the name of merchants. The biggest of the overseas merchants were not likely to become Puritans unless they had some special reason; a too severe moral righteousness would have deprived them of royal favor and hence of monopolies. But even the great Anglicans had a certain sympathy for the lesser Puritans, since they could see that the persecution of the best manufacturers and artisans would not work out for the good of commerce as a whole. To the harassing of heretics, one pamphleteer traced the current depression: "The nearest cause of our impoverishments" was the "ridgid Persecution upon the Trading Part of a land . . . We have gotten most of the Sober Trading Part of the Nation discouraged by Citations, Excommunications, Writs . . . they may remove to some other Country."

Of course business men of even the most orthodox persuasion grumbled under the taxation which kept up the Church of England. A contemporary wailer cried: "That the Trading Part of a Nation is devoured in this Prelatical Gulph, I shall demonstrate, by laying open to view the black back-door and sink that hath drained the Trading Purse dry." Thus economic interests and religious dissent began to nourish each other. And it was of especial importance that there was a determined religious dissenter in the heart of London's financial district, James Houblon the elder, "Father of the London Exchange," as he was called, *Pater Bursae Londiniensis*.

Houblon was a Calvinist of the strictest school, adhering to the severe dark robes and the observances of the little French Reformed Church in Threadneedle Street. A formidable force in London, the center of England's fluid wealth and stronghold of resistance to the King, this French émigré was in no mood to finance in his adopted country the same sort of Absolutism which had driven his family into exile.

Not all Puritans, however, opposed King Charles. A strict Protestant like Sir William Courteen, of a Flemish émigré family, could support Charles heartily, for he had secured from that monarch a license to trade in India as an "interloper," cutting in on the business of the East India Company. The ill behavior of the Courteen agents in India, stirring up natives and infringing on Company rights, so infuriated the merchant-directors of the latter, that they charged up to the Crown their resentment at Courteen. This was a contributory cause to the irritation between Crown and Company. Hence one source of the Puritan Revolution was the activity of a loyalist Puritan trader, who so angered Anglican monopolists that they broke with their monarch.

On the other hand, so complex was the situation, that a considerable group of wealthy Puritans had good cause to hate Charles for his pacifism. Charles hoped to avoid annoying the Spanish, at least in times of peace, and so he reduced the number of letters of marque issued to privateers. But privateering was a vested interest at London. A whole circle of merchants, accustomed to put their funds in such enterprises, rallied to the support of their chief, the bold Puritan pirate, Lord Rich, a courtier and malcontent.

Robert Rich, second Earl of Warwick, was descended from the "infamous Richard Rich," who had won a title for services rendered to Henry VIII. Robert owned many ships which he operated for the London investors, many of them Puritans like himself. He had been accustomed to obtaining sanction from his king for his exploits. But when Charles would not renew his rights, he was put to the trouble and expense of purchasing a license for freebooting from a Medicean duke of Florence. Another grievance of Rich was that he had had to pay more for a title than he thought it was worth.

Like the other Puritan, Courteen, Rich came into collision with the East India Company through his insults to the natives. The Company was desirous of friendly relations with the Indians, through whom it was just securing a foothold on the mainland. The Company had barely won privileges from the Great Mogul in 1616, when, as Craven tells the story, ships of Rich, scouring the Red Sea for plunder, gave chase to a splendid junk belonging to the Queen Mother of the Great Mogul. Had they taken it, the fortunes of the British Empire might have been very different. But it happened that ships of the India Company appeared in the nick of time and rescued from their piratical countrymen the distressed Indians.

Rich was incensed with what he regarded as unwarranted interference with individual liberty. His backers were robbed of dividends and he felt personally insulted. Recompense was demanded. The Company's representative apologized most humbly but explained:

> If you suffer rovers in these seas, there must be no traders. It is hard to prove to these people the difference of merchant and pirate, or if you could prove it, I am unwilling to lie for pawn until certificate came out of Europe.

Unmollified, Sir Robert brought his plea before the House of Lords and after years of altercation, finally obtained judgment for £4,000 damages against the Company which had cheated him of his prey. Here therefore was a case of a Puritan at odds with both king and Company. Around him formed an anti-royalist group, who assailed the pacific policy of Charles and demanded a free rein to fall upon Catholic Spain; it was natural, as Craven says, that these should be Puritans, having a religious as well as an economic hostility to Spain. They were an especially fearsome group of Charles' foes on account of their wealth.

It will be seen that the problem of the interaction of profit and creed is far from simple. Some men may have been fashioned into the likeness of successful business men by Calvinism; others turned to Calvinism as the instrument best suited to their interests and policies—as the cloak for privateering, in other words. The confusing blend of business and religion in those days may be illustrated by yet a third case, the attempt of courtiers of King Charles to make soap.

Soap, up to that time, had usually been brought to England from abroad. Only the poorest kinds had been made at home. In the hope of fostering production of that luxury in England, a royally privileged company, with funds raised chiefly among courtiers, was formed. Promising to use only English materials, it was given a monopoly for the realm, and foreign competition was excluded. But the product was poor and cost 200 per cent more than before. The buying public rebelled. True, soap-consumers in those days formed only an insignificant part of the population, but they were socially prominent. They forced an investigation. In its defense, the soap company presented 80 witnesses, among them even countesses, which shows that titled ladies were ready to testify for toilet goods long before American ingenuity made a racket of the practice. The charm of these lovely complexions appears to have confused the parliamentary investigators, who dropped the charges. The soap, however, grew no better. So at last there was nothing left for the disappointed consumers but to join the party of the malcontents with the stirring slogan, "Down with Popish Soap!" Thus the encounter of infuriated bathers versus boilers was another of the incidents leading up to the Revolution.

THE QUANDARY OF A PURITAN

According to Cromwell, the true-born Briton was free from pangs of conscience. In urging a trade-war to preserve English shipping in the Baltic, Cromwell called it a holy war, and told the English: "You . . . have not yet made your trade to prefer your profitt before your godliness but reckon godliness the greater gain." This loftiness of motive, this "purity of the profession" was, he admitted, often misunderstood by certain "bad men abroad who say, it is for money . . ."

Perhaps the British did indeed manage to smelt together "profitt," as those bad men abroad insinuated, with their godliness, never questioning the amalgam. But an occasional Frenchman was given to an un-British introspection. Thomas Papillon, who suffered from qualms, was one of those French Puritans who, like a younger Houblon and, much later, Fonnereaux, were highly connected with the British Navy as provisioners. Papillon's stock was pure Calvinist; his grandfather paid for his heresy in the St. Bartholomew Massacre. Naturally he stood on Cromwell's side, both as a Puritan and a man interested in developing the Cromwellian Navy.

Most of the time it was possible for Papillon to uphold his commerce and his faith together. He consistently defended the "rights and liberties of the City" of London against royal encroachment, and the monopolies of sundry companies against popular outcries; he further spoke for the merchant class, which sought to import cheap Irish cattle and lower the cost of living, against the English Royalist agrarians. And in line with this, he urged toleration in religious matters, for commercial reasons: "The unsettledness of men's minds in references to Religion was a great diversion and impediment to trade." Faith and economics coincided during the struggle within the East India Company, when Papillon led the Puritan group against the Anglicans, headed by Sir Josiah Child.

Still, he was not satisfied; he felt a tendency of his "carnal" mind to defeat his better nature. Sighing, he admitted, "The carnal mind is enmity to God, and yet this is the frame that too much takes hold on me; the Lord subdue it, and make me more heavenly." At times, in his joy over his good health, his "comfortable and affectionate relations with his wife," and "plenty of worldly good things," he neglected his "soul's concerns." Alas, too often had he allowed "thoughts of self-advancement . . . to mingle themselves in those transactions wherein I have been engaged." He had not been severe enough with Papists or kind enough to fellow-Puritans: "Certainly, God intends I should get my heart truly affected and humbled before him . . . O Lord, My God, enable me thereunto."

Papillon earnestly desired to become more "heavenly," but, with lovable frankness, he admitted it was uphill work. Try as he would to begin his epistles with lofty Biblical quotations and to dilate upon "the depravedness of my nature," he always slid rapidly down to earth, winding up, "I would willingly know how the affairs of the East India Company proceed; what the Stock is now worth." And he was unable to subdue his carnal nature at one point, when a nice question of ethics came up. When England in 1672 actually took Catholic France, the enemy of his fathers, as an ally in her fight over shipping against the Protestant Dutch, Papillon had to victual the fleet for the campaign. How could he reconcile that business, however patriotic, with his religious duty?

His wife and mother had all along expected something like this to occur. Even when he agreed to provision the Navy in 1668, the wife wrote to him, urging him to consider if there were not danger to his soul in that employment:

> As to the Navy business, truly I judge it may be well not to cast it off, since Providence does so eminently fasten it on thee; but . . . conversing with our good Mother she says to me, "what would he do if the Navy were employed against the Church of God?" This I thought to acquaint thee with; I am not fit to advise thee, but I earnestly beg the counsel of the all-wise God for thee.

His wife reminded Papillon of the high ethical standards of his forbears. When his father and his Italian Protestant uncle "were employed in such an affair against Rochelle," the Huguenot stronghold, they had refused to equip the fleet, regardless of profit, against men of their own faith. The stern model was held up to poor Papillon, who wavered none the less, and fell. He did provision the fleet to aid France, assisting the Crown which had exiled his family and slain his grandfather. But he did try to salvage his decorum, by refusing to go *on a Sunday* to get instructions for the job.

Most of the time, his conscience at least operated well enough to make him one of the best provisioners of the British Navy. The health of the sailors visibly improved, says Macaulay, while he delivered good meat and biscuit instead of moldly victuals, and at a cost no greater than before. Moreover, during his parliamentary career—he served thirteen years and sat on threescore committees—he did not abuse his position. He even fought *against* unreasonably large appropriations for naval supplies. Enough was enough, he would say: "A man is perfectly clothed though he has not three coats or three shirts; a ship is fitted though she has not three suits of sails."

In his long life (1623–1702), Papillon survived many changes of government and found it possible to agree with most of them and go on victualing the fleet. Once indeed, he was somewhat threatened, as a result of his stubborn defense of the London merchants against the Court party in municipal elections. He was banished for a time, in 1685. He did not suffer much in his purse, for he had cannily mortgaged his estates to a brother-in-law, and hence avoided paying the fine imposed on him. But he was very unhappy at the prospects of setting up business on the Continent, for he could find no place so suitable as England for spiritual and economic gain; there only could he keep both his stock and his soul high.

To France, he would not go, lest he be deprived of his faith; nor could he go to Luxemburg, where he could not trade. He tarried a while in Amsterdam, finding opportunity to prosper and worship as he liked, only, however, to find the Dutch atmosphere too massively materialistic:

> As to this place, it may be convenient in reference to trade, but as to all other things, I have no liking of it; there is no Christian society; getting of money, and saving of money, is the business; and there is little of the life, power, and spirituality of religion. . . . The preaching here is not generally as spiritual as in England.

He rejoiced greatly when he could return to England, the country where a business man would find profit and godliness most smoothly combined.

THE GATHERING OF THE FORCES

In seventeenth-century England, no other vocabulary than the Biblical was available for economic discussion. Professors of political economy and the argumentative Frenchmen had not yet come along to provide a solemn, scientific lay terminology in which to envelop the demands of business and labor. Men could not then appeal to economic "laws" above those of God. Even the biggest capitalists, in the Stuart Age, had to use the Bible as their source of authority like the humblest Diggers and Levelers and hill-billies. This unquestionably made the combination of many sorts of interests under the Cromwellian banner much easier.

In that time, the plaints of the poor against the rich, and of employers against workingmen, whether Puritan or Anglican, were indistinguishable in tone; all Englishmen, of whatever opinion or estate, employed the same Biblical imagery and spoke in the pure language of the King James' version. For instance, when the smaller merchants in the corporation of clothiers in London protested against the seizure of the best jobs in that body by the biggest cloak-and-suit men, they clothed their charge in religious metaphor; and in the same lofty tone, the jobholders replied, claiming that God, by concentrating light in the Sun and Moon, showed His approval of concentrated power in the garment trade. Not content with comparing themselves to the Sun and Moon, these important dry-goods dealers wound up by drawing a parallel between themselves and the Almighty, in their displeasure at "our dissenting brethren."

It was not difficult, therefore, for men whose interests were far from primarily religious to join the forces of Cromwell. Humphrey Chetham, a rich old bachelor cloth-dealer of the North country, was particularly aggrieved because the king had appointed him to the post of

High Sheriff of Lancashire, which was merely a pretext for screwing funds out of Humphrey for ship-subsidies; as he bitterly complained, this was a ruse "whereby I shall be made more popular and thereby more subject to the perils of the times." He was then forced to go into Parliament, which proved even more expensive. As his dislike grew for the monarch who had made him "popular" against his will, Humphrey became a vigorous advocate of the Puritan movement. During the upheaval, he was treasurer for his county and raised money for the Cromwellian commanders.

There were also several business men who joined Cromwell, not from personal grievance, but for financial reform. Henry Robinson and Samuel Lamb were merchants who wished to see a State Bank established to supply "imaginary money or credit"—a plan that had already been demonstrated in Italian towns, though the English still deemed it visionary. Lamb, an enthusiast for "imaginary money," urged upon Cromwell a genuine business administration for England. Let the Commander surround himself with trading men, he suggested: "What a glorious and honorable profession would it be, if your Highness's Court . . . were all merchants, and also your domestic servants every one venturing so much stock as he could spare into other parts of the world . . . It may make your Highness's court and domestics the most rich and flourishing of any potentate's in the world." At the same time, Lamb perceived the value of navalism to trade; the two, he thought, should develop together, as in fact they did under Cromwell:

> It is presumed, that that nation which hath most warlike shipping and mariners will command in chief at sea; and he that commands the sea may command trade, and he that hath the greatest trade will have the most money, which is of such value that it doth command all worldly things, both in war and peace.

His contemporary, Henry Robinson, also advocated the bank, and was a pioneer in working for religious toleration. Neither a Puritan nor a Catholic, he was foremost a business man, who believed fanaticism interfered with commerce. On his private printing-press, he published a tract, entitled "Liberty of Conscience," which his editor, Shaw, declares, antedated any attempt by any church "to anticipate the modern spirit." Shaw thinks it strange, though others might find it natural, that it should have been "a layman and a business man who was to be the first to point intolerant Presbyterian and fighting Independent to the true path of religious development . . . the path of tolerance in matter of religion." While Robinson did not see his religious ideal materialize, at least he rose under Cromwell to be Auditor of the Excise.

Thus the camp of Cromwell was filled with a vast variety of malcontents, often mutually opposed. For instance, some of the mighty monopolists were out of patience with the king because they felt themselves shamefully overtaxed, subjected to hasty levies, and compelled to pay excessive bribes for royal favor. Yet, rather unexpectedly, they found themselves politically joined with their own shareholders, who had been denouncing them as fraudulent bloodsuckers; with the small manufacturers, who had called them bloated octopi; and with the artisans, hostile to manufacturers, who dreamed of an English Republic. In short, the anti-royalist cause united the incompatibles; radical laborers and omnipotent magnates; shareholders and directors; army men and preachers; Puritans and Anglicans. For a time they were fused into a fighting whole by the accidental conjuncture of a confident leader, a magnificent rhetoric—and an economic depression.

COUNTINGHOUSE AGAINST CROWN

Perhaps it would be more correct to say that the English averted Absolutism than that they destroyed it; for monarchy, though theoretically called supreme in England as in France, had not in practice attained anything like the overweening powers of the French Crown. The wide-wandering "merchant-adventurers" of England could not be controlled so easily as the domesticated manufacturers of France, for one thing; and for another, English business men had no such reason as the French to support a strong State. They were not in the same situation as the French bourgeois, who were frightened by a tumultuous nobility into backing the Crown in self-defense. The English did not need to water the tender plant of tyranny with their wealth; and they did not provide the money to build up so strong a machinery, military and bureaucratic, as that in Spain, France or Prussia.

The English Stuart kings were not in fact Absolute; they were merely taking the first steps toward building up a military force and the necessary bureaucracy to establish Absolutism, when King Charles I sought funds with which to strengthen his army, navy and administration. Had he obtained them, no doubt England might have felt soon the heel of authority. But it was the good fortune of the English business class to see and fend off the threat in time.

On the other hand, the English were not naturally rebellious; the thought of armed upheaval was certainly far from their heads when they refused to give Charles the loans and subsidies which he demanded. The groups and interests opposed to Charles were, as has been shown, too incongruous to melt together except under strong pressure. The Puritan Revolution came to pass as the only way out of an intolerable muddle; it was not the premeditated attempt of business to seize sovereignty through the medium of a "strong man." Insofar it was not "Fascist," like, for instance, that little revolt in old Florence, when bankers set up the Duke of Athens as their puppet. In Florence, aims were defined and methods deliberate; but there was nothing of that old Italian clarity in the fog of seventeenth-century England.

Hence the parallels between Cromwell and Hitler must not be pressed too closely. Hitler has indeed called Cromwell his predecessor, and undoubtedly points of similarity can be shown. In either case certain capitalistic-monopolistic groups saw advantage in backing a leader who had the Army on his side. In both situations, a temporary and artificial union was formed between big and small bourgeois, during a period of economic stress. Cromwell, like Hitler, Savonarola and many another leader, was a "depression phenomenon." But the English, like the Americans and French, blundered into revolution, instead of performing a neatly timed coup, like the Italians of 1922 and Germans of 1933.

The dissatisfaction accumulating in many quarters was heightened by war, plague, rebellion in Ireland and confusion in the currency. It was brought to a focus by a rash royal act, the arbitrary seizure of merchant funds placed in the Tower of London for safe-keeping. So far did the business interests distrust the King that they would lend him no money, at any price, to strengthen his case against Parliament. The East India Company, forgetful of the rich privileges wrung from him in the past, stubbornly refused to lend him gold or spices. Nor would the other merchants of the City supply a penny. And when he appealed to bankers in Genoa, these astute financiers denied him also; in a conflict between a monarch and his own bankers, there seemed no sense in betting on royalty.

How sound was the Genoese judgment soon became evident. The business center of England, London, threw its force wholly behind Parliament and Puritanism. Its Council deposed the followers of the king and set up a Puritan in place of the royalist Lord Mayor. Forming a committee for defense, dominated by Puritans, the City raised funds by subscriptions. War-loans were popularized by a religious campaign in which all but Puritan preachers were silenced; and the Puritans defined the true Christian as a man who invested in revolutionary loans.

Naturally a Puritan leader like Houblon contributed heavily. He donated cloth and "a thousand payre of Pistolls and Holsters," and entered "one able bay gelding, his rider James Dandoe, armed with a Carabine, a case of pistolls, buffe coat and sword, all valued by the Commisarye, at 2.2.0." But the rest he handed to the cause not in the shape of a gift; it was a loan at eight per cent. And non-Puritans, of course, were even more impelled to regard their contributions as investments. They knew that if they furnished sinews of war to Parliament, they would get their money returned with interest, whereas, if they hung back, they might be entirely ruined. As Ranke points out, "the whole realm was their security."

London led the way in forming a fighting militia. The City rose in arms before the rest of England; but then there was a stir in the North as well, in the weaving and mining regions. A shrewd game was played by the Puritans in raising funds there; thus the adherence of Newcastle was assured by the foundation of a coal-mining and iron-smelting company in which Oliver Cromwell played a prominent part, as much for political as for economic reasons. Against a party with such resources and acumen, the King was pathetically poor and helpless. In vain he attempted to pump up loans among the landed gentry, only to find that these, for all their fine feathers, had little cash.

Thus, as the Venetian ambassador wrote home to the commercial patricians on the Adriatic, the Puritan Revolution united the power of gold to that of iron. The Puritan Republic was founded on the same forces; London finance and the Army supported the dictatorship of Cromwell. Then the Puritan movement, after the triumph, began to break up into its component parts: the radical Diggers and Levelers were shown that poor Puritans need expect no fraternization with rich Puritans. Big business assumed control and worsted the lesser business men and artisans who had assisted in the movement.

The first necessity of Cromwell was to repay the financiers of London for their contributions. This was done in raising a fresh loan to conquer Ireland by driving the Catholics away from some five million acres and distributing the land among the soldiers and the subscribers to the Puritan cause. Not much land came actually to the soldiers, for their officers and real-estate speculators, following the troops, bought up scrip at a fraction of its value and saw it redeemed in full. Many of the best Irish titled families were founded in this way. Houblon was particularly interested in the plan, whether because of his enmity to Papists, or his enthusiasm for the eight per cent. And Cromwell's own son-in-law, Ireton, was one of the chief beneficiaries of the scheme.

The manipulation of Parliament was handled as adroitly as the financial question. The monopolists of the great companies found it more pliant than it had been even under the Stuart kings. No more of those obnoxious investigating committees which had proved tiresome, were permitted to harass business men. When it was proposed to look into the activities of the East India Company, the directors quietly "lent" £60,000 to the Cromwellian Government—with the result that the report was shelved and a new charter was granted, making the Company for the first time a permanent institution. Nay more; England went to war on the Company's behalf. Thus the Dutch War of 1652 was started to exact damages for injuries done to the East India Company, as well as for injuries inflicted on the Russia and Greenland Companies. Stern Puritan moralist though he was, Cromwell fairly flew to arms to defend the monopolists, even to the extent of attacking his fellow-Calvinists, the Dutch, with whom he had blood-kinship. Cromwell's hatred for the Dutch was so intense that he was ready to ally himself with Catholic France against them.

Nor was the war against the Dutch competitors the sole combat pressed upon Parliament by Cromwell at the behest of business interests. The West Indies War against Spain over the right to sell slaves in the colonies was another case in point—a second conflict in which England had to seek a Catholic ally and sink religious differences in hopes of booty. To create the right spiritual atmosphere, Cromwell declared the enterprise a holy crusade: "Why, truly, your greatest enemy is the Spaniard. He is a natural enemy. He is naturally so; he is naturally so throughout—by reason of that enmity that is in him against whatsoever is of God."

Yet another business war advocated by Cromwell, though it never came to pass, was one to preserve shipping interests in the Baltic. Once again, he strove to dignify the naked rapacity of the plan with sentiment. In a free blending of religion and economic interest such as had not been so boldly attempted since the Venetian doges pressed their citizens into the Fourth Crusade, Cromwell explained that trade-imperialism would be to the advantage of purse and soul: "If they can shut us out of the Baltic sea . . . where is your trade? Where are your materials to preserve your shipping?" But, he added, the English would always reckon "godliness the greater gain."

The Puritan Englishmen, under Cromwell, smashed idols and stained glass windows, and cleared England quite thoroughly of precious art relics. But all the ornamentation which they removed from churches reappeared in their speeches. Beginning then, the British business man acquired an unction, which went on developing down to the "white-man's-burden" attitude of Queen Victoria's reign.

The Cromwellian dictatorship gave the English business men a chance to show their abilities in governing. They became the actual masters of the country, and sought also to be the titular heads. Cromwell, who had "hoped to live to see never a nobleman in England," was forced to confer knighthoods upon a good many merchants who were not content with using their Lord Protector to secure charters, crush labor troubles, and draw the nation into war on their behalf, but must needs become lords as well, through him.

The aims of the business men, as revealed during this period of dominance, were strikingly unlike those of the Stuart king whom they had beheaded. The Stuarts had been hesitant about proceeding drastically against cousins and uncles on the thrones of Europe; their international affiliations made them more pacific than the business men, who were national in their outlook. Business in power proved far more bellicose and imperialistic than the Crown had been.

It was under the Protectorate that English nationalism mounted, and the Navy assumed greater proportions. As it has been phrased, in the years when the English monarchy was in suspense, the English Empire came into being. Or rather, one should say, the English merchants had been gathering the overseas possessions during the monarchy, by exploration, colonization, privateering and trade; then, overthrowing the monarchy, they consolidated their gains into an Empire. Having worked so hard to make conquests, they realized the possibilities of imperialism better than the landed gentry, who stayed at home. England's imperialism, and the creation of a militarism adequate to the new needs, were largely the results of business administration.

THE FAILURE OF BUSINESS RULE

Though business supported and nourished militarism, it dreaded the force of the Army, and did not know how to manage the monster it was creating. Only Cromwell could manage the Army, and after he died, no strong man arose from the banking or shipping world to over-awe the troops. Moreover, the expenses of a business administration had been proven greater than those of the Stuarts; for the poor King had expended his money on finery, whereas business demanded the far more costly luxury of imperialist warfare.

Outcries against corruption increased. Soldiers and merchants were found as venal and spendthrift as monarchs and courtiers. In a remarkably short time, Charles II was welcomed back, with a general sigh of relief. True, the second Charles was unsatisfactory to business interests. Indeed, he was guilty of the same crime as his predecessor—seizure of merchant moneys in the Tower. In 1671, Charles closed the Exchequer, and this act brought down the credit of the Crown with a crash in which, it is said, ten thousand families suffered. As the crisis continued after the death of Charles II and the accession of James II, a more suitable monarch was sought in Holland, the bourgeois paradise across the Channel.

In bringing over the Dutch King, who knew bookkeeping and had some idea of contracts, the younger Houblon played a great part. The Houblon banking family took a rôle in regicide and kingmaking which entitles it to a place beside the Fuggers, who strengthened the Hapsburgs; or the Rothschilds, who helped overcome Napoleon. The Houblons, in fact, belong beside the very few men—Jacques Cœur and Thomas Gresham, for instance—who have known how to mold, as well as finance, royal régimes.

French genius has been especially exhibited in work within the State. Out of French bourgeoisie have come many impressive manipulators of State affairs, from Cœur to Colbert and down to Necker and Ouvrard. The Houblons brought some of this quality to England, and used their adopted land to further the strife of the French bourgeoisie against Louis XIV, the Absolutist Sun-King. A rich and influential group of Huguenot exiles filled London, thirsting for revenge upon the Sun-King, their relentless foe. In Dutch William, they saw their fitting tool.

It was Houblon the younger who brought the financial element of England squarely behind William. The land-poor gentry could not afford loans for the king, and so he was forced to rely upon the commercial City in which, like his father before him, the younger Houblon was master. Houblon was Lord Mayor, and with his brothers, ran the newly established Bank of England. Not only was he master of the City and of its wealth, but also was Commissioner of the Navy besides, and in this threefold capacity, a director of English destinies.

War against French Absolutism, personified in the Sun-King, was desired by Houblon, and his circle. Through the new Bank, funds were procured to help King William in this strife with France. Business men might not have lent directly to the Crown for such a purpose; but Houblon secured their wealth indirectly and kept a steady stream of gold flowing toward the Continent. Unswervingly, he fought to halt the onward march of French Absolutism, as his father had helped to lay English Absolutism low.

This was not accomplished without storms. Once one of the directors of the Bank, who went to take funds to Namur, was struck by a cannonball. Stocks went down and there was a flurry; some of the old-fashioned goldsmiths who loathed the new institution of the Bank, started a run on it, which was narrowly averted by Houblon, working with the aid of the philosopher, Locke, and the mathematician, Isaac Newton.

Speedily, Houblon put the Bank on its feet again, mobilized all resources, and demanded that the shareholders assess themselves 20 per cent. The shareholders were recalcitrant in mood, for they had objected to the use of the Bank funds for a war in the first place. But when Houblon stepped before them, he not only calmed their wrath —he got from them another big loan for William's war. Hypnotized by Houblon's massive presence, every hand in the hall went up in his favor.

Looking upon Houblon's portrait, which hangs in the Bank of England, it is easy to imagine such a scene. He must have been a magnificent-looking oligarch, in his robes and chains of office, with the sword of the municipality by his side. His heavy-jowled head in the great, curled wig shows power in every line; the jutting nose and bulldog mouth are those of a man who craves might—the drooping, disillusioned eyes belong to a Restoration cynic. Gazing at this face, one may well wonder what France would have become, had her tens of thousands of Puritan business men stayed at home, and taken the helm there, instead of in a foreign land?

XVI

THE HEYDAY OF THE MONOPOLIST
IN FRANCE AND GERMANY

A HUNDRED YEARS of social stability were experienced by Europe between the final "Glorious" Revolution in England (1688) and the French Revolution (1789). Both countries had taken decisive action, France by expelling the Calvinists in 1683, and England by installing a Dutch Calvinist king, five years later, who practiced toleration; the religious inclinations were exactly contrary, but the effect was the same: the religious contest was closed, and with it important social issues. In both countries, the commercial oligarchy at the top was unified and, its differences settled, could lean back to enjoy the spoils of victory. And these spoils were almost equally great in either country, for England and France were abreast of each other at last, and both had left Holland slowly fading in the rear.

In this century of social tranquillity and formality, in which even the wars were conducted with polite regard for etiquette, the wealth of the business classes seemed secure from threat; it rose enormously, with a profound effect upon the manners and character of men. Gradually this wealth won a new respect for itself; urban-commercial riches began to take precedence over landed property, and the cities of Paris and London outgrew the provincial nests. The business man, small or big, acquired a new sense of self-importance, and with it social and finally political ambitions.

On the heights, the very rich made their way into the aristocracies of either country, which became correspondingly commercialized. But there were important differences between France and England in this respect: in the former land, it was the financier who won entry to the highest social circles, whereas in England the merchant-monopolist was eligible for alliances; in both the manufacturer was still under the ban. In France, the rich man who acquired a title was practically obliged to retire from useful activity and become a seigneur; but in England he could continue to trade lustily, so long as he moved his home far away from his shop. The political and cultural relations of the two were likewise distinct: in France rich business men could create a culture of their own, more or less urban in character, though firmly debarred from all but very indirect political activities. It was otherwise in England, where business men accepted the standards and manners of the landed gentleman, instead of making their own cultural atmosphere, but, in return, joined with the gentry in exerting a most powerful political influence.

Of the two oligarchies, therefore, the English was in reality the more powerful, but the French more magnificent. When Englishmen traveled in France, they were amazed by the profusion of plate, the elegance of salons in homes of French bankers, especially *chez Laborde*. But when Frenchmen came to England, they heartily envied the respect and freedom accorded there to commerce. Both, however, were making complementary contributions to modern society: the French laying the basis for modern bourgeois culture, while the English were developing modern methods of representing special interests, through lobbying, debate and persuasive pamphleteering.

And though the one might be more resplendent or more tasteful than the other, both were in truth gorgeous enough. This period, in which commercial wealth and aristocracy were most nearly allied, was the time when parvenudom was particularly tasteful. Wealth from trade furnished the means for aristocrats to indulge their fancies, while at the same time they set a pattern for the rising trader; the interplay produced the utmost in self-adornment. Never before or since has the rich man looked so elegant and so imposing personally; even the most ugly and awkward *nouveau riche* could disguise himself successfully in the complete masquerade, from powdered wig and brilliant coat with swinging satin skirts, to the diamond buckles on his shoes. The ornate coaches, painted with the new coat-of-arms, the liveried footmen, the sumptuous châteaux and gardens, all assisted in providing him with an extraordinary background, so dazzling to the popular eye that individual shortcomings were blotted out. In this period, at least no one could reproach the rich man for having millions which were of no use to him, for never has wealth been more fully employed, and the maximum of enjoyment extracted from its powers.

THE VIE SCANDALEUSE OF THE BANKERS

In France, standards of living were steadily rising for all the business classes, the lesser as well as the higher. Shops, which had been dark little dens when Colbert took charge of France, had become fine gilded salons, adorned with mirrors, tapestries and screens in the rococo age. Homes altered correspondingly; more rooms, better furnished, were added. In 1606 the opulent Jean Gouault of Troyes had been compelled to receive guests in his bedroom, for only noblemen had a *salle;* most bourgeois merchants then ate in their kitchens. A generation or so later, the bourgeois Jean Michelin possessed a real *salle* with pictures, a buffet and curtains of green serge. But after that the middle class aspired to a *salon:* the rich merchant, father of the revolutionary heroine, Madame Roland, had a salon, which, however, his modest wife referred to as a *salle.*

The glitter of bourgeois life in the ancien régime has often been forgotten and attention focussed on Versailles. As a matter of fact, the homes of wealthy bankers who dwelled at Paris were a magnificent contrast to the narrow lodgings of courtiers at Versailles. Some of their country estates made the last Queen's Petit Trianon seem very modest; Paris de Montmartel, for instance, spent ten millions on his country place at Beauce and Laborde devoted fourteen millions merely to his English-style park. The marvel of Paris was the palace of the royal banker, Beaujon, filled with bronzes, Gobelins, and statues; his overflow of Sèvres cupids, marble clocks and other objects were sent to a country home, *La Folie Beaujon,* later bought by a Rothschild. Beaujon was, however, a sad case; though he spent millions on ornaments, he could enjoy nothing. He owned amazing gardens but was too fat to walk in them. He gave superb dinners at which he ate only spinach. He had countless splendid bedrooms and suffered from insomnia. The only way he could get sleep was by giving his famous evening parties, the *berceuses de M. de Beaujon,* which cost 200,000 livres a year; at these affairs he called in the loveliest courtesans of Paris to tell him little stories while he endeavored to doze off—a monstrous, bald, bloated old man in a bed sculptured and painted to resemble a gilded basket of roses.

Not only in Paris but in the provinces, the spectacle of opulence and gaiety was presented. At Marseilles, the Château Borelli was a spectacle; at Abbeville the Van Robais lived like lords; at Tours a damask-maker constructed a fabulous home with galleries, gardens and a private theater. The merchants of Lyons, an Englishman observed, lived as well as the courtiers of Versailles; another traveler, Mrs. Piozzi, said the rich folk of Lyons had 36 *plats* at dinner and 24 at supper, all served in silver vessels; after dinner, the ladies played the harp while the men sang gaily if not always in tune, and altogether she never had met so much cordiality in her life or found it more agreeable.

The two sea-ports of Nantes and Bordeaux were exceptionally noted for luxury. In the former, the tourist, Young, visited a theater five times as big as Drury Lane; the river banks were strung with homes having sculptured façades and iron-grilled balconies. Another visitor there, young Buffon, stated that the merchants could have bought their way into the noblesse had they chosen to do so, but they preferred "abundance in the bourgeoisie to famine in the aristocracy." Bordeaux had a reputation of its own for folly; there the rivalry among the rich families in outlay for silver and dress, and for gambling and the theater, brought many to bankruptcy. A special reason for the animation of that town was the residence there from 1758 on of the Maréchal de Richelieu, a grand-nephew of the old Cardinal, who was a magnificent monster, leading the bourgeoisie a merry dance through various shapes of corruption, and making the *vies scandaleuses* of Bordeaux bourgeois quite worthy to be set beside those of Paris bankers; both, indeed, yield in nothing to the chronicles of Versailles.

By contrast with the rich bankers of France, the courtiers of that small suburb, Versailles, cut altogether a poorer figure than the popular imagination has given them. Commonly they were land-poor and better known for debts than resources. The banker, Sam Bernard, possessed 33 millions, while the duc de Bourbon *owed* 5 millions. The duc de Choiseul made a stir by contracting 6 millions of debts, while the army-provider, Bouret, amassed 42 millions. The Prince de Guéméné won fame by losing 32 millions, but the financier, Paris de Montmartel, acquired 100 millions. In this state of affairs, it was inevitable that bankers should set the pace for the capital, and for the nation; it was no wonder that Marie Antoinette, when she wanted to enjoy herself, stole away from the dull Court, night after night, to the gay *bals masqués* of Paris.

ROCOCO AND THE FINANCIERS

That last refinement of the superfluous, the art of the rococo, owes quite as much to the tastes of business men as to the whims of aristocrats. It was not by any means the mere expression of the Court; at Court it was introduced by the banker's wife, the Pompadour, who became the king's mistress, but without severing her connections with Paris, over which she had already reigned as dictator of fashions, or with the great financiers and army-providers, who lent her funds in return for her amiable intercessions with ministers.

Bourgeois as well as the Court patronized opera and concerts; La Popelinière, the banker, had a symphony orchestra in his home, directed by Rameau. Circles of Bordeaux supported concerts which introduced the music of Gluck and Mozart to France. In the field of painting, the inroads of bourgeois demands became conspicuous, as, instead of the aristocratic Poussin, favor turned to the homelier Watteau, who lived with, and on, the merchant Crozat. There were two brothers Crozat of Toulouse; the elder, a banker and trader, enjoyed exclusive privileges in dealings with the New World. These rights he cannily sold to the speculator, John Law, and so made money while nearly everyone else lost in the Law Bubble. He tried to break into the aristocracy by marrying his pretty daughter to a Count whose mother, the haughty duchesse de Bouillon, called her "my little gold-ingot." The mother later advised her son, the Count, to dissolve the marriage on the ground of inequality of birth; and as soon as he had made money by speculating with the dowry, he did.

The younger Crozat, perhaps dismayed by that experience, did not attempt to climb the thorny path to social eminence. Instead, retiring from business in 1703, he devoted his fortune to the patronage of art and music. In his town hotel and wonderful country villa, housing works of Michelangelo and Veronese—one of the richest private collections of all France—he invited the painter Watteau to make his home, and every Sunday he received artists and musicians of Paris in true Medicean style.

Another of the influential business patrons of art was the German banker, Jabach, the leading connoisseur and purchaser of art in Paris, whose collection formed the nucleus of the Louvre Museum. His cultivated taste, upon which Colbert relied, assisted the formation of French industrial art in the Baroque. But the bankers were not all fitted for such a rôle; some of them, like the brothers de la Reynière, gave their attention chiefly to the culinary arts. The gastronomy of the *ancien régime* owes much to the army-provider, Bouret, who taught the nobility of France how to eat.

Bouret stood close enough to the State to hold the postal service and many tax-gathering rights, while in private, he indulged in speculations in salt and grain. With his colossal wealth and vanities, this man had rather more than the usual eccentricities of the great. His annual dinners to the king and entire Court of Versailles defy description. Each guest was served his favorite dishes in golden vessels and given costly presents—on gifts of jewels alone, Bouret spent eight millions a year. The flowers on the tables were artificial, made of gems. For the festivity, a fabulous pavilion was built, containing a statue of Louis XV, adorned with verses by Voltaire. All this, however, did not win the respect of the king; but the invitation of an army-provider could not be rejected by the haughtiest Bourbon, and so he always went, until Bouret, at last, bankrupted himself by display and died a ruined man.

Bouret had not lived in vain. His example greatly assisted in the culinary education of the French noblesse which, in its old-fashioned state, had cared almost as little about its sauces as the British. Indeed, the divergences in the two aristocracies are in part due to the fact that the latter was rivaled only by merchants, who have ever been more homely in their tastes than financiers; had Britain had an army-provider like Bouret, perhaps she, too, would delight in subtle ragouts. Only in France, however, were such gentry so ostentatious. From the sixteenth century on down, they challenged the oldest families by their extravagances. Thus a candlemaker's son, Bordier, had become provisioner of the forces and a financier of the State and was known as the most pompous parvenu until Richelieu disgraced him. Buying a huge château and the title of M. de Raincy for his son, the two rode about in carriages emblazoned with crowns. The story is told that they adorned their horses with red pompons such as only gentlemen of the highest quality were supposed to display. When someone raised this point with M. de Raincy, as he was setting out on a journey to Rome, he simply opened a casket by his side, showing its brimming contents of louis d'or, and replied: "A gentleman who has this much to spend on a trip to Rome may put whatever he likes on his horses."

A more agreeable sort of parvenu was the famous Sam Bernard, born in 1651, the son of a painter to the king. He became enormously rich as a financier, and was so useful that, even though a Huguenot, he could not be touched by proscription. He married his daughters and granddaughters, at least the legitimate ones—George Sand was a descendant of his—to high titles, thereby causing much gnashing of teeth among the noblesse; and he had himself painted in dangerously near-royal poses, with velvet swathes behind his gilded chair. As Hénault, also of a financial family but far from friendly to Sam, described him: "He is not M. Jourdain, he is not Turcaret, he is like nothing that has yet been played in a comedy, because there has never been before a fool of his species; he had an extravagant pride, which in some manner ennobled him, for he was insolent with good faith. . . . He had loved the most beautiful princesses of Germany (where he had never been); he recounted the fêtes he had given them. . . . I ought to add that he was generous." With open purse and bearish gallantry he haunted corridors of Versailles.

Greater even than Sam Bernard were the brothers Paris, the financial rulers of France at the opening of the eighteenth century. They were close friends of the Pompadour, and like her, befriended the literati, with such good effect that Beaumarchais and Voltaire, whom they admitted to some share in the army-provisioning business, obligingly shifted their ridicule away from the racket of army-victualing and attacked merely the titular masters of the nation. The wealth of the brothers was a favorite theme for stories. A merchant at dinner is supposed to have asked the younger Paris, "If I needed a thousand louis, would you refuse them?" "No," was the answer, "and if you needed

30 millions, you could have them in eight days." Not a witty retort, perhaps, but as much so as most anecdotes about bankers, who seemed close-mouthed even in that age of sparkling quips.

Yet, behind this sumptuous façade of France, there was decided uneasiness. True, under Absolutism, a banker might mount more swiftly and higher than in a relatively democratic system; through the favor of a noble courtier, a mere barber might become a financier, with astounding rapidity; and the old tax-farming system of France, besides the constant opening for war-furnishing in so bellicose a State, allowed a banker an extraordinary power in the government and over society. He could be magnificent, insolent, perhaps more than others of his day. But these opportunities were balanced by the ever-present possibility of a tragic fall, like Bordier's. Though no English man of wealth has made quite so startling a parade of possession as the French financier, Fouquet, it was also true that none there fell so low, from such a height, as that financier. All the time even the most fortunate of men in France were more at the mercy of royal displeasure than those across the Channel.

When Colbert died, example was immediately made of several of the leading business men who had been his assistants in the economic development of France. He had brought in many foreigners, Swedes and Germans, to exploit mines and cast cannon, Dutch to treat tobacco, Milanese to make silk and Venetians to start the manufacture of glass and lace. One of these, the right-hand man of Colbert, was a naturalized Italian, Bellinzoni, a diplomatic, suave, ingenious and much suspected adventurer. His wife, described by La Bruyère as the perfect type of the parvenu's conquettish spouse, perhaps aroused animosity too. The king disliked this agent intensely, and no doubt Bellinzoni was feathering his own nest well; he could hardly have drawn a line between his private undertakings and the public affairs in which he engaged. He was inspector of manufactures, director of merchant companies and general purchasing agent for the State. He traveled on tours of inspection, discussed business-codes with silk-makers, bought hemp for the Navy and recruited sailors, negotiated with Spain for a hat-maker competent to teach his art to the French. Naturally he confused, at times, his activities for the State, the Companies and himself. The moment the protecting hand of Colbert was withdrawn, the king sent him to the Bastille, charged with using treasury funds to speculate in East India stocks.

At about the same time another capitalist and friend of Colbert suffered disgrace. Pierre Formont was one of the Huguenots shielded by the Minister because they were sharper buyers and bidders than orthodox Christians. No man could purvey munitions for the Navy or

swans and orange-trees for the gardens of Versailles like this strict
Calvinist. For twenty years, Formont was the chief agent of the State;
he contracted to deliver materials for building Versailles, and brought
marble and lead piping for the fountains at a handsome profit. For the
Army and Navy he found food, equipment, metals, Barbary horses or
English donkeys. On his private account, as well, he was a great merchant, participating in the French East India Company, speculating
in lead, tin, salt, vinegar, glass, leather. His ships sailed to Guinea and
America; his agents were in Calais, Madrid, Rome, Venice, London,
Amsterdam, Hamburg, Danzig, Vienna. The extent of these interests
made him very useful to the State, then devoid of an efficient consular
service. Wherever the State made payment abroad for pictures or
military subsidies, his firm handled the transaction; and when secret
information was desired about enemy Powers, he also obtained it. His
son Nicolas and two brothers in Danzig besides his brother-in-law in
Hamburg wrote letters on trade and politics for the king, acting as
secret agents. With such aids, Formont was able to announce the movements of enemy fleets in the English-Dutch War in 1666. Like Bellinzoni, however, he may have forgotten the boundaries between private
and public enterprise in such a position; certainly his son Nicolas
served two masters, informing the Germans about French military
operations as well as vice versa. And no doubt his stubborn Puritanism
stood in his way. He was dismissed; his widow and sons were beggared
and sent into exile to live on the charity of strangers.

Upon the most powerful men in the realm, the royal hand might
fall heavily and unexpectedly. And even when they were not victims
of royal caprice, they were at every turn bound down by governmental supervision, far more than was the case of the English. This is
illustrated by the career of François Martin, a prominent figure in the
East India Company, a whirlwind of efficiency and a man after Colbert's heart. Hardly another French business man of the period so
clearly deserves to be set beside the English and Dutch merchant-
adventurers who were then carving out trade-empires. Martin was as
versatile as they, never at a loss, whether gathering up a cargo under
extreme difficulties, finding a lion as a present for the King of Siam,
or leading troops of rajputs with elephants to win a trading concession.
Though a man of mettle, who gave France a new place in India, he
could not enjoy a free hand like his rivals in India, the English and
Dutch; he received conflicting orders from home, whereas they were
given the utmost latitude; he was the harassed servant of the king, but
the Englishman, Sir Josiah Child, had tied the Court to his pocket.

The English and Dutch India Companies were managed by business
men, who owed but a nominal allegiance to the king, and had charge

of their own troops, the right to make treaties and war in distant parts. The French Company, like the French State, was full of discordant elements; the king could never make up his mind whether he preferred glory or profit, and demanding now one and now the other, in the end lost both. The king would not give troops over to a mere merchant; the military element remained quite independent, and made a great deal of trouble for Martin. Piquing themselves upon gentility, they refused to associate with traders; and one irate major wrote back from India:

> The merchants who have been in India several years have lived in places where, in the absence of troops, they found themselves on top and regarded as great lords by the poor miserable blacks . . . homage which so flattered them that they find it very strange if anyone has the boldness to dispute any point with them. However nothing could be more absurd than that gentlemen of good birth should be subordinated to such men. . . . They have already usurped enough of the rights of troops which are not due them . . . and demand military honors at their funerals as though such pomp was invented for folk who never were warriors; nothing is more mortifying for an officer than to conduct a troop of soldiers before the bier of an agent or a merchant.

While Martin endeavored to soothe the choleric majors, he was also hampered by religious quarrels between the Jesuits and Capuchins who carried their rivalries into the East and quarreled constantly with the natives and one another. It was as impossible to bring them to view all matters in the light of good business as it was to convince the military. Their zeal stirred up the natives, whom the placid Dutch refrained from annoying on matters of faith. Once, for instance, the French priests determined to burn all the idols of Pondicherry; the weavers and others, about 15,000 persons in all, prepared to leave the city and go out to the more tolerant Dutch. At the moment of departure Martin managed to head them off and shut the gates; he saved his colony by effecting a compromise: the workers were to keep their idols but not carry them on the streets.

Again, Martin once struck off a coin showing the deity of riches, the goddess Lakmé, and it proved very popular. But the priests objected to this heathen abomination and when the directors approved of Lakmé they appealed to the king. The monarch finally decided to go ahead with Lakmé, adding, however, his own *fleur de lys*. Vainly Martin kept calling attention to the fact that the English, Dutch and Danes did not let religious convictions interfere for a moment with a good bargain. He even suggested: "Perhaps we in France do not render enough justice

to the natives of the Indies for their intelligence and good sense. . . .
They are not behind the nations of Europe." But the king desired to
spread the light of the true faith as much as to drive a shrewd deal; his
faith, as well as his pride, prevented that single-minded attention to
business which carried the English so far.

Lacking the capital and organization, or the free hand, all that Martin achieved was the more remarkable. He had indeed won an almost
royal position for himself in the East, this once poor grocer's apprentice; and at seventy-two, after forty years' service in the Company, he
died at Pondicherry, the town he had built and fortified, quite sure in
his last moments that he had laid the "foundation for the French Empire in the East and of the Christian religion." But he had attempted
too much; the English fared better by attempting less.

If the regulations of the French Government were so crippling to
merchants in foreign parts, they were much more serious for those at
home, directly under the eyes of the bustling bureaucrats. Innovation
in industry was repressed by the Crown, after Colbert died, with increasing severity. Control was tightened over every phase of commercial life. But, as it was impossible to extract enough wealth in taxes from
an industry so confined, the Court turned to the money-lenders; and
so the kings who despised the trader became the bankers' prey. This
led to an ever-tightening relationship between Crown and business, on
both sides.

Business men found it more profitable to hang about the Court, waiting for contracts and subsidies, or the chance to loan large sums in return for tax-gathering privileges, than to produce goods. The manufacture of goods did not pay so well as speculation and the manipulation
of privileges. One example illustrates the situation. In 1757 the Government determined to win away the Near Eastern cloth-market from
the English and Dutch. It sold to manufacturers, therefore, the privilege of making the cloth to be shipped. A feverish speculation in the
papers ensued. "The mistresses of MM. the bureaucrats, the valets and
femmes de chambres, and *comédiennes,* made a thousand écus here and
two thousand écus there," says Martin. "One may imagine what man-
euvres, seductions, corruption were necessary to obtain the right to
work." After this fantastic little boom collapsed, those who did have
the right to work made such a botch of it that the Turks would buy
none of the cloth.

The tendency of the French to seek riches by intriguing for State
aid was of course very old, an inheritance from the Italian financiers
who taught the French natives the art of absorbing public resources.
Now, however, in the *ancien régime,* this tendency became fixed. Despotism encouraged such intrigue. The English traveler, Arthur Young,

noticed the inclination of French business men to operate in groups or cabals, instead of acting on their own individual initiative. And not only were they trying to dip into the State treasuries or obtain personal favors; they were also seeking tax-exemption through the purchase of government posts and titles, which automatically freed them from this burden. The most eager desire of a rich business man in France, as the English observer, Josiah Tucker, noted in the 1750's, was to retire from trade, buy himself a title and land, and place his sons in Church and Army. In England, Tucker commented, no man need leave his trade to pass for a gentleman, whereas in France the wealth made in commerce was spent upon agrarian properties, or display at Court, and withdrawn from business enterprise.

Some French merchants greatly regretted this turn to aristocratization. One citizen of Bordeaux, writing an "Apologie du commerce" in 1777, bewails the fact that business houses could no longer erect dynasties: "Hardly does one see a business house passing to the second generation. A son who inherits the fortune of his father, wishes to enjoy the fruits . . . in idleness. Scarcely does he deign to admit that his fortune derives from commerce."

BOURGEOIS AND ARISTOCRATS

Both speculation and the urge toward aristocratization took funds away from productive industry, thereby impoverishing national economy. This would not have happened to such an extent in France if the nobility had been permitted to engage in trade. But as things stood, if a Breton nobleman, for example, wished to enter commerce, he had to hang up his sword in the Chamber of the Peers and he could not resume it until he had purged himself of the trading taint. The only form of manufacturing which a gentleman might safely pursue was glass-making, legalized after 1727. The great feudal estates had forests to burn for this business; when the forests dwindled, however, what then? Some impertinent persons suggested that the gentry burn coal, like the English, whereupon the blue-blooded glass-makers haughtily replied: "It is not possible that gentlemen engaged in glass-making should be able to endure the thick smoke coming from coal." So the art fell into the grasp of bourgeois with less sensitive nostrils.

Of course the prohibition could not be absolutely enforced. Special dispensation was sometimes granted by the king. In 1739, for instance, Sieur Jean-Baptiste Michel, the king's Secretary, successfully begged that his son might run a bleachery without losing his title. When privileged to open plants, frequently manufacturers were specifically allowed to sell shares to nobles. Mining, pursued on the estates of the great nobles, was sometimes permitted; thus the Mirabeau, Lafayette, and d'Entragues families, and the duc de Charost too, headed societies for mining. Occasionally nobles had the right to erect mills and forges on their estates; for instance, the Duchess of Mazarin had a cloth-hall and the Sieur de la Chaussade made anchors for the navy. Nevertheless such activities did not provide an extended opening for profit-making on the part of the aristocracy.

Many of the nobles, the lesser ones particularly, wished to go into business. Led by practical interests, they delved into technology, read papers at the Academy, and corresponded with bourgeois on scientific matters. A few voices were raised to propose a thoroughly Anglicized trading-aristocracy. Thus l'Abbé Coyer, in a tract called "La Noblesse Commerçante," wrote: "The French noblesse, in time of peace, is a paralytic body, without movement or action; should I say? without ideas." And he suggested: "Let us enrich the nobility by commerce, and it will contract marriages," increase and flourish.

Such propaganda was without much effect. Generally the French aristocracy remained "above" useful pursuits. This fact was emphasized as one of the striking differences between France and England. A London pamphleteer in 1691 remarked: "It is very rare to see a French Gentleman turn to Merchandizing. . . . It is something surprising, they should so much disdain Merchandizing, their King *Lewis le Grand*, not to mention his other Commodities, being the greatest salt-merchant in the known World."

If it had followed the English road to riches, the French aristocracy might have survived as a class—at least for a long time. Or, it might have maintained itself in the German manner: while the German Junkers likewise kept aloof from trade, they lived simply on their landed estates or earned their living in bureaucratic civilian and military posts; thus they kept health and power and made a little money. But the French would not follow either course. They wished to have their cake and eat it: they wanted to be more exclusive than others; they would neither go into business nor accept dirty office-jobs. At the same time they insisted upon living around the Court at Versailles where they were in dire need of funds for their extravagant display.

So idle an aristocracy would have collapsed sooner than it did, had it not been able to "fertilize its fields with gold," as the saying went, from the dowries of burgher-daughters; and if its ranks were not filled constantly with recruits from the bourgeoisie. This social climbing went on for many generations; Louis XIII ennobled members of a company for developing Canada; Henry IV sold 1,000 letters of nobility; in 1696, 6,000 letters of nobility were sold. Louis XIV ennobled Van Robais, and Louis XVI offered to honor the cotton-maker, Oberkampf.

In 1773, Jacques Gouault of Troyes obtained a title, in honor of "his fathers who have pursued commerce for two hundred years." The satirists were quick to perceive the comical side of such transactions; they described the decay of the noblesse, from the days of Dancourt and d'Allainval down to Boileau, who wrote of a certain rich man, that the genealogist would help him:

> *If he has no title and no memories,*
> *D'Hozier will find him a hundred ancestors in history.*

How far this embourgeoisement of the aristocracy had gone by the end of the *ancien régime,* may be judged from a fact stated by Babeau: in 1789, on the eve of the Revolution, the king's genealogist, Chérin, said that out of every 100 noblemen, no less than 95 were of bourgeois origin. By the time the "national razor" spilled the blood of French aristocrats, that blood was already very far from a true blue.

The bourgeois, however, though he joined the aristocracy, did not alter its views. Though the noblesse was so largely diluted, it remained quite as disdainful of trade as before. This was because the roturiers were so eager to hide their origins and adopt the grand manner. They usually severed connections with their old lives, left business ventures, snubbed their former friends, and lived in sterile leisure. Thus, when the son of one of the great bankers, the Paris brothers, became a Marquis, he could not see any of his former cronies. Yet no aristocrat would stoop to visit him. So he sat in his gorgeous dining-hall, under crystal chandeliers, and was served on golden platters—quite alone. When the solitude became unbearable, he used to ask his liveried servants to sit down with him.

Of course, the bourgeois might have refused to toady to such supercilious gentlemen; in that case, they would not have needed to make a Revolution. A few business men, like some slave-dealers of Nantes, were indeed proud of their trade, and would not stoop to buy titles. But for the average rich man, the lure of nobility, carrying tax-exemption, was strong. Moreover, in a time when life-insurance was undeveloped, it was a good way to secure the future of his family. And, after all, the bourgeois was only secondarily a business man—first of all, he was a human being, who smarted under social inferiority.

For generations, the bourgeois struggled to win more esteem in France; at last he gained the right to be addressed as "Monsieur," as though he were a gentleman; his wife, formerly "Mademoiselle," became "Madame," like the queen. But this victory was insufficient. The barrier at Court remained. Though business men could buy posts in the magistracy which conferred legal titles, they were not as a rule admitted to the table of the king. Worse yet, their wives were merely saluted by His Majesty. That is to say, when they were presented at Court, declares Sénac de Meilhan, the king did not

> approach his cheek as though to embrace them . . . he made them a simple salute. This difference was humiliating to the distinguished families of the magistracy. . . . The Magistrates preferred that their wives should not appear any more at Court, if they were treated with less consideration than others.

It is this sort of thing which makes revolutions. No doubt, there were more serious grounds for an upheaval. But in all probability, most of the other, merely economic, issues might have been settled by compromise; the Crown was yielding on such questions as tariffs, taxation and financial reforms. Only on one point was the king adamant: he would kiss no green-grocers' wives. And who shall say whether it was not precisely this which sealed the doom of the French monarchy?

CHURCH AND BUSINESS

Rarely invited to Court, the business man was none too comfortable even in the Mother Church. The clerics had to uphold the Absolute Monarchy, in heaven and upon earth. God, declared the Jansenists, was beyond the reach of reason, and of anything except faith. But the business man was not enthusiastic about unconditional surrender of reason and his rights in spiritual or temporal matters. Protestant writers, therefore, who were the first to question the authority of the Throne, according to Sée, appealed to the bourgeois more than the Jansenists; but Calvinism, with its revolutionary tendencies, was driven out of France. For the business man who did not choose exile, there was no remaining spiritual comfort.

The orthodox clerics, as Groethuysen relates, did not know how to appeal to the middle classes. They could console the poor, or alternately scold and praise the aristocrats, for their awful vices and splendid repentances. But the bourgeois did not suffer like the poor or sin like the aristocrats. He was not even much afraid of Hell, because he was sure that he was very good.

For a time, the Jesuits undertook the task of converting the French business men, as they had won the heathen in savage lands, by subtle compromise. Their long experience in business fitted them to appreciate the economic viewpoint, for their Order was one of the chief financial and commercial powers of the world, engaged in Oriental trade, banking and manufacturing; at Angers, for instance, they had a sugar-refinery, which they had to defend against jealous competitors, who denounced it as unhygienic and a menace to public health.

With this wide experience in practical affairs, the Jesuits knew the proper dialect as well as dialectics. Said one: "Alms may be not badly compared to drafts drawn on eternity; on one's arrival they are payable at sight." In a sermon on usury, Father Hyacinthe de Gasquet, in 1766, announced:

> Not only is Jesus Christ himself your endorser, but it is between His divine hands and on His adorable head, that you place your capital. Could you make any placement more solid and profitable? This sort of stock can never perish . . . the interest thereon will be perpetual.

In this fashion, the Jesuits could appeal to the small-town shop-keeper. But even they, for all their casuistry, could not make a place in Heaven for the grasping, speculating plutocrat. They could find no words to excuse wholesale extortion and monopoly. Indeed, they were compelled to denounce brazen graft as much as the other clergy:

> Hands that amass from every side, that accumulate with such haste, are not very clean. Fortunes made almost in a moment, savour of the marvelous; is it God who has wrought the miracle?

Since they did not attract the great merchants, or please the aristocracy either, the Jesuits were expelled from France in 1764. Now that Calvinists and Jesuits had fled, the field was left in possession of the extreme upholders of Absolutism, both of God and of the king. Still the bourgeois would not yield one iota. Instead, he turned skeptic. He laughed at the excesses of the clergy, when they refused to palliate his own. With scornful words, on the eve of the French Revolution, a financier dismissed religion as something useful merely for the poor. Necker, the great Swiss banker at Paris, wrote:

> The more the extent of taxes retains the people in subjection and misery, the more necessary it is to give them a religious education.

As the bourgeois in France moved out of the folds of the national Church, and as their magnificence outshone that of the nobility, men began to question how long this curious state of things could last? How long would a busy, aggressive bourgeois remain under the red heels of the disdainful and impecunious aristocrats? And in what shape would the final eruption come? A foretaste of the disorders in store for French society was given at the opening of the century, in the notorious Law Bubble.

LAW: THE SCOTCH WIZARD

French society lacked three of the things which assured stability in England: an aristocracy hospitable to traders, a church with open portals for the erring business man, and a national bank. England's bank had been founded by a Huguenot and a Scotchman, John Paterson; but no such institution was erected in France itself as a bulwark of the public credit. It remained, therefore, for a remarkable Scotchman, John Law, the boy-wonder of finance, to attempt the establishment of such a foundation. With his Scotch blood, Law had a more natural affection for the Crown of France than that of England; he was an intense believer in Absolute Monarchy, and proposed to save it in France by turning the French State into a holding-company. It is probable that he was sincere in his intentions, but, whereas the Huguenot had saved England, the Scotchman all but ruined France.

He appeared at a propitious time in Paris for such a venture. After the old tyrant, Louis XIV, had died, leaving an immense debt and a debased coinage, the advisers of the new king, Louis XV, recommended a swift and wholesome declaration of bankruptcy and a fresh start. But at this juncture emerged a young adventurer, "a very tall, black, lean man; well-shaped . . . big-nosed, and speaking broad and loud," who had fled from London after killing a man in a duel, and had studied finance in Amsterdam and gambling in Venice. Speaking from the accumulated wisdom of his thirty years, this magician, Law, said that what France needed was not bankruptcy, but a bank.

For a sample, Law founded one in Paris. In glowing terms he described the benefits of banking, as exhibited in Holland and England. It would increase the circulation of currency and encourage foreigners to invest in France. Hitherto there had been "banks," to be sure, which lent money; but France had not progressed to the point of having institutions which issued "imaginary money" on the strength of deposits. Law offered to make the Monarchy itself such a Company, and issue stock upon the basis of royal privileges.

He bought up the privileges of the royal companies founded to trade with the Cape of Good Hope, the Red Sea, Persia, Mongolia, Siam, Japan and South America. He got possession of the Louisiana Company, promising to go on converting the Indians. On the foundation of these somewhat shadowy rights to the universe, Law issued shares. He also purchased the tax-gathering rights in France by lending 1,200 millions to the Government, against the opposition and frantic bidding of the Paris brothers. Determined to gather in more power, Law was willing to turn Catholic in order to be made Comptroller of Finances.

His propaganda was masterly. The old prospectuses written for the royal companies by hired savants were outdone by Law's gaudy prospectuses enriched by engravings of feathered Indians, explaining:

There one sees mountains filled with gold, silver, copper, lead, quicksilver. Since these metals are common there and the savages do not imagine their worth, they exchange them for . . . a swallow of brandy.

With his issues, Law commenced to play. One set after another appeared, known respectively as mothers, daughters, granddaughters. One might subscribe to the granddaughters only by showing possession of four mothers and a daughter. This brought a lively trade in all issues, for old stocks were bought up and sold at 1,000 per cent gain to those who needed them to purchase new issues. Prices rose in some cases 800 per cent above par.

Excited crowds so filled 'Change Alley, the Rue de Quincampoix, that troops had to clear it at nightfall. Before Law's house, mobs stood night and day, and many died in the crush. His antechamber was crowded with ladies as well as lords; a prince, needing a chaperon for his daughter, was told to go to Law's where all the duchesses were gathered. Law moved to a greater mansion and rented the space in the garden to stock-jobbers, at 500 livres a month for the privilege of setting up a tent. There were 500 pavilions, gay with ribands, forming a *Vanity Fair* to which rich came in palanquins, and beggars to catch the crumbs.

Vast wealth was won overnight. The Duke of Bourbon made 60 millions; the banker Leblanc reaped 100 millions; a hotel-waiter got 30 millions. Valets became bourgeois and bourgeois turned aristocrats. Whoever gained riches bought jewels, plate and houses; looms were humming day and night to turn out gold brocade for parvenu chambermaids and lustrous satins for speculators. A marvelous illusion of prosperity cast its glow over the decadent royal régime.

Since the aristocrat is not distinguished from the bourgeois by a disdain for money, but only by an ignorance of thrift, simple noblemen became mad harpies. The old Duke of Saint-Simon, however, kept insisting that a sensible bankruptcy was better than an insane prosperity. And the old soldier, Marshal Villars, riding by the stock exchange in a carriage, stuck his head out of the window, and reproached the crowd for its disgusting demonstration of avarice.

At the height of the madness, a young nobleman, Count d'Horn, committed a terrible crime to obtain the coveted shares. Like a robber baron, he lured a rich broker into his toils, murdered him and stole his stocks. When he was caught, the aristocracy as a body begged that the youth be given an honorable death by execution. But Law, who had been a friend of the slain broker, insisted that the Count be broken on the wheel.

Try as they would, the intellectuals of France could not all stay out of the general mania. Voltaire did so, but he was an exception. The story goes that two very sober philosophers, M. de la Motte and the Abbé Terrason, congratulated each other that they, at least, would never be caught. But a week later they met, at the stock-jobbers, M. de la Motte coming out and the Abbé rushing in. They shook hands, and laughingly agreed that philosophy was no protection against unreason.

Philosophers, however they might buy, could see that the boom was without foundation. Law was pledged to pay 12 per cent on the nominal worth of his shares. But his original capital of 312 millions was now expanded to 1,797 millions, and in order to pay even 4 per cent on this, his Company must make 72 millions profit. Where were the savages willing to part with so much precious metal for a few swallows of brandy? To quiet one panic, the Government paraded a few thousand beggars, carrying picks and shovels, as though about to leave for New Orleans, to mine gold in the bayous. The market was buoyed by the prospect.

Counterfeiters added to the confusion by adding millions of livres of fake shares to the already super-abundant genuine ones. This caused some nervousness in the buying public, but the majority still hoped to make just a little more profit before withdrawing to safety. A few wiser heads stole out just before the day of doom. One clever stock-jobber, Vermalet, got a million livres in coins, packed them on the bottom of a farmer's cart, covered it with hay and dung, and, attired in a dirty smock, drove it himself into Belgium the day before the market broke.

For break it did. Promptly the flight of capital was forbidden. Hoarding was declared illegal. Law was banished and his property confiscated. Gleefully, the Paris brothers returned to power and wound up his affairs, finding billions of deficit.

The reaction was hideous. Corpses were laid before the house of Law, where, but a short time before, silken dandies had jostled past the gay, beribboned tents. Rioting mobs called for victims. Amid general repentance, various solemn warnings against the speculative evil were issued. A caricature of the times, reverting to the "triumph" theme, depicted the Goddess of Shares seated on a triumphal car, drawn by traders along a way paved with the crushed ledgers of reputable firms. About the chariot a wild throng leaped and snatched at bubbles. At the end of the path stood a building with three entrances, one of which the crowd must choose, labeled, "Insane Asylum," "Hospital" and "Penitentiary." But, all unperceived by the men of that age, the building had another door: Revolution.

GERMAN FINANCIER-MONOPOLISTS

Curiously enough, two of the German financiers who won entry to the French aristocracy had previously failed to attain any such social recognition at home. The Schicklers and the Rothschilds found acceptance abroad that was denied the merchant or banker, however rich and powerful he might be, in the German States. For the situation of such men was still much more difficult in Germany than in France. Relatively, France might put up more barriers to the climbing business man than England, but she offered a paradise by contrast to Germany in the eighteenth century, and part of the nineteenth as well.

True, some court bankers exercised much influence in Germany, like the "Jew Süss" and Gotzkowski. The latter advised Frederick the Great in industrial matters; his private wealth was so large that he could sustain the public credit of Prussia abroad merely on his own account; by his large contributions and personal pressure he was able to prevent the Russians from plundering Berlin in the Seven Years' War. Even so, admired and even feared as he might be, he was not "accepted." Neither were the Schickler brothers, who engrossed so much of the commercial activity of the raw young State-in-the-making, Prussia, that for a long time nothing could be done without their aid. They lent money for the pet projects of Frederick the Great. Luring entrepreneurs and foreign workers to the boom town of Berlin, procuring gold and silver for the royal mints, they also manufactured glass and guns, refined sugar and imported anything needed by king or country, from buffalo-skins, tobacco, copper, coal, wax, salt, indigo and wine to old iron. They were advisers as well as bankers, meeting every wish of the king, whether for larks, balsam, shoe-leather, dancers and painters, or the company of the French jester, M. Voltaire.

Theirs was a strategic position. Close to the king, they urged him to make a commercial treaty with France in 1746 and assisted him with plans for founding trading companies. His military might depended on their contribution: guns. At Potsdam their factory remains, surmounted by heroic statues of blacksmiths and the motto: "Officina Cyclopam, Marti Sacra." Steadily their output increased from 1719, when they turned out 2,000 muskets at 3½ Thaler apiece with a tidy profit of 1,000 Thaler clear. A state monopoly for their products allowed them to employ orphans without pay, and no legislation hampered them.

By 1756 their turnover had increased to 97,000 Thaler and by 1762 it was 882,000 Thaler. Their profits from arms-making alone between 1767 and 1785 amounted to 90,000 Thaler.

Men of such significance in France or England would have mounted high in the State. But this was impossible in Germany, where the richest and most influential "royal merchants," though they might sway political decisions, could not expect high social titles such as adorned the Englishman, Josiah Child, or social prestige comparable to that of the bankers Law and Necker in France, or Robert Morris in the United States. The Schickler brothers could not marry high; the king arranged their weddings himself and saw to it that these were bourgeois and advantageous. When this family rose to the aristocracy it was in the hostile foe of Prussia, France. It had happened that, deeply involved in loans to the French Government, they were alarmed to the core when the Revolution voided their claims; and they eagerly provided Frederick William III with arms to be used against Napoleon. But, though pressing war against France, they also took care to find re-insurance in France, by uniting one branch of their family with a French family of Bordeaux, so that they could claim special protection when the French invaded Prussia. Eventually members of the family made Paris their home.

A similar fate marked the career of the Rothschilds. The founder of the house, Mayer Amschel, had close connections with the Kurfürst of Hesse, whose riches he saved by transferring them to London, out of the reach of the invading French. But Mayer Amschel and his son Amschel did not acquire distinctions from grateful princes. Indeed, the latter was pointedly ignored on one humiliating occasion by the Prussian king, Frederick William IV, a king above "sordid commerce," filled with romantic dreams, such as that of founding a bishopric in Jerusalem. He despised monetary concerns. When he once came to Frankfurt-am-Main, His Majesty was besought by his councillors to speak to the great moneyed man, Amschel, in the hope that this recognition might benefit the disordered finances of Prussia. But the king would not condescend to notice a mere banker, or even glance in the direction of Amschel, as he stood all evening in the Assembly. Accustomed to that sort of aristocratic slur, Amschel bore no grudge against the king; he merely regarded the incident a bit wistfully. Afterward he remarked to the king's councillor: "He might have spoken to me. After all, I'm a practical man, I am, and perhaps I could have said something he might have found useful."

It was left for Mayer Amschel's sons who went abroad to gain honors as well as powers. James helped to reestablish the Bourbons in France and became a baron. Of his king-making activities, Metternich said: "The House of Rothschild plays in France a much greater rôle than any foreign government, with the possible exception of the English." Under Napoleon III this family's influence was at its height: a Rothschild had access to the Emperor's private chamber and his children belonged to the court circle.

Another branch of the Rothschild family was no less successful—in England. True, the first to come, Nathan, so-called king of the London Exchange, perhaps did not wish to be in politics too conspicuously and an English contemporary declared he was not adapted to "the high direction of public functions." But his son Lionel sought power openly and stood so well in the estimation of men in the City that they elected him regularly as their representative, despite the fact that, as a Jew, he was debarred from taking his seat in the House. As he refused to change his creed, and his City friends would not alter their votes, it became imperative to mend the British Constitution in 1858; after that Lionel could enter upon a public career. How far both the English and French representatives of this house went beyond the native branch is illustrated in a description by Bismarck, who visited the old Amschel at Frankfurt and found him:

> A poor man in his palace, a widower, deceived by his servants and badly treated by his elegant Frenchified and Anglicized nephews and nieces who inherit his treasures without thanks and without love. In spite of that, his business sense was still very keen.

Social cleavage was indeed far more marked in German States, and particularly in Prussia, than elsewhere. This was often symbolized visibly by a cord stretched at receptions across palace ballrooms to separate the meek herd of burghers and their wives from personages of rank. At the opera, the bourgeois took a back seat. He was taxed systematically out of his surpluses, in most places, and forbidden to rival his betters even when he could afford it: in some parts, as in Hildesheim down to 1799, merchants were not allowed to wear lace, satin or silk. Thus the German merchant class of this century—always excepting a few free ports, like Hamburg and Bremen, from the picture—did not share in the opulent ostentation of France and England.

Of course, this was partly due to simple poverty. Prevented by localism from enlarging their industries to the greater scale of France's manufacturing establishments, they could not make such fine profits, or obtain such subsidies from the State coffers. A vivid sketch of the relative impoverishment of Berlin as late as the Napoleonic era—in striking contrast to contemporary Paris—is given by a letter of Field Marshal Gneisenau to the historian, Niebuhr. The latter wished to open an exhibition of German paintings in that town, but the Marshal warned him that Berlin lacked money for the muses and would not even buy an engraving. Noblemen, he said, lived in feudal seclusion still on country estates which they did not trouble to adorn, while the bourgeois made heavy feeding his chief pleasure. An "Esslust," an eating-mania, had seized upon Berlin, causing people to lose time, money and spirit at the table. The average upper-class Berliner who had "given a number of banquets during the year and outfitted his wife and daughter with laces . . . needed the utmost thrift to get through the year without debts, and nothing is left over for the arts."

Though not all towns were so poor as Berlin then—Leipzig, for instance, was rather elegant, with flourishing fairs and fur and other industries—the German merchant generally lacked the means to dazzle the German aristocracy. He could not buy his way into the nobility and bureaucracy as the French did; he might possibly marry his daughter to a Junker officer where a ruler permitted such a mésalliance, but that was frowned upon in Prussia by Frederick the Great, who would not have a trading father-in-law even in the background of his army officials. Nor could the German bargain for a compromise after the British fashion.

There was a constant clash of interests in Germany between the mercantile and the military-agrarian classes. The latter grew grain on great estates, much of it for export, and wished to sell the products of these "grain-factories" as dear as possible to townsmen. Their attitude was therefore somewhat like that of the French; both aristocracies had agrarian interests antagonistic to business claims. No harmonization in Prussia was possible like that in England, where wool-growing landed gentlemen met wool-traders half-way. Nor were both elements brought together in merchant-companies as in England. A few concerns, especially in mining, might bring such a nobleman as Prince Wittgenstein into line with bourgeois, but there was no such constant familiarity as existed in English coffee-houses and directors' meetings. Neither were there salons in Germany, like those in Paris, where financiers and their wives blended diverse elements. Relatively late, one such home in Germany, that of the brilliant daughter of a Jewish banker, Rahel von Varnhagen, née Levin, attempted such a formidable task. But one salon could not change all the German States.

THE RELIGIOUS FACTOR IN GERMANY

How far the religious factor should be considered along with the economic and political aspects, in accounting for the character and fate of the German business man, is a debated question. Various writers, following Weber, have declared that the Lutheran Church failed to give the self-confidence and spiritual push to business which the Calvinist doctrines tended to provide. Luther's deity, said Weber, was easily propitiated by repentance and love, and did not care whether a man worked hard or enjoyed himself; his material success indicated nothing about his salvation. On the contrary, the Calvinist God insisted that His Elect should labor to His glory, and pursue their callings with heart and soul.

Capitalistic development did indeed seem to proceed farther where Calvinists were settled in Germany, than in the Catholic or Lutheran parts. Perhaps twenty per cent of the population were of that creed, many of them exiles from foreign lands. Hamburg, the magnet for French refugees, received 14,000 and had besides English and Dutch Reformed and Jews from Spain and Portugal. Bremen adopted the Calvinist faith which came from its customer, Holland. Both cities were remarkably prosperous. Then there was the great Ruhr region around Essen and Elberfeld-Barmen, now the heavy-industrialist center of Germany, dowered with natural resources and water-power which attracted manufactures; Calvinist doctrines seeped in from nearby Holland and, when the Brandenburg Electors were to inherit this part as a marriage portion, they turned Calvinist to win it. Perhaps this Calvinism accounts for the royal driving power in a measure; possibly the thrift, energy and business acumen of Frederick William the First were increased by the shift in faith. But Prussia proper did not turn Calvinist like its monarchs.

While one might expect so active a Calvinist leaven to work politically for the business man in Germany, actually this was not the case. Since the refugees in Hamburg and Bremen were handsomely received and these cities were free and merchant-governed, there was no necessity for them to organize a revolt. In the Ruhr region the nobility was not aggressive and the Prussians granted bourgeois manufacturers many privileges, exempting them from military service for instance, so slight urge to revolution existed there also.

While the most hustling body of merchants, the Calvinists, were disinclined for one reason or another to make much trouble for German autocrats, little was to be feared from the Lutherans either. In most parts of Germany, Lutheran pastors were dependent for their livings upon pleasing princes and were able to set themselves apart from the bourgeois, claiming precedence. Accordingly, their doctrinal views were somewhat different from those of English Puritan divines, after the Glorious Revolution, who held their pulpits largely at the good will of merchants, and had the most pressing reasons for blessing the pursuit of gain.

Hamburg was exceptional in that there Lutheran pastors were compelled to curry favor with trading men, and in that city Lutheranism underwent some practicable modifications. Lutheran preachers in that port had to console bankrupts and comfort nervous brokers in fits of depression; in booms they permitted their flocks to sing Hymn Number 351, a praise of commerce included in the Hamburg Hymnal: "Thou givest the ships their courses on rivers and seas, and maketh Trade to bloom." This relaxation was gradual, however, and reluctant. In the 1600's, Lutheran pastors tried to prevent their flocks from doing business with dissident refugees and thundered against the cordial welcome of Catholics, Calvinists and Jews. But at length the Church gave in to the inevitable, and Pastor Schupp absolved merchants of evil-doing in associating with blasphemous immigrants; grateful traders filled his pews and made him popular. Nevertheless, the Pastor was discontented. Though he had won them over, he could not inspire them. He complained that they held whispered conversations about the price of shares in Amsterdam, behind their big hats, even during his sermons.

In Hamburg, too, was achieved a measure of cooperation between church and business in missionary endeavor which was otherwise slow to appear in Germany. Foreign missions had been neglected in that country while French Catholic fathers were busily acting as diplomatic agents for trading companies in the Far East, and Englishmen were sailing out with Bibles likewise, obeying the injunction of an East India Company director to consider religion as a necessary prop of trade. This idea took root in Germany late, not until the latter part of the eighteenth century, when the Hamburg exporters got interested in missions. In 1782, a Hamburg wine-and-leather-goods man offered financial aid for the work. But the relations between business and missions never became so warm at any stage as in France, Great Britain and the United States; in 1899, a Hamburg business man wrote to a newspaper about the violent death of evangelists in China, saying: "One would almost rejoice that two missionaries were murdered."

Another religious group in Germany resembled the Calvinists in its share in capitalistic development. German Quietism, or Pietism, produced some of the most important early capitalist entrepreneurs. Yet it taught political withdrawal; it might make good bourgeois, but not good bourgeois revolutionists.

XVII

THE HEYDAY OF THE MONOPOLIST: EIGHTEENTH-CENTURY ENGLAND

WITH THE GREAT PEACE of 1713 there was ushered in for England a time of social tranquillity. Business had had its chance to govern, and the gross failure under Cromwell, with the taste of a "strong man" and fear of army dictatorship, made it well satisfied to accept a reasonable political compromise with the landed gentry. On its side, the gentry, more practical than the more punctilious French and German noblemen, accepted the rich profits which accrued to it under this alliance, with cheerful Restoration cynicism. Perhaps the situation and the temper of his age were best phrased by that grand monopolist and *de facto* ruler of the East India Company, Sir Josiah Child.

Child was under no illusions about his own class of business men, whom he considered narrow in their views and unfitted by their special interests to conceive of broad designs in politics. Nor did he entertain a high opinion of the county families; once when some of his doings were criticized as contrary to English law, he snorted and called the laws of England "a heap of nonsense, compiled by a few ignorant country gentlemen, who hardly know how to make laws for the government of their own families, much less for the regulation of companies and foreign commerce." Yet, put the two together, he insisted in 1681, and each would ideally complement the other, both in commerce and in politics:

Trading merchants . . . although they be very wise and good men, are not always the best judges of trade, as it relates to the profit or power of a kingdom. The reason may be, because their eyes are so continually fixt, and their minds intent upon what makes for their peculiar gain or loss, that they have not the leisure to expatiate or turn their thoughts to what is most advantageous in general. This I am told was the opinion anciently of M. T. Cicero . . . The like may be said of all shop-keepers, artificers, clothiers, and other manufacturers, until they leave off their trades, and being rich, by the purchase of lands, become of the same common interest with most of their countrymen . . . I am of the opinion, and have found by experience, that a mixt assembly of noblemen, gentlemen, and merchants, are the best constitution that can be established.

No doubt the calm was disturbed by small tiffs and squalls; one of the worst moments was caused by the hesitation of George I, the new king fresh from aristocratic Germany, to admit wholesalers to his Presence; but at last, to the relief of all, he accepted the strange sort of newly varnished nobility at his Court and made Smith-Carrington a peer, "the first man engaged in trade," according to Namier, whom he could bring himself to admit to the nobility. Again, much later, some dismay was occasioned when the so-called "Bengal Squad" of gilded Indian nabobs rushed to Parliament, where their unseemly haste after the perquisites of office produced murmurings among older and mellower members. But on the whole, differences were adjusted with a wonderful smoothness, for several generations. More perfectly in England than anywhere else in the world did

> . . . jarring interests of themselves create
> The according music of a well-mix'd state.

The literature of that age in England has been called "Augustan," for excellent reasons, since it sprang from a sociological basis which was not without analogies to Imperial Rome. In eighteenth-century England, as in second-century Rome, a part of the condition of the compromise was the acceptance, on the part of business men, of the social standards of the agrarians. So far as possible, they conformed to the life of the nobility, bought estates and hunting-packs, strove for political power for themselves, peerages for their sons and good marriages for their daughters; and in order to fill their atria with ancestral masks, like the Romans, they commissioned Reynolds to paint them enthroned against rock or tree. Again, as in Rome, the lords condescended, while the bourgeois rose; they met them half-way, admitting the merchants into fat government contracts in return for inside tips on 'Change Alley, and all the favors which the great Companies delighted to show. Such operations were described by a pamphleteer in King William's time, when the new East India Company was disputing with the old organization:

The Members of both Companies, with all the Trick, Artifice, Cunning and Corruption, that Money and Interest could arm them

with, bestirred themselves to be chosen Members . . . Brokers rid
Night and Day from one end of the Kingdom to the other, to engage Gentlemen to bribe Corporations, to buy off Competitors,
and to mannage the Elections.

Yet the analogies must not be pressed too closely. The harmony in
England was in fact greater than in Old Rome; it was unique. In part
it may be explained by the more thorough renovation which the English aristocracy had undergone than any other; in the Wars of the
Roses, old families stamped one another out, until few prominent representatives of the most ancient lineage survived. For that reason obscure county families have so often a longer lineage than the chief
houses of England. It was necessary for Henry VIII to create a nobility of his own in the sixteenth century, and being himself the son of
"plain Mr. Owen Tudor," and married at one time to Anne Boleyn,
the daughter of a rich and ambitious merchant, he naturally recruited
it largely from commercial wealth. On the other hand, merchants had
been acquiring titles ever since the Hundred Years' War had produced munitioneers capable of buying them. But, as an article in H. G.
Selfridge's "Romance of Commerce" so elaborately shows, other trades
contributed no less.

From the clothing trades came Earls of Bathurst; Earls of Bath with
a lineage running back to a fourteenth-century draper; Dukes of
Leeds; the Earl of Wemyss, whose maternal ancestor, one John Robinson, was a clothier; the Earl of Warwick, offspring of a family of
Gloucestershire wool staplers; the Duke of Northumberland; Earls of
Dartmouth, Earls of Coventry, of Holland and Warwick, Earls Fitz-
william, Dukes of Sutherland and Earls Verney. The Earls of Essex descended from a merchant tailor of 1509 and the first Earl of Craven
traced himself back to a merchant tailor of 1611. Indeed the Veres de
Vere, whose name is so often thought synonymous with noble birth,
had connections with a clothier who became a "gent" and had his son
made a lord.

From other branches of commerce came families no less illustrious.
Peerages for the successful exploitation of mines were awarded to the
Pelhams, ancestors of the Dukes of Newcastle and Earls of Chichester,
and to the Sackvilles, Earls of Dorset, the Ashburnhams, Nevills, Sey-
mours, Lowthers and Dudleys. The Earls of Cranbrook owed their
original fortunes to a mining speculator of low degree. From other
branches rose the Earls of Holdernesse and of Nottingham, with those
of Dover, descended from a skinner. The Earls Verney went back to
Sir Harry Calvert, a brewer, who bought the name, arms and estates
of his predecessor. Lord Salisbury's lineage might also be traced to a

brewer, Sir Crisp Gascoyne. The Earl of Romney had a grocer for an ancestor. From merchants descended the first Earl of Aucaster, Earls of Caledon, of Ravensworth, of Arran, and the Earls Temple of Stowe, Earls of Leicester, of Lonsdale and of Jersey. These are but samples taken at random from the higher circles; the infiltration was earlier and far more thorough among the lesser orders of nobility.

Of course, this meant a considerable flow of capital from city to land, very much as in France. A good many complained of it, as did one pamphleteer of 1691, who pointed out that things were much better in Holland, where merchants, even as they retired, left their funds in shares, whereas: "Our English merchants, having the Opportunity of Injoying the Fruits of their Industry in a spacious, delicate, fruitful Country, are apt to yield to the Temptation, and to exchange the hurry of Trade for the pleasures of a Country-life." For this condition, Sir Josiah Child blamed women. Dutchwomen, he said, were bred to business, and he wished English girls were likewise taught to appreciate trade and be "as knowing therein as the men, it doth encourage their husbands to hold on in their trades to their dying days." And he remarked upon the fact that the back-to-the-land movement deprived English business of dynasties: great merchants like the Houblons, and Child himself, left heirs in rural obscurity.

But this condition was not so serious in England as in France, for the reason that English squires grew wool, not so exclusively grain. In France and Germany, lords raised grain, in Prussia for export; this brought them into perpetual conflict with the urban bourgeois who demanded cheap food for themselves and their laborers. Some of this conflict was unavoidable in England too, but there the gentlemen increasingly produced wool for the expanding industry and commerce of the country, and their interest merged with that of the exporting merchants. Accordingly in England there was less antagonism between birth and money, between town and country, than on the Continent. Only in England was presented what Ehrenberg calls the "solid phalanx" of social forces lined up together flawlessly.

SEA-POWER AND THE ENGLISH MERCHANTS

Yet a further reason for the "solid phalanx" in England was the fact that her strength rested upon the Navy and not upon an army. The feudal noblemen of the Continent, and the old Romans too, were belligerent, and constantly threatened the State with their swords; but the English gentlemen, after the old feudal animosities were exhausted in the Wars of the Roses, became tamer, and moreover, with the feudal lord's dislike for water, they distrusted naval warfare. As we have seen, it was the merchant class, traditionally the friend of the Navy, which sought the imperialistic naval campaigns of the Cromwellian period and after; the English country gentlemen were more pacific than the traders.

From the first, the Navy was a merchants' affair. They had most of the ships originally, for which the Tudors had to bargain; the English State conducted its warfare on a contractual basis with them. Thus Queen Elizabeth invested heavily in John Hawkins' company, giving him four warships of the State to add to his own fleet in exchange for a third of the proceeds. In this way her Navy operated free of State cost and with a clear bonus of £1,000 for the exchequer. The queen had also the double pleasure of seeing the Spanish maltreated and of disavowing the deeds as the activities of private subjects. Such was for a long time the method of the Government; it issued hundreds of letters of marque whenever war was proclaimed, thus making the merchants an intimate part of the fighting strength. Like feudal lords, they undertook the defense of their sovereign in expectation of titles, loot, grants and vast rewards.

And they were rewarded like feudal lords, by grants to enormous domains, greater in extent than those of landed dukes at home, but which lay overseas, in Asia and the Americas, where they could not be supervised. A true feudal duke might be deprived of his estates, or even his head, if his sovereign were displeased; but these realms won by the merchant princes were too far away to be touched, or well supervised. Over these territories they reigned almost supreme, acknowledging only a limited allegiance to the Monarchy. They paid fealty and tribute to the king, it is true, but their restrictions ended there. Occasionally one of them might lose his post through Court disfavor, as John Churchill, later Duke of Marlborough, was ousted from the directorate of the Hudson's Bay Company, for being in the wrong political camp. But once in favor, their charters endowed them with "large and loving privileges," and freedom to explore, conquer, colonize. They could make treaties with heathen potentates, declare and wage war on their own account, enjoy rights of ruling and taxing their heathen subjects. They were in a sense more Absolute than the Stuarts, in the Canadian wilderness or the Indian Archipelago.

A supreme example of this mercantile feudalism is provided by the East India Company, not managed by the State "but rather having the State itself in its debt." In exchange for bribes and loans, amounting at one time to perhaps £400,000 a year, the merchants of this Company received the entire rights over all of India that they could bring under their sway. Their enemies complained that they "have half the known world in their charter, and that's too much for any Company."

As its director, Sir Josiah Child, once boasted, the India Company was "a sovereign state" itself. It declared war on the Mogul Empire; it had a fleet, an army and fortified settlements; it could coin money and make laws. Business men administered India in their own fashion, and a very lively fashion it was for a long time; so noisy was the Company riff-raff that "there has been files of musketeers sent for to keep the peace at dinner-time"; and the rowdies spent their days gambling and drinking, until a despairing director sighed: "It is a wonder to us that any of you live 6 months to an end . . . if half the liquors he charges were really guzzled down." The higher officers of the Company built mansions, kept slaves, lived like dukes in their conquered domains, and returned to England—nabobs—to transmit their garish splendors. The climax of this merchant-rule came in the late eighteenth century, under Hastings, whose "employment of personal severities, with the superintendence of British officers, in order to extract money from women and eunuchs," brought censure in the homeland.

This business administration of India was not ended until Victoria's reign. It proved ruinous to the conquered people; the profiteering of the Company's servants who bought up rice in famine times, the terrible revenue laws, and the sanction of slavery, had a dire effect on the social fabric in a large part of India. Only in 1749 did the absentee lords, who directed the Company, write out to India: "We cannot approve of putting any slaves to death"; and not until the nineteenth century did they send to India a Governor-General who had the slightest notion that the welfare of the natives might be an interest of the Company. With entire ruthlessness, the Company destroyed the marvelous handicrafts which had been the admiration of the world since Roman days, and flooded the land with cheap and ugly Manchester cottons.

In this East India Company British lords were glad to take shares. In the second joint-stock venture of 1617, for example, those who subscribed, out of a total of 954 members contributing a million and a half pounds were: "15 dukes and earls, 13 countesses and other titled ladies, 82 knights . . . 18 widows and maiden ladies, 26 clergymen and physicians, 313 merchants, 214 tradesmen, 25 merchant strangers." If the Company maintained its rule over India so long, it was because the dividends were highly satisfactory to the noble shareholders.

A great fleet had to be maintained to preserve such extensive possessions, and garrisons had to be supported in all corners of the earth; the outfitting of fleet and garrisons presented remarkable opportunities for gain also to the merchants; those who had friends at Court or in Parliament could secure rich government contracts, and usually the same relatively small circle of men with capital shared the spoils of directorates and contracts among themselves, with favors to spare for their noble patrons. Through naval contracts, the business world was drawn closely to the Government.

A pretty picture of this relationship is drawn by Pepys, the immortal diarist, who, in his job as supervisor of naval provisioning, was well acquainted with the banking family of the Houblons. He liked to visit James Houblon, in his charming home with a musical wife and "most excellent discourse." In fact he admired "all the five brothers Houblons, and mighty fine gentlemen they are all . . . We were mighty civilly merry, and their discourses, having been all abroad, very fine . . . A fine sight it is to see these five brothers thus loving to one another, and all industrious Merchants." But he was drawn to their company for profit of a substantial as well as social kind; Pepys helped the brothers to evade the embargo on merchant ships in 1665, for a tidy sum. At that time he wrote: "I did also give a good step in a business of Mr. Houbland's about getting a ship of his to go to Tangier, which during this strict embargo is a great matter, and I shall have a good reward for it I hope." He was not disappointed, for by and by "comes in Mr. James Houbland . . . a man I love mightily . . . He told me in my eare this night what he and his brothers have resolved to give me, which is £200 for helping them out with two or three ships. A good sum . . . and I did expect little less."

Such men as the Houblons "having been all abroad," were far more readily accepted by the English gentlemen than grimy manufacturers would have been. There was an air of magnificence and a suggestion of adventure about the overseas merchant, and especially about those who had made fabulous riches, no one knew quite how, in the East, which rendered them perfectly eligible to society. The genteel Addison admitted their respectability. In one of his essays he finds the overseas merchants admirable; they find work for the poor, make the rich more wealthy and the lords more lordly, and, in short, do the will of God. Addison was sure such economic operations, so beneficial to Britain, must be pleasing to Heaven. And he could not repress his awe at the power of these "private men, who, in times of our ancient kings, would have been the vassals of some powerful baron," but who now "negotiate like princes, for greater sums than were formerly to be met with in the Royal Treasury."

MONOPOLISTS AND CONTRACTORS

During the long stretch of over two centuries between Elizabeth's reign and Victoria's, the big British business man was a company-monopolist or a contractor; he was less apt to be a financier than the Frenchman, since only in France did the banker have the chance to buy the tax-farming privileges and so make the whole nation his tributary. The type of the Englishman remained accordingly the same, but there was a steady development none the less in his character and political methods. Constantly he refined his ways of approaching power, and entered politics more and more directly and effectively.

In Elizabeth's day, of course, the rich monopolist-type was comparatively simple. Sir Thomas Smythe, one of the leading men of that reign, was a plain royal-merchant who depended on Court favor. A haberdasher and skinner to begin with, he was later Governor of the East India and Muscovy Companies, a treasurer for the Virginia Company, "Prime Undertaker for the Discovery of the Northwest Passage," a principal commissioner of an expedition against pirates, as well as Ambassador to the Grand Duke of Russia and to the King of Sumatra. Abroad he was received as the equal of monarchs; Sumatra welcomed him with a procession of elephants and a shower of golden gifts. At home he entered the nobility; his widow married the Earl of Leicester and his son was united to a daughter of the Earl of Warwick. He himself stood close to two monarchs. Elizabeth acquitted him of complicity in the Essex case, because of his exceeding usefulness. James I condescended to dine aboard his biggest vessel, *Trade's Increase*, which was to carry on British trade with India on a new scale. On that occasion the king flung "a gold chain, worth better than £500," around the merchant's neck.

Another of these splendid and ambitious monopolists was Sir Giles Mompesson, in the reign of Charles I, who was caricatured under the name of Sir Giles Overreach, in a play by Massinger, "A New Way to Pay Old Debts." Here he is shown trying to climb into society and marry his daughter to a nobleman. To the prospective son-in-law, Overreach is made to say:

> *Nay, when my ears are pierced with widows' cries,*
> *And undone orphans wash with tears my threshold,*
> *I only think what 'tis to have my daughter*
> *Right honourable; and 'tis a powerful charm*
> *Makes me insensible of remorse, or pity,*
> *Or the least sting of conscience. I am marble.*
> *Nay more, if you will have my character*
> *In little, I enjoy more true delight*
> *In my arrival to my wealth by dark*
> *And crooked ways, than you shall e'er take pleasure*
> *In spending what my industry hath encompassed.*

In the Restoration period, under Charles II, a more complicated personage appeared, Sir Dudley North, not merely the friend of the king, like Smythe, or a purchaser of place, like Mompesson, but a political leader and a persuasive pamphleteer, consummately skillful in his handling of men and interests. This art, no doubt, North learned in the Near East, as agent in Constantinople. There he found out how to win cases for his company with more than Oriental skill, bribing judges and traducing witnesses, and he penetrated the secrets of seraglio politics. In this Eastern society, said his brother, North became "an exquisite judge of adventures," and so sharp that no man ever cheated twice in his company. If there was any cheating to be done, the Director attended to it himself:

> As to all the mercantile arts or guiles, and stratagems of trade, which could be used to get money from those he dealt with, I believe he was no niggard; but as for falsities, such as cheating by weights and measures, or anything knavish, treacherous or perfidious . . . he was as clean as any man living. He transacted and dealt in all respects as a merchant of honour.

On North's return to England from the East, only forty years old, rich and full of stratagems, he tried his skill in English affairs, and with such success that he became Sheriff of London and a director of the African Company. He was a good mixer, said his admiring brother: "A gentleman ever brisk and witty, a great observer of all incidents, and withal very friendly and communicative, which made him be generally beloved." But he was not beloved by the Whigs, at least, for his severe prosecution of that party, in his capacity as Sheriff, was notorious. Macaulay says:

> His juries never failed to find verdicts of guilty; and on a day of judicial butchery, carts, loaded with the legs and arms of quartered Whigs, were, to the great discomposure of his lady, driven to his fine house in Bassinghall Street for orders.

For this coolness in the exercise of power, which he may have increased by observing Eastern potentates at work, North received a knighthood. When James II ascended the throne, North was made financial expert of the Commons, and henceforth was as active in politics as in business, laying imposts and elaborating his views on economic subjects in excellent pamphlets. As befitted so splendid a person, he made aristocratic pretensions; he married Lady Gunning, daughter of a rich merchant, Sir Robert Cann. Cann and North, his son-in-law, used to make display of their wealth: "The old man . . . often said to him, 'Come, son, let us go out and shine.'—that is, walk about the streets, with six footmen in rich liveries attending."

In private, however, North preserved many of the simple traits so characteristic of millionaires from the times of Cosimo de' Medici down to Andrew Carnegie. This was not due to puritanic inhibitions, for North was an Anglican. But he naturally relished rustic ease, as much as he enjoyed "shining" in city streets. On his country estate, he had a room for woodworking, where, when he wearied of Whig-butchery and mercantile stratagems, he amused himself by making his own tables—truly, an idyllic picture:

> This morning work before dressing, he coming out with a red short waistcoat, red cap, and black face; so that my lady, when she came to call us for dinner, was full of admiration what creatures she had in her family.

In the afternoon, the labor was resumed:

> It was not a little strange to see with what earnestness and pains we worked, sweating most immoderately, and scarce allowing ourselves time to eat. At the light works in the afternoon he hath sat, perhaps, scraping a stick, or turning a piece of wood, and this for many afternoons together, all the while singing like a cobbler, incomparably more pleased than he hath been in all the stages of his life before.

A contemporary of North, Sir Josiah Child, was richer, perhaps more influential, and quite as vocal, although not directly a participant in the work of Government. Like Smythe and North, he started poor, rose through trade with the East and official connections, and bought a title, setting an example of lavish display on his immense estate. Child was interested in the provisioning of the Navy under Pepys' administration; he also managed to work his way to a dictatorial position in the East India Company. Bestowing enormous bribes on high personages, and pulling political wires, he succeeded in ousting Puritans, like Papillon, "getting others into the company and choosing them of the Committee, though they understood no more of trade than I of physic; also naming ships by great men's names," to court their favor. In such devious ways did Child become a despot, ruling "over the company as absolutely as if it had been his private business."

Even in that golden age of merchant-companies, when the peak of dividend-outpouring was reached, the East India Company was the most tremendous, paying 400 per cent to the original investors between 1683–92. In the management of the Company and its funds, Child showed his genius, inventing new forms of manipulation as he went along, which excited the horror of conservatives. Defoe, in 1719, called Child the "Original of Stock-Jobbing," and blamed on him, with his naughty "machines and contrivances," the evils of the new generation:

> It would be endless to give an account of the Subtilities of that Capital Che . . t, when he had a Design to Bite the whole *Exchange:* As he was the leading Hand to the Market. [He juggled his own stock chiefly,] tho' there were other Stocks afoot too . . . the *Hudson's*-Bay Company, the Linnen Manufacture Stock, Paper Stock, Salt-Petre Stock, and the others, all at this Day worse than nothing, tho' some of them then jobb'd up to 350 per cent.
>   . . . If Sir *Josiah* had a Mind to buy, the first thing he did was to Commission his Brokers to look sower, shake their Heads, suggest bad News from *India* . . . and perhaps they would actually sell Ten, perhaps Twenty Thousand Pound; immediately the *Exchange* . . . was full of Sellers; no Body would buy a Shilling, 'till perhaps the Stock would fall Six, Seven, Eight, Ten *per Cent.*, sometimes more; then the Cunning Jobber had another Sett of them employ'd . . . to buy, but with Privacy and Caution, till by selling Ten Thousand Pound, at Four or Five *per Cent.* lost, he would buy a Hundred Thousand Pound Stock, at ten or twelve *per Cent.* under Price; and in a few Weeks by just the contrary Method, set them all a buying, and then sell them their own Stock again at Ten or Twelve *per Cent.* Profit.

Into his schemes, Child drew lords, and involved the political leaders of London. As Defoe, in his pamphlet, "The Anatomy of Exchange Alley," called it in 1719, it was a collusion of the great: "The principal leaders in the jobbing trade . . . are Whigs, Members of Parliament, and Friends to the Government." The wretches whose aim was to "stock jobb the Nation, couzen the Parliament, ruffle the Bank, run up and down Stocks, and put the Dice upon the whole Town," were personages of the highest rank, who wanted "to be Rich at the Price of every Man they can bubble." Among them, said Defoe, were "Persons even too big for our Reproof":

> To see States-Men turn Dealers, and Men of Honour stoop to the Chicanry of Jobbing; to see Men at the offices in the Morning, at the P. House (Parliament) about Noon, at the Cabinet at Night, and in the *Exchange-Alley* at the proper Intervals, What new

Phaenomina are these? What fatal things may these shining Planets . . . fortel to the State, and to the Publick; for when Statesmen turn Jobbers the State may be jobb'd. In a Word, I appeal to all the World, whether any Man that is intrusted with other Mens Money . . . ought to be seen in Exchange-Alley.

As the government became increasingly involved in the toils of the financiers, and the technique of the latter improved, the poet Pope cried:

> *Bless'd paper credit! last and best supply!*
> *That lends corruption lighter wings to fly! . . .*
> *A single leaf shall waft an army o'er . . .*
> *Pregnant with thousands flits the scrap unseen,*
> *And silent sells a king or buys a queen.*

Pope's prophecy was borne out later by the power of Rothschild, who indeed "wafted an army o'er" with a scrap of paper, to defeat Napoleon. Corruption's light wings had become necessary to England's defense and imperial enterprises, as they had been to Old Rome. But English satirists, like the Romans they were so fond of imitating, grumbled sometimes that the price of empire was too high, if purchased by the degradation of the agricultural classes and the general demoralization of the people by money-power:

> *At length corruption, like a general flood . . .*
> *Shall deluge all; and avarice creeping on,*
> *Spread like a low-born mist, and blot the sun;*
> *Statesmen and patriot ply alike the stocks . . .*
> *And judges job, and bishops bite the town,*
> *And mighty dukes pack cards for half-a-crown.*
> *See Britain sunk in lucre's sordid charms . . .*

But many of the penmen of England, including the poet Gray, and the prophetic Defoe himself, were themselves caught in the strange aberration of the South Sea Bubble.

SOUTH SEA BUBBLE

Perhaps the corruption in and around Exchange-Alley was a less serious factor than the wildly insubstantial character of so many of the projects floated there. They were often pure flights of fancy, Shakespearean clowning, possible only in a country like England which, by the

1720's, had not even yet buckled down to industrial enterprise with heart and soul. In the equally destructive bubbles blown in France, just five years before, and in Holland earlier, the objects of speculation were at least ostensibly reasonable. The Dutch tulips could be seen and grown; and much of the Dutch frenzy centered not merely around tulips but perfectly plausible-sounding insurance and trading-companies; so, too, in the Law-delirium in France, the original idea of Law was not at all ridiculous. But the English share-buying public was first attracted by a fantastic dream.

One William Phipps had found a wrecked Spanish plate-ship and returned to his shareholders 100 times their investment, bringing home bullion such as had not been divided in England since Drake's celebrated voyage. This occurrence touched off the spark of imagination in the public; it seemed possible to restore the lost golden days of Elizabeth: if it was no longer so easy to prey on plate ships, it might still be possible to salvage them. So no less than 150 companies were founded to raise Spanish galleons from the deep. The English, and also the Scotch, romantic enthusiasm was raised to fever temperature by this treasure-hunting and wreck-raising excitement, which seemed to promise fortunes with the least semblance of toil. If treasure could only be taken from under the water, instead of upon it, it would be possible to postpone industrialization for some time—but alas, this boom marked the end of that old, wild, freebooting dream. It was the last gleam of the Elizabethan spirit.

Notwithstanding the inevitability of the collapse, other schemes, even more baseless, were attempted, many of them obviously "fake" projects to get oil from sunflower seeds, to build ships to proceed against pirates, to cultivate silkworms in Surrey, to make a *perpetuum mobile.* A company was even organized for "better funerals." In a list of bubbles, published in 1721, are contained such propositions as these: for Radish Oil; Mother Wyebourne's Machine Conundrums; Briscoe's Transmutation of Animals; Pollington's Plan to melt saw-dust to deal-boards; Curing of Lunatick Persons; Curing of broken-winded horses and mares; Office for Maintaining Bastard Children; a Coral Fishery; and the memorable "Subscription of 2 million pounds to a promising scheme, the details of which will later be made public."

The South Sea Company itself, around which these lesser insanities appeared, was indeed a purely exploitative enterprise, although not wholly without prospects of profit. It promised to secure the British State debt and pay high dividends, in return for a monopoly of trade, particularly of the slave-trade, to the Spanish West Indies. According to its plans, slavery would be made to serve the State and enrich capitalists alike in a single beautiful operation, requiring anything but hum-drum labor.

This prospect boosted shares at one time up to 1,050 per cent. 'Change Alley was choked with the coaches of the grand folk and the crutches of the poor, for everybody came to snatch shares in the millennium. As the London *Journal* described it:

> The hurry of stock-jobbing bubbles has been so great this week as to exceed all ever known. Nothing but running about from coffee-house to coffee-house, and subscribing without knowing what the proposals were. The constant cry was, "For God's sake, let us subscribe to something; we don't care what it is."

All the aspects of human greed and folly that such blooms reveal were there displayed. Parliamentarians engaged in speculation heavily; beggars became richer than earls for a moment; vain ambition soared so high that one man, determined to buy the throne of Poland and lacking but a few hundred pounds for the millions he required, held on just two days too long. The crash brought the would-be King of Poland to actual rags again, and with him countless other dupes. Literary men, caught as well as dukes and dames, porters and serving-wenches, lamented their fate and the general calamity in many a doleful stanza:

> *Behold a poor dejected wretch,*
> *Who kept a South Sea coach of late,*
> *And now is glad to humble catch*
> *A penny at the prison gate.*

> *Fools lost where the Directors won,*
> *And now the poor Directors lose;*
> *And where the South Sea stock will run,*
> *Old Nick, the first projector, knows.*

The severe headache of her awakening helped to sober England; henceforth she began to harness her exuberant imagination to more reasonable enterprises, and to admit that the Age of Drake was really over. That catastrophe, as much as original Calvinism, encouraged the bourgeois virtues in her people. And it was of important moral effect, also, that the investigations and punishments after the Bubble burst were so severe. If her speculation had been in many ways more childish than that of the Dutch and French, she made up for it by a more thorough house-cleaning afterwards, and drastic sentences, which reached high in the Government, and caught such distinguished individuals as the grandfather of the historian Gibbon.

CONTRACTORS IN POLITICS

Though the association of business men and politicians in the stock market was not so flagrant after the mopping-up of the South Sea Bubble, amid national repentance, their connections in Parliament grew steadily closer. Here public opinion could not pursue them for a long time; nor did the eighteenth century, cheerfully venal, see anything reprehensible in the eagerness of an M.P. to recompense himself for his election expenses by allotting government plums to his friends and himself. It was taken for granted in "Augustan" England as in America, when the next century opened and the Tweed Ring commenced operations. This corruption was, however, of the sort peculiar to democratic countries; the give-and-take of politicians and contractors under parliamentarism was radically different from the autocratic corruption of France in the *ancien régime*, where the favors were distributed by courtiers and ministers in still more devious back-stair intrigues, but the pretense of an open and honest government was not so zealously upheld.

Naturally, the closer the contractor could come to Parliament, the better; if he could get in himself, it was ideal. The latter position he attained more and more as Namier has shown in his illuminating study of politics under George III; at first, business men entered Parliament through "pocket boroughs" in out-of-the-way corners. Bristol, Liverpool and the City of London were indeed willing occasionally to elect men of commerce, but the other large English towns showed a decided "preference for the 'well-born' "; even trading-centers were insistent upon electing lords, though these were often sons of trading fathers. The best chance for the ambitious merchant was in exploiting the corrupt election system of the times; merchants who came with sufficient wealth from the East, could buy up districts with a minimum of voters, as the original Pitt, Madras representative of the India Company, purchased the furrowed fields of Old Sarum, the most famous "pocket borough," from which his heir went to Parliament. Another of these Eastern nabobs was Clive, who flourished in the same Company and acquired similar boroughs. In one way or another, a chosen few of the richest and most ambitious did get into Parliament; in 1761, as Namier estimates, there were 50 merchants in that body, of whom at least 37 may be proved to have had governmental favors, like the Fonnereaux family.

The Fonnereaux family, a Huguenot dynasty, used the capital won in the West Indies trade and in Africa to obtain three seats in Parliament; they were costly, but the contracts for naval provisioning which could be secured thereby seem to have been worth the outlay. Zachary

Fonnereaux thought it good business to pay as high as £30,000 on elections. As the Duke of Newcastle remarked about Zachary: "I suppose, his price is some valuable remittance to Minorca, etc.; when a man knows himself that he is bought, one had nothing to say to him."

The winning frankness with which such new parliamentarians awaited an immediate reward was typical of the age. Thus, Chauncey Townsend, who worked up through linen-drapery to contracts for victualing the fleet, once wrote to his party chief saying that, since his elections had cost him £6,000, he needed a plum: "Mony support I allways declined when hinted—half Gibraltar was my object." But apparently, it was not always the desire to "take Gibraltar" or some other garrison which animated English merchants in their drive toward political careers. Some of them sought parliamentary immunity from investigations. "It was the regular practice of nabobs returning 'from India's plundered land,' to insure against inquiries into the origin of their fortunes by providing themselves with seats in Parliament," says Namier. Among these in the late eighteenth century were members of the Bengal Squad, whose activities so shocked the statesman, Chatham; his own fortune came also from Eastern trade, though he was removed from it by one gentlemanly generation. It also appears that one of the greatest manufacturers of munitions during the American Revolution, Anthony Bacon, sought a seat in Parliament to escape his creditors.

The poet Pope satirized these concession-hunters in his portrait of Sir Balaam, who yields to the temptations of Satan and sells his soul for a company directorship. Then he must needs buy a title; he "leaves the dull cits," bows at Court and joins the lords in Parliament. But Pope mercilessly brings Balaam to an end that was certainly anything but typical, for Balaam

> *takes a bribe from France,*
> *The house impeach him, Coningsby harangues;*
> *The Court forsake him, and Sir Balaam hangs.*

This pleasant harmonization lasted for a very long time, quite untroubled by rude cries from press or people, and not affected by the occasional epigrams of a biting poet. In the course of time, the characters of both lords and merchants were altered by such close association; both became traders, both became politicians. The lords took a more amicable interest in the aims of business than any other aristocrats, and of course many of the distinguished political families, being of business origins, remained sympathetic to arguments from that side. Among the Lords Chancellors, for instance, stood Lord King, aspiring heir of an Exeter grocer and an Earl of Eldon, son of a Newcastle coal merchant. Lord Cowper was the descendant of a London dyer. Others springing from trade were: the Earl of Chatham, grandson of Thomas Pitt, a competitor of the East India Company; Sir Robert Peel, groomed by his Manchester manufacturing father, and himself in business; Sir Henry Campbell-Bannerman, of shopkeeping fortune; Disraeli, Lord Beaconsfield, grandson of a Venetian Jewish shopkeeper, and both the Gladstones. John Gladstone, father of William Ewart, was a corn and flour merchant, three times an M.P.

On the other hand, the business man in England benefited through contact with the political classes. He was indeed far more independent of state control than the French or German, but he was not powerful enough to rule as an open oligarch, like a Dutchman; he had to compromise, win good-will by ingratiating himself with aristocracy and the share-buying public. He had to become adept in social as well as political compromises. In the great trading-companies, better mixed than those of other nations, he had to work with many types, and so in the directing board he learned the political arts. Since he got his charters and privileges from Parliament very often by appealing to public interest, he required all sorts of arguments, economic, religious, patriotic. He had to become vocal, persuasive. Whereas the French manufacturers at that time were operating invisibly, behind scenes, in search of Royal favor, the English-monopolists openly advertised for support, inviting everyone to invest in their enterprises and uphold their pretensions to charters.

The British merchant had thus a twofold aspect. Abroad, he was predatory; at home persuasive. Overseas, he might be a privateer; at home he must be a pamphleteer. This contradiction accounts for many baffling phenomena, the combination of ruthlessness and righteousness, so often amazing to foreigners and explained by them as hypocrisy induced by an overdose of Calvinism. In fact, all the circumstances of the Englishman's life and labor led to such a pose; he was the only business man of Europe who had the need to assume it.

ENTER THE SHOPKEEPER

Below this solidifying upper crust of merchant-princes and princely merchants, there gradually began to form an intermediary group, the shopkeepers. This lesser and lower business stratum filled in the gap between the mighty monopolists and contractors and the simple rural folk who still formed the overwhelming majority in England. England thus was learning to keep shop before she developed manufacturing to a very high degree; a hundred years after the South Sea Bubble, Napoleon could say contemptuously, of the English, "They are a nation of shopkeepers." As a matter of fact, although he was not aware of it, they had just then begun to be a nation of industrialists, and their shop-keeping era was drawing to its close.

Shopkeeping, however natural to the English it seemed in the time of Napoleon, did not come easily to them at first.

The Englishman was not naturally an ideal salesman, and he felt humiliated by the position behind the counter. As Defoe expressed it, in his "Complete Tradesman": "What impertinences, what taunts, flouts . . . he must bear in his trade, and must not show . . . the least signal of disgust: he must have no passions, no fire in his temper . . . he must be a perfect *complete hypocrite*, if he will be a *complete* Tradesman."

Many Englishmen found it quite beyond their powers to be polite in the shop, under such conditions. Or, if they managed to swallow their wrath in the presence of customers, they vented their wrath savagely on their families:

> There are men who have by custom and usage brought themselves to it, that nothing could be meeker and milder than they, when behind the counter, [but] the provocations that they have met with in their shops have so irritated their rage, that they would go upstairs from their shops, and fall into frenzies, and a kind of madness, and beat their heads against the wall. [One of these would] beat his wife, kick his children about like dogs, and be as furious for two or three minutes as a man chain'd down in Bedlam; and after the fit he would go down into his shop again, and be as humble, as courteous, and as calm as any man whatever . . . in the shop meek like the lamb, but in the family outrageous like a *Libyan* lion.

The French, it will be recalled, felt the same dislike of customers, but they had solved the problem to some extent by employing feminine salesclerks whose gifts of forbearance and palaver indicated that the "perfect complete hypocrite" so badly needed in trade was clearly the woman. It was a long time before the "natural man" in either country was subdued so far as to accept the fact that "his customers are to be his idols; so far as he may worship idols . . . he is to bow down to them." Nowadays, accustomed to the effusive verbiage of the American Selfridge in London and the elder Wanamaker in New York, whose columns in the press assure customers that their lightest whims must be law for the shopkeeper, we have almost forgotten the painful début of the modern salesman.

When he did learn, however, the English shops became marvels, "perfect gilded theatres," as Addison called them, and the men who managed them were "positively the greatest fops in the kingdom; they have their toilets and their fine nightgowns; their chocolate in the morning and their green tea two hours after . . . and their perfumes, washes, and clean linen equip them for the Parade." Not only were they well-dressed, and washed behind the ears like a lord, but they also had as fine manners as a French courtier. With a flourish, they would hand a lady from a coach and spread silks before her with a droll patter: "This, madam, is so diverting a silk. This, madam, my stars! How cool it looks! But this, madam—ye Gods! Would I had 10,000 yards of it!" And when she protested the price, the patterer would gasp: "Fan me, ye winds, your ladyship rallies me!"

But this immoderate and fantastical line of talk was also displeasing to Defoe. He thought it necessary indeed to be polite, but could not a salesman "talk to his customers like a man of sense, and not like a mountebank and merry-andrew"? Was it not "a scandal upon trade, to pretend to say that a Tradesman cannot live without lying"? Could there not be an art of salesmanship without such gross distortion of the truth?

> Our shop-rhetorick is a strange kind of speech . . . 'Tis composed of a mass of rattling flattery to the buyer, and that fill'd with hypocrisy, self-praises, falsehood, and in short, a complication of wickedness; it is a corrupt means to a vicious end . . . The shopkeeper ought indeed to have a good tongue, but he should not make a common whore of his tongue . . . Tradesmen ought no more to lie behind the counter, than parsons ought to talk treason in the pulpit.

Salesmanship, however, once embarked upon, carried the shopkeeper to the wildest extremes, and before long his ballyhoo spread to the magazines. The Englishman was becoming a glib advertiser, a canny writer of prospectuses. This was not entirely a new thing, for even Ben Jonson had noted the advertising expert, one "threadbare shark" named Shift, who wrote blurbs for pay. But by the time Addison created his satirical sketch of "Isaac Bickerstaff, Master in the whole art of advertising," the dim outlines of the modern sales promoter had become perceptible.

Perhaps it was a Greek merchant, descendant of an ancient race of salesmen, Pasqua Rosee, who may be said to have introduced Oriental eloquence into modern advertising. His new drink, coffee, was, he proclaimed, "a simple, innocent thing . . . good against sore eyes . . . excellent to prevent and cure the dropsy, gout and scurvy . . . hypochondriac minds, and the like." In his advertising campaign he carried on a lively dispute with the vendors of that other curious beverage, tea, for which miraculous performances were also claimed.

Before long, English imagination had outstripped the Oriental, and native eloquence was turned to pushing the "Apoplectic Balsam," a preparation for "coaxing hair to grow on bald heads." A lively campaign was soon in swing against "B.O." or "all smells arising from bad Teeth, etc." Noisier and noisier grew the conflicting claims and aspersions of truss-makers. Addison reported:

> Half the advertisements one meets with nowadays are purely polemical. The inventors of Strops for Razors have written against one another for several years, saying, "They will give razors . . . such an exquisite, fine, smooth, sharp, exact and durable edge, that the like was never known, which has been experienced by thousands of gentlemen in England, Scotland and Ireland," a claim hotly contested by the Right Venetian Strops Co.

This sort of rivalry had gone on for a long time when good old Doctor Johnson finally let loose the whole force of his ponderous verbiage to stop it. He declared that the public was tired of the ballyhoo and warned business men, in 1759, that they would have to mend their ways if they desired public respect:

> The man who first took advantage of the general curiosity that was excited by a siege or battle to betray the readers of news into the knowledge of the shop where the best puffs and powder were to be sold, was undoubtedly a man of great sagacity, and profound skill in the nature of man. [However, the trick had grown stale:] Advertisements are now so numerous that they are very negligently perused, and it is therefore become necessary to gain attention by magnificence of promise, and by eloquence sometimes sublime and sometimes pathetic. . . . Promise, large promise, is the soul of an advertisement. I remember a washball that had a quality truly wonderful—it gave an exquisite edge to the razor. . . . There are some, however, that know the prejudice of mankind in favor of modest sincerity. The vendor of the beautifying fluid sells a lotion that repels pimples, washes away freckles, smooths the skin, and plumps the flesh; and yet . . . confesses that it will not restore the bloom of fifteen to a lady of fifty. . . . The zeal shown by the seller of the anodyne necklace, for the ease and safety of poor teething infants, and the affection with which he warned every mother that she would never forgive herself if her infant should perish without it. . . . The trade of advertising is now so near

perfection, that it is not easy to propose any improvement. But as every art ought to be exercised in due subordination to the public good, I cannot but propose it as a moral question to these masters of the public ear, whether they do not sometimes play too wantonly with our passions? . . . And whether the advertising controversialists do not indulge in asperity of language without any adequate provocation? As in the dispute about strops for razors, now happily subdued, and in the altercation which now subsists concerning Eau de Luce.

Despite the heavy artillery of Doctor Johnson, the "masters of the public ear" went on unfolding new and unsuspected marvels of their art. Advertising was fully developed before the Machine was ready to supply mass-wares. The technique of cozening readers was prepared while inventors of mass-production methods were slumbering. Englishmen first learned how to sell goods to the masses and then how to make them.

THE RISE OF SUBURBIA

The shopkeeping part of the population became a small bourgeoisie with habits and sentiments prophetic of the present-day. It vied as well as it could with the great merchants and the greater lords; when it could not afford country estates, it moved to the suburbs, and bought a "Box." As one of the literary journals of the age, the *Connoisseur*, remarks:

The object of this "Box" was the better avoidance of the Sabbath, to attain which desirable consummation one half of Saturday was lost in papering up cold chickens, bottling brandy punch, sorting clean shifts and nightcaps for the children . . . And one half of Monday was wasted in undoing the same packages and putting away the things on their return to town.

The Box, as this journal described it, "enjoyed a beautiful vista of two men hanging in chains on Kensington Common, with a distant view of St. Paul's cupola enveloped in a cloud of smoke." The entrance hall was adorned with a map of London and a colored print representing "The Death of the Stag." The family did not lack portraits for the parlor. There sat the shopkeeper himself, "bolt upright, in a fullbottom'd periwig . . . a snuff-colour'd velvet coat with gold buttons . . . one hand stuck in the bosom of his shirt, and the other holding out a letter, with the superscription, 'To Mr. . . . '" His wife, slightly superior to him socially, had herself depicted "in the habit of a shepherdess smelling a nosegay, and stroking a ram with gilt horns."

All this represented new strivings and cravings in a class which had hitherto been remarkable for its coarseness of manners. The appalling drunken bouts which Sir Walter Besant represents as typical of the tradesman's life—and of his family's—in an earlier day, began to yield to more refined, more "exotick" and therefore more expensive amusements. The daughter was given French lessons and music; a few books were bought; much more attention was paid to dress and frequenting of balls and the theater. In 1732, the "citizens and young Tradesmen" were outnumbering the gentlemen at the gay resorts of London, and had donned a genteel costume, appearing "with their long wigs and swords, rather than with aprons on."

At home, "not a family, no, hardly of the meanest Tradesman," but set out a tea-table and poured chocolate for friends; port was offered instead of humble home-brewed ale. When "very ordinary Tradesmen" were keeping at least two maids, the grander had to advance to footmen: "Witness the infinite number of blue liveries, which are so common now, that they are called Tradesmen's Liveries; and few gentlemen care to give blue to their servants for that very reason."

The grand bourgeois game of "keeping up with the Joneses" had begun, and with some demoralizing, as well as refining, effects. A tradesman was apparently ruined by the cost if he tried to keep up, and ruined by social failure if he did not, for "such is the expensive humour of the times":

> Tradesmen cannot live as Tradesmen in the same class used to live . . . In short, there is a Fate upon a Tradesman, either he must yield to the snare of the times, or be the jest of the times . . . in a word, he must spend more than he can afford, and so be undone; or not spend it, and so be undone.

As this middle class increased in wealth, its rivalry began to affect not only its own ranks, but that of the lesser gentry as well. Grocers and herring-dealers were now seen buying faked heraldic emblems in order to establish reputations; they were seen "coming every day to the Herald's office," to find some coat of arms, and to trace their pedigrees. Few must have been turned away; somehow, they acquired the coats in abundance "to paint them upon their coaches, and engrave them upon their plate, embroider them upon their furniture or carve them upon the pediments of their new houses."

Growing more ambitious, traders married genuine titles:

> Trade in England makes gentlemen, and has peopled this nation with gentlemen . . . 'Tis very probable, a few years will show us

still a greater race of trade-bred gentlemen, than ever England yet had . . . How ordinary it is to see a Tradesman go off the stage, even from but mere shop-keeping, with from ten to forty thousand pounds estates . . . How are the sons of Tradesmen rank'd among the prime of the gentry? How are the daughters of Tradesmen at this time adorn'd with the ducal coronets? . . . How many noble seats, superior to the palaces of foreign princes . . . we see erected within few miles of this city by Tradesmen . . . while the seats and castles of the antient gentry, like their families, look worn out, and fallen into decay!

Hard cash was becoming the measuring-rod of life and distinction as never before. The poor gentleman was already an object of ridicule, and gentility without means was scorned in England. As a pamphleteer wrote in 1691, this was a "New State," and for his part he rejoiced: "Who would not rather be a substantial honest Trader, so as to stand upon his own legs, and make some figure in the World, than . . . starve with a point of Honour . . . in this Age especially, when Poverty is so little pitied, and grown so contemptible?" But another in 1701 put it less pathetically, more pungently:

> Wealth, howsoever got, in England makes
> Lords of Mechanicks, Gentlemen of Rakes;
> Antiquity and birth are needless here;
> 'Tis impudence and money makes a Peer.

THE NEW SELF-ESTEEM

As trading wealth became an increasingly important factor in English society, the self-esteem of the business man rose. He had indeed respect for titles, but he was confident that they could be his, and he was inclined to a cocky attitude, like that London trader who, when a lord "bad him hold his tongue, for he was no gentleman," smartly retorted, "No, Sir, *but I can buy a gentleman*, and therefore I claim a liberty to speak among gentlemen." Some went even farther, and would agree with Sir Dudley North, that eventually only the busy business man would count in England. North, the Restoration merchant who had risen into the aristocracy, castigated the class to which he climbed, and pronounced any trading men better than lords or bishops:

When it is said that "people are the wealth of a nation," it is only meant, laborious and industrious people; and not such as are wholly unemployed, as gentry, clergy, lawyers, serving-men, and beggars, etc., or, which is worse, employed only in disturbing the industrious and laborious, as pettifoggers, informers . . . thieves; though the first may be necessary, as harmless spurs to consumption, learning or virtue . . . yet the fewer such the better.

One may trace the gradual raising of this self-esteem among business men both in France and England during this century, finding it greater in the latter. At the commencement of the period, in the mid-seventeenth century, the Frenchman and Englishman seem equally apologetic for their humble occupations, and appear very much on the defensive. Selecting two specimens in each land, one discovers them both arguing rather hopelessly against prejudice. The Frenchman, Oudard Coquault of Reims (about 1655), was not unlucky, for he had managed to keep five houses through civil strife, but he was full of complaints, a constant old grumbler, without a ray of hope in his system. Scolding the scandalous behavior of priests and courtiers, and the "always insolent" laboring men, Oudard reserved his choicest venom for the local nobility. He had once been victimized by the soldiers of the Duke of Lorraine, who stripped him of cloak and horse, and he could not get over the vexation:

> Beyond comparison, the honorable bourgeois of the towns and the good merchants are nobler than all of them; for they are more decent, lead better lives . . . their family and homes are better regulated; each . . . does not cause anybody to murmur, and pays everybody who works for him.

Oudard stated this conviction merely as a private opinion, his own defense against an outrageous world. Similarly, across the Channel, a Puritan trader, the father of Thomas Papillon, was rather hopelessly defending the respectability of the trader to a landed squire. He wished to procure the hand of the squire's daughter, Jane, for his son, Thomas, The squire had rejected the plea very loftily, not only because business seemed to him unsavory, but because he thought it unsafe; there was no future in it. London City, he declared, was in a "very tottering condition" and "trading more hazardous than ever," and, in brief, he intended to keep Jane on the land. The elder Papillon summoned eloquent arguments from history to assist him in the struggle for his son's happiness:

> I answer . . . Trade must be supported by the State, or the State cannot subsist: for Trade is the pillar of a State . . . How will the great landed men receive their rents? They will certainly fall into

greater streights than the merchants. For industrious merchants can live gallantly in all parts of Christendom; so cannot great landed men if they are deprived of their rents. For the 3rd—the fears of the ruin of the city are mere chimeras; for the ruin of the city will draw after it the desolation of the whole nation . . . The condition of the man that hath some land and some industry is far safer than the condition of a great landed man who hath no industry.

For proof, Papillon invited the squire to consider the case of "Peter de Medicis, Duke of Florence," who would certainly have starved, when he was expelled from his dukedom, had he not "in his youth been brought up in the trade of merchandize; but by his industry he maintained himself and his family very gaily during his abode at Venice." Such an historic argument was, it is to be feared, less potent than Papillon's final offer of 84 acres of good meadow land, which at last won Jane for his Thomas. Since London did not collapse, after all, the marriage turned out much better than the bucolic gentleman had imagined in his simplicity.

A hundred years later, if we dip in for samples of prevailing mentality, the scene seems vastly altered. The bourgeois is no longer so timid; indeed, he is aggressive, standing on his "natural" rights, and inclined to trample on those of the agrarians. Babeau, in his study of the evolution of the French middle class, presented a striking contrast between the soured, grim, narrow-minded, black-coated grumbler, of the type of Oudard Coquault, and the gay, progressive merchant of Le Mans, M. d'Ardenay, in the late eighteenth century. D'Ardenay was full of ideas, bright in his outlook as in his choice of waistcoat-hues. He engaged in efforts to uplift society by music, the betterment of agriculture, education and hospitals. He was on local boards and societies; in 1790 he was Mayor of Le Mans. Slightly sentimental in the fashionable Rousseau vein, he dabbled in verse; he also studied law and economy, and became an ardent believer in the Revolution, when it opened. The Terror months, however, he spent in rustic seclusion, for the future then appeared a little darker than his dreams had pictured it.

A suitable comparison for d'Ardenay might be discovered in the person of an English clothier, Mr. William Temple of Trowbridge, who published a pamphlet in praise of commerce in 1758. This was on the eve of England's Industrial Revolution; already, however, the mind of Mr. Temple seems "machine-made." He derided culture, humanism, labor, rural life; his estimates of life-values are as purely monetary as those of "The Man Who Knew Coolidge." Without his periwig, this estimable clothier would be at home in most smoking-cars today.

What had enraged Mr. Temple was a prize essay of a Cambridge student, a hymn to agrarian virtues. This was old-fashioned and absurd in Mr. Temple's view, and he advised Cambridge University to renounce its ridiculous humanistic studies, which were unprofitable, and take up practical science in the interests of commerce:

> The sciences are of no manner of service, but so far as they aid and assist commerce . . . The settling of the text of an author; what is the true reading of an inscription upon an antient coin; how the Romans made their fibula . . . are matters of no consequence to society . . . The noble architecture of card-houses and dirt-pies among children is of a piece with such learning.

The highest good to humanity would not come from such pottering of academicians in Cambridge, announced Mr. Temple, but from commerce, which alone had been able to "humanize mankind, make the difference between the *Moors* on the *Niger*, and *Britons* on the banks of the *Thames*," and "lift brute nature to contemplations of the deity." Certainly, he declared, it was not agriculture which made men virtuous. Let the Cambridge youth who "entertains such a great opinion of the temperance, sobriety and purity of manners, which prevail in the country," go to the country and watch the rustics: "We fancy if he were to attend to the manners, behaviour and conversation of a crowd of haymakers," he would be horrified. It was not true, said Mr. Temple, that the rich merchants of London were vicious because they lived well; there is a vicious luxury, that of the poor, and an innocent one, that of the rich:

> A porter may be viciously luxurious on fat bacon, tobacco, red herrings, gin, malt-spirits, and with a nasty bunter, or stinking dirty fish drab; whilst a nobleman may be innocently luxurious on ortolans, pine-apples, Tokay and the richest wines, and foods, accompanied with a fine lady flaunting in jewels and brocades, and "fragrant as Chloe issuing to an evening mask."

Finding it difficult to dispute the Cambridge thesis that agriculture would feed the people better than commerce, Mr. Temple argued that feeding the people well would only demoralize the brutes. If once they had their bellies full, the poor would lie down and snore:

> If a labourer can procure by his high wages or plenty, all the necessaries of life; and have afterwards a residuum, he would expend the same, either in gin, rum, brandy or strong beer; luxurize on great heaps of fat beef or bacon, and eat perhaps until he

spewed; and having gorged and gotten dead drunk, lie down like
a pig, and snore till he was fresh. This is the common consequence
of high wages and plenty.

M. d'Ardenay and Mr. Trowbridge were both confident for the
future. But the Frenchman felt that the millennium for business must
come through some immense social transformation; the Englishman,
without envisaging a régime of "liberty, equality and fraternity," felt
sure that it would come without upheaval, and without concession.

THE ACCEPTANCE OF A BUSINESS DESTINY

Yet there were some uneasy consciences at the time. Defoe, for instance, looking with keen and disillusioned eyes upon the world of
affairs, perceived that the rise of the lower trading-class, to which he
himself belonged, was chiefly due to war and luxury, rather than to
its native virtues. War, he declared, was basic:

> How many more families among Tradesmen have been rais'd to
> immense estates . . . by the attending circumstances of the war . . .
> And by whom have the prodigious taxes been paid, the loans sup-
> plied, and money advanced . . . Has not trade and the Tradesman
> borne the burthen of the war?

Nor could luxury be abolished:

> The nation's prosperity is built on the ruin of the Nation's morals
> . . . in short, Virtue would be really, in the very letter of it, a
> SINKING FUND, for it would in a word sink the value of many
> of our most important funds . . . And the wealth of the country is
> rais'd by its wickedness, and if it shou'd be reform'd it would be
> undone.

That is no Calvinist dogma, and yet Defoe's book, which describes
and even in a measure justifies the rise and extravagance of the new-
rich, is generally taken as proof of the coming into play of the so-called
bourgeois virtues. Weber and Sombart, and a host of other writers,
quote Defoe to indicate the growth of a Puritan-bred morality in England. All sorts of other things could be proved by Defoe, who seems
not only to be distributing moral advice but also to be lamenting that
there are so few to take it.

In any case, Defoe had few illusions about the value of the bourgeois virtues. He did not pretend, like a Samuel Smiles, that the merely

virtuous man must succeed in business. He knew better. Had he not
gone bankrupt himself in the brick-business? He declared that there
must be a certain amount of guile: "There is some difference between
an *honest* man, and an *honest* Tradesman." And after all, a tradesman
had better rely upon the fickle Etruscan deity, Fortuna, and not upon
the guidance of God alone. For it all too often happens that men

> in spite of good understanding . . . in spite of the most indefat-
> igable industry go bankrupt, while some plodding weak-headed
> wretch that can't look a quarter of a mile from his shop-door into
> the world . . . yet rises apace . . . and this fellow shall get money
> insensibly and grow rich even he knows not how, and nobody else
> knows why.

What Defoe undoubtedly does represent is a turning-point of business development. He was gazing backward with nostalgia to the enforced thrift and modesty of the old-fashioned petty tradesman in
straitened circumstances; yet he could not help but rejoice in the splendor and power now manifested by his class. Rather shocked to consider
how that wealth was won, in pandering to luxury and provisioning for
war, still he was dazzled by it. Instead of looking forward to still greater
strides of capitalism, he stopped short, awed and alarmed. He feared
the "Engrosser," the "Oppressor, indeed, a meer Trading Dragoon," who
"by the strength of his Cunning and the Strength of his Stock united,"
destroyed more than he created, and gathered up the trade from the
small men. Such powerful money manipulators, "that can buy cheap
and sell dear," would prove "a general calamity to the whole Nation. If
they grew mighty, the poor would grow poorer and consume less."
In the end one would see "the Rich devour the Poor, the Poor starve
the Manufacturer."

In short, the writings of Defoe express the wail of the passing generation of petty grocers and brick-dealers, who still felt pride in their
former simplicity, and meditated on the future with mingled trepida-
tion and amazement. They watched trade waxing every day, overshadowing agriculture, making a mock of gentility. They beheld England changing into a commercial power of mighty proportions. At the
parting of the ways they stood, loath to give up the past entirely, fascinated by the prospect of things to come. They saw the destiny of
England determined by her trade: ·

> The whole glory and greatness of England then being rais'd by
> trade . . . the only fountain from whence we all, take us as a nation,
> are rais'd . . . The very name of an *English* Tradesman will and

does already obtain in the world; and as our soldiers by the late war gained the reputation of being some of the best troops in the world, and our seamen are at this day, and very justly too, esteemed the best sailors in the world; so the *English Tradesman* may in a few years be allowed to rank with the best gentlemen in Europe; and as the Prophet Isaiah said of the merchants of *Tyre* that her traffickers were the honorable of the earth . . .

But they could not know that the greatness of England would be won in a way unlike that of Tyre or Venice, or all her other predecessors; that the mellow harmony of shopkeepers, merchant-monopolists and contractors was soon to be shattered, as soon as the roar of machinery in the North of England began. Then a strange race of grimy manufacturers, thirsty for power, would descend upon London, defeat the grand old oligarchy of landed gentlemen and merchant-princes, and claim for themselves the future of the nation. And even while Defoe yet lived, the very first signs of the new capitalism were being manifested around Manchester.

PART FOUR

THE INDIVIDUALIST

XVIII

STIRRINGS AND STEAM IN EUROPE

TOWARD THE CLOSE of the eighteenth century a challenging figure appeared on the horizon: the manufacturer. Long as he had been at work, perfecting his methods and enlarging his plants, he was still far from rivaling the older dominating types of the sea-merchant and the financier. He had yet to carve out his place in society. Lacking the social graces or traditions of traders and bankers, he had not won aristocratic acceptance and, without it, remained outside on the periphery, away from the government treasury, and the best favors and places. Though he had received subsidies, he did not enjoy such rich sinecures, such fat contracts and monopolies, as his betters.

The ranks were closed against him, and the hostile front was composed not merely of monarchs and courtiers, but of other business men. Satisfied with their triumph, forgetting what revolutionary disturbances they had created in their own struggle for power, as Puritans or Huguenots, the sea-merchants and financiers had formed too remunerative an alliance with the nobility to welcome newcomers. Serene in possession, and already aristocratized in manners and mentality, they desired no more "progress," no more upheavals. But just as this society seemed to be settling into a most formal mold, with a pacification and consolidation of groups, it was threatened by the manufacturer, who was in turn a revolutionary element.

Steam, of course, was to be the great propulsive force that would carry the manufacturer to the heights; and puffs of steam were already rising in England by 1773, and a little later, shortly before the French Revolution, in Bordeaux, that port of France where the most Anglophile merchants lived. But steam alone, harnessed to the most marvelous of machines, would not suffice to win a triumph for the aspiring producer; another volatile element, oratory, ideology, was required. If he was to make himself heard, the entrepreneur must push his way to the center of power, elbowing and shouting, demanding liberty for the individual and free play for Nature. Steam and wind together were to break up the mellowed *ancien régime* in France and the "Augustan" poise of England, and burst a way through for the modern capitalist.

Individualism was necessarily the chosen philosophy of a business man who could find no rich and powerful group ready to support his pretensions. As no one would cooperate and combine with him, he denounced cooperation and combination. But, clearly as the main line of thought was forced upon him by his situation, the actual development of his arguments and ideals was a very complex matter, requiring altogether as much ingenuity and time as the perfection of his steam-looms and other contrivances. And in this mental as well as in the mechanical progress, men of many races shared: France, Germany, England, even Italy, had their varying parts to play in the eighteenth century.

To France fell the formulation of the sacred doctrine of laissez faire, which demanded liberty of action; liberty of personal character-development was, however, the claim of the Germans, who perfected individualism from within while the French elaborated it as regards the external world. Laissez faire was first put to the practical test, nevertheless, by a third people; it was Florence, the old cradle of individualism in the Renaissance, that tried out the idea of economic freedom. And finally the English, receptive to currents of foreign thought, observed the French phrase, the Italian practice and the German ideal, and added to them, not only steam, but, characteristically, political genius and organization.

"LET NATURE DO IT"—THE FRENCH SLOGAN

The first determined and sweeping effort to alter the protective system of Mercantilism came in Florence, though it was applied there by Austrian rulers, the successors of the Medici. Realizing that government regulation had become oppressive, these sought to inject a fresh shot of business individualism, and so, by 1770, the privileges of Church and State were to a large degree withdrawn; taxes and restrictions were lifted from industry and trade, and professional schools of the crafts were founded. The result was a remarkable little boom in the harbor of Leghorn, where the grain trade was liberated, and millionaires soon developed. French and English observers watched this little demonstration of free trade with the keenest interest; although earlier systematized in French theory, this was the first radical application. But the Italian upswing was brief; almost immediately the French armies under Napoleon, supposedly carrying the torch of liberty, had trampled out freedom in Tuscany and most of Italy. Still the example was of effect in many places, and had repercussions in Austria and Russia; it showed what "Nature" could do, upon occasion, when let alone.

When and where did the theory arise that Nature could regulate the affairs of men better than man himself? Who first announced belief in the miraculous restorative powers of Nature, her tendency ever to preserve balance and maintain health in men and states? Benjamin Franklin thought some business men had coined the phrase, laissez faire. When Minister Colbert asked grumbling merchants of Lyons how the State might assist them, they churlishly replied, "Let us alone"—"Laissons nous faire." So the classic story went. But, of course, it is now generally believed that the slogan was first employed *against* big business; it was used by a nobleman who sought freedom for Nature in the agrarian cause. Agrarians first raised the chorus of praise for Nature in France. Moreover, it is obvious that faith in Nature's beneficent workings is much older than the French nation. It goes back to antiquity; it is, in fact, as old as worship of Fortuna.

In a brilliant essay on the origins of the doctrine, Stephan Bauer has traced it back to the ancients. It can occasion no surprise to learn that it was formulated, to all appearances, in the great trading-city of Alexandria. There, sciences and particularly medicine, were cultivated; a famous doctor of Alexandria, Empiricus, urged that Nature should be left as far as possible to work her own cures. But the ancients did not apply the notion to economic affairs.

When ancient learning was revived in Europe, in the Renaissance, classic medicine was also restored to favor. Bauer has shown how Montaigne, in the sixteenth century, animated by the Renaissance Humanist's interest in medicine, repeated the Alexandrian idea in French: "Laissons faire à la Nature; elle entend ses affaires mieux que nous." But still it was not generally maintained that Nature "understands her business better than we" in economic matters, until the French agrarians began to protest against state control of their grain-production.

Calling upon Nature, those who clamored for freedom first in France were the landed gentry. They felt unjustly discriminated against by the State, which, since Colbert's time, fed the big commercial cities at the expense of the countryside, by laying strict regulations upon the sale and export of grain. Quesnay assailed royal privilege and called for liberty, from the agrarians' standpoint; he was not interested in striking the shackles from merchants, whom he considered a "classe stérile." Perhaps it may be suggested, in support of Bauer's thesis, that Quesnay, as a doctor, was the more easily persuaded of the truth in the antique medical theory of Nature's benevolence.

Only gradually did merchants join with agrarians in a movement against royal authority. They shouted for freedom too. But instead of setting up their own deity, Fortuna, the old goddess of trading men, they followed the agrarians' lead, perhaps cleverly, and laid incense upon the altar of Nature, a divinity more appropriate to farmers. This could happen in France, more readily than elsewhere, because so many merchants had themselves agricultural interests, a phenomenon typical of France to this day.

The very revolutionary merchants of Bordeaux, for instance, as Leroux shows, were growers as well as sellers of wine. One of the men who first formed a union of commerce and agriculture for the purposes of propaganda, was Dupont de Nemours, whose "Journal de l'agriculture, du commerce et des finances," founded about 1765, crusaded for liberty. Though a business man, Dupont was also a conservative land-holder, uniting in his person as in his ideas two apparently irreconcilable interests. Indeed, according to Mathiez, when the liberal section in the French Revolution proposed to abolish the old feudal dues upon serfs, in return for an indemnity, no one was more vehemently opposed to such a compromise than Dupont. In the Assembly, one of the richest noblemen of France, the Duke d'Aiguilon, proposed the peaceful settlement of the issue of feudal rights, and possibly his measure might have been adopted by the other members, who were deeply moved by the appeal of this noble lord; but the bourgeois, Dupont de Nemours, prevented such accord by springing to the defense of this side of feudalism. Many rich business men in France who also owned estates were seemingly less sympathetic with their serfs than their older seigneurs; through Dupont de Nemours, these bourgeois demanded utmost severity through local tribunals against unruly peasants.

The term "revolutionary" must be used, therefore, with extreme caution when applied to the French business men of the *ancien régime*. Dupont was radical in some ways, ultra-conservative in others. So, too, his son, Irénée, had a dual rôle in the United States; on the one hand he set up a gunpowder-making plant to help the American Rebellion against royal authority; but on the other, he pleaded for state aid for his own plant from the new Republic, in the most old-fashioned French monopolist manner.

An attempt to discover what part the business man actually took in preparing for the French Revolution must lead the seeker into all sorts of contradictions. For instance, business men's wives would seem to have been more helpful in laying the ideological groundwork than their husbands; they entertained the literati who undermined the authority of the State. But these literati, though they pressed for greater liberty, were not as a rule very friendly to big business and few of them dreamed of stripping all bondage from capitalism and leaving high finance to Nature. Nor were the laboring people, who brought revolt at last, in any way eager for laissez faire—their most urgent wish was to retain the old codes and statutes, which set some bounds at least to the demands of industrialists. Yet, consciously or not, all these were working for the business men, the agrarians who called upon Nature, the literati who called upon the ladies, and the poor who lit the torches of Liberty.

FRENCH WIVES AT PLAY WITH DANGEROUS IDEAS

Against the will of the Absolute King in France, said Bishop Bossuet, the subject had no possible recourse save "prayer and patience." Even a mild protest at excesses of royal authority was considered impious in the seventeenth century, when it was believed that God had sanctioned governmental control over the behavior, beliefs and industries of citizens. The notion that business might prosper without such interference was heretical. One might as well have preached rugged individualism to a Bolshevist as to the Bishop.

As murmurings constantly mounted, however, against State and Church, the idea that economy should be freed from authoritarian trammels and left to the all-wise goddess, Nature, whose other name is Fortuna, found more and more acclaim. In the eighteenth century, many a "salon red" was expatiating upon laissez faire from the security of some marquise's sofa, and giving vent to cynical laughter at state-management of utilities. "Let Nature do it!" said the radicals.

But who were these radicals? Some business men were friendly to the philosophical movement. Helvétius, for instance, was an apostle of skepticism as his wife was a Diotima for philosophers. Henri Watelet, the banker, was also painter, poet, sculptor and a collaborator of Diderot on the Encyclopedia. But such examples cannot be multiplied indefinitely. On the whole, it does appear that women of business circles toyed more enthusiastically with dangerous ideas and, through their salons, did more than their men to propagate criticism of the status quo.

While the honor of developing the pleasures of the table and the opera may go to the rich bankers and merchants, it seems that patronage of literary and philosophical innovation belongs to their wives and daughters. Thus, while Laborde made a hobby of banqueting and gardening, his daughter had one of the most intellectual salons. As the doddering manufacturer, Pierre Geoffrin, was sinking in silence to the grave, his wife was mothering the wits of Paris. While the financier, de la Live d'Epinay, devoted himself to theater and gallantry, his wife turned to philosophy and befriended Duclos, Diderot, Voltaire and other forthright critics; and she built a rustic hermitage for her pet lion,

Rousseau. Rousseau was given the task of educating the son of another financier's spouse, the feminist wife of Dupin de Chenonceaux. She delighted in Rousseau's attacks on urban over-sophistication and the status quo, though her banker-husband, Dupin, feebly remonstrated and even composed a defense of his brethren, the gens de finance. But Dupin's work was suppressed, gossip said, by Madame de Pompadour, queen of Paris financial circles, who ardently fostered criticism of the society for which she herself set the pace.

La Pompadour was supposed to be the illegitimate daughter of the vastly rich financier, de Tournehem, and married his nephew, also a money-lender, d'Etioles. She was one of the reigning beauties of Paris bourgeois circles when the Dauphin, later Louis XV, laid eyes on her. After she became his mistress, and a marquise, she shaped the goût of France, and supported the literary and philosophical gentlemen who were undermining royalty and finance. The Pompadour assisted the Paris brothers, the fabulously rich money-lenders, to control of French tax-gathering, and to fat government contracts, but she was sympathetic with those who, like Montesquieu, assailed gens de finance. She was the most extravagant woman in France, and spent 37 millions of the nation's money on her whims, yet worshiped the rough apostle of simplicity, Rousseau. A marquise and the king's mistress, she protected Quesnay, the physiocrat, whose ideas were instrumental in overthrowing Absolutism.

Was bourgeois woman unaware of her economic advantage? It would seem so. No matter how closely men of the commercial classes may be shown to have followed the dictates of their pocketbooks, the same clear line of reasoning cannot be traced among their feminine counterparts. Commerce and finance provided the ladies with astounding fortunes, leisure and unheard-of luxury. But they were devastated with boredom and given to fits of the vapors. Restlessly, they applauded innovators. Possibly, this was because the status of woman was changing in that period: the woman of the rococo was a creature of the transition between feudalism and capitalism.

The martial-heroic epoch had closed, and though the romantic culture based upon feudalism survived, it was without genuine foundation. Yet woman was not ready to accept anything like pure utilitarianism, and become "emancipated" as a "business girl." Rather, she hung between the two. As far as she could, she preserved the past heritage of art, though it had shrunk to a pretty puppet-show and had become, in the rococo age, "the art of the superfluous"—only a little later, art would itself be thought superfluous. On the other hand, rococo women admitted the forces of the coming era to their hearts, and many of them managed their intrigues according to the coolest mercenary speculations—they introduced calculation to love, but had not learned to love calculation.

The critics who enjoyed the protection and assistance of the restless rich *bourgeoises* of France were not, by and large, seeking in return to free finance and business from all governmental control. It is true that the result of their cogitations was the overthrow of Absolutism, and that another capitalism emerged out of the ruins, but this was not exactly the outcome which the philosophers had envisaged. Rousseau, for instance, the ladies' darling, the stern Swiss moralist of a Geneva Calvinist background, opposed the artificiality of the *ancien régime*, but would not have accepted in its place the artificiality of urban industrialist civilization.

Thoroughly anti-capitalist was Fénelon, one of the earliest strong critics of the Monarchy, who told Louis XIV that his "creaky old machine," la France, was about to collapse. In his utopia, Fénelon pictured a millennium based on agriculture, wherein wealth is cut down and business regulated by the State. So, too, the Marquis d'Argenson, supposedly the first man to use the phrase, "Laissez faire, laissez passer," was a stern opponent of complete freedom for business. He was a nobleman, and therefore suspicious of commerce as the churchman, Fénelon. Indeed, he assailed industrialists as robbers of the artisans; he called financiers cankers on the body politic. And, as Foreign Minister, he wished to stop warfare for markets. Neither Fénelon nor d'Argenson intended for a moment to cut down the Monarchy in order to give capitalists a free hand and assist to unqualified power the foes of their Church and class.

So, too, one of the great thinkers, Montesquieu, of Bordeaux, was as firmly opposed to unbalanced commercialism as to unrestrained monarchy. To be sure, he was realistic enough to see that French prosperity did not rest on agriculture alone, and he believed in a wider measure of freedom for experimentation in business. But he was afraid that great fortunes, made in trade, would prove to be the chief danger of the balance of powers in the State he admired. In his "Esprit des Lois," he insisted that some means must be found of lopping off incomes in the highest brackets, and maintaining some sort of balance between poor and rich. He believed in fostering finance, yet in controlling its extravagances, even though, personally, he admired the Pompadour.

But at least one major prophet, Voltaire, may be allotted to the business man's side. He liked business men. He was one himself. Not only did he engage in manufacturing silk stockings, which he sold to his fair acquaintances, but he was generously admitted to various munitioneering deals by his friends, the Brothers Paris. Perhaps, indeed, Voltaire learned a measure of his cynicism from them—or was it the other way around?—for at least both he and they escaped the general contagion of the big Law boom and bubble. In 1719, when most of Paris was seething with speculative fervor, the Paris brothers were standing aloof and Voltaire was writing from a rural retreat:

> Are you really all gone crazy at Paris? I hear only millions spoken of; it is said that everyone who was well-off is now in misery and all who were mendicants are opulent. Is it reality? Is it chimaera? Has half the nation found the philosopher's stone in paper-mills? Is Law a god, a rascal, or a charlatan who poisons himself with the drug he distributes to the world? Will all be content with imaginary riches? It is a chaos which I cannot pierce and . . . as for me, I shall not deliver myself to chimaeras other than that of poetry.

The greatest wit of France saw through the Stock Market as readily as through the Absolute Monarchy. Yet unhesitatingly, he preferred the evils of the former to those of the latter; at least, he spared the money-changers when he let fly his poisoned darts. He might laugh at misers or take a fling at a petty bookkeeper, but he left the big financiers, like the Paris brothers, unscathed, while he jeered at Crown and Church.

As Voltaire summed up the Rights of Man, he condensed the demands of the restless intellectuals into a Magna Charta which bourgeois could support. He demanded: "Entire liberty of person, of property, of thought, of religion, of press, of being judged in a criminal affair by a jury only, and only according to the terms of the law." He did not add: entire liberty for business; that was left to the imagination of his supporters. Liberty was naturally extended to economic enterprise by all those groups in France who needed it: merchants of Bordeaux, slave-dealers of Nantes, grumbling manufacturers of Paris and Lyons. And thus the slogans of agrarians and philosophers in time were adapted to the purposes of French businesses.

GERMAN BUSINESS AND CULTURE

German business men did not join in the tremendous scramble for colonies, markets, mechanical improvements and speculative gains which engaged the energies of their contemporaries in the eighteenth century. On the whole, they lagged behind the rest. But this was of the most far-reaching consequences for European culture—it meant that there was at least one country in the heart of Europe which was not then dominated by hustling traders. In this land, if hardly anywhere else, speculation might take philosophic instead of financial forms—where the economic imperative was lacking, the categorical imperative might be discussed.

With business men sitting at home in a semi-comatose condition, the practical aims of life were not so constantly in view as in England, France, Holland and America, where "go-getting" merchants were devoting their lives to the ever-swifter transport of sugar and cotton, the elaboration of machinery, the exploitation of empires and the guillotining of aristocrats. In such business countries, intellectuals felt the prevailing atmosphere and bent their minds to the problems of economics and social adjustment. Only in Germany, where there really was no use in thinking, was thought cultivated as a fine art.

Hustling Britons, churning the seas with their cargoes of rum and slaves, were under the impression that they ruled the waves and had no time to wonder whether, after all, the leading influence might not be that of the Moon. It took a German, Leonhard Euler, to perfect marvelous tables showing the lunar influence over tides. At a time when they had no navigation to speak of, Germans observed the sea with scientific detachment.

Instead of a practical mechanic like Watt, the Germans produced so majestic a theoretician as Leibnitz. Or, to be accurate, they had indeed a Watt, but he was not honored. The born Frenchman, Papin (1647–1710), a professor of physics in Germany, was, it now appears, the real inventor of the modern steam-boiler and made early experiments with the steamboat. But his boat was smashed and nobody noticed the boiler. At this stage, German rulers discountenanced mechanical progress; they wished only to preserve the status quo. In 1681 and on other occasions, improvements in weaving were forbidden by imperial decree, and even in progressive Hamburg, a free merchant city, some descriptions of new inventions were solemnly burned by order of the Senate. This was entirely at variance with English practice; there, the Government encouraged invention by patent laws and prizes, while aristocrats joined with manufacturers in promoting change. From the 1600's onward, England was looking forward to new things, while Germany was suppressing them.

This repression of economic and political activity in Germany, meant a diversion of energies of the business classes to other fields. German business men went to the theater of Schiller, because they could not go to Parliament. They hearkened to Lessing on the Laocoon, since they could not make speeches on the wool tariff. They listened to Beethoven's "Eroica," expressing the spirit of the French Revolution, since they could not knock their own aristocracy on the head. Unable to win laissez faire in the economic world, they proclaimed spiritual freedom, and, having no chance for mechanical development, they emphasized the unfolding of the human character. The poignance, the sentiment, the romanticism of the Germans were the expression of middle classes denied channels of activity; they idealized the wandering, carefree artist, the Bohemian genius, who was not so bound down as they.

And because the Germans pondered and dreamed, ransacked world literatures, dug into ancient documents, poured out matchless music, all without any immediate and profitable aim in view, they were naturally regarded with surprise abroad. They seemed incomprehensible and even a bit mad, to the business-enveloped and politics-absorbed Anglo-Saxons and the industrious French, who had put mysticism sternly behind them.

GOETHE AND BUSINESS

Only in a land of such leisure as Germany could a Goethe have found time to write a "Faust." Faust took many years to fathom the meaning of life; through drinking, dueling, mocking with Mephistopheles, consultation with Helena, exploration of earth, heaven and hell, he arrives in the final moment at a vision: the glory of labor and constructive effort for the social good, exemplified in the digging of canals and the building of cities in the wilderness. Only a German would have reached so utilitarian a result by so devious a process. Anglo-Saxons were too busy making canals and cities to ponder the process.

Only the German middle classes were asking themselves: what shall we do with our lives? Other men knew. They turned their faces to the profit-making opportunities of the hour. But the German had a choice between absorption in his small, tedious, slow-growing business or the improvement of leisure hours and of himself. This is the problem at the basis of Goethe's novels of "Wilhelm Meister." In this story, Werner Meister personifies business; he is an iron-manufacturer who can think of nothing but his furnaces. Crassly materialistic, he proposes to sell the paternal mansion with its art collection assembled by the grandfather, for he wishes to have no coach, no pictures, no rich furniture, or any superfluities in his life. Every penny, like every moment, is to go into business. This entire practicality disgusts his brother Wilhelm, the hero, who calls it sheer "brutality," and asks, "What shall it profit me to manufacture good iron if my own soul is full of slag?"

Wilhelm Meister, through whom we hear Goethe speak, does not condemn the manufacture of iron as an occupation. Not business *per se* is vulgar, but business divorced from the honor and respectability of public office and rank. Goethe, who became himself a minister in a petty German State, was far from a blind foe of commercialism; he was no enemy of the rising manufacturer of his age. But he had no use for a man who would not aspire to public affairs. Certainly he did not ask very much of the business man after all; he did not want to make of him a savant, a genius, a Faust. He sought only a certain air of cultivation, poise, a graceful levity, such as the British brewer or tack-manufacturer could easily assume by acquiring a landed estate, imitating country squires and buying a title. This personal charm, this irreducible minimum, was within the grasp of the Briton or Frenchman, or at least of their sons; but it was not easy of attainment for the home-bound, subjected business man of the over-governed German principalities.

"I do not know how it is in foreign lands," writes Wilhelm, "but in Germany a certain broad personal development, if I may say so, is possible only to the nobleman." The bourgeois dared not practice freedom of speech and behavior, lest it be regarded as impudent presumption in him. And that, thought Goethe, was the real reason why he concentrated on money. "He may not ask: What are you? But only: What have you?" This question, which is so often associated with "Ford civilization," was considered by Goethe inseparable from his own Germany.

If the bourgeois would not devote himself to grim money-grubbing like Werner, he would find escape difficult from his class; he might marry a countess, which is Wilhelm's final solution to the problem, but this was admittedly an exceptionally "happy" outcome. Another Goethean figure, hero of the "Sorrows of Werther," come to a more tragic end; Werther shoots himself, ostensibly because his love for the country Lotte is not returned, but in reality because he was afterward snubbed by the *grandes dames* of a pint-pot principality—it is this which finally causes his act of desperation. For the rest, there remained only the magic world of make-believe and counterfeit victory, behind the footlights.

The Theater was for the German bourgeois, precisely as for the Japanese traders of Osaka and Tokyo during the same period—a substitute for achievement in the real world of action. "On the stage," as Wilhelm explains to his brother, "the educated man appears personally as splendid as in the upper classes." If the bourgeois could not marry an aristocrat, or even behave like one, he might find temporary relief in playing a king before the footlights. In this mimicry, moreover, he might develop what the bourgeois had heretofore lacked: a personality.

Wilhelm, joining the Bohemian back-stage circles, found that "Through bodily exercises, I have won much since I saw you . . . also I have developed my speech and voice."

Thus the German, who could not achieve that apparently ideal amalgamation with the noblesse which was possible for the rich elsewhere, would not rest in his striving until he had discovered a substitute in the cult of the individual. If he could not wrap himself in a feudal aura, he would become a personality. The Goethean movement, aiming at the unfolding of the character, flowered in a way long afterward in America, where business men most enthusiastically adopted it. They, like the Germans, lacked aristocratic models and were forced to mold themselves. They came to believe fervidly that a "pleasing personality" is a "business asset," to be attained through athletics, a five-foot-shelf and courses in salesmanship. The German-descended, so-called "Smiling Charlie" Schwab explains at length in his autobiography that his success has been to a great extent the result of "that indefinable charm that gives to men what perfume gives to flowers," and which, he thinks, may be "acquired" by the persevering aspirant in commerce. Thus the heavy-industrialist of today, Schwab, accepted as an essential part of the iron-business that personal development which the old German ironmaster in the story, Werner, rejected with scorn as a fantastic new whim of his idle brother.

HAMBURG, CITADEL OF BUSINESS CULTURE

The chances for the unfoldment of the business man remained greatest in the free port of Hamburg. In other cities, to be sure, some favoring circumstances were also to be found; Bremen was as free as Hamburg, but its citizens had turned Calvinist and were too Puritanical to countenance the theatrical diversions in which Hamburg delighted. Leipzig was gay enough, and its elegance in dressing and housing led Goethe to call it "A little Paris," but the tone was strongly influenced by the frivolous Saxon court. Frankfort-am-Main had a certain prosperity, but exercised no cultural command. Berlin was a dump. The other towns where the bourgeois might have asserted himself were university places like Göttingen or seats of courts like Weimar, and in either case he was overshadowed by classes more sure of themselves than he was.

Only Hamburg was wholly mercantile, very wealthy, full of Puritan push but not too dominated by Puritans to be interested in cultural matters. Here no aristocracy, no ministry, no prince, could shut the pathway to the sea. Even when other ports were as good as closed, during time of war, Hamburg remained the outlet for the whole country, and the receiving-center for foreign goods and ideas. Since there was so little manufacturing beyond linen-making in Germany, the principal sources of wealth lay in shipping and wholesaling, and this was concentrated in Hamburg, which accordingly became the richest of the towns.

In Hamburg the merchant ruled for a long time. Lawyers and preachers, of course, made a considerable parade of importance, but even these were gradually submerged as the wealth of the trader rose. The town remained dominated by the native-born Hamburgers who formed a jealously closed clique. It was the burning ambition of all the newcomers, English or French, to break down the gate to this Patriotic Society; there was no other place to climb into in Hamburg, and as foreigners they had the social-climbing instinct so ingrained that they strove with feverish intensity to prove themselves worthy of the native club. They built impressive homes, splurged in coaches and cellars, and angled for marriages—usually in vain. The Hamburg Patriots as a rule would only open their doors after several generations of assimilation had produced offspring with a Hamburg style.

Though the tone was set by the natives, the wealth was largely in the hands of the parvenus. The richest men of the town were not native-born, but nearly all were immigrant Dutch, French or English Reformed, and Portuguese Jews. It was they who imported trader-pride from abroad and thus refreshed the ancient tradition of Hanse independence. These émigrés, flocking by the thousands, insisted upon maintaining the profitable policy of free trade and neutrality; since they came from many countries, they were as neutral as the Swiss. They knew how to avoid taking sides during the long English-French hostilities, and provided each party with grain and war-supplies.

The French formed a particularly resplendent group in Hamburg, living in the style of princes. Indeed, of the great piles built by the two Godeffroys, Jean and César, a contemporary remarked: "They are palaces with which few of the *Residenz* castles of the little German princes may be compared." Pierre His, another Frenchman, built his home in more or less distant imitation of Versailles, about the same time that Frederick the Great was erecting another version in Potsdam. Frederick hated the rich and ostentatious traders of the free city, who thus frankly rivaled him; against a French émigré in Hamburg, Pierre Boué, the king wrote an invective poem: "Ein Kapitel gegen die Werten Herren Blutsauger, auf Griechisch: Philokopros." (A Chapter Against the Honored Lord Bloodsuckers, in Greek: Philokopros.)

Splendid as were some houses, like the Hammerhof residence of the French trader Chapeaurouge, they all remained bourgeois homes. No matter how well-to-do, Hamburg men were not ashamed of dwelling beside town-offices and keeping in close contact with underlings. Even their country villas were near to trade, for the shipping-lords built them along the high cliff that runs seaward beside the river Elbe; from their stately porches and gardens, merchants could look far down to the broad flood on which their vessels were sailing away, saluting with guns as they departed, to Mexico and Africa.

The Hamburg shipper was a merchant-patriarch, who did not try to imitate another caste. Such a man as César Godeffroy knew every captain and every cook on his vessels; he named his ships after his children and took the same personal interest in them as in his own off-spring, being fond of the good and lucky *Sophie*, eager to outfit the *Charlotte* with handsome cannon before her voyage to the Pacific, and to see that there were plenty of provisions "so that things will be done handsomely aboard, as becomes the ship of a Godeffroy."

Most of these free-spending, high-living traders were Puritans. The richest men were Reformed like Chapeaurouge, the Godeffroys, John Parish, who were Genevan, French and Scotch Calvinists. In the group of French Huguenots were the His, Ami Boué, Ochs, Diodati, Des Arts and Vidal. As Weber himself is forced to admit, this seigneurial display and worship of the flesh in Hamburg ill accords with the so-called "Puritan-entrepreneur" type which he wished to set up, who supposedly leads an ascetic life that he may concentrate his whole soul on money-grubbing.

The Hamburg Puritans spent lavishly during booms, like anybody else, if the truth be known, and failed just as foolishly in crises. During the early half of the 1700's, while England and France were at war, neutral Hamburg reaped profits. English and French merchants, in the safety-zone, sold grain, sugar, wood to the belligerents, on credit; they attracted capital from the war-zones and, on this new money built a high and fancy credit-structure. These war-years were times of great gayety, in which the dourest Puritan relaxed. But then of course, de-spite the famed canniness of Puritan capitalists, crashes came. The terrible crack of 1799, caused in part by the flooding of the markets with goods from the United States, and in part by the removal of the war-scenes to Italy, was devastating. Within six weeks there were 136 bankrupts and the city was paralyzed. Gold was hastily ordered from abroad, but just as the ship bearing it drew near and all hopes were rising, the ship sank, with man and mouse and every bar of gold, off the Dutch coast. After that the crisis raged with greater fury. And in the depths of it, many persons felt that the whole world must surely profit from the lesson of this terrible disaster arising from speculation; a learned Dutch historian of the period cried: "Must then every new generation of business men pay out apprentice-money, in order to acquire afresh the necessary foresight and keenness?"—the after-thought of every crisis, as stereotyped by now as the incidents of the crises themselves.

By the 1800's, when Hamburg had recovered, the merchants were again spending profusely on coaches, silver, wines, Christmas and gambling. This splendor is mirrored in the Godeffroy account-books; in one year the head of the household won 43,000 marks at the gaming-table and lost it a little later, being not too Puritanical for cards. In one year, 1822, the family expenses were:

	Thalers
Equipage (horses, coaches, liveries)	7,500
Wine cellar	2,500
Dockenhuder country estate upkeep	9,000
Domestics	1,200
Town House in Hamburg	2,200
Christmas	1,600
Heating	1,300
Children's tutors, clothes, toys	3,200
Family of wife	7,126
Travel, theater box, silver from Paris	3,350
Extras	15,449
	54,425

In this city of good spenders, where there was no other class to set the prevailing patterns, it was natural that the materialism of Hamburg should become notorious. One scornful aesthete called it *Stomachopolis*, and another the *Beefsteak Paradise*, much as Thackeray spoke of "the monstrous belly worship" in the City of London. Banqueting, gaming, dressing, were the amusements of the rich. Money alone had influence among them, as one writer in 1802 wrote: "Whoever pays up his notes is here esteemed an honorable man; a well-filled purse is the best adornment; elegance itself lies in being able to calculate the curve of stocks; to have luck in business means to have talent and wit; to play a rôle at the Exchange is to hold the highest post of honor: for at this Court of Plutus, esteem and admiration are measured only according to the bank account."

Nevertheless, it was in this Court of Plutus, this Beefsteak Paradise, that the bourgeois awakening in the eighteenth century commenced in Germany. Hamburg afforded the earliest refuge which artists and intellectuals could find outside the courts. Thus she sheltered Klop-stock and Lessing, long before the courtly Weimar was ready to receive Goethe and Schiller. Later on Hamburg had Heinrich Heine for a time—until he failed in the banking business there—and Brahms and Hebbel.

But it was not merely in the protection of genius that the importance of Hamburg lay. There the merchant class itself perceived a need for self-cultivation. The influence of such English middle class papers as the *Tatler* and *Spectator* was felt early in the port of Hamburg, with its English connections; one of the most flourishing of the "moral weeklies" was founded on the English model, to teach codes of etiquette, elevate family life, and improve the art of conversation.

In these periodicals, merchants discussed their position in society. In the early 1700's, a Hamburg paper, the *Patriot*, boldly campaigned against the pretensions of professional men, and insisted that the business man was the equal of any. The bourgeois also vented his wrath against the nobility, condemning it for immorality and extravagance. The aim of the German bourgeois was not to ape the fantastic courts, but to develop a superior society.

Gradually, Hamburg merchants began to lift up their voices and express themselves. Up to the 1750's, German merchants not only did not write much, but could hardly read. They had not the "Grand Tour" habits, and seldom gave their sons a liberal education. The chief German literary productions had been lengthy euphuistic novels and accounts of the scandals of courts. But then, at the middle of the eighteenth century, the business man appeared in literature; his diaries, letters, reflections, showed his awakening. Cities, refreshed by prosperity, slowly took up again their chronicles, which had been dropped since the Middle Ages. Fostered by the trading cities, and particularly by Hamburg, German literature recommenced.

Naturally Hamburg merchants began to write on themes near to their experience, on law, banking, navigation, a history of the Exchange, prison reform. A library and an academy were opened. At last a wine merchant began the collection of paintings. And finally, toward the close of the eighteenth century, a writer could rejoice that Maecenas was born again: "Hamburg's nobler merchants have discarded the petty tradesman's mind that can only count and reckon. They have called the arts that rejoice and beautify life, and have gathered around the artists and wise men, not as princes do in forming a court, but as friends and companions." Among these, the French émigré César Godeffroy was especially admired as "one of the group of most distinguished citizens of his father city and one of the most morally ennobled through taste and aesthetic education." It was hoped that the Genius of well-earned Repose might long continue to bless him, whilst the joyous Goddess of Social Converse still proceeded to scatter her most beauteous and perfumed blooms of *esprit* in his path.

Merchants' sons took to literature, and gave expression of their fathers' tastes. Michael Richey (1678–1761), son of a rich Hamburg trader, wrote elegies in a curiously commercial spirit. A remarkable example was his "Victory of Love," in which Cupid is seen vanquishing a reluctant merchant, who protests:

> *to be in love*
> *Brings no penny in;*
> *A merchant has other things to do.*

The singularly canny Eros, however, points out another merchant,

> *To whose keen energy and honesty*
> *The best place on Hamburg's Börse belongs,*

who has nevertheless admitted the tender passion. So the hero submits gracefully to a non-lucrative pastime.

Another scion of a rich house of Hamburg, Brockes (1680–1747) a jurist, expressed the sentiments of the commercial city; much of his verse indicates a better understanding of economics than poetical inspiration: "The true use of metals is, that they ever circulate." But he was extremely popular among his fellow-townsmen with such verse as this, in which Pegasus appears hitched to a delivery-wagon:

> *Whoever considers, finds,*
> *That upon earth only Gold*
> *Binds together human society.*
> *Gold has the merit of aiding the peoples*
> *To help, improve, serve, protect one another,*
> *And to write, print and teach,*
> *How best to honor the Creator.*

Or:

> *To the merchant the world appears only a counting-house,*
> *An exchange-bank, a fair,*
> *Full of hope of gain, full of fear and anxiety before loss.*

Long before Goethe discovered the ideal escape for the bourgeois was the theater, German trading cities had led in building it up, promoting its gradual evolution from the opera, which remained the aristocratic art. The initial step was to give opera in the German language instead of Italian or French. The first German music in an opera was given under bourgeois auspices at the trading-city of Leipzig. In 1728, the "Musical Patriot" proudly announced that "where the best banks are, the best operas also are to be found." But opera was too formal for the business man; in the theater he discovered in Germany, as previously in Holland and France, a make-believe nearer to his tastes.

The excitement over the theater in Hamburg was comparable to that in England over newspapers and politics. It formed almost the only outlet for emotion outside the church. At first, the bourgeois was not ready to make his own drama; he went to see the bold woman director, the Neuberin, who presented aristocratic plays about knights and shepherds, with a faint attempt to adapt them to her merchant audiences by a prologue in which the trader's God, Mercury, appeared and praised Hamburg. Her visits to Hamburg were financed by merchants like Poppe and Krohn. Money for later attempts came from such men as Caspar Voght, the first Hamburg trader who "brought coffee from Mocca, tobacco from Baltimore, and rubber from Africa," and who gave freely to charity and agricultural improvement. It was another group of business men, such as Ochs and Buber, who engaged Lessing in 1767 and Lessing at last brought true bourgeois life on the stage.

In Altona, the twin-city of Hamburg, a grand theater was built in 1754 on the splendid Palmaille, where the palazzi of merchant princes stood. In 1783 a larger one was erected by the rich merchant Johann Schleppegrell, who himself emphasized the connection between economic boom and drama: "It was in the years of the war between England and America, which favored the growth of the trade and industry of this city." Soon business men even wrote for the stage, if not with lasting luster. George Behrmann (1704–56) wrote a "Horace"; another, Menz, indited "Merchant, a Friend of Humanity." In 1707 a bank-cashier, Cuno, published an opera text. While this obsession continued, the Church thundered in vain, even at times forbidding communion to recalcitrants. But nothing could halt the dramatic fever—except depression.

The theater remained the chief art developed under the active patronage of German business men. Architectural development continued largely in princely hands; so did painting, despite some experimentation with portraits of merchant families and caricatures of bourgeois life, like Chlodowiecki's "The Bankrupt."

Hamburg showed the German bourgeois the way to emancipation. It defended the merchant against the disapproval of the clergy, and the pretensions of the lawyers, helped raise moral standards after the excesses of the Thirty Years' War, and encouraged idealism; in short, it was the hot-bed of the cultural movement. Yet it remained a thor-

oughly commercial city, in which business came first and artistic temperaments were always baffled by the colossal phlegmatism of the
natives. Indeed, the babbittry of Hamburg was assailed by the poet
Heinrich Heine, whose revilement of its heavy complacency was
more scathing, and certainly more filthy, than anything Sinclair Lewis
ever said about Gopher Prairie, or John Ruskin about Manchester.

Heine was sent up from Düsseldorf to Hamburg by his business
father, who wanted him to go into banking. His rich uncle, Solomon
Heine, set him up in an independent business. But the firm "Harry
Heine and Company" was insolvent in a few months; before long the
exiled poet in Paris was pouring out his vials of wrath on the vulgar
Hamburg worship of the flesh. Yet Heine loved Hamburg; he felt
deep affection for the fog-wrapped sea-city, with its patriarchal "solidity," its beefsteak-hunger, and its superb self-satisfaction.

With as great an appreciation of the realities, but a milder amusement, Thomas Mann, the modern novelist, turned to Hamburg for a
hero in his "Magic Mountain." He found him in one of the great
merchant families, dwelling on the lake-front in the row of patriarchal
palaces: a smooth, correct, dull young man, with that unique Hamburg
pride, belonging to burghers who never aped an aristocracy or bowed
to any conqueror less than Napoleon. In this epitome of Hamburg merchantry, Mann perceived wistful stirrings; he brought his hero up to
the rarefied atmosphere of the Magic Mountain, showed him visions
and then, mercifully perhaps, instead of sending him back to the
countinghouse, let him die.

It was Hamburg's good fortune that Thomas Mann, like Heine, at
least in a generous moment, could view the bourgeois spectacle with
penetrating sympathy. Mann does not estimate it more highly, perhaps,
than sharp critics rate American business society. But whereas Carol
Kennicott in "Main Street," fails to find salvation on her flat prairie,
the hero of the *Zauberberg* is raised by a kindly author from the low
marshes of Hamburg to a mountain-top.

ENGLISH MERCHANTS AS MOLDERS OF OPINION

While French and Germans sought liberty, outer or inner, for deeds
or souls, and in the process were advancing large and splendid theories,
the English men of business, being freer in both respects, could concentrate upon more specific interests. They were also more vocal; not
depending upon literati to express their ideas, they became active and
effective propagandists for their own causes.

Commercial men in other lands, to be sure, have been their own
advocates: mercantilism in Italy was defended by the banker, Belloni;

in Holland, the merchants Usselincx and de la Court made themselves heard. Laissez faire was pushed by Dupont de Nemours, and another French business man, Richard Cantillon, wrote a work "Upon the Nature of Commerce in General," in 1755, dealing with the production and distribution of wealth, which influenced the physiocrats and has indeed been called one of the most important works foreshadowing the "science" of Political Economy. But, granting this, the array of English business writers is more imposing: Malynes, Mun, Misselden, Child, Henry Robinson and Samuel Lamb, Slingsby Bethel, William Paterson, Defoe, Dudley North and Child, began a tradition which was continued to modern times, when Ricardo, economist and stock-broker, and John Stuart Mill, clerk in the East India House, erected their theories. Political Economy is now, however, so generally considered a structure reared by pure theoreticians, wholly objective and removed from the strife of the marketplace, that its origins in the disputations of business men are sometimes overlooked.

In appealing to a public so largely agrarian as the English, the ambitious man of business there had to give his arguments the appearance, at least, of broad principles. Addressing himself to slow-minded country squires, he had to put his arguments on a "commonsense" level, without intricacy. And he had to present his scheme, whatever it was, as sensible, national, rational and agreeable to God. Invoking the commonweal, the defense of sovereignty on the seas, or religion, he tried to explain that the welfare of the whole people of England depended upon his plans. "National interest" was employed for many generations as the most potent argument for all sorts of purposes. From the seventeenth century mercantilist-merchants, like Mun and Malynes, down to the fiery advocates of Manchesterism and laissez faire, Cobden and Bright, the English men of business have generally succeeded in identifying their causes with the fortunes of the nation, in a fashion unequaled by anyone else, except possibly the American. In so doing, in representing themselves as patriots, they wove garments of righteousness which they learned to wear continuously; thus the Briton was set apart from other men, not so much because of his true nature, as by his need to embellish his true nature before the public eye.

The first of the men who pleaded were very simple. Misselden, a member of the Merchant-Adventurers and a negotiator for the East India Company, merely begged for government favors. Thomas Mun, who became governor of the East India Company, produced an impressive defense of that organization in 1621—a "Discourse of Trade from England to the East Indies"—urging the export of bullion to the East as beneficial in the end to the national trade balance; this was the burden also of his "England's Treasure by Foreign Trade." In a pamphlet designed for King James, Sir Walter Raleigh, monopolist and state-merchant, maintained that his own type should be encouraged:

A state-merchant will roundly and effectually bring all the promises to pass, fill your havens with ships, those ships with mariners, your kingdom full of merchants, their houses full of outlandish commodities, and your coffers full of coin . . . and your people shall have just cause to hold in happy memory . . . Your Majesty.

A friend of Raleigh, Gerard Malynes, propounded a Natural Law unquestionably operating toward an English millennium. Far from a success in business himself, he was finally lodged in jail when, as appointee to a government financial post, his scheme to coin brass farthings went awry; but he was undaunted. In his "Canker of England's Commonwealth," issued in 1601, he insisted that his preachings held good even if, as he confessed, he could "hardly maintain my own little family."

A flood of pamphlets from that time on urged a more serious consideration of business on the part of the government. A colleague of Paterson in the Hampstead Water Company maintained that "Laws should be so contrived as never in the least to discourage or check any conception or endeavor of the venturous merchant." And he wanted more business men in high posts, as it was "impossible for noblemen and gentlemen, by short debates . . . ever to arrive at a perfect understanding" of trade. "How can the divines, lawyers, nobles, and great gentry of the kingdom be nice judges . . . between the clashing and tangling interests of so great a mystery as universal trade?"

Defense of monopolies, of one kind or another, called forth eloquence also, and Sir Josiah Child was supreme in that field. Himself the greatest of monopolists, Child boldly shielded his order against all comers and in terms that would to this day meet the exactions of any large utility corporation. Ensuing writers down to the most modern apologists have, in essence, but repeated the arguments of this remarkable man. The charge that his Company was dominated by a few over-rich leaders was refuted: "If it be thought . . . that some few men of the company are too rich and powerful in the committee . . . for the sons of such men were never known to succeed their fathers in the painful fatigue of the company's affairs; but did always settle themselves upon the easier course of life by a revenue in land." Furthermore, the more stock a man had, the keener was his concern for the affairs of the company. To detractors who complained that "the present stock is ingrossed into a few hands, some single adventurers having £16 or £17,000 principal stock in their own names," Child answered:

> The more an adventurer hath in the stock, the more he is engaged to study and promote the good of it, by all possible means within his power. An adventurer that hath the smallest interest may be as just and true to the stock as he that hath the greatest: But I can never believe that a small interest will awaken a man so often in the night, nor keep him so long from sleeping, in the meditation of any business, as a very great and principal concern will do.

Summing up the opposition, Child bluntly condemned all his critics as rank communists:

> The complaint would sound better out of the mouth of a leveller, than a merchant's, living under a free and royal monarchy. And yet to give the maddest of men their due, neither the late English levellers, nor their elder brethren, the people of Rome . . . none of them ever had that excess of indiscretion, as to pretend to stint, much less to level personal estates, which if they could be made even at noon, would be unequal before night.

By many another clever argument, the inner ring of control as well as the whole monopoly was defended by appeals to "national interest" in a "Treatise wherein it is demonstrated that the East India Company is the most National of all Trades, that the Clamours, Aspersions, and Objections made against the present East India Company, are sinister, selfish, or groundless." In 1681 Child was boasting that the Company, by using "great warlike English ships" of 50 guns apiece, was conveying war stores and hence forming an integral part of the defense system of the country.

Other business men and disgruntled shareholders attacked Child's monopolistic thesis by declaring it led to dangerous concentration of wealth: "If all the trade of this Kingdom were carried on by such exclusive joint-stocks as those of the East India and Guinea Companies, this nation might produce half a dozen men of estates equal with most dukes, and all other traders must remain their slaves, their vassals." Sir Josiah was accused of the baldest trickery; his financial jugglery, it was said, "laid the Foundation of an Opulent Family, and initiated the Crowd of Jobbers into that dexterity in tricking and cheating one another, which to this day they are the greatest Proficients in, that this part of the World ever saw."

A sarcastic merchant went so far as to claim that the Company had not discovered new trades, as it boasted, but had lost several; all it had done was to find "a great vent for our manufacture, if the lives of poor Englishmen may be called a manufacture." Instead of benefiting England, the Company had proved a liability; in that hour, the Indian Empire was not even a vision, and it had not yet occurred to a Company member to urge Britons "to carry on your trade, sword in hand," and lay a "sure dominion" overseas. The waste of lives so far seemed useless; in thirty-six years, the Company had vainly lost "several hundred poor Englishmen's lives, which have been sent thither to die like dogs."

Beside the pro and con of monopoly, a project for a bank to print "imaginary money" provoked merchants to public expression. Some were quite sure it was a scheme of the radicals to seize the government: "Another comes and tells ye, that he, or his grandsire . . . have been abroad . . . and in all their peregrinations they never met with banks nor stocks anywhere but only in republics; and if we let them get footing in England, we shall certainly be in danger of a commonwealth." But others were as sure that a bank was a scheme of monarchists to crush democracy: "rich and monied men, we find by experience, are naturally timorous and fearful" and will be a prey to a tyrant king.

One of the most far-sighted writers of the business world, and an advocate of broader schemes, and not merely his own narrow interest, was the Scotchman, William Paterson. Paterson almost alone stopped one unsound paper-money scheme from going through Parliament, he also saw through the Law Bubble in France, and his pamphlet exposing it was publicly burned by infuriated clerks of the English Stock Exchange. One of the earliest of his countrymen to awaken Scotland to her business destiny, Paterson advocated the union of Scotland and England. As a balladist, describing the stimulating effects of Paterson's propaganda on his native land, put it:

> I who know this and see what has been done,
> Admire the steady soul of Paterson;
> It is no common genius can persuade
> A nation bred to war, to think of trade.

The Darien Company formed by Paterson, which was to bring Scotland into the world-stream of trade, collapsed ignominiously, it is true, partly owing to his ignorance of the New World, and partly to the jealousy of the English Parliament which sabotaged the Scottish concern. After the disastrous failure, Paterson issued an eloquent plea for indemnification of the losers in his Company; but around this specific proposal, he wove such a general discussion of economics as to render this pamphlet decidedly noteworthy.

Paterson urged the creation of a "brain trust" to be composed of business men and nobles, which was to meet and plan the economy of the nation, for the benefit of both commerce and agriculture. This "new deal" of 1700 would, as the author was aware, require the best minds: "The qualifications . . . of those who shall compose this Council will be such, that the whole collective wisdom and experience of men in the kingdom, will be but little enough to choose and continue the succession of persons fit for so weighty a management and trust." Alas, yes.

The Council was of course to assist the Darien Company, but it was also to encourage English business in the large: to reform the penal code for debtors; to standardize weights and measures; to appoint consuls abroad for the service of trade; to set low tariffs and maintain a set price level of products by purchasing surpluses with government funds; to improve roads, bridges and harbors, and reduce the interest rate to 3 per cent or less. In short, it was to formulate a grand plan of national economy; so sensible did this appear to the Scotchman, that he could only wonder at the previous obtuseness of the British; surely, he said, it was very odd that people had gone on so long merely muddling through:

It is very strange that some of the many straits and necessities this nation hath been under have not produced some such national care and economy long ere this. It is true such great and unwieldy societies of men, as considerable kingdoms or states . . . seldom ever made any good or fundamental reform but by accident or necessity.

It was time, in 1700, thought Paterson, that there was "stirred up and awakened the very mass of mankind to some such national care and economy as is hereby proposed." And, to push popular thought in this direction, he founded one of the earliest libraries on commerce for the study of State and business relations and the consideration of "management, or influence of government." He also wanted this library to serve for research into the problems of periods of plenty and want— for Paterson had already discovered the "business cycle."

Needless to say, Paterson's work had no direct effect. Instead of calling an economic council, the Government promptly decided to save national credit through the South Sea Bubble plan of a speculative slaving-company, which failed more dreadfully than the Darien concern, and drew the monied classes of England into the maelstrom. Then, as the evils of muddling incompetence became more glaringly evident than ever before, and the revelations of ignorance and corruption in high places had shocked all England, the idea of preventive planning no longer seemed a curious fantasy of a business man. Then there was lifted a poet's cry with a ring as modern as the voice of Paterson. Pope wrote:

> *O impudence of wealth! With all thy store*
> *How darest thou let one worthy man be poor?*

THE IDEA OF INDUSTRY IN ENGLAND

So far, these were the voices of traders. The idea of industry was slower in penetrating the feudal layers of the English mind. But, from time to time, pamphleteers discussed the possibilities of going to work. Unpleasant as it might be, England could not avoid it forever. As one writer in 1675 put it picturesquely, the English had managed to thrive so far without toil, like the hornets which "by their rapine, bring to their nests more honey at once, than the industrious bees can in many times." But when there were no nests to rob, the bee becomes the better model.

Since the bee was not so romantic an insect to the early English mind, in spite of Mandeville's bright presentation of its virtues, the business men of that age were still casting about for some method of making work much less painful than it had been for the grubbing Continentals. And perhaps this long period of theoretical discussion among men of commerce was a decisive element in England's immense modern advance; for, there only, thought about industry preceded its great unfolding. In France, state reason had managed the promotion of manufactures, and the government had provided teachers, and forced them upon the people. England, before going to work, considered the matter from every angle, to see if there were not some way of escaping too arduous an effort—and stumbled upon the Machine.

Over a century before the harnessing of steam to the processes of industry began, the question of invention was occupying the minds of some English merchants. Still full of Elizabethan fantasy, and faith in miracles, they kept hoping for a sublime discovery to rescue them from grim labor. A merchant in the Cromwellian Age, Samuel Lamb, urged attention to inventiveness. This, he said, was responsible for much of the success of the Dutch, besides their honesty and mass-production methods:

> Their true and faithful making their manufactures without deceit ... thriving with the less profit, by selling much greater quantities abroad ... and having quicker returns and greater stocks

than the English . . . giving countenance and encouragement to new designs propounded to them . . . which whets the invention, and occasions new discoveries.

While the Germans were still solemnly burning designs for new devices, and the French were muffled in red tape of officialdom, which would not permit radical and sudden alterations, the English men of business were eagerly combining to offer prizes for all kinds of new appliances, while gentlemen also rewarded suggestions in the agricultural sphere, and the Crown encouraged new methods in navigation. The English patent-system safeguarded inventors. Of course a number of superlatively cracked-brained wizards responded to the invitation, and their devices for perpetual motion and other wonders were floated among the South Sea Bubbles, on the Stock Exchange. But it has been ascertained that most of the epoch-making inventions of the seventeenth and eighteenth centuries were made in answer to such prize-contests. The astounding burst of mechanical genius in England was far from fortuitous: the English were very consciously searching about for a way to escape hard work.

There were, of course, strong aristocratic prejudices to sweep away before even machines could be put to labor. The balladists found Holland, "that scarce deserves the name of land," extremely ridiculous because it honored successful inventor-manufacturers; any bog-dweller, they jeered, could "invent a shovel, and be magistrate." But laughter at the Dutch for their industry began to die down by 1666, when Admiral Tromp sailed right up the Thames under the very noses of the astonished citizens of London. He produced an effect somewhat like that of Perry, two hundred years later, upon the similarly feudal-agrarian island of Japan. The threat of an enemy who was more developed commercially than they, forced the English islanders also to rub their eyes, commence studying, adapting, the methods of the menacing foreigners, trying to ward them off by economic as well as military efforts. As John Evelyn said a few years later, England must recognize Dutch achievements:

We will yet give them their due; they are *gyants* of stature, fierce in beard and countenance, full of goodly towns, strong in *munition*, numerous in shipping; in a word *high* and *mighty-states*, and all this the product of *commerce* and *navigation* . . . Commerce alone . . . to which not only the neighboring parts of Europe contribute, but the *Indies*, and *Antipodes*; so the whole world (vast as it appears to others) seems but a *farm*, scarce another province to them.

And though he was a gentleman, with interests in agriculture, Evelyn thought that Dutch industry should be imitated. Let England shed her aristocratic and religious prejudices against the commercial worker. Let the public forget that "Our Saviour scourged the money-changers out of the temple," and remember instead that "commerce taught us religion." Business men were "a useful race of men" who could "employ hands for regulated salaries" and so increase the national wealth. Rightly regarded, they were the "pillars of all magnificence." And if England would but stoop to spin and weave, thought Evelyn, she would gain another sort of pride, in recompense for her lost aristocratic hauteur—the pride of labor. This was something she had not known, but it was worth having:

> The lillies, which spin not, and are yet so splendidly clad, are not in this respect, so happy as an industrious and prudent man; because they have neither knowledge of their being and perfections.

And he was quite right: scarce a century after John Evelyn had begged England to spin and weave, Bolton and Arkwright appeared to teach her how; steam was arising on the Northern rugged frontier of England by the last quarter of the eighteenth century, and it would not now be long before England, having cast aside her feudal pride, would envelop herself in that mantle of Victorian self-satisfaction which, as Evelyn prophesied, would more than atone for any shattered complacencies. Winning ever more applause from their countrymen and the world, British industrialists of the age of Cobden would then acquire the "sublime sense of their own perfections" that so readily distinguished them from Solomon's lilies.

XIX

BUSINESS FERMENT ON BRITISH FRONTIERS

ALTHOUGH THE AIR was filled with discussion of impending change in France, Germany and southern England, the actual debut of the modern industrialist entrepreneur took place in none of these regions. He came, not in one of Europe's old, long-flourishing cities, center of consumption, experience, and technical skill and revolutionary ideas, but in the raw, bleak, North country of England, at that time one of the most backward parts of the Old World.

The North country had not been touched by the bloom of mediaeval or Renaissance culture, but had remained roadless, almost townless, indeed, as historians call it, "semi-barbaric." Even rural prosperity had passed it by, for in large areas it was too barren for the plough; this part of England, long the poorest and least penetrated by civilization, was inhabited chiefly by scrofulous cottagers, inured to a diet of watery porridge, enlivened only on festive occasions by treacle. The windowless huts of mud and straw generally lacked the luxury of floors and often had "an iron pot as the only furniture." In places there, as also in Scotland, people could sometimes be seen living in primitive dugouts, *underground*.

INDUSTRIALISM LAUNCHED ON THE ENGLISH FRONTIER

Upon this remote frontier which, up to the eighteenth century, had produced nothing of significance, occurred, however, one of the mightiest conceivable revolutions in human life and thought. In breathtaking succession, appeared shrewd inventors and improvers of the Power-Machine and exploiters whose organizing ability created the factory-system; these were followed by social and political crusaders of the first magnitude, Cobden, Bright and Owen, expounding theories of Manchesterism, Darwinism and Socialism, and providing ideological accompaniments for the mechanical revolution.

Why did modern capitalists arise in such a backwoods? Why not in the rich city of London, among the ambitious class of mercers, whose luxury was pictured by Addison and Defoe? Or why not on the Continent where, at the momentous time that the steam-machine was evolving, Voltaire, Mozart and Goethe were living? Certainly there were natural advantages in the North of England in unique combination: coal, iron, waterpower, good wool and a damp climate suitable for spinning, close to harbors ideally situated for transatlantic trade. England had also captured the best sea routes and colonies and was socially more stable than other countries. More thoroughly than her neighbors she had been cleansed of historic relics of the past; more fortunate than they, she had escaped the constant fear of invasion, avoided spending her riches upon land-armies to nourish a race of cavalier-officers for the defense of her soil. But to these numerous reasons belongs another: the spirit of business enterprise loves an open frontier.

Again and again the spirit of enterprise has passed by richer and older regions to settle upon some desolate rim of the world, such as the bleak coast of the Baltic and the dunes and marshes of Holland. It seems to prefer virgin soil to that which has been heavily encumbered by vested interests and prejudices. The civilized parts of Europe, therefore, were perhaps too rich, too skillful, too experienced, by the mid-eighteenth century. Initiative on the Continent there was hampered by overgrown bodies of regulations; jealous gildsmen and torpid monopolists sought to preserve the status quo. Liberty of action could be found only in the grim, rough North country.

It was a lawless country, comparatively speaking. The Lancashire villages were too small to have developed gild regulations; this was discovered, as business men moved up from the better controlled South of England. Shippers, grown weary of London red tape, hailed the delights of tiny fishing ports without an officialdom. Huguenot weavers set up their looms in the countryside, where no gildsmen could bar them from work. And so, long before the fine term laissez faire was imported, men were accustomed to doing as they pleased in Lancashire.

Scant heritage of technical skill, to be sure, was at hand. The highest ability was unquestionably not in England at all, but on the Continent, where marvelous clocks, porcelains and telescopes were then being produced. The most intricate machines, up to the era of steam, were the hand-operated or water-driven contrivances for weaving silk in Italy; their secrets were so well guarded that once, when an Englishman stole plans and fled, he was pursued to England by Italian assassins and murdered. By comparison, the men of the North country were crude, but, as it happened, this was an asset.

Only cheap, rough articles were made in Lancashire, such as black mugs, boot-straps, fustians for yokels and checked shirts for sailors.

But, precisely because these were goods for the masses, they were suitable for the application of modern factory methods. Mass-production could be made to count in these branches, but not in the manufacture of fancy satins and pretty "cherry-derries" or marquetry tables for the rich few. The challenge of the mass market had been ignored by European mercantilist-statesmen, blinded by the theories of the Age of Colbert.

The relatively greater mechanical ingenuity of Europe was used for the adornment or entertainment of the moneyed minority. Thus at Mozart's city, Salzburg, a rivulet was harnessed to make water-power, quite as cleverly as any Englishman could have done it; but the only labor it performed was playing tinkling tunes and animating puppets upon a toy stage, for the diversion of the archbishop's mistresses. So, too, there was sufficient passion for regimentation in Goethe's Germany to have revolutionized factory methods, but it was diverted into military channels and served to standardize grenadiers, not products. The spirit of innovation flamed brightly in Voltaire's France, but circumstances directed it toward social and political, instead of technical, upheaval.

In Lancashire, however, the blue-blooded families were few, and these were relatively unspoiled by contacts with the leisured Southern aristocracy. Instead of sinking into indolence, they frequently continued in activity, unlike noblemen elsewhere who tended by their example to lead the middle class away from commercial pursuits. Little temptation existed in the North of England to cease money-making for a life of enjoyment or intellectual pleasures. There was really not much to think about except money, or, as they called it up there, "t'brass." "Keen on the brass" became their watchword.

In yet another way, the poverty and rudeness of the frontier was an asset to capitalistic development. An unlimited supply of "cheap labor" was present for the new machines. At hand, ready for Lancashire's call when the immediate labor market was exhausted, were thousands of English reduced to beggary by the greed of great lords, who raised "sheep instead of men." For a similar reason, clan chieftains of Scotland were ousting their followers; while, still lower in the scale of living standards, the Irish had been thrust from their furrows by the English conquerors. With this uprooted labor, plus the Machine, it was possible for the business men of Manchester and other cities to undersell the flourishing old cities of Europe, and spread a wide wake of ruin to the Far East, where even the craftsmen of ancient India were unable to compete.

The point is of vital importance, in order to arrive at a just conception of the deeds of the English business entrepreneur. He is often condemned for wrecking a previously established society of happy and aesthetically-productive yokelry and artisans. In a measure, this is true, for there were many regions in Europe where life was definitely more cheerful and beautiful than in the North of England at that time. For instance, in the more prosperous parts of Holland, Denmark, Friesland or Bavaria, in the 1700's, a veritable bloom of peasant culture was to be found; the richer peasants were painting pictures, carving furniture, designing holiday costumes, putting up tile ovens in big, gaily-painted houses which were much more comfortable than the chill castles of English lords. Among such a population, even if a Watt or an Ark-wright had arisen, he could hardly have found a proletariat sufficiently wretched for his purposes; these folk would not willingly have herded into filthy towns, toiling sixteen and eighteen hours a day for four-pence, sleeping in damp cellars without beds or even bedding. The English coolie-laborers had never known much better, and that was why the horrors of the early industrial revolution were not so horrible to them.

Certainly it cannot be maintained that the life of all Europe, much less of Asia, was an idyllic dream on the eve of the modern mechanical era. Huge numbers of the French and German serfs lived in depths of wretchedness, but they were still soil-bound, and hungry for land. They were not a houseless and homeless multitude, driven from the fields, like the English, Scotch and Irish wanderers. One may say, there-fore, that the capitalist entrepreneur did destroy some local societies of remarkable charm in Europe; moreover, he underbid Indian artisans, and thus wrecked the wonderful crafts of India, which had excited the admiration of Europe since Roman days. By exploiting cheap labor and technical devices, Lancashire did upset the balance of the older worlds, precisely as nowadays China and Japan threaten to underbid and under-mine the living standards of the Occident. Japan, with a still keener application of technique and by virtue of yet more reduced living standards, has endangered today the economic foundations of Lanca-shire, and has turned back the weapons of Westerners upon the West.

In the land of its birth, nevertheless, the Machine did not appear as a hideous apparition in the midst of joy and plenty. In Lancashire there had never been a fat and jolly farmer-folk, attired in elaborate gar-ments, dwelling in snug, stout homes. No more culture existed in the neighborhood of Manchester to be destroyed than there was around the later Pittsburgh or Magnitogorsk. The usual dictum must be reversed; it is more proper to say the Machine arose *because* Lancashire was wretched, *because* the people were callous to suffering and indifferent to aims beyond profit. The gospels of bustle and laissez faire, and the avid pursuit of gain, represented in Lancashire no sudden change of mind and heart, occasioned by a fortuitous invention. The North of England had never erected cathedrals to another God before it turned to worship the Machine.

FATHERS OF THE MACHINE

The men who lived on this frontier had laissez faire in their blood quite as much as the American pioneers. It was natural to them to do as they pleased. Other virtues of the frontiersmen were theirs by inheritance; ingenuity, hustle, shrewdness, hardness.

The average well-to-do merchant of Manchester and its environs was in fact simpler than the richest of the corresponding type in the overseas colonies of America. Plain little Manchester in the 1770's could not be compared with elegant Boston in the same period; her marketplace, adorned solely with a pillory and town pump, had nothing so dazzling as Faneuil Hall. Moreover, such a prosperous wool merchant of Manchester as Titus Hibbert was quite unpretentious: he did not keep coaches and give balls, like the wealthy privateers and real-estate speculators of New York and Philadelphia. He entertained with home-made cider, whereas the colonial Americans often had the best French wines.

For the most part, the Northern Englishmen lived as rudely as their apprentices. They rose at dawn and rode horseback over the trails of the English wilderness. Energy and bustle marked them off from the more indolent brethren of the South of England. Indeed, a Southerner remarked of Birmingham: "I was much surprised at the place, but more at the people. They were species I had never seen. . . . I had been among dreamers, but now I saw men awake: their very step along the streets showed alacrity."

These spry, gold-hungry "men on the make" were destined to exploit the new devices and, eventually, to dominate for a time the markets of the world. The Lancashire folk were not passively waiting until some genius loomed on their horizon with an invention. No indeed, they were out looking for new methods, new ways to gather in "t'brass." They were revolutionizing the routine of business even before the Machine came.

By the first part of the eighteenth century, they had laid the groundwork of industrial capitalism in the so-called "putting-out system." That is, they provided the capital and raw material, and the cottagers did the work. As they took this step forward in production, they pulled up distribution as well: and went upon the highroad as the first modern traveling salesmen. In the 1740's, a good two decades before the era of great invention could be called open, these Manchester "chapmen," or "Manchester men," began riding about England with sample cases.

An outcry against Manchester then arose, although the Machine had not arrived as yet. For the chapmen were disrupting the old system of periodical fairs. They cheapened prices to the consumer, but threw out of work a multitude of carters, handlers, middlemen. Rage and distress grew; Manchester chapmen were attacked for their unnatural thirst for profit and blind indifference to the commonweal. And thus, even before they had modern mechanisms in their power, they were objects of opprobrium to conservatives, and were regarded as "enemies of established society."

About the same time, efforts toward standardization appeared. One of the milestones on the road to modern factory-management was set by Josiah Wedgwood, of Staffordshire, who, eager as he was for chemical and mechanical improvements, owed his fortune even more to his interest in organization. He was a self-made man in the approved Samuel Smiles manner, who left the humble potter's bench to become owner of a factory called "Etruria." He continued to act as his own superintendent, clerk, warehouseman, laboratory-head and maker of models. Early perceiving that "the want of system, the dirt and muddle" of his fellows was a serious drawback, he introduced absolute exactness and conformity to pattern. His plates could be piled. His lids fitted. Nothing enraged him so much as to find deviations from a model. As he stumped about on his wooden leg, looking for mistakes, he chalked on any unlucky workman's bench: "This won't do for Jos. Wedgwood."

Ingenious and aggressive, Wedgwood was not daunted by the lack of designers in this raw North country. He set about "adapting" the designs of Greeks and Romans. In this manner, he was spared the cost of original patterns and could undersell the Dutch, who were still creating fresh fancies; the entrepreneurs of Delft, even by starving their artists, could not compete with wares by Wedgwood, adorned by scenes filched from the past. This innovation was very helpful to the budding English industry, for it enabled manufacturers to exploit museums and exhume dead "periods." Desire for cheap patterns thus led to the horror of Victorian eclecticism.

As the first manufacturer to provide England with a first-class article of wide exportability—in addition to woolen cloth—Wedgwood became famous and admired. After his first half-million pounds, he got a knighthood and had his picture painted by another parvenu knight, Sir Joshua Reynolds, a favorite of upper middle class sitters because he lent a gentlemanly touch to portraits of mercers, brewers and their wives.

In many ways, Wedgwood illustrated the best quality in early Staffordshire, its lively curiosity. His activity was constant in many fields. He corresponded with artists and archaeologists, read Rousseau, staunchly defended American independence and opposed slavery. Such awareness was quite general in the North country, as it was in pioneer America; the word "gumption" is as good Manchester-ese as it is Yankee. Long before the power-machine era, gumption set the Lancashire men to studying chemistry in order to improve dyes. They imported Dutch craftsmen in the effort to capture the tape market from Holland. Their spare shillings went for lectures on phrenology and electricity, and to support wandering cranks who proposed to establish perpetual motion "from the joint of gravity and lateral ethereal motion." And many of them, like Titus Hibbert, were forced, before the end of their lives, to flee from the results of their own curiosity: gasping and choking, they had to move out of Manchester to escape the acrid fumes from their cranky protégés' factories.

The first two men who may be styled the "godfathers" of the industrial revolution were sufficiently wealthy to indulge their curiosity, at considerable expense. It may seem odd that "the first great Manchester man" was a duke. But in the North dukes were often business men, whereas in the South of England, business men aped dukes. There was little to distinguish the Duke of Bridgewater from a commoner. He had the boundless optimism and the hustle of the frontier. Stories are told of his ignorance in aesthetic matters which might still pass current in Hollywood—the farthest frontier today. It is said, for instance, that his Grace first came into contact with Art in the home of the Duke of Sutherland. Struck by a Van Dyck portrait, Bridgewater banged the table with his fist and cried, "You must take me to that d—d fellow tomorrow!" And forthwith he started the first big art collection in the North country.

Bridgewater's zeal for change led him to invest £170,000 of his own fortune in revolutionary improvements in mining, and in connecting his mines with Manchester by canal, a project carried out under his own supervision and pushed through by his indomitable energy. It ended in cutting the cost of coal in half and assuring that city's industrial future. In his mines, however, as the shafts were sunk more deeply, new problems in pumping and ventilation were encountered. These were met by experimentation in mechanical devices. The quaint and cumbersome steam-pump of the inventor, James Watt, was at length installed by the Duke, and the Industrial Revolution had begun.

This particular pump was made possible through the patronage of another rich capitalist, Matthew Boulton, who, like Bridgewater, might have retired upon a comfortable income; the son of a Birmingham "toy-maker," he might have spent his days hunting foxes, but, instead, chose to stay in business. Wishing to wipe out Birmingham's bad reputation for shoddy, Boulton built the large Soho works about 1759, a model factory to produce the best kinds of ornamental metal-wares. Full of curiosity and thirst for change and improvement, Boulton busily inquired into scientific lore and political economy, studied antique models for his bronzes, corresponded with the astronomer Herschel and the chemist Priestley. A patriarchal type of oldfashioned business man, Boulton did things in a grand manner, "more like a sovereign than a private manufacturer." At family festivals, his workmen came in procession, headed by a band, to dine on whole roasted oxen; he himself, tall, handsome, fastidious, prided himself upon keeping to the powdered wig long after others abandoned it. Like the later mechanical wizards, Ford and Krupp, this early patron of the steam-machine, Boulton, was as conservative in his habits as he was revolutionary in his work, and delighted in retaining details of the handicraft quaintness, even though he destroyed the basis of that older society.

Boulton and Wedgwood, the two manufacturers who stood at the threshold of the new age, took a wide interest in aesthetics and science because their type of businesses demanded both. They were inclined to liberalism, providing libraries and benefits for their workmen, who were skilled adult artisans. And they kept up a pretty rivalry which was more chivalric than the bulldog competition of a later age. Thus, when Boulton thought of invading pottery-making, Wedgwood wrote to a friend, in 1768:

> If Etruria cannot stand its ground, but must give way to Soho, and fall before her, let us not sell the victory too cheap, but maintain our ground like men, and endeavor, even in defeat, to share the laurels with our conqueror. It doubles my courage to have the first manufacturer in England to encounter with. The match likes me well. I like the man, I like his spirit.

Certain feudalistic traits thus clung to these godfathers of the Machine, Bridgewater, Boulton and Wedgwood. But soon a new crop of men arose, self-made entrepreneurs, who spoke a different language, and represented another kind of life. The chief of these was Richard Arkwright, that "bag-cheeked, pot-bellied" "barber-knight," who so excited the derision of Carlyle and the wonder of Samuel Smiles.

Arkwright began as peddler of women's hair to make wigs. When wigs were going out of style, he turned to spinning-machinery and, with the aid of a liquor-merchant as patron, Mr. Smalley, invented the spinning-throstle; perhaps, as alleged, he stole it. Year by year he enlarged his patents and built mills to exploit them. Finally, like Wedgwood, he too received the seal of social success, being made a knight by George III. For his bearings he chose a bee, *volant*, and for his crest an eagle soaring with a sprig of the cotton-plant. He commenced building a castle and entered local politics; though never so acceptable to the gentry as the more literate Wedgwood, he did enjoy some triumphs, such as the one described in the Manchester *Mercury* of March 27, 1787:

> On Sunday last, Sir Richard Arkwright, Knight, High Sheriff of the County, arrived at Derby . . . his javelin men . . . dressed in the richest liveries ever seen there on such an occasion . . . all rode black horses. . . . The trumpeters were . . . elegantly dressed in scarlet and gold. The High Sheriff's coach was very elegant and fashionable, with . . . rich decorations, designs, and arms. We must not forget to inform our readers that Sir Richard during the whole of the Assize provided a plentiful table, with the choicest wines, etc. for such gentlemen as pleased to partake of the noble banquet.

But Sir Richard was about the only inventor who was canny enough to exploit his own devices, if indeed they were his own. The other successful business men usually seized upon the designs of others. Lancashire and the counties round became populated with manufacturers who were blossoming into knights and mayors and erecting "elegant mansions" set "amid pleasure-grounds." But they were, in character and activities, far from the leisurely and seigneurial "Princely" Boulton. They followed the methods of Arkwright instead, and employed pauper infants, rather than skilled adult artisans.

Arkwright had discovered that the adults around Lancashire were generally clumsy and unacquainted with mechanical processes, like the Russian mujiks who represented another such problem to capitalism. They rebelled at the monotony of the factory and could not "conform to the regular celerity of the machine," as Arkwright complained. It was to take generations of effort to make engineers and good laborers out of Englishmen, and in the meantime Arkwright solved his problem by taking on very young children, "their small fingers being more active." His example was followed immediately by other factory-owners. Machine-industry was hailed by statesmen because it gave employment to babes.

The signs of a revolution were soon observable far and wide. In 1792, an indignant country gentleman from the South, Sir John Byng, was touring in the North country. As he leaned from his coach-window, he was annoyed by the changes in the familiar landscape: "Why, here now, is a great flaring Mill," he cried. "With the bell ringing, and the clamour of the Mill, all the Vale is disturb'd." What would become of gentlemanly sightseers, if these "vicious, unwholesome Trades" prospered further? "Sir Richard Arkwright may have introduced Much Wealth into his Family, and into his Country, but, as a Tourist, I execrate his Schemes, which having crept into every Pastoral Vale, have destroy'd the course, and Beauty of Nature." At Manchester, his ire could not be contained. "Oh! What a dog's hole is Manchester!" he cried, beholding only "gloom and dirt. . . . Wander'd about Town till Dinner Time, without seeing anything that I should ever wish to see again."

But scold as squires might, no one could now undo the work of the business duke, Bridgewater, and the barber-knight, Arkwright. The new industrialism had taken root and begun to grow, and the tempo of its unfolding was amazing, was in fact what we are accustomed to regard as American.

BRITISH FRONTIERSMEN SYMPATHIZE WITH AMERICAN FRONTIERSMEN

Near the middle of the eighteenth century, when North-country men were preparing to upset the old balance of business powers at home, Great Britain had another frontier where troubles were brewing. That frontier lay in the thirteen English colonies on the American seaboard. Although most of the emigrants to the colonies had gone from the South country, they soon developed, especially in New England, many characteristics that seemed like those of the hustlers in the North country—the new business frontier of Britain. Indeed the likeness of the Lancashire men to the "Yankee" has been too striking to pass unnoticed. They both speak a variety of English that is sharp and nasal in twang. Both "reckon" and utter dry witticisms in a funereal tone. Those who read such novels as "Harvest in the North" greet as familiar types the domineering, capable woman, the rich business man with sentimental heart and tied tongue, or the traveling salesman with his flashy clothes and unquenchable humor. Like Lancashire men, the Yankee and his rivals in other parts of America have been "plain fellows," irked by cultural poses and scornful of idleness and leisure.

Anecdotes of successful money-makers in both countries betray a decided similarity of temperament. In Manchester, one story is preserved with particular affection, concerning John Reid, a well-favored man, to whom a friend one day admiringly remarked, in a broad Lancashire dialect, "Ah, thou art a pratty lad!" To which Reid drolly replied, "Ah, my lad, thou hast the prattier pocket!" This is on the same level with the toothless jests compiled in the American Encyclopedia of Commercial and Business Anecdotes in the same period. It belongs with the story of the Yankee, Budgett, who heard a man wish for more money and snappishly said, "Do you? I do not. But if I did wish for more, I should get it." Or the tale of the New England merchant who, when asked how much money would content him answered, "A little more."

On their own part, the Lancashire men were not slow to recognize an essential kinship with the hustlers in the New World frontier. During the American Revolution, nowhere were more eager defenders of the colonial rebels than merchants of the North country such as Hibbert and Wedgwood, who saw their own cause fought overseas, in a way— since North-country districts were then about as little represented in the English Parliament as were the Americans. Such influence as they had was obtained through lobbying. In the Civil War also, when Northern manufacturers of America were having their struggle with the planters of the South, Lancashire men continued to sympathize with their cousins in the North, who had obtained the full manhood suffrage for which they were themselves still striving.

Liverpool formed an exception to rules in the American Civil War, for that old center of slave-dealing and privateering recovered its youth for a time in outfitting blockade-runners who supplied the South with luxuries and munitions at tremendous profits. But Manchester produced at least one manufacturer, John Bright, the cotton-spinner, and the famous associate of Cobden, who did perhaps more than any other single man to keep the sympathy of England on the Northern side. He felt the call of class to class and was as ready to oppose Virginia gentlemen as he had been to campaign against the lords of Devonshire. To complicate the situation in England, moreover, lay the struggle over grain; Bright wanted the cheap grain produced by the Union side, to lower the costs of British industry. While the North-country men stood almost solidly for the cause of the American Union, the landed aristocracy of Great Britain and the London financiers, in the main, wanted to see the American Republic broken to pieces.

In this way, the ties of interest bound the two countries in a complex fashion, and prevented a too-simple rivalry between the two industrial frontiers, in the Old and New Worlds. In fact, Lancashire men not only saw their own social and political struggles duplicated overseas, but felt that the Yankees would some day inherit their industrial crown. On the broad American continent, and not in narrow England, the full possibilities of the Machine would ultimately be unfolded. Robert Owen, for example, the cotton-spinner and reformer long associated with Manchester, went over to America to set up his utopia, which, though ill-fated, gave as remarkable an impetus to the American trade-union movement as Owen gave to that of his own land. So, too, Richard Cobden viewed with the utmost enthusiasm the prospects of industrialism in America. Reaching the Mississippi Valley in 1835, he predicted a destiny for American business more splendid than that of his own region:

> Here one day will be the head-quarters of agriculture and manufacturing industry; here will one day centre the civilization, the wealth, the power of the entire world.

Unlike Dickens, admirer of country squires, the English business man, Cobden, was immediately attracted to Americans:

> I find myself in love with their intelligence, their sincerity, and decorous self-respect . . . The very genius of activity . . . They have not, 'tis true, the force of Englishmen in personal weight or strength, but they have compensated for this deficiency by quickening the momentum of their enterprises. All is in favor of celerity of action and the saving of time. Speed, speed, speed, is the motto.

Cobden pictured the Americans as supreme utilitarians, going a step further than Lancashire men, by dispensing with sleep and food, while their machines quickened, and so performed "miracles 'till panting time toils after them in vain." Encouraged by the sight of America, where individualism seemed more classically exemplified in many respects than in Britain, Cobden went home refreshed, to formulate his philosophy of rugged individualism for campaign purposes in England.

All along, therefore, the two frontiers developed together, and were regarded in much the same light by English of aristocratic views. In both Northern regions, the Power-Machine could be watched at work, least trammeled by governmental authority or previous prejudices; both showed a disregard for the tastes of landlords and squires. Those who hated the one, could not but loathe the other. Thus Dickens and Mrs. Trollope, for instance, feared the new industrialism almost equally at home and in the United States. Touring in America, such critics of rising capitalism found support for their case against the industrialists of England. Conversely, visitors such as Harriet Martineau, daughter of a utilitarian manufacturer, of Huguenot origin, who sympathized with the aims of English business men, regarded the uncouth towns of the American pioneers with a more indulgent eye. Impressions gathered in the United States were employed on either side of the great battle between agrarian and mercantile classes in England.

America served England as an example, dreadful or inspiring. Her development heartened the English manufacturers in their fight against the gentry over political representation and legislation. In return, they paid Americans back in many commodities: out of the grim North of England came models for American machines and factories, and a huge stock of ideas as well: individualism, business morality, utilitarianism, political economy, Manchesterism—methods and Methodism. And that is not all, for they likewise exhibited to Americans the trade-union movement as well as business enterprise.

But the Americans were slower to recognize any ties with Lancashire. One rare exception was Nelson B. Aldrich, the big business man of Rhode Island, who was a politician of stature as well as a magnate in industry; in the American Senate, Aldrich stood for the Northeastern manufacturing groups against the South and West, and their embattled farmers. He knew very well how nearly this combat resembled the strife of North and South in England, Manchester and London. And so he frankly patterned his life upon that of the great cotton-spinner politician of England, Robert Peel.

Most Americans, however, sentimental pilgrims going abroad for purposes of ancestor-worship, flocked to the pleasanter Downs and cathedral towns of South England, so long the seats of the inveterate enemies of industrialism. Less often did they make their way up North, to that dark region of soot and fog, home of modern manufacturing capitalism, which America was to imitate, after she fought a Revolution to free herself from the colonial ban upon her industries.

THE SOUTHERN ENGLISH PUT PRESSURE ON THE AMERICAN FRONTIER

In time North-country Englishmen were to march on London, frighten Tories into giving their towns representation in the House of Commons, force Parliament to give the vote to factory workers, and upset both the Whigs and Tories. But before the frontiersmen from Birmingham, Leeds, Bradford, Burslem, and Manchester were ready for their fray, indeed just as they were getting well started, American frontiersmen in business developed a quarrel with the old merchants and landed gentry who controlled the British government and headed in the direction of revolution, considerably against their will.

Although this dispute had many sides, there is scarcely any question that business men were the immediate instigators of it, as A. M. Schlesinger conclusively shows in his "Colonial Merchants and the American Revolution." By 1763 "overproduction" was a problem in England, even before steam had become a serious factor; that is, British business men and shareholders were looking for bigger outlets for goods and capital. As in France, so in England, business men were turning out more goods than consumers could buy, at least under the existing social arrangements. Pressure of production was straining the framework of society. In France business strove for an extension of inner markets by relaxing laws and regulations which reared domestic trade barriers. But Britain had little to expect from such an inner expansion, for her gilds and internal trade regulations were less hampering than corresponding institutions and measures across the Channel.

On the eve of the business revolution in the English North country, before the power-machine had gathered momentum, all countries in Western Europe were threatened by the stresses and strains of internal business. With the great American frontier available, it was natural for British business men to indulge in fond speculations about the possibilities overseas; they fancied that the American Colonies could be forced to remain agrarian, simple producers of onions, tobacco, beef and turpentine, which, by some magic of transfer, could be exchanged abroad for ever-increasing quantities of British-made manufactured articles. This dream was not an evidence of a singularly blind or ruthless mentality; indeed it was almost precisely like that of American consuls from the McKinley to the Hoover Age, who solemnly calculated the surpluses to be unloaded upon Latin America or the Far East, if every coolie or peon could be persuaded to buy a telephone, a four-door sedan or an extra shirt—but did not consider the question of how this was all to be paid for. In either case, the difficulties of matching products of the soil against those of refined industry, and effecting an exchange favorable to both, were unseen, or, if considered, they were left for the future to solve.

America, in the formula of Pitt, was not to be allowed to make a nail or a yard of cloth for sale abroad. She was to be compelled to remain a perpetual purchaser of British products. This was not merely a policy formed by the Crown; indeed it was often forced through by lobbying business interests against the better judgment of the gentlemen on the government's Board of Trade. Whenever they felt the pinch of hard times, British hat-makers, ship-builders, iron and wool men, rushed to petition the Board, demanding an outlet in the Colonies and insisting that budding industries overseas must be crushed before competition began. But manufacturers were as yet not dominant in England; their squeezing of the Colonies was only one of many pressures put upon the Americans. Wool-growing lords were as interested as wool-manufacturers in restraining the Colonists. Merchants, powerful in the Parliament, had an even larger interest in holding the sea-trade of Asia and Europe with the Colonies; when the East India Company dumped tea upon the markets cheaply, it was not an injury to American consumers at all, but to American development in trade and shipping. Viewing Boston and Salem, as they advanced in seamanship, with a jealous eye, Sir Josiah Child, master of the East India Company, declared that Colony to be "the most prejudicial plantation to this kingdom." But tea was not the only commodity dumped upon the Americans. There was also human freight to be disposed of.

Ever since England had wrested the slave-trade from Spain and France and become the world's leading purveyor of Negroes, she was frantically searching for new markets. She beat down Virginian resistance to slave-importation and that of South Carolina as well. In the latter Colony, in 1734 and again in 1760, the Governor, Council and Commons of Charleston strove desperately to halt "the greedy British merchants seeking to defeat the province's efforts to check slave-importation." But the slave-dealers had joined forces with the French money-lenders of that city in floating a grand speculative orgy in land and slaves: land warrants were issued, giving each settler fifty acres for every slave, and the slaves were to be supplied on credit. The flood of Negroes—5,000 in a few months of one year—meant the pushing out of white settlers; old frontiersmen were dispossessed by real-estate speculators. Thus one part of British business was really defeating the other: for the slave-dealers, by forcing slave-labor upon the South, made tobacco cheaper, and hence it could buy less and less of the products of European shops and factories.

At the same time, the Americans were being exploited by the British sugar-planting interests. They were ground between the upper and nether millstones of British business and British agriculture—the ten thousand lords and merchants who governed England—and it was this which rendered their situation serious. The big planters of the West Indies were agrarian gentlemen who had an even greater influence with the Government than merchants, and held seventy-four seats in Parliament when the hated Molasses Act was passed which compelled the Americans to buy that necessary ingredient for their rum exclusively from British island possessions. As these did not produce nearly enough molasses to keep American distilleries running, the Colonists were compelled either to surrender or to smuggle from French and Spanish islands.

This combination of forces pressing upon them drove Americans into risky and speculative ventures in the desperate effort to find something salable abroad. Since they were forbidden to manufacture almost everything, their energies were diverted into money-lending, land-exploitation, fur-dealing, smuggling and privateering which sometimes verged on piracy. And that in turn brought on fresh troubles: for instance, the fur-traffic, though it yielded profits up to one hundred percent, involved continual warfare. The various fur-dealers were jealous of one another, and it was said that Virginians armed the Indians against South Carolinians and vice versa; all attempts to rationalize the business, like that of Thomas Welch, the trader who dreamed of a vast forest-empire with a center near what is now Muscle Shoals, were shattered by such rivalries. Moreover, as the business was conducted, credit was extended to the savages, who periodically arose to balance their books by murder. Business men were not at all eager to exterminate the Indians, for they needed them badly as animal-catchers; they intended only to put down these strikes of redskin-labor, so to speak. But this policy meant continual harassing forays; the traders had to call in British troops, and soon there were more war-debts than ever to pay, and so still more furs had to be obtained to pay them, and the vicious circle started again.

Paper-money might have broken the circle at least temporarily; an efficient banking and credit-system, established in the Colonies as it had already been done in Britain, might have aided the development of the frontier. But American merchants were quite as eager as British to prevent payment in "imaginary money." Rich traders of Boston, like Hutchinson, stood firmly against the cry of farmers and small mechanics for land-banks and inflation; they rejoiced when England extended the Bubble Act to cover the Colonies, and so shut the small banks which were starting up. The father of Sam Adams, the Boston patriot, was almost ruined by the sudden closure of his bank. Moreover, American merchants had supplied the armies which fought in the various colonial wars of Britain; they were quite as determined to be paid in specie as any British army-purveyors. Thomas Hancock, uncle of the patriot, John, had amassed one of the greatest fortunes of New England largely through selling food to British troops—what was left over he swept up and sold to France for convicts. He did not want recompense in paper, nor did men like him in Charleston, after the Yemmassee War was concluded.

In Charleston, the planters pushed through a bill to issue £40,000 of paper money to pay the Indian War debts in the 1720's; there was a furious tussle, and twenty-eight business men who protested against this inflation were put into jail for contempt. Their friends, the British purveyors and merchants, lobbied more effectively in London and succeeded in stopping the measure. But the Colony was then on the verge of dissolution, with rioting and uproar, and at last the Crown stepped in and decided in favor of paper. It felt that to retire the issue would ruin nineteen-twentieths of the people and would actually enrich only a score or two of the biggest merchants.

Thus it would be entirely false to assume that there was a "united front" of British capital against American business. Both were in fact interlocked, and that is why the Rebellion was such a long time a-brewing. European capital was poured into American lands; Huguenot money-lenders of Charleston cooperated with British slave-traders; Norfolk shippers, who were mostly Scotch, were connected with Glasgow firms. Some Englishmen took a lively concern in smuggling as well. Old letters of a Rhode Island family show a Bristol merchant, Henry Cruger, expressing his entire sympathies with the Americans in 1767; he was aware of his correspondents' smuggling—"I do not much like it, not from Conscientious Scruples, but fear . . ."—but he understood that the Colonists must have some means to pay men like himself—"If I am not paid how can I pay?" And indeed many British business men were as angry as Americans against "Plantocracy's" Molasses Act. Moreover, a number of Manchester men, who, as budding capitalists, might be expected to favor oppression particularly, were in reality the warmest supporters of the Rebels—they were not represented in Parliament any more than the Colonials, and were as filled with resentment as Bostonians.

On the other hand, it must not be imagined that Americans were really thirsting at that moment for a chance to start manufactures. Black labor was inefficient and white labor was rare and dear; the idea of trying to compete on these terms with Britain made men like Otis of Boston laugh aloud. Almost the only revolutionary leader who vociferously demanded this inalienable right was Sam Adams, the homespun-clad Gandhi of the home rule resistance, the friend of brawny longshoremen and foe of respectable business men, who had failed dismally in every commercial venture and could not even make beer.

The American Revolution, accordingly, falls into no very simple scheme. It is an unhappily common error to suppose that an "economic explanation" must necessarily be simpler than a psychological one, but in fact the ascertaining of "interests" in the minds of a distant day, and their grouping, is very difficult. In that period, when business men were not specialized, they were apt to have many and often contradictory lines of enterprise. Only in a most general way, therefore, may the economic conflicts behind the American Revolution be summed up; it was not a war "caused" by British business men alone, or "started" by angry American traders alone. It was not a revolt of would-be manufacturers. But it was indirectly a product of the mental unrest and the industrial and commercial pressure of pre-Machine Europe. The mutterings of the coming storm had been growing louder on the Continent for several decades, when this first clap of thunder came on the rim of the civilized world—on the British frontier in America.

XX

THE AMERICAN REVOLUTION—BLAZING
A WAY FOR THE MANUFACTURER

THE BELOVED PHRASE, "business pioneer," is misleading as a special characterization of the American, in so far as it tends to suggest unusual endurance of physical hardship and danger. To make this distinction is to ignore contemporary developments in Europe. In the Colonial epoch, while Manchester chapmen were struggling with their sample-cases over roadless mire and inventors of the North were bending over their grimy machines, the ease-loving merchants of the American Colonies, in the principal ports, were not under the necessity of stooping to labors so distressful. Indeed, as early as 1663, a British merchant who voyaged overseas, John Josselyn, was awed and even disgruntled by his visit to Boston. "Some of their Merchants are damnable rich," he wrote, and "inexplicably covetous and proud."

Admiring the "fair buildings" of masonry, "joyning one to the other as in London," along streets paved with cobble-stones, Josselyn was especially impressed by one erected by "Mr. Gibs, a merchant, being a stately edifice, which it is thought will stand him a little less than £3,000 before it be fully finished." Considering the purchasing power of money in the seventeenth century, Mr. Gibs' home would be valued at about £30,000, or $150,000 today. Nor was he alone in his grandeur; the rich Edward Breck of the same period had even a bath-tub among his numerous possessions. A score of silversmiths, who of course also engaged in money-lending, were active in Boston by 1680, including John Hull, whose wealth was proverbial. Ministers' sons were eagerly studying trade, said a Dutch traveler, and former Puritanism was already waning before the advance of commerce: "As to truth and true godliness, you must not expect more of them than of others." A hundred years later, on the eve of the Revolution, the coast was strewn with centers of riches and fashion. North as well as South, slaves were common in households and the display of coaches and balls was so lavish as to offend backwoodsmen whenever they came to town. The Hugers and Manigaults of Charleston, the Jays and Philipses of New York, or "King" Derby of Salem, had passed beyond manual toil. Gentlemen of much leisure, correctly periwigged, brightly buckled and buttoned—even attired in crimson velvet with diamonds, like Hancock—their greatest tests of endurance were lengthy banquets of turkey and meringue, capped by interminable toasts in the best Madeira. So far was John Hancock of Boston from riding horseback, like a Manchester man, that he not only had a coach furnished with plate glass and a coat of arms, but was frequently too much crippled with gout to enter it.

On the whole, therefore, the American business man has suffered relatively little, compared to the militant traders of the Old World, the Dandolos, Castorps or Stroganovs, who carved out trade-empires with the sword, struggling savagely over every route and parcel of primeval wilderness. Even in Colonial times, the American could win vast tracts of land with a stroke of the pen in an Eastern office, as Frederick Philipse, the Dutch merchant of New York, took 205,000 acres from the Indians by altering a phrase in a contract. Nor did they have to defend their acquisitions; notoriously unable to hold their fur trade by their own efforts, Americans called upon the professional soldiers of Britain to put down the Indians, whenever these animal-catching laborers of the forests rose to wipe out indebtedness by murder.

If this was true of the earlier stages, it remained so as American business developed later. Of course, examples could be piled up of men who went through battle, like Asa Peabody and William Grey, or saw deck service, like Girard and Handasyd Perkins; or, as engineer-promoters, pushed railroads through wastes and forest-jungles. But the fact remains that the major business men, with few exceptions, were born in the long-settled East where they faced no hardships more excruciating than rising at dawn to sweep out the store. The dominating masters of business, to whom the word pioneer is applied, remained largely remote from personal threat: the greatest shipper of them all was "Commodore" Vanderbilt, whose seafaring was mainly confined to ferryboats; the supreme fortunes in war were made by men in the rear, like Armour and Du Pont; the chief railroaders, like Gould and Hill, followed tracks only from a private car; the richest mining claims were bought by others from the pick-and-shovel men, and, after the Gold Rush, California belonged to the "Big Four," three grocers and a peddler, who had not wielded tools but sold them to the miners, and supplied peaches at $96.00 a tin to the gay sisterhood of the Barbary Coast.

Yet, when all this is discounted, there is a quality about the American business man which the word "pioneer" endeavors to express. It is compounded of industrial simplicity and readiness to take speculative risks. Until very recently, he has been a perpetual beginner, easily dropping one thing and taking up another, finding more romance as well as riches in roaming forward to the frontiers of business than in remaining behind, in the ruts of a complex industry, tediously perfecting the manufacture of, say, optical instruments. He has left such refinements and taxing routine to others, while he pressed on, plunging and scheming, jockeying with controls and powers, attempting audacious corners, engulfing thousands of miles of track, millions of acres, billions of gallons of oil, with an appetite as herculean as that of Paul Bunyan for flapjacks.

From 1700 to nearly 1900, the American managed to avoid the necessity of thorough research and painful application to the more difficult and delicate branches of industry. He made more money in the mass-production of simple articles, or in combination and speculation. But that, at the same time, meant far more deadly risks, not physical, but financial, for himself or his "investors." In the wild combat of American individualistic society, less restrained by regulations than in older regions, he had to develop an "Indian-face," which became the admiration of Europeans, as he braved a swifter rise or fall of fortune than other men, and a more merciless rivalry. This has kept the American essentially closer to the Elizabethan, or "natural man." He has been a hulking anachronism in an otherwise sobered bourgeois world. This character, however, was not due merely to the crudities of the frontier, but also to the original cultural lag of the Colonial epoch; in the seventeenth and eighteenth centuries, when Europeans were learning how to manufacture, the Americans remained largely barred from such enterprise. They were forced into speculative channels, compelled to engage in such risky, not to say violent, trades as that in fur or rum. And this, in turn, made Revolution—the supreme risk—easier for them to face.

THE COLONIAL PANORAMA OF PORTS

Retarded in development in the early period, kept back to a more primitive stage of methods, the American business man began as a gambler in commodities, instead of a producer of goods tamed to toil. Restlessly casting about for some way to make money without making anything, he grew accustomed to queer ventures and odd "notions." A typical product of this milieu was the roaming, ingenious Yankee trader, who did what no one else would think of doing, selling warming pans to the West Indies to ladle molasses, or carrying cargoes of ice all around the Horn to Calcutta to cool fevered Maharajahs, or, like Barnum, piling up money out of publicity for a thing which did not exist or even have a name, the famous "Zip-What-Is-It." Equally typical was the great speculator, New York style, who learned how to inveigle European capital into often somewhat shadowy schemes of "development," or the Huguenot financier of the South, who held the surrounding planters in his relentless grip.

In the American towns, some of the best business talents, Huguenot, Quaker, Scotch, Dutch, were to be found. Each of these groups, thwarted in the manufacturing field, found some other outlet according to native bent. The French naturally turned to fur and mortgages, the Dutch to investment in land and cows, the Quakers and Scotch to smuggling and privateering. And, in time, all along the coast from Charleston to Salem and Newport, there was presented a spectacle of commercial ports, widely various in cultural and racial aspects, but akin in the fact that their business energies were diverted into some non-manufacturing field.

At New York, the first permanent settlers were Huguenots, and as late as 1716 it was said, "The French have all the privileges that can be, and are the most in number here; they are of the Council and of the Parliament, and are in all other employments." French families like the Jays divided honors and profits with Dutch clans like the Schuylers and Philipses and individual Englishmen like Gouverneur Morris. Their main commercial enterprise was shipping to England and the West Indies, which included a good deal of smuggling and even piracy, involving such merchants as Auguste Jay and Philipse.

But the characteristic outlet for New Yorkers was gambling in land. It was a peculiarity of this colony that land was on private sale and not, as in New England, assignable by communities. So easy was the game that Robert Livingston could buy 2,600 scattered acres and by the simple act of calling them contiguous, obtain 175,000 more for which he never paid. In dealing with such huge areas, European capital was drawn in by big speculators like Robert Morris. In part, the Revolution was favored by those seeking to enter the yet more westerly territory newly wrested from the French by Britain, which the Crown withheld from such traffic, lest it be involved in more Indian wars.

In this "first paradise of speculation," as Dixon Ryan Fox calls New York, a greater proportion of lawyers than anywhere else was needed to draw up deeds. Lawyers formed an important group, closely bound up with the business families, and assisting them politically, a fact of much weight in determining the new government after the Revolution. Not only did the land game produce a peculiar legal caste in the city, but it also tended to make New Yorkers more "aristocratic" in temper, agrarian-conservative, than other business men. With their enormous estates, they acquired a grand patroon manner, and a certain heavy somnolence crept over them as they devoted themselves to eating and drinking, combining Dutch and French cuisines. In this semi-comatose condition they remained until the waves of Yankees, Irish and mid-Western trust-makers burst in upon them.

Nowhere was banqueting a more serious rite than in the home of William Walton, President of the New York Chamber of Commerce in 1775; his three-storied brick house was the finest on Pearl Street; his carved lions' heads and stone armorial bearings were the most imposing and his stair-case rail was the darkest mahogany in town. Though Walton's entertainments, at which "forests of decanters" gleamed, were the "most sumptuous," other members of the Chamber did their best to rival them. When John Adams came from Boston in the previous year and was given "the most splendid dinner I ever saw" by the Chamber, he was amazed at the profusion of silver, the delicacy of the viands. Yet he did not like New York business men's manners:

> With all the opulence and splendor of this city there is very little good breeding to be found. We have been treated with an assiduous respect; but I have not seen one real gentleman, one well-bred man, since I came to town. At their entertainments there is no conversation that is agreeable; there is no modesty, no attention to one another. They talk very loud, very fast, and all together. If they ask you a question, before you can utter three words of your answer they will break out upon you and talk away.

It was not only Bostonians who objected to New York manners; so did the surly tenants of New York State, ever restive on the estates of the patroons and the lands of the speculative buyers, who formed a hinterland of antagonism to the port on the Hudson. They contrasted their grubbing, log-cabin existence with the fine mansions of the city-gentry, and were filled with venomous envy; so also were the agriculturalists around other ports, Charleston and Boston in particular. There too, the contrast between the struggle of the pioneer in the backwoods and the gay, amiable life of the merchant-townsman was so glaring that it excited hostile movements.

The city of wide-piazzaed Georgian homes, Charleston, was said in 1750 to contain 5,000 citizens who had "plenty of the good things of life." Residences along "The Bay" rented as high as £700 a year, and chaises, spinets and silver were common. The ruling influence of the city was French Huguenot; few of these exiles were aristocrats by birth, but they were inclined by French tradition to extreme formality; when wealth was achieved, they acquired plantations and coats-of-arms, attempted to dazzle one another by display of millinery and, as far as possible, made the town an imitation of Bordeaux or some other French merchant-port. They supported a theater, the best in the Colonies; one of the oldest libraries and a college were founded and maintained by merchants; and the social life of their ladies was if anything too sparkling, at least for the backwoodsmen. These debtors in the hinterland raised a howl in 1767 against their urban creditors, declaring that "The sums trifled with in a playhouse there would have raised us fifty new churches," and protesting against the "£60,000 voted lately for an exchange of merchants and a ballroom for the ladies of Charleston, while nearly 6,000 back settlers have not a minister or a church."

The money-lenders of Charleston, holders of mortgages on the countryside, were French Huguenots largely, who had been denied the right to found industries. Originally, when the first group came over in 1679, they had been given permission by England to start silk manufacturing, in which they were well-versed; many of them succeeded in growing the raw silk on their plantations, as did Isaac Mazyck, who brought much wealth of his own, and Gabriel Manigault, backed by capital of rich refugees in London. But when the latter set up a factory to spin the silk and make rugs and shawls, the entire budding industry was suppressed, and it was no longer profitable even to grow the silk.

The Huguenot families, the Hugers, Mottes, Legendres and Legares, accordingly, were compelled to become agents for the planters, conveying their tobacco to England, and incidentally extending credit to the planters; they also embarked in the West Indian traffic and in fur dealing, and many a sizeable fortune was piled up in these ways. Foremost was that of Gabriel Manigault, owner of many ships, stores, and a "barony" of 14,000 fertile acres; one of the three richest men in America, he left an estate of $845,000, which would have been larger had he not grown so enthusiastic about the Revolution that, in his seventies, he lent $220,000 to the Government, little of which was repaid.

Not only in Charleston did the refugee Huguenots show at first an eagerness to found manufactures. In Newport, Gabriel Bernon, who sought refuge from French religious persecution, and indeed had escaped from jail, set out to make leather and hats; but the London hat makers managed to ruin such activities in America, and then Bernon, having relatives in London, worked hard to obtain permission for other sorts of industry. As this was in vain, he became a trader, a partner of Ayrault in the West Indian traffic. Doubtless it was this experience which turned him into an early revolutionary sympathizer. Nor was this example isolated; again and again, at the foundation of an industry, as in the case of textiles at Middleton, Massachusetts, a French name appears. This is not surprising, for the French were by far the most technically competent group in the Colonies in early times, surpassing the Germans who, though good craftsmen, were not industrial organizers. In fact, the French were so many-sided that, when their industrial efforts were blocked, they could turn to law, trade and finance, becoming fur dealers as at Detroit, founders of banks and insurance companies, like Peter Chardon and Stephen Girard, or merchants of note, like the Devereux, Jays and Peter Faneuil, who left Faneuil Hall as his memorial. Two of the greatest fortunes founded in the eighteenth century were French, though not Huguenot, those of Stephen Girard, the first giant of American business, a mighty shipper, director of the United States Bank, and of Du Pont, the gunpowder maker who was only remotely descended from Huguenots. By stretching a point, one might even include the half-Huguenot, Alexander Hamilton, the most ardent advocate of industrialization for America, whose genius for finance and propaganda finally did pave the way for manufactures in the new country and thus managed what other Frenchmen had failed to achieve.

To the French yet another debt is owed: the extensive preservation of family papers of business houses. Their family sense has apparently been stronger than that of other groups—witness the clan-dynasty of the Du Ponts; and even in Rhode Island, it is the papers of the Ayraults and Champlins which shed the clearest light on early traffic. This is particularly lucky because of the great dearth of other Rhode Island letters, many of which were destroyed, it is thought, by descendants who could not bear the memory of their ancestors' dealings in slaves and rum, a traffic that was indeed the "main hinge" of that State in the beginning.

The Rhode Island hinterland was poorer than that of other states in suitable products for foreign exchange. It had iron, it is true, and at first the Colonists endeavored to exploit that one resource: the Jenckes family embarked on iron manufacture, the Greenes began to make anchors, and the Bissells turned out nails and cannon, while the Hopkins and Browns put in a furnace at Scituate. But this promising development was cut short in 1750, when British iron interests succeeded in stamping down Colonial manufacture. Thereafter little else could be done except engage in the rum-slaves-molasses traffic, and make continuous triangular voyages to Africa with rum to buy slaves, thence to the West Indies with the slaves to exchange for molasses, and back to Rhode Island to turn the molasses into rum, and so commence another cycle. Distilleries were put up instead of smithies; by 1764 there were 30 running full blast, one managed at Providence by a minister and two deacons.

The second settlement in Rhode Island was made in 1638 by a Boston merchant of dissenting opinions, William Coddington, together with the religious leader, Anne Hutchinson, and other followers. He had been a member of the upper house of the Massachusetts Assembly, and Treasurer of the Colony, but his views on religion did not coincide with those of any majority. He soon found Anne too liberal and established himself at Newport, where his family remained. For a time his sense of importance made a good deal of trouble; he went to London and obtained an appointment as Governor of Rhode Island for life; but Roger Williams and others rushed to England and won an annulment. Incidentally they brought back to the Colony the first commission for privateering, which furnished one of the supplementary sources of income, along with distilling, and in which the Coddingtons also engaged.

Privateering, verging upon piracy at times, together with the rum-and-Negro trade, might have supported this congenial society of traders for an indefinite time. Certainly they were well satisfied with the situation, when the Molasses Act was forced through, in 1733, putting legal barriers in the way of non-British molasses. The Act, however, was hardly a halt to business, for if the law endangered commerce, so much the worse for the law. With the best conscience imaginable, the devout smuggler slipped his contraband cargo into harbor under cover of night and, next morning, serenely passed the plate in church. As there was but one customs house to 400 miles of coast, and as the New Englanders all up and down the coast were extremely taciturn, few hitches were found until 1760 and again in 1764, when more active efforts were made by Britain to enforce the Act. It could not be done: in 1763 there were 150 vessels bringing 14,000 hogsheads of molasses, but only 2,500 hogsheads were British; the rest were illicit.

Smuggling seemed comparatively free from moral taint in an age when all seafaring nations were constantly engaged in privateering and were so generally careless with colors at sea. The Rhode Islanders, however, sometimes went farther. Not only did they take out letters of marque against French and Spanish, during war-time, while they were occupied in buying illicit molasses from the same parties, but they also sold provisions to the French fleet to be used against British forces during King George's War, in return for the precious molasses. This was a very awkward situation, and it even happened that Rhode Islanders engaged in this treasonable business were captured by New York privateersmen who were honestly working for Great Britain.

Owing to the complexities of trade in that time, it was a common practice of masters to equip ships with several sets of papers, signed by various owners. Thus Captain Thomas Hazard, who sailed from Hispaniola for Newport, carrying molasses and indigo worth $12,000, had two sets of papers, American and French. When chased by the *Young*

Eagle, of Boston, each party trying to outguess the other in the matter of flags, Hazard threw his American papers overboard; too late, he found his captor was an American and he was hauled to Charleston as an unlucky prize. Similarly, up to a late date, after slaving had been forbidden in Massachusetts, one eminent Boston firm continued, says Morison, under Danish papers.

The borderline between such guessing-games at sea and outright piracy was as hard for Americans as for others to trace, and it must be said that neither New York nor Newport tried very zealously to find it. New York was a kind of headquarters for selling pirate prizes. In Boston also, Robert Harding disposed of the booty of the successful buccaneer, Thomas Cromwell, and Charleston was often enlivened by pirate visits. But it was left to Newport to open society's gates to a pirate. Captain Thomas Tew, setting out as a privateer, turned pirate, making headquarters at Madagascar. Coming back at last, very rich, he paid to the owners of his first vessel fourteen times the value of their ship and outfit, and settled down as one of the first respectable millionaires of Newport.

Newport was cosmopolitan. It welcomed Genoese, Portuguese, Norwegian and Spanish merchants, as well as French, among them Stephen Decatur, grandfather of the Commodore. Aaron Lopez of Portugal was one of the richest shipmasters, vying with the Coddingtons and Browns. Owing to the destruction of their old papers, however, these personalities are vague. Color clings only to the names of their privateering and smuggling ships, the *Charming Sally*, the *Jolly Bachelor*, and the *Wheel of Fortune*; and there is a certain charm in the puritanic nomenclature of other vessels so employed: the *Content*, the *Diligence, Humility, Happy Expectation* and *Willing Mind*.

Rhode Islanders led this traffic but they were far from being alone in it. Up and down the coast others had been forced to seek profit in the Indies; at Norfolk, for instance, a group of active Scotchmen had found it difficult to penetrate the great agrarian hinterland of Virginia for business. The richest planters had their own wharves along the riverfronts, to which vessels from England came direct. This precluded the early growth of a town business class in Virginia; and disappointed Norfolk turned extensively to smuggling, although of course it managed some of the tobacco trade as well. Salem was another port subsisting largely on the West Indian trade in rum and Negroes; it was relatively a simple town of merchants who had begun as captains and never lost their ship-shape tastes. The rivalry of the Crowninshields and Derbys was not in dress or dinners; the Salem folk gave few balls, enjoying nothing so heartily as chowder parties. They were an easy-going group, so much more sociable than the stiff Bostonians that some who moved to the larger town quite startled it by their affability, until "they got some Cabot wives, who shut them up." This plainness of living, thinks Morison, was responsible for the remarkable longevity of Salem families. Assuredly it was not due to poverty, for "King" Derby, who left one and a half million dollars, was one of the richest men in Colonial America.

Boston did not depend as heavily upon smuggling as Providence, Newport and Salem. There were indeed threescore distilleries, which could be kept running only by illicit traffic; and at Boston lived the richest and mightiest of contraband-runners, the "Prince of Smugglers," as he was known, the patriot John Hancock. Left a fortune of £70,000 by his uncle Thomas, the war profiteer, he became one of the wealthiest men of New England, but he was not wholly welcomed by the solid families of Boston, who found his brains as shallow as his pockets were deep, and did not like his manners. These other, more reputable merchants were not, it is true, altogether unaware of the practice themselves; one authority thinks that the majority of the leading American merchants were cognizant of smuggling and that one-quarter of the signers of the Declaration of Independence winked at it. But at Boston there were many other things to do.

A certain amount of wool manufacturing went on around Boston, despite the interdictions of Britain. Forbidden to transport wool to their factories, Colonists simply drove the sheep to the gate to be sheared. Boston, moreover, very early threatened Britain with rivalry in shipbuilding and sea trade. By 1675 the town had thirty merchants worth £10,000 to £20,000 apiece, and 430 large vessels at sea; "so that there is little left for the merchants residing in England to import into any of the plantations." Paying little attention to English laws, they sent their vessels to Guinea, the slave-mart, and to Madagascar, the pirate rendezvous, and to every port where a bargain might be had. They also engaged in privateering; the Quincy family made one of the greatest hauls, in 1713, a Spanish treasure ship "worth the better part of an hundred thousand pounds Sterling." By the eve of the Revolution a very well-to-do upper-caste of traders had formed, a set of "gay Idle people" whom Sam Adams never tired of denouncing for their display, pointing to the "Decorations of the Parlor, the Shining Sideboards of Plate, the costly Piles of China."

Foremost among the Bostonians stood the merchant, Thomas Hutchinson, who was also a historian of the Province, a judge and Lieutenant-Governor, and an unshakable advocate of sound money. Hutchinson managed to divide the higher government posts between his own family and the allied clan of the Olivers, and thus ruled the Colony by a nepotism which resembled that of a Dutch oligarchical régime. Other towns, New York or Charleston, were also run by rich merchant families, but they were not so dominated by a single family, a solitary figure, as was Boston for a time.

Around the shipbuilding industry, however, grew up the most dangerous proletariat of the Colonies—a proletariat that threatened the reign of Hutchinson by its constant disturbances. The brawny carpenters, the "brassy and hardy" longshoremen of the town found their greatest delight in tavern brawls and cudgel play between Catholic and Protestant factions. It was not difficult for the politician, Sam Adams, to organize them into clubs, to control the lower jobs of the town as completely as Hutchinson held the upper positions.

Between the latter and the former existed a sharp animosity. Adams was the problem child of a business man who had been ruined by Hutchinson's sound money policies. Adams had been given a thousand pounds by his father to go into business, and had immediately lent the sum to a friend, who lost it. Then Adams had been taken into the paternal brewery; but he never cared for such endeavors. As he naïvely confessed: "I get out of my Line when I touch upon commerce; it is a Subject I never understood." He was sure, however, that he hated it; never weary of decrying luxury and vain display with a moral fervor to which conversion by a Wakefield revival meeting had contributed, he especially pointed to Hutchinson, whose "soft words, fair promises, and other tickling blandishments" were designed to mislead the plain people. When Hutchinson appeared lukewarm in patriotism, Adams' cudgel-boys set upon Hutchinson's house and sacked it.

As fate designed it, Adams united his forces with Hancock, the Prince of Smugglers, who had cause to denounce the tyranny of Britain. Hancock was very unhappy because the East India Company had begun to ask such low prices for tea that smuggling was no longer profitable. This seemed an intolerable interference with Liberty—or at least with the *Liberty*, as one of John's sloops was named—by the monopolistic British Government. It was the final outrage on the part of Britain that at last provoked open Rebellion. Individualistic tea drinkers, defying State interference, refused to drink a beverage so inexpensive. The smugglers themselves resorted to reprisals; John Hancock had been supporting Adams' "Sons of Liberty" with a free hand. He also gave employment to a thousand families by opening new wharves and works, and his thoughtfulness had benefited him in 1768, when his sloop, the *Liberty*, had been seized for a cargo of illicit wine; then the populace had arisen in wrath and stoned the revenue officers' houses. This second incident was more serious: Sam Adams organized the Boston Tea Party and dumped into the water the tea which the Company had sought to dump on land.

Hancock had good reason to be pleased with the ensuing troubles after the Tea Party. "At the exact hour of the shedding of blood at Lexington," he was appointed to appear before the Admiralty Court of Boston to answer charges of smuggling which, if sustained, would have cost him $500,000 in penalties. John Adams was his counsel. It is no wonder that Hancock wrote his name under the Declaration of Independence in letters so large that, as he boasted, King George could read it without his spectacles. Or that Adams signed too.

BUSINESS AND REVOLUTION

If the lack of manufacturing opportunities had tended to turn so many rich merchants into law-breakers—smugglers who took risks and accepted violence as all in the day's work—it also made the common people unruly, for they found no relief in industrial employment. Farmers and planters were drawn into debt to the city merchant class; but the business men, though they might buy up their beef, grain and tobacco, could not offer the sons of farmers ample mechanic employments, and the imported cloth and hardware they offered in exchange for agricultural produce were necessarily too dear for the pioneers. Business was not tied in with the other interests of the country; class-antagonisms had been created which were to prove dangerous. Both elements of society, the risk-running smugglers and the riotous "Sons of Liberty," could bring about a revolution when they were drawn together in a common cause, as happened when the Stamp Act, coming in an economic depression, hurt everyone alike, including the vocal lawyers.

Beyond a doubt, the most influential and respectable merchants of the Colonies were far from contemplating a revolution, when they agreed to put up resistance to the Stamp Act. In fact, the most pro-British of them all, the New Yorkers, led in that movement. By agreeing among themselves to refrain from importing British wares, including slaves, they did indeed help to force a repeal of the Act. Thereupon they tried to stop resistance at once; but a storm had been raised which could not be laid again immediately by calm words from the counting-house.

New York patricians managed at first to get a controlling influence in patriotic committees, and so modify the enthusiasm of the Mohawks. On the other hand, the popular bands of Boston, organized by the adept Adams, advocate of inflation and an anti-business radical, could not be swayed by merchants any longer. Always growing more tempestuous, they continued their wild meetings and threatened any business men who seemed likely to cool off. Trembling, fearing that buckets of tar would be "decanted" over their "pates," the shop-keepers withdrew the offending wares, and agreed to sign patriotic agreements brandished under their noses.

In Rhode Island, merchants had also taken the lead in a provocative act and were prevented by popular fervor from backing down afterward. A smuggler ship, the *Prudent Hannah*, was prudently dashing for port when the *Gaspee*, a British revenue cutter, gave chase and, turning Namquit Point, ran aground. In the dusk, angry natives, led by the richest merchant of Providence, John Brown (benefactor of Brown University), rowed out and destroyed the craft. Nor was the British Government able to secure the name of a single guilty party. Defending their right to smuggle rum, the Rhode Islanders met under the "Liberty Tree" and proclaimed their defiance to governmental regulation; later, when they found this diminished their stocks in trade, and would have moderated this attitude, it was too late.

Meanwhile, merchants of Charleston had slowly been turned to thoughts of war by similar interference with their smuggling. Henry Laurens detested the rioting of the crowds as much as the tyranny of the Crown and in 1765 he refused to sign a non-importation agreement, telling a band that burst into his home and menaced him and his sick wife, that he would not affix his name, though "you may barbecue me." Just a little later, however, some of Henry's ships were set upon by customs officers for having the wrong kind of molasses aboard. This was a shock to his loyalty, and in 1769 he wrote an acrid pamphlet, addressing to the world "A Few General Observations on American Custom House Officers." The following year he was a willing cooperator and, as President of the First Provincial Congress, pledged his all for liberty. During the Revolution, he was commissioned to seek a huge loan in Holland, but was captured and held in the Tower of London, while his son, John, upheld the martial end of the family's resistance.

When Rhode Island, Charleston and Boston had all been aroused over the smuggling issue, and the folk in town and country had taken up the cry, it was clear that business would have to make the grave decision at last. Some were not long in doubt. William Grey, one of the most highly respected merchants of Boston, was not; he marched with the embattled farmers to Lexington. Gabriel Manigault and Haym Solomon offered large loans to the Government, most of which were lost. Merchants such as Josiah Quincy and Elbridge Gerry gave assistance, and so did the bold sea-trader of New Hampshire, John Langdon, who announced himself ready to gamble on freedom.

I have a thousand dollars in hard money; I will pledge my plate for three thousand more. I have seventy hogsheads of Tobago rum.

They are at the service of the State. . . . If we succeed . . . I will be remunerated; if we do not, then the property will be of no value to me.

By and large, however, business men did not support the war with whole-hearted enthusiasm; so the necessity of resorting to issuance of paper money to keep the soldiers going pressed upon them. Nor did British business men seem any more eager to come over and fight for their markets; they preferred to hire Hessians. A good deal of vacillation and anguish was undergone by the Tories in the Colonies, like those at Norfolk, who dallied with decision until the Rebels were at their doors. Snatching up a few possessions, they rushed aboard their schooners and hastened to the shadow of British warships, from which, looking back, they saw their homes and shops ablaze. Those were fortunate who escaped with capital enough to begin again in New York.

New York remained Tory, although such merchants as Henry Cruger and Isaac Roosevelt withdrew to give their adherence to the Revolution. In their loyalty, however, these "Tory" merchants were much disturbed by Britain's attitude toward privateering. Rebel ships, with letters of marque, kept swooping down upon their wares at sea. Vainly the Chamber of Commerce begged for British privateers in retaliation. His Majesty's Government did not favor such irregularity. Disappointed, the Chamber stiffly replied that they were "exceeding sorry," for undoubtedly, privateering was one of the chief marks of American genius:

> Nor has any maxim obtained more universal assent than that all wise Governments should assiduously consult and attend to the Temper and Genius of the people, and it is notorious that the Genius of no people was ever more peculiar or conspicuous than that of the Americans for privateering.

BUSINESS PRIVATEERS

Genius enough the Americans might have for that form of sea-sport, and gladly they welcomed the chance to indulge in it again, more than 1,500 letters of marque being issued in Massachusetts alone during the Revolution. But without large capital, the privateersmen could not be outfitted. Where were they to obtain it? It was fortunate for the American cause that British capitalists opened their purses so generously at this point, assisting the Rebels in their fight on Britain. Arms were smuggled through from Britain by a ring of British business men, with Robert Walpole, son of the statesman, at their head, and through the agency of the Yankee, Silas Deane. Others invested in privateering; and not only did they outfit ships but, says Fortescue, in his *History of the British Army*, they even "spared no pains to seize sailors from the Royal Navy to man them." How business interests may cut across national boundaries was excellently illustrated by the Rodney incident in the West Indies.

The clearing-houses for such transactions, to which London investors sent their funds, were in the West Indies. Jamaica was one. The Dutch island of St. Eustatius, through which munitions passed to George Washington, was the heart of the business. Fortescue, explaining the defeat of the British forces in the war, lays heavy blame upon "the greedy, traitorous merchants of Barbadoes, Jamaica, and of London itself," who "consigned every kind of supplies that could benefit the enemy." The whole island was "one vast store of French, Dutch and American goods, the very streets being piled with bales for want of space in the warehouses." So profitable was this risky trade that the annual rents of the waterfront, "of a space not greater than eighteen hundred yards long by two hundred yards broad, exceeded a million sterling." And a contemporary wrote: "The Bay is covered with them Rhode Islanders."

These busy traders neglected to preserve complete impartiality. They refused a sale to the British Admiral Rodney, who was aggrieved; the very least that could be expected of his countrymen, the Admiral thought, was that they should sell to both sides. So he sailed right into the harbor in 1781 and took the town with scores of vessels and goods to the value of four millions. Being a simple sailor, he fancied he had made a good stroke. George Washington thought so too. For a moment it looked as though this death-blow aimed at the contraband-trade had sealed the doom of the Revolution. But a roar of rage went up— in England.

British merchants were furious at this interference in their dealing with the Rebel and enemy privateers. In Parliament, Burke and Fox fumed over the iniquity of Rodney's act, and, as Fortescue bitterly reflects: "Since it was revealed in the course of debate that over six score merchants of Liverpool, including at least one member of Parliament, had lost very heavily over St. Eustatius, the source of their indignation is not very difficult to trace . . . inasmuch as there was hardly a British trader in the West Indies without some venture in St. Eustatius." The angry business men stirred up so much trouble in the prize courts that they stripped the Admiral of much of his loot.

American merchants gladly accepted the help from the English side and did not forget the debt later on; in the War of 1812 some American business men repaid it by assisting the British against the United States.

The center of that contraband traffic was again St. Eustatius. And to make matters more complex, a privateering vessel was built in England for Americans to prey upon the American merchants thus illicitly trafficking with England.

Among the renowned Colonial sea-fighters who managed to aid the cause of independence and, at the same time, lay up a substantial capital as the basis for future business expansion, was the privateering-officer, Asa Clapp. After the War he advanced to shipping and banking, acquired political distinctions, and at eighty-five was the richest man in Maine. Israel Thorndike, a poor apprentice boy, rose from privateering to the then enormous fortune of nearly two million dollars. Another hardy leader, George Cabot of Boston, with his brother, directed a fleet of twenty privateers, one of them called the *Pilgrim*, and captured rich booty which formed the basis for later merchandizing and a career as Senator. Among them all, none was more picturesque than Joseph Peabody.

Peabody, son of a deacon and a staunch Puritan, embraced the patriotic cause, naming one of his sloops the *Bunker Hill*. As energetic as he was devout, he must have cut a fine figure as he brandished his boarding-spike, yelling amid the smoke of naval battle: "We've sunk one, my boys; now let us sink the other!" In recognition of his valuable services in the cause of freedom, he was presented with a boarding-spike richly mounted in silver by the grateful merchants of Alexandria, where he marketed his loot.

After the war, Peabody was only too glad to invest the proceeds in other activities; acquiring a fleet of eighty sail that skimmed the seven seas, he settled down in Salem to a patriarchal old age. Known for conspicuous charity and modest refusal of public office, he became one of the early models of success for aspiring youth to follow. In his little book of maxims, a "Guide Through Life," Peabody set a fashion later followed by Carnegie and other expounders of sound morality.

Of course, not all privateering paid. The risks were high, and the Dutch merchant, Alexander Gillon, who, assisted by Henry Laurens of Charleston, attempted one of the most ambitious projects, sank his entire fortune and failed to recoup. Nevertheless, when peace came, much wealth had been won. Though many figures disappeared, they were replaced by new faces; the Hutchinsons of Boston, ruined by Tory sympathies, were not missed when the clan of Stephen Higginson became as dominating as the old family. The problem, therefore, was now one of consolidating and preserving gains for the future. And in this none was more concerned than William Bingham, who had made an impressive sum out of privateering himself.

When the Rebellion broke out, Bingham happened to be in a strategic position, as commercial agent for the British Government in the West Indies, and he continued in the same capacity for the Rebels. His fortune, partly made in privateering, was augmented by land speculations and an alliance with Anne Willing, daughter of a prominent banker and merchant, and partner of Robert Morris, in Philadelphia. When Bingham joined the high circles of that city, becoming a powerful influence in the first Bank of the United States and finding his way to the Senate as well, he worked to strengthen the ties with British business which had been weakened by war, though kept up as well as possible at St. Eustatius.

Bingham was a most enthusiastic admirer of the British financial system which he desired to see copied in America, and urged upon Alexander Hamilton, as James O. Wettereau has pointed out. With this attitude was connected a social striving; his wife, as simpler patriots complained, was very elegant but "too much dissipation and frivolity of amusements . . . have weaned her from her native country and given her a passion and thirst after all the luxuries of Europe." Immense wealth enabled the Binghams to import fashions, and copy the Duke of Manchester's residence in Philadelphia, exhibiting the first stairway of marble and Italian paintings; against the background of this resplendent establishment they gave the first masquerade ball in the city, encouraging what soon became a mania among the American rich—a passion for dressing up as aristocrats.

The Binghams finally achieved their ambitions by uniting two daughters to foreign aristocrats; one to Count de Tilly, and the other to a member of the London banking house of the Barings, who later became Lord Ashburton. The Willings as well as the Barings were of German origin, it appears, and both were among the families most instrumental in maintaining cordial relations between the two Anglo-Saxon countries; Lord Ashburton helped to avert a possible war which would have disturbed business harmony. By these and other money powers the business basis of the new country was soon laid, setting bounds and brakes for democracy.

At first, London business men feared that their investments would be lost, as they saw private property overseas threatened by popular upheavals, like that of Massachusetts farmers demanding agricultural relief. In 1788 an agitated Parliamentarian cried: "What will become of the most useful, and one of the most respectable bodies of men in the nation, the merchants, and particularly those of the city of London, who have now, nearly two millions of property lying in America?" But they were reassured by Mr. Stanhope, who, with sanity and calm, and perhaps a twinkle in the eye, begged leave to doubt that the Colonists would defy London finance as they had the Crown:

Independence . . . that Sir, I think, will very much depend upon the manner in which the continental paper money shall be funded. . . . All the moneyed men there will be interested to support the funds. And then the high tone of prerogative and supremacy will cease there, as it has done here, and in its room the milder voice of influence will be heard and attended to.

And so it came to pass. The "milder voice of influence" in the mouths of men like Hamilton and Robert Morris, both English by birth, and Bingham, the admirer of all things English, made itself heard at length; the new-won wealth and opportunities for enlarging it were safe-guarded by setting up a strong government with adequate powers and revenues, and a sound credit system on the British model. This was achieved by a compromise between commercial leaders and landed gen-try, a self-styled "aristocracy" resembling that of eighteenth-century England itself.

THE COMPROMISE OF LAND AND BUSINESS

The very backwardness of American economic life was perhaps so-cially an advantage, for it permitted, at least for a time, an alliance or compromise between landed and commercial interests, while the Con-stitution was being prepared and national institutions grounded. This fortunate balancing of forces was only possible in a land not yet dis-turbed by the pressure of manufacturing, by the threat of great in-dustrial cities; the manufacturer would have been a type too uncon-genial for the landed gentlemen to tolerate. Suspicious as they were of simple trade, they would have been ten times more hostile to pushing entrepreneurs. But, as it happened, America was still in a stage where an oligarchical union of lordly merchants or bankers and speculative landlords, on the model of the old régime in France and England, could still be effected, and could last for the critical decade.

As yet, American business men of wealth and influence were of the sort considered somewhat eligible by country gentry: men of money, with large investments in the soil. Contact with sea and land ennobles, and they had both. Such a man as Benjamin Franklin, considered by European critics the very embodiment of the Puritan entrepreneur mentality, had in fact won a large part of his riches through happy ventures in land; similarly, the land-speculations of men like Gouver-neur Morris or William Bingham were so vast that it is hard to classify them as either business men or landed gentlemen. Moreover, the Ameri-can was not yet a plodding specialist in a narrow field. Holding widely diversified interests, ranging from ironworks to whaling, he had a broader outlook upon political affairs than the limited factory entrepreneur; and, despite his manifold activities, he retained a great deal of leisure for politics. Business men in the early period had much energy left over for campaigning, for careers in the local and national scene; they were even unashamed to retire, like Philip Hone, when they had a sufficiency, and turn to political battle. In politics, they appeared as equals of the landed gentry, for they were likewise seigneurial in their habits; not ex-foremen, or parvenu mechanics, as the early manufacturers were apt to be, these merchant-shippers aspired to be aristocrats. They affected powdered heads and red cloaks; their coats-of-arms were no whit fresher or more cheaply purchased than those of the self-styled "Cavaliers" of Virginia.

On their part, the owners of landed estates were not so far from business as they often pretended to be. Not only did rich planters, for instance Robert Carter of Virginia, frequently have mills and shops on their estates, but their land itself was acquired as a speculation. George Washington, though apparently the pure type of the military-landed gentleman, was constantly augmenting his domains by ventures in real estate, partly with his friend Robert Morris. The richest man of Colonial America, Washington was not the old-fashioned British squire, set upon a paternal estate of limited extent, tilling it in a routine way; indeed, he called himself "merchant," not "planter." Nowhere were the planters and landlords content with their estates. Like the humble plough-boys, they all looked Westward for extension. All were caught in the fever of speculation, so that a tranquil agricultural society in an Old-World manner was impossible.

True, many of the agrarians continued to think about business with a simplicity which really belonged in the seventeenth rather than the eighteenth century; they could not understand the complexities of the contemporary European economic structure, any more than Shakespeare had understood the intricacies of Venetian finance in his day. Thus that stubborn Jeffersonian, with an eye to rural votes, William Maclay, was horrified at the mere notion of shareholding companies, such as were springing up daily around him; shareholders, he felt, were "unproductive drones" who should be done away with. Nor did he admit that Britain's adoption of a national bank and a public debt system had assisted her social stability; he thought it had only led her into expensive wars and "the commotion of the world."

Equally hostile to such schemes was Charles Pinckney of Charleston, who desired America to reject a paper currency; that would prevent her from doing any foreign business, but foreign trade was the chief threat to agrarian society. Without it, America would have few luxuries; however, that was the price of the bucolic virtues:

There are three ways for a nation to acquire wealth. The first is by war, as the Romans did in plundering their conquered neighbors; this is robbery. The second is by commerce, which is generally cheating. The third is by agriculture, the only honest way.

Of manufacturing, Pinckney did not seriously think. He was speaking in terms of bygone moralists; like Plato, St. Francis and Machiavelli, the Carolinian believed that the one alternative to the domination of business was modest poverty, heroically accepted. The choice lay between a business America and a Spartan America. In reality, the choice had long before been made. Poverty, the grim antithesis to Business, was never greeted with enthusiasm by any considerable party of Americans. Least of all were the agrarians content with frugality and the status quo. Patriarchal as they might appear in manner, the Southern planters were exhausting the soil of their plantations as ruthlessly as later capitalists exploited the mineral resources, and had already begun to look ever Westward for more land. That was the chief trouble with Virginia, for instance, which now could do little but breed slaves for other states, and had thus entered in reality upon trade, the slave trade. In New York State the Dutch patroons, the Schuylers, Van Rensselaers and Van Vechtens, were indeed building mansions and assuming feudal airs and graces toward their tenantry, but they were also busily negotiating for new tracts of wilderness, and were ready to join with merchants of New York in lobbying for canals to open up and develop this hinterland. Let Jeffersonians hammer Hamiltonians as they would, rich agrarians clasped hands with the realtor.

The Revolution had only unleashed this land speculation, for the territories wrested from the French, hitherto withheld from traffic by the British Crown, were now given over to the state legislatures and to Congress, which began to fling open these and other possessions, as a way to pay their debts. In 1787, five million acres north of the Ohio were sold at two-thirds of a dollar per acre, the first great "land job" of America; the next year six million acres in New York were sold to Oliver Phelps and Nathaniel Gorham; two years afterward, gigantic territories were granted by Georgia to several companies, under conditions constituting one of the first flagrant scandals. And in these and other gambles were invested European as well as American funds; Dutch merchants joined with French noblemen, eager to transfer their capital from war-torn centers of Europe, and Boston fish dealers, anxious to rescue their funds from the perils of the deep. This imperial game, of claiming, boosting and unloading territories, rich in ores and furs, regal in extent, had already deeply altered the bucolic virtues. Long before the big trust-builders of modern times—the barons of oil and railroads—had appeared, the glib-tongued auctioneer of land parcels—the realtor—had undermined agrarian democracy. In fact, agrarians themselves were caught in the same speculative tendency and soaring ambitions that they deplored in others; hence America, where agriculture had always been a frantic business, could least hope to shake off Business.

For the opening and development of this mighty hinterland, the assurance of claims and titles, a strong government was as necessary to the landed gentlemen as to the business men. Moreover, both classes were drawn into speculation with the depreciated government paper, issued during the Revolution to pay war expenses. These and other ties bound them together until a Constitution could be formed. Playing upon such sympathies, the Hamiltonian bargain was made, whereby both elements were to support the adoption of a new Constitution and the establishment of a centralized and powerful government, able to pay in full the debts issued by the states and the War Congress. Gambling on this prospect, agents for sponsors of the plan bought up huge amounts of the almost worthless paper scrip from penniless veterans and farmers. On the new Stock Exchange, founded in New York, a lively marketing of this paper commenced. At least forty out of the fifty members of the Constitutional Convention, according to Beard's estimate, were holders of such securities, who naturally expected to benefit from their political work, and in fact did so. When the new financial system was set up under the Constitution, security holders and speculators won no less than forty million dollars.

Although this was a "business" deal, it was not confined to business men, by any means. Of the fifty-five men regularly present in the Convention of 1787, only eleven might unequivocally be called business men; the majority were lawyers or landed gentlemen. Nor were all merchants everywhere agreed on the entire wisdom of paying the speculators to the last penny; indeed the autocrat of Boston, the merchant Stephen Higginson, feared to drain the bucket to the last drop. He thought it would "sour" a "vast many people," and perhaps seriously antagonize the people to business at the very start of national life. In a letter rescued by Wettereau, he expressed his grave anxiety to Alexander Hamilton:

> Rich men are in all countries, and at all times, objects of Envy with the common people; but they become more so, when it is believed that the poor are depressed to increase their wealth. Everything which operates a great fluctuation of property & tends rapidly to transfer it from the poor to the rich will naturally excite irritation.

Nevertheless, the deal to fund the old debts went through, despite the embittered opposition of such Jeffersonians as Maclay. Vainly Maclay, who was paired with the financier, Robert Morris, the other Senator from Pennsylvania, strove to reason with his fellow-legislator. This plan would indeed secure the national finances, but to the profit of private speculators and the anguish of impoverished veterans and farmers. Morris smilingly replied: "The broad side of America was able for it."

For a moment, Maclay fancied that his party of small agrarians could defeat the tremendous interest of the rich landlords and merchant-speculators. The funding bill was temporarily defeated. Senator Robert Morris, finding himself in danger, grew so angry and excited that "his collar fairly choked him"; he sat down in confusion; then he got up, apologized for his "confusion, but declared it did not arise from the personal interest he had in public securities; that, although he was possessed of some, he was no speculator." And Maclay added, "I wish he had not made this last apology, for I fear it fixed the matter deeper on him." Maclay observed with delight the panic on the visages of other speculators, whose first thought was the sinking of their funds on the Exchange: "Fitzsimmons reddened like scarlet; his eyes were brimful." Clymer resembled "a turkey or goose nearly strangled in the act of deglutition." Gerry, always cadaverous, emitted consumptive coughs. Then the merchant, Fitzsimmons,

endeavored to rally the discomfited and disheartened heroes. He hoped the good sense of the House would still predominate . . . the Secretary's group pricked up their ears, and Speculation wiped a tear from either eye. Goddess of description, paint the gallery; here's the paper; find fancy quills or crayons yourself.

The agrarian victory was short lived. In due time the bill passed, creating the "national" public debt. Defeated in the following election, Maclay retired mournfully from the arena where Business had taken the chief prizes. "Let me deliver myself from the society of such men," he sighed, "for I verily believe the sun never shone on a more abandoned composition of political characters." But he persisted in blaming everything upon the business man in politics, for it "seems as difficult to restrain a merchant from striking at gain as to prevent a spaniel from springing at game." Candor and integrity, those jewels of the human soul he still supposed resided only in "the plain and sober countryman; never . . . in the sordid clown."

The candid countryman and the "sordid clown" none the less continued to play games with each other, dickering and dealing over every point. The location of the national capitol on the banks of the Potomac was another one of their compromises; business men secured the final part of their debt-program—the assumption of the state debts by the national government—in return for permitting the Southern gentry to have the capitol where they could watch over it. Morris wanted to keep it in a commercial city, preferably his own, Philadelphia. But he acquiesced; and the landed gentlemen, including his friend, Washington, found themselves benefited, personally and as a class, by the change.

One of the prime moving forces in this struggle of the elements, Robert Morris, was ideally fitted to guide the commercial party, since he was interested in manufacturing, finance, shipping to the Indies, and giant land schemes alike. He was an Englishman from Liverpool who had risen from poverty to a commanding position as "financier of the Revolution." Though he remained silent throughout the debates of the Convention, and opened his mouth only once, to nominate his friend George Washington, he did give quiet dinner parties during the Convention, at which important matters were arranged, confidentially, in the old English manner. "No man," in the estimation of Beard, "contributed more to the establishment of the Constitution and the stability of our national institutions" than this business man, who saw to it that Washington, the landed gentleman, was chosen President, and remained his intimate companion, suggesting to him the appointment of Alexander Hamilton as Secretary of the Treasury. While he refused that post himself, he went to the Senate, where he worked tirelessly for business protection, outmaneuvering Maclay, who retaliated by private remarks upon his venomous appearance: "I could see his nostrils widen and his nose flatten like the head of a viper," whenever a commercial interest was at stake.

THE FIRST AMERICAN ARISTOCRACY

This alliance between commercial and landed interests, personified in the harmony of Morris and Washington, lasted long enough to permit the creation and adoption of a superbly designed instrument of cohesion, the Constitution, for the reluctant separatist states; it also allowed the passage in 1792 of Hamilton's tariff bill to favor new industries, which, he eloquently argued, would employ infants "of tender years" who might otherwise be idle. Thus Hamilton, the half-French Colbert of America, could assure the future of great industry in the new country, and protect "infant industries," if not infants.

But this alliance was not entirely without dangerous influence upon business; for it tended to "aristocratize" the manners and political thinking of business men, and so estrange them from the common people. It was not simply the opposition of business to agrarianism which created this situation, but the cohesion of rich business men with rich landed gentry. By nature, of course, the shippers of New England were inclined to authoritarian habits; they ran their cities like their vessels with "quarterdeck" tones and were not compelled, like manufacturers, to consider problems of conciliating labor. If their labor struck it was a "mutiny." Hauteur was vastly increased where, as in New York, business men associated with patroons.

The growing aristocratization of temper and manners astonished French travelers, who came from a country where, in the 1790's, an ancient régime was falling in ruins, to find another aristocratic régime rising in a young Republic. America was already "decrepit," they announced; Americans were coveting patrician honors, trying to distinguish their families, affecting "the ridiculous airs of our old noblesse," if on a basis purely of gold: "There the rich blockhead is more considered than the first magistrate," and money established rank. Mrs. Robert Morris was led in first to supper in Philadelphia, "as the richest woman in the city; all ranks here being equal and men following their natural bent by giving the preference to riches."

How long a Republic would last under such conditions seemed dubious to the French Minister at that time. He had found "rich merchants . . . do not blush to say it would be better to live under a king, whose domination would guarantee the peaceable enjoyment of their property." Forgetting hatred of Britain, they turned anew toward London; they were already fatigued by a brief trial of equality, much as Puritan revolutionists in England after Cromwell welcomed the return of monarchical security.

Nevertheless, it was a Republic in effect, although not named as such in the Constitution, which was framed amid the secret debates of 1787. Out of fifty-five members in regular attendance, the majority in that august assembly were landed gentlemen and lawyers, with no representative of the "common man"; only eleven could be called clearly business men, and these were in agreement with the rest that democracy must be restrained. It was, thought James McHenry, heir of a business fortune in Maryland, "synonymous with confusion and licentiousness." Jacob Broom of Pennsylvania, engaged in banking, insurance and textiles, demanded restrictions on popular elections; so did George Clymer, of the same State, a wealthy shipper, who declared: "A representative of the people is appointed to think *for* and not *with* his constituents." A strong judiciary as a check was urged by Rufus King of Massachusetts and Oliver Ellsworth of Connecticut, a speculator in securities and interested in mills and banks. The latter was one of the firmest antagonists of a "levelling democracy" and at one time advocated patrician titles for American business families after the pattern of old Genoa and Venice.

Patrician upper houses were urged by Elbridge Gerry, active merchant and speculator in land and government securities, proud to be a stock-jobber, and a bull on America. Declaring, "The people do not want virtue, but are the dupes of pretended patriots," he thought they should be guided by the true patriots, presumably the stock-jobbers, who "kept up the value of the paper. Without them there would be no market."

By far the most outspoken "aristocrat" in the Constitutional Assembly was Gouverneur Morris of New York, who later lived in Europe and sympathized with its upper caste, and who believed that business could be saved by a permanent consolidation with land. Having himself joined his interest in shipping and ironworks to land speculation, in the New York manner, he dreamed of an oligarchy, assured by a landed qualification on office holding. This need never bar rich merchants, for, "if they have the wealth and value the right, they can acquire it. If not, they don't deserve it." Again and again his cynicism about human motives and nature shocked even that hard-headed gathering, and at last Madison, though generally in agreement, had to protest against Morris' "forever calculating the utter political depravity of men, and the necessity of opposing one vice and interest as the only possible check to another vice and interest."

Morris expressed the common attitude of this commercial class when he pictured the dangers of future manufacturing in America. All these shippers, like the landed gentry, feared the rise of a type of business man who, to them, seemed a mere greasy mechanic, a shirtsleeved fellow unworthy of their company. And they foresaw a time when the manufacturer would control the votes of the populace and oust them from their power: "This country will abound with mechanics . . . who will receive their bread from their employers. Will such men be the secure and faithful guardians of liberty?"

In the same tone, later on, other New Yorkers showed their apprehension of manufacturers, with their "crowds of dependents," who would, so it seemed, vote as they were told. When the New York merchants and patroons opposed the extension of manhood suffrage to the landless in the 1820's, they voiced their dread, not of the common man so much as of the manufacturer: "Under the pretense of giving the right to them, we in fact give it to those who employ, clothe and feed them." They did not wish to open their ranks to goods-producers any more than did the eighteenth-century oligarchies of France and England.

But with their sublime self-assurance, they failed to consider the question of anchoring themselves in a democracy; the shrewd Hamilton propounded to them a broad plan of propaganda, to enlist support for the Constitution and "the Christian religion," by pamphlets, clubs, especially benevolent societies on the Tammany model, and by work among immigrants, but the Federalists of New York would not accept it. They were too cold and formal in their manners to unbend so far, though Isaac Sebring, the wealthy New York shipper, organized the Washington Benevolent Society in 1808, made up in part of old soldiers, and it held grand processions with banners and relics of George Washington borne along with the utmost ceremony. Sebring went further and built Washington Hall, the first edifice for party purposes in America, according to Professor Fox; this hall was in grand contrast—perhaps too grand—with the tavern, familiarly known as the "Pigpen," where the Tammanyites foregathered.

New York merchants willingly gave financial support to the Federalist party. Since four out of five of the trustees of the New York Stock Exchange in 1801 were members of the Federalist party, money was available. Cornelius Ray, foremost financier, Elisha Tibbetts, insurance man, bankers such as Nicholas Low, merchant-shippers such as Murray and Gracie, gladly assisted the party. When the party was called upon to put up a ticket in 1806, a conclave of business men, meeting under the chairmanship of John B. Dash, importer of hardware, and including such merchants as Wynant van Zandt, nominated for Congress the banker, Fish, and a flour merchant, John B. Coles. But they still admitted the overwhelming influence of the landed gentlemen, the lordly figure of "The Patroon," Stephen Van Rensselaer, a grave squire and the richest man in the State, and the ponderous Abraham Van Vechten, or the "Prince of Schaghticoke," Herman Knickerbocker, who had acquired a beautiful "Habit of Command" from lordship over slaves and tenants. These feudal figures dominated Federalist politics, notwithstanding the fact that business men contributed money, and they would not stoop to a "jovial, social, Democratical-Republican-how-do-you-do Suavity."

Under such tutelage, the American business man was hindered in finding his political place. Vainly he protested his devotion to the Constitution and Washington. Soon he had to surrender the name of Federalist, which had become too much associated with aristocracy, and cautiously adopt the name Federalist-Republican, and at last—with a sigh—plain Republican. At the same time, a clearer line of propaganda had to be thought out. At first, Sebring required candidates in his Society to swear eternal opposition to "the inroads of despotism, anarchy, aristocracy, and democracy"—a pledge so inclusive as to bewilder the novice, who could only agree to be "agin" everything. But the Benevolent Society disappeared, and its place was taken by a "People's Party" seeking to identify the interests of business and of the people, without such squirearchical condescension as the word "benevolent" implied.

This momentous change occurred when the economic basis of the old oligarchy was threatened. The upstate manufacturer, taking advantage of the canal-building of the old patroons, to carry his goods to port, was elbowing his way into politics. And mere land speculation and merchandising were proving insufficient sources of wealth to maintain such an oligarchy.

THE WEAKENING OF ARISTOCRACY

In reality, this "aristocracy" of America was founded too late. Similar oligarchies of England and France were being unsettled by the rise of manufacturing, while the Americans made their futile attempt to prolong the eighteenth century into the nineteenth. They were anachronistic in their thinking, as they continued to be in their methods for some time.

The early towering fortunes made by the first "colossi" were amassed by men resembling figures out of the European past, rather than modern American capitalists. Thus Stephen Girard, the one-eyed French ship-agent from Bordeaux who took advantage of the Revolutionary confusion to sell his master's ship and cargo and set himself up in the wine business, shipping, and finally banking, was a survival of the Voltairean Age, a mocking cynic. During his lifetime he aroused resentment by his refusal to contribute to charities. Then he confused the public still more on his deathbed, by leaving a fortune to an educational institution which no minister of the gospel was ever to visit, even as a guest. The second tremendous fortune was amassed by a German, John Jacob Astor, butcher-boy from the village of Waldorf, gruff and rough-hewn, who grasped the potentialities of the wilderness and of the city alike, and, cornering furs in the one and lots in the other, made money in much the same way as old Hanseatic patricians had done. The third titan, Vanderbilt, was a Dutchman who might have stepped from the company of bulldog-jawed burgomasters in the seventeenth century, having the Dutch gifts for political action and love of boats.

If there was a flavor of past epochs about these mighty personages, it clung also to the shipping-owners of Boston and Salem into the 1850's. Still turning restlessly for fresh trading opportunities and new adventures, they had pressed for the opening of the Canton market, where Salem shippers vied with British and Parsees in the opium traffic, and likewise sought admission to the markets of Russia and Japan. Entering the Far Eastern routes, establishing a new "triangular traffic" like the old one in rum and slaves, but this time with ginseng, Oregon furs and Chinese tea, they developed the swift clipper ship. If it was the most graceful handiwork of man, none the less it was an anachronism, an emblem of a dying ancient régime in business. For even while the splendid craft were darting around the Horn, the soberer manufacturers of Scotland, with an eye to the future, were turning out unpoetic but more practical ships—of iron—and hence laying a secure foundation for British naval superiority. The eighteenth century died harder in Boston than in Glasgow. In Boston the "aristocracy" of America kept its course, like a proud old clipper, her sails filled with the winds of pride, but for all her speed, behind the times.

This aristocracy was not really shattered until after the Civil War, when it met the opposing "aristocracy" of the South, based on cotton planting, and both were defeated by the rising railroader and manufacturer. But severe disillusionment was experienced in the 1830's when the turbulent tide of Jeffersonian democracy broke over the White House. During the next decade or two, observers from Europe were astonished to find the rich in America trembling under democracy, as the poor of Europe shuddered under autocracy. In America, it was the millionaires who "look upon the law with suspicion," said de Tocqueville; and they were learning to keep their aristocratic ideas to themselves:

> Mark, for instance, that opulent citizen, who is anxious as a Jew of the middle ages to conceal his wealth. His dress is plain, his demeanor unassuming; but the interior of his dwelling glitters with luxury, and none but a few chosen guests whom he haughtily styles his equals, are allowed to penetrate into this sanctuary. No European noble is more exclusive in his pleasures, or more jealous of the smallest advantages which his privileged station confers on him. But the very same individual crosses the city to reach a dark counting-house in the center of traffic, where everyone may accost him who pleases. If he meets his cobbler upon the way, they stop and converse; the two citizens discuss the affairs of the state in which they have an equal interest, and they shake hands before they part.

The American Crœsus was beginning to shed his eighteenth-century garb at last, realizing that he would never win political power unless he took to shirtsleeves, or found some new manner, different from that of the Old World which he had at first thought to transplant. But he was still rueful about it, in the opinion of Tocqueville:

At the present day the more affluent classes of society are so entirely removed from the direction of political affairs . . . that wealth, far from conferring a right to the exercise of power, is rather an obstacle . . . The Wealthy members of the community abandon the lists, through unwillingness to contend, and frequently contend in vain, against the poorest classes of their fellow-citizens. They concentrate all their enjoyments in the privacy of their homes, where they occupy a rank which cannot be assumed in public. . . . They submit to this state of things as an irremediable evil, but they are careful not to show that they are galled . . . it is even not uncommon to hear them laud the delights of republican government, and the advantages of democratic institutions when they are in public.

But beneath this artificial enthusiasm, and these obsequious attentions to the preponderating power, it is easy to perceive that the wealthy members of the community entertain a hearty distaste to the democratic institutions of their country. The populace is at once the object of their scorn and of their fears. If the maladministration of the democracy ever brings about a revolutionary crisis, and if monarchial institutions ever become practicable in the United States, the truth of what I advance will become obvious.

This attitude of watchful waiting seemed to other observers decidedly ignoble; they would have preferred a more dashing appearance. Thus a petty nobleman from Germany, married into a Boston merchant's family, was amused around 1839 to find a society in which ladies were in grand imported toilettes, talking loud and quoting Latin, while men were sometimes hardly washed and nearly illiterate; he felt that the ambition of the former was one of the great causes of business activity in America. According to the German, these lovely creatures assume that "after they have been *genteel* awhile they have the right to become *exclusive*," even if they buy on the installment plan, and "help a young beginner only by spurring him to triple his industrial activities." At the same time, the women did not appreciate such enterprises, but "on account of complete distance from business and trade," were "richer in fantasy, spirit and even patriotism." Pushing business men forward, they yet turned from business.

The German, like the Frenchman, felt the thwarted hunger of power in the rich, and declared: "You love magnificence and have not the courage to show it. Your aristocrats do not understand how to dazzle the lower classes." He condemned the whole puzzling American attitude as "moral poltroonery." And so also did an Englishman who followed him. The rich only chafe and irritate the masses, said

Thomas Grattan, by their "efforts to establish by secret and insidious means what they have not the manliness openly to advocate." Missing the grand manner of his countrymen, he bewailed the fact that even corruption was less well applied in America than at home.

> Even that they manage badly. They have no boldness in their measures; no liberality in their expenditure. They cabal and coalesce to carry a point, and when defeated they sneak out. They do not show a daring front to the foe their own false pride has created. They are usurpers without spirit. A tyrant should be brave, and a conspirator prodigal. Coriolanus scorned the mob. Catiline bought them up. The "aristocratic" cotton spinners or ship-owners of New England or New York do a paltry business with a trembling hand. The people are too strong for them. Defeat is their desert and their destiny.

To such foreigners the American business man had merely failed to imitate European successes. They did not visualize the possibility that in the Old World, as in the New, the coming of mass-democracy would bring similar phenomena, and create there also that type which then struck them as so strange overseas—the trembling millionaire who hesitates to exhibit sovereign power or even to grasp for it openly, the Crœsus in shirtsleeves, more humble than the rich of any previous age, endeavoring in silence, apologetically and benevolently, to find a safe spot in democracy. As yet American business men themselves were not fully conscious of the trend, but, while they were sloughing off the eighteenth-century heritage, they were fumbling for the new rôle—to be played after the combination of Eastern industrialism and Western agrarianism had broken the dominion of the planters at Washington.

XXI

THE FRENCH REVOLUTION AND THE STRUGGLE OF THE INDIVIDUALIST AGAINST ARISTOCRACY

POSSIBLY Europe might have effected the transition to a capitalist society more peacefully had not the blaze on the distant American frontier cast sparks into the powder-magazine of France. But the more highly developed business becomes, the more susceptible it appears to revolts of consumers on remote outposts who are apt to be of a rougher disposition and better armed than the population at home, and so tend to extremes. Thus the World War started in an agrarian land, Serbia, heavily indebted like Colonial America for manufactured articles, and determined to force its pigs on a reluctant Austria in payment. So, too, the more recent Spanish Rebellion, flaring up on one of the remaining frontiers in Europe, soon involved more capitalistically advanced countries that had sought to exploit its ores. The American Revolution was in essence like these later rebellions—a mere blaze in a woodshack, which, however, could easily enkindle all of Western society.

The French Revolution, which soon followed the American and then, carrying its slogans outward through Napoleon, drew the whole of Europe into a welter of warfare, precluded any quiet unfolding of capitalism. Yet this outcome was hardly envisaged by the business men whose demands for more liberties were so largely responsible for the catastrophe. In this the French Revolution resembled its predecessors, the American and the Puritan in England. In all three upheavals, the grievances of business classes against governmental control, and their resistance to regimentation, lay in the background; in each, business men furnished motives and a driving force, and all worked out to the ultimate advantage of capitalist enterprise. But none was "started" by men of commerce; the forces of popular rage were let slip, as it seems, by accident, and speedily went far beyond the control or aims of business.

On the whole, the Americans may be said to have purchased their emancipation most cheaply and rationally. Their Revolution was much more frankly a struggle over economic matters, taxes and tariffs, and less beclouded by ideologies, Puritan or Voltairean; the aims, being better defined, could be secured more easily. Moreover, the War came early, before an aristocratic or military caste had been formed; it was in the nature of a preventive operation. Both in England and France, the might of monarchy was imbedded too deeply to be removed by a single slash; two revolutions and a restoration were required in the former, and more than three convulsions in the latter, before stability could be assured to bourgeois life. And neither the English nor the French Revolutions were an unqualified success; both were followed by aristocratic reactions, and both failed to efface completely the stamp of aristocratic tastes from the business world.

The chief trouble with the French Revolution was the heterogeneous character of the business groups that had been clamoring for the "Rights of Man," and Liberty, Equality and Fraternity. Business did not form any unified front against the *ancien régime;* and those who opposed it the most did so for singular reasons.

SLAVE-DEALERS AND THE RIGHTS OF MAN

Active advocates of the Rights of Man, firm believers in the beneficence of Nature, resolute opponents of Tyranny, were the slave-dealers of Nantes. Among them, the revolutionary seeds sown by the philosophers fell upon most fertile ground. This is indicated, for one thing, by the names which they gave their ships. The vessels of the slaving firm of Montaudoin Brothers were called *Paix, Amitié, Fidélité, Voltaire* and *le Contrat Social.* Other hulks, into which the living black cargo was packed so tightly that the captives could scarcely turn over during the whole nightmare voyage, were sentimentally labeled the *Tendre Famille, Bons Enfants* and *Saint Francis.*

These merchants of Nantes, slave-dealers who applauded the principle of equality and fraternity, and who tore black mothers from their infants and shipped them to servitude in vessels like *The Tender Family*, were the very loudest of all denouncers of the "abuses of the ancien régime." This was particularly odd because their business had profited more than most others by the loving care of the same régime.

The Absolute State had been very careful to foster slaving, which was supposed to be an ideal form of business enterprise from the point of view of "state reason." It did not take money out of France, but instead sold French products in Africa for captives, who in turn were exchanged for West Indian indigo and coffee. Not a penny left the land, whereas the Indian trade drained the nation of specie. Mercantilists praised this traffic and the slave-dealers themselves echoed the theorists; a document of the Nantes Chamber of Commerce exclaims: "What commerce could compare with that which results in obtaining men for merchandise!"

But this theoretically ideal form of enterprise held dangerous seeds. Capitalism had reared its head at Nantes before it invaded other businesses, for, by its very nature, slave-dealing entailed heavy investments. To send an armed armada for at least 18 months, perhaps 7 million francs were needed, and insurance in addition at from 7 to 35 per cent. Forts must be kept up in Africa and "slave-parks" in the West Indies to fatten such captives as survived the voyage. Months elapsed before returns came in; more than a year was spent in sailing to Africa and twice across the Atlantic, with dickering and barter at both ends. But the returns were attractive: between 1715 and 1728, the captains of Nantes handled 35,986 blacks, of whom 6,497 died before they could be sold, 633 were lost to pirates, and the rest disposed of at a good price. The peak of the trade was reached in 1751, when 35 ships carried 10,003 slaves.

Petty individuals could not hope to engage in such large dealings. Hence slave-trading companies were formed, reckoned among the first signs of capitalism in France. The most daring plan was that floated, not by a Puritan—as a Weberite might expect—but an Irish Catholic. Anton Wailsh, a refugee from Ireland on account of his faith, settled at Nantes, among Scotch, Dutch and other Irish (the firm of Murphy also does not sound very Calvinistic). He made so much money that by 1763 he retired with a fortune and bought a title; from him descended the Counts of Serrant.

Perhaps if Weber would not claim Wailsh as a Puritan, Sombart might explain him as an exile, for exiles are notoriously successful and pushing business men. At any rate, Wailsh had plenty of pioneer virtues and vision. His society had more than a million and a half livres of capital. A rude, hard, haughty, insolent man, he worked longer than his own sailors and, by preference, lived like them. So thrifty was he that the mortality on his ships was unusually high, because his captains were ordered to pack their human freight to the suffocating point.

Out of such a milieu rose a belligerent French capitalism, and with it the urge for political expression. The slave-dealers of Nantes were determined to achieve self-government; they captured municipal offices, and by 1740, the royal functionaries were superseded by merchants themselves, such as René Darquistade. From 1760 on, men of Nantes were electing deputies to the Estates of Brittany and played a leading parts in debates. They kept a permanent lobby at Paris, fighting for their rights against tax-officials. Constantly, they deluged government offices with pamphlets and petitions urging war for the preservation of their trade, or special clauses in treaties, if "peace is to be made on solid and durable foundations."

During war, they aided the Government. Since it was difficult to carry on the trade at such times, they turned their ships readily into men-o'-war and rendered patriotic service. In return, they demanded favors. Thus, they complained that the royal Guinea Company was privileged to sell Negroes to the French colonists; this seemed to them a wicked piece of autocratic interference. Amid cries and lamentations, they upheld the sacred cause of free trade against government operation of utilities.

So valuable a business, and one so essential to colonial development, was fought over by France and Britain. The Dutch and Spanish joined the fray; all were quarreling in Africa, arming the natives against one another, or robbing cargoes on the high seas. The monopoly of this form of traffic was a principal objective of the warfare of the period. First France won the precious right from Spain to furnish Negroes up to the number of 38,000 to the Spanish overseas colonies. Then jealous Britain waged relentless war until she had snatched this privilege from the Sun-King by the Asiento in 1713. She thenceforth rapidly outdistanced France, and even smuggled to the French colonists, who forgot their patriotism when they saw the British could deliver fatter captives on easier terms than their own countrymen.

When Britain, with her stout ships and keen traders, began to cut down French business, the men of Nantes were thrown into ever deeper distress. They were in the depths of despair, and there seemed no way out for them but some violent upheaval in the social situation. And so, declares Sée, on the eve of Revolution, when the Estates all over France were drawing up *cahiers* of grievances for consideration by the State, those written by the slave-dealers of Nantes were outstanding in eloquence and knowledge of the literature of revolutionary ideas.

MINING EXPLOITERS VERSUS SERFDOM

The development of mining was strangely similar to that of slave-dealing. Both were favored by a paternalistic State, and each outgrew the State, producing revolutionary figures. Mining societies, like the slave-companies, showed capitalistic trends by the late eighteenth century. They used complex machinery. Some were organized on a large scale, like that of Creusot, which on the eve of the Revolution had 4,000 shares at 2,500 livres the share distributed in the highest circles; mining was often permitted to the noblesse since it exploited treasure from the soil.

One of the mining-men well-protected by the Absolute State was Tubeuf who was granted a sweeping concession to the minerals of Languedoc. But when he came to take them up, he encountered a furious opposition on the part of peasants, nobles and clergy, loath to permit a great capitalistic enterprise to rob them of their individual rights. They had sunk countless little shafts, each making a petty profit. They did not intend to be dispossessed by an exploiter from Paris despite his royal letter.

To clear the ground for his company, Tubeuf expelled peasant owners by force. When they rioted, he prided himself upon offering them bread instead of sending them to the galleys as they deserved. He tried to conciliate aristocrats by offering them shares in his corporation, which was as shaky as a wild-cat bank. To mitigate the wrath of the clergy he gave them gifts. But his efforts were in vain. He began to see that one could not open up the territory without a revolution. One would have to sweep away local prejudices; and thus the "abuses of the ancien régime" came to appear as detestable and antiquated to a mining-exploiter as to a slave-dealer.

Perhaps the picture of aristocrats and clergy, as protectors of the peasants against the big business man of Paris, conflicts with more conventional views of the French Revolution. But there is a wealth of illustration to show the complexity of the real situation. The grumbling inhabitants of Alençon, for instance, said on their cahiers of grievances, just before the Revolution, that they hated the new-rich squires more than the old noblesse: "We are ready to keep lands for the descendants of old warriors who have shed their blood for the country, but not for an enriched puppy with a well-lined purse." During the Revolution, it was clear that the business classes lined up to repress the revolting peasantry, often with more severity than the aristocrats desired. This was especially true at Lyons, where the merchants saw with dread that their contumacious laboring population was assisting the serfs to destroy old property rights.

Absolutism, therefore, was not merely the oppressor of the serfs. In a way, it protected them. Tubeuf was a "modern" type, a great exploiter who rode roughshod over petty folk, creating bigger and better business, tearing out wealth from the earth at whatever cost, hating stagnation, oblivious to the immediate effects upon society. He lined up for the Revolution.

But Tubeuf miscalculated, like other business men who have called in the terrible force of mob violence to further private aims. The Revolution went too far. No revolutionary tribunal would confirm his concession. His always shaky structure collapsed. So he emigrated to America. This hard-boiled promoter was himself taken in—by a prospectus of the wonderful copper resources in Virginia. He bought a huge tract, sight unseen; when he went to occupy it in 1795, he was killed by the Indians.

UNREST IN INDUSTRY

In industry, similar changes appeared. Two generations before the Revolution, France, though definitely behind England, had great spinning plants in which mechanization had arrived, reaching ever-widening markets.

This possibility of expansion in consumption, however, had not been visualized by the statesmen of Absolutism, like Colbert. They had assumed that industry should purvey silks and mirrors for aristocrats and plain stuffs for the plebeians; that the number of the former consumers of fancy wares would remain small, and that the level of taste among the latter would not greatly rise. Colbert, to be sure, had hoped to increase bourgeois luxury, but his successors were men of more rigid outlook, who frowned upon rapid changes of fashion in middle class circles. In any case, the older Governmental regulations rapidly became obsolete. As the Amiens Chamber of Commerce complained, shortly before the Revolution, only the oldest and plainest females were still willing to wear dark, simple stuffs, such as had contented most bourgeoises of Colbert's day. Under Colbert,

> The citizens . . . were divided into classes; no luxury then; no one wanted change; the furniture and clothing had to be durable; the good and substantial were called for. The regulations were admirable for the time, and necessary, but now all conditions are absolutely different.

Nowadays, declared the manufacturers, the masses yearned for bright novelties, the flimsier the better: "It is notorious that people nowadays buy only with the intention to renew as soon as possible." But the Government disliked the proposed deterioration of quality; the State wished to preserve the old standards of durability, and resisted the trend toward the cheap-and-shoddy, which the people, and hence the business men, seemed to want. From this we see, that it was not the frivolous expenditures of Queen Marie Antoinette alone which caused the Revolution, but the craze for fantastic novelties in Mrs. Average Citizen. Her thirst for shoddy stuffs helped overthrow the Bourbon régime and bring on the reign of terror.

Among the restless spirits in the manufacturing class was the Bavarian émigré, Oberkampf. With royal permission, he had set up a cloth-printing works in the valley of Jouey not far from Versailles, where he designed, and printed, the delightful *toiles de Jouey,* now sought after by collectors. But he wished to print cottons in the Indian manner, and such stuffs had been barred from France, in order to protect home industry from Oriental competition. To enlarge his sales, Oberkampf had to array himself against the system which had helped him in the beginning. And in his fight for laissez faire, Oberkampf was aided by the theoretician, Morellet.

In this contest, Oberkampf won, and the king yielded. Soon his printed cottons were sold in France and abroad. Then he began to spin and weave, sent to Persia and India for patterns and processes, and laid the basis for an industry occupying 20,000 workers, which drew to France an annual revenue of 240 millions. So brilliant an argument for freedom in industry brought applause from the king himself, who proposed to ennoble the manufacturer. But Oberkampf modestly refused it.

Though willing to accept the theory of liberty when it happened to coincide with his needs, and to work against the royal interference of Louis, Oberkampf was not so dogmatic that he could not shift his views when it seemed advisable. He was ready to shake hands with a *duce,* Napoleon, even more autocratic than Louis. Napoleon, delighted to see Oberkampf underselling England, gave him a decoration and declared: "We are both fighting England, and your campaign is more important than mine." But the dictatorship which seemed to favor Oberkampf at first, brought him ruin, for it was inseparable from war. Foreign troops, after Waterloo, ravaged the valley of Jouey, destroyed the factories and burned the homes. Seeing the work of sixty years undone, and his workers starving, Oberkampf gasped, "Ce spectacle me tue," and died.

MANUFACTURERS VERSUS FINANCIERS

Munitioneers and financiers had little cause to seek an overthrow, or even alterations, in the existing régime; their complaints were chiefly against social discrimination. Economically, they held the State in pawn, and were more powerful in France than in England or Germany.

England had a strong national bank, which gave credit to the Government without recourse to usurers. The Prussian king, while refusing to allow such an institution, had decided to live parsimoniously and not run into debt. Both countries, for differing reasons, had avoided the difficulty that has weakened French society ever since the days when Italian leeches fastened upon the State.

So long as Colbert himself could direct the course of Absolutism, he restrained the financiers. But even the Colbertian program called for enormous loans, to finance the new industries. Millions were required to set up new plants; millions more were needed to build up a State strong enough to supervise an industry so fostered. Then more millions were called for to wage warfare for markets. Yet the State never managed to get adequate return from industry, so long as the big industrialists could buy titles and obtain tax-exemption. So the royal régime was committed to a costly patronage of business, for which it failed to win repayment or even gratitude.

Imperialist warfare is usually out of proportion to its results. How many millions of pounds did not England expend in order to obtain, as the chief practical gain of the Treaty of Utrecht, the right to carry a few thousand Negroes overseas! How many millions did it not cost France to strive, in vain, to recapture this monopoly! Such wars, waged with or without ostensible economic ends, brought the plague of the army-providers. Possibly Colbert could have done something about these also, but he was denied the portfolio of the Army.

The problem of munitioneering could not be solved so long as aristocrats held military power. True, even in the middle of the eighteenth century, attempts were made sporadically to clean up the mess. One doomed effort was that of the Ministry of Choiseul to put war-industries under State control. But this was a brief struggle; the financiers and army-contractors were more powerful than Absolutism.

To the other bourgeois, therefore, the evils of finance seemed inseparable from the Monarchy. Merchants and manufacturers loathed the bankers. Of course, the two classes were not strictly separable; financiers joined in the merchants' enterprises, and both were more or less allied with the Government. But nevertheless, there was serious friction, economic and social, between the two groups. The merchant was often dependent upon the Government for subsidies and he accepted the supervision of its agents; whereas the financier was a part of the Government, often an administrative official with lucrative posts, titles and enormous privileges. Under the French tax-gathering system, a banker might be an official revenue-collector, and hence, doubly hateful to the bourgeois.

Socially, moreover, thinks Normand, the two classes were set apart by a deep gulf of custom and origins. Financiers typically arose from the kitchens and antechambers of the great, where, as valet or lackey or barber, they learned the servile acts of flattery and intrigue. They were more subtle, and yet more crude, than the thrifty, sober, narrow bourgeois. And their ostentation was more aggressively vulgar.

The bourgeois abominated the licentious displays of the most flamboyant of such financiers, who flaunted the treasure they had squeezed from the State and in taxes from the people. However, the resentful business man did not pause to reflect that his own generous tax-exemptions, his tariff-privileges, his colonial warfare, and immense subsidies were drawing the Bourbon State into debt, forcing it to have recourse to such bankers. He saw instead the extravagances of the queen, who indulged her fancies at State expense—though, in fact, the whims of the merchant-banker Laborde were far more costly. Much as the business men grumbled at the indebtedness of the State, it never occurred to them that they might renounce the exemption system which protected the largest incomes, and accept a cut also in subsidies for their manufactures.

This growing animosity toward the financial circles in France was mirrored by the literary satires. So long as Colbert kept the banker Fouquet in jail, the dramatists merely smiled gently at the vanity of the rich. Molière led the chorus; his gold-thirsty *Harpagon* became the classic miser, who lives on in the pages of Zola. Dancourt portrayed, in 1690, the house-parties of bankers, in his "Coquette's Summer." But these were harmless jests, directed at excess of greed or folly.

It was Lesage, creator of *Gil Blas,* who drew the devastating portrait of the "public robber," in *M. Turcaret,* the pompous imbecile, vastly shrewd in money-matters, easily misled in affairs of the heart—in short, a French version of the Venetian *Pantalone.* Lesage had himself served in tax-offices. He was sympathetic with the better sort of merchants, whom he had seen, in the hard winter of 1703, at St. Malo, giving millions, largely derived from South American shipping, to feed the starving in the region. At the same time, he had witnessed the heartless ostentation of the financiers, who exacted taxes without mercy, and could not spare a sou for charity from dice and the opera. All his social grudge is poured, molten-hot, into the shape of *Turcaret,* "voleur publique."

Turcaret takes the savings of artisans and loses them in wildcat schemes, and organizes bankruptcies to defraud the public. He slips agents into industrial companies to pocket the funds. He is the evil genius of commerce as well as of the State. But he puts a fine face on the matter and gives himself seigneurial airs. At the opera he appears habited in gold brocade, with a long cane. His table is open to poets like poor *Gloutonneau,* who never opens his mouth save to eat. *Turcaret* himself writes amateur verses in which love and arithmetic are confused:

> *Be assured that my soul*
> *Will forever preserve an eternal flame;*
> *It is as certain as that three and three make six.*

For such a type, the very real army-contractor Bonnier de la Mosson might well have stood as model. He preened himself upon writing poetry, which his unwilling guest and auditor, Voltaire, said was so execrable that it deserved to be crowned by the Academy.

After *Turcaret's* death, Lesage depicts the valet, who has learned all the tricks, ready to follow in his master's path. *Frontin*, the valet, boasts: "See, now the reign of *M. Turcaret* is over; mine is just beginning." So, as Etienne says, in his study of finance and French theater, Lesage leaves his audience with the sarcastic reminder that the individual rascal may die, but the race of rascals is immortal.

This play created a scandal. The banker-financiers offered Lesage 100,000 francs if he would withdraw the piece. He refused. They protested to the Minister. Lesage went to the dauphin and got royal protection, for the Bourbons enjoyed a joke on the bankers as well as the common people. Eventually, however, Lesage was forced from the chief stage in France and took up the proletarian literature of that time —for that is, of course, what "Gil Blas" and other picaresque tales of the underworld represent.

At times the State endeavored to reform the financial situation by investigations. In 1716, a huge list of fines was imposed upon leading financiers. Sombart says that 726 persons were burdened with fines totaling 147,365,433 livres. Some individuals, such as the banker Crozat, were subjected to as high a levy as 6 millions. This might have crippled them, had they paid much attention to the matter. But only a small part, perhaps 20 millions, was ever collected.

This antagonism within the ranks of business men themselves, this cleft between the manufacturing-commercial class and the big *gens de finance* who strove to manipulate commercial companies, was one of the factors in the pre-revolutionary era which contributed deep unrest. Popular resentment, thus, was not solely against King, Church and Nobility; the common people clamored for the blood of bankers as well.

The guillotine took a toll of these victims during the Revolution. The people, not sated with the executions of aristocrats, or of the queen, had to see at least a few moneyed men die. And so, on May 8, 1794, twenty-eight financiers were brought to the scaffold, among them Lavoisier, father of modern chemistry. Their goods were taken by the State. Grim wits of the times called this process, "battre monnaie sur la Place de la République."

THE ABUSES OF THE ANCIEN RÉGIME

When the business men cried out against the "abuses" of the Bourbon system, they were railing at a creation for which they were themselves to a considerable extent responsible. The merchant class had given the Crown originally its strength; merchants had grown rich under its shadow, and indeed, at the expense of agriculture. Part of the wretched plight of the serfs was due to the fact that grain-prices were consistently held down to provide cheap bread for factory-workers.

In the glories as well as in the evils of the period, the business man had a share at least as large as that of nobles. Commercial wealth outshone the fortunes of all but the highest nobility. The swift pace led by bankers in Paris was responsible for the ruin of many an old family. Bourgeois patronized opera, opened salons, shaped cultural expressions, and assisted in the refinement of French civilization. If the bourgeois were as lavish as aristocrats, they were also certainly as corrupt. The graft of bourgeois administrators was fully as harmful to the economic system as the frivolity of marquises. The tax-exemptions of the larger manufacturers was weakening to the State, like the tax-exemption of feudal nobles. Moreover, as has previously been shown, there was no such real gulf between bourgeois and aristocrat; for the noblesse was constantly being recruited from contractors, slave-dealers and stocking-manufacturers.

If any heartless observation was responsible for the final outbreak of the Revolution, it was not the famous "Oh, can't they get bread? Why don't they eat cake?" imputed to the queen, but the remark of a successful wall-paper manufacturer of Paris, one Révillon, that "a workman could live on 15 sous a day." His home was pillaged by furious mobs and the sack lasted until troops were summoned and many rioters killed. That incident was a storm signal of Revolution. It occurred before the mob marched against the the Bastille, and the queen.

Moreover, though the Court at Versailles has been justly blamed for its supineness and lack of plan, the same charge might be leveled at the planless, emotional bourgeoisie. The business men were, after all, in contact with reality as courtiers were not. They had every opportunity to evolve purpose and leadership. But they were filled with vague ideas, catchwords of the hour, slogans about "liberty" and enthusiasm for "Nature." With much less experience in the arts of self-government than the British, they thought they could make up for everything by their own self-confidence and the perfervid oratory of their lawyers.

Nor could business men complain with truth that they had not been listened to, whenever they had advice to offer. The record shows how patiently the Crown listened to economic theoreticians and modified its policies incessantly. In fact, the whole sorry march toward ruin and revolution in the eighteenth century is marked with the bones, and books, of business experts.

DEPRESSION AND REVOLUTION

The first of these experts had been the Scotch wizard, John Law, whose panacea did not work. Though the creaky machine of the Monarchy managed to pull through the débâcle caused by his advice, it was finally undermined by hearkening to the pleas of manufacturers for free trade and freedom of initiative. It was the first tentative practice of laissez faire that brought depression—then Revolution.

Manufacturers had been insisting that they could prosper if the Government would only remove its protective hand from labor. And so, in 1774, Minister Turgot made the experiment. He abolished the Six Guilds of Paris, which had limited the number of artisans and maintained wage levels. Work was declared the "unalienable right of humanity" and labor was told it must not try to restrict jobs: "We owe to all our subjects the assurance of the full and complete enjoyment of their rights." Lest they hug their chains, workers and apprentices were forbidden "to form any association or assembly among themselves under any pretext whatever." The Six Guilds feebly protested, but Turgot warned them that revolt against liberty was useless: "We shall not be halted in this act of justice by fear."

The chaos ensuing upon this too-sudden reversal of systems was insupportable. The transition from strict royal regulation to the anarchy of Dame Nature brought confusion. After two years the Crown had to step in between labor and the liberty-loving manufacturers. But though some of their domestic operations were once more brought under control, the manufacturers were permitted to have, at least, the fling at free trade for which they begged. Free trade, they said, would give them foreign outlet.

Obligingly the Crown formed trade treaties with various powers and lowered its tariff-walls. In 1786 a treaty with England gave either country a greater measure of freedom in exchange of goods. But the outcome was the reverse of what the business men had expected.

England was now far ahead of France industrially. Once the bars were lowered, France was promptly flooded with articles of English manufacture. And then, when depression settled down over industrial centers in France, the industrialists began to wail piteously for protection. They blamed their woes upon that unfortunate treaty, which had left half the looms of Troyes silent, and increased unemployment throughout France. Unanimously, the Chambers of Commerce at Rouen and Amiens condemned the treaty; but they did not blame Nature, or their own technical backwardness.

In that depression, which came on in 1788, the French Revolution was born. Obviously, it cannot be considered as a movement simply for laissez faire. That had been tried on a certain scale, and nobody was more disappointed with the outcome than the manufacturers. Rather, the howl of the business classes was for salvation, without a clear program. The Crown could not offer one; nor could it imagine how to please a bourgeoisie which shrieked for free trade at one moment and protection the next, which was furious when the State supervised its enterprises, and enraged when the State withdrew its paternalistic subsidies. In that crisis, the Crown decided to let the greatest business man of France take complete charge of economic life. The King left everything to the Swiss Puritan banker, Jacques Necker, in whom the commercial classes of the nation had the utmost confidence. And it was under Necker's hand that the storm broke.

THE BANKER'S TRAGEDY

The simple King went hunting with a carefree mind. He did not know much about business, but he wanted to please his subjects; and he was only too glad to receive advice from experienced men of affairs. So he picked out the most popular expert in economics and finance, the great merchant and banker, theorist and all-around business success of the day, who had been expounding his ideas so brilliantly. And Necker was permitted to show what he could do.

Necker's ability seemed proved by his riches. He had been a director of the French East India Company and, though charged with graft, defended his administration by an able pamphlet. As partner in the bank of Thelussen and Necker, he had made huge sums by lending to the Government and in grain-speculation. People believed that he had made many millions out of a clever, if shady, deal; a French statesman, aware of impending peace with England in 1763, was said to have offered to Necker the chance to buy up British shares at a low figure and profit by their rise as soon as peace was signed. Necker bought heavily and realized 40 per cent, but, so the story went, since the little deal was not put in writing, he refused to divide the spoils with the diplomat. This sort of thing inspired the greatest popular confidence in Necker, among business men. Obviously he was a regular fellow, as smart as anyone.

Likewise impressive was his reputation as an economic theorist. Had not his works been crowned by the Academy? In the salon of his clever wife, intellectuals crowded to view the great man, and were much awed by his important silence. In that age of flowing chatter, the spectacle of a taciturn man was overwhelming. Business men pointed out to any skeptics who might be left unconvinced, that the administrative record of Necker was flawless. Between 1776–81, he had been director of the Treasury; and he had done well, although his task was favored then—as was that of Andrew W. Mellon during the Coolidge boom—by fortunate circumstances. Necker had even initiated reforms, cut down the expenses of the Court, relaxed the bonds upon business enterprise, and favored a certain degree of political expression in the nation. Besides this, he had met the huge expenses of the war with England, in defense of the American Revolutionists, by the most painless of methods—not taxation, but loans raised among his rich friends.

Necker believed that confidence was the vital asset. "He floated his loans by representations of the state of royal finances so flattering that charity can hardly suppose him to have believed them himself." Though he knew that the credit of the Monarchy hung upon a thread, he was sure that all would be well, if the business elements could preserve optimism. His roseate pictures of the fiscal status, moreover, could not well be disputed because, in those days, budgets were not made public and no outsider, not even the King, knew enough about national finances to discuss the matter.

With an abyss of debts skillfully concealed, Necker issued a report in 1781, which contained no hint of trouble. "He drew an imaginary picture of revenue and expenditure in a normal state of affairs"; which was wholly irrelevant to the abnormal conditions then existing. Because he managed to point a fictitious surplus, the nation regarded him as a savior. And he would have continued to hold the post had he not, led on by a fatal vanity, demanded the title of Minister, which could not be accorded to a Protestant heretic, like himself. Denied his request, he resigned.

He was escorted home by the nation. His country house became a court whither all who wished to be thought enlightened, humane, and lovers of virtue divorced from power, thronged to pay their respects. Many nobles came to wait on the banker, and even the Archbishop of Paris and other prelates paid formal visits to the Calvinist.

After this resignation, he stalked through his salon, in enigmatic silence, while his successors committed one blunder after another. Since they had to flounder in the hopeless muddle left by Necker, there was no hope for them. Finally, when the crisis had deepened, in 1788, Necker flung back the veil of mystery and published a book, "The Administration of the Finances of France," which sold like wildfire and was hailed with rapturous joy. Nobles and merchants, women and men, pleaded with the king to restore their wizard, and so the "greatest secretary of the Treasury" was given more rope.

The adoration of Necker faintly suggests that of Herbert Hoover. To the laborious, upright savior-expert, Calvinism gave the same religious sanctification that Quakerism lent to Hoover. That he was a foreigner was no disadvantage to Necker in Paris, where heretics were busy in financial affairs; there were, for example, the Swiss Panchaud, the Scotch Clouard and Huguenots returned from exile like Perregaux. But this idol of the populace, Necker, suffered from a fatal tendency to vacillation. He was constitutionally unable to speak out the worst about a given situation. He did not like to make up his mind on thorny subjects. Sometimes, it was claimed, he even sat waiting in his carriage for a quarter of an hour before he could decide where he wished to be driven.

Such was the personage summoned from the realm of business to guide the destiny of the nation. He was not the first who had come from such a background to a position of national influence in France. Long is the line of moneyed men whose plans have been received by the French State. Laffémas, the merchant-tailor, originally advised the close cooperation of Crown and commerce, which the bourgeois, Colbert, made so profitable to both parties. The banker, Law, proposed to perpetuate that compromise by turning the Monarchy into a business corporation, a stock-company. Then the banker, Necker, by summoning a meeting of the States General, endeavored to bring about another reconciliation, but, by his indecision, brought ruin on both sides.

Nor was that the end of banking influence over the French State. After the chaos of the Revolution, arose the mightiest of financial wizards in French history, Ouvrard, who set up Napoleon and helped found the Bank of France; after Napoleon, the banker, Lafitte, assisted the Bourbon Restoration. And again, a banker, Rothschild, supported the Imperium of the "Umbrella King," embodiment of the bourgeois ideal. But it so happened, that the weakest of this long line of business leaders was Necker, who faced the severest trial—which, perhaps, he himself brought on the country.

As Necker looked about him, observing the effects of the severe winter and the depression, he decided—to investigate. Much as Hoover planned his famous study of the state of the social sciences in America, so Necker decided to let the people of France draw up cahiers of grievances. For months, France was filled with discussion of wrongs and rights. Partisans and demagogues shouted one another down. Peasants, merchants, agitating lawyers, offered countless conflicting recipes for universal prosperity. But Necker believed a Minister should not interfere in the matter. It was his duty to let the people speak themselves out.

When the elections for the Estates-General took place, Necker did not interfere. He did not even prepare a program for the Assembly to debate upon. Indeed, he did not even determine in what order or in what rooms it should sit. Nor did he endeavor to see that the deputies should be men of good sense and experience. He had allowed the whole country to vote; every man, and many women, above 25 years of age on the tax register had a ballot; this included artisans who paid a workers' tax. "Roughly it may be said that only the poorest laborers and downright paupers were excluded from the franchise."

This vast mass-balloting resulted in the election of an overwhelming number of provincial lawyers, in the bourgeois class, or Third Estate. Only 130 were merchants and bankers, and only 40 were farmers; the remaining 360 were mostly legal rhetoricians. When they all arrived, Necker had called a caucus of the most intemperate elements in France, with neither candidate nor platform to present. He had not even a good building for the show. Finally he had to face the democratic phenomenon he had summoned up. He rose to open the meeting. The might of France was represented before him, the nobles in glittering costumes, the prelates and the black-gowned bourgeois. Necker began by reading a report which falsified financial matters and suggested a few petty and inconsequential reforms. It was a report so long and windy that, as moments went by, his voice weakened and finally faded out altogether. He handed the sheets to a secretary to continue. He had stood up the idol of France—he sat down, deflated.

At once the huge assembly got out of hand. In the awful confusion that ensued, men kept coming to Necker and pleading with him to do something. But he always "declined on principle all private communication with members of the Estates General." He kept his seat and watched, hoping apparently that some divine wind would sweep into harmony these country lordlings, petty lawyers and hedge priests. His goddess was Fortuna.

But the poor King, who saw to what lengths the ineptitude of his banker-prophet had led matters, told Necker to leave France in a hurry and never come back. He fled to Geneva, where he lived on, a forgotten and embittered man, writing endless explanations. Later on, he sent to Napoleon two propositions for governments, one adapted to a monarchy and the other to a republic. Apparently, he had not decided which was preferable. To his dying breath, Necker was unable to make up his mind.

THE FRENCH STATE AND FINANCE

It was many a decade before business prosperity was restored in France after the storm of the Revolution. Ruin and chaos had been left in its wake. The exports of France dwindled almost to the vanishing point during the height of the Terror. Out of the anarchy, the first successful men to emerge upon a new foundation were those who understood inflation. With the rapidly depreciating Government currency, they bought real goods. Acquiring fortunes in this manner, they undertook to furnish the armies. The real profit-makers of the Revolutionary epoch, accordingly, were munitioneers, who continued in a fateful rôle in the French State.

Thus the French people's ancient grudge against the moneyed forces was not suffered to subside for a moment. Even during the Terror, when aristocrats were dying daily, the people could see the elegant carriages of bejeweled parvenus, no whit less gorgeous than those of the old aristocrats, rolling up to the theaters. To express their sentiments of contempt, fish-wives called after them: "Place for His Honor the Provisioner of Prisons!" "Room for His Excellency the Army Feeder!"

Supreme among these new men was the extraordinary financial genius, Ouvrard. The son of a paper-mill owner of Nantes, this bright young man, just nineteen in 1789, perceived what a Revolution would chiefly produce: words. He knew that, given the nature of the French, there would always be argument, come riots, come war, come ruin. The one commodity the nation could not do without was paper upon which to print words. Gambling upon democracy, as the stimulator of the paper business, he contracted for all the paper the chief mills could supply for two years ahead. With the gains, he speculated in colonial products and became so wealthy he was denounced as a profiteer. He saved himself from jail by becoming an aide-de-camp to his good friend, General Boivin, and moving to Paris.

In Paris, Ouvrard became a giant power, with wires of social, diplomatic and commercial intrigue in his hands. As naval contractor, he gathered in 15 millions in a throw; making use of the inflation, he bought some huge palaces of the doomed aristocracy which the State was selling cheaply. His influence was employed to rescue his big business friends in Nantes from radical revolutionary tribunals; one of these, a factory-owner, gave him his daughter in gratitude. But Ouvrard's hostess in his château was the superb Madame Tallien, who created a salon for revolutionary leaders of all sorts. Politicians met there with the traders and bankers, Perregaux, Bazin and Récamier, the financier whose charming wife, Madame de Récamier, was goddess of fashion.

Able as he was to form and direct the affairs of France, Ouvrard at first hoped to make a kind of business democracy work. He watched anxiously while the visionary agrarians were brought to defeat. St.

Just, who dreamed of a luxury-less utopia wherein all men up to the age of fifty would be compelled to plough the fields and bear arms, was executed. So was Robespierre, who likewise wanted to establish a puritanic, martial commonwealth of embattled farmers, and denounced the usurers and grain-monopolists in violent terms. Such radical agrarian schemes were defeated, thanks to the efforts of such friends of trade as Anacharsis Cloots, the banker of German origin, and self-styled "Mouthpiece of the Human Race." But still the Republic was a long way from stability.

Ouvrard offered the Directorate a scheme for putting the new government on a business basis, by establishing a public funded debt and issuing paper money. But this plan was far in advance of his age and, like similar proposals in England and Prussia, was rejected with horror at first. Unable to see hope in the revolutionary movement any longer, Ouvrard was turned toward dictatorship. He gambled on the young Napoleon to the extent of lending him 10 millions for the Egyptian campaign. The strong man, he fancied, would be good for business, and especially his own business. For he had gigantic plans for profit-making on an imperial scale. In the shadow of Spanish windmills, Ouvrard dreamed of business conquests as vast as Napoleon's military visions before the Sphinx.

The ambitions of Ouvrard were boundless; thus in 1804, he offered France 50 millions and offered to procure thrice as much, in return for a grip on the national tax-collection; soon after, he found 400 millions for the State in return for the power to provide the armies and navy. Soon he wished to manage not merely France, but Spain and the New World. He formed a project to extend credit to Spain by arranging a loan in Holland and, as a price, obtaining a free hand in reorganizing that country and its colonial empire. He proposed to sell the goods of the clergy in Spain, against a reimbursement in the form of pensions, and use the money to put the Spanish Monarchy on a business basis; with a monopoly of overseas trading rights, he fancied he could draw inexhaustible treasure from the Americas. For this audacious enterprise, Ouvrard needed the Napoleonic signature; but, as it turned out, the "strong man" he had elevated was one of the most primitive of Italian tyrants, a pure soldier with no heartfelt sympathy for trade or the trader—even though of Tuscan ancestry.

Whereas Ouvrard wanted to reorganize France and Spain on a basis of public credit, it was the aim of Napoleon to break the independence of business. He was filled with loathing for army-purveyors, who corrupted his generals and demanded high prices on account of the risks of warfare; among them, he hated Ouvrard most of all. For ordinary business men, Napoleon had only contempt; he was fond of taunting

French merchants with their lack of statesmanship, saying, "I know your business better than you do mine." Again he would remark, as he did to a Dutch delegation: "I love merchants not; a merchant would be ready to sell his country for a dollar." The worst thing he could find to say about the British was, "sono mercanti"—they are shop-keepers.

The determination of Napoleon to build a purely military state, with business under its thumb, and his ignorance of economic matters, led him to violent methods. He refused to understand the function of credit, for he loved the clink of actual coins. He would not suffer the Parisian Exchange to fluctuate, for as he said, "The rising of public papers ought to be naturally continual; there ought to be no bearish speculation." Of any large fortune, he was jealous: "in a revolutionary time, no man ought to have over 3 millions, and even that is too much." This "Arch-Enemy of Trade," as the infuriated Dutch called him, prevented the Spanish scheme by simply declaring Ouvrard bankrupt for 427 millions. And he excused himself by growling: "All these munitioneers are rascals. . . . They had millions and displayed their wealth when my soldiers had neither bread nor shoes."

Although the military genius struggled madly against the financial genius, both were bound together. Napoleon tried to be independent of provisioners, by taking his armies abroad to feed, but he was always in debt to munitioneers like Barras, and always needed Ouvrard, whom he jailed but had to release. When he tried to conquer Russia, without the hated provisioners, his ill-fed armies fell victim to the Russian winter, and the result was a hideous débâcle. Despite his fury against that class of men, opulent army-contractors formed the principal social life around the parvenu Emperor. The chief salon in his reign was held by Madame Hamelin, wife of the very rich munitioneer-banker.

In the end, both Ouvrard and Napoleon failed. They were both primitive geniuses, the latter utterly untutored in economic matters, and the former, Ouvrard, almost illiterate and hardly able to read state papers. Ouvrard wrongly supposed that he could manipulate a dictatorship by the power of finance alone; Napoleon was in error when he fancied he could regiment business by the sheer force of the sword. Ouvrard failed to turn militarism to the interests of business; Napoleon was unable to bend business indefinitely to the purposes of militarism. Both ended in ruin, as exiles.

Yet the heritage of both survives. France was formed anew by the efforts of the two colossal plungers, economic and military. Napoleon centralized the State, making it so unified and strong that for a long time it could pursue a consistent, far-sighted diplomatic course more easily than any other government. The Banque de France focussed economic power to an extent unknown elsewhere; controlled by financiers and munitioneers, it directed economic life until 1936. The two merged forces, the State using the Banque to foster its political designs through foreign loans, and the ostensibly non-political bank, at times, exercising overshadowing influence over decisions of statesmanship.

The relative weights of high finance and high politics continued to form the supreme issue in France, from Napoleon to the Blum Cabinet and beyond. Which should obtain predominance? The issue was squarely posed before Napoleon one day by his minister, Mollien. Coming from an interview with one of the Emperor's financial enemies, the banker Lafitte, Mollien declared: "The question is, whether the first duty of politics is to serve every convenience of commerce and perhaps of every business man, or whether . . . those who hold first place in commerce could not bend their convenience and their calculations to serve those of high politics." This remained the question, despite all the changes wrought in France by modern developments.

THE SWING BACK TO CONSERVATISM

In France, the home of the phrase, laissez faire, competition was restrained until far into the nineteenth century. Strongly protectionist until the 1860's, France never did accord her industrialists anything like the astonishing freedom enjoyed for a time in England. Her conservative rulers viewed innovations with suspicion, and the weaving-masters of Lyons were reluctant to try out a new machine, like that of Jacquard, until they saw Englishmen reaching for it. And so, although modern capitalism grew in France, it did not cause a break with the past so radical as the excesses of the Revolution seemed to forecast.

On the whole, French industry continued to a large extent along the lines laid down under Absolutism. Luxury-trades formed a mainstay, and the national exports were kept up by maintaining the old monopoly of fashion in Europe; this was not cracked until the 1880's, when foreign competition grew stronger in many lines, and the balance of trade slowly began to turn against France. With few exceptions, therefore, French industrialists were not pioneers on the Anglo-Saxon or even German model. The crude, bluff, self-confident individualists who erected towering structures elsewhere had counterparts in France only in the fields of finance and munitioneering, to which French genius continued to turn, as in the days before the Reign of Terror.

Some outstanding Frenchmen endeavored to burst through the tradition of catering to the rich few; one of these was André Boucicaut, a humble clerk who created the first really modern great department-store, to offer wares to the masses. In his *Au Bon Marché*, the idea of selling cheaply for cash was developed as never before, and advertising, including window-displays, was perfected. Embarking upon cut-rate competitions and sending mail-order catalogues to the provinces, he slashed across the routine of retailing and shocked not only French but Americans as well. Back in 1893, *Harper's* was blaming Paris and Boucicaut for the shocking standardization of life. If America was growing more commonplace, said *Harper's*, it was the fault of Paris which cheapened styles: "The great vulgarisers of fashion at the present day are the large drygoods stores like the Louvre." Already, "the roller of industrialism, of bureaucracy, of the mode, has passed over the world and erased originality." Thus what France now blames on Ford, America then blamed on Boucicaut.

Like Ford also in his philanthropy, Boucicaut set a new standard in handling personnel as well as wares. Indeed he started a system of profit-sharing among his employees; his wife, who had been one of his clerks, turned over the entire concern at her death to the force, leaving a large part of her private wealth to Pasteur. Thus the pair were pioneers in humanitarian enterprise and not only stimulated the mass-consumption of goods but sought to form new patterns in mass-management.

In more modern times, André Citroën, the "French Ford," perhaps the best advertised industrialist of France, also tried to tap the greater markets of the classes with lower purchasing power. His cheap cars were offered amid terrific publicity, Sahara-crossings and electric signs on the Eiffel Tower. His similarity to Ford was most marked in his effort to keep his concern independent of finance and within his own family. But the effort to steer clear of the financial oligarchy ended in ruin.

In the main, French industrialists persisted in their age-old caution, their reliance upon the State, their tendency to retire as rentiers. This natural conservatism was reinforced by the fact that modernism brought to perfection industries like the processing of wines and champagnes or cheeses which were based upon agriculture; thus science produced a most influential class of agrarian-merchants, proprietor-salesmen, living on large estates in considerable leisure, forming dynasties and handing down wealth and lore to long lines of descendants. Moreover, their way of life attached them to the country gentry and even to the lesser nobility, whom they resembled in love of routine and stability.

The country gentry accordingly retained much prestige and business men still liked to retire and join them. In the deep country, priests still turned toward the pew of the local comte to say "Dominus Vobiscum." One cartoonist depicted the heartrending encounters in a rural church, where the comte refuses to bow to the sugar-dealer, M. Poton, in the adjoining pew. The comte's son pointedly lifts his hat to the beggars at the door but simply cannot see the Potons. The merchant, however, consoles himself with the reflection: "Let the little Potons grow up, and our sugar will catch the vicomtes yet."

When industrialists went into politics, as the satirists loved to point out, it was in the guise of country gentlemen, possibly with cravats a shade too high, whiskers too glossy, and voice too deep when they intoned their references to "the soil, the family and society, the honesty of the countryside and the pestilential atmosphere of the cities." Provincial business men were still humble toward the capital, still dominated, as ever, by financiers and the returned noblesse. Some independent patriciates retained traditions, as at Bordeaux and Marseilles, comparable to similar groups of overseas-merchants in German Hamburg or Bremen. But in manufacturing cities like Lille and Lyons, new methods had evoked new men and the parvenus who floated to the top were more like the self-made industrialists of Birmingham and Glasgow, fervently pious and very energetic, but lacking in polish. They did not have the campaigning ardor, the political will to conquer, of such Englishmen, however, and remained overshadowed by financial Paris, socially and politically.

Their servility toward aristocratic groups was the subject of many a jest. In the "Comédie de notre temps," written in 1874, the mocking *Bertall* reveals the ballroom of *M.* and *Mme. Big Purse.* Conspicuously set is a huge glass dome, under which repose the wooden shoes in which *Papa* originally walked to Paris to find work. But this past is now put behind them as mere decoration by the *Big Purses*, who invite the cream of Paris to their functions and warn the flunkey at the door: "Roar titles, acclaim judges, resound *la grosse banque,* delicately distinguish the industrialists—and glide over the rest."

The consuming ambition of *Papa,* as he tells *Maman,* is to rise beyond trade: "When one has one's millions out of the business, one may marry one's little *Niniche* as one will." He says to his daughter, "My mouse, you may choose." And when the petulant *Niniche* finds the "marquises too rococo and the princes a bit faded—papa, I must have a duke," her indulgent parent replies, "My little rat, I will buy you one."

What the *Big Purses* achieved, the *Little Purses* dreamed about. They might not be able to embroider coronets on their kerchiefs or buy ancestral portraits "with and without cuirass," in dozen lots, but they managed to be bourgeois gentlemen and ladies, not too different from those in the time of Colbert. When the biographies of the nineteenth-century leaders of business in France, assembled for the Universal Exposition of Paris in 1901, are examined, there is an impressive scarcity of business men in public life. Apart from an occasional cotton-spinning deputy, like Ernest Loyer, or a municipal reformer such as the naturalized German, Leven, office-seeking was rare; it was left to lawyers. The majority apparently sought no other distinction than a blue ribbon or gold medals; one or two ventured into self-expression, like Paul Leprince, who sold a million kilo of coffee a year and was the author of Alexandrine verses, crowned by a provincial academy, which describe "the usefulness of flowers, inseparable companions of our existence." He was also the author of a novel, "Lover and Mistress," written in "a very high moral tone," in which, we are assured, he unhesitatingly declared himself "a partisan of the institution of marriage."

The caution of French business was indeed beneficial to economy in many ways. Lack of over-speculation and dependence on outside markets was an element of safety in some of the most dangerous of crises. The extremes of depression that broke the morale of business classes elsewhere were less obvious in still agrarian France. The bulk of the peasantry formed a strong counter-weight to urban labor, such as increasingly industrialized Britain did not preserve. Businesses in France were built up as far as possible by family dynasties, in the most solid way, and control of banks was avoided by keeping concerns small enough. As Calmes has shown, small and medium-sized firms predominated, and the majority of these did not take the form of stock-companies floating shares on the open market. The coal industry in particular, elsewhere the region of immense combinations, offers in France the spectacle of many companies, some going as far back as 1757, of which one only, the newest, enlarged its original capitalization up to the last few years. Many decreased capitalization instead, in striking contrast to the German coal-companies, which all enlarged theirs, and one by more than 2,000 per cent.

Keeping to this policy meant that business in France did not catch the savings of the people to anything like the extent in Anglo-Saxon countries. French banks were notoriously loath to lend to native companies, and the public was suspicious of enterprises, partly, perhaps, because there was no independent press to offer even ostensibly impartial judgment as a guide to investors. And so the frugal French offered their wealth to the State; in 1850, for instance, the Paris Bourse yielded 24 foreign loans and only 4 industrial papers. The result was that classes with money to invest tended to identify their interests with the State rather than Business.

Business accordingly stood outside politics, leaving legislation to the same caste, the *noblesse de la robe*, which had acted for it ever since the fourteenth century. Socially it accepted the canons of the returned émigrés. And far from capturing public confidence and the government, business men as a whole were gradually overawed by the forces of finance and munitioneering, closely allied with the mighty and willful French State, almost as though no Reign of Terror had intervened.

CANNON-KINGS AND FINANCIERS

Very soon indeed after the Revolution, appeared two munitioneers as mighty as those who flourished under Absolutism. The brothers Schneider in 1836 bought up the desolate village of Creusot, and presently enlarged their steel plants to supply locomotives, steamships and armaments. In the latter field, we are told, they were more fortunate than Krupp in Germany, who faced the hostility of bureaucrats—the Schneiders had an uncle who was Minister of War. The two brothers also went into public life, one managing the town as Mayor and the other rising high under Louis-Napoleon. In Creusot, they erected a seigneurial dwelling, guarded by artillery pieces and armed men; the environs were in a state of feudal submission, with schools and municipal offices controlled by the family and churches named for its various members—there was built a St.-Henri for Henri Schneider, a St.-Eugène and a St.-Charles, giving an air almost of apotheosis to the house. Schneider I had his statue at one end of town and Schneider II planned to set his at the other, showing himself with workers recumbent at his feet, and, for emblem, a cannon.

But the despotism of the first and greatest Schneider, and his use of state troops for private ends, to subdue recalcitrant laborers, roused such a storm that he was forced to retire from public life. Ever since, the family was kept under heavy fire from political opposition, until the most recent times, when it was accused of assisting Hitler to power in Germany, to promote the armament-race in Europe. This hostility was also spread to another gun-king, François de Wendel, Senator and a regent of the Bank of France; this family, controlling the French armaments trust, was especially suspected because of its international affiliations which enabled it, before the War, to play politics on both sides of the Rhine.

Along with figures such as these, reminiscent of the overthrown régime, towered the financiers, who learned to use their high and independent position to levy toll on industry. They had themselves appointed to the directing boards, entitled to the cream of the dividends, the so-called tantièmes. The tribute so exacted from French business by directors has been estimated at as high as 10 billion francs yearly. In other lands high salaries were paid to executives, but, said Habaru, the tantième-system gave French directors often "a remuneration a hundred times larger than that of their Anglo-Saxon colleagues." In some companies, the annual share of the directors reached 24 per cent of the dividends, and in a few family concerns it might run up to 45. As some directors of one company might be engaged in twenty or thirty besides, the total of their benefits assumed formidable proportions.

In return, the Bank would reply, that the financiers guided the State through crises and controlled economy to its good. But as some French business men, Lucien Bailly for instance, complained, the tendency ran toward stagnation, the old French trouble. For over a generation, said Bailly after the World War, the chief activity had been not the creation of new firms but the formation of filiales and subdivisions; lords mounted over vassals, exacting tribute, until French business began to assume a feudal aspect, with many fiefs, but a small aristocracy at the top. The general cry against the "financial oligarchy," the 200 or 300 men said to control national destinies, was based on this charge: in effect, their foes declared, they had restored the *ancien régime*.

In fact this "feudal plutocracy" has been composed to a remarkable extent of old names. Many titles of the elder nobility still lingered on the lists; and until 1936 the most influential group of the Banque de France consisted of long-established families like the Vernes, Rothschilds, and the Calvinist Mirabauds. Among the few manufacturers in the sacred circle was Voguë, but he was not a newcomer, for his ancestors had been helped to affluence by Minister Colbert over two centuries before. It was the effort of the Blum Cabinet in 1936 to bring manufacturing to more influence in the Bank.

Financiers not only intimidated manufacturers, but outshone them in political ambitions. Sometimes the ramifications of their investments persuaded them to take office; thus André Lebon had interests as wide as a colonial empire and his relatives were as strategically disposed as his funds. He became Minister of Colonies, but as supervisor of Devil's Island, his severity toward Dreyfus brought such a boomerang of hostility that his career was ended. Another public character was Octave Homberg, supposed to have been highly connected in some capacity with 52 societies ranging from salt, silk, electricity, Indochinese rubber, Saigon cotton, gems and perfumes of Madagascar, distilleries and mines to West-African water-power. This imperial financier owned a daily paper and conducted wide political campaigns; he was the author of works defending finance and warning the public against American predatory imperialism.

In Paris, therefore, the top-crust remained to a large extent what it had ever been, a mixture of financiers and aristocrats, with social authority lodged among the latter. True, there was much rivalry between the two elements, a strife of salons, in which bankers like Lafitte, the king-maker, plotted with administrators and literary lions against the pretensions of the nobility. But these remained skirmishes because, after all, under any system, finance and aristocracy found a common ground in France.

Although financiers, munitioneers and aristocrats formed again a constellation around the French State, the State managed as before to assert its will in certain fields against even the strongest economic forces. It would be false to conclude that the French State was overmastered by finance merely because a series of "affaires," from the Panama to the Stavisky, revealed corruption. Despite intrigues involving politicians, the State managed to keep an independence, based on the financial strength gained through the savings of the French people. As the wealth of the folk was offered to the Government, or invested in foreign loans approved by it, the State could fling the weight of capital in the diplomatic scales of Europe. It could, for example, prevent the flotation of German shares on the Paris Bourse before the War, and bar certain kinds of American industrial shares as well. Instead it could direct the national funds to Russia as the chosen military ally. With such power, French statesmen could pursue set courses, following "state reason" rather than commercial expediency; and thus French imperialism was as consciously dictated from above by politicians as shaped from below by forward-pushing industrialists.

On the whole, therefore, it cannot be claimed that the violence of political upheaval, or the ensuing technical revolution, radically altered French society in the nineteenth century; it is at least as true to say that the old forms of French society determined the flow of modern capitalism. The character of France, fixed during the Renaissance and Baroque, could not be broken up by steam-engines in a few years. Nothing, therefore, is more misleading than to suppose that the thread of history was cut in two when the machine appeared; the machine worked differently in each country, according to the social pattern left by historic forces. The economic individualities of nations were blurred, perhaps, but not lost.

DIFFERENT TYPES OF BUSINESS REFLECTED IN LITERATURE

The widely various results of the change to modern machine capitalism in England, France and Germany were mirrored clearly in the three literatures in the nineteenth century. In France, where industrialism was not so highly developed, the novelists were on the whole sympathetic with the goods-maker. Zola was not entirely antagonistic to the big department store and Daudet dealt gently with business men in "Froment jeune et Risler Aîné." But toward the financier the literati were pitiless as they had been in the Renaissance, depicting them as bloated monsters who controlled the strings of politics and opinion, ruining victims for pleasure out of a "sadisme plutocratique," or collecting loves, like art treasures, with a cold cerebral calculation. The power-maniac, the Nabob of Daudet, pours out millions to buy deputies, while Zola's money-master in "L'Argent" exults in conquest like Napoleon. In this procession of fictional ogres, as studied by Leblond, few Jews appear, and these were by no means so vehemently attacked as the true Frenchmen. Jews were admitted to have at least family attachments, whereas the rest were portrayed as incapable of human emotion save lust for power, love of hazard; in this the fiery, volatile men of the South were represented as more prone to excess than the more massive and moderate Northerners.

The social-literary situation was reversed in England, where two camps, industrial and agrarian, had been formed in the 1830's by the campaigns of the Manchester manufacturers for cheap grain. On the whole novelists took the side of country squires, leveling their lances at machine-capitalists as fiercely as the French penmen at financiers. This attack on business was not in the beginning radical so much as genteel; not socialists set their faces against Manchester but lovers of old-fashioned rurality. George Eliot's picture of the narrow-minded *Harold Transome* may be recalled, with Charlotte Brontë's inflexible mill-owner, *Moore*, and Mrs. Gaskell's utilitarian who reasoned "as if commerce were everything and humanity nothing." Thackeray launched darts at "The Newcomes," and so did the idolized Dickens, whom nowadays the bourgeois takes close to his heart. To be sure there are some pleasant-visaged business men in his works, like the *Cheeryble Brothers;* but against these may be set the mass of his caricatures; *Mr. Sparkle*, the parvenu who sat shamefacedly at dinner in his new palace, hiding his hands in his cuffs; the "Mudfog Association," with its uproarious miscalculations of the chair-market; the speculators, *Wilkins Flasher* and *Mr. Merdle*. Above all stands the study of English industrialism and speculation in "Martin Chuzzlewit," which evoked such resentment in America on account of stray shots in that direction also, but was primarily a denunciation of home business even more than of transatlantic manners.

The full-length portrait of the Manchester Warehousemen, *Anthony Chuzzlewit* and his son, expressed Dickens' distaste for utilitarianism. "There's another thing that's not easily overdone, father," says the younger of the pair, and that is "a bargain. Here's the rule for bargains —'Do other men, for they would do you.'" Their establishment left no room for the punchbowls and mistletoe or other symbols of squire-archical joviality, beloved by Dickens; stripped of Victorian genteel clutter, it was a den for rationalists:

A dim, dirty, smoky, tumble-down, rotten old house it was . . . but there the firm of Anthony Chuzzlewit and Son transacted all their business and their pleasure too, such as it was; for neither the young man nor the old had any other residence, or any care or thought beyond its narrow limits.

Business, as may be readily supposed, was the main thing in this establishment; insomuch indeed that it shouldered comfort out of doors . . . in the miserable bedrooms there were files of moth-eaten letters . . . and meagre bedsteads, washing-stands, and scraps of carpet, were huddled away into corners as objects of secondary consideration, not to be thought of but as disagreeable necessities, furnishing no profit . . . The solitary little table for purposes of reflection and social enjoyment bore as fair a proportion to the desk and other business furniture, as the graces and harmless relaxations of life had ever done . . . to their pursuit of wealth.

While English writers were assailing industrialists, and Frenchmen were denouncing financiers, two exiled Germans, Marx and Heine, entered that atmosphere. Heine, at Paris, lashed fiercely at the Paris financier, Rothschild, from whom he won cash at times by threats of literary violence. Marx, knowing both countries, united their hatreds of both types of business men in his excoriations of the bourgeois. But within Germany itself, where neither finance nor industrialism grew up until much later, the tone of writers was on the whole much milder. Generally the novelists viewed with respect the rising of the German middle classes, whose solid representative was still the merchant. The German merchants, as it happened, carried over a romantic tradition from Hanseatic times, which suited the medium of art. Moreover, novelists like Freytag found in them qualities superior to those of the aristocrat. A Liberal in politics, Freytag emphasized this past tradition as an encouragement for the future, and sought to elevate the self-confidence of the business men and strengthen their resistance to the nobility, by writing "Soll und Haben" and "Die Ahnen."

If it was the hope of Freytag in the earlier part of the century, that business men, inspired with pride in their ancestors, would become a mighty factor in German life, the close of the period saw a more melancholy picture, the "Buddenbrooks" of Thomas Mann. Like Freytag, Mann found much to admire in the Hanseatic sea-merchants, but in this novel, the greatest piece of literature with a business man as subject, Mann describes the disintegration of a grand old firm, which cannot be sustained by tradition alone, when vigor is gone.

XXII

GERMANY–LAND WITHOUT A BUSINESS REVOLT

THE RICHEST MEN of England, America, France and Russia, at various times, have been of German origin. Thus John Jacob Astor stunned the New World by his prodigious fortune; Rockefeller was of German descent; less known but perhaps the wealthiest business man who had ever joined the gallery of American millionaires was the German lumber man of the West, Weyerhäuser. In France, the German Rothschilds represented for a period the peak of financial power. The unrivaled giant of Eastern Europe, founder and master of modern Russian industries, was the astonishing Ludwig Knoop of Germany. And the vastest fortune ever made in the British Empire, estimated at more than £40,000,000, was produced in shipping by Sir John Ellerman, son of a poor German bookkeeper.

Many another poor immigrant from the same land found elsewhere the opportunities denied him at home and founded other families, only a little less eminent, as did the Protestant Barings, world-renowned bankers, or Beit, who stood close to Cecil Rhodes with a South African fortune. All these helped show the world what forces lay yet dormant in Central Europe, even while Germany itself lagged industrially behind the Anglo-Saxon lands and France. Germans themselves did not really join in the tremendous scramble until after the Franco-Prussian War in 1871. But it was clearly for other reasons than lack of ability.

Business men in Germany encountered great difficulties when they sought to assemble. Cut off by countless boundaries which parceled the German land, they lacked a meeting place like the Parliaments of England and France. In the Reichstag, where they aired their grievances in the Middle Ages, they had now practically no voice. The last assembly of the Hanse cities occurred in the seventeenth century, and thereafter the last political training-grounds were gone. In the territories, often of a miniature size, there was little room for industries on a large scale; denied economic victories, upon which depend social and political conquests, the Germans remained without upheavals corresponding to those

abroad. Tremors of the three revolutions which freed business elsewhere did indeed reach Germany, but without creating a similarly violent break-up of strata.

Indeed the effect of the French Revolution was to retard the emancipation of business in Prussia, by frightening the Prussian rulers into a
renewal of their restrictions upon enterprise. In this north-eastern part
of Central Europe, there was in any case no tradition of a bourgeois
independence or prosperity; even in the Middle Ages, there had been
no flowering of towns. Instead the land had been owned by a caste of
Junker-landlords who raised grain and soldiers as their principal products. They were the chief surviving representatives in the modern era
of the feudal military virtues and the feudal scorn of burgher ways. It
was much easier for a commoner to break through the barriers at Versailles or Buckingham than at Potsdam. And it was this caste, and this
realm, which was destined to bring all Germany under Prussian sway in
1870–71.

Business was an imported and artificially stimulated plant in Prussia,
carefully tended by the kings and entirely dependent on royal favor.
It also happened that a great proportion of the capitalist bankers and
entrepreneurs who built up Prussian industries were foreigners, invited
by the king and living in Berlin only on sufferance. A steady stream
of French Huguenot refugees brought talent and funds to that town;
the Jews had not found anything attractive about Brandenburg until
they were urged to come as guests. When modern Berlin, swayed by
Hitler, turned against the Jews, it was under a misconception: in
Prussia, Jewish capitalism was not a "parasite" that had fastened itself
upon an Aryan realm. The Jews had been urged by the Great Fritz to
create a commerce in the poor and crude country settlement of Berlin, and had doubtless come with misgivings.

Though Frederick was eager to increase the fluid wealth in his barren land by bringing in industries and capital, after the example of the
French royalty, he was determined to keep the upper hand over the
invited bourgeois. In his view, business must remain the tool of the
State; the State itself must be military. Junkers were barred from trade;
and no merchant was permitted to marry into the nobility or even buy
a *Rittergut*, a feudal estate. The sternness of these decrees was relaxed
in time, but never enough to affect seriously the social stratification in
Prussia; the agrarians continued there to hold bureaucratic power and
monopolize the high posts in army, diplomacy and government.

Business elements did not yield without a struggle. In the first part
of the nineteenth century, just after the defeat of Prussia by Napoleon,
financial chaos was spreading and demands for enormous reparations

by the French had to be met; in this crisis, the commercial groups, upon whom this disaster had fallen, were determined to make themselves heard. In 1810 they drew up a plan to put the country on a sound business basis, by establishing a national debt and a national bank on the model of the French, English and American schemes. This they proposed to the State through Prince Wittgenstein, a high nobleman but an entrepreneur interested in Silesian coal-mining, and politically ambitious.

But the agrarian caste in Prussia was determined not to allow such a plan to go through. The Junkers had learned from historic events abroad that the result of banks and debts was invariably a growing predominance of the capitalist class. Finance Minister Freiherr von Altenstein knew very well what had happened in England, where the founding of the Bank had led to the overweening influence of its directors over the Crown. Had not the scheme of John Law for reorganizing the finances of France helped on Revolution? And was not the horror of that upheaval still fresh?

Minister von Altenstein refused even to discuss the matter with merchants. Obviously, they would be prejudiced in favor of a matter so clearly in their interests, and so it would be better to ignore them. And he did not, in any case, like to meet such middle class persons. As he wrote disdainfully to the King, he had occasionally consulted bankers—being Finance Minister, this was sometimes unavoidable—but he preferred to have his underlings gather their opinions and spare him direct associations. In this situation, at least, he saw no necessity for listening to advice from business men. The following letter to the King, penned on March 18, 1810, is a hitherto unpublished document in the Prussian State Archives:

Your Majesty wishes perhaps that I should speak with Jews and bankers which Prince Wittgenstein is supposed to have heard . . . I have not seen such . . . On weighty matters I have always consulted bankers. My underlings are well acquainted with such men, and can obtain and have obtained their frank views. The result always was that they made demands in their own interest, a trend of thought which brings no shame upon a merchant as such, but should not have any influence over my measures . . . The Finance Minister can hear business men on the subject of commercial conditions, but in the questions of the government of the State and upon the more important operations touching the whole nation, surely it was never proposed to a Finance Minister in any State, to put himself in the hands of merchants and seek advice from them.

Free from the prejudices of vulgar traders, therefore, and following only his Junker conceptions and the demands of state reason *à la prussienne*, the Minister unconditionally rejected the plan. The very notion of a state debt, a state bank, though tested means for achieving national cohesion, filled him with horrid visions of ambitious merchants insisting perhaps upon parliamentary representation. And where would that lead? Possibly to the death of Hohenzollern princes upon the scaffold. He asked the King to consider why the business men were demanding that the state loan should be raised in the name of the nation instead of the Crown? "The Prussian Nation as an entity exists only through the Throne, and its existence ceases with the destruction of the Throne." Surely, therefore, the business men must "reckon upon the continued existence of the Prussian State under a different dynasty . . . I am far from supposing that Prince Wittgenstein has such intentions; he is led to this only by shortsightedness. But it is postulated . . . and the bonds between Your Majesty and his folk are loosened in the public eye."

He begged the King to consider what he owed himself and his family and to refrain from placing "the sovereign power under such self-made guardians as would be the directing group of the new National Bank, which is to be declared independent of Your Majesty." If once a group of business men were put in control of any public institution, free from royal grasp, the end could only be disaster. As the example of Sweden and other foreign lands had only too shockingly proved, the outcome would be a democracy:

> The plan of a National Bank will lead to a National Parliament that approves and guarantees such a creation. This is entirely unavoidable and is inherent more or less in all plans for such an institution. A meeting of the Estates of the Kingdom is already proposed here and there with more or less urgency. It seems that public opinion has been worked upon intentionally to this end, and if the plan laid before us does not clearly express this, it is only because the author knows Your Majesty's dislikes on this point and is convinced that such a thing will come to pass of its own accord . . . What history teaches about all such assemblies whenever a Regent in a time of need has surrendered to them, is, that they almost always have had a revolution as a result, and at the least the most terrible scenes for the governing family.

This curious document has exercised a fateful influence upon the history of the business man. In a sense, its results are still observable today; it is even possible that the entire modern capitalistic system may be brought down with a crash because Prussia was thus carefully preserved, as a feudal-military anachronism, in the heart of Europe. The opposition of Minister von Altenstein kept the King away from commercial-democratic channels; Prussia was developed without the device of a national bank, controlled by a powerful and independent clique, and without that parliamentary discussion which had helped to mold other countries. So the feudal spirit of Prussia was prolonged and, even after the whole of Germany was united under the Prussian king, with a very limited parliamentary system, the Prussian Army preserved its high position and would yield allegiance only to the king.

To be sure, as the nineteenth century swept along, business unfolded in Germany and eventually the German business man was "emancipated" from absolutism. But such freedom as he won was not a thing he obtained by his own determined struggles. Though merchants clamored for the Zollverein, the abolition of the hundreds of petty customs-lines, they did not achieve it by their own strength. Laissez faire in Prussia, moreover, was not the rallying cry for business interests; rather, it was a foreign notion that the king himself adopted and applied by pressure. Minister von Hardenburg, the rival of the hide-bound conservative, von Altenstein, put through reforms giving greater freedom of person and property in Prussia; but, as he said: "We must achieve from above, Majesty, what the French have done from below up." Bureaucrats decided freedom would be better for the business man, and so they gave him a shadowy and paternal liberalism.

For a moment, of course, around 1848, it looked as though Germany would have a revolution backed by commercial interests. But German business men did not then make common cause for very long with the revolting proletariat, as the French, English Puritans and Americans had previously done for opportune periods. Instead they were persuaded that their true interest lay in clinging to the strong State, and not in overthrowing it.

The emancipation of the German business man, like the enfranchisement of the German woman after the World War, was a gift; in both cases, the recipient had not worked for it with revolutionary ardor, and was not prepared to exercise it. Even when the way was opened for political expression, the merchant did not make himself offensive to the Prussian Government. He bowed to it and concentrated his energies largely upon his own economic affairs. Traders and bankers generally neglected political action. Some other groups, it is true, especially the heavy-industrialists, showed a tendency to exercise indirect influence over German politics. Thus, as Kehr has shown, a tremendous "deal" was consummated before the World War, whereby the makers of armor-plate and cannon secured a big navy, while the Junker landlords at the same time obtained high tariffs for their "grain-factories."

Both parties united on the program of tariff protection *plus* armaments, which was profitable to each, and forced it upon Germany by an expensive publicity campaign, financed by the interested business concerns. But this was merely a harmonious working together of business and Junkerdom. They did not clash. Never, before the World War, did a dangerous force spring out of the commercial sphere to thwart the military-agrarian caste of Prussia, wrest away its monopoly of government functions, subdue its agriculture to manufacturing, and limit its freedom of action in military affairs.

DEVELOPMENT OF GERMAN BUSINESS CHARACTER

Certainly Prussia was not all of Germany—merely its ultimate master. Other parts retained more of the older tradition of commercial pride. Up to a very late time, until 1874, for instance, the city of Bremen had enough Hanseatic spirit left to govern itself, and, as Gustave Pauli has told it, they did well. Up to that date, the Bremen citizens taxed themselves, at their own estimation of what they could afford to pay, but without making any declaration of income, and with no legal control over their decision. At stated times, they delivered the amount of money which they thought they owed the City in sealed packages, always in cash, at the beautiful old Rathaus. When the City became modern, under Prussian influence, it erected the new system of governmental tax-declarations. It was naturally expected that a great increase in municipal revenue would be the result, but, to the general surprise, no more money was sent in than before. The Bremen citizenry had paid up in full, even without publicity on incomes and fear of condign punishment.

This sort of surviving pride did not, however, make for positive political action. German business men in general lacked too many of the motives which animated their contemporaries. Devoid of Calvinist religious compulsion on the whole, unable to scale a social ladder, barred from political meetings, limited in economic opportunity, they were thrust back upon themselves. Their place was the home. And home-life, accordingly, became *gemütlich*, placid, and unlike the driving "domesticity" of the upward-straining parvenus abroad. It was more openly and without pretense, bourgeois.

Even very rich Germans continued to live near, or at times above, their offices until well into the nineteenth century. They had no such reasons for pretending to sever connections with trade as the English; by the sixteenth century, Englishmen were building separate residences in the snobbish hope of bettering themselves. Frenchmen of means not only moved away from the shop, but shut up the shop altogether. Only the Germans remained quite honestly what they were, since there was but the slightest chance of becoming anything else.

The idea of the Frankfurt merchant was to be "stillreich," "quiet-rich." The Hamburg phrase, "solide," indicates a similar state of torpid affluence. This unruffled atmosphere was conducive, however, to the concentration of energies. Doubtless, as Sombart maintains, it was partly responsible for the tremendous push exhibited by German business men when, in the late nineteenth century, they did get openings at last for capitalistic expansion. Under Absolutism, according to this theory, German merchants learned to be supple and adaptable; hence they later showed themselves more ready to please foreign customers by concessions and a study of their wants than prouder and more rigid Britons. It is probable that many of the forces which, in England, were diffused in politics and, in France, were diverted into *rentier* leisure, were focused in Germany upon the immense modern drive of pure business.

In his intensity, the German business man came, therefore, to resemble the American particularly. The German, who could not easily climb into his aristocracy, devoted himself to the pursuit of gain as whole-heartedly as the American, who had no upper class to bother about. Neither was affected by the wish to imitate landed gentlemen so much as the English and French. The country week-ends and leisurely delays which often render business dealings with these latter peoples irritating to Yankee "go-getters," are really the concomitants of their social climbing.

In a sense, in modern times, the German has been even more absorbed in business than the American. Men like Stinnes worked with an almost superhuman concentration, and often shortened their lives by neglect of rest. The German has known less golfing and club-life than the American; he has also felt less social compulsion for entertaining, philanthropy and community drives. There was not so much necessity for him to be a good mixer or a good giver. Moreover, the industrial activities of the Germans tended to involve more technical preparation; the American has made money on the whole more easily in speculation and in natural resources, rather than in slow perfection of elaborate processes. The German has had to give a steadier attention to technology and to emphasize thoroughness.

This earnest air has, however, come recently upon the Germans—in the mounting pressure of the capitalistic age. In the eighteenth century, opportunities for business expansion were still strictly limited by the stern rules of Absolutism. Business could not grow and seek foreign outlets; it could not absorb the energies of the middle classes to such an extent as later. In the circumstances, a great proportion of the surplus time of the early German bourgeois turned to philosophic speculation, pure science, the arts and especially the theater. Thus the economic backwardness of Germany produced a rare bloom of culture.

This background of cultural exploration differentiated German business men from Anglo-Saxons bred to economic exploitation. Out of Germany have come some of the most acute and refined intellects in the world of business, men like Rathenau and Engels, with a far higher education than would elsewhere be considered "good form"—men with a more serious, broad and keen awareness of the whole capitalistic process. In German business may be found lower depths and greater heights than in other lands. On the one hand, stood men devoted to money-grubbing and heavy feeding, and yet, on the other, some of the most talented and sensitive figures in business history.

The Anglo-Saxons and French have followed on the whole a middle path, comparatively easy. They could win material success and at the same time an agreeable social distinction; as a result, they became neither remarkably crude nor unusually subtle—merely "acceptable." The German was more variable in type and might swing to one extreme or the other. At one end of the scale appeared the early Rothschilds, of whom Bismarck said in 1879: "I have known many members of this house. Striking to me always was their pursuit of money." The Rothschilds, when they left their Frankfurt nest, were considered crude in England. Nathan was described by a Londoner: "The things to be bought with money had in themselves little worth to him. He had no feeling for that goal to which every Englishman tends, when he possesses enough money to acquire it, for 'Comfort' in the widest sense of the word. His ambition consisted in reaching a commercial goal quicker and more effectively than others." The total lack of sympathy for art on the part of Nathan, and of his Paris brother, James, was the subject of constant jokes. Once Nathan is supposed to have jingled the coins in his pocket and said to the musician Spohr: "That is *my* music. That is what we of the 'Change understand."

Nor was this attitude exemplified merely in the Jewish family, for it could be seen as well in the Protestant emigrants to London who founded the great banking-firm of Baring, and were notorious for their beggarly and unkempt appearance, and lack of regard for English gentlemanly proprieties in dress. John Jacob Astor in America, also a German emigrant, may be taken as yet another example of titanic disregard for cultural amenities.

Against such pictures may be set, however, the family of the Berlin bankers, the Mendelssohns. The philosopher, Moses Mendelssohn, who was in the silk-business, was taken by Lessing as the model for his "Nathan the Wise." He was followed by Abraham, who, through banking connections with the Prussian State, made enough money to support the genius of his son, Felix, the great musician. Members of this family exercised a great influence in the romantic movement in Germany, and acquired the friendship and admiration of artists and intellectuals. But the brilliance of the Mendelssohns was as foreign to the Anglo-Saxon tradition as were the barbarisms of the Barings. The English tried to maintain the "golden mean" which so often becomes a gilded mediocrity, whereas the Germans ran to extremes, complete absorption in profit-making, or a broader range of cultural interests.

GERMAN BUSINESS MEN AND THE STATE

The keenest thinking about the relationship of business and the State, on the part of practical men of affairs, has been done across the Rhine, in Germany. The German in business has been generally ahead of others in power and lucidity of thought and expression; he has been by far the most brilliant theoretician in modern times. This was partly owing to the difficult situation of the relatively poor and disunited German region in the early part of the nineteenth century; from the first, German business needed to make the strong State, instead of to overthrow it, like French and Englishmen. Besides, coming on the scene so very much later than either French or British, the German could critically observe others before he set out to rival them in world commerce.

Up to the 1850's, very little was stirring in Germany in an industrial way; the full tide of prosperity and manufacturing did not come until the 1870's. During many a decade, accordingly, the German merchants could travel abroad, weighing and judging the mechanical progress in other lands, much as the eighteenth-century English studied Dutch and French methods before embarking on their own career as industrialists. Friedrich Engels, the cotton-man who lived long in Manchester, strenuously warned his fellow-countrymen against adopting the pure doctrine of Manchesterism. So, too, Friedrich List, another business man, advised Germany to avoid too close an imitation of England, and to study instead the working-out of the Hamiltonian principles in the United States. List was an enthusiastic apostle of German unification; he pressed for railroads, as one means of breaking down the localism of Germany; as early as 1819, he conducted a big meeting of business men in Frankfurt-am-Main, out of which came a great organization to work for the Zollverein, the customs-union of the German states. List's commercial interests took him to America, where he saw protectionism and union impressively operating in a new country. Formulating his theories, List became the first popularizer of the science of political economy in Germany.

A third German business man, exponent of Liberalism, was the noted

David Hansemann, who became Prussian Minister and advocate of a constitution and a parliamentarism for Germany on the Belgian model. Originally the son of a Lutheran pastor, Hansemann began as a poor apprentice in a retail firm, and grew rapidly in wealth and political vision. Seemingly gifted with second sight, any novelty he took up, from steel pen-nibs to fire insurance and railways, yielded large profits; at sixty, instead of retiring, he had just begun to form a great bank. Travels to England gave Hansemann the firm conviction that a humanitarian movement must accompany the expansion of industry in Germany; he devoted a large part of his fortune to experiments in education of workers. From private philanthropy, he branched out into politics and was active during the dangerous revolutionary period of 1848, urging compromise.

Hansemann earnestly strove to bend the stubborn Prussian State toward a milder Liberalism. As Treitschke complained, Minister Hansemann considered the "army and bureaucracy as annoying parasites of the merchants and manufacturers." Boldly he laid his views before his Sovereign. Probably, says Wantoch, it was the first time in Germany since the days of the Fugger that a bourgeois had adopted so firm a tone toward a monarch as did Hansemann when he announced that "the country's strength no longer rested on feudal principles, (on) the military autocracy."

Men such as these dreamed of reforming, compromising, Liberalizing. They sought a mild régime, combining the better features of several systems, in a State both strong and comparatively free. But their aspirations were balked by the Prussian bureaucracy and Army. These old historic forces raised themselves anew; they knew how to turn to their own advantage the hopes and organizations of business men. Though merchants might agitate for a Zollverein, it was the bureaucrats and army men who actually achieved unification; their military triumphs brought the tremendous upswing of the 1870's, in which opposition was almost stifled.

Business men did not yield easily to this powerful State; many fought bitterly against the budgets proposed by Bismarck for the Army. But the Junker caste arrogated to itself the highest posts in the diplomatic service, the Army and Government. And its members were of a character peculiarly hostile to urban culture and commerce. They would only engage in what they considered respectable trades, such as horse-dealing, beet-sugar raising or distilling liquor from potatoes. Still living largely upon remote estates, they were not burgher-minded. Nor had they such training-schools as Eton and Harrow to mold "gentlemen," the odd, specifically English hybrid of feudal lord and bourgeois. As a matter of fact, the Prussian Junkerdom did not even acknowledge the binding force of religious faith to such an extent as the Catholic aristocracy of Poland, the Orthodox Russians or the Anglican British. A proud, pagan, Spartan caste, resolutely rural and none too highly educated, the Junkerdom of Prussia was without a parallel in Western Europe.

For a time these agrarians and business men agreed on a mild program of laissez faire. The victorious Junker, Bismarck, was willing to leave the barriers low while German grain was selling well abroad; but, after the crisis of 1873, and as American grain was competing seriously, the German agrarians shouted for protection. So did the iron-industries. And so the doors were slowly shut, and German business as a whole was subjected increasingly to the demands of the agrarians.

Since they saw no way to escape this situation, German business men were inclined to join the upper ranks of society as far as possible. They tried to buy landed estates; one member of the Siemens family, great in the chemical and electrical fields, wasted huge sums in the unprofitable upkeep of a castle, much to the disgust of the business-like relatives. Sometimes the ambitious business man joined the Army as reserve-officer; his sons, if possible, entered the exclusive student fraternities of the universities, which really held the keys to high governmental and diplomatic posts.

The son of the great Liberal, David Hansemann, turned "governmental." Adding the noble "von" to his name, he became Adolph von Hansemann; he acquired the dignity and uniform of an Austrian General Consul, so resplendent that, half in pride and half in irony, he called it his "Lobster Uniform." Unlike his father, Adolph did not care who ruled the State, so long as he was profitably employed in building it up. He steered his father's Disconto-Gesellschaft through three wars, the formation of an Empire, and successive booms and crashes, to his death in 1903. Incidentally, he assisted the Government in colonial schemes, particularly in New Guinea; he had a romantic weakness for ventures in China, Brazil and Venezuela, which cost his institution millions.

In this Hansemann, the North German Hanseatic type lived on. His giant frame, grown heavy with wine and banqueting, clad in the Lobster Uniform, would have been ideal for an old-time burgomaster. He had a solid and genteel background, bought good paintings and read Livy. A powerful tyrant over men, conceited, shrewd, bull-headed, he was fond of terrifying stockholders. Once, when asked for a report on a railroad under his control, he merely formed his big hands into a trumpet and bellowed the single syllable, "Foul." Rarely did he deign to explain his plans; when asked for his reasons in a certain course of action, on one occasion, Hansemann replied: "We thought it necessary." Thereupon the impertinent stockholder collapsed, saying meekly,

"Thank you for the exhaustive reply. I never expected so much."

The powerful "Pasha," as he was known, however, used his strength for the State, not against it. So did others of a similar stamp. Heinrich Wiegand, for instance, eager patriot in Bremen, was absorbed in the ancient rivalry of Bremen and Hamburg over shipping. To his mind, the local strife loomed greater than national politics. And there was yet another reason for the single-minded devotion of so many business giants to their enterprises; when the Germans entered the world race for markets, they found the cream skimmed off by the British. Only by a greater ingenuity and a more dogged persistence, could they hope to forge ahead. Quick returns and easy speculations, in which the American might trust, were denied to the German. The latter had to be willing to undergo scholastic preparation and slow maturing of plans. The result was that German businesses were often more solid when they were finished; fewer obsolescent plants burdened Germany, and she was spared some of the risks of speculation and peculation which endangered both England and America.

A herculean worker, the German had little time to enter noisy political campaigns. And often he was entirely blind to the need for political action; Emil Rathenau, for instance, was one of the men who revolutionized the surroundings of the human race, but never considered ultimate consequences. He was a sort of Jules Verne in electricity; he could see far into the future of business, and was fond of spinning wonderful yarns of the years to come. As his son Walter said of him, men "came from far to ask him what would come out of this technique, that form of communication, this economic structure . . . And then he quietly answered them and wondered only that they were not disgusted by the obviousness of his remarks."

Yet this forward-pressing spirit was unconcerned with social transformation or political adaptation. His whole soul was in production. Exhaustless in energy, he drove his technicians to sanatoria by the problems he set, and lived in a continual delirium of nervous excitement. But there were strange incongruities in his mind: he would build plants big enough for generations to come, but rode on trams to save the wear and tear on his automobile tires; he could invest millions in a wild dream, but he quarreled fiercely about the bill for every strip of linoleum in his office. He changed the life of man, but ignored men.

Thus the Germans, though in many ways so different from their French neighbors, were like them in refraining from politics. And on both sides of the Rhine, the one industrial element which achieved effective influence with the State was that of munitioneering. In Germany, as in France, the makers of armaments attained a greater power than ordinary merchants and manufacturers. But the German heavy-industrialists were not merely eager to outfit the Prussian Army; they urged the building also of a big Navy, which would use yet greater amounts of steel. And, combining with the Prussian agrarians, they forced the Navy upon the reluctant remainder of business men, who did not stand to profit by the arrangement, but had, instead, everything to lose.

One of the chief munitioneers with direct political influence was von Stumm. His family had been working in coal and iron in the Saar ever since the 1600's. At last, in the Wilhelminic times, one of them took the title of "Freiherr von Halberg Stumm," and merging into the higher caste, became a friend of the Supreme Junker, Bismarck. Controlling a big newspaper and entering the Reichstag, von Stumm was a driving force behind the armament of Germany. He was a reserve officer in the Army; so he stood high with the military forces, made armor-plate, and voted for its purchase.

Von Stumm was famed for his fierce resistance to any sort of social measures, however mild. This, it is fair to say, was not the attitude of all the coal-barons. His rival, Röchling, was a national-liberal, ready to compromise with democratic forces. The two titans battled in the Saar over economic and political policies for many years. In fact, their feud shook the earth. Once even a duel occurred, from which the two coal-barons emerged unscratched, but angrier than ever. Eventually, von Stumm won the contest, with the help of Bismarck's bureaucrats; that Röchling had married his daughter into the Government availed him little.

The heavy-industrialists did not propose to manage the military powers which they were helping to enlarge. They were not thinking about civilian control over the vastly increased Army and the new Navy. Nor did they even make it a condition of their help to bring the Prussian Army to the point of swearing allegiance to the bourgeois constitution. They left the forces of militarism irresponsible, while they, thinking purely of economic advantage, augmented them incessantly. So little were they concerned with possible explosions that, as Hallgarten shows, they extended their control far into French armament-industry as well, and profited also by the budgetary increases for defense in France. At the same time, the French armament-family of de Wendel had representatives on both sides of the Rhine.

Krupp, representative of a very old, partly Dutch Calvinist, burgher family, and the mightiest steel-magnate of Germany, appears to have wavered between Germany and France as potential customers for his monstrous cannon. According to the new biography by Bernhard Menne, he was incessantly struggling to win French favor; in 1843, he sought intervention by the Paris house of Rothschild to offer weapons and defensive armor for the French Army. Again and again, as Menne indicates, when the tides of feeling were at a height between the two nations, Krupp was imperturbably pressing his deadly wares upon France. Probably, he would have erected a plant there, had not the pressure of the Schneider House, his colossal rival, been too strong upon the French Government. So, despite his years of wooing, all Krupp received was membership in the French Legion of Honor.

Thrown back upon the home markets, Krupp devoted his energies to upholding the military forces of Germany and helping to pass their big budgets through a reluctant Parliament. At one time, when the liberal element in Parliament seemed determined to cut down appropriations for armaments, Krupp offered to lend the State the necessary funds to buy his products. But he was not an obvious propagandist like von Stumm; only late in his life, in 1887, did he send his son to Parliament, bidding his workers vote for him "purely in order to support the government's military estimates" and so bring orders to Essen. Always, however, Krupp kept insisting that he knew nothing about politics, and would not venture into any branch of administration. He preferred a background position.

To a large extent, this one individual was responsible for the thorough-going militarization of Germany and for the British-German naval race which led ultimately to the World War. He was far more than a simple purveyor of munitions; he was a driving force to rouse up the slothful and parsimonious, unprogressive Junker officers. They did not want to spend the vast sums required for his crucible steel products; they really wished to make war more cheaply. But Krupp's unbaffled determination forced "progress" upon the Junkers. Yet Krupp, representing so mighty a force in European history, was not a sinister figure. Personally, there is something irresistibly touching and wistful about him. But through his refusal to consider the social consequences of his profession, he helped to bring immeasurable disaster upon the Continent.

Not for vices can Krupp be condemned; rather, it was his virtues and especially his humility, which endangered world peace. Had he run casinos, the fault would have ended with his life, but his shirking of responsibility for invention endangered Europe. As he said of himself, he was "a passionate gun-maker." He did not have to make armaments; nobody wanted the new kinds he turned out at first, least of all the army officers. Gun-making was not as profitable as spoon-pouring. Not even the forgivable lure of vast gains, or patriotic necessity, led Krupp into munitioneering. What was his motive? Sheer technical pride in performance, it would seem. Proud as a Lucifer amid the smoking furnaces of his Essen, he admired the burnished hammer,

"Fritz," weighing 50,000 pounds, smiting an anvil weighing two million pounds. Happily he crowed that no one in the world, not even his French rival, Schneider of Creusot, had such a monster as this, "which must wake the Antipodes from their slumbers."

Like a King of the Underworld, Krupp flourished amid lurid flames. Once a humble laborer in a tiny plant, he had swallowed the whole town with his steel works, much as Schneider had engulfed Creusot. He rejoiced in the acrid fumes of his establishments, and was wretched because his feeble son acquired coughs, and his wife preferred Baden-Baden. Vainly the Steel-King tried to detain her by building a palatial home with a game-cover and riding-track, and even cascades; he had all the "miserable hovels" which might offend her view swept away, in the hope of creating a substitute for the "expensive visits to watering-places." But Persephone would only spend a season in Krupp's Underworld.

Proud of his fine guns, Krupp longed to have the whole world admire them. But the rigid old conservatives in the German army caste wanted to be left alone; they snubbed the "passionate gun-maker." To wake them up, Krupp endeavored to sell his weapons to France, Britain and Russia, enemies of the Fatherland. As he explained, it was pure patriotism which led him to persuade the Crown Prince of Germany to introduce him to the British Admiralty, that he might sell his colossal cannon to the foes of Germany.

As soon as he won a little success in Britain, Krupp wrote to the German military officials, pointing out that "The Royal Prussian Navy should not draw its guns from abroad . . . for me a matter more of honour than of financial interest." He begged them to let him equip a battleship for them free of charge. In this way, Krupp unleashed the British-German naval competition, arming both sides and playing each off against the other. Following the same policy, he armed the Austrian antagonists of Prussia, and when, on the eve of war, the incensed Bismarck urged him at least to delay delivery of guns to the foe, Krupp recalls, "I said that we must safeguard our reputation abroad." He then told Bismarck to order more than the Austrians.

After he assisted the German Army to defeat France in 1870–71, Krupp was recognized by the Junkerdom at last as the chief support of their power. Then the king would have given him orders and gifts, but he modestly declined them. He had acted only out of the purest motives and was satisfied. If the king insisted upon rewarding him, it might only be with a pair of horses for his wife—"Young horses jumping about in a meadow, that is a delightful thing to see!" Horses were "something tangible, from which one gets pleasure daily, and more solid than little crosses and stars and titles and such-like cheap goods."

If there was anything Krupp was prouder of than his guns, it was his own humility. Overwhelmed by the recognition of his own limitations, he wrote one of the most extraordinary documents ever penned by a business man. Seldom has so clear a light been cast upon the inner workings of a steel-titan's mind as by this letter, directed to the great scholar, Alexander von Humboldt, in 1858. In this, Krupp makes deep bows, admitting "my profoundly-realised insignificance in the face of intellectual eminence," and admiring Humboldt's "selfless and pure philanthropy." He would not dream, he said, of pretensions himself:

> Having chosen a completely retired existence, divided between business and domesticity, having a sincere contempt for all the ostentation of public and personal distinctions, and having no further ambition than the desire to reap the comforting consciousness of duty performed.

In the simple mind of Krupp, however, as he offered tribute to the magnanimous scholar, there was a certain stirring of self-reproach. He felt bound to insist, in the letter, that he had derived his principal profits from railroads and steamships, not guns. Why, then, had he made guns? It was, he explained, in order to do something for his country:

> Alongside these appliances of peaceful intercourse, those of warguns are also provided for. The ideal is the highest degree of indestructibility; in the former case, for furthering the safety of property and human lives, in the latter for increasing the capacity of destruction. The former assumes the leading position, and must provide our living. The latter I cultivate at a great sacrifice, in the interests of progress, and this work will not achieve a value in my eyes until I can serve the fatherland with it in time of need. For the blessings of peace, however, I gladly renounce such an opportunity for proving what a home industry can do, as well as my pride therein.

So, too, in his old age, still anxious to further "progress," Krupp rushed about Europe trying to make reluctant military men accept his newest improvement, pivoted guns behind great forged shields, which made deadly sea-engines out of battleships. Everybody asked nothing better than to be left alone in the old rut. But modest old Krupp, selfless old Krupp, out of pure technical pride and humble hope, tormented military men into accepting his darlings. It almost exhausted him physically and was a drain on his resources. As he sadly wrote to a general: "It is well known that I have sunk the greater part of my fortune in the plan required for the manufacture of guns . . . As the result of the progress along the road to the creation of a great industry entirely with the object of honorably serving our great nation (not from the desire for gain or ambition)—I have expended a great fortune and fallen into debt."

Thus, it may be said with some assurance that, single-handed, the gun-maker of Essen did more to upset the balance of Europe and the budgets of nations, destroy the whole political set-up of the world, and endanger the future of capitalism itself, than the soldiers and politicians put together. Yet, even while he undermined the old social order, he anxiously desired to preserve the ancient forms intact. He was always peevishly protesting against even small changes in the life about him. Bedridden and querulous, signing himself the "Old Man," he scribbled endless notes to his workers: "People so spoilt are beyond helping . . . women in the journeyman's family wear lace-up boots nowadays," whereas when he was young, he wore wooden clogs, costing only a silver groschen a pair: "I wore them at the damp dripping hammer, on the cold earth, and warmed them every now and then by shaking inside them glowing ashes from the fire." Why could not the world go pleasantly on, adopting his latest pivoted guns, but wearing wooden shoes?

Brooding over the depravity of the world, the Old Man decided the Socialists were entirely to blame, and said Lassalle had done more to corrupt the "simple wants and ways" with his "devilish philosophy and his doctrine that men should get used to a style of life" above their station. "The wretch has sown evil seed," complained Krupp, and he was glad to say, "I am acquainted with only a few of his writings." It never occurred to Krupp that he, and men like André Boucicaut, could have done as much to corrupt the old simplicity with armaments and department-store advertising as a preacher of change like Lassalle.

The Old Man felt that repression was the answer. Manhood suffrage must be abolished in Germany and the penal code stiffened. All progress should be halted except in the field of warfare. Much as he rubbed his hands at the prospects of trying out his guns in a sea-battle between Britain and Russia, he rejected with horror the notion of altering the people's footgear. And at last, he decided to set an example to the world of the ancient simplicity in manners. He refurbished his little childhood hovel and dedicated it to the future. His little old house was to be preserved as "a warning not to despise the humblest thing, and to beware of arrogance."

His last hours were spent in going over the plans for building a whole colony of little houses, exactly like the hut in which he had been born seventy-five years before. Surely, he thought, if good workers were housed as he had been, they would be modest as he was. Like Henry Ford, who also changed the world and spent the proceeds upon romantic dreams of the horse-and-buggy days, erecting a model village devoted to barn-dancing, so Krupp set up insanitary old-fashioned dwellings as a pattern, while he waited to die: "I am . . . nearly only a skin with some bones, the rest is gas. It may happen that one fine day, the gas overwhelms by its lightness . . . the weight of the poor bones and suddenly . . . I shall go up directly into Heaven."

The last recorded letter of Krupp was about the blue Ratisbon slate which was to be duplicated upon roofs of the new hovels, his lasting monument. With this touching tribute to the ancient world he had left broken behind him, the soul of modest, sentimental, kindly old Krupp left his poor bones and winged "directly into Heaven" from the Hell of Essen. He left behind him a Germany well-armed, facing a France prepared by his business rival, Schneider of Creusot, and an England whom he had helped stimulate to imperialist enterprise.

XXIII

FROM NATURE TO EMPIRE—THE ENG-
LISH INDUSTRIAL REVOLUTION AND
THE STRIFE OF MANUFACTURERS
AGAINST LANDED GENTRY

THE REPERCUSSIONS of the French Revolution had entirely opposite effects upon Britain and Prussia; in the latter, the horror of the
Reign of Terror produced an aristocratic consolidation against the ambitions of business men, while, in England, the upheaval proved a stimulus to the machine-industry already implanted there. Napoleon's Continental system, which was to bar all Europe to British-made goods,
was the threat which at last aroused the manufacturers of the Manchester region to unfold their utmost energies.

Cheaper and cheaper should be their wares, made by pauper labor,
in order to underbid anything made on the Continent; and in a frenzy
of haste, the Manchester men turned to any promising new invention.
When even the cheapest textiles were unsalable, as Napoleon's political system was strengthened, there could be only one answer: war.
No other groups in England were more eager for the prosecution of
that retaliatory warfare upon France than the budding industrialists.
They not only intended to open Europe by force to their goods, but at
the same time hoped to rid themselves of the hordes of starving jobless
in their growing cities by enlisting them in the armies, thus dumping labor as well as wares abroad. To attract the unemployed to the army in
the crisis, recruiting sergeants paraded Manchester streets with loaves
of bread stuck on their bayonets. But that was not the only profit which
the war held out; the industrialists of England also helped to arm
France, while fighting her. Questioned about his patriotism, a Mr. Gill
of Birmingham, who made 2,000 daggers for the French, said he hadn't
known their destination, but, even if he had, "My Neighbours in the
Sword Trade really are not more virtuous in this Dagger Business than
myself."

The War was over in 1815, and the English industrialists confidently
awaited the immense prosperity which they had predicted: Europe,

they thought, would pant after their wares, and in a moment they would recoup themselves for all the blood and treasure spent by England upon that terrific combat. But the expensive war, so it seemed at first, had been a gross miscalculation. The crisis did not abate, and the expected markets did not materialize, for the Continent, so long cut off from England, had in the meantime developed some machinery of its own and had begun to make its own goods; for the rest, it was too poor to buy freely, had it so desired. Also, during the long Continental War, a Corn Law had been passed in Britain which kept up the bread prices for the benefit of the landed gentry—it was the only way to interest country gentlemen in the War as well as manufacturers—and this had raised the cost of living in the manufacturing cities, until they could no longer compete so well with the Continent. As a prominent business man put the case: "Manchester, which urged on, with an almost savage earnestness, that long-protracted and disastrous conflict, was the severest sufferer by its continuance!"

Yet, a few years later, new markets were found after all, in Spanish America, and the upswing began; a prosperity blossomed which surpassed the hopes of the manufacturers and proved their efforts had not been in vain. Then the fear of social upheaval and industrial ruin faded; a humming activity began, and speculation spread in cotton, iron, shipping and mines. Harriet Martineau described this period, which presented most of the classic features of the perfect boom. Shops displayed finer goods; canals and tunnels were projected, machinery was ceaselessly perfected. Standards of comfort also rose; merchants whose fathers had lived in dark alleys above dingy shops, toiling until midnight over accounts, now became leisured as well as rich and took regular vacations by the seashore. They began to order carpets, porcelain and other furnishings for the home, until then the rarest luxuries in the bleak North.

Rapidly the march of mechanization passed from field to field, from water-power to steam, from spinning and weaving to other industries, from industry itself to transportation by sea and land. Wonderfully subtle grew the Machine, able to catch and twirl in its iron fingers the tiniest slivers of cotton to make the finest thread; it also acquired strength, for lifting, stamping, and drilling and smoothing the mightiest engines, the hulks of locomotives or the sheaths of ironclads. And all the while its speed increased, like its power and finesse, until from the flying shuttles poured out hundreds of millions of yards of cloth, enough to envelop European masses and to turban and gird the teeming populations of Asia.

Each lunge forward meant a dislocation of industries based on previous processes; hence "progress" took a zigzag course. There was a continuous dying and rebirth of manufactures—a perpetual companionship of misery and triumph. Workers, deprived of a living by the swift strides of invention, turned to rioting, smashed the looms and trampled the webs into the mire, while alarmed employers took refuge behind troops. Manufacturers of the older type themselves, seeing their profits snatched by the few mighty possessors of new patents, wailed in unison: "Shall the welfare of forty thousand useful subjects be put into competition with forty?" But the victorious members of society heard none of these protests, which were drowned in the roar and surge of untrammeled industrialism:

> *Hark! what a sound! Art's pond'rous fabric reels,*
> *Beneath machinery's ten thousand wheels:*
> *Loud falls the stamp, the whirling lathes resound,*
> *And engines weave, while hammers clatter round . . .*

And so, once more, a revolution of Frenchmen had resulted in a commercial benefit to the English. Much as the movement of the French Huguenots in the seventeenth century, though shattered at home, had ultimately worked out to the assistance of English Puritans, so, at the opening of the eighteenth century, the upheaval in Paris had stimulated England's manufacturing class to extraordinary efforts. Napoleon, when he said the English were a nation of shopkeepers, did not realize that his own efforts were already turning them into something else—the world's supreme manufacturers.

LAISSEZ FAIRE IN OPERATION

No control over this process was established for a long time. Governmental supervision was furiously resisted by the large manufacturers, who wished no law but jungle law. At Manchester, these men insisted that police officers would only be spies upon their trade secrets and that "An influx of such gentry to disturb the harmony and arrangements of their manufactures, to deprive them of personal liberty, and the free exercise of their property, is UNWISE, IMPOLITIC and UNJUST." They defied inspection.

Free from plan and supervision, the industries shot off sprouts and, as factory barracks were set up in country valleys, the general development of the regions was left to Nature's management; roads, canals, press and post were rushed through recklessly; villages were enlarged to towns and towns to cities—ugly, sprawling, haphazard in construction as in layout, ill-lighted, unpoliced, without sanitation. On the outskirts rose the gingerbread "mansions" of the successful; at times, in a sudden outburst of yearning for culture, a "Grecian marketplace" would be set up in the heart of the medley. Thus, in the first part of the nineteenth century, Manchester transferred the Exchange from the old tavern on Penniless Hill to a new building with eight Corinthian pillars; but not far away from the glory of this classic edifice, a whole row of crazy buildings, together with a soap-works, collapsed and fell into the river.

The speed of the cities' transformation gave utmost delight to the inhabitants. Birmingham folk began chanting: "I can't find Brumma-gem!" A proud historian of the town in 1783 recorded in his annals: "The Traveller, who visits her but once in six months, supposes him-self well acquainted with her; but he may chance to find a Street of Houses in the Autumn where he saw his horse at grass in the Spring. A pitiful Market Town, in an inland Country, by pure industry, in a few years, surpasses most of our Cities!"

That there could be cause for dismay in the growth of these filthy, congested, crime- and plague-breeding spots, whose soot was "making a new Heaven and a new Earth—both black," seldom occurred to the enthusiastic witnesses of the transformation. Full of happy faith, they agreed with the bard of Birmingham, Mr. Moffitt, who thus apostro-phized his native town in 1818:

> Pride of the Country! Glory of the isle!
> Europe's grand toyshop! Art's exhaustless mine!
>
> . . . . . .
>
> Thy swords, elastic, arm our heroes' hands;
> Thy muskets thunder in remotest lands;
> Thy sparkling buttons distant courts emblaze . . .

All these wonders, the bard declared, were due to laissez faire. Bir-mingham, "from chartered fetters free," had now a "soul, as lib'ral as the breath of spring." In order to preserve this precious freedom, the various cities refused to grow up politically. Birmingham, as a protec-tor in Parliament declared, was "a village . . . its glory was in its village situation and he wished to preserve it." Down to Victoria's time, to 1853, Manchester continued to resist a city status; it preferred to have no official higher than a constable, and went on electing a swineherd every Michaelmas. Liverpool, pretending also to be a hamlet, developed no more efficient police-force than that afforded by fifty ancient men, known as "Old Charlies," even after it had become a huge city. The cities knew very well that, so long as they remained minors, they would be indulged and spoiled. The result was an industrial Peter-Pan-ism.

But though industry and building-speculation were free, or, as the poets put it, "un-charter-cramp'd," this complete freedom was judged too dangerous for workmen to share. As early as possible restrictions were imposed upon them; combinations among workmen were made illegal. Such anti-labor union laws could be enforced in towns like Manchester because there were few existing old gild-laws or regulations protecting artisans; some statutes governed the position of apprentices, but these were easily set aside. Labor was declared "free" from mediaeval fetters, and the anti-combination laws were explained as efforts to protect individualism.

Beyond this, nothing was done about the education, amusement or supervision of the mass of immigrants who poured into Manchester and Liverpool and other towns, by cart and boat and afoot, from the remote hovels of Ireland, Scotland and Wales, as well as from English parishes. For the most part, these were starved, illiterate folk, accustomed already to the foulest conditions, tamed through centuries of submission, eager to accept any pittance as preferable to a famine-death. But they formed a festering mass; unable to read, given no parks or diversions, they spent their pennies on strong liquor. Typhus raged among them; "consumption, distortion and idiocy" as well as brutal crime, were common; there was a fear that revolution might flare up in such a scene as it had done in France.

The horrors of the early industrialism have been told often enough, and reports of investigating committees and travelers have depicted the conditions among which infants labored in the cotton mills. According to these reports, poor-law authorities delivered pauper children, in batches of 50 and 100, to factory-owners, making no accounting for their welfare or even survival, and stipulating only that a certain percentage of idiots should be taken along with the normal ones. Sir Robert Peel had a thousand children in his plants. Children were the chosen operatives of the cotton-industry. Often they were left in the hands of real Simon Legrees, to be underfed on rancid bacon, worked as many as 18 hours a day, put in irons or whipped, kept prisoners. Blindly ignorant, stunted "infants" as they were called, stood whimpering at their machines from dawn until deep at night, with scarce a pause to eat. Their one friend, death, was a constant visitor to the mills.

In the mines as well, children toiled along with half-naked men and women, pushing up steep and slimy tunnels the heavy coal-cars, the weight of which made sores on their tender foreheads. They seldom saw the light of the sun. If they survived to become adults, their lot was hardly improved. A country parson described the towing-men along the canals, "fastened to their lines as horses to their traces," and distinguished from the brutes "only by this: horses are indulged with a collar to save their breasts." Real coolies were these; the main difference between them and the Asians was that they stupefied themselves with gin instead of opium, and went staggering and raving in their free hours, instead of lying in a dreamy somnolence. Indeed, the English were more uncouth than, for instance, the Chinese; as late as 1901, when the merchants of Manchester held a festival in honor of Queen Victoria, the whole roasted beeves and plum-puddings were cut in pieces and the dripping fragments were hurled among a crowd which fought and tumbled for the scraps. Indeed, an even nearer analogy was pressed by the great cotton-manufacturer of New Lanark, Robert Owen, who had risen through the old system himself and deplored it. He very bluntly said:

> Bad and unwise as American slavery is . . . the white slavery in the manufactories of England was at this unrestricted period far worse than that of the house-slaves whom I afterward saw in the West Indies and in the United States.

But such a voice as Owen's was rare in the North-country. There the bulk of industrialists were full of optimism, thrilled by the speed and growth around them. With a beatific satisfaction in their progress and creativeness, they speak of their deeds, in writings and manifestos, as "great and extraordinary" and "unexampled in the world." They look forward to making "great changes . . . in the appearance of the civilized world," and are sure any change must be an improvement. They foresee the glorious day when Manchester goods must be "spread in ten thousand forms and colours, not only in these kingdoms, but all over Europe, and even into distant continents." And they felt no qualms about the backwash of progress, as they marched confidently forward, crying, "These are thy blessings, O Commerce! These are thy rewards, O Industry!"

CULTURE ON THE ENGLISH FRONTIER

These rising business men had at first no gentlemen's clubs, hunting packs, or other uses for leisure than parading and drinking. Feudal customs were almost as absent on the English frontier as in the American wilderness. Hence the manufacturers of Manchester and other expanding towns became addicts of fraternal organizations of a noisy kind. They were fond of marching in orange capes "having on beautiful emblematic buttons, manufactured by ingenious gentlemen of the town," and of giving uplift banquets. One may readily picture the old English ancestor of the American, *Mr. Babbitt,* back in 1788, recognizable despite his disguise of knee-breeches and powdered hair, joining in the chorus of fellow-realtors, pounding on the table as they sing the boosters' song:

> *Sons of Trade, for mirth prepare,*
> *Banish sadness, banish care . . .*
> *Builders now your plans extend,*
> *To your projects there's no end,*
> *Noble make the town appear,*
> *Large and lofty mansions rear.*

Even before the next century opened, it was observed that the "whole stock of hands, money, and intellectual abilities" in that corner of England was in trade; people had forgotten agriculture and had never known diversions, but "speak of spinning jennies, and mules, and carding machines, they will talk for days with you." With simple and unabashed frankness, the Englishman measured life and achievements in terms of t'brass; how much a bride was "worth," was quite commonly advertised in the social columns of the press. Thus, one paper reported: "On Monday last was married . . . Mr. Harfurd, an eminent merchant of Bristol, to Miss Scandarett of this Town, a young lady of great Merit, with a Fortune of £10,000." Karl Marx, who watched the later industrial changes of England, declared that the main difference between Englishmen and Americans was that the former thought more of gains, the latter of gaining.

English utilitarians, quite as much as Americans, objected to the intrusion of aesthetics in secular or religious life. The strait-laced, commonsense attitude of Richard Cobden, touring the museums of Europe, reminds one closely of Mark Twain's "Innocents Abroad." For example, when this rich cotton-spinner visited the treasures of the Vatican, he was shocked by the Laocoon group, which, to his unspeakable embarrassment, he found draped only in serpents. He said: "I am not able to feel the enthusiasm which some men feel or affect for the 'crack' pieces of sculpture." Much more agreeable to him was a "pleasing and sweet" modern representation of "Modesty," clothed fully, if not in Manchester goods, and hence more attractive to a prominent cloth-manufacturer.

A moment lost in dalliance with Art was, to the new industrialists, that much cash wasted. As a eulogist of Birmingham warbled in 1783, the Muses must be practical:

> *Hail Birmingham . . .*
> *The useful article and the pleasing Toy,*
> *Its fertile Geniuses alike employ:*

> *Which to complete they do no labour spare,*
> *That Merchants through the World may send their Ware,*
> *And Orders bring to carry on the Trade ...*
> *But Idleness will find no sanction here,*
> *For men of Business they all revere ...*

Theaters seemed an encouragement to idleness. This lack of toleration for drama, so unusual among business men, might be explained by the fact that Northerners were not "frustrated" and eager for romantic compensation like more illusion-thirsty bourgeois. At any rate, they disapproved of it wholly for workers. In 1773 a Bill was before Parliament to establish a royally licensed theater in Birmingham; Edmund Burke warmly espoused it, saying: "I look upon Birmingham to be the great Toy Shop of Europe, and submit to the Members of this Hon. House, to consider if Birmingham on that account, is not the most proper place in England to have a licensed theatre." Around that same time, a number of noble Anglican lords were advocating such theaters for other towns on the ground that a little fun would be good for the utilitarians, and prevent them from falling into Methodism. "Methodism," said the Earl of Carlisle, was "daily gaining ground, particularly in the manufacturing towns," and he hoped that

> playhouses, well regulated, would be the means of dispelling those gloomy thoughts, and that melancholy state of mind so favourable to the propagation of the dangerous doctrines ... There is no way so effectually to eradicate that dark, odious, and ridiculous enthusiasm as by giving the people cheerful amusements to counteract their methodistical melancholy.

But utilitarians resisted such efforts to impose fun upon them from above. A group of worried industrialists rushed up to London to protest:

> Whereas on the mature consideration of many respectable Manufacturers in this very populous and important Town, the Exhibition of Plays have been deemed extremely prejudicial to the Manufactures carried on here, having a Tendency to promote Negligence, create Expense, and corrupt the Morals of the Industrious; the said Manufacturers are come to a Resolution to do their utmost to prevent such Exhibitions in the future.

In their stand, the manufacturers had the support of those who feared revolutionary ideas might creep across the footlights. "The Beggar's

Opera, for instance," a speaker declared, "had brought more unhappy people to the gallows, than any one thing he could name." The Archbishop of Canterbury agreed with the Bishop of London that a playhouse was a menace in "a great trading manufacturing town . . . It is impossible to get them [laborers] to their business for two or three days after they have been at the theatre."

But, no matter how they frowned upon diversion, these busy utilitarians managed to find a good deal of time for potations. Their laborers were commonly too befuddled to work on Monday; the managers of mills were so generally given to bouts that Robert Owen, though a mere lad, was engaged on the spot to handle a huge plant when he announced that he did not drink. The industrialists themselves yielded to nobody at the flowing bowl; as Prentice, a prominent Manchester manufacturer, recorded in his memoirs: "It was no uncommon sight, in those days, to see well-to-do manufacturers reeling down Marketlane, in the broad daylight of a summer afternoon, trolling their drunken catches." Another depiction of local politics, as late as 1865, reveals "bribery, corruption and treating" at the political headquarters, where men crowded in, "stuffed themselves full and guzzled champagne in streams . . . for 8 days there was free drinking in all the alehouses."

Foreign visitors to this section were filled with deep alarm, as well as surprise, at the barbarism of early industrialism. One German, Wendeborn, visiting Manchester in 1788, exclaimed: "Imagine, in this great, rich city, not a single artist of any kind!" and added, "I don't believe there is a single statue, good or bad, private or public." According to him, the business men of all England, even of London, were hardly much better, for they thought the noblest works of art were the portraits of kings on their coins. A second German, J. G. Kohl, in 1842, decided that Birmingham and Leeds were "the most destitute of taste, ornament and enjoyment" among the raw manufacturing towns; as to the former, "it may be questioned whether in the whole world another town of equal extent and importance could be found so destitute of public monuments."

Two years later than Kohl's report, a documented indictment of the evils of early industrialism was produced by yet a third German, Friedrich Engels, who was representing his father's cotton-firm in Manchester. In "The Condition of the Working Classes in England," Engels warned Germany of the social menace of untrammeled enterprise, and advised his countrymen, if they must turn industrial also, to establish government regulation in the beginning.

Just a little before Kohl and Engels, two Germans, were expressing their shocked dismay at Manchester, a prominent manufacturer of that city, Richard Cobden, went to Germany and other parts of the Continent. Cobden was, of course, the supreme Free Trader, the shining exponent of industrialism, the man who gave Manchester her Manchesterism. If any man in England was filled with enthusiasm for his native province and its works and ways, it was Cobden. Nevertheless, he was aware of the mental backwardness, and especially the peril of intemperance, among his peers. As a young man, traveling for a cotton-firm, he had had occasion to see the low life on the road, and was constantly endeavoring to elevate the conversation in taprooms. In his maturity, as a celebrated business man, he drew his fellow-citizens' attention to the superiority of foreign men of commerce.

Traveling abroad in 1838, to study the state of industry, preparatory to launching his great campaign for free trade, Cobden was astonished to find that workmen in other lands could be more sober and decent than "the miserable and moping mechanic that pines in his dark alley in our English cities on the Sabbath-day." And what was more remarkable, even business men were civilized on the Continent:

I do hope the leather-headed bipeds who soak themselves upon prosperous market-days in brandy and water at the White Bear, will be brought to the temperature of rational beings by the last twelve months' regimen of low prices. And then let us hope that we may see them trying at least to bestow a little more thought upon their own interests in matters beyond the range of their factory walls. It humiliates me to think of the class of people at home, who belong to the order of intelligent and educated men that I see on the Continent, following the business of manufacturing, spinning, etc. Our countrymen, if they were possessed of a little of the *mind* of the merchants and manufacturers of Frankfurt, Chemnitz, Elberfeld, etc., would become the De Medicis, and Fuggers, and De Witts of England, instead of glorying in being the toadies of a clod-pole aristocracy, only less enlightened than themselves!

Eagerly, Cobden encouraged the cultural awakening in the industrial centers. When the Athenaeum was opened in Manchester, he hailed the new institution with joy, and reminded his audience of business men that there would be, ultimately,

but one test for the future greatness of Manchester, and that will be a mental test, not a material test; that our destiny will be decided, not by the expanse of bricks and mortar, nor by the multiplication of steam engines, nor by the accumulation of wealth, but just in proportion as mental development goes forward.

At each stage, in the unfolding of machine civilization, critics came up from the South of England to watch the spectacle in Northern and Midland manufacturing districts. With each new thrust of industry, a chorus of groans was heard from disgusted country squires and dismayed aesthetes. When the transformation was just beginning, a country gentleman from the South declared that in places where wealth is quickly obtained "it is ignorantly spent; for the upstart man of Riches knows no better." Just about a hundred years later, when the Machine was triumphant, John Ruskin traveled through its realm and announced:

> The two most frightful things I have ever yet seen in my life are the south-eastern suburb of Bradford (six miles long) and the scene from Wakefield Bridge, by the chapel; yet I cannot but more and more reverence the fierce courage and industry, the gloomy endurance, and the infinite mechanical ingenuity of the great centres, as one reverences the fervid labours of a wasp's nest, though the end of it all is only a noxious lump of clay.

About sixty years after Ruskin, another traveler, Priestley, took the same way, and observed the squalid rows of sooty barracks, variegated by pubs and fish-stalls, surrounded by a country covered with sulphurous slag. But he came in the after-War depression, and found even the "fervid labours" admired by Ruskin were lacking to animate the scene. Even the hope which illuminated the darkness before, had gone with the paralysis of industry:

> Grim and ugly as might be, nevertheless if this riverside had been black and shattering with the smoke and din of tens of thousands of men hard at it . . . I think I could have found it wildly inspiring . . . but what chiefly caught the eye there were evidences of past greed, now satiated here and ravening elsewhere.

THE POLITICAL EDUCATION OF THE ENGLISHMEN

Similar as the character and situation of the North-Briton and Northern American might be at an early stage, the two began to diverge toward the middle of the nineteenth century. Then the American discovered breath-taking possibilities in railroad and mining developments; with extraordinary chances for gorging and gambling, a race of titanic speculators grew up in America, surpassing the wildest dreams of wealth among Lancashire men, who still had to go on working and pinching pennies. It was the Briton who remained the Yankee, if one may so phrase it.

Though the North-country man was slower to win big fortune, he kept it well, partly because he often went back to the land to renew his strength, as the American had not yet learned to do. To approximate a real English gentleman, he knew that he must show some expert knowledge of pigs and poultry, and exhibit porkers at the county fairs like the Duke of Devonshire. He also knew that he must become a sheriff or mayor—he must farm, and he must govern. Hence the striking difference in the stories of successful Englishmen. They start out like tales of Americans. The Englishman goes through the classic tribulations and wins out by the inevitable grit and family virtues. But the end is unique. The American just dies. The Englishman is draped with the robes and chains of office, and passes away on his estate amid mourning retainers. The account of the Englishman's climb to wealth is fairly sure to lack the pungent and startling details which may enliven the biographies of American plungers; but he makes the handsomer corpse.

One autobiography of a typical self-made and self-satisfied British business man, illustrating the urge to office, may be cited. Sir Joshua Walmsley of Liverpool, born in 1794, had a hard youth, keeping himself alive on sour bread and watery porridge. By grit and gumption he rose; he learned to tell Irish from English grain by the feel of it, as he plunged his hand in the bag. A man so clever and persistent was sure to win the amiable daughter of a wine-merchant; but Walmsley retained the lower-bourgeois frugality and industry, persisting in eating his lunch from a tin box and still giving an encouraging nod to employees. So far, so American.

But a very un-American faith buoyed up Walmsley. His father kept saying, "Jos will be Mayor of Liverpool." No American boy would have planned to be anything less than President, and had he become a millionaire he would hardly have bothered to be that. It was, however, the ambition of an Englishman; and Walmsley felt it quite as necessary for him to rule Liverpool for a few years as to become a country squire, and teach old farmers, to their rage and disgust, how to farm.

In Manchester, this high regard for municipal offices was most evident. To be Mayor, set the seal of arrival upon the new-rich. Such upward-strivers as Neild, a poor calico-printer who had made good, coveted the post; it was held also by an erstwhile farmer's boy, Sir John Potter; by Sir Elkanah Armitage, a poor maker of bed-ticking who developed one of the largest weaving factories in the world and was knighted for "bravery" displayed in repressing the rioting poor in 1848; by Abel Heywood, son of a putter-out to weavers who built a great wallpaper concern; by Sydney Grundy, a German immigrant, and others.

This political tendency was not, however, a mere fawning imitation of the gentleman. It was forced upon the Briton by the sternest kind of necessity. The deepening crises, the narrowing of the frontier, and the growing animosity of the landed gentlemen, all helped to push him in this direction. The American, quite to the contrary, always managed to escape direct political action throughout this century; in his crises, he found fresh resources to develop, and when he struggled with the landed gentry of the Southern States, the issue was settled by the sword. The American could remain the carefree pursuer of riches for a longer time, while the Briton was turning into a popular orator, a formulator of domestic and foreign policies, a mighty crusader for his "rights."

In these fencing exercises, the Briton grew supple and personally powerful, unlike his American cousin who was never called upon to defend his ideas upon the public platform. Thus Bright and Cobden of the North country, though far less rich than Vanderbilt and Astor, were men who assumed power as well as possessed it. They were men who by "logic" persuaded a public to follow their leadership, instead of soothing the public with benefactions. And in the course of their fiery campaigning, they elaborated the thesis of laissez faire and business individualism which was adopted by Americans without further parley. As the revolutionary French had fought out the ideological battles for the British in the eighteenth century, so the politically pugnacious British in the nineteenth century fought the same theoretical battles for the American traders on the soil of England.

MISERY THE MOTHER OF THOUGHT

At first the rising class of industrialists in the North followed the dictates of expediency, rather than those of a theory. They acted as they pleased, and did not even know it could be called a law of nature. They had not learned to justify their actions by grand phrases from the French—plenty of them, in fact, were still taking lessons in English pronunciation. More than one crisis was needed to mobilize their minds.

A terrible crisis was, however, at length brought on by their over-expansion and over-optimism. A childish hopefulness, said Martineau, had filled their souls. Impossible and infantile dreams danced before their eyes. They spun fantastic projects for mining in the Cordilleras and fishing for pearls on the coast of Colombia, and selling bed-warmers from Birmingham to Rio de Janeiro. In the year 1824–25 more than a hundred companies with a capital of over a hundred million pounds were formed for railroads, banking, insurance, shipping. Millions of pounds were lent abroad to Brazil, Chile, Denmark, Mexico, Peru,

Naples, Portugal, Russia and Spain at high rates. And, seeing the industrialists of the North and the financiers of the South so jubilant, the middle classes rushed to invest their savings.

A beautiful example of the infatuation of the times was the butter-project in La Plata. It occurred to some business men that there was a glorious opportunity to start an English butter company in Buenos Aires; the people of that city had no butter, and yet herds of cows were abundant in La Plata. They sent over a shipload of Scotch milkmaids; the unhappy maidens found the wild animals of the pampas intractable, but the initial difficulties were got over by hiring crews of gauchos to hold the beasts. At length butter was produced—but not bought. Too late, the Company found that the people of Buenos Aires had no butter because they simply preferred to cook with oil.

The hour of doom for this and other speculations was drawing nigh. The Ministry endeavored to keep up optimism. In a Throne Speech on July 6, 1825, the King closed the parliamentary session on a cheery note, congratulating the realm upon its prosperity—almost instantly came the crash. No income arrived from the pampas or the pearl fisheries to keep the companies afloat. London houses toppled, provincial houses followed and the people ran to the banks. Only the invincible optimists went on as before. "The press, with very few exceptions, laboured earnestly to persuade the public that the distress was only temporary. Trade was always to be better next week or next month. In winter it was to be better than in the spring; in spring, it was to be better in the summer; in summer it was to be better in the autumn. The writers seemed to think, that all that was wanted was 'confidence.' "

Nevertheless, the joy and cheer of England was ebbing. Rich people gave up the second coach and cut down on concert subscriptions. Pawnhouses filled. Labor began to riot, though manufacturers held meetings to create an atmosphere of calm and trust. And by 1829, the pit of despair was reached. It was necessary to find a way out, and the manufacturers decided to blame the landed gentry, whose greed, they said, in keeping the Corn Laws, was really responsible for the nation's woes.

Although the crisis had been produced by the folly of their over-confidence quite as much as by the Corn Laws, business men declared themselves guiltless. The cure for the people's ills was to give the manufacturing North political representation and free trade. The ill-effects of partial laissez faire could be counteracted by complete laissez faire. It was difficult to prove such a statement, since complete freedom had not been tried at any time within the memory of man. Only brilliant theoreticians could render the scheme plausible, but these, it happened, were at hand.

Adam Smith, at the beginning of the industrial revolution, had brought over the fine French phraseology to England, transforming the ugly "go-and-grab-it" of the North country by its magic. But, though he attacked the mercantilist monopolies, he was never an advocate of complete non-regulation. Moreover, he died before the results of industrial change were evident. But enough could be found in his work to assist the Manchester men.

Several sons of business families, like Bentham and Mill, were also useful in elevating the grim purpose of the industrialists to a law of nature under the name of Utilitarianism. Professor Malthus, of the East India Company's college, by teaching that the population tended to outrun the food supply, and that the better off it was the faster it multiplied, encouraged the manufacturers in their resistance to aiding the poor. A broker on the London Exchange, of Dutch-Jewish extraction, Ricardo, was another of the guiding influences in forming the new science of political economy. And of course, it was Darwin, grandson of old Josiah Wedgwood, who crowned the labors of the rest by his interpretation of the "struggle for existence" and "survival of the fittest"—a hypothesis which he borrowed from Malthus and "found" in nature.

Darwin was not only descendant of the pottery-maker of Etruria, but he married a Wedgwood, his cousin, and it was the wealth and encouragement of the Wedgwoods which kept him in scientific pursuits. On his paternal side he was the grandson of Erasmus Darwin, who had written about the early industrial changes in rhapsodic vein, thus describing Arkwright's spinning-mill on the river Derwent:

> ... where Derwent guides his dusky floods
> Through vaulted mountains and night of woods,
> The nymph Gossypia treads the velvet sod,
> And warms with rosy smiles the wat'ry god;
> His pond'rous oars to slender spindles turns,
> And pours o'er massy wheels his foaming urns;
> With playful charms her hoary lover wins,
> And wields his trident while the monarch spins.

It remained for the young Darwin, thus related to the early industrialism, to accept the full competitive doctrine of the North country and transfer it to the animal kingdom. In Nature he saw the tooth-and-claw struggle which had produced Manchester. As Marx, writing to his friend, Engels, who was in the cotton business at that city, said in 1862:

It is remarkable, how Darwin recognizes in beasts and plants his English society with its division of work, competition, opening of new markets, "discoveries" and the Malthusian "struggle for existence"!

THE STRUGGLE OF NORTH AND SOUTH ENGLAND

Armed with theories, energy and plenty of t'brass, the North-country men took the stump against the landed gentry of England. And there began an epic strife, the greatest combat in all the story of the business man. Never was so remarkable a wordy battle fought between agrarianism and industrialism. Never had business men emerged so boldly into the open, as advocates of their own cause, and showed themselves figures of such imposing format. To dethrone the haughty landed gentlemen of England peacefully, by arguments, was a mighty feat. Years were spent in whirlwind oratorical campaigns; the thinkers and writers of the nation divided into camps. Consuming passion was exhibited. The people was verbally at war, with the future of capitalism at stake.

At first the landed gentlemen took the onslaught lightly. How could anyone pretend to set up industry as a paramount interest of England? Agriculture reared "hardy honesty," while trade supported "enervating debauchery." What would become of a trader England in a war— "What could the sons of the Shuttle perform against the followers of the Plough?"

It was rank absurdity to suppose a manufacturer gifted with political acumen, said the serene agrarians. Let the business man keep his hands off politics. What experience had he had in statesmanship? Up to that time, the notion of rich industrialists dictating national policies seemed the height of madness. There were, in 1828, only nine members in Parliament representing the manufacturing interest; and when it was then proposed to increase that number very slightly, the lords denounced such treason. The Marquis of Salisbury "called the attention of their lordships to the words of the preamble of the bill . . . 'Whereas, on account of the great wealth and population of Manchester, it is expedient that it should return burgesses to parliament.' " That was a horrible, dangerous doctrine, said he. Since when had England sunk so low that mere money, mere mob, could entitle a place to send deliberators to London? "In that single sentence were embodied all the wildest doctrines of reform . . . he had determined to enter his protest against such doctrines being smuggled into a bill to ruin the constitution."

Against this adamant position of the lords, the up-and-coming class of the manufacturers had to make their drive. Their chief advantage over the agrarians lay in their energy. The landed gentry were torpid

and sure of their hereditary grandeur. As one country gentleman, Sir
Charles Bunbury, picturesquely phrased it in 1788, his rural fellows
were as quiet as the mutton they grew, whereas traders were rambunc-
tious as wild boars:

> The landed gentlemen were like the flocks upon the plains; they
> suffered themselves to be shorn without resistance; while the trad-
> ing part of the nation resembled the boar, who would not let a
> bristle be plucked from his back without making the whole parish
> echo with his complaints.

The result was, said Bunbury, that the "honest simplicity and patience of the sheep" was imposed on by "specious pretences and fair
words," and the noisy hog got all the "treasury acorns." And so it
turned out in the middle of the century, when the wild boar, anxious
about his bristles, made all the parishes of England echo with his complaints. The sheep could think of no adequate reply to such roarings.

Gathering together thousands of pounds in campaign funds, and
forming a network of organizations, the manufacturers opened a propaganda offensive. They turned to "educate" the poor whom they had
hitherto scarcely deemed fit for the ABC's, but whom they now pressed
to study political theory. By explaining that laissez faire would open
the closed plants, they roused the mill-town masses to the rioting point.
"Cheap bread!" was the cry. And to win over country yokels to the
gospel also, these were offered a chance to escape the control of the
squires and enter cities and mills, should free trade be established. Such
energy soon showed astonishing results. As one of the organizers of the
movement, Richard Cobden, declared:

> The aristocracy are afraid of nothing but systematic organization
> ... They know that the only advantage we of the stirring class have
> over them is in habits of persevering labour. They fear nothing but
> the application of these qualities to the business of political agita-
> tion.

Directed by Cobden, the "stirring class" brought determination to
the business of propaganda. Hundreds of manufacturers from the industrial towns came up to London to plead with Sir Robert Peel, a
Manchester manufacturer like themselves, to remember his birth and
occupation and abstain from permanent alliance with the country lords.
London "witnessed the astonishing spectacle of this crowd of manufacturers in top-hats and frock-coats walking as a 'demonstration' arm-
in-arm from the Strand . . . struggling with the police . . . crying out

for 'Cheap food'!" And under Peel in 1846, the Corn Laws were indeed repealed. The landed class, losing tariff protection, relinquished much of its power to the ascendant manufacturing interest. All went blissfully in the Black Country—until the next crisis, which happened to come after hardly more than a year.

SPREADING THE GOSPEL ABROAD

Out of this hurly-burly of campaign oratory the British nation emerged with the conviction that industrial aims were intertwined with the very purposes of Deity. The manufacturers who led the charge against the camp of the agrarians had to whip themselves into such orgies of sentiment in order to carry along the masses and wring tears of repentance from hardened fox-hunters, that, incessantly proclaiming the holiness of their mission, they converted themselves as well. The spirit of the crusader in God's war then remained, after the battle was over, as a permanent acquisition of the British middle classes, affecting those who depended on them. The wonderful Victorian complacency, which was thus partly a product of expensive propaganda, settled down over city and land.

Eloquence and faith alone had not won the victory, of course. Not all the political aspirants were gifted prophets. The rich Thomas Attwood, of a business family of Birmingham, who organized a Political Union in 1830 to agitate for the enfranchisement of propertied men, announced flatly that the trade of Birmingham was falling off, and taxes must be reduced. Richard Potter, an equally blunt citizen of Manchester, decried also the "immense load of taxation," which they laid "to the account of the aristocracy." They wanted places in Parliament where "there are no men of business," in order to do something about taxes. This frankness was common, for the *Birmingham Morning Chronicle* in 1830 decided that "interest, and interest alone, in the vulgar sense, determined nineteen out of twenty" of the agitating bankers and industrialists.

The evangelist fervor in the North country was largely the work of a few eager spirits who identified their cause with that of humanity-in-the-large and thirsted to save the whole world as well as themselves. Such was John Bright, the "radical cotton-spinner from Rochdale," who arrived at a comfortable income through industry and then, putting business more or less in the background, cleared his decks for political action. Sincerely, it seems, John Bright learned to regard himself as the messenger of the Lord. Disclaiming selfish motives, he declared his "love of what I have believed to be the truth" led him to an "unchangeable hostility to the selfishness and fraud" of the agrarians. His self-assumed mission was to overthrow that landed gentry, and he fulfilled it with the ardor of a true prophet. His pictures of the starved rustics who suffered under the tyranny of squires haunted England. Of course the squires replied with an equally virulent attack on the manufacturers' abuse of urban labor, through their mouthpiece, "Bully" Ferrand, as well as through Dickens, Trollope and other defenders. But Bright was not ruffled by such retorts—he insisted that was not the same sort of thing at all. Personally, he indeed believed that a ten-hour-day was long enough in mills, but he resolutely opposed any law which would establish such a maximum, or in some other way hamper industry. To oppress manufacturers by such regulation, Bright said, would injure workmen also in the long run.

Hard as John Bright was in his home territories, he was full of compassion and benevolence for suffering humanity abroad. Peace was his ideal—and a free hand in his factories. His famous "Angel of Death" speech during the Crimean War moved the crustiest of Victorians to a sigh or tears.

Even more impressive was Richard Cobden, greatest of the Free Traders, the Richard Cœur de Lion of British industry. At a comparatively early age, he had risen from clerking in a warehouse and commercial traveling to part-ownership of a cotton-printing works in Manchester and, owing to the fine quality of design in "Cobden prints," his income and position were assured. At this point he relaxed his money-making efforts and went on extensive travels to seek confirmation of his views of laissez faire. From traveling he turned to pamphleteering, entered local politics and got a seat in the Commons. Through the Anti-Corn-Law League, which he dominated, he exerted powerful pressure upon public opinion.

As spokesman for his class, Cobden bore down opponents with fervor and statistics. Yet he did not view himself in such a limited rôle. In promulgating the program of his fellow-manufacturers, he thought he was doing the work of Heaven. What he preached was the plain tooth-and-claw struggle devoid of any such qualifications as, nowadays, the stoutest advocate of rugged individualism would take for granted. Absolute free trade, absolute freedom from regulation in industry, were in his opinion the clear dictates of Almighty God: "We advocate nothing but what is agreeable to the highest behests of Christianity—to buy in the cheapest market and sell in the dearest."

The plight of English labor in the Northern mill-towns was, to him, really not involved in the matter at all. He advocated Repeal on the ground that, by making bread cheaper, it would enable manufacturers to pay lower wages and thus put England in a position to beat the rest of Europe at the competitive game. The query, whether England could continue indefinitely to underbid her neighbors apparently did not occur to him. In the view of Cobden, as in that of old Colbert, the economic character of nations was static; he pictured peoples like the Americans remaining permanently agricultural, feeding Britain and buying British woolens to all eternity. And therefore, he felt sure that universal laissez faire must result in a happy competition, guarantee of perpetual peace. Passionately pacifist, condemning the old balance-of-power politics, Cobden worked for international arbitration and proposed the mutual reduction of land-armaments among European peoples. At the same time, he urged a big British Navy as the protector of world harmony.

Exhausting himself and his private fortune in the holy war for Repeal, Cobden gave everything freely, not to the cause merely of his class, but to God and Humanity. When the battle was won, an organization gathered up voluntary contributions for the leader—"The nation owed him," it was said, and certainly the industrial regions did. A handsome purse of £80,000 was presented to the great free-trader and pacifist. With that he might have rested on his oars, but instead he determined to diffuse Manchesterism through all the world. Receiving the tribute of his countrymen in 1846, he responded:

> Well, I will, with God's assistance . . . visit all the large states of Europe . . . If the public spirit of my countrymen affords me the means of traveling as their missionary, I will be the first ambassador from the people of this country to the nations of the continent. I am impelled to this by an instinctive emotion such as has never deceived me.

As the apostle from the British people to the yet unenlightened universe, Richard Cobden sailed off to new conquests. He visited royal courts, addressed banquets, cemented trade treaties and everywhere drummed up a tremendous interest in the English industrial experiment and its philosophy. Seldom has a business man been accorded such a triumph. This magnificently sure, self-appointed envoy of Manchester was greeted with a serious attention greater even than that accorded in modern times to another manufacturer, Henry Ford of Detroit, with a similarly simple recipe for relieving the world's ills.

According to the pure gospel of the Cobdenites, the formula for permanent world prosperity had been miraculously revealed by God in the North of England. It was now only necessary for peoples desiring a bliss like that of the Black Country, to import Britain's machinery, methods and utilitarian credo. And thus, within a brief period, the summit of evolution would be reached, and the age-long struggle of mankind upward from primordial ooze would end—in the murk of a universal Manchester.

On second thought, most of the peoples addressed by Cobden decided not to take this missionary of "buying in the cheapest market and selling in the dearest" at his own estimation. They bought new machinery but declined to tear down entirely their old protective structures to admit the flood of English goods. Pure laissez faire, foreign and domestic, was not adopted by mankind as a whole, and indeed did not last very long even in England. But the credo was of immense effect upon the life of the nineteenth century. Men who would not practice the jungle competition in classic form, yet echoed its phraseology. Those who refused to accept the Cobden premises, and go over to pure freedom, yet believed heartily in his conclusion: that mankind was destined to speed salvation through the new machine-business. And so, though Cobden did not convert humanity, as he had dreamed, he warmed it with the glow of his imagination, and for many a day, the blaze of enthusiasm, kindled in England, lingered cheerfully on the horizon.

NATURE'S ERRORS

The jubilant men of Manchester, hailing Nature as their deity, had no sooner won the main victory for free trade in 1846 than, a year later, on the heels of victory, came the terrible panic of 1847, followed by an agony of unrest in which the radical Chartist movement crystallized. This panic was especially shocking to Nature-lovers since it was largely due to unregulated business expansion, unchecked competition—in short, to laissez faire in railroading.

England at that time dreamed of connecting cozy suburbs by rail with the industrial towns. Spanning England with tracks would increase democracy, it was presumed: "the peer, the manufacturer and the landlord shall now meet and talk together on the same railroad wagon." The railroad in the age of Dickens was expected to disrupt the English caste-system, much as it was, a generation or so later, presumed to destroy that of Kipling's India. And England was willing to share the benefits with the world; writers prophesied: "the ruined hills and broken altars of old Greece will soon re-echo the whistle of the locomotive, or be converted to shrines sacred to commerce."

The chief manipulator of these railroads was the "Railway King," George Hudson, the massive Yorkshire farmer's boy, who so imposed on everyone by his mere appearance, his "extra-aldermanic bulk . . . with a tendency to develop every way but upwards," and the round bullet-like head set without a neck on the square shoulders, from which came "a thick utterance, as though the voice had to be pumped up from cavernous recesses." This remarkable man was the English figure most nearly comparable with Vanderbilt or Gould in America; of overbearing nature, he frightened stockholders out of their wits by his roars, and could even silence the Prince Consort. Like Gould, he was fond of cutting a dash.

Probably, thinks Lambert, he was "the first self-made provincial millionaire to settle in Victorian London," besides Crockford the gambler. By his publicity, which was akin to Barnum's, and the immensity of his establishment at Albert House, his palace, he woke up the capital in 1846. He loved golden wine-coolers, reckless gas-illuminations, bean-feasts, table-thumpings and dashing about in private trains amid incessant celebration. For one of these railroading-festivals, he even persuaded Queen Victoria to enter a special train, fitted with rare woods and filled with flowers. And when she looked about her and said, a little bit fluttered, "Really, this *is* beautiful!" his cup was filled.

This Yorkshire man, who was doing everything he could to bisect and blacken the estates of country gentlemen, with his tracks, was nevertheless profoundly loyal to the old gentry. He fancied himself one of them when he finally bought an estate, and took the part of "our aristocracy" against the "wild, visionary cotton lords" in the Corn Law struggle. Although economic interest might well have allied him with the free-traders, whose products were to roll over his lines, his mind was made up by bucolic origin and social ambition instead. And although he was defending his conception of laissez faire, the right to build or buy wherever he chose and make no accounting to State or shareholders, he was politically opposed to their party. Not only did he denounce them; indirectly, unintentionally, he all but ruined them: for railroading was diverting money from industry and creating a speculative danger which involved even sound enterprises.

Aware of approaching peril, Parliament intervened, to fix a deadline before which all proposals for new lines had to be submitted. A fantastic race to stake out claims ensued. An army of writers composed prospectuses, while hundreds of Belgian lithographers were imported to illustrate them alluringly. Coaches drawn by foaming horses were still galloping up with sheets damp from the presses when the chimes struck. Outside the closed doors, excluded schemers attacked one another with their fists.

Just after an optimistic speech from the Crown, reassuring the public, the Railroad Bubble broke. Banks failed; factories shut down; multitudes were thrown on relief. A parliamentary investigation failed to obtain much satisfaction from George, however; vainly a patient, and annoyingly persistent, Quaker pestered him, "Does thee remember" this or that? George could remember nothing; he failed entirely to recollect "with precision any of those expressions or acts which have impressed themselves on the memories of others." It was impossible to punish such a victim of amnesia, but he staggered out of the committee as a ruined man.

Ominous were the reverberations of the panic, as it swept out from England to Paris, Amsterdam, Hamburg and St. Petersburg. This was a sign that, owing in part to railroading, the world was now so united that panics could not again be readily localized. And the next convulsion produced by a railroad-orgy was a genuine world-panic, originating in the New World.

If anyone supposed that the English people, awakened by such terrible experiences at home, would be chary about entrusting funds to far-away American railroad speculators, even more untrammeled than Hudson, that expectation was without warrant. A mere ten years after the English railroad crash, came a collapse of "the American dream," involving huge amounts of English and German capital. Revelations of astounding corruption left a long-lingering taint upon the air.

To heighten the feverish symptoms in the public, the gold-mania had been added to the railway-delirium. The latent Elizabethan lust for ingots had been once more aroused by the glitter of gold-dust in California. Sober Britons lost their balance as they calculated profits to be won by selling fancy shirt-goods to the "Forty-Niners" on the Pacific Coast. Factories were hastily built in Lancashire; huge shipments of luxuries were dispatched. And between railroading and gold-mining, according to Wirth, 153 new companies with a combined capital of 500 million gulden were formed in Europe during the first five months of 1852. But a serious miscalculation had been made: the miners had to pay so many nuggets for beefsteaks and laundry that they had little left for elegant wares from Europe. Gold-mining, it was discovered, did not pay. When the costs of transporting men and equipment to the Coast and maintaining them were reckoned, the Californian venture with all its shining metal was found to have been less profitable than more humdrum employments like selling groceries.

At all events, the crash in America brought down Canadian firms, followed by the slipping of London houses. Vainly the *Times* besought the public to keep its nerves steady. A bank failed in Glasgow, dragging Scotch houses after it, and spreading ruin to Liverpool and the whole iron and cotton district. Before long the threat reached the nation. Then the terror spread to Germany, where Hamburg resembled a stricken city for two weeks. It passed to Christiania, Stockholm, Copenhagen, Rio de Janeiro, Port au Prince. Few places were spared. Bremen, which had not indulged in excessive speculation, escaped; the

Swiss, who had been conservative, remained firm; the French were hurt later than other peoples.

A striking feature of this panic was the absence of a scapegoat. Most unusually, no plague, famine, war-debt, wicked law or political move was available this time upon which the distress could be blamed. In these circumstances, the ineptitude and lack of judgment on the part of business men who had pinned their faith on unregulated expansion could not be overlooked. The lesson was so plain that the fear of doom amounted to agony. To be sure, men always tend to believe that the Day of Judgment is at hand when stocks are low, but now they questioned the very theory of laissez faire.

Perhaps Friedrich Engels was the only truly happy and confident business man in that dreadful time. A representative of his German father's cotton firm in Manchester, Engels welcomed the "downfall of the capitalist system." Every fresh symptom of disaster made Engels the gayer, as it supported his pet thesis. In the highest good spirits, Engels watched his father's and his own money vanish. He penned letters of cheer to his German friend, Karl Marx, the little-known scrivener whom he constantly supplied with pocket-money. However, Engels gave Marx more than cash and encouragement, for so closely did the business man work with the theoretician that the ideas of the twain are not always distinguishable today in their publications. It appears that the original draft of the Communist Manifesto, for instance, was made by Engels himself, and in such crises as this of 1857, Engels furnished both practical advice and descriptive material.

Marx wrote back to Engels, when the doom of capitalism seemed assured: "Despite my financial distress, I have not felt so cozy since 1849." In that year he had expected the downfall; now he was sure. Engels agreed. Taking up military studies, he prepared for the wonderful revolution which would arrive, provided the masses had not become too "damned lethargic during the long prosperity." In proportion to the mounting misery of the cotton-men in Manchester, the smile of Engels brightened. He teased his fellow-capitalists:

> The general aspect of the Exchange here was most delicious in the past week. The fellows grow black in the face with rage at my suddenly rising good spirits. Indeed the Exchange is the only place where my present dullness changed to elasticity and bouncing. And yet I naturally always prophesy the gloomiest things; that angers the asses doubly. On Thursday the state of affairs was most pitiful, Friday the gentlemen were puzzling over the possible effect of the suspension of the Bank Act, and since cotton rose another penny, they thought: now we are past the worst. But by yes-

terday the most-to-be-rejoiced-over despondency appeared again; the whole story was just phraseology and hardly a being wanted to buy.

Rubbing his hands with glee, Engels reported that his fellow-countrymen, the Germans, had also been caught in the toils of the Yankees, who "have swindled, as always indeed, with foreign capital, but this time especially with continental capital. The bureaucrats and rentiers who in Germany have bought up everything that was American will have to bleed for it now." And so would his father:

> We are involved with £6000, that's £300 for my share! . . . In these circumstances I shall probably have to make some new agreement with my Old Man.

It was plain, thought Engels, that crises were intensifying and extending to the farthest zone, taking in agricultural as well as manufacturing processes. He laughed at the trusting faith of his contemporaries: "In his heart every bourgeois still believes that his special branch of business and his own in particular has been thoroughly sound." But for Engels the hour of trial was at hand; raucous and dingy Manchester must soon be purified by tears of repentance:

> The bourgeois filth of the last seven years has stuck to me; now it is washed off, and I am again another man. The crisis will do me as much good as a sea-bath.

With gusto, in letters full of dramatic detail, Engels poured forth his impressions to his dear Marx. However wrong he was about the outcome, his vignettes form a unique record of a great crash:

> Today I hear that the Cookes, owners of the colossal factory in Oxford Road (Oxford Road Twist Comp.) have sold their hunters, fox-hounds, grey-hounds, and so on, that one has discharged his servants and left his palace to be let . . . Another fourteen days and the dance will be in full swing here.
> The London and Liverpool produce-houses will do a somersault next. In Liverpool it looks ghastly, the fellows are completely dazed and hardly have the energy to go bankrupt. The faces on the Exchange there, I'm told, by someone who was there Monday, are three times longer than here.
> Among the Philistines here the crisis leads to heavy drinking. Nobody can stand it alone with the family and the sorrows. The

clubs are enlivened and the consumption of liquor rises greatly. The deeper a man is sunk, the more strenuously he tries to make merry. The next day he is then the most striking example of moral and physical *Katzenjammer*.

But even while Engels was getting ready for the hour of barricades, the clouds began to lift, and the sun presently shone again over England. And, puzzled and disappointed, the revolutionary capitalist confessed to his dear Marx that his prognostications were wrong again:

> I must say that the ways and means by which the over-produced masses of wares, heaped up by the crisis, have been absorbed, are not at all clear; such a quick ebb after so violent a storm-flood has never been witnessed.

The world-crisis did not bring the end of the machine-system after all. No, but it did mark the close of the first era of old-style competitive capitalism. The fine early flush of triumph had faded. During months of terrified doubt, the industrialists of England had veered toward the State; they could see that France escaped many of the scars of panic because her officialdom wielded a strong stabilizing influence, and the example of what governmental control could do in ameliorating a crisis was impressive. Besides, other forces were pushing industry toward more regulation. Private means could not cope with misery in a huge industrial population; state relief seemed to offer the only way out of a dangerous hole. And so they were willing to dicker with their ancient foes, the landed gentlemen, and the State. Turning from Nature, who had so failed them, and was again to shock them in 1873, they groped about for some new abstraction to replace the old. Empire seemed more reliable than fickle Nature. Hallowed by tradition, dowered with the divine attribute of permanence in a changing world, Empire was accordingly adored by the generation from 1880 to 1914, until the World War made the slogan, "Imperialism," a byword and a reproach, as "jungle law" had previously become.

THREE BUSINESS IMPERIALISTS

Presently men of the two classes that had been locked in the almost revolutionary struggle over free trade and the theory of Nature, were now found united in using government, laws, armies and navies in the prosecution of activities which brought trade to industrialists and orders to armament firms, and at the same time furnished administrative posts to the unemployed scions of old houses—demonstrating feudal might and shedding luster upon Victoria's Crown. Thus was achieved a new compromise, like that of the eighteenth century, between business and land, parvenu and aristocrat, in England.

Delightful to the seeker for historical parallels is the thought that it was a descendant of a "Merchant of Venice" who helped to cast a romantic glamor over the concept of Eastern Empire for the British public. Benjamin Disraeli's family came originally from Venice, the home of magnificent imperialism in the thirteenth century. The grandfather made a fortune rapidly in England and retired to build an Italian garden, where he

> played whist with Sir Horace Mann, who was his great acquaintance, and who had known his brother at Venice, as a banker, ate macaroni which was dressed by the Venetian consul, sang canzonettas . . . lived till he was nearly ninety, and then died in 1817 in the full enjoyment of a prolonged existence.

As often happens, the next member, Isaac, was a rebel against business and wrote diatribes against commercialism; but the grandson, the celebrated Benjamin, inherited the ancestral inclination for business operations. He entered the Stock Exchange and merrily gambled on Spanish-American mining shares. Out of the crash of 1825, the youth, barely twenty, emerged with debts amounting to thousands of pounds —and an increased respect for business acumen in others.

This unusual bankrupt then drew on his painfully acquired knowledge to write novels in which he described successful business men so wistfully that the Manchester manufacturer, Cobden, said gratefully of Disraeli:

> I believe he is the first man of distinguished genius who, in a work of imagination, has assigned to a man of my order something like an honourable status in his pages . . . I remember his "Milbank," and I thank him for it.

Business educated Disraeli for politics, as he insisted himself. In an autobiographically tinged paragraph in "Tancred," the character *Fakredeen* declares that ruin schooled him to statesmanship. He was

> fond of his debts; they were the source indeed of his only real excitement, and he was grateful to them for their stirring powers . . . "What should I be without my debts?" he would sometimes exclaim . . . "All my knowledge of human nature is owing to them: it is in managing my affairs that I have sounded the depths of the

human heart, recognized all the combinations of human character, developed my own powers, and mastered the resources of others. What expedient in negotiation is unknown to me? What degree of endurance have I not calculated? What play of countenance have I not observed? Yes, among my creditors, I have disciplined that diplomatic ability, that shall some day confound and control cabinets."

The flamboyant attire of "Dizzy," the bankrupt broker, and his dreams of empire in the magnificent East, were bewitching to the sober business classes of England, who were themselves too timid to express such desires, perhaps, but who felt within them the revival of the old Elizabethan mood, poetic and violent. Under the magic touch of this Jewish descendant of a "Merchant of Venice," the English envisioned themselves recapturing their lost youth, turning conquistadores once more. And as the Italian lagoon-city, in the thirteenth century, had carved an Oriental trade-empire, so London, now proudly accepting the title of "Venice of the Ocean," proposed to hold the East, Near and Far, in fee.

The Midland industrial district sent into the direction of empire a powerful imperialist politician successor to Dizzy. "Joe" Chamberlain, screw-maker of Birmingham, was a leading spirit in the British aggression against the Boers of South Africa. The munitions interests, in which he was at least indirectly involved, appear to have assisted both sides in that memorable conflict. According to Hallgarten, it was shown in legal proceedings before a court that Chamberlain's brother, wife, daughter, his son, Austen Chamberlain, and other relatives, owned about six out of every seven shares in a Birmingham trust which sold dynamite to the British government at prices higher than those charged by other firms. At the same time, Birmingham plants affiliated under this trust were delivering arms to the Boers. It was little wonder, therefore, that the wits of the time cried: "The more the Empire expands, the more the Chamberlains contract."

Like so many Englishmen, Chamberlain was able to put aside a neat fortune at an early age and devote his maturity to political action. Before he was forty, he had exploited the possibilities of screw-manufacture in Birmingham and retired to try orchid-fancying and statesmanship. As he blossomed into a Colonial Minister, "Joe" assumed a monocle. But this impeccably tailored Midland manufacturer was just a trifle too correct, too studied in manner, to please the slouchy lords of seasoned families.

The first step in his political career was to wipe out the effects of laissez faire, as far as he could, in his home-town of Birmingham. Entering the Mayor's office, he announced, "In twelve months by God's help the town shall not know itself," and remade the community as rapidly as he had monopolized the screw business. Initiating municipal control of light and water, clearing slum areas, reducing the death rate 30 per cent, and helping to found an art gallery and university, Chamberlain soon had "transformed the festering growth of accident, negligence and greed" left by an earlier generation. As far as possible, he strove to heal the scars left by the lawless anarchy which his forebears had proclaimed as the will of Nature.

After renovating his birthplace, he entered the national sphere as an advocate of housing-regulation, workmen's compensation and other pieces of social legislation. Breaking with the Cobden doctrine that a manufacturer owed no responsibility to labor, Chamberlain warned his fellows that such protection was "the tax prosperity must pay to society for security." Much as Chamberlain attacked the competitive ruthlessness of older industrialists, however, he also punctured their sentimental pacifism. Fine ideals at home but war abroad was his formula—just the reverse of the Cobden creed, calling for arbitration among nations while denying it to labor.

The powerful "Jingo from Birmingham," as Cobdenites called him, undid the lifework of the earlier Manchester men. He urged a preferential tariff on grain, the sacred free bread for which Bright had wrought upon the passions of England. Chamberlain helped to cement British possessions into an economic whole protected by tariff walls and thus complete the work of binding down Nature. Urging imperialist expansion and consolidation, Chamberlain took the position that humanitarian projects at home would be necessary to content the English masses and rally them to the support of Empire. In the future, he felt, exploitation of subject masses should be carried on in foreign colonies instead of on British soil.

This was the view of Cecil Rhodes as well, another giant among business imperialists, who cooperated with Chamberlain in furthering the Boer conflict. The Empire, said Rhodes, was simply a "Stomach-Question." Business men must face it as such: "If they don't want civil war, they must become imperialists." Rhodes is said to have told a friend in 1895:

I was yesterday in London and visited a meeting of the unemployed. And as I came home, after hearing the wild speeches, which were only a cry for bread, I was more than ever convinced of the importance of imperialism . . . My great idea is the solution of the social problem, that is, in order to preserve the forty million inhabitants of the United Kingdom from a murderous civil war, we colonial politicians must open new provinces to take up the surplus in population and to create new markets for the goods which they produce.

Thus a great cycle swung to completion in England, which had taken from 1780 to 1880 to run its course. In that hundred years, the rising class of manufacturers had battled for laissez faire and defied the landed caste; then they had subsided, muttering feebly, and come to a composition with the aristocrats, disavowing Nature and accepting the State once more. But in this new phase, they still thought they had a message for the rest of the world. Chamberlain declared that

Providence . . . intended us to be a great governing power—conquering, yes conquering, but conquering only in order to civilize, to administer, to develop vast races on the world's surface, primarily for their advantage, but no doubt for our advantage as well.

And Rhodes called it "God's purpose" to "make the Anglo-Saxon race predominant" and "so bring nearer the reign of justice, liberty, and peace."

EMPIRE-GATHERERS

Light-heartedly setting out to follow Nature's call, Englishmen furnished capital to build railroads in America; then a flood of cheap American grain and meat, cheapened by the railroads, ruined British agrarians who in turn could not buy so much cotton. Next the British money-lenders built railroads over France; the Continent, growing more self-sufficing thereby, bought less from Manchester also. Finally the British helped lay tracks in the Far East and sold machinery to Orientals who in turn prepared to underbid Lancashire.

More or less inadvertently, also, British business men acquired enormous territories in various parts of the world. The careless adventures of merchants, often banded into trading companies, who enlarged the British Empire in the nineteenth century, much resembled those who gathered in the domains for Tudors and Stuarts. The East India Company was the largest of these; it informally absorbed the Indian States and, bringing on the Opium War, helped to win Hong-Kong. So, too, the North Borneo Company under Sir Alfred Dent and the Nigeria Company collected imperial spheres which the Government later took over. Led by Sir William Mackinnon, the British India Navigation Company assumed management of Zanzibar and adjacent regions; Sir William also organized the Imperial British East African Company to keep Germans from the Nile and to explore and conquer, it was said, for the "material improvement of the situation of the natives and their civilization." On the death of Sir William, the Government bought out the Company. Another outstanding adventurer was Taubman Goldie, formerly of the National African Company; after ruining French competitors, Goldie annexed large parts of lower Nigeria with a wealth of tin, cotton and palm-oil, which then became a British protectorate. Goldie's purpose was "to create a situation which offers sufficient security for a great commerce and the necessary transportation-routes. When that is achieved, the time is reached for the taking over of the company by the British government."

A formidable aggregation of lands had thus been picked up by business men and handed over to the Government. Early Free Traders urged the abandonment of many such colonies, but after 1840, when the Continental markets dwindled, English manufacturers became increasingly dependent upon Asian and African outlets. Yet, though they might seize colonial domains, through jungle law, a more conventional legality was necessary to bind them together and defend their borders. This drew England also into the business of arms-manufacture, in which, at length, she outdistanced both Germany and France; moreover her Imperialism excited other nations to rivalry.

Empire thus proved as dangerous as Nature to business. A device potent in rousing masses to cheer for war and support a capitalism which seemed to serve some higher purpose than profits, it had its menacing aspects. The symbol of Empire awakened dark forces of blood-lust, irrational mysticism and pride of race. Above all, it gave increased power, in England as in Germany and elsewhere, to the old foes of business, the warriors, and shed a fresh glamor upon coronets, steel helmets and massed banners. In this lay portents beyond the estimates of actuaries.

XXIV

THE VICTORY OF AMERICAN BUSINESS OVER PLANTOCRACY AND ITS CELE-BRATION IN THE GILDED AGE

WHILE THE MANCHESTER MEN were struggling over the Corn Laws in England, and denouncing the selfishness of country squires, they were indirectly responsible for rearing a new race of yet more stubborn agrarians, overseas, in the Southern half of the United States. The demands of Manchester's machines for cheap cotton accelerated the spread of the slave-holding system in the South; by 1860 the area under cotton produced a thousand times as much as it had when the country opened, and on the basis of this rural wealth arose an "aristocracy" or "plantocracy," which challenged the powers of commerce and industry in the American North to a combat far more deadly than that so peaceably settled in England.

Not by political argument, but only on the battlefields of the Civil War, could the issue between business and agrarianism be decided in America. The American landed gentry were more intransigent than the European; like all things in the New World, "aristocracy" was also carried to hitherto unknown extremes. With a hauteur greater than that of Louis Quatorze, the planters of the South repudiated trade without giving it at least a patient trial; they showed less comprehension of economic matters than Prussia's Great Frederick or even the ancient Romans, whom they so often invoked.

Incongruously, this new agrarian conservatism was developed in the nineteenth century side by side with machine civilization, and indeed dependent on it, for no previous agricultural society had been so little self-sustaining as that based on cotton. Yet the planters would not recognize that the basis of their wealth was the Machine; they prepared to defy industry and business in the United States. In this movement, a decisive leadership was assumed by Charleston, the early center of Secession sentiment, the home of Calhoun and other political figures who, it has been said, probably had, for good or evil, a larger influence on American history than any similar number of people in the country.

Oddly enough, in this city merchants, turned "aristocrats," were out-

Bourboning the Bourbons. Like New Orleans, it was French in tone, but Huguenot instead of Catholic, and proud of it. As a Charlestonian wrote, the Cavaliers and "Huguenots who settled the South, naturally hate, contemn and despise the Puritans, who settled the North. The former are master races; the latter a slave race, descendants of the Anglo-Saxon serfs." The tendency of the French to become bourgeois *gentilshommes* added to this pride. Scorning their own business, the rich merchants strove to emulate the planters about them and outvie them in displays of imported millinery and coaches; adopting the duelling and hunting codes of the surrounding gentry, buying plantations, they managed indeed to impress the squires of Georgia and even Virginia. Though few of them had noble ancestry, they all became, by common consent, "French aristocrats," notorious for extreme hauteur and regarded with general awe. Thus the French *ancien régime*, destroyed at home, was revivified in the Machine Age in America, home of survivals.

Around 1816 Charleston was second only to New York in export trade. The State of South Carolina exported $10,000,000 worth of goods, as compared with the $16,000,000 of the latter. Charleston banks, directed by families such as the Legaré and Petigru, were well managed, and in fact remained more solid than Wall Street up to the Civil War; they furnished a large part of the financial strength of the South in that conflict. Next to New Orleans, Charleston was the most populous city of the South, and in proportion to number of inhabitants, the wealthiest. But for various reasons, the city early began to sink, as planting declined. South Carolina, like Virginia, was rapidly exhausting its soil by ruthless methods long before the War came, and suffered from a drop in production; both states lost sons to the new regions farther South and West. Whole sections of Virginia were reduced to breeding slaves for more fertile states; Charleston wished to revive the slave-importation traffic, but could not force the measure through, across Virginia's opposition. Vainly the slave-trading interests of the former argued in conventions in the 1850's. At the Charleston Democratic National Convention in 1860, a champion of lower trade barriers declared:

> I tell you that the slave-trading of Virginia is more immoral, more unchristian in every possible point of view, than the African slave-trade, which goes to Africa and brings a heathen and worthless man here, christianizes him, and sends him and his posterity down the stream of time to enjoy the blessings of civilization. . . . It has been my fortune to go into that noble old State to buy a few darkies, and I have had to pay from $1000. to $2000. a head, when I could go to Africa and buy better negroes for $50. apiece.

Under these conditions, the wharves of Charleston received fewer and fewer bales; there was less noise of bidding in the great iron-gated "Mart" where slaves were sold. By the 1830's the "mournful silence of premature decay" was visible there, with "the very grass growing in our streets and houses falling into ruins." Many enterprising spirits left the city, taking their funds North. Certainly matters were not improved by the social climbing of the French merchants, who poured out their wealth in ostentation and yielded to leisured ideals until it became disgraceful not only to engage in trade but to admit one's grandfather had been a "ham-slinger on the Bay." Nor would the Charlestonians permit the inroads of machine-industry; steam engines were forbidden, and until 1844 the scent of magnolia was kept practically free of contamination by the reek of factories in South Carolina. As a merchant, William Gregg, sarcastically remarked,

This power is withheld lest the smoke of an engine should disturb the delicate nerves of an agriculturalist; or the noise of a mechanic's hammer should break in upon the slumber of a real estate holder, or an importing merchant, while he is indulging in fanciful dreams of building on paper the Queen City of the South,—the paragon of the ages.

Owing to aristocratic ambitions, which had appeared in mediaeval communities, such as Lübeck, only after centuries, this American town rapidly exhibited symptoms of social decay. The narrow pride of the Charlestonian patriciate remained unbroken by increasing poverty. Even more bitterly than Virginians, its members blamed the greed of Northern manufacturers and shippers for their plight. Stoutly defending the Southern system, indicting the Yankee capitalists as the cause of all their woes, hot-heads of Charleston, like William Rhett, sought to draw the rest of the South into their plans for revolt; as intransigeants from other regions were attracted to the city, it became the citadel of the Secession movement. The dying port would not succumb without dragging the whole nation into war.

In Charleston the antithesis of business and agrarianism was personified in William Gregg and Edmund Ruffin. Gregg, a self-made man from Virginia, with a fortune made in the jewelry business, devoted his days to breaking down the prejudices of Southerners against industrialism. Pamphleteering, fighting in the legislature, seeking to arouse interest in the problem of educating and employing the idle poor whites, he finally crushed Charleston's opposition to the steam-engine and opened mills. No child under twelve years of age was employed; temperance was strictly enforced; education and improved standards were turned to raising industrial efficiency. Gregg was not, however, a pure philan-thropist, though he toiled for years without profit; he believed, and finally proved, that the South could produce at a lower cost than the North, owing to the fact that "Capital will always be able to control labor, even in manufacture with whites, for blacks can always be re-sorted to in case of need."

Gregg's plant was on the verge of paying well when he died, from exposure, after working waist-deep in water to repair a broken dam. Although it proved to be one of the mainstays of the Confederacy in the War, it did not inspire imitation in the South, as Gregg had hoped it would. Grumble though the South did at Northern power, it was content to leave nearly eighty-five per cent of the country's manufac-turing to the North. Nor was it able to organize transportation to com-pete with the railroad system swiftly spreading and combining in the North and West. In part its failure was due to the furious local jeal-ousies, as between Richmond and Norfolk, which left little lines trail-ing into space and prevented any grand linking of the Southern cen-ters. No titan appeared, equal to a Northern Gould or Vanderbilt, to override the petty community corruption by his Napoleonic private frauds. Likewise the growth of banks was hampered by the angry re-sistance of mortgage-ridden planters to "that meanest, most odious, and most degrading" of all governments, "the domination of an irrespon-sible money oligarchy."

Naturally, the wealth of the South did not swell as fast as that of the North: by 1859 the return from the activities of the former amounted to only 204 millions, while those of Northern manufacturers brought in nearly two billions; Southerners as a whole owed up to $400,000,000 to Northern capitalists by 1860. If in numerical strength the two classes were nearly matched—350,000 slave owners, large and small, as against 460,000 income-tax payers under the Civil War Act, mainly in the North—the South did not as a whole perceive that it was economic madness to challenge the North. Men like Ruffin believed that material advantages counted for little against martial prowess, which superior-ity, "as well as many others, social, intellectual and moral, we owe to our institution of slavery." Business men, they thought, had ever been timid fighters, easily overcome.

Feeling themselves akin to the old Romans (though they did not, like the old Romans, use their slaves as business proxies), the Southern agrarians thought they could defeat the North, viewed by them as a degenerate commercial Carthage, too greedy for profit to "waste mil-lions in dollars and men to gratify the abolitionists." Or if it should fight, they pictured it easily overthrown in a second Battle of Zama. Unacquainted with technological affairs, they did not realize how warfare had changed in two thousand years, and how helpless even Scipio Africanus would be in the nineteenth century if he lacked a swift train to take him to the front.

The stern old Cato of the Secession was Ruffin, subduing all men by his fierce eyes and the dignity of a hoary mane floating to his shoulders. Finding Virginia was too calm, Ruffin left the state and adopted Charleston, city of gentlemanly extremists, as his home. Preaching enmity to nearly everything that Gregg had advocated, except improvement of the soil, he attacked the whole business system of the North. Machine Industry, he prophesied, would end in appalling misery, and socialism, destructive to efficiency and initiative, would probably be the outcome. Better by far was Negro slavery, the ideal arrangement: "In the institution of domestic slavery, and in that only, are most completely realized the dreams and sanguine hopes of the socialistic school of philanthropists." After years of crusading, the hour sought by Ruffin drew near: Charleston's rebels prepared to fire on Fort Sumter, the act which rendered the civil conflict unavoidable. And Ruffin, the old war-horse, gleefully received permission from General Beauregard to blaze away at that symbol of Yankee commercial despotism.

THE EMPIRE OF NORTHERN BUSINESS

While landed gentlemen of the South, with leisure for politics and the formulation of a philosophy, were crusading in their own behalf, Northern business men were saying very little in direct reply. Boston men backed the lawyer, Daniel Webster, who defended their cause in tariff controversies at Washington, but they themselves preferred to work in quiet. A form of the indirect reply was the "underground railway" along which fugitive slaves were helped to escape to free territory, and one of the "stations" on the route was the home of Peter Sylvester Holden, a Puritan-descended cotton merchant of Massachusetts; another was maintained in the house of Nathaniel White, New Hampshire stagecoach magnate and prohibition candidate for State Governor. A leader in the abolition movement was Robert Purvis, wealthy cottonbroker of English birth who married a beautiful Moorish slave named Dido; his son was on the board of directors, so to speak, of the illegal Refugee Railway.

The American situation thus reversed the English, where landed gentlemen refrained from taking up arms, while cotton spinners like Cobden and Bright were preaching to the people, claiming their rights on high moral principles. Northern business was, however, far from unanimous on many points, and the protective tariffs sought by manufacturers were often assailed by exporting and importing merchants almost as angrily as by planters. Perhaps, also, Northern business men had no breath left for political oratory, since the special gifts for rhapsody they possessed were extensively employed in boosting western lands for sale.

As the South consolidated the planting system, capitalists of the Northeastern seaboard were stretching their dominion farther and farther into the West, buying up enormous areas rich in resources, and building railroads, along which cities sprouted, to bind their purchases together. By swiftly combining their railway lines, although a heavy price was paid in corruption and tremendous losses were borne by investors, the Northerners were steadily beating the South in the race for empire. As was estimated in 1861, $500,000,000 was spent to "change the direction of the commerce of the Mississippi." Not only were they mortgaging the wilderness, and carrying settlers to the frontiers, but they were also bringing the wheat and pork of the West directly to the Eastern cities, making possible the avoidance of the long slow route down the Mississippi to New Orleans. Thanks to railroads, farmers became dependent upon the credit of Eastern merchants, not that of the Southern port.

How much of the opened continent was thus taken by business men of the East has hardly been realized until our own time, so much has the popular imagination been occupied by pretty pictures of buckskinclad pioneers pressing back the frontier. Actually, the engineer-surveyors for the business men and their companies preceded the settlers as a rule. This was inevitable, as the Colonial land-speculator, Gouverneur Morris, early remarked, for it was "absurd to suppose that a person with scarce a second shirt to his back can go two or three hundred miles" or more, to survey a farm and return to clear the title, before he took possession. "The conflict of title is generally between men able to stand the shock." Merchants with large capital, or railway promoters, early sought out the desirable lands. By the time the humble settlers arrived, they were apt to find the best spots picked over and those with the most valuable resources already monopolized by companies, which had purchased deserts and forests in advance and were holding realms for a rise. The great problem of the settlers was not "wresting America from the wilderness," as the saying goes, but reclaiming it from the business man.

Only a small part of the American continent has ever been "free," that is, taken by the individual adventurer for the price of his labor. According to Gates, "actual homesteading," under the Act of 1862, "was generally confined to the less desirable lands distant from railroad lines," and up to 1890, homesteaders had acquired less than 3½ per cent of the land west of the Mississippi. The best and most accessible lands were sold for cash by companies. True, even at company prices, land was relatively cheap. It was low enough to lure millions of European immigrants. But the myth of the "free continent" is now dispelled in part by the researches of Gates and Shannon, who have shown the prodigious extent of the business man's holdings.

The reach of his imperial enterprise is indeed staggering to contemplate. In Colonial times, surprising areas were tossed over the counter: a Boston merchant, Robert Usher, sold the entire territory which is now the State of Maine to a development company. But if they were reckoning in hundreds of thousands of acres in that period, by the nineteenth century the dealing had progressed to millions. It has been estimated that 155,000,000 acres, containing some of the finest natural resources, were handed out in a few years to companies proposing to build railways and canals. Referring to the course of empire under the Homestead Act, Shannon shows that by 1890 four times as much land had been given away by the Government to railroads as to homestead settlers.

Still the railway domains formed only a part of the business man's possessions. The Indian lands, for instance, it now appears, were mainly sold in large blocks for cash to capitalists as individuals, or in syndicates. Another source of speculation was the area granted by the Federal Government after 1862 to various states, to be used by them in providing funds to erect and maintain educational institutions; immense stretches of this land were sold at auction to the highest bidders, including Eastern bankers and merchants, such as Blair, Sage and Cornell. The grants to railroads and canals totaled more than 150,000,000 acres; the Indian lands comprised 100,000,000 acres more, and those sold for educational and other purposes totaled 140,000,000 acres. Large companies took the cream of the tracts; most of the public domain, ostensibly thrown open to homesteaders gratis, actually came into the possession of speculators from whom the pioneers had to buy it.

The gigantic expanses conquered in the Southwest should be included in the business man's winnings. Here a number of capitalists became great landlords, for example William S. Chapman and Henry Miller, each of whom owned a million acres at one time. In Texas the Farwell Brothers made a proposition to the State, by which they were to build a capitol costing $5,000,000 in Austin in return for a cession of 3,500,000 acres in the Upper Panhandle. This region they disposed of with more than royal absolutism, building cities and railroads at will, and gradually selling their holdings away.

How breath-taking was landed empire of the business man in America may be realized by comparison with his puny holdings in the past: with the estates in Egypt won by Roman speculators; with the towns defended by mediaeval merchants. Never before had such reaches of the earth come into the possession of men of affairs; always, in previous times, the soil had to be taken by the sword, and the merchant, less martial or less interested in the furrow, had not wrested great dominions from feudal chivalry. Hitherto only upon the ocean had his empire been broad and undisputed. In sixteenth-century Russia a parallel might be found in the Siberian empire achieved by the merchant family of the Stroganovs; the Stroganovs, however, had to employ Cossack armies and the founder of the family was slain by wild Mongols. For the first time, and in America, business men acquired territories of regal extent, without lifting a battleaxe.

This domestic imperialism was an easy "proposition." Merely from his office in Boston or New York, or in a lobby chamber at the capital, the speculator could purchase forests, prairies or mountain ranges, and trust to the United States Army to clear the way for him by removing Indians and squatters. Unlike a Spanish conquistador, he did not need to set foot upon even the hem of the land or lake to which he laid claim. Nor did he have to kneel before a sovereign lord, like a feudal vassal, making humiliating obeisances to "acquire title." He was not put to the trouble of governing his provinces, for he could populate his broad domains with inarticulate, non-existent "dummy" settlers. And he could unload his empire before it became an unremunerative burden.

Large capital was, of course, required for such enterprises, and this naturally came from the business cities of the East, where wealth had long been accumulating, rather than from the relatively poor Southern planters. As even the East could not supply all the funds, the savings of Europe were tapped. In the development of Chicago, for example, a mining-venturer from Maine, Daniel H. Hale, took an important part; going abroad, he formed both a Scottish and an English company with large capital, and lured immigrants as well as money to his favorite project in the wilderness. One of the most tremendous speculative companies, which took huge slices of California forests, was based on English capital primarily. The combination of such capital resources enabled land-seizure to proceed with amazing rapidity; by the 1830's the company-agents were selling off the Middle-Western States; by the end of the next decade they had reached the Coast and begun to knock down desirable wharf-sites at auction; in the 1850's they were boosting and building cities over the breadth of America, until, a year or two before the Civil War, the wealth invested in urban and industrial property had come to equal rural riches.

Then at last, when it was too late, the South challenged the North. A half-century before, the Northern business man might have been even glad to see it go out of the Union. During the War of 1812, when the South supported a campaign that was paralyzing sea-borne commerce, some of the leading merchants of the North dallied with thoughts of Secession themselves—with plans for retiring to form a small but compact business nation, comprising New York, Pennsylvania, and New England. Thus the commercial North had considered leaving the Union before the Southern planters, in 1832, made their first premature attempt at withdrawal. Each section had grown impatient with the other; but by the 1860's, only the South remained enmeshed in localism; the Northern business men had then come into possession of a vast Western empire, and a rich Far Eastern trade. They held gold mines, railroads, growing new cities and expanding industrial plants. It was no wonder that they were thinking in continental terms, and were ready to throw the weight of their wealth, and the man-power of the newly opened West, into the scales against a South engaged in disrupting their dream of "magnificent destiny."

Clear as the main dividing lines appear, there were yet some minor confusions of purpose and deed among business men. For instance, it was a Yankee business man and inventor, Eli Whitney, who gave the South the cotton-gin, which really made possible the reign of King Cotton. When the North battled with the South, a Virginian inventor and business man, Cyrus Hall McCormick, aided the triumph of King Wheat with his reapers; harvesting could go on while millions of men were in uniform. Moreover, many an exporting and importing merchant in the North, aided by his bankers, was in sympathy with the Southern planters who supplied him with produce to sell and orders for foreign goods in exchange.

THE SPIRIT OF THE REALTOR

In the pre-Civil War period, in the age of city-planting and of exuberant boosting and booming, the promoter of real-estate values, the "realtor" as he afterward liked to call himself, appeared on the horizon. By two novelists, Charles Dickens and Sinclair Lewis, he has been made the symbol of American enterprise. The former's "Martin Chuzzlewit" and the latter's "Babbitt" were built around this glib-tongued business man, who was made to appear characteristically American, thus arousing storms of protest against that view of American business.

Dickens visited America in the 1840's, in the aftermath of a speculative fever aroused by the opening of mid-western lands. The fantastic spectacle of this boom was described by another contemporary: "The more absurd the project, the more remote the object, the more madly were they pursued. The prairies of Illinois, the forests of Wisconsin, the sand-hills of Michigan" were all dowered with "supposititious villages and cities . . . Some wary operator would ride day and night until the place was secured at the government price. Then the miserable waste of sand and fens . . . was suddenly elevated into a mighty city with a projected harbor and lighthouse, railroads and canals, and in a short time the circumjacent lands were sold in lots. Not the puniest brook on the shore of Lake Michigan was suffered to remain without a city at its mouth." Center of this trading was the log-cabin settlement near what is now Chicago; the delirium lasted until 1837, when prices had been driven skyward and wild-cat currency was issued on the basis of inflated land-values. Then Chicago went bankrupt. One unlucky victim, who failed for one hundred thousand dollars, was heard to remark regretfully that, had the collapse been postponed only another week, he could have failed for a million.

But no crash could halt the hopes of the public; as soon as one region failed them, another was flung open. Immediately throngs abandoned legitimate trade, as the critics moaned, to hang around the auctioneer's booth and bid up the price of choice corner-lots in a wilderness newly staked out. Before a month was gone, prefabricated housing, no modern invention, was rushed out by railroad, and a roaring town was rising, with saloons and churches side by side. In a decade or two, a city had appeared, more populous than many a mediaeval town which had taken centuries in the building. And there were always a few who made fortunes out of the rush.

In this milieu, Dickens' nefarious realtor, *Scadder*, operated. His office was a mere shanty and his attire negligent—with a shudder of repulsion, Dickens noted that he did not wear a collar. But such shortcomings were more than offset by the florid prospectuses and maps of "Eden City," in which a few wonderful bargains miraculously remained, all because the Eden Land Company would not sell to any but "Aristocrats of Natur'." Dickens' innocent British hero was sure he was one of Nature's aristocrats, and paid over his last penny for a water-front lot which turned out to be on a lonely malarial swamp. Quite forgetting that this great game of land-speculation had been introduced to America by British courtiers and ignoring the rôle of foreign capital in such companies, Dickens launched into his famous tirade against American commercialism, in which the vice was represented as indigenous:

> All their cares, hopes, joys, affections, virtues, and associations seem to be melted down into dollars . . . Men were weighed by their dollars. Life was auctioneered, appraised, put up, and knocked down for its dollars . . . The more of that worthless ballast, honour and fair-dealing, which any man cast overboard from the ship of

his Good Name and Good Intent, the more ample stowage-room he had for dollars. Make commerce one huge lie and mighty theft. Deface the banner of the nation for an idle rag; pollute it star by star; and cut out stripe by stripe as from the arm of a degraded soldier. Do anything for dollars! What is a flag to them?

At that time, it is true, American swindling had not kept pace with the refinements of British speculation; the Eden Land Company's shanty-office lacked the elegant appointments of the equally baseless "Anglo-Bengalee Company" of London, caricatured by Dickens in the same novel. But even after a more perfect American finish was acquired, Sinclair Lewis was still discontented. His realtor was indeed not a cold villain like *Scadder;* he was a babbling *Babbitt,* pathetic rather than malevolent.

More complex than either fictional character was the living American realtor, George Francis Train, who strewed new cities over America and Australia with godlike carelessness. With the shrewdness of a Barnum he united the mellifluous oratorical periods of a Southern Senator, and could sway any audience into a mad stampede for subscriptions. One of his original ideas, a rapid trip around the world, taken to boost Tacoma as a port, inspired Jules Verne to write a novel based on the realtor—"Around the World in Eighty Days," with Train figuring as *Phineas Fogg.* Decidedly bizarre in his habits, Train was noted for dispensing champagne over marble counters to his prospects and for refusing to shake hands lest he lose some of his electrodynamic energy; he also invented pencils with erasers attached, and created the word "crank" which he so eminently illustrated.

Yet Train was neither so coldly unscrupulous as *Scadder* nor so foolish as *Babbitt.* He was rather an artist often carried away by his own oratory, as appears from his book, written after the great crash of 1857, "Young America in Wall Street." In this work, the American realtor expressed his amazement at the blind hopes of his country: "The most surprising thing to me is that an intelligent community, a mercantile people, could march on with a steady tramp to the brink of the precipice, blindfold their eyes, recklessly advance, step over, and fall into an almost universal bankruptcy, without being aware of it themselves." He confessed with a sigh: "The truth is we are a fast people, bound to beat the world, even in the abysses of our insolvency." Nevertheless Train displayed a knowledge of business history and a wide comprehension of speculation in England and France in the same period, which enabled him to point out international contrasts: "The press of France is voiceless; hence French bubbles are seldom seen floating upon the waters." England was more mature and steady—"the only nation that understands the art of raising the wind, and growing richer and richer the more she owes to her own people." So terrified was Train by the prospects of unregulated speculation, in a land so given to hysterical hopes as his own, that he proposed a strong governmental assistance thenceforth, and a public works project which should "extend to the State, the county, the city, and the town" and prevent such shocks for the future.

Among other city-fathers of the time a wide variety of character was exhibited. Plain rascals abounded, like that Rathbun who made Buffalo "an elegant town," and yet in 1843 was himself "in Auburn penitentiary for his many acts of swindling and forgery—the means by which he for a long period carried on the improvements of the place." Some realtors, especially in the Far West, became attached almost in spite of themselves to a particular locality which they then boosted with a genuine passion. Such was the picturesque Indian-fighter, engineer and promoter, General William J. Palmer, who helped to fling the Union Pacific across the desert. Along the way he espied ore-bearing deposits, seized them in haste and ran tracks to them; he formed industrial companies to exploit these resources, knit them in primitive trust-formations and built towns around them. For most of these towns he had no real affection, but he was completely captured by Colorado Springs where he developed a health-resort. There he ran hotels, fed guests from his irrigated farms and endeavored to control the growth of the community and fix the moral tone by imposing temperance and religion upon it with seigneurial obstinacy. In the mountains near by he owned silver, coal, iron and water-power and an estate of hundreds of thousands of acres in the so-called "Garden of the Gods" where he built a Tudor castle, complete with every luxury of the age. Occasionally, however, catching sight of Pike's Peak on the horizon, he would remove his broad-brimmed hat and humbly declare that it impressed him with the insignificance of man. No ordinary mountain could thus have dwarfed the General.

More pathetic was the career of William Ralston, who so devoted himself to the promotion of San Francisco that he forgot profit in excess of civic pride. Through his Bank of California he sought to give his chosen town everything overnight: not only steamship lines, a railroad and factories, but art, a reform movement and a lavish society life. Opening a quarter-million dollar theater with a masked ball, at which he appeared garbed as a doge of Venice, he proudly displayed his chosen decorations: "At the base of one pillar on the left is the Tragic Muse; at the base to the right is the Comic Muse. Beneath the balcony is a medallion on which appears the incoming Pacific Railroad." He commissioned Bret Harte to write a play for the theater; he brought the Shakespearean actress, Adelaide Neilson, to the Coast and presented her with a $10,000 diamond necklace, exhibiting so much romantic devotion as to estrange his wife, Lizzie.

Feeling that San Francisco must have a "Society," he constructed roads and reservoirs on his vast land-holdings, hoping to start a colony of the region's richest families; as an architectural model he erected a palace with a peerless ball-room; for its crystal, marquetry and ornaments, Lizzie ransacked Europe. Often this palace was the scene of masquerades, at which Ralston was fond of appearing as a French marquis. Gleefully watching his guests, he would stand on the side, cranking his new mechanical piano.

Unfortunately for Ralston, other millionaires refused to rise to his bait. When they would not come to him, he went to them and started a six million dollar hotel in the city, to be called "The Palace." Unhappily it burned before completion. Another blow fell when strangers duped him with a "salted" diamond-mine in the desert; valiantly he returned the money to those who followed him into this mad scheme and kept the canceled checks under glass in his office. Finally his bank was ruined in a competition over the Comstock Lode with men more single-minded than he. Then the restless Ralston sought peace in the waters of the Bay.

It was on the Pacific Coast, where the ocean brought to a halt the westward sweep of the land-speculator, that the realtor's imagination achieved its last lush flowering. Realizing that he could go no further, that this was his final opportunity, he made the most of it. The supreme frenzied exhibition of self-hypnotism took place at Los Angeles, where the booster-brethren, pulling together with unexampled cooperative enthusiasm, rushed up hotels and an opera house and prepared for the millennium, while they chorused, "Buy Acres Here and Wear Diamonds!" This was the climax. Henceforth the boom-spirit, cramped and bound at last, was to move in ever-narrower fields. Closer and fiercer became the struggle over the development of the cities so hastily scattered and over the possession of their harbors, transport-lines, industries and political offices. Now a truer city-building epoch unfolded.

BUSINESS AND THE CITIES

The story of the business man's share in city-construction is full of gaps, despite its brevity. So much newer than Lübeck or Florence, the origins of American towns are nevertheless enshrouded in much the same obscurity. American chroniclers, like mediaeval monks, tended to record trivial incidents and ignore vital economic matters, such as the strife of realtors and contractors over down-town shopping districts and the sites of public edifices, or the rise of merchant families and their ramifications with legal and political castes; nor did they always think it worthwhile to mention the occupations and interests of early mayors and other officials. As a result of this indifference to foundations, our Dark Ages will be as much of a puzzle to future historians as that of Europe to the historians of today.

Certainly, however, the business man's share in the upbuilding of American towns and cities was hardly less than that of his prototype in bygone centuries in Europe. Some American towns and cities were the conception of a single man, notably Pullman, built and owned by the sleeping-car manufacturer, and Hersheyville set up by the candy-maker. Often urban centers were dominated in the beginning by one personality, as in the case of New York, for a time so largely swayed by Astor, and San Diego, once run as a "one-man town" by John D. Spreckels, who perhaps inherited a Hanseatic tradition from old Claus, the Hawaiian Sugar-King, originally from the region of Bremen. So, too, Chicago was for a period overlorded by William B. Ogden, banker, realtor, merchant and "Railway King of the West," promoter of everything from canals to harvesting machines, and mayor of the city. The strategic position of Denver, as the hub of a railway-wheel, was to a large extent the idea of David H. Moffat, storekeeper and banker, who pushed lines in every direction to open surrounding mineral resources. Best remembered is his terrific battle to take a line to Salt Lake across the Rockies, with his crew fighting incessantly against the rival gangs of Harriman, trying to lay parallel tracks.

Occasionally a single family dynasty, the Du Ponts in Wilmington being a striking instance, overshadowed a center long after the pioneer stage was left behind. But usually the shadow was that of a group of families, sometimes hardened to a caste, as in some New England mill-towns, and again open to constant renovation. The crystallization of such business "élites" might be observed in the tiniest towns, where the blue-bloods could "trace their lineage to the first subscribers to the town bridge." When it reached the mightiest, usually a "millionaire residence section" was developed, such as "Nob Hill" in San Francisco, the seat of competition in mansion-building among the gold-rush prof-iteers, until the prize was borne off by Jim Flood, the Bonanza King, with his $30,000 brass fence kept perpetually bright by a squad of polishers.

In the earlier stages, especially, there was a considerable difference in make-up and methods among these patriciates: in Salt Lake City, the Mormon trader-saints formed a closed corporation; thrifty and cohesive New England business men made a "Little Boston" of Seattle and a "New Connecticut" of Cleveland. In St. Louis and Detroit the tone was French for a season, as it had been Dutch in Albany and Schenectady, the latter built on the lands of the merchant, Killiaen van Rensselaer. Everywhere, of course, the tendency was for new races to efface the older; thus Germans almost overwhelmed the Yankee stratum of Cleveland.

As in past times, American commercial wealth manifested itself in private display and public benefaction. The natural thing was for the American to copy his predecessors. So Huntington imitated a Venetian palace, Palmer an English castle, and one of the Vanderbilts a château of Jacques Cœur. However, the obligation of civic benevolence was also felt: the American gave parks, asylums, libraries and "cathedrals of learning" and joined committees and boards for reform and charity. Very often canals, port-enlargements, waterworks and other "improvements" were conceived in the two-fold aspect of good business and civic betterment, and in pushing them the leading men of commerce identified their private interests with the interest of the community. Such projects brought business men together in boosting and benevolent brotherhoods, filled with mediaevalism, as far as emblems, banquets and frolics were concerned.

Of all the modern business men, the Japanese excepted, the Americans became the most clubby. The basis of this fraternization, however, they did not create. At least one of their fraternal organizations, the Masonic, was a genuine survival, although its source in the Middle Ages was a secret organization of laborers, socially far below the rank of merchants; European business men in the eighteenth century had revived this Order. They had also resorted to other clubs, the Illuminati for example, partly to seek distinctions denied them by the absolutistic States, and partly from political motives. It is now claimed that Masonry played a considerable part in the making of the French Revolution. Americans transplanted the Masonic organization before that storm broke.

Pittsburgh, in 1785, became one of the strongholds of this Order. Its Lodge Number 45 was "the most influential social organization in the village. Nearly all the leading citizens were members." The great civic event of the year was their parade, distinguished by the cocked hats and aprons of their craft and the Bible carried before the marchers on a cushion. This tradition persisted. Although almost all compilations of city biographies are filled with mentions of clubs, offices and titles, those of Pittsburgh seem especially conspicuous in this respect. One notes that a magnate of screw-manufacture is a member of the Ancient Arabic Order of Nobles of the Mystic Shrine; another in the furniture business, is Grand Chief of the Electric Star Castle of the Knights of the Golden Eagle. And so the roll-call continues, reminiscent of the solemnity with which the old Germans took their clubs of Bears and Cats.

Feuds, as characteristic as fraternities in mediaeval life, also enlivened the years in early American towns. Furious inter-city rivalry occurred over trade-routes and ports; embattled citizens of Cleveland and Ohio City, in 1837, seized guns to fight about a bridge, which one or the other party blew up. The enmity of St. Paul and Minneapolis, Portland and Astoria, Los Angeles and San Francisco, might appropriately be set beside the ancient jealousies of Florence and Siena, or Hamburg and Bremen. Within the towns, as well as between them, the struggles of commercial factions were merciless—illustrated by the war of Gould and Cassatt for the railway terminus in Pittsburgh, for instance, or the epic fare-battle in San Francisco, city of hysterical gold-rushers, ruled by almost barbarically jealous moguls.

A good deal of Renaissance grandezza and venom characterized the masters of the latter city—Adolf Sutro and the so-called "Big Four" who had made that port the terminal of transcontinental railway lines. With Medicean lavishness, they competed in display and in adjectives, proclaiming the "magnificent destiny" toward which they were guiding their city. Adolf Sutro's imagination knew no bounds; a once-poor immigrant become a plutocratic mine-owner, through his technical training and ingenuity, he achieved fame as "King of the Comstock"; he bought the Duke of Marlborough's library in England and presented it to the city fathers, though they had not the least idea what to do with it. Then he built the Sutro Baths to dazzle the public—a park in which was exhibited his engineering skill in tunneling and blasting, as well as his collections of zoological and aesthetic rarities. But Sutro had to enter politics, to win a five-cent fare on the trolley-line to his Baths, and in this connection he hurt the jealous pride of one of the Big Four, Huntington, who had intended to eclipse everyone else through his Venetian splendors. Huntington would not yield a point on the fare issue. So Sutro enlisted the aid of George Hearst; thus was secured the bitterest pen in America, that of Ambrose Bierce, to defame Huntington. Bierce called him the "surviving thirty-six" of "our modern forty thieves." This verbal war, waged by literati, in the best old Florentine manner, was finally ended in the defeat of Sutro.

Yet such resemblances to the past were superficial. Huntington and Sutro did not establish themselves as oligarchs, like the last Medici. Nor was city politics their ultimate interest. The Big Four had to keep their eyes on Washington; masters of enormous domains and interests, covering the continent, they wrangled over city affairs merely in their spare moments. That was one of the reasons why American business men failed to rule the cities they had built; they were too busy, as a rule, with wider games. There were exceptions, of course, especially in the first stages. The first Mayor of Chicago, Ogden, was a "Railway King," and in Pittsburgh he was a dry-goods merchant, Ebenezer Denny. Occasionally, arose a figure, such as Russell Sage, who might have graced Old Amsterdam; in his official capacity as City Councilor of Troy, Sage wrecked the railroad which he was empowered to supervise; then he sold it cheaply to himself, in his private capacity as railroad man. So an oligarch of an elder time would have managed the entire operation, instead of working through lawyers; but this perfect coalescence of civic and economic activities was comparatively rare in America.

Another reason for the failure of American business men to dominate the scene was lack of family continuity. In coming to new Western towns, men had left their relatives behind; no flock of clansmen was at their heels. Scorning tribalism and exalting the individual, they could not weave such fine-meshed political nets as those originally cast about municipalities by the many-headed merchant families of Europe. And then the flood of immigrant labor presented peculiar problems to American business rule. The story of Pittsburgh is especially instructive in that respect.

Pittsburgh began as a trading-post, around which developed mining and industries. At first merchants and employers did hold municipal offices, much as in embryo towns of mediaeval Europe. They built churches; their residences clustered together on Market Street; their Masonic fraternity was a patrician brotherhood of men in power. Among these burghers were persons of military and even noble origin, eager to direct the community: the Indian-fighter, General Richard Butler, who kept a store; a French aristocratic émigré who sold wines; a third storekeeper, the son of a Belgian baron. In short, by the early 1800's, there was a nucleus for development in a European fashion. Then, however, politics took a new, an American, turn.

In their commercial-political battles, business men resorted to the practice of importing aliens, naturalizing them in lots and making them useful as voters and laborers. But such masses had to be managed by men of their own race—by bosses. When the business men yielded municipal offices to the bosses, they grew dependent upon the *demos* they had imported. Since the chief Republican politicians dwelt in Clapboard Row, which now disputed power with Market Street, "Clapboard Row politics" became a favorite descriptive term for the boss-system wherever it was manifested.

For a short time, a business family reasserted strength in Pittsburgh. Thus the Bigelows divided the functions of money-winning and governing among their several members. Edward Manning Bigelow was city-ruler, while his brother Thomas, a street-car magnate, supported his fight against the opposing boss-machine. The Bigelows formed a Citizens' Party, with the assistance of Senator Quay, and for a political moment had an imposing steam-roller of their own. But Clapboard Row politics revived in Pittsburgh. Neither there nor in other cities was it easy to erect powerful, well-ramified and inter-married patrician circles—in a society so mobile. Moreover, when big business men attempted to campaign directly, they met hostility in the swarming industrial centers. The harvester-magnate, McCormick, was defeated in Chicago; the millionaire merchant, Abram S. Hewitt, only won in New York, even on a Tammany ticket, against the Henry George labor candidate, by the most corrupt tactics.

Though they used bosses of necessity, big business men often resented this indirect kind of government. Their scorn is mirrored in a story told by Charles Norman Fay, manufacturer and former utility head, who was for a time leader of the National Manufacturers' Association and a vehement pleader for direct assertion of business in politics. Though Fay wished to venture forth himself in Chicago as open opponent of a certain blackmailing politician who had been overcharging him for "protection," he met no sympathy from his fellow-business men:

> One of my directors used to say to me contemptuously, "Why waste your time? I would just as soon buy that kind of alderman as a pound of beef. If the people will elect such men, the shame is theirs; and they must pay the bill! So pay that rascal his blackmail; and spread the cost over *their gas* bills. That is democracy!"

But of course it was not "democracy" alone which was responsible for the corruption of the Tweed Ring era; even if they had been spared popular elections, American business men could hardly have taken time for petty municipal concerns. The era of localism, which had endured for so many centuries in Europe, ended in America before the cities were finished; no generations of leisure were given to business men for dwelling within their walls, molding a tradition and practicing government in miniature. That deepening experience was denied them. Before their crude booming and boosting could mellow into a burgher-spirit, the age of business adventure on a national scale had opened, with the conclusion of the Civil War. Business men neglected the cities they had made, for a whole continent lay before them, waiting "development." Though a few politicians of the first magnitude emerged from the business world, like Aldrich of Rhode Island and Mark Hanna of Cleveland, they were not content with a local stage.

THE GREAT AMERICAN SPECULATOR

The Civil War left neither side unchanged. By their own triumph, the dominating business groups of the Northeast were shaken to the core; the small, compact, slow-moving patriciate of New York was especially overwhelmed by the tremendous economic transformations caused by putting the country on a war-basis.

In the good old Knickerbocker days, New York bankers had enjoyed "abundant yawning time between breakfast and dinner." Business was broken by chats, and concluded by big home dinners. Scarcely anyone dined out save a few bachelors calling themselves the Jolly Fellows and led by the old merchant, Colonel Nick Saltus, an "abrupt and dictatorial" man until "mollified by his duck and olives, accompanied with copious libations of Madeira." On Sundays, respectable citizens paraded solemnly on foot: the ladies in quiet attire, revealing their financial status only by a lace kerchief "carried by its exact centre between forefinger and thumb"; and the gentlemen all in black. They donned black gloves, black shoes much too tight, black stocks that choked the throat and wing-collars that prevented them from turning their heads, black frock coats that were a "marvel of disproportion and discomfort," and heavy beaver hats that gave them headaches. Carrying European fashion to extremes, as usual, they wore black trousers so excessively tight that they could hardly bend the knees; this inclined them to walk gravely and made them reluctant to sit down. In fact, the sartorial elegance of Old New York is one of the clues to a very vexing problem in economic history—the question why American business men put their feet on desks.

Possibly Eastern merchants might have gone on hardening into a yet greater Old World rigidity, had they not been struck, in the 1830's, by the Bankruptcy Acts, forced upon them by Jeffersonian Democracy and curtailing the power of the courts to uphold "the sanctity of contracts." Such Acts had been demanded by farmers as well as by small business men who fancied that they would free themselves of the loads of debts upon their holdings, in making bankruptcy easy. Farmers also supposed they would do serious damage to their hated foes, the capitalists of the East, holders of mortgages on their lands. Indeed this was the immediate effect, for many New England merchants, having invested heavily in Western lands, were hard hit. But the Bankruptcy Acts had results quite unforeseen by the proponents: they undermined commercial honor and paved the way for an unparalleled speculative age.

Bankruptcy had always been a dreadful idea in the Old World—a sin tinged with religious horror. Effigies of bankrupts used to be displayed in Florence; in mediaeval Germany, the victims had to wear special caps. Down to modern times this attitude persisted; in early America, especially in the New England states, the courts retained a merciless grip upon the goods of defaulters. So the new Acts and their interpretation by Jacksonian federal judges were in fact revolutionary. Now a man could "sponge the slate" three or four times and yet rise imperturbably. After he had cleared his debts by a "settlement" in bankruptcy, he could no longer be pursued for "debts of honor." As the realtor, George Francis Train, phrased it:

Germans hold a debt over a man for forty years . . . In England a man who fails seldom again rises above low-water mark. In America, where ninety-five out of the hundred come down, everybody floats in on the flood.

An American stops once in five years and pays fifty cents on the dollar; while an Englishman breaks once in ten years and pays nothing.

Honor in American business was irreparably hurt by these Acts. And none were so affected by the ultimate consequences as the small folk who sponsored them, for great railroaders, after the Civil War, took advantage of such legislation to go bankrupt as often as they chose, mulcting the little investors by the thousands.

Since the courts were prevented by bankruptcy legislation from serving as stern referees over competition and Jacksonian Democracy would not set up such a regulative institution as the Bank of England, struggle for survival assumed cut-throat forms. Moreover, it was immensely extended by an expansion of credit and flotation of "securities" which threw open the doors more widely than in Europe to the small man. Swarms of petty jobbers and storekeepers were enabled to attempt enterprises far beyond their means, and thus swell the speculative frenzies beyond any bounds known to a more rigid Europe. For most of these small pioneers, the end could only be ruin; in 1888, General Dearborn observed: "Among one hundred merchants no more than three ever acquire a competency." Even the biggest could only preserve their positions in that arena by unceasing combat and, as these titans measured strength, their Saturnian warfare shook the earth.

To add to the confusion, European investors took advantage of the moral and legal laxity in the New World to pour in their funds for canals and railways that could hardly have been built without them. Europe thus heightened the melodramatic character of American business life in which, as many observed, booms were more bloated and crashes more resounding than anywhere else—at that time. And the odd thing, as Dickens remarked in the 1840's, was that they seemed to be going on simultaneously:

"You have come to visit our country, sir, at a season of great commercial depression," said the Major.

"At an alarming crisis," said the Colonel.

"At a period of unprecedented stagnation," said Mr. Jefferson Brick.

"Well," returned the Major, "I expect we shall get along some-how and come all right in the end."

"We are an elastic country," said the Rowdy Journal.

"We are a young lion," said Mr. Jefferson Brick . . .

Martin knew nothing about America, or he would have known perfectly well that if its individual citizens, to a man, are to be be-lieved, it always *is* depressed, and always *is* stagnated, and always *is* at an alarming crisis, and never was otherwise; though as a body they are ready to make oath upon the evangelists at any hour of the day or night, that it is the most thriving and prosperous of all countries on the habitable globe.

Even before the Civil War, therefore, the background was well pre-pared for an unparalleled speculation; and then came the pressure of military demands, transforming the methods of business in all lines. Railroading paid as never before, through the carriage of troops and supplies; iron-production was hastened not only for railroads but also for arms-manufacture in which Sam Colt of Hartford applied mass-production methods. A similar drive to large-scale enterprise was en-couraged in Chicago meat-packing and in New England textiles; the readymade garment industry began to flourish and able organizers like James Talcott in New York overrode the small, routine-minded mill-men who could not rise to the war-need for clothing a mass-army. In-dustrial patents doubled during the War, as labor-saving devices were sought to replace men at the front. McCormick's reaper was one of the first of these to yield a fortune; but the more abundant harvesting of wheat that he made possible produced a mighty whirlpool of specula-tion at Chicago, in the Wheat Pit, dominated at the close of the War by "Old Hutch," Benjamin P. Hutchinson, who came from a Massa-chusetts farm to make himself Wheat King of the West, having cor-rectly guessed the effect of the conclusion of peace on the market.

Such operations were conducted, of course, on a continental stage, and as such were far vaster than enterprises in contemporary Europe, cut apart into so many national entities. Opportunity provoked gam-bling on a superhuman scale in America. There was the further factor of unique resources available, like petroleum, such as no European state possessed within its own borders. Only Germany with her potassium had a chance to form mighty capitalistic combinations based on domestic resources analogous to the combinations taking shape in America. By 1861, one of the earliest significant attempts at manipulation of American resources, the Michigan Salt Combine, pointed the way to the exploitation of the peculiar American riches, soon to become an American characteristic. The most old-fashioned of cities in many ways, New York, became the center of this giant speculation.

At first New Yorkers thought they could halt the trend. "A few rich, grey-headed old fogies frowned down the more enterprising but less wealthy 'Young America' element, which went in for bold, dashing moves, cliques, corners and the like." Young America, however, as it was proud to be called (hence the title of Train's book, "Young America in Wall Street"), opened up a cellar exchange, the "coal hole," in 1862, and soon an Old and a New Board were bitterly contesting. By 1869, the old "fogies" gave up and the two American forces were consolidated. Around that time, as the reminiscent broker, Fowler, wrote, the basements of lower New York became burrows of "singular animals—mostly rodents . . . gnawing at the vast cheese of speculation." They would sit blinking at their holes, frisk about, pick up a few choice bits and dive back again to darkness. Presently the venturers grew richer and bolder; they selected "more ostentatious offices, glittering with plate glass and garnished with the most arabesque of black walnut furniture," where they offered magnificent claims to non-existent gold-veins in purely putative mountain-ranges.

Upon this well-set stage, the Great American Speculator could now appear—a type as uniquely American as the earlier real-estate promoter, but in many ways possessing exactly the opposite traits. Gifted not with glibness but with silence, he was noted above all for the amazing Indian stoicism with which he accepted fortunes and reverses alike. He might grasp a swifter and dizzier success than the contemporary European, but he also faced terrible losses with undaunted calm. As an Englishman wrote in the 1860's:

> Most of the fortunes at New York have been made and re-made over again. Millions rise and fall by turns, like the waves of a troubled sea. Men get seasoned by this spectacle, and are neither surprised to find themselves after a few years princes in the finance world, or beggars at the end of a few days' commercial crisis.

In those tumultuous years, business was not envisaged as something to be stabilized and held on an even keel of "normal prosperity"; it was regarded as a faro-game for giants and only those with healthy nerves were expected to "sit in" at the tables. Possibly this very expectation of reverses steeled men better than the modern philosophy of optimism, which offers a dream of perpetually avoiding crises by interventions of one kind or another. Probably also, as researches by Taussig and others have shown, more strength fresh from the old-fashioned farm managed business in those days, exemplified in men like Gould, Little, Drew or "Old Hutch." At any rate, when something went wrong and they dropped a few millions, such old masters of the market did not grow pale, rush to Washington, or jump out of a high window. With impervious calm, the jut-jawed Vanderbilt stared down his foes; and the fashionable Leonard W. Jerome, prince of the turf, answered a fall with the springy, "I am all right, boys; I'll be with you in a jiffy." Accustomed to losing fortunes, the Rhode Islander, Jacob Little, leading "bear," and brusque as that animal, was always at bay, facing an army of bulls. Again and again he was tossed; over and over he tricked the throng; and just when they thought they had cornered all the "Erie" in the world, he would wave a fresh bundle under their noses. True, he lost once too often, but he never gave up; a "broken, weird looking old man," he continued to haunt the Board Room, offering five shares of stock in concerns he used to own entirely. So, too, "Uncle Daniel," the ex-circus proprietor, emitted his funny short laugh, "like the cackle of a hen," whenever the boys had "taken a slice out of him." And before the day was out, he would be revenged. "What glee on that queer old face, as he drew the string to snare the game!" exclaimed a contemporary broker. A victory was "good as nuts and cheese" to Uncle Daniel.

The severest ordeal which the New York Exchange had yet encountered was the notorious attempt in 1869 of Gould and his associates to corner all the gold in America. On that "Black Friday" in the Gold Room, when the price of the precious metal was driven up and up despite bullion from abroad, the tension among the fear-crazed speculators was such that Gould fled, barricading himself in his headquarters at the Grand Opera House. When President Grant gave government aid, if tardily, and the storm subsided, Edmund Clarence Stedman, a literary stockbroker on the floor, saw some of the stoutest gamblers close to the breaking-point: "a leading gold bull," Israel Freyer, had gone glassy-eyed and kept shouting hoarsely for "any part of 5,000,000 at 160" long after the price had fallen to 135.

Even New Yorkers, seasoned in the 60's and 70's, held their breath when the "Chicago crowd" of "high rollers" brought their horsy spirits to town in the 1880's. They were the "biggest gamblers the modern world has known." Out in the grain-pit of America, on LaSalle Street, the gambling was quite as wild and vast, in its way, as that on Wall Street, illustrated by the attempt of "Crazy Harper" in the 80's to become Wheat King of the World; looting a bank of its last dollar, he bought wheat, though it poured upon him from a seemingly limitless cornucopia; at last a paltry million dollars was all that stood between him and a universal corner. When the delirium subsided, he was led to prison. But where Crazy Harper failed, "Old Hutch" almost immediately succeeded; right after the Civil War he had made himself master of the nation's market; but, losing heavily in the Chicago fire, he had to climb up again; in 1888, he won a world corner on wheat. With grim joviality surveying the sweating crowd of operators, milling before him like livestock in one of his own slaughterhouse pens, he called out to them at last: "Step up to the captain, boys." And step up they did, to settle, many of them utterly ruined in the process.

Old Hutch was a New Englander who preserved some fragments of classic lore and was fond of quoting Euripides: "Life is a tale told by an idiot, dancing down the wind." When he could find no one to laugh at life with him, in the correct circles of Chicago, he would go out and invite crews of Italian sewer-diggers to come in to dinner. In general, these speculators and combiners, in the West, exhibited more personal idiosyncrasies than the regular Easterners. Not so impervious as Vanderbilt, so frosty as Gould, were "Joe" Leiter, who wanted to buy the Great Wall of China to preserve it, or Daniel G. Reid, who used periodically to regale himself for a week with wine and song, then call for an axe and smash everything in the establishment, after which he would pay the bill and relieve the Loop of his presence. The most unconventional millionaire couple of America were probably "Bet-a-Million" Gates and his wife, "Ma" Gates.

The popular story about Bet-a-Million—that he wagered a small fortune on a raindrop coursing down a window-pane—is an old one, told also about British aristocrats in the eighteenth century. It may be regarded as a folk-myth. Legends also persist about Gates' betting on Texan cock-fights, in his early days as a barbed-wire salesman in the cattle country. There seems little doubt that he introduced to New York poker for astonishing stakes; settling down at the newly-opened Waldorf Hotel, as Crockett describes it, Gates and his friends, Herman Frasch, the Sulphur King, Sielcken, the Coffee King, and the coke man, Henry Frick, ran all-night games in which the turnover was as high as $150,000 in a session; at the same time they ate prodigious quantities of *crêpes Suzette*, for which Gates' appetite seems to have been Homeric. But it was more than a heightened gambling gusto which Gates and the "Chicago crowd" brought to the East when they bought out the "Pittsburgh crowd." Gates appears to have studied the methods of the rollicking Irish speculator of contemporary London, Ernest Terah Hooley, expert in amalgamating companies and issuing super-securities. Out of the West, therefore, Chicagoans carried the merger-idea, and saw it flower in the mighty United States Steel Corporation which, with the Eastern money of J. P. Morgan, bought out the hugest combination so far seen, that of Andrew Carnegie, and became the first "billion-dollar" corporation. The era of trusts and Big Business was now wide open.

Greatest of manipulators as they were, the Chicagoans also brought to a close the period of primitive speculation; thenceforth it became so immense, so complex and abstract that it could no longer be classed with the picturesque, personal adventuring of the earlier decades. No longer was business strife to be visualized as the struggle of individuals, mighty, lavish, pious and ferocious, in the style of Renaissance princes like the Medici and the Strozzi. It became more and more the maneuvering of great corporations, whose heads were no longer visible. Gone were the days when Fisk and Drew escaped in a green coach loaded with satchels of cash and bonds; gone was the time of colossal gambling in gold and wheat. The glitter of the precious metal, the rustle of certificates, which had made the rivalry of the simpler players in Gold Room or Wheat Pit appear so sensuously exciting, like the buccaneering of Drake in the age of Elizabeth, now vanished, as modern titans began to wrestle behind scenes, over intangibles.

BUSINESS CLAIMING A CONTINENT

As the land-speculator pushed back the frontier more rapidly than throngs of private pioneers could do, and as the real-estate promoter made possible the swift tempo of the city-building epoch, compressing centuries of "Dark Ages" into a few decades, so the Great American Speculator in stocks, rails and commodities achieved an amazing unification of the economic continent within a few years. Never before had such a task been performed by business men. Smashing localism, binding together petty units, standardizing rules and methods, building up by privileges and charters a large-scale industry capable of serving great masses of people—that work which, in Baroque Europe, had required the armies of monarchs, was here finished by men of commerce, with government as a beneficent assistant.

Promoters and exploiters, the Vanderbilts and Goulds, played parts in America which had once fallen to the lot of the Valois and the Tudors, whom indeed they much resembled in reckless pride of authority and a certain negligence about the finer shades of ethics. Just as the European era of nation-building, the era of eighteenth-century absolutism, was one of extreme corruption in which ministers and monopolists conspired together, confounding public and private affairs, so the American decades of centralization were marked by the ceaseless complicity of legislators and manipulators—a "graft" more astonishing than that of earlier Europe only because a continent was here being exploited, and not merely nations.

Such business men, reaching out for increasing mastery of lands and lines of transport, resources, gold, industries, managed to create nation-wide complexes super-regal, indeed Napoleonic, in scope. At first they sought to grasp lines of communication in order to develop their territories. Thus John Jacob Astor, organizing his fur-trading company to battle in the Northwest against British monopolists, planned to sell his furs to China in return for tea and porcelain; he needed sea-power to make his forest-domains pay. J. J. Hill, planning to open the rich wheat region of the Red River, embarked on a vast scheme to connect his empire with world markets by American transcontinental rails, by ship to the Orient, and onward by rail through Russia to Europe.

To take a less known example, Patrick Calhoun, grandson of the Southern statesman who had failed so dismally in railroading as to die indebted, organized the Calhoun Land Company and then branched out to railroading; at the age of thirty, without means or friends, solely by persuasive eloquence like that of his distinguished ancestor, the young Calhoun got capitalistic backing and gained control of the great Terminal Company of the South, with 8,000 miles of track. Soon he had two extensive systems. Then he went to the United States Senate where influence to preserve his interests could best be exerted. For similar reasons two other land-speculators turned to railroading and a political career; the "Shovel King," Oakes Ames, developer of the Union Pacific, who, though a Congressman, was censured for corruption incidental to his activities; and Leland Stanford who, likewise seeking to exploit territorial and mining interests in California, battled for railroad control and carried his fight himself into the Senate.

Many men changed from one type of communication to another, or tried to tie several together. Ebenezer Henry Virgil, founder of the National Express Company, began with stagecoach lines and branched into railroads and steamships, until by 1853 he had some 10,000 miles of lines in the East; at the age of eighty he was turning to the dream of coast-to-coast mastery—that obsession of so many American business men. Others came to railroading from canals and trolley lines; Vanderbilt the First moved from ferryboats to steamships and then to land-transport. As the strife went on, the size of the combinations increased; ever more gigantic complexes were built, wrecked and remodeled, amid a great squeezing and wailing of shareholders. Some men, notably William Thompson Walters, who flung a long vertical line between the iron region of the Great Lakes and the Gulf of Mexico, tried to claim the Mississippi Valley for their own: others sought to hold the Southwest or Northwest; many, like Virgil, were dominated by the horizontal, cross-country vision.

Gradually this struggle over surfaces of the earth grew more involved as men delved below the ground for gold and coal, copper, iron and oil. From problems in plane geometry, they moved to solid geometry. This again was uniquely American, since European nations, as has already been said, lacked such domestic resources to serve as the basis of monopolies. The American commodity-kings were peculiar to this country, whereas the railroad-kings could be paralleled abroad. But the commodity-kings, in their turn, fought among themselves: the three poor immigrants, Daly, Clark and Heinze, tried to resist Rockefeller in the battle for the control of the "richest hill on earth," the gold-bearing deposit at Alder Gulch; sugar kings wrestled over Hawaii and Cuba; out of similar strife arose the Packing Trust, the Whiskey Ring, the Armor Plate Trust and Powder Trust. In other quarters appeared lesser barons and dukes of plumbing, steam laundries, and the like. There was, for instance, Ferdinand Schumacher, the German immigrant who became President of the American Cereal Company, ruler of oatmeal and, incidentally, Prohibition candidate for governor in Ohio. With him might be classed the American "Peanut King" so-called, Pembroke Decatur Gwaltney of Virginia, who, after inventing a peanut-stemming machine, developed with his partner, Augustus Bunkley, the mighty firm of Gwaltney and Bunkley, producers of forty-five million pounds of immaculate, standardized goobers a year. Gwaltney became a Baptist deacon, superintendent of a Bible class and, as he recorded, devoted himself to his favorite recreations of "yachting, fishing and rose culture, and reading Shakespeare."

The masters of commodities warred not only with one another but against the transport men. The Second Vanderbilt, manipulator of railroads, went down to defeat under Rockefeller, ruler of oil; Rockefeller extended control from oil to coal, iron, copper and then to railroading, finally taking the next step to banking. Railroad men, on the other hand, often reached out for commodities, as the Vanderbilt and Morgan interests fought against Philadelphia groups for Pennsylvania's coal. While the trusts and railroads carried on their terrible combats, cutting rates and wages, misery spread widely, mounting in the high period of distress and strikes extending from 1873 onward; thus economic centralization was won on economic battlefields comparable to the political and military arenas in which the nations of Europe were organized.

Out of the welter of conflicts between interests of transport and resources, while men like Hill, Harriman, Rockefeller and Vanderbilt were plotting and maneuvering their aldermen and senators as kings their troops, emerged a new type of dictator aspiring to manage both commodities and communications. J. P. Morgan the Elder was a supreme manipulator, arbiter and king of kings—in brief an Emperor of Business. Indeed, in 1889, Morgan invited eighteen railway presidents and bankers to dinner, at which he told these mighty magnates that they could no longer "take the law into their own hands," and send armed trainmen to gun-play in the battle over lines: "This is not elsewhere customary in civilized communities, and no good reason exists why such a practice should continue among railroads." Morgan's fiat, tremblingly accepted by his satraps, closed the era of rough-and-tumble individualism, and Morgan went on to reach the zenith of attainable personal power.

Before Morgan's climb men had controlled but a few branches of business; he held scores together. After Morgan, however, the structures of capitalist enterprise became too vast for a similar domination by a single personality. Or at least business personalities tended to become dwarfed by their impersonal corporations. Like kings of Egypt, the later business men were buried under their own pyramids.

Morgan stood at the Great Divide. Behind him lay the era of simple railroad-rovers; before him stretched the epoch of impersonal and invisible direction of power. In character discreet, aloof, cynical and luxurious, he was as far beyond the First Vanderbilt or Astor, in outlook and methods, as the sophisticated Emperor, Charles the Fifth, was removed from the struggling dukes of the Dark Ages. Morgan controlled companies valued at seventeen billions, including the entire outfit of Andrew Carnegie, which he bought at a single stroke and made over into a billion-dollar Steel Trust holding ore deposits, fleets of steamers and miles of tracks. In addition, as the banker closest to the Government of the United States, aiding it by selling its securities, laying down the law to it under President Cleveland, he had a financial might which he could employ in developing the latest phase of American business: large-scale corporate manufacturing.

Backed by the strength of Eastern financiers like Morgan, great industrial corporations reached out to capture both resources and transportation in complicated and shifting frames. Soap and cocoa men acquired plantations in the tropics; packers turned to subsidiary plants making by-products; utilities branched out, such as the International Paper and Power Company which bought newspapers to stabilize the sale of paper, besides timber tracts and electric power and paper mills. William Randolph Hearst, who raised a public tempest over this particular combination, was himself, through his own newspaper syndicate, trying to reserve the practice and control timber and power. Manufacturers pushed farther into marketing, opening chains of stores, as did book publishers, the shoe and tobacco and candy men. Then manufacturers fought among themselves for survival in the manner of early transportation men. The National Cash Register Corporation, for instance, according to its President, Patterson, in 1897 was "going to absolutely control the competition of the world," by the most drastic methods: "We do not buy out; we knock out." In the same tone, a Du Pont denied that he was entering a combination to dictate prices, saying that it was unnecessary: "We do our own dictating."

By 1907, the forces of centralization had won out in manufacturing as in other fields. Incorporated firms were annually producing goods amounting to ten times the value of the commodities made by business enterprises, individually owned. Twenty years later the concentration movement was still growing and some two hundred of the corporations had already absorbed about half the corporate wealth of the country. The huge holding company loomed above the trusts; pyramids were built in utilities, motion pictures and artificial silk. Perhaps the most awe-inspiring edifice was that of the Du Pont family, which gathered under one scepter the manufacturing of some 11,000 articles, ranging from silks and paints to munitions of war. At the beginning and at the end of this century of development—between 1815 and 1915— two outstanding fortunes—those of Girard and Du Pont—were French-American.

THE AMERICAN HUSTLER

Owing to the pressure of competition, the American was constantly compelled to increase his push and pace, scrap machines quickly, think up new stunts. Naturally he took up the telephone and filing systems before the Continentals found them useful. A Yorkshire manufacturer, at the opening of this century, decided that the American could not relax even if he would; that he had to keep sober and swill ice-water instead of drinking like a leisured Briton. He needed a clear brain to invent his startling forms of advertising like the golden goddess presiding over Siegel Cooper's soda fountain. Nor could the poor fellow get time to dine on sound beef and mutton; he merely snatched a sandwich. Another commiserating Englishman, Bristed, in the 1850's, commented on the exhausting pace of American life:

These men present a singular contrast and combination of strength and weakness. They can work at their desks all day for days together; they walk like locomotives, when they do walk. . . .

But they are continually bilious, dyspeptic, and altogether seedy; are subject to rheumatism . . . require strong excitement to amuse them.

The ever-accelerating tempo and craving for novelty made the "go-ahead man" of America feared abroad, while pitied. Octave Homberg, French imperialist financier, warned his countrymen against the predatory character of the newcomer. Germans, hard-driving as they were themselves, issued such plaints as that conveyed in "Anti-Ford; or the Dignity of Mankind." Britons, admitting that "in adaptiveness, in resource, in ingenuity, in whole-souled keenness to succeed, the average American manufacturer is by far the superior of his British compeer," began to wonder whether this restless fellow might not, eventually, undermine the sacred British week-end?

The driving spirit carried the American ahead so easily that he did not need to buckle down to the tedious toil of nursing to maturity complex industries requiring patient technical preparation and yielding slow returns. He could still win fabulous sums by swift throws in reckless games. The manufacture of violins or precision instruments, for instance, he could afford to leave to the Germans, while he supplied cheap watches and revolvers *en masse*. Elegance was very well for the French, long masters of good cabinet-making; for the American there was more money in Grand Rapids suites. Henry Ford could offer "tin lizzies" to the multitude instead of catering to the high plutocracy with a Rolls-Royce, like Sir Frederick Royce.

The contrast of Ford and Royce is significant. Both men began as poor boys, ingenious tinkerers. But the Englishman reflected an old mechanical artisanry left behind in America. The United States had a vaster mass-market than England, and free trade throughout. The two men of the two worlds were as different as their products—the "Model T," and the "Silver Ghost."

Disregarding exceptions in both worlds, the American has been described as comparatively "slovenly" and "amateurish," by careful students of business enterprise. He could not have been otherwise in a land where millions of acres awaited the appropriating genius and hordes of settlers clamored for the first necessities of life, soon to include the automobile. It was possible for the American to avoid toil and study to a large extent. He made a quick fortune in rationalizing industrial processes; in mechanizing the processes to which machines could not be applied abroad, such as pea-shelling and hog-slaughtering; in combinations of ten-cent stores or cheap restaurants; in the mass-sale of shoes, oil burners, chewing gum and cosmetics. He perfected refrigerating cars and other equipment needed only by a continent as

unified as the American; or he cleverly adapted inventions made by
foreigners but not fully utilized abroad, such as the automobile, sewing
machine, and typewriter; moreover, he was prolific in nifty gadgets,
such as the zipper and the pencil sharpener. For such reasons the
American got into the habit of expecting a fresh miracle every morning. More hopeful than other men, confident of saving himself by
some happy thought, some gift of fancy, he became the *Micawber*
among business men. Consequently, when things went wrong with him
he was more prone to jump out of the window.

The competitive conditions promoting a subtle order of intelligence
were lacking; it cannot be proved, of course, that the level of average
mentality was comparatively low in America, but it may be maintained
that the heights of theoretical speculation were not represented. Many
able politicians, Hanna, Aldrich or Platt, for instance, operated successfully, but none of them reached the full stature of a Rhodes, Cobden or Stresemann. No theoretician appeared in business to match
Rathenau or Engels. Instead, America had a surplus of amiable fellows,
of a smooth brightness and sureness, who brushed theories aside im-
patiently. Many samples of frontier cynicism may be adduced, but the
"History is bunk" of Ford and the classic "A sucker is born every
minute" of Barnum, only illustrate the cheery nature of its homespun
business philosophy.

Even the American freaks were entertaining in a less macabre fashion
than the European. They were "amoosin' cusses" like the Maxims, or
George Francis Train, instead of inspired madmen, such as Rimbaud,
Schliemann or Meyrink. And where in the history of the United
States can a parallel be found for the mind of the Austrian munitioneer,
Backfrieder? His hobby it was to persuade the military men whom he
supplied with arms to insert provisions in their wills ordering their
bodies buried on his, Backfrieder's, private estate, near Vienna. Backfrieder's gruesome pleasure in his expanding collection of mortuary
monuments was a constant irritation to the aged General Radetzky.
Radetzky said he himself had no intention of becoming a corpse soon,
or of giving it to Backfrieder in any case; yet he could not dream of
offending the most efficient of his contractors and, humorously com·
plaining, he postponed his decision about a will from battle to battle.

To continue comparisons, the nineteenth-century American, according to critics, was more corrupt than the Europeans, not only because
he actually handled vaster sums of money, but because the people more
readily condoned any transgressions that might be uncovered. The
general public, it seemed, did not seriously mind any excesses a business
man might commit, if he appeared to be doing something big. He might
"go broke" often and loudly, pocket legislatures, shear his shareholders

and engulf domains so long as he appeared to be building up the country.

In the United States, as de Tocqueville early declared, the European scale of values was exactly reversed. Thus temerity was a social virtue in the New World and leisure was an anti-social vice. More stabilized Europe, on the contrary, had come to value quiet leisure and to fear adventurous deeds. It could not be denied that temerity had once had a social worth in Europe when the wild and brutal sea-robbers of Elizabethan England, for example, were fêted for their cruelties because they were forming the British Empire; no fraud seemed inexcusable in the light of that holy purpose. And even during the nineteenth century, as a matter of fact, many of the "empire-builders" of Britain, like Harry Johnston and Rhodes, were accumulating enormous territories with scant regard for human life or the ethical niceties. The "Opium War," brought upon China by the efforts of English merchants with American aid in a determination to force the drug upon a reluctant Celestial Kingdom, was certainly as bold as the most bare-faced adventures of American "robber-barons." Britons and Americans were both excused by their respective publics when they were building empires. The difference was that the American was making his empire at home, while the depredations of the Briton were tolerated only in distant lands, in colonial territories, and no longer among his own fellow-citizens.

European States had become so strong in the nineteenth century that they could act as umpires; their bureaucracies stood apart from and somewhat above the business world, and hence were often able to bring the more flagrant swindlers to justice. Orgies of speculations swept Europe throughout the same period, but the mopping up afterward was generally more thorough there than in America. The American public, having not yet known the meager stability of Europe, was for a long time less easily angered by adventurers who upset the balance of society. It permitted Vanderbilt to escape with a mild censure for "negligence," in selling leaky vessels to the Government during the Civil War, whereas the English public howled for vengeance on those guilty of fraud—on Fauntleroy, for instance, who was hanged publicly in 1824.

The prevailing attitude of Americans toward the battlers in their midst was expressed by Stedman, lyrical stockbroker of New York. A sensitive nature, he longed, like the bankers Walter Leaf of London and James Loeb of Germany, to take refuge in the classics. A broker *malgré lui*, he wrote "Pan in Wall Street," a pathetic effort to depict the woodland god touching the hearts of his fellow-speculators. In his telegraphic code, "Cancel order to buy" was KEATS and "Select and sell at discretion" was SHELLEY. Revolted by the "enormous crowd of vulgarians" created by the Civil War and appalled by the successive storms he had been forced to weather, Stedman lashed out at the public for its acclaim of any gambling "Clown" who appeared big enough to buy judges and a legislature, and its susceptibility to "swindle on the large, respectable, white-cravated, Philistine scale." With rare prophetic vision, he portrayed, in "The Sacking of New York," the approaching panic of 1873. But none heeded him.

Nevertheless, Stedman refused to frame a blanket indictment of the Street, for which an editor once begged. Even he found something heroic in "the great operators who make the market and are unmade by it—who direct the battle—and above all the 600 traders and brokers" on the floor of the Exchange: "These men, in their direct panics, *must* be Spartan, and hide the foxes tearing in their vitals: they must smile and talk composedly, even jest, while doom is on them . . . They are husbands, sons, brothers, and do not 'turn a hair' while dying by piecemeal. Don't I know it all?" Authorship and gambling, he was wont to say, are the only pursuits fit for gentlemen: "I laugh when I lose, and when I win, I laugh a little more, like Beecher's gambler."

By the time Stedman was ready to retire from the Exchange, toward the turn of the century, however, he and the public-at-large were beginning to hunger for more quiet and security. They began to dread temerity, lest it endanger all the gains so far made. Moreover, the excuse for gambling, that it made a nation, was less readily offered now that centralization was so nearly complete, with the result that the Stock Exchange had, as Stedman said, become "the focus to which all currents of American purpose and energy converge." An impressive symbol of this concentration was the ramification of telegraph wires, in those days unconcealed, as they converged on the Exchange: "Hundreds, seemingly thousands, of these wires stretched toward the Exchange. No bird could fly through their network, a man could almost walk upon them; in fact, they darkened the street and the windows."

Now that America became so well linked, it vibrated at every shock. Meanwhile also the great speculator had left the visible arena to hide himself behind a corporate personality; the people no longer watched him in wheat-pit or Gold Room, taking the "swag" or a fall with equal composure. They did not know so well who or where he was when he operated behind brokers; nor did they fully understand his maneuvers, for these had become cold and abstract like the calculations of a professor of theoretical physics. The public, which had not minded being sheared so much when it could keep an eye on the man himself, grew distrustful when he veiled himself from view. Paradoxically, in that dangerous period of transition in the 90's, when the admiration for the mighty speculator began to wane—and the small man for the first time was losing hope of growing big himself—the big business man made his boldest bid for political power and his most audacious display of unbounded riches.

Retiring from the visible stage in business management, he invaded Washington as a public personality. By amazing excesses of expenditure he fixed himself in the public mind now as a fellow of sultanic tastes and reckless disregard of public opinion. His direct and conspicuous political and social methods did not, however, correspond to his new indirect and concealed economic tactics. This period, 1890–1912, in which he exulted openly in power and riches, won by national centralization, may be called the business baroque.

THE BUSINESS BAROQUE

From the triumph of Jacksonian Democracy in 1835 to the end of the Civil War thirty years later, business had operated more or less behind the scenes, where it managed to buy government officials according to fixed tariff rates. In the 1850's, the La Crosse and Milwaukee Railroad, when investigated, admitted that, seeking land grants, it had paid $872,000 for brokers, judges, editors and law-givers, including such items as the following:

One governor	$ 50,000
State comptroller	10,000
One private secretary	5,000
"A certain Smith"	10,000
Thirteen head of Senators	175,000
First Secretary, Upper House	10,000
Ditto, Lower House	5,000

In such circumstances, business men tended to despise their hirelings too much to join them frankly in political life, even had the tide of popular feeling been running their way. So Sam Colt wrote to his brother:

Don't, for the sake of your own good name think again of being a subordinate officer of government. You had better blow out your brains at once and manure some honest man's ground with your carcase than to hang your ambitions on so low a peg.

This situation the Civil War altered by reducing the power of Southern statesmen; after the period of lush expansion and concentration, business men with mounting wealth sought office increasingly. Among the opulent law-givers now figured Senator Clark, the mining-man with a bizarre taste in architecture; Guggenheim of Colorado, Knox of Pennsylvania and Foraker of Ohio; Stephen B. Elkins, owner of gigantic Southwestern tracts, and the Nevada Bonanza King, James Graham Fair. The Senate in Washington became known as a Millionaires' Club. When McKinley was elected in 1896 as "Advance Agent of Prosperity," he gave cabinet posts to Cornelius Newton Bliss, banker and dry-goods man, and James A. Gary, a power in cotton, gas and finance. Behind the White House hovered the shadow of Mark Hanna, who had left a business career in Cleveland's coal and iron region to organize the Republican Party on a business basis.

Hanna's machine was stupendous. Bringing advertising methods into politics, Hanna used clever slogans, distributed tons of "boilerplate" to local newspapers, set up posters and conducted local canvasses. For his renovation of political methods he required at least ten million dollars, an unprecedented sum levied upon various firms according to their ability to pay and their interest at stake. So honest was his accounting that, after the campaign, he was said to have refunded great sums to contributors such as the Standard Oil; this inspired deep confidence in his management, and gave him the appearance of a mighty wizard bringing incredible order into the democratic turmoil. By long practice, he became so attractive to audiences, so affable, so quick in humorous retort, that he was the most effective business personality in politics.

Possibly Hanna might have gone far in public life. He was apparently entertaining hopes of running against Theodore Roosevelt for the Presidency, when this plan was cut short by premature death. Still his career was hopelessly damaged by the attacks of another business man, William Randolph Hearst, who, through his newspapers, managed to fix Hanna, the chief political talent of the business world, in the public eye as a dollar-mark and the horrible ogre of Eastern capitalism. Hearst's attack was to a very large extent responsible for the hostility which prevented Hanna from stepping out as a candidate himself for any federal office to be acquired by popular vote; or indeed from accepting a post in McKinley's Cabinet. It might have counted against him had he run for the Presidency.

The horrid fate of Hanna, target of mudslinging, tended no doubt to make other business men hesitate about entering national politics. Nor were they reassured by the career of Nelson B. Aldrich, who ruled the Senate for many years at the turn of the century, in alliance with other senatorial business men. From the business point of view, Aldrich was immensely successful: through his skillful maneuvers he managed to win for big industry the protection it sought; he increased tariffs, assisted sugar-refiners against agrarian sugar-growers, defended railroads against regulation, defeated attempts to tax incomes and supervise foods and drugs; he was the supreme champion of the Eastern manufacturers against the agrarian West and, later in life, the spokesman of centralized banking and foreign commercial expansion. Nevertheless his victories, as in the case of Hanna, evoked a popular fury and no ordinary, timid business man could envy Hanna and Aldrich their exposed positions on the battlements.

Not being skilled in forensics, Aldrich made no attempt even to reply to invidious attacks. Somewhat taciturn, as business men had tended to be since the days of Crassus and Cœur, he could at best utter shrewd arguments and dry jests. He could not sway masses. His true genius lay in back-stage strategy. As he once said to a rival during a senatorial battle over railroads: "You may talk and we'll keep still." His attitude of aloof disdain was partly the result of a lifelong admiration for Sir Robert Peel, the mighty defender of English manufacturing, whose rôle had been analogous to his own. He aspired to become a country gentleman like Peel as soon as he left the grocery business behind and made a fortune in Rhode Island traction and sugar. But the high and chilly manner of an English lord, which the erstwhile grocer assumed, did not endear him to the American public. It was "aristocratic"; and the quality, ever provoking suspicion in a democracy, was the more dangerous in politics because, at that time, the spenders of great wealth were doing everything to appear exclusive or, as the age called it, "swell."

Between the pranks of Western nabobs and the stilted pretensions of New York, the last two decades of the nineteenth century offered a spectacle of parvenudom without a peer. Ostentatious display was given the utmost press publicity, for a man like "Silver Dollar" Tabor was only too anxious to have the world know that even the door-knobs in his palace were of silver. No more abashed in their magnificence than royalty of the European baroque, were the American business men who had, like kings, made a nation; but the splendor of kings had seemed, not personal, but an integral aspect of their office, whereas the magnificence of the millionaires remained private and without the justification of a governing position. It was this difference which caused the naïve whims of the new-rich to exercise so fatal an effect on the public mind of America.

Their effulgence occurred at a time when home-life was yielding to the lure of public life; hotels and restaurants were springing up like mushrooms. In Waldorf's "Peacock Alley" and in San Francisco's "Poodle Dog," millionaires paraded in their newest finery. San Francisco was no whit behind New York in its display; indeed it had the reputation of being the most formal town in America as far as dress was concerned. The very streets of the cities became filled with visions of elegance: ladies "like butterflies . . . with their brilliant and vari-colored dresses, their glittering jewels, their air of sprightly and reck-less extravagance." Beside them stalked imposingly solid men: "glossy-headed old nabobs with rubicund noses, bald foreheads, heavy side whiskers, portly bodies, and great watch seals, types of prosperous sons of commerce; there are dapper little dandies and ponderous big dandies."

The castles of the new-rich were rising everywhere, to the astonish-ment and envy of the public. In Chicago, in 1880, the "new family residence" of the McCormicks was opened with a tremendous recep-tion, revealing a salon in Louis XVI style opposite a hall frescoed like a castle of Henri IV, but managing to include a reaper in the motif. Along the Hudson sprang up Rhine castles with grottoes about them; on the lawns the new-rich danced like any court or indulged in straw-berry-festivals. In upper New York, as an English visitor in 1870 dis-covered, a whole section was being built by "lucky bankers . . . large stuff-merchants and sugar-manufacturers . . . Traders in jewels and teas . . . speculators in city lots and western lands; men who made sudden fortunes during the civil war by government contracts, pur-chases of gold and silver mines and petroleum wells." He was dis-tinctly impressed:

> Solemn, lofty mansions, some "swell-front," many built of beau-tiful brown stone, and even marble, growing more and more luxurious as you progress, apprise you that you are among the upper ten thousand. . . . This is the region where dwells in osten-tatious splendor the moneyed aristocracy of Gotham. The equi-pages in the streets have become uniformly showy and ornate . . . clattering vehicles, through whose windows you discern puffy masses of silk and satin, and fair heads graced with flowers and glistening with tiaras. . . . There is something in the tranquillity which prevails that induces the wealth worshipper to walk softly, and to regard the high portals and the lofty windows with a sort of awe.

At Newport, this foreign visitor found the decorations "almost op-pressive." He would not have qualified the adjective had he returned a decade or so later, when the rivalry in construction really began. At Newport one millionaire erected a Tudor mansion, and, to make the effect complete, interlarded his conversation with Tudor words, beginning every other sentence with "prithee." Still he was outdone by a coal baron's reproduction of Buckingham Palace, which cost five millions and was the only house in that "seaside Valhalla of swagger-dom" to possess *three* carriage entrances.

In food, as well as in homes and clothes, extravagance was manifest. The well-to-do broker at Delmonico's lunched off partridges, stuffed with truffles, "washed down by a bottle of Château d'Yquem," and, undaunted, turned up again for a dinner of "nine courses of fish, flesh and fowl, flanked by the most toothsome of entremets, and wines that could make a Mussulman forswear his creed." Licking its chops, the public read the menus. It might not have begrudged the successful self-made man his nourishment, however, had he or his wife not taken to giving "monkey dinners" and banquets on horse-back, at which cigarettes were passed around wrapped in hundred-dollar bills.

It was in the matter of conveyance that the rich utterly exasperated the public. Not content with appearing in a "tall Belmont, with a flunkey in livery, on the back seat," whirled by a "pair of spanking bays, tandem" through the park, the rich of Newport at last bought motor-cars. And instead of observing the speed-laws of that district, prohibiting any vehicles from moving faster than ten miles an hour, they burned up the roads at the insane pace of *twenty* miles an hour, choking the public with dust no less than themselves. What was more: a devil-may-care set of "idle rich" clubbed together to hold races near Newport, at which even *thirty* miles an hour were attained; and so great was the power of wealth over the majesty of the law that the local sheriffs did not dare arrest the malefactors. It was then, in 1901, that a radical arose in wrath to ask how long this should continue? Re-calling the reckless insouciance with which a French marquis, before the Revolution, had ridden down a child of the poor, he cried: "It will probably be but a short time before a man with a 'machine' will enjoy the God-given right of 'doing what he will with his own'!"

It was of course impossible then to foresee business giving a swiftly moving equipage to multitudes of Americans and enabling the "average citizen" to be as much of a public menace on the high road as the mil-lionaire. The process by which the luxuries of the rich seeped down to become the commonplaces of life had just begun to function. Still in its youth were the readymade garment industry and the cosmetics-trade, eventually to spread comforts and conceits of the urban rich to the backwoods farms. The canned-foods industry and chains of cheap res-taurants, destined to make dining in public on varied fare a popular cus-tom, were just starting. Even so, Charles Dickens, coming to America from England where mill-girls could be sharply distinguished from ladies, by their clogs and shawls, had been surprised to see girls of the humbler classes, as in Massachusetts, dressed in veils and high-heeled shoes like women of the upper classes; the blurring of social lines had long been under way and smashing breaks were to come. The interlude, however, was both shocking and dangerous. The business man had become a "corporate personality," bewildering to the critics; he had not yet gone very far in sharing his luxuries through large-scale enterprise with the wide mass of citizenry or offering shares in his business undertakings to millions of investors. In the interval of doubt and suspicion, he did not exactly know himself or his purposes. Somewhat bewildered, he decided to join his wife and sons and daughters in taking on the raiment of European royalty at masked balls in New York and other places. His public assumption of crown and scepter helped to bring on the real "trust-busting" storm of the twentieth century.

THE QUEENS OF BUSINESS

How much this display was due to the influence of women in America is a moot point. But throughout the ages women, like the Church, the Feudality and the Army, had been a problem for the business man. On the whole, the feminine mind, conservative and family-conditioned, has not conformed to the dynamic individualism of the business man. Wives of well-to-do men of commerce revealed little enthusiasm for their husbands' enterprises matching the zeal with which the noble warrior's womenfolk applauded his feats at arms; ladies who leaned joyously over the balcony to watch the knight cleave his enemy's skull with a single blow, at a mediaeval jousting, turned coldly away from the intricacies of the countinghouse. The middle-class wife, far from being content with her standing, has ever aspired to that of the warrior's wife; she has accepted the traditions and patterns of aristocratic ladies; in the hours of idleness provided by a soap-boiling or beer-brewing husband, she has wept over chivalric romances.

But the business man, having had scant time for frivolity, could do little about providing other occupations. The financier was often allied with court-circles and compelled to seek contracts with the State through feminine favor; his work, more intermittent than that of the heavy-industrialist, sometimes allowed him leisure for the ladies, between coups. For one reason or another, to the financier cannot be ascribed a lack of gallantry. But the merchant and manufacturer, on the whole, have had less time for their families, though they showered them with gifts. Thus the increasing complexity of business merely heightened what was an old trait. Through the ages—from the grumbling mediaeval merchants casting accounts by candlelight with not a moment to spare, to the Dutch, "too busy to keep mistresses," and on to the moderns, such as the elder Rathenau, whose wife sighed that "there were not so many novels in the world as she needed for her vacant hours"—the business man has generally been too occupied to offer large place to women in his scheme of life and labor.

The soldier, the priest and the farmer had a well-defined rôle to offer woman, often a low one, it is true, but at least a rôle complementary to their own. On the contrary, the business man left his wife to her own resources; frequently in this situation she entertained the philosophers, priests, novelists and poets who flouted business. Who could imagine a parson's wife surrounding herself with atheists or a soldier's wife leading pacifist societies? Yet the business man's wife encouraged business critics. In the Victorian Age, this disparity of interests became acute when the business man, with his factories, took away much of the work from the home, thereby diminishing woman's former sphere of productive employment. His philosophy of individualism bereft her of her semi-matriarchal family position as old as human society. His hostility to the priest, that historic ally of the landed gentry, drove away woman's traditional friend, the man who recognized the primacy of emotion over reason. In short, the range of woman's beliefs and domestic occupations was at first narrowed by business. When she had to accept the Machine, she at last endeavored in large numbers to enter the competitive arena, as the good sport, the business and professional woman. The business man offered her positions, but no position.

The business man, however, in the Anglo-Saxon countries, differed from the Continental in that his enterprises were apt to be more speculative and gargantuan, less technically refined. Especially in America, where business early outgrew the stage of the family-firm, it was more difficult for wives to find a place in it than was the case in France or even in Germany. The "Veuve Cliquot" in France, who continued the champagne business of her husband, and Margarete Krupp, widow of the last male of that iron dynasty, who directed family-businesses, had fewer counterparts in America. As business outgrew the family in America, the family was less often conducted on business principles. The American, like the English woman, was in general less thrifty and penny-pinching than the French, Dutch or other Continentals, who felt themselves a more intimate part of their husbands' enterprises and were proud to run their homes on the business model.

For various reasons, the American woman felt especially at a distance from business. Yet she was given far larger sums to spend than her sisters of any previous age had enjoyed. At the same time, she had less masculine interference in the spending of money. Whereas on the Continent or in England, men generally had some idea of what they wished to do with their profits, desiring to become a country squire or a Herr

Geheimrat, the American titan was usually helpless in default of mod-els—despite exceptions such as Clark, Gould and Morgan. With a hu-morous smile, old "Phil" Armour confessed: "My culture is all in my wife's name." The later J. Ogden Armour is depicted by Dies as sneak-ing off from parties given by his wife and quoted as saying: "I don't suppose I shall ever be happy. Perhaps no one ever is. The thing that would make me happiest just now would be to know that I could get roaring drunk and wander about the Loop for two days with no one paying the slightest attention to me."

Another of these indecisive colossi was Stuyvesant Fish, called by his wife, "The Good Man." Being very plain and sober, refusing to play cards on a Sunday, he felt out of place at Newport; wistfully he used to take guests to see the tiny bedroom where he had slept as a boy and say to them: "None of the maids will sleep in it; it is not good enough for them; yet I spent some of the happiest hours of my life here." When the Good Man happened to come home unexpectedly, finding a party in progress he would shrug his shoulders and murmur: "It seems I am giving a party. Well, I hope you are enjoying yourselves." Then he would slip quickly and silently away, while "Mamie" Fish proudly an-nounced: "Where would he be without me? I made him. I put him on the throne."

Infinitely sad, from all accounts, was the life of the silent titans at Newport in the days of gilded extravagance, despite appearances of reckless gaiety. Business men preferred Saratoga, where "King Cor-nelius" held court, where there was a bowling alley and pistol-shooting; on the broad veranda, they not only "*talked* stocks" but "*sold* them. Little knots of dealers stood on the piazzas of the United States Hotel, the Union and the Congress, and traded in Erie and Harlem." For ac-tual buying Newport early became too "swell"; and "papa" was there reduced to reading financial reports in the papers, a plight for which an Englishman pitied him:

It is both melancholy and amusing to watch the poor man of commerce as the "long, long, weary day" drags slowly on. He can, for the life of him, find nothing to do. He gets desperately hungry for his breakfast, which, at home, he is wont to have at sharp seven; and the first day he was at Newport he afforded a fund for a day's amusement among the waiters by incessantly asking if he couldn't have his breakfast as early as nine. He wanders about the vast hotel and through the streets, hands in pockets; his disconsolate face now and then looms for a moment at the door of a billiard-room; he is seen haunting the reading-room for hours before the arrival of the mail; and the only morsel of comfort which he enjoys the livelong day is when his *Herald* comes by the evening boat, and he may sit crouched up at one corner of the piazza, and gloat over the "Money Market" and "Trade Report." The poor man finally becomes desperate with so indolent an existence, and frantically tries in succession the round of seaside amusements; is in everybody's way at the stables; gets sea-sick on a short yacht excursion; is woefully beaten at billiards; and makes the ladies of his family heartily ashamed of him by his incorrigible awkwardness at the picnics and in the ball-room.

This unhappy situation was not improved with the passage of time. Elizabeth Drexel Lehr, reared in that atmosphere, has told about the men of her family coming home more exhausted than field laborers to sit silently chewing at the head of long dinner-parties: "The Newport millionaires . . . might hold up the market but they could not prevent conversation from slumping rather heavily at their own table . . . They were prepared to spend their last cent in justifying the whims of their womenfolk, but they were incapable of amusing them themselves." In this manless world, the "queens" of Newport, striving to create a society, had to bring in such eccentrics as Harry Lehr.

Over the heads of their weary titans, the social queens fought their battles for precedence, during the six or seven weeks of the season, spending up to $300,000 per week or per ball, according to the resources behind them. One of the fiercest tussles was waged between Mamie Fish and Mary Harriman, wives of railroad magnates, who severed their husbands' business friendship. They gave one another no quarter, these powerful women whose rubicund faces, with bold chins and big eyes, stare at one from many an old tintype. Their strife went on until, with a flounce and a flashing triumph, one of them would deseat another on the red cushions of Mrs. Astor's divan, known as "The Throne." Thus, with their merciless campaigns, conducted regardless of expense, they formed a competitive social life mirroring the economic warfare of their lockjawed menfolk.

The defiant exceptions to the generality were Bet-a-Million and Ma Gates of Chicago. Bet-a-Million was the only self-made millionaire who could not be stopped from spitting wherever he happened to be—a habit arousing great animosity in the best hotels of Europe; whenever the social error of ruining Aubusson carpets was pointed out to him, Bet-a-Million would draw his checkbook gallantly to make amends— and then fire another shot. Only the formidable Ma Gates could have induced him to stop, but she was practically the only woman in America, except Hetty Green and Calamity Jane, who did not care to improve herself or anybody else. She was only too happy to take off her diamond stomacher at the end of a hard social day and flip pancakes in the kitchen of her palatial suite at the Waldorf.

AFTER THE BALL

Had more millionaires resembled Ma and Bet-a-Million, the course of American business might have flowed along more smoothly, if in narrower channels. Popular animosity might have been avoided during a dangerous period; but the popular imitation which led to the spread of wholesale markets in luxury-goods would also have been cut down. Both were growing in the 1880's, when alarmed onlookers decried the spread of demoralization from Newport down to the people:

> Through the great thoroughfares of our city *fashion* rolls along in one steady stream . . . In and out of the great silken and dry goods warehouses . . . crowds pass in and out, with the spirit of determined rivalry on flushed faces, the petty spirit to outvie one another in the display of bracelets, or gorgeous pins.

Surely, wailed one business man, "a rosebud half hidden on the veiled bosom, a stray curl" would be sufficient for the good wife who wished to "guard her husband's credit 'on change' as she would his honor at home." He hoped it was not too late to stay the tide by an appeal to the heart of Mrs. Croesus:

> Is there much enjoyment in the anticipation of an entertainment which is to cost the poor devil of a stockjobbing husband most of the profits of his haphazard speculations? Not a bit of it. The shining moire antique, the costly lace, the regal gem, the contraband bouquet, may pass muster for a time in the crowded salon; but Madame Croesus, you must come to grief in the end . . . for *Madame Nouveau Riche* will surely cross your path . . . Her scarf alone cost thousands, the plume that decks her chignon was the gift of a Russian prince . . . For mercy's sake, fair and beloved American ladies, do set your faces against this reckless riot in extravagant display . . . Serious thought may perhaps induce some to exercise that moderation which will commend itself even in this railroad age.

Mere display of gowns, had they all been of the latest fashion, might have remained harmless. But the "queens" of society hankered after the costumes of royalty. In this mood, the wife of Vanderbilt III appeared at the opera with a crown, costing £300,000, patterned after that of

Queen Victoria. Mrs. McCormick had herself portrayed before a tasseled portière, wearing a satin hoop-skirt. Then, in the depths of economic depression, two very new-rich, the Bradley-Martins, gave a ball at the Waldorf, made over in the period of Louis XIV, at which the hostess appeared wearing a $50,000 crown, while her husband represented a courtier. This spectacle aroused a fury in the public which was soon increased by another, this time given by the son of a business man.

Sons of business men have ever had a tendency to turn out social rebels like St. Francis or Gandhi, Fourier, Ruskin, Engels, Piatakov or Léon Blum (while daughters may follow St. Catherine of Siena or Jane Addams). Or, at the opposite extreme, they become gilded playboys, a menace to traffic. In the 1880's, George A. Baker, Jr., pleaded with the rich to do something about the latter, "noisy, conceited, and intrusive" little cigar-smoking youths. Let them be sent to college, where they would learn baseball, not poker:

> Are there no asylums, where at an early age he can be secluded. . . . Indeed there are . . . Harvard, Yale and Columbia—these are the proper receptacles for the gilded youth . . . Oh, business-engrossed fathers, and foolish mothers, deliver us we pray you from this sore affliction; and send your sons to college and rid New York society of the gilded youth.

A gilded youth, James Hazen Hyde, eight years after the Bradley-Martin Ball at the Waldorf, gave one more brilliant at Sherry's which was transformed into the Palace of Versailles. But where Mrs. Martin had chosen the period of Louis XIV, Hyde selected one with yet more unfortunate associations, and greeted his guests in the robes of the ill-fated Louis XVI. Promptly the people intimated that they knew history too, and were prepared to play their part, if drama was desired. Amid the general roar of rage, a sweeping investigation was started which uncovered startling frauds in the Equitable Life Insurance Company, a concern bequeathed to Hyde by his father. Hastily abdicating, the "last of the Capetians" fled to France. But the popular storm, gathering volume, swept on to the muckraking and trust-busting explosion that carried Theodore Roosevelt to triumph.

The American Baroque was over by 1910. If fond of displaying themselves in the robes of Bourbons, it must be said that the American rich were not so blind. They swiftly wrapped tissue paper about their crowns and put away their royal robes in moth-balls. Indeed it was a member of the sacred group, Frederick Townsend Martin, who pronounced the "age of arrogance" ended and his set as ready for repentance. In "The Passing of the Idle Rich," he declared: "Idleness is doomed as a vocation." More rapidly and eagerly than any dominant class before, the American descended voluntarily from the heights and gave evidences of regret: checks to charities enormously increased; débutantes joined the Junior League, which provided them with social work; and sons were packed away in college, as Baker had long ago advised. "Queens" of society gave balls for worthy and charitable ends, not, however, creating a fashion so much as following one set by a lawyer's wife, Mrs. Harrison Gray Otis, in the 1850's. Everyone was glad to appear busy, and for the first time, according to Martin, people began to ask one another "what one did for a living. . . . I constantly hear that very question asked, without rebuke, in the most fashionable clubs of the city." Volumes of humble apology were written by the titans of business themselves, explaining how active they had been and how simple their tastes really were. Even Bet-A-Million faded away into the distance, and was last heard of lecturing to a meeting of Texas preachers, imploring them not to drink or gamble.

For the second time, the formation of a solid "aristocracy" of riches was blocked. The first defeat had occurred a century earlier, when the would-be aristocrats, American merchants and land-speculators, had been menaced by Jefferson and overwhelmed by Jackson until they withdrew, muttering but humble, from the public stage. Now the new business royalty at Newport and Nob Hill was humiliated by the crusading fervor of the trust-busters, under Theodore Roosevelt and Robbert M. LaFollette, who swept business politicians such as Aldrich from the arena of Washington. Once more, the American was forced to renounce the high altitudes, display simple manners, practice the appearances of reticence and benevolence, and find his place in democracy.

This pushed the American ahead of the European in social respects, if he was still a laggard in some industrial techniques. While the business man in the United States was struggling with the problems of adjustment to public opinion, the European was still secure in his coalition with the more or less genuine and militant aristocracy—an alliance which was to have calamitous results in the World War. The American at least knew when to take off his Louis-Quatorze ruffles and hide away his wig and sword.

Probably he did so the more readily because he was really more at ease in shirtsleeves. A century before, his heart had been bursting with ambition; this time, he had not wholly enjoyed the extravagance of "conspicuous waste." Indeed he began to smile more and more broadly as the shutters were put up at the château and his family scattered to various employments. Best of all, he found two things to do with his leisure. He took up golf; by 1910 Henry Frick was leading Taft around the links at Myopia, the oddly named resort now more favored than Newport by the rich who sought retirement. And he took to the motorcar. But Papa Croesus was not to enjoy his first bout of real fun very long. Scarcely had he sneaked out of the Newport mansion with his golf clubs and climbed into the old bus, pointing her nose toward Myopia—when the World War blew in also upon him.

XXV

BUSINESS AND UPHEAVAL IN RUSSIA AND THE EAST

WHEN THE PEOPLES of the earth had been taught modern business methods and had all been linked together in ceaseless intercommunication, so ran the Victorian thesis, the world could not fail to become happy and at peace. To hurry the process of civilizing the backward and distributing the lore of new technology was the clear duty of the enlightened. In the haste of this pedagogy, to be sure, such severe pain was occasionally inflicted upon pupil-peoples as to draw indignant protests from Liberals like Gladstone; but even such humanitarians, though they deplored the Opium War for instance, felt sure that the ultimate result of universal commerce must be universal peace.

This doctrine, that world trade spelled happiness to humanity, was attractive to the mechanically minded Victorians because it appeared beautifully automatic. But the Victorians did not invent it. Back in the sixteenth century, the French writer, Bodin, explained that God had divided resources among many lands in order to make nations dependent upon one another and hence to render warfare damaging to all parties. In the late eighteenth century also, the yearning for cosmopolitanism was strong. Adam Smith announced that the capitalist ought to be international and that whoever has money to invest is a citizen of the world. Contemporaneously, the German bourgeois, who were still shut off from outside contacts, had visions of internationalism, both cultural and commercial. Kant declared in a famous pamphlet that commercial intercourse between peoples was the surest foundation for peace and Goethe led in the conception and formation of a "world literature," based upon the noble traffic of ideas. And so, as the creed grew, from Bodin to Kant, Smith to Cobden, it acquired the blessings of religion, philosophy, literature and finally of science.

But in the meantime something unforeseen by Bodin and Kant had happened: the industrial revolution. This altered the condition of world commerce, for even if all nations could conceivably become highly developed capitalistic societies, could they live by taking in one another's pig-iron and typewriters? The pressure of competition might grow acute and generate friction as easily as good-will. But such a state is hardly realizable, since some peoples, possessors of coal and steel, must under modern conditions have the advantage over others. Would the intercourse of superior and inferior be conducive to everlasting peace?

If universal industrialism were impossible, and a part of the world were doomed to perpetual "backwardness," the question of international relationship would be far from simple. As Zimmermann has so painstakingly shown, the "vegetable civilizations" found the utmost difficulty in making enough by labor in fields and plantations to pay for imported wares, cloth and machinery, bought from the industrial or "mineral" civilizations. The agony of the Balkans, for instance, was largely caused by the hopeless indebtedness to more advanced societies. "Darkest Africa" had a hard time paying for goods from darker Manchester. Unless the vegetable civilizations could be helped to enlarge their wants, and increase their yield, they would not offer expanding markets to the factory-lands. If not—could business exist without exploitation?

Highly complex and flourishing business had not been built, in the past, upon the mutually profitable exchange of wares between peers. Previous ages could offer little practical illustration of the grand Victorian hypothesis. On the contrary, the chief trade-empires were founded upon exploitation of some sort of monopoly, whether of skill, routes or raw material. The creators of such dominions were men who knew how to take advantage of more ignorant or weaker races. Alexandria, for instance, held the keys to the Indies and sold goods to the simple Romans who craved luxuries but did not know how to make, obtain or transport them. Heir to Alexandria was Venice, long flourishing upon a similar monopoly of Eastern luxuries which she distributed to the backward feudal nobles of Western Europe. Lübeck lived upon the relative innocence of fourteenth-century England and the wildernesses of Russia. Florence sucked France dry. Then France, as inheritor of Italianate culture, created a monopoly of taste; for a long time France found wealth in distributing her fine, exclusive products to the rising new-rich aristocrats of seventeenth-century Europe, in less industrialized lands.

In modern times the exploitive character of business became more, not less evident. Holland "took the world for a farm," because she could build and sail better ships than anyone else; her "waggoners of the waves" carried the world's goods. England, her successor, even more brilliantly demonstrated the erection of economic power upon the seizure of colonial markets and routes, the quasi-monopoly of wool-production and utilization of unique skill in technology. In short, there had been no static epoch in Europe, a time of saturation and pause. Instead, there had existed a glaring contrast between advanced, talented peoples and the simple and underdeveloped folk. Commerce was built upon this fact.

Even the United States offered only an apparent exception to this generalization in the nineteenth century. For many generations, a vast continent was to be taken, settled, civilized. Absorbed in this work, and satisfied with its magnificent rewards, the American business man scarcely lifted his eyes abroad until late, in the era of McKinley. But though Americans were so busy at home, it did not follow that their experience was wholly different from that of the Old World. America was unique principally in having exploited her own backwardness instead of that of other peoples. The Eastern seaboard cities of New England lived upon the rustics of the West quite as much as old Florence and Venice depended upon the uncouth feudal agriculture of Northern Europe in the Middle Ages.

Up to the late Victorian Age, in short, the Western lands had still contained backwoods, fields for development. They had not been fully organized and penetrated by business. But by the opening of the twentieth century, Western Europe had few regions still primitive from a technological standpoint; opportunities for such exploitation had passed in that area, as the melancholy German, Spengler, observed in 1912. He had then begun to compose the "Downfall of the West," resting on the thesis that, since European peoples had become peers in commerce, and could no longer live by exploiting one another's weaknesses, there was really nothing left for them to do but to cut one another's throats. This they proceeded to do in 1914, while Spengler looked on gloomily, even though he reckoned on a German victory.

Of course, the glutting of Europe need not have led to such a crisis if only the needed new markets could have been found in the vast stagnating areas outside Western Europe. From the purely statistical standpoint, it was absurd to speak of a "saturated" world at that time, when only the fringe of the gigantic Europo-Asian land-block was darkened with smoking chimneys and noisy with clattering cars. Beyond Belgium and the clusters of manufacturing towns in Germany, stretched the enormous territories of the agrarians—the Balkans, Austria-Hungary, Poland and Russia. Farther away lay Africa, India, China, South America, also very imperfectly transformed by business enterprise into either makers or consumers of goods. But these regions had not been brought securely within the capitalist scheme despite the rampant imperialists and the persuasive salesmen of the West.

The transformation of such agrarian lands was left to chance; the West supposed that mere machinery could produce the machine society, and ignored the psychological and social factors in "progress." Mental preparedness for machine capitalism, however, which had taken centuries in Europe, was lacking elsewhere. Russia, the Balkans and India had never known a Renaissance, teaching individualism, or a Reformation, instilling self-reliance, or social revolutions to free business from the handicaps of custom. Only in Japan had a certain historic foundation for modern industry been laid. Without such preparation, however, Eastern business men in general were too few, too inexperienced and timid, to seize resolutely the guiding authority within these societies, when older forms began to dissolve.

THE FAILURE IN RUSSIA

The worst defeat of the business man was in Russia. Conceivably, the Czar's mammoth dominions might have given employment to Western Europe for many a year. But Russia missed the stages of development undergone by the West; she knew no cultural bloom of trader-towns, no religious upheaval, no movement able to overthrow autocracy and raise the standards of living for the masses; she lacked Renaissance individualism and Baroque centralization. Mills and offices were planted here and there in a giant agricultural region, devoid of almost all historical preparation.

Up to the 1800's there were few free laborers for hire. One of the earliest "free" sources of industrial labor in Russia (as also in Prussia) was the womenfolk of the soldiers in the big garrison-towns. For the rest, when the State needed mines and factories opened for munitions, it had to deed crowds of serfs to privileged entrepreneurs; troops were sent to round up peasants, drag them away from their families and fields to the various plants, where they frequently were not paid, but were expected to toil hard "to work out their taxes." At times, entrepreneurs could buy large blocks of land and serfs who went with them, though this was stoutly resisted by the landlord-nobility. Amid extreme cruelty and misery, accordingly, business began in Russia. It commenced at a far lower depth than it had in Western Europe. The chaining and flogging of starving workers, the savage repression of desperate revolts, left in Russia a heritage of folk-hatred against business unlike that anywhere else. Business did not appear to be ameliorating life in Russia even as much as in Asia.

The first Russian business men did not work up and out through cities, like those in other lands both of Europe and Asia. On the contrary, they commenced as territorial lords, absolute rulers of destitute serfs. The Stroganovs, for instance, were wild viceroys of uncivilized domains. The family was founded by a Christian Tartar, a fur-trader named Spiridion. After he was done horribly to death by wild tribes-men, his three sons enlarged his enterprises under Ivan the Terrible and operated in salt, furs and mining, importing German craftsmen, book-keepers and officials as organizers. Ivan promised them Siberia if they could take it; the grandsons hired Cossack hordes, seized the immense wastes and ruled over them until Peter the Great stripped them of au-thority. As an aristocratic family they survived into modern times. Titles were readily purchasable under the Czars.

As landlords, other entrepreneurs proved themselves eligible for the Russian aristocracy. The Demidovs, miners of the Ural, made fortunes in munitioneering under Peter the Great, and bought titles. Their mines were scenes of peculiarly dreadful revolts by masses of serfs who had been taken from their families and dragged to living death. Becoming aristocratic was an advantage to the Demidovs, because they could then own serfs and were not so dependent on the Crown for their labor-supply.

Foreigners on the borders of Russia, Jews and Germans on the West and Chinese on the East, strove for centuries to reach into the benighted land but with little effect. Not until the nineteenth century did foreign capital begin to flow in sufficient measure to alter the old life. The man who probably did most, as an individual, to alter the old economy, was the German, Ludwig Knoop, a man of prodigious energy, who started as a clerk in Manchester, studied English methods and took them to the undeveloped wastes of Russia, where he built up gigantic power and wealth. By 1857 industrialism had so far grown up in Russia that she could feel the effects of a world crisis.

This late and swift industrial revolution in Russia was not ameliorated either by the humanitarianism of the West or by the immemorial cus-toms which acted as a brake in Asia. For a long time, the Russian manu-facturers resisted the slightest infringement of their authority by the State in the shape of labor laws. Only occasionally could the Czars force some restraint upon them. Harshly driven, the enlarging masses of uprooted peasants in the industrialized towns presented new prob-lems to the stability of the despotic system. Their grievances against the manufacturers added to the agrarian discontent which produced the upheaval of 1905.

At that time, the famous petition of Father Gapon, offered on a Bloody Sunday to the Czar, was directed especially against the exac-tions of business men. The petitioners who ventured to approach the throne with their grievances were massacred. The cruelty of the Czar sent a shudder through the world. But the cruelty against which the crowd had come to protest was that of the industrial autocrats, the manufacturers:

We beg little: we desire only that without which life is not life, but hard labour and eternal torture. The first request which we made was that our masters should discuss our needs with us; but that they refused, on the ground that no right to make this request is recognized by law.... Every one of our requests was a crime ... Sire, here are many thousands of us, and all are human beings only in appearance.

Peculiar savagery and suffering furnished the ground out of which again Revolution arose in Russia. But though such circumstances may explain the bitterness of the people against business, which invaded their land in such alarming shapes, they do not suffice in themselves to explain the triumph of Communism and the removal of Russian territories from the sphere of private enterprise. For this, the character of the Russian business man must be considered.

The Revolution of 1917 came, removing the Czar and his family, sweeping away the old régime of the landed aristocracy. But, as Lenin has told the story, the Moscow revolutionists were terrified by the unexpected swiftness of their success and the size of the monstrous tasks before them. They had no comprehensive economic plan ready. In eagerness and humility, they approached the middle class elements and vainly begged them to suggest a program and take power.

No capitalist arose in Russia at that hour, with the daring of an old Stroganov, to seize upon that collection of nations which is Russia, and rule it in the interests of business. Perhaps this was the most dazzling opportunity ever offered at a single swoop to a business man. But business men were afraid or incompetent. And so, almost against their will, the revolutionists had to take the helm and steer the course of Russia out into unknown waters. Ironically enough, one of these was Piatakov, son of a rich business man, a sugar-manufacturer, who refused to touch a kopek of the millions left him by his father. Willy-nilly, however, he inherited his father's business genius and showed such remarkable leadership in the economic reconstruction of Russia that Lenin, in his testament, recorded that gratefully, as well as his courage and honor. He was directing the heavy industries when Stalin struck him down.

BUSINESS AND THE INDIAN CASTES

India, unlike Russia, had a high culture, but of a character decidedly less adapted to capitalistic business enterprise than those of China and Japan. So extraordinarily difficult was the penetration of industrialism into this mighty land-mass that, even today, according to Buchanan, only two per cent of the population are employed by factories.

Indian crafts had indeed a long and splendid tradition; a kind of putting-out system had been developed in parts which was not unlike that preceding capitalism in Europe. But the artisans of India toiled for courts rather than for city-burghers, and lacked the broader markets which China's stimulating urban life supplied. Another reason for the conservatism of Indian business was the fact that this region had all the types of commodities needed by the people. From the days of Caesar, the West tried in vain to tempt India with wares, but she coveted little except pure gold and silver.

India's religion was the philosophy of poverty, the negation of ambition. Among her social castes, that of the merchant was low. The dominant types, priests and warriors, were supposed, according to Hindu scriptures, never to lend at interest. Land-holding and administration were alone respectable. The Mohammedans in India also had a repugnance to taking interest which unfitted them for business enterprise. Only the Parsees could be called spiritually prepared for the coming of the new industrialism.

Of all business men in Asia, perhaps, the Parsees were most akin to the Victorian business men who went out to "hustle the East." Their rôle in India was remarkably like that of the Jews and Huguenots in Europe, for they, too, were an oppressed religious minority in exile. Forced to leave Persia and seek refuge abroad, they had been unable to purchase land and merge themselves into native Indian society. Denied citizenship rights, they could not become soldiers. Almost all that was left for them was to take up the despised commercial pursuits.

Parsees were outside the caste structure. Unlike the good Brahmin, they could travel without contamination. Able even to mingle with laborers, it was possible for them to manage factories. Their fire-worshiping faith instilled hope in them, instead of the Hindu's gloomy nihilism. The strict observance of its religious tenets led, as in the case of Puritanism, to reinforcement of the virtues of thrift, hard work and attention to material success. So well did they manage their affairs that vagabonds and thieves were rare among them. Their women were comparatively well educated. In short, the Parsee attitude, earnest, benevolent, righteous, was readily appreciated by the European. And Parsees quickly proved themselves fully the equal of Western merchants by joining them in the business of forcing opium on China.

There were only about 150,000 Parsees amid the millions of all India, but they had already managed to conquer the Indian States more effectively than any armed hordes that had appeared before the British occupation. Thus they were the only group on the spot able to take instant advantage of the new industrialism, and to win a certain social acceptance as well from the British. Thackeray described the high position of a typical, though imaginary, *Rummun Loll* in the phony bank of the nabob, *Colonel Newcome*. In real life, one of the most famous Parsees was a mighty plutocrat, Jamsitjee Jeebehoy (1783–1859). Beginning life as a "bottle-wallah," poor and industrious as a Carnegie or Krupp, he became a railway-promoter and amassed prodigious riches which he distributed among Parsee religious schools and for female education. From the British he received the title of baronet. Later, the Sassoons appeared, also a Parsee family, contributing first to British wealth and then to literature.

Acting as brokers for the Europeans, the Parsees soon learned the new methods and branched out as pioneers in the Bombay cotton-industry. The establishment of cotton-plants in India meant disaster for the native craftsmen, who had already lost their foreign markets after Europe found out how to manufacture printed stuffs cheaper than the poorest artisan of the most wretched land. When the Parsees set up mills in India, the home markets also were closed to the native artisans. Thus the coming of industrialism did not bring a widespread awakening of business enterprise among the native population, but benefited very largely the alien money-lenders, the Parsees.

THE CHINESE BREAK-UP

The Western business man who sailed to the East in the past century was generally quite unaware of his own history. It never occurred to him that his own ancestors once were very much like the exotic, long-robed merchants whom he met in Canton. A patrician of old Venice or Augsburg in the Renaissance would have been perfectly at home among such wholesalers of China as the dignified Houqua. But the Victorian Westerner, divorced from his own past, felt chiefly amusement or worse, ennui, among the Celestials. "Very wearisome" to British merchants, reported C. Middleton Smith, were those

> Chinese dinner-parties which commence at 6 P.M. and continue until 1 A.M. The Chinese merchants are in the habit of doing all of their chief business in the places of joy, amidst the glare of a thousand lights, the din of native music, and in an atmosphere which may be called "gay." Their outlook on life is not our outlook; they have a very keen appreciation of "having a good time" . . . Recently a wealthy British merchant discussed this aspect of Chinese trade with the writer. He said that he simply could not stand that sort of life, and he knew that he lost a good deal of business in consequence. He liked to have all his business transacted in the office.

Americans in the East, as Smith observed, were "more popular with the Chinese because they are rather less of what they call 'the high-brow,' type than the average Briton. They do not hesitate to mix freely with the Chinese." But though the Yankees were perhaps glad to shake hands with the natives, they, too, distrusted too "gay" an atmosphere. Business had become a solemn affair to all Westerners since Puritanism stamped out the old frivolity of the West. A Medici would not have minded gongs and bright lights, nor would a Lübeck wholesaler have objected to the flowing bowl; up to the Renaissance, most European merchants would dicker together amid happy gossip over fine clothes, jewels and children. And Chinese merchants were still in that stage.

When the Chinese began to deal with the Europeans, they had not advanced to the consolidated and all-powerful State; they were still, like Renaissance Europeans, primarily city-men. Development in China had gone parallel with that in Europe up to a certain point, and then stopped dead. The Han Empire in China had been formed about the same time as the Roman Empire, and crumbled almost as Rome "fell." A Dark Ages ensued in the Asian world as in the Western, during which business men had to shift for themselves. Without a strong State to assure them continuous protection, they built high ramparts about their towns, ruled independently and developed a culture more refined than that of mediaeval Europe.

Through the gilds, merchants of China governed themselves and, incidentally, their apprentices. Gild offices were elective, to be sure, but naturally the richest and oldest men formed an aristocratic element of power; they fixed prices and rules of conduct and punished offenses of members in their own courts—from the "tong" justice of these secret tribunals, no appeal was possible to another authority. Each gild worshiped with feasting and dramas some patron saint such as the God of Riches or Lou Pan the Technologist.

So smoothly and secretly did these corporations function that there was little necessity for the State to intervene. Occasionally a Mandarin might meddle bureaucratically with this self-regulating commerce, but it was within the power of the gilds to strike most effectively and paralyze economic activity by boycott. As a rule, the gilds did not call upon the State for aid, but when trouble drew nigh they levied taxes on themselves and raised hireling armies. In peaceful periods, they supported fire brigades, gave rice to the poor, and edified the public by processions with a tremendous show of banners and drums. Almost the only threat to their authority came from labor unions, journeymen gilds, but these, says Morse, they generally managed to repress.

The Southern city of Canton was run by the mightiest of all these self-governing merchants. By position and history, Canton was fated to play a major rôle in business development. Founded by refugees from Central China who settled in a strategic point on Pearl River, it could monopolize the trade with India and Persia and even receive ambassadors from Rome. By the third century A.D., it had become the richest trading-center of China. From this belligerent city went out seafarers to navigate the typhoon-swept seas as far as Singapore and Manila; its burgher-lords fought and intrigued to keep their wealth from the preying warriors of the more feudal-agrarian and less cosmopolitan regions of the North.

The animosity between the two different areas, South and North, began early. Several times the Cantonese merchants supported a Southern dynasty against a Northern contestant, and in all ages they took an active part in political strife. Their hostility to the North was enormously increased when the Manchus swept down and absorbed China, making Peking their capital. Canton was the last city in China to surrender to these barbaric hordes; in 1644 it held the Manchus at bay for a whole year and only succumbed when its gates were opened through treachery. Then the Manchus slew 80,000 victims there. Those who survived the horror, and their offspring, never forgot or forgave. No friendly feeling could exist between the victimized Cantonese and the Peking rulers.

Canton and Peking disagreed over opium. The Northern Emperors refused admittance to the insidious drug, and to the Western "foreign devils" who brought it. Had it not been for the Cantonese merchants, avid for gain, regardless of the results to the country at large, Westerners might have knocked long in vain at the gates of the Celestial Kingdom. But the profit-seeking Southerners let the European salesmen in through the back-door and, growing wealthy themselves on the illicit traffic in poppy-juice, extended their financial power over the rice-fields, banks, shops and ships of the rest of China.

When the foreigners were well-established at Canton, in their "Factory" near Hog Lane, the colony included 162 British and 62 Parsees from India, besides 44 Americans and a few Portuguese. All were impressed by the gorgeous palaces, and also by the business acumen of their Cantonese hosts. On Chinese shop-walls, they read cheerful slogans of which they could approve:

> For idle persons there is no admittance.
> Customers come in numbers like the gathering of clouds.
> Rich customers are perpetually welcome.
> From a single cash, may 10,000 be derived.

Some of these Chinese, even according to Western standards, were immensely rich. Old Houqua, who died in 1843 at the age of 74 was the dean of them all, worth about 26 millions, a sum equal now to 52 millions of Chinese dollars. His home was fabulous, though he lived in its simplest rooms with a frugality like that of Jacob Fugger, Crassus or Cosimo de' Medici. In Houqua, as among his fellows, a high sense of honesty, or "honor" as the Westerners somewhat inexactly called it, was particularly striking.

This commercial "honor" was rightly respected by the Westerners, for without it the opium trade would have ceased abruptly. The traffic in the "foreign mud" was forbidden by the Government under penalty of death. If a merchant therefore refused to pay for wares, no redress could be sought in courts. But the "high sense of honor" of the Cantonese could be trusted. It was these honest gentlemen who managed the "squeeze," the costly bribes which induced the Mandarin officials to look the other way. As old Houqua used to grumble: "Have got muchee bad news. Have spillum too much."

Vainly the Peking Government attempted to appeal to Western public opinion. To the British Sovereign it addressed a long document begging help in stopping the opium traffic. But the British were highly amused at its florid exhortations:

> In dealing with opium, regardless of the injury it inflicts upon the Chinese people, an inordinate thirst for gain controls the action of these foreign devils . . . Hitherto we have heard that You, Honoured Sovereign, whose heart is full of benevolence, would not do to others that which you would not others should do to yourself.

Failing in this sort of protest, the Chinese Government took drastic measures and confiscated chests of the forbidden "mud." In a rage, Captain Elliott reported in 1839 this "unprovoked initiative in aggressive measures against British *life, liberty* and *property*, and against the dignity of the British Crown." The British *Nemesis* moved in and blew up the only Chinese warship. The Opium War began, which cost China untold suffering and finally an indemnity of 21 millions of dollars.

The Opium War was not the only violent movement to disrupt China which came from the great trading center of Canton. From that city started also the T'ai-Ping rebellion, the most terrible civil war of history, whose ravages were felt up and down the Yangtze Valley; throughout Central China, immense and rich cities, filled with palaces and libraries, were utterly destroyed. By sword and flame, the seats of ancient culture and merchant leadership in the heart of China were blotted out, with fatal consequences to the future development of the land. At last, out of Canton swept the revolutionary forces, backed by merchant loans, which finally cast down the hated Manchu monarchy and elected Sun Yat-sen, who came from the neighborhood of Canton, as President of a Republic.

Thus in China, as in England, France and America, business men had a hand in the revolt against royal autocracy. But the Chinese were not able to form a stable bourgeois society like those of the West. True, the Cantonese who had finally achieved revenge upon the Manchus were excellent and venturesome merchants, fit to be set beside Europeans. They provided immigrants to Hawaii, the Philippines and the United States, and the score of Chinese millionaires who owned tin-mines and other concessions in the Malay States. But even this race of fighters, adventurers and bargain-hunters, could not take over the great State which they had brought to ruin, or produce order in the chaos of their making.

Many Westerners rejoiced at the establishment of the Republic, sweeping away the old régime of literati who had governed China for two thousand years. It was supposed that merchants could of course rule better than literati, bureaucrats chosen only on the basis of literary examinations. But merchants had never managed so vast a dominion in the West, and much less could this be expected of the Chinese, where merchants have always entertained the lowest possible opinion of the soldier. The Chinese merchants soon found themselves the tools, or taxpayers, and not the masters of the war-lords. Moreover, the T'ai-Ping rebellion had wiped away so large an urban element from China that the agrarians overwhelmingly predominated, and for them the merchants had nothing substantial to offer in place of the old Confucian order.

Thus it happened that the Chinese business men failed to dominate their society. They had indeed learned self-government in limited urban spheres and developed a culture and discipline of their own through the ages; they had the will to assail and at last overthrow autocracy by revolution, but from that point they could not go on and follow the Westerners to high-pressure capitalistic methods.

THE BATTLE OF BUSINESS WITH FEUDALISM IN JAPAN

The astounding feats of the Japanese in assimilating Western capitalism in the nineteenth century was the marvel of the world. How was it possible for a people so long swaddled in bonds of agrarian feudalism, and so long isolated from contacts with foreign societies, to spring up in a moment, grasp everything vital the West had to offer and rival the haughtiest powers of Europe in war and industry? Why were the Japanese so much more successful than other Easterners? The answer lies deep in the history of the Japanese business man.

It is of course true that Japan was a "hermit nation" and to all appearances sunk in a trance when the black ships of Perry cast anchor off her coast. She had been cut off from nearly all trading with the world for 250 years. But before that time, very long ago, Japan had been more nearly like Western lands; she had stored up a large fund of knowledge which was not lost or forgotten when intercourse was cut off by the Shoguns.

Indeed, no other Easterners were such daring seafarers as the Japanese overseas-traders in distant ages. They had surpassed the Indians and the Siamese and also overawed most of the Chinese on the coast. Up to about 1600, these adventurers of Japan had been in contact with other cultures, both in China and, through the Portuguese, with the West. In fact, Japan had assimilated more Western methods and ideas than had China or India, up to the moment when the famous exclusion act of 1635 was passed, severing most of the ties with the outer world.

Until close to 1600, accordingly, the development of business in Japan was not unlike that in Western Europe. True, there was no Renaissance in an Eastern land, and the Japanese, like all the Asians, missed the experience of individualism. But this, far from being altogether a disadvantage, may have been a permanent asset, enabling Japanese capitalists to cooperate better in clans and associations and with the State.

Rather remarkable parallels in time may be drawn between the flowering of the business cities in Japan and China, from the 1100's to the 1400's, and the similar unfolding of Western towns. The Japanese centers, however, were less splendid and rich than those of China, or the West, during the Middle Ages. It is often mistakenly assumed that Japanese have been silk-workers "from time immemorial." In fact, they took up silk-production rather late; in the fourteenth century they were behind Florence or Bologna in this respect. But if they were not such booming sites of large industries, the Japanese towns were akin in character to those of Europe.

In both hemispheres, the rôle of religion as city-builder and trade-fosterer was unmistakable. Markets often grew up under the shadow of sacred edifices in Japan. The Buddhist Church, as a great land-holder and money-lender, was usually ready to help merchants against the lordly governors when projects to remit debts were announced.

The feudal gentry in Japan as in Europe were apt to grow impatient with merchants who regularly charged 30 per cent of ordinary citizens and asked 36 of the Government. Merchants took the weapons and armor of the fighting men in pawn, sometimes; it could happen that a lord had to take almost naked troops to battle. Worse, perhaps, merchants speculated in grain during famines. To counteract these tendencies, the Government occasionally issued *tokusei* proclamations, remitting debts, not unlike the *seisachtheia* of Greece under Solon. By these periodic decrees, all but 10 per cent of the original sums owed was wiped out; the knights rushed to get their swords and plated-shirts out of hock. By way of justification the Government declared that it intended to equalize the distribution of wealth:

> Those who possess a large stock of rice and coins, or take mortgages in order to make a profit, would not face starvation even if they were deprived of their property, and the rich are only one or two among a hundred people.

This confiscatory policy was stoutly resisted by the Buddhist temples who appreciated the business point of view. Priests, moreover, bought up large domains upon which they wiped away toll-privileges—an action also in line with the needs of commerce. Finally, it was under Buddhist auspices that trade began with China in the fourteenth century. According to Takekoshi, who has recently done most to illuminate the background of Japanese business history for Western readers, temple priests managed the flotillas which carried goods between Canton and Peking for about two centuries. As learned men, they acted in negotiations with the Chinese Court, which merchants could hardly have undertaken alone. And they helped merchants to hoodwink the feudal lords of Japan, who were averse to such commerce. The chief product proffered by the Japanese was the wonderful swords, made from peculiarly excellent ore by superb armorers—in 1483, no less than 67,000 such swords were bought by China. Swords, together with sulphur and fans, yielded large profits. But unluckily, the Chinese would only buy them on condition that Japan admitted herself a vassal State and allowed her trade-ships to be called tribute-bringers. The feudal lords would not have submitted to such a humiliating position, thinks Takekoshi, had not the priests helped to conceal the full extent of this subjection from the knights who were too illiterate to read the documents.

Not only was the Buddhist Church of assistance to Japanese business men but the native faith, Shinto, also offered aid. Some of the most flourishing towns grew up around its shrines; merchants purchased from the priests the rights to hold markets and monopolies, and often, growing more powerful, reduced the authority of the shrines to a minimum. Such towns were, like mediaeval European seats of trade, fortified by walls, defended by hired soldiers, and virtually self-governing.

Waxing proud, the towns leagued together to uphold their rights, conducting forays and burning down nests of robber barons. Particularly anxious to sweep away toll-barriers, they at last brought under their control the principal highways. This was a step in advance of Europe, for in Japan, feudal lords had to pay toll along roads owned by merchant corporations.

This movement, in which the sea-coast towns led, has been compared to that of the Hanseatic League. In these Eastern centers, a patrician class of merchants was formed among the men who contracted for the China trade. Sword-salesmen and importers of face-powder grew mighty in commercial councils. The town of Sakai was governed by the rich traders who owned waterfront warehouses. In Muro, the money-lenders predominated and kept so strict a rule than a man would as soon die as shirk his debts on New Year's Day, for if he had not paid, the whole populace could see that there were no ceremonial decorations at his doorway.

Relatively wealthier than land-poor feudal lords, these rich sea-traders were expansionist and quick to catch at new fads and ideas. They would trade or talk with anyone. The patricians of Sakai, it seems, were the first to introduce the famous tea-ceremony from China to Japan; they sold the precious bowls, kettles and paraphernalia to the feudal gentry and courtiers who copied urban styles. The same folk were eager to induce the Dutch to deal with them, and agreed to adopt the Catholic faith of the Portuguese in order to set up traffic.

Innovations were gladly welcomed in other coastal towns, as at Hakata, whose people imported pig-iron from China and revolutionized economic life in Japan by improving mining. Others studied new types of cloth, imitating the coveted European velvets and setting up weaving-mills. Among such imported processes, none was more important than the fine foreign art of manufacturing gunpowder and firearms. For a time, therefore, the Japanese merchants seem to have just such a monopoly on modern weapons as their fellows in Europe, and like them, sold guns to their feudal foes. In return for money and promises, Japanese munitioneers purveyed the new armament to the knightly class—with the inevitable result that the feudal lords laid low the merchants with their own weapons and abolished foreign commerce in the opening of the seventeenth century.

Far from passive recipients of culture, however, were these bold coast-merchants. They ventured far and wide in Eastern waters, rivaling the Cantonese in capturing the carrying-trade of the Siamese, who were as timorous about water as their own cats. Japanese raiders fought to obtain posts and footholds in Formosa, the Philippines and South

Sea Islands. They so harried the coasts of China that the Ming Government hardly knew whether to defend first its Northern boundaries against the Manchu barbarians, or its long shores against Japanese pirate-traders. The worst of the matter, for the Peking Court, was that unsympathetic Southern Chinese assisted the Japanese; there were merchant-pirates in Fukien and at Canton who helped the invaders for a good share of the profits. So hearty was this Sino-Japanese cooperation that, quaintly enough, a Chinese pirate introduced the piratical Portuguese to the rich Japanese financier of piratical expeditions, the merchant Ouchi. Converted to Catholicism at a fortunate moment, Ouchi opened the way for foreign penetration of Japan.

In short, during the period 1300 to 1530, the Japanese carried on their traffic in much the same fashion as seafaring peoples of the West —the early Genoese and Venetians, the later Dutch, Elizabethan English and finally the American privateers and smugglers of pre-Revolutionary days. All these violent merchant-adventurers seized treasure by force when they could not obtain it by bargaining; they stored up fortunes and used them to buy titles and lands, build city residences and develop economic life.

Like the Puritan Englishman, Lord Rich, who outfitted expeditions for plundering, or the American family of the Jays who backed Caribbean privateering, the Japanese employed the gains from sea-exploits to found respectable families. Many of the old "noble" lines of Japan, it appears, descended from such fishermen-salesmen-explorers. The family of Ouchi, for instance, engaged in the China trade, dealt with the Portuguese, financed pirates, and so at last could buy old court titles in Japan and become dukes.

In fact the Ouchi were far richer than most of the landed lords themselves. They could make dazzling presents to the sovereigns and obtain remarkable power in court intrigues. With their commercial and social contacts, they developed the art of good living to a higher degree than the poorer country gentlemen. Wearing Chinese robes of utmost magnificence, they surrounded themselves with a small court of their own. Broad in their tastes, they became Catholic at the behest of Francis Xavier and by so conforming diverted a valuable flow of Portuguese trade to their town, Oita. Eventually, the Ouchi became involved in a war over the possession of silver-mines and were ruined—a sign of Heaven's displeasure, said Buddhist priests.

Other instances, from the variegated pages of Takekoshi, show how close the resemblances were between Western and Eastern traders. Like a Yankee, it seems, was the salt-merchant, whaler and part-time pirate, Owatari of Hirado, in the fourteenth century, whose ambition was to own 99 ships to trade with 99 islands. The patrician abodes of some ancient families survived into modern times, such as the gold-enriched temple of Toanji in Sakai, which was once the dwelling-place of a great China trader, Sukezaemon.

Evidently, when the Westerners first came into contact with Japanese in the sixteenth century, they encountered equals, not inferiors. These were no country bumpkins, timid and ignorant, who greeted the Portuguese merchants and missionaries, the Dutch and later the agents of the British India Company. Instead, the countrymen of Ouchi were bold, shrewd and rapacious as Europeans themselves. As Kipling says, "A man is a man, though he comes from the end of the world."

EXPERIMENT IN ISOLATION

While the national States in Europe were being created or consolidated by kings in the 1600's, a similar development was taking place in the Eastern island. Japan was undergoing a national unification under the Tokugawa Shoguns, those martial conquerors who pushed the Imperial House into the background and assumed the real power. As a result of their deeds, Japan passed beyond the stage of city-localism, a fact of far-reaching consequence.

The only country of the Far East which did reach this level of nationalism was Japan. The Shoguns centralized commerce, built roads, freed others from the control of business gilds, and encouraged intercommunication. They destroyed the pretensions of independent merchants as ruthlessly as they crushed the claims of feudal knights or the Buddhist Church. And before they had done, the Japanese became, unlike the Chinese or Indian, a bourgeois, a citizen or subject of a strong State—and in brief a fellow to the European. This was slowly accomplished, of course. Cities yielded gradually; in order to diminish their resistance, the Tokugawas built up two new centers, Tokyo and Osaka, to which they brought merchants from other places. Over each of these towns they erected magnificent and impregnable castles, reminding the merchants in their shadow of omnipresent State power.

At the same time, the swashbuckling merchant-adventurers of Japan were cleverly stripped of their weapons. On the pretext that he needed iron for nails to build a colossal wooden Buddha, the Shogun Hideyoshi smilingly requisitioned the swords of the merchant class. But he found he did not need the blades of the samurai, and so these knights were left the sole sword-bearers in the land. To complete the mental conquest, the Shoguns also brought over Chinese scholars and bade them preach Confucian doctrines which glorified agriculture and left commerce shorn of a halo. Shinto, the faith of the Emperors and of Kyoto merchants, was discouraged; even Buddhism, the old friend of trade, was not much assisted. Only the pure agrarian philosophy of Confucius was deemed favorable to the new State.

Realizing that a growing commerce with foreign lands would sooner or later endanger this hierarchical and agrarian society, the Shoguns sternly severed the ties which bound Japan to the outside world. By 1635 the Ordinance of National Isolation shut the doors to foreign trade. No more ships might sail to China. The Portuguese were driven away and the Christian heresy extirpated. Only the Dutch were permitted to continue in a confined fashion on a small outpost, because they were notoriously indifferent to religious proselytizing. Most remarkable of all, the settlements established abroad by Japanese were left to their fate; more than 100,000 Japanese, it is thought, happened to be trading and living in various parts of the Pacific world at that time, and these were refused permission ever to return to their homes. Thus an absolutist sword cut down trader-imperialism.

In this manner, military lords managed to give Japan peace for 250 years. Neither domestic upheaval nor foreign war disturbed the miraculous calm which descended on the island kingdom when the business man, eternal fomenter of discord and disorganizer of static societies, was subdued. This unbroken record of tranquillity, which seems so abnormal to Westerners that it is generally dubbed "stagnation," cannot be paralleled in the history of any other great nation, save possibly in ancient Egypt, where the trader was also held down for a long time.

Though socially humiliated, merchants were not wholly out of the picture in Japan under Absolutism. They might not wear swords, give themselves family names and other airs, or dwell in mansions with aristocratic decorations on their gates. They could not attend meetings on politics and their reading-matter was severely censored. But they waxed fat, none the less, and at last contrived to bring down in ruins this mightiest of all attempts in modern times to throttle business.

The stronger the Government grew, the richer became the contractors who carried out its projects for roads, canals and castles. Its power, moreover, was to a large extent based upon public ownership of mines. But such factors as the Gotos, who operated the mines, became richer than many a duke. Soon, too, the ingenuity of merchants devised more perfect ways of getting around the agrarian system; Osaka men, early in the seventeenth century, issued paper money and, shortly after, one of the early members of the Kyoto house of the Mitsui put into circulation bills of exchange. Grain-exchanges and banks were opened in that century in Japan, just as they were spreading in Europe, and reached England, at that time. With increasing mobility of wealth, merchants acquired new power over the land-poor nobility whose income was largely in rice and vegetables.

Not only did the merchants draw dukes and knights into a hopeless state of indebtedness, but they also tempted these feudal gentlemen to forget the Spartan simplicity which should have been their ideal. Vainly the Shoguns forbade the knights to set foot in the theaters and inns of the business men, lest they be caught by the contagious love of luxury. Bourgeois example was too enticing for many a gentleman. After all the bourgeois had nothing to do but play, in his leisure moments, since he was forbidden administrative posts; and his demoralizing spectacles undermined the old manners. Much the same sort of thing was happening in Japan in the eighteenth century that was going on during that period in France, in the *ancien régime*. Gay bourgeois financiers, Eastern and Western, were corrupting the aristocrats who lost prestige as they sank into a morass of debts.

The theater was the chosen vehicle of expression for the business circles of Japan in the eighteenth century as it was, contemporaneously, in Germany. Like Hamburg, the Eastern sea-city, Osaka, went mad on drama. How much the theatrical enthusiasm there was affected by the influence of the Dutch traders, is difficult to say; but some sort of mutual influence appears probable. The Osaka stage showed plays to the taste of the merchantry, depicting for instance the deeds of the terrible seafaring adventurer, *Koxinga*. Eventually, Tokyo caught the dramatic fever from Osaka.

Of course, the bourgeois does not always wish to see himself upon the stage. He thirsts for illusion as well as realism. It was so in Hamburg, where stolid brokers in herrings and wheat were delighted by cloak-and-rapier romances which made up for the hum-drum quality of their lives and recompensed them for political inactivity. So, too, the Japanese drama contained poetic and romantic themes; warriors whirled in stamping death-dances, wielding long lances with surgical dexterity, and drew applause from audiences composed of plump and pacific eel-dealers, who not only had never brandished a sword or lance in their lives, but would have landed in jail had they even possessed one.

A favorite theme of the Tokyo stage was the conflict between marauding gangs of knightly desperadoes, who made the streets of the capital unsafe at night, and brave bands of citizen defenders. The delight of the Tokyo bourgeois in such tussles was much like that of the Germans at the same time in Schiller's "The Robbers." In both, the oppressed bourgeois found a thrill of vicarious satisfaction in beholding bold *Robin Hood*, a bohemian vagabond, or some other rebel, unashamed of his plebeian origins, making sport of high authority. Revolutionary implications were contained in the Japanese dramas of the "machiyakko," or city gangsters, as in Schiller's play, which made the latter still uncomfortable to the Government in Hitler's régime.

The more cultivated aristocracy in Japan remained superciliously aloof from this theater. Its patronage was given instead to the Noh, which resembled, with its formal music and stiff ballet, the Grand Opera beloved in European courts. East and West, in fact, a similar division of tastes existed, the business classes as a whole preferring the more realistic and homely theater, while the grandees in general supported the pompous and artificial opera, especially before the theater had developed to its highest art.

In the case of the wood-block prints, most celebrated product of bourgeois Japan, a comparison between the hemispheres is equally impressive. The print, a mass-product of mechanical devices, was essentially a favorite of business circles; the burghers of German cities in Dürer's time bought prints, and so did the merchants of Osaka and Tokyo delight in the genre scenes, the gay grotesqueries of Hiroshige and Hokusai. The trader has ever tended to look at life realistically, with its humors and horrors, and not so much as the aristocrat through a veil of convention. On their part, the Court noblemen of old Japan were inclined to be contemptuous of commonplace prints. To them only sublime brush-strokes upon scrolls of pure silk, no picture exactly like another and yet all conforming to strict canons, brought aesthetic gratification.

Commercial interchange between East and West was mirrored in these Japanese prints. Artists in Japan were in some degree influenced by examples of Western products brought by Dutch traders, suggesting a greater realism and teaching perspective. On the other hand, the art of the East was also shipped back to Amsterdam and was responsible in part for the vivid colorings of Dutch paintings. The blue plates of Delft were direct imitations of Oriental wares; the interior scenes of the Delft painter, Vermeer, showing series of rooms in sunny recession, also indicate probable influence from Japanese models. In Vermeer's pictures, Delft patricians appear in all their dignity, surrounded by the bright porcelains and knickknacks imported by the Dutch East India Company. Thus the bourgeois circles of Delft and Osaka, half a world away, testified for each other.

Additional similarities may be traced between various trader-communities of history and their cultures. In love of theatrical show, the great sea-ports of Alexandria, Venice, Hamburg and Osaka were akin. Realistic treatment in painting and sculpture was favored by most of the commercial cities from Rhodes and Piræus in the antique world down to the mediaeval towns of Europe and the Tokugawa cities of Japan. Societies which suppress the trader, like the old Egyptian, remain conventional; those which almost dispense with him, like the old Hindu, are slow to develop pictorial representation of the secular type. The business man, in his sober moments, wishes to gaze clearly and steadily at the world which he is striving to possess; best of all, he likes a photograph of it.

In many cases, this aesthetic realism was definitely an instrument of social criticism. Thus in German Nürnberg, some of the wood-engravings illustrating the verses of Hans Sachs, the cobbler-poet, were scurrilous jibes at feudal lords, and appealed to the trading-fathers of that city. The same mood was evidenced in Japan; one striking instance was the case of an illustrated book, "A Hundred Women," issued under the patronage of a rich merchant, Kinokuniya Bunzaemon, satirizing the wives and daughters of high feudal lords. The artist was banished for his audacity but Bunzaemon, being a government contractor, remained unscathed.

This particular millionaire, whose story is related by Takekoshi, was one of the jolly apparitions of business history. A plebeian orange-seller, unacquainted with the names of his parents, he somehow rose to gambling in lumber and engaged in government contracts for building and coinage, making a huge fortune for himself. His rival was another contractor, equally rich, and quite as boisterous, Naraya Mozaemon. The two vied in extravagance and notoriety-seeking, much like some of the more notorious financiers in Old France. Bunzaemon had a burning thirst for personal advertisement; when balladists poked fun at him, he paid them to sing all the louder, judging that any notice, however ridiculous, was better for the lumber-business than none.

It was in the tea-houses of Tokyo, or Edo as it was then known, that epic battles for publicity were waged. The two men outdid each other in banquets and riotous horseplay. Finally Bunzaemon came off victor from the luxury-duel. He hired a poet to write a song celebrating his triumphs in love over Mozaemon, and persuaded the handsomest courtesan of old Edo to trill it to her *samisen*. Soon the whole city, even the nation, was singing in chorus.

Singing, feasting and jesting in the tea-houses accompanied Japanese, like Chinese, business. In many ways, the amusements of Osaka society recall the pleasure-seeking of commercial Alexandria in classic times; in both cases, there was the same drifting about in barges between banks lined with torch-lit inns, where, in interminable leisure, Easterners discussed ship-insurance and exchange-rates, over banquets of inexhaustible variety, amid laughter and song.

A variety of reasons led the Japanese business men to concentrate their activities and even their ostentation in tea-houses. For one, other forms of public assembly, save the theater, were forbidden; they could meet only under the guise of pleasure, and many a political intrigue was spun by contractors and financiers behind the painted screens of inns. For another, the sumptuary laws restrained the middle classes from decking themselves, or even their homes, as they liked. This was not generally true in China, where a millionaire like Houqua in Canton could build anything he chose, extending his gardens and carved pavilions and filling his rooms with jade-backed couches. The Chinese left their sing-song houses comparatively tawdry, and lavished most of their wealth on homes. Quite on the contrary in Japan, the utmost refinement appeared in tea-houses.

"Conspicuous waste," dear to the Western millionaire from of old, was dangerous in Japan. A Japanese merchant was not permitted, at some periods, to inhabit a mansion rivaling a castle of a duke. So he rented banquet-halls in an inn. He could not adorn his wife, who was restricted in her choice of colors and sleeve-lengths, but his mistress could flaunt lacquered pins and rainbow robes. Citizens were forbidden by a Spartanic Government for a long time to wear socks, or *tabi*, even in the dead of winter, but courtesans could appear in them.

When sumptuary laws did not restrain the merchant, he was haunted by another fear. The jealousy of the Shoguns was easily aroused, and they were quick to break and banish any money-lender who seemed a trifle too conspicuous in his "waste." Violent might be the end of a spender who overstepped the bounds of good taste. If a banker let himself appear obviously rolling in wealth, his noble debtors were sure to feel reluctant to pay up on loans and mortgages. It was always extremely easy for a knight or duke to default anyway, for the law afforded no recourse to a merchant; at best, he could paste up public notices which deprived the debtor of "face." This legal rule was adopted by the State because it wished the feudal gentry to avoid borrowing and to live within their means—if they did resort to the merchant, let the merchant beware!

Scores of the most successful financiers of Old Japan were ruined in this fashion. Ishikawa Jian was a magnificent banker of Kyoto, whose home was a veritable museum of art treasures; the lords repudiated their debts and he was destroyed. Gorgeous Nawaya of the same city was undone by too splendid banquet-giving. Incautious Itoya Jurozaemon built a shrine plated with gold, and also succumbed. Among the many who were similarly threatened was an ancestor of the famous house of Mitsui, who managed, however, to pull through such a crisis.

Yet the laws, which left a faithless debtor of noble blood unscathed were merciless to the bankrupt merchant. Sometimes the unlucky man was crucified. Even if spared, he could seldom if ever raise himself again to positions of trust. Hence the ever-present fear of ruin and death kept the business man's ostentation within limits. And it is to this, very largely, that the exquisite good taste of Japan is due: the business parvenu did not dare to give too many "monkey dinners" lest he end up prematurely, nailed to a cross.

Nowhere in the world, accordingly, did a more delicate restraint in decoration prevail among bourgeois circles than in Japan. Merchants' wives could not wear cloth of gold, in view of legal and social penalties; so they permitted little flashes of color to appear in linings of their subdued robes, with the result that, willy-nilly, they acquired the subtle insinuations of refined elegance. So clever were they in dodging restrictions that even noblewomen imitated their styles. It was a rich merchant's wife of Kyoto, the lovely Nakamura Kuranosuke, who besought an artist to advise her on dress and, at his suggestion, appeared only in black and white. So astonishingly elegant was the effect that soon all followed her, and even the grandest court ladies assumed black —which has remained even to this day the prescribed hue of ceremonial costumes. Thus in the eighteenth century, a bourgeois woman in Japan was setting the mode for the aristocracy, as the banker's wife, La Pompadour, was doing in France. The difference was, that the Frenchwoman could be as extravagant as she liked, whereas the Japanese, with keener ingenuity, turned her restraint into an asset.

Many features of the culture developed in eighteenth-century bourgeois circles of Japan lie at the basis of Western aesthetics now. Modern decoration in homes and dress has been fundamentally influenced by Japanese examples of tonal subtlety, emphasis on surface and lines instead of ornament. And if this old "new" art seems sympathetic to our millionaires, it is largely because they, like the old Japanese, are more eager than before to shun notoriety. If not the law, they dread envious public opinion. When they desire extravaganza they go to hotels, as did the inn-loving people of Edo. They shrink from building palaces in the Medicean manner, but instead seek ways to express their power, like Japanese contractors, by expensive simplicity.

THE JAPANESE BOURGEOIS REVOLUTION

A fate curiously similar befell Japanese, Germans and Italians during their middle periods. Their three lands were filled with proud, bold, seafaring merchants around 1400, who were quite independent of feudal lords. The Hanseatics ruled the North Atlantic and Baltic, the Genoese and Venetians terrorized the coasts of the Levant, and the Japanese roamed the Pacific waters—all three merchant-adventurers were regarded with awe by their neighbors. But in each case, the business men at length lost their trade-routes, markets, dependencies and succumbed to autocracy, though in different ways. By 1600 a long night had settled down upon the traders of Italy, Germany and Japan;

agrarianism and absolutism appeared to have extinguished their power.

In the nineteenth century, each of these countries had a "come-back" of bourgeoisdom, brought about by social upheaval. Germany's unification began in 1864; Japan's was finished in 1868 and Italy's in 1870. Following one upon the other in such quick succession, these three movements established parliamentarism and gave new liberties and opportunities to business men. Business interests supported in some measure all these efforts at liberation, restoration and national unification, but most definitely, perhaps, the Japanese Restoration.

It is considered more than probable that a rebellion of the middle classes would have taken place in Japan even if Perry's black ships had not swum upon the horizon to signalize the end of the old Shogunate. Forces of discontent had been gathering throughout the eighteenth century, and already the unrest of business was endangering Absolutism. The Mitsui family, for instance, was violently anti-feudal ever since one of its early members was nearly ruined by negligent noblemen. This Mitsui, Takafusa, wrote a testament, the "Choninko," in which he urged merchants to unite in order to make their associations as strong as the clans of their hereditary foes, the sword-bearers. Force, he thought, would not avail, for "in business warfare between the samurai and the merchant, the samurai handles a very sharp sword and the merchant has only a bamboo spear." Guile, wariness and combination were the answers:

> However desirous the merchant may be to take advantage of the samurai's lack of economic knowledge, to make money out of him and withdraw just at the right moment, it is very difficult, or rather impossible, for the merchant to get the better of the samurai in their business or commercial warfare, for the samurai is the head of the four classes of people.

In answer to such appeals, organizations of business interests were forming, such as the Wholesale Merchants' Association. And these aroused traders were fortunate enough to discover an ideology for their revolutionary aims. It was under the guise of a religious purification movement—to sweep away corruption from the Buddhist Church as from the Shogunate—that Business finally swept to triumph in Japan. Hence the Japanese Restoration is most closely comparable to the English Puritan Revolution which took place two hundred years before.

For over a century before the actual revolt in Japan, the spiritual preparation went on. Shinto was the new, or rather revived creed, around which the middle class rallied. In a striking way, Shinto was to Buddhism what the English Puritanism of the Roundheads was to the

High Church elaboration of the Cavaliers. It was a faith without idols, without dogma, devoid of ornament and incense, appealing alike to the common man and to the business man, uniting momentarily lower and middle classes against the reigning powers.

Shinto had been in the most ancient times a faith widespread among traders. The old pirates, or *wako*, had been adherents. In this, too, another parallel with English merchantry may be found, for the Japanese *wako* and Shinto are comparable to the British blend of Puritanism and piracy. Moreover, Shinto, like Puritanism, encouraged revolution. Shinto, the faith of the Emperors, persisted in Kyoto, where these powerless monarchs continued to dwell; it was accepted by the very best business talents of Japan, which at the right time happened to be those of Kyoto, the Mitsui among them. These Southern traders, who had moved in numbers to Tokyo and reached high positions, kept their natural loyalty to the Imperial House, as well as their suspicious hatred of the feudal lords. They were Shintoists as well as revolutionaries.

The trouble was that by the 1700's, scarcely a soul knew any more what genuine Shinto really was. The pure old faith had been almost extinguished, and even the Emperors sometimes neglected its rites. A mass of meaningless ceremonies, it lacked even a native name, for Shinto is Chinese. To be useful, Shinto had to be re-created and this was done largely by guesswork. The most expert mental-tailors in the eighteenth century refitted it to contemporary needs. As Mabuchi, one of the men who "rescued" Shinto, explained, it would be easy to attract peasants away from a Shogun, who lived amid gorgeous Chinese pageantry, to an Emperor who was worshiped in simple, rustic shrines where the poorest farmer would not feel abashed.

Ruthlessly, Shinto was stripped of every ornament and dogma. Almost all that was left was a belief that the Imperial Household was descended from the Sun-Goddess and that all Japanese were also offspring of gods. This doctrine, now official, and apparently forming an innate and immemorial part of the Japanese psyche, was in fact, Satow declares, ridiculed by scholars in the eighteenth century as fantastic. What, every Japanese a god? Absurd! The scholarly skeptic, Ichikawa Tatsumaro, declared that the legend of the Sun-Goddess was a myth, and that the ancestors of the Japanese had been men like those of everybody else. But the "every man a god" movement swept the land; and in the forces of the insurgents, who tore the images from Buddhist temples, clerks of the Osaka countinghouses marched to battle.

It may seem at first glance odd that the business men of Japan, heading a movement for modern capitalism and parliamentarism, were the very ones who put across the most primitive tenets, appealing to the mysticism of blood and soil. But the analogy with modern Germany and Italy is too apparent to call for further comment. The Fascist movement in Italy told the people that they were sons of the old Romans; the Nazis declared that every German was the offspring of Nature's noblemen, the Aryans. And the Japanese, as usual more thorough than the Westerners, merely went a step deeper and explained to the peasants that their ancestors were divine.

BUSINESS AND THE ARMY IN JAPAN

To all appearances, the business men of Japan were vastly more successful in dominating society and refashioning the State to their desire than other Easterners, in India or China. But, in fact, their ultimate position is by no means assured even today.

Feudal sword-bearers, the samurai, proved very good business men too. Their old experience as administrators gave them posts in the new régime and even in businesses. And they continued to look down upon the plebeians as before. Moreover, though the merchant class was freed of old trammels, and could expand at will, it was not able to outweigh the combined interests of army and agriculture. "In no other land on earth," an observer says, "is wealth concentrated in so few hands as in Japan." Six or seven major concerns tower above all other companies, and two among these are giants: the Mitsui, descendants of the rebels of Kyoto, and the Mitsubishi, who between them control most of Japan's textile, shipping and banking interests. With economic power, they united political influence, for, each family supporting one of the two principal parties, they made reasonably sure of all but a handful of votes in the Diet.

Not only was wealth amazingly concentrated in these two families, but the families were themselves united in an extraordinary cohesion. The older and greater, the Mitsui, have a family council and a constitution which is 250 years old. This document was written by Hachirobei Mitsui, founder of the first fixed price dry-goods store in Tokyo, and it forms an instructive comparison with lines of advice given by or to business men in Western history. Overtones of Morelli and Savary, Defoe and Carnegie may be heard in the Oriental voice:

> Know that over-expansion, which you may covet, will beget confusion and trouble . . . Thrift enriches the House, while luxury ruins a man . . . The life work of a man lasts as long as he lives. Therefore, do not, without reason, seek the luxury and ease of retirement . . . He who does not know cannot lead. Make your sons begin with the mean tasks of the apprentice . . . Employ men of great abilities . . . Practice mutual caution and counsel.

The two giant families have been somewhat different in their interests and policies. The Mitsui, who founded the first modern munitions
plant in Japan and aided in the Restoration, have remained closer to
Army circles and tended to expansionist aims. The Mitsubishi, more involved in finance, nearer to the Navy, as it is said, and more international in outlook, have been on the whole more conservative.

The power of this pair of business families is unique; to find a parallel one must go back to the Medici or the Bickers brothers. But the
Japanese family-dynasties do not rule like the old Italians and Dutch in
open pomp. On the contrary, they must exert influence as invisibly as
possible over often recalcitrant politicians. They do not control trading-cities merely, but instead are in the midst of a great peasant nation,
with a decided hostility to capitalism. The Army, recruited largely
from this peasantry, is more independent of business men than were
the armed forces in the days of the Medici and Bickers.

Great is the power of the two families, indisputably. Even in France,
where power is so concentrated, at least "200 families" manage affairs,
and not, as in Japan, merely two. But it may still be debated whether
this makes business strong or imperils it. For though the giant houses of
Japan have no rivals, they have also few consumers; the rest of the
bourgeois are too weak to oppose them and yet also too poor to absorb their wares.

The triumph of business in Japan led therefore to a serious dilemma.
On the one hand, business cannot hope to raise the standard of living
among peasants in order to make more consumers at home, for then labor would be dear and Japanese industry might be wrecked by the
undercutting of the yet poorer Chinese. The other choice is to keep the
levels of living in Japan down below at least those of the West and
close to those of the East as a whole. Here the rôle of the rituals, art,
doctrines and systems of the past becomes vital, for they inculcate patient endurance and national morale among the people. As a leading
textile man in Japan said not long ago, the strength of Japanese industry lies in the precious heritage of the so-called "Japan Spirit." Triumphant business has had to turn back and study the methods which
those dextrous manipulators of the mass-mind, the Tokugawas, had
learned from Chinese scholars.

But though business may preserve the Spartan simplicity of the old
régime a while longer, it cannot also preserve the national isolation of
the Tokugawas. Wares must be sold abroad, if markets do not widen at
home. To support expansion, the Army must grow. But the Army is
far from the tool of business. Composed of peasants, inimical to the
commercial giants, it is not altogether different from the old merchant-
baiting crowd of feudal knights and retainers. Bushido, the creed of the

warrior, inculcated still in the soldier, praises the rash man of action and scorns the timid bargainer. By encouraging love of glory instead of careful calculation of results, bushido might lead to unprofitable adventures and unleash primitive forces.

Of all lands in the Far East, Japan is the one in which the outward forms of capitalism have been most successfully transplanted. But even there, as in Europe and America, the business man is far from being undisputed master in the house, despite his revolution. The capitalist has not extirpated feudalism, after all, as he was so confidently planning to do.

Feudalism, so recently considered the incompatible foe and predestined victim of capitalism, has somehow survived with and through capitalism. Indeed, the capitalist could not do without it. The feudal force of Army assists him to markets abroad. More and more he is compelled to rely on ancient rites and symbols to stimulate the loyalty of the folk, a loyalty which is as indispensable to a modern industrial society as it was to the mediaeval order. Stability in Japan still requires incantations, flags and Fuji-worship.

As psychological factors in business are being increasingly emphasized, even in the West, the Japanese have been inclined to re-appraise their own heritage of loyalty. The little shrines which used to provoke smiles because they seemed like such anachronisms in the heart of the Tokyo skyscraper district, are now viewed with new respect as perhaps more essential to the smooth operations of capitalism than the tall office-buildings themselves. Business can be conducted after all in one-story buildings. But it cannot long endure without social stability, ensured by emotional contentment among the masses.

It is true that George Bernard Shaw, visiting the East, advised the Japanese to rely "on machinery, not bushido." But high business men, quaintly enough, rushed to defend bushido against his criticism; the romantic sentiments so airily discounted by the Irish playwright were, they said, full of economic value. Mr. Koyata Yamamoto, a prominent textile manufacturer, declared that only the old family-system and patriotism made possible a drastic general cut of 50 per cent in wages; this enabled the Japanese textile mills to be remodeled and fitted with new machinery, to compete with those of Lancashire. To give point to his announcement, Mr. Yamamoto gave free lessons in tea-ceremony, ethics, music and religion to his operatives, for as he explained:

> One of the fundamental factors which enabled the Japanese cotton industry to carry out substantial improvements is spiritual. It can be described as the Nippon Spirit . . . And this Spirit is peculiar to Japan alone.

So far, the Japanese merchants think that they have fared well by thriftily preserving the emotions of the past. They have even been able to smile at the over-confident Westerners who, relying entirely upon technical progress and material efficiency, dismissed everything mystical or picturesque in the East as "impediments" to modernization. Now they behold these pep-filled salesmen who once tried to "hustle the East," seeking about with frantic dismay for a mythos of their own, a patriotism, a Fascist symbol, a sentimental slogan, anything to fill the awful void in the Western mass-heart, and create loyalty. The Japanese congratulate themselves upon having saved a genuine feudalism which is richer than Fascist substitutes. But how far Japan can prolong the past is dubious. After all, Europe likewise presented just such a picture of incongruities in the last century, as capitalism grew amid feudal remnants, and modern entrepreneurs consorted with the antediluvian figures of dukes and generals. In the West, the curious mixture of elements proved inflammable. It blew apart with the detonation of the World War.

XXVI

THE APOGEE OF THE INDIVIDUALIST:
1880–1914

DURING THE AMAZING CENTURY stretching from the Napoleonic conflicts to the World War, the size and scope of commercial activities increased so far beyond previous concepts that contemporaries had the utmost difficulty in grasping or describing this expansion. Awed statisticians exhausted their ingenuity in estimates of tonnages and volumes; they draped the moon, figuratively, with telegraph lines, or computed how far the earth's railroads, if laid end to end, would project into interstellar space. Borrowing adjectives from Barnum, they strove to portray the "staggering" dimensions of modern business, and the power of its master, the modern capitalist, the "titan," "king," "colossus" and "glittering man-mountain of gold."

Surveying the advance in wealth and display of wealth between 1837 and 1857, the American real-estate speculator, George Francis Train, expatiated on the changes in society which had taken place in that brief time: marble and brownstone mansions, "gilded churches for gilt-edged sermons," "crinolines, hoops and diamonds, fast horses, and brandy smashes have been introduced *since that day!* . . . The brandy of bubbling speculation has stupefied our reason, and *delirium* tremens has overtaken the nation." But it was after recovery from the world-crash of 1857 that the true "âge d'or" of prosperity and reckless spending dawned upon the Western countries. Then riches were won more rapidly than ever and scattered by a race of parvenus such as the earth had never seen, men and women who came to millions direct from the smithy and washtub, unpracticed in the arts of leisure, but filled with heady delight in their swift success. They snatched at the gaudiest objects before them, and their revelry and rivalry made possible the strange excesses of the "kolossal" in Wilhelminic Berlin, the coarse nabobery in Victorian London, the feverish "danse des millions" in Paris, and the raucous competition of Bonanza Kings in Gilded Age America.

By the 1880's, the world presented a spectacle of rejoicing and parading among business families of many races, comparable to the Renaissance when the oligarch had celebrated his gains with sumptuous pageantry; or to the colder glitter of the *ancien régime,* in which the magnificent monopolist took his pleasure. For the third time, the business man had reached a high peak of success; and for the moment the stability of his riches seemed perfectly assured. Like his predecessors, he could see no possibility of failure before him, but solemnly believed in the permanence of his conquests and virtues and the essential soundness of his trolley-car stocks. When he built châteaux, accordingly, it was not merely out of vainglory, but with a sincere trust in the future: he made his staircases wide and his ballrooms high to hold the fawning courtiers of his children's children.

This third period was by far the briefest; scarcely more than a generation was given to all this exultation before the cataclysm of the World War. Unlike the oligarch and the monopolist before him, the nineteenth-century capitalist lacked a chance to mellow his riches over a long space of years, to refine his tastes, and deepen the gilt to gold. Yet, while his celebration was so short, he had much more wealth to display as long as it lasted.

Never had there been similar riches in the world. By 1900 Paris had a hundred men with revenues of more than a million francs, where there had scarcely been a dozen such in the *ancien régime,* and not half a dozen in the whole sweep of the Middle Ages in France. Still France was far from the richest land in the nineteenth century; an earlier estimate, at the opening of the 1880's, on the basis of fortune, not income, and in dollars, not francs, gave France only seventy-five millionaires as compared to one hundred in Germany and Austria, one hundred in America, two hundred in England, besides fifty each in Russia and India, and one hundred twenty-five more elsewhere. Below these seven hundred millionaires of the world, extended a great plateau of rich families whose fortunes were hardly to be computed in an age so heedless of income taxes or passports.

Not only was this wealth vaster, but it was sapped by fewer claims, whether of Church, State, community or clan. In the past, feudal lords had supported retinues of clansmen and warriors for protection and power-display; now that the State assumed police-duties and the rich man avoided the appearance of open power, this was no longer necessary. He could spend his riches upon himself, if he chose. Besides, the chief luxuries, such as sugar and silk, had been cheapened to a ridiculously low figure, and the items which bulked so large in a Renaissance budget were negligible in that of the new nabob. Feeding fewer dependents on less expensive dishes, the share of food in the expenditure of the rich sank rapidly: in 1788, the duc de la Tremoille spent 90,000 out of 286,000 francs, nearly a third of his income, merely for food;

but a Croesus of 1888, no matter what exalted ideas of cuisine he might have, would never approach that proportion. And there was a further saving in wardrobe: the modern rich man does not adorn his person with brocades and plumes, or costume a throng of bodyguards and lackeys with hauberks or wigs and other elaborate equipment. In the nineteenth century, this fashion display had in the main to be concentrated upon the solitary, if ample, hour-glass figure of the millionaire's wife.

At the same time, the old standards and traditions which had hitherto guided parvenus were weakening. The tastes of the agrarian, once so noble and imposing, appeared for the first time ridiculous; the advance of urban industrialism had left agriculture the weaker party, dependent upon the will of the railroader or the speculator in a distant grain-pit; and the Cato of the furrows had become a figure of fun. Royalty, basing its power upon the swords of the agrarians, but also dependent upon commercial loans, no longer dared to frown down a millionaire; instead, it promoted business, in the manner of Albert the Good or the Emperor Meiji, or benevolently encouraged its citizens, as did Louis-Philippe: "Enrichissez-vous." The few remaining autocrats, sultans or pashas, had become entangled in the toils of financiers; only in a remote corner of the world could they still assert their primacy, as did a native prince of India, who harnessed two bankers to his chariot and drove them himself around the streets of his principal city.

Nor was the claim of religion to regulate the gaining or spending of wealth so confidently proclaimed as before. In 1830 the Roman Church reversed its age-old stand, admitting that, in some circumstances, the charging and taking of interest might be consistent with the soul's salvation. Closing the thousand-year quarrel with the business man over usury, the Church made at least a truce with the progressing capitalism; and by 1905, as the Montagnini papers disclosed, M. de Rothschild had become papal banker. Though Methodism in a sense took up the struggle where Catholicism temporarily dropped it, all the Churches accepted business aid for foreign missions, and, in the East, however unwillingly at times, helped to open the doors for trade, insisting upon modesty and Manchester cottons; moreover, none of them carried the scholastic doctrine of the "just price" to the heathen.

Had the Church continued to defend her right to restrain the selfish instincts and ameliorate human strife, in the interests of a supra-national Christian commonwealth, that would have involved a broader discussion of values than Victorian bishops were willing to launch. And there was little use in mentioning emotion, mystery, revelation or other "unreasonable" elements, so long as the scientists formed a hollow square about the business man, defending laissez faire in the animal and human world. The scientists were still cock-sure about their newly formulated "laws," and were charging into "superstitions" hampering the cotton-brokers of their day; with Huxley, they carried Manchesterism into biology, seeking to prove that jungle law was the will of God for the perfection of the human species. In effect, they were assailing the old Christian view of a planned society; science and religion were quarreling over the body of the business man. And for the moment, the formidable logic of the evolutionists seemed unanswerable; the ministers of the Anglican Church drew back, and even the loftiest bishops were reduced to sputtering and gasping about "monkey ancestry" in the face of Huxley's smiling calm. None could then have fore-told how soon confusion would overtake the scientists in turn; how, growing silent and absorbed, they would leave the public arena and turn to stare through their instruments at baffling new phenomena, finding errors in Newton and inexplicable hitches in the universe.

Before the gospel of Manchesterism, the doctrine of the "cheap and shoddy," handicraft standards were dissolving. Some conservative firms stood out against the tide, maintaining a degree of prestige, or yielded only with distaste, as did the Chocolate King, Cadbury, who finally allowed the public to have the sickly stuff it preferred to his best Dutch blends. Some newspapers refused to cater to the lowest and largest publics; some stores kept quality goods; some manufacturers, in the Far East especially, refused to adulterate their purest silks. But the times were against this attitude and everywhere artisans were being demoralized under the pressure of hustling bargainers who had no tradition to preserve.

At this period of breakdown in old values, the business man had himself very little to offer. The Renaissance individualist had won his emancipation by pointing to the Greek and Roman classics; these not only supported the individual but taught him how to face success and celebrate his triumph. The modern individualist on the contrary was buttressed chiefly by science, which had no use for art at that time, or by a puritanical religion which disapproved of leisure. His philosophy of rugged individualism was ideal for getting money, but was silent on the subject of spending. Spending had become, therefore, not only secularized and private, as never before, but planless.

It was this lack of pattern and plan which made the nineteenth century seem so selfish, so money-mad to those who looked backward. Men had indeed worshiped *pulchra Laverna,* the old Roman goddess of profit, through many ages, quite as earnestly, but never before had all scales of values been so overtipped by sheer mass of gold; never before had birth, breeding and office counted for so little; nor had the ideals of seigneurial dignity, aesthetic proportion or religious asceticism, ever seemed so pallid as in the glare of the Gilded Age. As yet, though the business man gave to charity and good works, he had not discovered the more recent formulae of "service to the public," "loyalty to the firm," or "the responsibility of great wealth." He had shed the old humanitarian robes and found no new covering ideology. This age, between the collapse of ancient moralities and the building up of "business ethics," was one of candid covetousness.

Certainly the business man was not more callous or selfish than the unscrupulous pagans of the Medicean Age, or the ribald financiers of the Voltairean Era. Indeed he was much more apt to be humane, devout in a Quaker or Methodist manner, modestly aware of his humble origins and often a bit intimidated by his own good luck. He gave enormously to churches, charity and education, far more than his predecessors, but as a private individual and according to a private whim. It was not in a public capacity or following a clear, if absurd, social model. Hence his actions were not hallowed by institutions, like those of bygone successful men. When the mediaeval or Renaissance oligarchs indulged in pageantry, it appeared as a community-demonstration in which the city-society took part. In the *ancien régime*, rich men seemed to be imitating the pattern set by kings, and so even their grossest displays were forgiven and their excesses only merged into the general romantic glamor around the State. It was otherwise in the nineteenth century, when millionaires outshone kings and spending was neither regulated nor sanctified by superior institutions, models or traditions; the business man's sins or generosity alike were too personal and accidental to appear magnificent.

THE LAVERNIANS RELAXED

In animalic gusto, at least, the three periods of spending—the sixteenth, eighteenth and nineteenth centuries—were akin. Conceivably, the Gilded Age was the last in which wealth could be so heartily enjoyed, without the dread of popular disapproval or the stale taste of boredom. If mechanization up to 1914 was indeed producing tension and nervous exhaustion was rife among Americans, there was still plenty of leisure for spacious dining and long drives in the park; fireworks and circuses continued to amuse generations which the cinema, radio and swift motorcars had not yet made blasé. Nor were the pangs of conscience disturbing. Though the new capitalist, taken as a type, was kinder than the dissolute cynics of the Restoration Period, for instance, or the slave-dealers of old Nantes, he felt optimistic about the future; even the most radical reformers among business men, like Owen or Engels, were almost as sure that all wrongs could be adjusted automatically, some day, as were those who left everything to Nature, Evolution and Providence. There seemed no reason why the business man should not go on forever like this, the glossy and God-appointed ruler of the habitable earth. What need had he to elaborate plans for government, when the stars fought for him? Why should he direct his destinies, when the ultimate victory was ordained by scientific law? Who would be so foolish as to reject the full platter before him?

The atmosphere of confidence lay thick and rich upon the age. The neo-Lavernians, the worshipers of Gain, were quite sure that the world, whether by Nature or Reform, would eventually be made over according to their desires, and all peoples brought under the same religion and moral code. A civilization built up of such various components as French styles, British parliamentarism and utilitarian philosophy, German organization and scientific research, American plumbing and "efficiency," would cover the earth, while the East should provide "Nippes" for the mantelpiece. Prophets depicted mankind, shaking off its ancient sloth, marching toward a wonderful dawn in which every nation would have a Black Triangle as busy as England's, and trains would arrive and depart on schedule between cities so nearly identical as to make travel for the purpose of sight-seeing quite superfluous.

The happy radiance of that bygone age, so securely wrapped in its Victorian dream, has been ideally captured in verses by the elder Rockefeller, read at the opening of a Poets' Room in Rockefeller Center:

> *I was early taught to work as well as play;*
> *My life has been one long, happy holiday,*
> *Full of work, full of play—*
> *I dropped the worry on the way—*
> *And God was good to me every day.*

Naturally, each milestone of this march toward perfection had to be celebrated by jubilees, ovations, and world-expositions. The opening of canals and ports, the laying of cables and the launching of liners, all proceeded amid wild huzzas, gas-flares, the waving of banners and draining of loving cups. Gargantuan banquets were held, as was natural in an age when business enterprise had cheapened the most luxurious foods, improved champagne and most wines, and brought the rarities of every clime together. At such feasts, warmed by "deafening cheers" and successive bumpers of "bubbly," the self-made business man relaxed his old tradition of taciturnity and, without waiting for Samuel Smiles to explain the secrets of his success, gave away the mystery himself.

After-dinner oratory assumed strange and wonderful forms on these occasions. Cotton-spinners of Lyons waxed eloquent in references to the sacred soil, until no eye was left dry; in a bluffer and broader British manner, George Hudson, the Railway King, introduced by an ecstatic chairman who cried, "Mr. Hudson is just the sort of man who *ought* to be rich," invited the boosters of Sutherland to indulge in visions: "Gentlemen, there is something in imagination. I don't say that it ought to govern us; but . . . let imagination have a little play, and let us imagine we are going to be the Liverpool and Manchester of the world."—On the other side of the ocean, the Americans at length found their voices also, and eventually, through the banker, Jacob Schiff, introduced the Japanese to speaking at their meals, thus breaking through the reticence of the "silent East."

In intervals between banquets and expositions, the millionaires gave balls, preferably in costume. In aristocratic England, they dressed up as cooks and chambermaids. The desire to masquerade in robes of royalty was much stronger in America, where there was none, and in France, especially after the Emperors were discarded. Even the fantasies of Newport parvenus, in that line, were outdone by the make-believe of the French, when there was no longer a court to set the social tone: they garbed themselves as Oriental potentates and were brought to the ballroom in palanquins borne by Nubians to the clangor of gongs.

This sort of incessant celebration by pageantry and festival was reminiscent of the Renaissance, and there were reminders of the *ancien régime* as well. The horsiness of the rich was a hangover from that age of aristocratic amusements; the hunting, coaching, racing and parades of turn-outs in Hyde or Central Parks and the Champs Elysées, were reminiscent of the earlier efforts of a Fugger to prove himself eligible for the society of dukes by writing a learned work, in fact the first learned work, on Hippology.

The gambling at extravagant new casinos, as in Monte Carlo, and the formal spectacles of diamond horseshoes at the operas, costly fashion battles, continued rococo methods of competition in display, led by imposing women like Lillian Russell, often connected with the theater, who could be trusted to guide puzzled millionaires in the disposal of superfluous funds. The homage paid to such personages was often remarkable. The coldly correct Philip Hone, merchant Mayor of New York, remained calm through the great conflagration which almost consumed the city, and allowed no intemperate word to creep into his diary—except when he saw Fanny Elssler. Heening, the Australian millionaire, draped Anna Robinson with $160,000 worth of diamonds. But it remained for a German, in whom the fantasy of mediaeval chivalry best survived, to display the most imagination: a Berlin banker, by the name of Hirschfeld, one day appeared in trousers patterned in an extremely broad check, and in each vacant square was a tiny image of the delightful dancer, Pepita.

If such resemblances to the past may be heaped up, the spending of the new rich did not exhaust itself in pageantry and masquerade, as in the Renaissance, or in hunting and spectacles, as among early courtiers; it was much more than ever before concentrated upon the home and personal comforts. Private spending, rather than public display, was the characteristic of the age. This, to be sure, was an old trait of business men; they had used riches to achieve comfort, whereas the seigneur sought self-advertisement instead: the aim of the one was to pamper himself, the aim of the other to exhibit his pomp. But generally before, the business man had united the two, and had been controlled in disposing of his wealth by the models of feudal grandeur. Now, for the first time, he was free to indulge his love of the Home to its fullest extent.

Through the ages, the business man had endeavored to find comfortable beds, delicate food and some mode of conveyance less irksome than horseback-riding. Not for him the hardships of the lord, the chilly castle, the hard saddle and heavy armor; he had desired a pleasant existence for himself and his family, ever since commercial Lydians first lolled on couches at home, and were carried downtown, still lolling, in litters. But he had always been a bit restrained by the severe taste of the Roman nobleman's cold atrium, the Greek agrarians' frugality, the feudal lord's disdain for the soft "peppersack." Now for the first time, he produced a home that was unlike anything seigneurial, that was all comfort, and that made the palaces of a previous time seem unbearable by contrast. Today the simplest clerk in a business office would be miserably unhappy, and probably fall mortally ill of a croup, were he to spend a winter month in the gilded cells of unheated and unwashed Old Versailles.

This love of comfort had brought peculiarly demoralizing effects upon business men in the past, whereas luxury left unharmed the feudal lord, for the extravagances of the aristocrat did not impair his lust for action; no matter how many louis d'or he flung away upon wine and women, he was ever ready for the trumpet of war. A slighter sum, however, invested in a good bed and a stove could have much more devastating results upon the burgher's morale. In their torpidity, the Lydians and the Carthaginians forgot how to defend their gains from the hungry soldiery of less satiated lands, and Renaissance city-fathers, growing unused to martial handiwork, hired condottieri who became tyrants. The temptation had now become infinitely stronger. Never had the business man leaned back in so soft a self-indulgence, feeling that he could afford to relax his vigilance over his hired tools, the armies and navies—until the World War broke in upon his privacy.

At the early stages of this growing comfort, a warning was issued by de Tocqueville, addressed to America but generally applicable. Men who lived so daintily, he declared, would soon forget the charms of action and over-emphasize its risks; they would find it harder and harder to rouse themselves from smothering ease:

> The men of the eighteenth century scarcely knew this kind of passion for comfort, which is the mother of slavery . . . a passion which is compatible with honesty, but makes heroism impossible, and all whose greatness consists in producing men of great respectability and no public spirit.

The Victorian, however, had a special reason for clinging to the Home, because it was a haven of security, as business became increasingly subjected to the uncertainties of competition and the strain of great enterprise. By building up insurance companies and the Home, the modern individualist strove to provide against the nerve-shattering effects of individualism. There, he could feed his optimism: behind the heavy portières and paravents of his ornate parlor, the noise of the jungle law in operation outside seemed muffled and far away, even if his feet rested on a tiger-skin.

SPECULATING AND SPENDING

Undoubtedly there was a marked difference in the manner of spending wealth between those who made it slowly, and in industry, and those who won it overnight in speculation. The former were loath to part with pennies acquired so painfully and they tended to retire from public gaze, into the home. The latter were not only more reckless but were under the necessity of speedily acquiring credit for themselves, and this they could do best by ostentation and alliances with the aristocrats, or, as the age phrased it, putting up a "front."

There is no easy way of determining which element had actually the larger wealth. Certainly the speculators made so much splash that they gave the tone to the whole age; but a number of the greatest fortunes in Europe were built on solider foundations. Krupp was richer than any German of his day, except Rothschild, and he was the plainest of men, caring nothing for display. In England, the richest man in 1936 was Joseph Rank, a miller, wealthier indeed than the Caesars, but engaged in the same occupation as the old Roman, Eurysaces, who left the most imposing ancient mortuary monument to a business man.

Rank, throughout his long life, was so modest about his missionary efforts, his charities and general style of living that few people even in his own country were aware of his importance. Following him in point of fortune, the shipping-magnate, Sir John Ellerman, left behind him over £40,000,000; but he was almost as little known; and the only item of interest revealed about his heir is the fact that he seemed fond of keeping porcupines as pets.

In the first decades of the nineteenth century, the self-made entrepreneurs of the simple, cautious *Samuel Smiles* type held the field, men who rose from the humblest beginnings with considerable effort, like August Borsig, the German mechanic, mighty builder of locomotives; and James Baird, the Scotch iron-master, who expanded from a single tiny shaft to a wide control over the metal trades and became "the wealthiest commoner of England" in his day. Such characters were apt to retain the frugal habits of a lifetime for a great many in England were Quakers; and the most they aspired to was retirement to an imposing estate, like Baird's dwelling reputed to cost two million pounds, or that of Samuel Cunliffe-Lister, the spinner, whose country home was surrounded by 35,000 acres. Some of them, like Lister, the first peer to come direct from the factory, accepted titles; others refrained even from that, like Bass, of Bass's Ale, who refused to become a peer— better "first in the beerage, than last in the peerage," as he phrased it himself.

A great many of these figures, who had had to tussle for success, did not lose the bitter memory, and so felt obligated to make some accounting to the public. Thus the department-store men, Boucicault in France, Wanamaker in America, and later Selfridge in England, became known for their emphasis upon morality and ethics; so did various shoe men, Johnson, Filene, and Bata. The candy men, Lombart in France, Cadbury in England and Hershey in America, felt impelled to use a part of their wealth in making model communities, as did the industrialists, Titus Salt, creator of "Saltaire," and Zeiss in Jena. Such lists could of course be enormously extended. Flamboyant flaunting of luxury came in rather with the speculators, whose activities presently, with the turn of the century, began to overshadow those of the old-style entrepreneurs.

The new race of speculators was of a different stamp. The early manipulators of railroads and canals, for instance, like Hudson, Gould and Péreire, were known for extravagantly pretentious mansions. That of Hudson was the first exhibition of overweening nabobery in Victorian London. Not only was the Newport mansion of Gould an incredible spectacle, but the palais of Anna Gould in Paris exceeded it; her first home she aptly called "only a warehouse," promising the next would be "like the staircase at the Opéra, only bigger." Still grander was the Paris hôtel of the financier from Bordeaux, Isaac Péreire, who floated the Crédit mobilier. He seems to have been a bit dashed by it himself: leading awed guests through his salon, where the gilt coruscated in a thousand forms under enormous gas-chandeliers, he would murmur in modest deprecation: "There is too much gold in here." And waving a hand toward his gallery of Flemish masters, he was wont to add, "simply": "These are my true treasures."

Naturally the real-estate speculators exhibited the same trend to the spectacular in domiciles. At the opening of the century, large cities were few; but within three generations, the million-headed hives of to-day had been created. All over the world men began to put up imitations of Western industrial centers: Lodz became the Polish Manchester, and Hankow the Chinese Manchester. One after the other, huge metropolises appeared, much alike in formlessness and general unfitness for human habitation, since all were erected with an avidity for profits that ignored welfare or permanence. All had their construction-booms in which miles of gingerbread façades and acres of insanitary tenements were spread out at top speed, to the enrichment not only of the contractors, but often of the aristocratic landlords also who cooperated with them—dukes of London, daimyos of Tokyo, princes of Vienna. In the latter city, one of the most monstrous scandals of the sort exploded in the 1870's: the builders had bought up enough land, at ten times the normal price, to enlarge Vienna to three times its existing extent, and built gigantic rococo palaces upon it. Yet Vienna, unlike most other places at that time, did not grow, and soon the palaces were left untenanted.

The growth of insurance companies throughout the period was likewise accompanied by gaudy display, often intended to cover fraud. The ball of James Hazen Hyde, it will be recalled, capped the extravagance of the "idle rich," in New York, and wrecked the Gilded Age. Earlier, however, insurance companies had been associated with pomp. In New York in the 1860's, according to Fowler, these concerns "had a *hankering* for an imposing office" and tried to inspire confidence by their "solid mahogany doors," frequently the only solid thing about them, and the big iron chest always in view, supposed to contain tremendous assets. In London, as Dickens relates, monumental façades were erected by similar firms, including his immortal "Anglo-Bengalee Company." As he describes it:

The offices were newly plastered, newly papered, newly countered . . . newly fitted up in every way, with goods that were substantial and expensive, and designed (like the company) to last. Business! Look at the green ledgers with red backs . . . the court guides, directories, day-books, almanacks, letter-boxes, weighing-machines for letters, rows of buckets for dashing out a conflagration at the first spark, and saving the immense wealth in notes and bonds belonging to the company; look at the iron safes, the clock, the office seal . . . Solidity! Look at the massive blocks of marble in the chimney-pieces, and the gorgeous parapet on the top of the house! Publicity! Why, the Anglo-Bengalee Disinterested Loan and Life-Insurance Company is painted on the very coal-scuttles . . . Lest with all these proofs and confirmations, any man should be suspicious of the Anglo-Bengalee Disinterested Loan and Life-Insurance Company . . . there was a porter on the premises—a wonderful creature, in a vast red waistcoat and a short-tailed pepper-and-salt coat—who carried more conviction to the minds of sceptics than the whole establishment without him.

The creator of this Disinterested Company was the very pattern of the Victorian fraud-floater: "He had a world of jet-black shining hair upon his head, upon his cheeks, upon his chin, upon his upper lip . . . Flowers of gold and blue, and green and blushing red, were on his waistcoat; precious chains and jewels sparkled on his breast; his fingers, clogged with brilliant rings, were as unwieldy as summer flies but newly rescued from a honey-pot." This florid creature, "satanic, gallant, military Tigg," was at his best in a jovial mood, behind locked doors, "in conference":

"What," asked the secretary, bursting into another laugh, "What will be the paid-up capital according to the next prospectus?"

"A figure of two, and as many oughts after it as the printer can get into the same line," replied his friend, "Ha, ha!" . . .

"What a chap you are!" exclaimed David, admiringly . . .

"Say genius, David, genius." . . .

"Ha, ha," cried the secretary. . . . "When I look at you, and think of your property in Bengal being—ha, ha, ha!—being amenable—to all claims upon the company: when I look at you and think of that, you might tickle me into fits by waving the feather of a pen at me. Upon my soul, you might!"

"It's a devilish fine property," said Tigg Montague, "to be amenable to any claims. The preserve of tigers alone is worth a mint of money, David."

David could only reply in the intervals of his laughter, "Oh, what a chap you are!" and so continued to laugh, and hold his sides, and wipe his eyes, for some time, without offering any other observation.

The operations of these and other financial speculators increased with the spread of cables, telegraph and telephone lines, linking Paris over the Pyrenees and the Indian Ocean to Bombay and binding Vienna, Moscow and Tiflis with London and New York. More variegated herds of innocent sheep might be rounded up through these agencies: a speculator in London could rip the wool and hides from victims in every corner of the earth in an hour or two. Still so irrepressible was the confidence that, despite every experience of that kind, the circles of amateur gamblers seemed never to shrink. In the sanguine interval between the crises of 1857 and 1873, the "founding-fever," as the Germans called it, was well-nigh universal; in the years 1871–72 alone, it is estimated that new firms with a total capital of more than twenty-eight billion gold francs sprang up in Germany, France, England, Austria and America. Gold-miners, bubble-blowers, marketers of new inventions, plied the public. And it responded with Renaissance optimism, or shriveled in a night before the blast. Péreire, trying to explain why the public fortunes of France had fallen away some $200,000,000 in five months in 1857, remarked: "The budget of fear almost equals the budget of France!"

As the century wore on, the players in the pits and exchanges of the world began to climb upon the shoulders of other types of business men, gathering into their hands the rewards of all fields. Then it was seen that, though the chess-board had been enlarged to world dimensions, the rules of the game, despite the name of "modern capitalism," were not altogether new. Many of the pieces and moves were after all familiar. And despite the power of the "early capitalist entrepreneur," with his Puritan virtues, the ultimate master of the situation was a man whose predecessors were in control of Florence, old Rome, and Hammurabi's Babylon: the financier. And through all the ages, he retained the same tastes; he remained more flamboyant than the green-grocer, the shipper, the merchant tailor and the weaver.

The overshadowing, socially as well as economically, of other commercial types by the speculative genius was apparent everywhere before the 1880's arrived. In the United States, for instance, the discreet traditions of Back Bay and Bowling Green were quite buried under the notoriety surrounding the speculators, such as Jim Fisk, or the later "Chicago Crowd" which invaded the East with a whoop. The efforts of New York's "Four Hundred" to close the gates against the newcomers were in vain; the new wealth could not be shut out. And about the same period, a somewhat similar change was occurring in Victorian England.

Up to the middle of the century, the manufacturing North of England preserved its atmosphere of grim moral purpose; and so long as its iron-masters and spinners held sway over the country, their Puritanic code of manners prevailed and the inhibitions which had originated in the provincial towns of the North became so general as to be called Victorian. But this Northern morality relaxed, as wealthy families moved to London, yielding to the insidious gaiety of the Southern aristocracy. Brokers became respectable, thinks Mottram, when Edward VII surrounded himself with representatives of finance, the Rothschilds and Sassoons. Presently, inroads were made on the North itself by nabobs with treasures from Africa or India and a splendid manner caught directly from foreign potentates. Thackeray, in his "Newcomes," pictures the effect upon the Manchester region of *Sir Barnes Newcome*, whose Indian riches are symbolized by the silver cocoa-tree on his dinner-table, and whose magnificence dazzles the population—until the "Bundelcund Bank" blows up. The process of demoralization was hastened by the speculators, each more gorgeous than the last, gulling the public of England with few intermissions.

It was more dangerous to defraud the English public than the American, certainly. Whereas a mere admonition, or at most an "investigation," threatened the "robber baron" of the Gilded Age in the United States, his like in England faced severer penalties: Ernest Terah Hooley, the rollicking rogue, was twice imprisoned; the building speculator, Jabez Spencer Balfour, got fourteen years in jail; Whitaker Wright, author of the fanciful Ivanhoe Mining Company, took cyanide of potassium in court. After the smash of 1824, the elegant banker, Fauntleroy, was hanged outside Newgate Prison. Twenty years later, the dapper Sir John Paul was deported, and the forger, Watts, only escaped a similar fate by hanging himself in the prison lavatory. As a matter of fact, a crew of American adventurers, led by the devout George Bidwell, who tried to make themselves at home in London, received penal servitude for life. Only one American proved too "sharp" for the City; that was H. H. Warner, patent medicine salesman, who gathered considerable loot by an expedient which afterwards remained famous as the Warner Bear Squeeze. But this was rather a case of shrewd practice than of palpable iniquity.

Nevertheless, though a British rogue might be in keener danger of trial than the American, he was more welcome to enjoy himself up to the last hour. At any moment, he might have to escape abroad in a black beard like Mr. Bevan, or take prussic acid like James White. In the meantime, he was free to sit in Parliament or a mayor's chair, spend a fortune on racing studs and champagne, as Bottomley did, and cultivate the manners of a "sporting peer," as far as so-called public opinion was concerned. He could swagger with greater impunity than the American, even if he found it riskier to swindle.

Most of these adventurers surrounded themselves with the best society, in order to keep up their credit. Hooley was one of the first to recognize the uses of the aristocracy in England. He not only kept noble company and was well on the way to a baronetcy when he was arrested; he also knew how to make use of titles and, as he explained in his "Confessions," he put decoy dukes on his boards of directors to snare investors—the "guinea-pig system":

> I got hold of an earl and said, "Now look here, I'll give you £10,000 for a Duke, and £5,000 apiece for a couple of ordinary peers." "Right you are, my boy," he replied breezily.

The same system was already well-known and practiced on the Continent where "revelations" were periodically made, showing the golden stains which spread through the topmost tiers of society. It was familiar to Vienna where the aristocracy was very ready to lend its prestige to all sorts of schemes; the world-crisis of 1873 started in a crack of a Viennese credit-institution (repeated in 1929), by means of which, as a later trial revealed, ministers and noble lords had put millions into their pockets, and left little for good materials to be used in the railroads and bridges they were supposed to be building.

In Germany, also, the rather simple and "solide" merchants such as Hansemann or manufacturers such as Krupp were outshone by financiers: by Felix Sommerfeld, for instance, whose banquets, the most fabulous yet seen in that land of good eating, united noblemen and artists around the host, who played Maecenas—until he had to shoot himself. Another would-be patron of the arts was Henry Strousberg, in the 1860's, the first great speculator of that country, dazzling everybody by châteaux and painting-collections, before he ventured too far in Rumanian railroads. Again, there were the pious bankers, Schulz, Romeick, Sanden and Terlinden, who played on the religious sensibilities of the Empress, thus winning entry into Potsdam society with a view to finding victims. Gerhard Terlinden set above his office-door in golden letters, "Honest in Trade, Christian in Life." Sanden erected a statue of Christ in his garden and he and his wife gave spiritualist séances for Potsdam nobility. After the crash of 1900, when customers lost every pfennig and clamored for relief, the Sandens imperturbably emphasized the efficacy of prayer.

The union of high finance and aristocracy was only different in France in that it was not a characteristic of the modern epoch, but a survival of the *ancien régime*. It was merely a continuation of one of France's oldest traditions when speculators, abetted by the noblesse, dazzled the public—Mirès, for example, the poor journalist who mysteriously acquired the control of banks, railroads, and gas companies, announced a capital of seven hundred millions, allied his daughter to the princely family of Polignac and had everybody gasping; then he suddenly went bankrupt and was arrested. Equally in the grand old manner was the explosion of the Union générale of Eugen Bontoux, a little later, whose railroad schemes, extending over Eastern Europe, involved the clergy and high aristocracy. From their longer experience in such matters, the French knew how to do these things best.

Relatively, the speculation in France was small compared to that in other countries. As an American stockbroker from Wall Street, Fowler, who had seen Gould and Drew at work, observed in the 1880's, there were even more gesticulation and other forms of frenzy to be seen in the Paris Bourse than anywhere else, though it was all about nothing; the wild-eyed men were just passing around five hundred francs' worth of Chemin de Fer du Nord—"Pshaw! So the old women in the Rue St. Honoré sell you a plate of fried potatoes—price one sou." That is true, and yet the style of the splendid old financiers, the Paris brothers, John Law, Sam Bernard, remained to lend a special glamor to even the most picayune "affaires" in France. If behind the Anglo-Saxon countries in great fortunes—millionaires were actually scarcer in Paris in 1890 than in Cleveland, Ohio—Paris employed her funds so skillfully that she seemed the most dazzling city in the world, the supreme capital of fashion, luxury and enjoyment. So it was necessary for the mightiest Americans, and for Englishmen as well, to learn from the French how to spend their millions.

Pathetically poor, beside the "queens" of Saratoga and Newport, was the Frenchwoman, but she had not forgotten the arts of the ingenious Pompadour, and she made more out of such wealth as her husband possessed. Only she would first have thought of appearing in flame-red coats with cut-glass buttons as big as butter-plates; and when she did, her sisters all over the world were smitten with awe. They could only compete in quantity, as did the American millionairess of Newport, who ordered from Paris a hundred costumes, complete with millinery and boas, for a single week-end on a yacht. Nonetheless, it was necessary for Anna Gould to marry a Parisian, Count Boni de Castellane, to find out how really to wear such creations.

Through wit and tradition, therefore, rather than gold, Paris became the arbiter over the international pageantry of the "newcomes." Paris had changed least of all, perhaps, in spirit, since the eighteenth century; she was still the citadel of feudal-financial formality. Her leadership in fashion and frolic meant the guidance into ancient ruts of the teeming ambitions in the new age of modern capitalism. It meant the worship of an anachronism by men whose business activities were revolutionizing human life. Winning their wealth through blast-furnaces, locomotives and iron liners, they were prevented from seeking equally novel ways of spending it; instead, following French dictates, they squeezed themselves into tight kid gloves, struggled to memorize "purée" and "hors d'œuvre" and to balance on the edge of rococo gilt chairs; thus restricted, they became embarrassed, then bored, and felt positively relieved when they went bankrupt and could begin money-making again.

Through French tyranny over modes, oddly coupled with the puritanic morality of the Anglo-Saxon countries, the whole age acquired a curious stiffness of manner, a pompous air that seemed falsely assumed, in view of the raw gusto of the "newcomes" and their essential naïveté of heart and mind. Their display was less purposeful than in any previous age, and that is why the crowded drawing-rooms, the galleries of dead masters, lighted by the harsh glare of gas, arouse no emotion among their descendants but surprise. The impression left by the epoch is, in sum, that acknowledged by M. Péreire in his own salon: *il y a trop d'or ici.*

GENIUS AND BOURGEOIS

Partly because of this meaningless pretense, the relations of the business man to the artist were never more unsatisfactory. Though the business man was the dominant figure of the nineteenth century, master of miraculous inventions and riches beyond count—though he had apparently vanquished his oldest foes, Church, State, the soldier, the aristocrat, the agrarian and, through Science, the intellectual—though he was preparing to remold human society from the Thames and Ganges to the Mississippi—still, try as he would, he could not get his portrait painted.

Previously, artists had always managed to shed a certain charm or dignity about the homeliest grocers of Bruges or butter-dealers of Amsterdam or the grossest of plutocrats in Paris, such as Sam Bernard, the Huguenot tax-farmer. Now before this new type, painters dropped their brushes in despair. Only a very few good semblances of business men were executed, some of them by a nobleman, von Kalckreuth, who portrayed Hamburg patricians. But in general, the artists turned away to limn the toilers in factories, miners and peasants. With a sympathy unapproached in art up to this time, men like Millet and Liebermann depicted the acts of labor; those more advanced in technique discovered how to paint the Machine itself, and gloated upon whirling cogs and the light breaking and glancing on myriad surfaces. Workers and mechanisms, bridges and belching chimneys, were represented with power. But not a soul knew what to do with the master of the machines, employer of the workers, and supreme controller of the Victorian universe himself—the business individualist.

Nor was he luckier with the writers. Despite his technical triumphs and his brand-new name, the capitalist entrepreneur could not for a moment startle the literati of the century into taking him for a fresh species of mankind. They persisted in regarding him as the eternal blundering parvenu, who had reappeared in all ages for at least two thousand years, now in classic Rome as *Trimalchio*, in Renaissance Italy as *Pantalone*, and in Baroque France as the *Bourgeois Gentilhomme*. One might have expected that figure of fun to die out in France, at least; Molière's comic *M. Jourdain* was created to amuse French courtiers, convulsed by the antithesis of bourgeois and *gentilhomme* in the very title. But even after the courtiers went to the guillotine, and the bourgeois dominated France, the merry parvenu lived on. The Genius used him as the foil for his own exceeding perfections—and made the bourgeois pay heavily to laugh at himself.

Indeed, at the very close of the period under review, in 1914, appeared the most melodious representation of the immortal theme: the opera, "Ariadne auf Naxos." The librettist, von Hofmannsthal, came from a rich Jewish financier's family in Vienna, while the composer, Richard Strauss, married into one of Munich's best "Aryan" beer-brewing families. Between them they concocted a fantastic vision of "the richest man of Vienna," who wants to have a grand tragedy performed simultaneously with a clowning show. The *Genius*, hero of the opera, is persuaded by the pretty soprano to debauch his art, and he agrees to mingle the noble strains of *Ariadne's* sorrow with the swift tumbling of *Harlequin*. The "richest man" and his guests are shown applauding on the sidelines, while the hero all but expires of grief.

Gradually, the literary type of the parvenu assumed more solemn aspects (as in Ibsen's *Peer Gynt*), and was developed into full symbolic height. The German, Karl Marx, coming from a land hardly as yet turned to business, learned to hate the new unregulated capitalism of England, and pinned responsibility for everything wrong in the world upon the bourgeois. The bourgeois retained a certain humorous aspect when he became *Babbitt* in America. Then in Russia he took on the terrifying lineaments of the Antichrist. There the Bourgeois was detested, as by Marx, because he was the unfamiliar, wicked alien who was bringing suspicious artificialities into a largely rustic society.

Such a cleavage as developed between Bourgeois and Genius was not due, as is often thought, merely to the former's neglect of Art. On the contrary, business men provided nourishment for art in this century of munificent endowments of museums and libraries, marked by the mushroom growth of printing and engraving, which opened mass-markets to artistic production. Instead of condemning beauty entirely, the business man did a very great deal to restore it to the world.

The pitiable state of the arts after 1815 was due quite as much to the war-machine of Napoleon as to the steam-machine which hurt handicrafts. As the flood of revolutionary warfare ebbed, leaving much of the splendor of the Continent in ruins, a state of barbarism existed in many parts of Europe. Consequently, as the machine was introduced, manufacturers had difficulty in procuring adequate designs—in France, for instance, where the whole Colbertian edifice of art-schools had been razed by the Revolution.

It was not the outraged Artist who first tried to reform the ugly products of the Machine. In point of priority, the business man has the better claim. As early as 1750, manufacturers of Edinburgh, Dublin and London were investigating the pattern-problem; Manchester organized a study of the situation in the 1830's; in the 1840's a commission examined 56,000 English designs and found not one hundred which showed the slightest signs of originality, a fact viewed with alarm by the manufacturers, aware that the Continent might yet beat their machines with craftsmen. Under private and governmental auspices, schools and museums were opened, with such effect that, two decades later, the country's wares were selling in foreign markets by virtue of good design as well as cheapness. And then, after the crass materialists had been shouting for better craftsmanship for a century, the artists themselves began to campaign for more beauty in mechanical output; Morris Craftsmen exhibited in 1877, and the Ruskin Guild of Handicrafts in 1880.

French industrialists were hard hit by the English competition in design; by the 1850's they harassed the French Government with pleas for action. As one Frenchman wrote, the taste of France must be reconstructed and the art-school system rebuilt, lest France lose her markets to the British who had fashioned the perfect teapot and the chair which would not tear clothes. Gambetta responded; the French Government tried to regain the strong leadership in commercial art it had possessed in the seventeenth century, when Colbert declared: "We must conquer Europe with our taste and subject the world to ourselves through the Mode."

Similarly, in Germany and Austria artists did not struggle to their feet alone. Prince Kaunitz observed that French artists were more profitable to that State than its generals, and urged Austria to stimulate designing. In Germany, it was not until the World Exposition of 1851 revealed to manufacturers how badly they needed better patterns, that the art-in-industry movement commenced. Up to the 1870's, as Waentig says, the best-designed German product remained cannon by Krupp.

But, thanks to royal patronage and business men's interest, in large part, German wares showed a tremendous advance by 1904.

America possessed a certain artistic heritage, in the pottery of the Pennsylvania peasants, for instance. But in the Gilded Age, such simplicity was not appreciated, and it was long before business men realized the money-value of art. Indeed the World Exposition of 1851 disclosed to them, as to the Germans, their backwardness. There they saw to their shame that the only original products they could present to the universal audience were a few hatchets, knives, saws and axes which, a traveling European declared, had the same rude charm observable in Stone Age relics. Awakened by such criticisms, the exhibiting committee reported that America would be bankrupt if she continued to export only pork and import beauty, because the work of six men in a year growing pigs would not pay the salary of one clever technical designer in Europe, working on porcelain or rugs. Strenuous efforts were then made by Americans to balance their budget with beauty; museums and technical education were fostered by business men in the race for world trade. Only comparatively late did artists themselves take up the propaganda; their arts and crafts movement reached a peak in the 1890's.

The fact is, therefore, that business men throughout the world were trying desperately to put more aesthetic value into the products of the machine. But their efforts did not win them the gratitude and appreciation of artists. This was partly due to the increasing aloofness of the purchaser of artistic works. The entrepreneur of a great plant did not trouble himself to meet a designer personally; the wealthy business man might hire an artist to paint his portrait, but did not entertain a Michelangelo constantly at his table, in the Medicean fashion. The art-dealer interposed between patron and creative worker, giving the latter indeed freedom from the old servility, but making him more conscious of his status as employee.

Perhaps, too, the artist was unable to read significance in the carefully expressionless faces of the Victorian business men. These were, as a rule, men of soft lives, not weathered by battle and sea-storm. Nor were they burgomasters, admirals, ambassadors, true public men. A man whose chief care in life was to avoid public notice and posts of peril could hardly be presented very dramatically or nobly in portraiture.

Finding the business man not worthy of worship, and dissatisfied with everyone else, the Artist very naturally began to admire himself exclusively. Byron, at the commencement of the century, as an aristocrat and poet, felt above the bourgeois, and set a pattern of self-deification. The cult of the Genius was developed with increasing preciosity between 1850 and 1900, culminating in the "fin de siècle" vagaries of Oscar Wilde and the Yellow Book circle. Believing with Tennyson that the poet's soul was too deep for ordinary folk to fathom, the artists tried to set themselves apart from the Philistine by Bohemian costume and pose. But, finding that the temple of art was too holy for the laity, the latter lost interest in it, and turned to sport or science instead. So the genius and the public were moving farther away from each other.

When the artist faithfully tried to depict the achievements of the business man upon canvas, the latter was shocked. Much as the laissez fairist demanded jungle law in life, he hated to confront it in art. Even while he was destroying the old social order, he refused to see the savage beauty in the explosions of Futurism. He wrecked the basis upon which old-fashioned womanhood was formed, denying the sovereignty of emotion, symbolized by Venus, and breaking up the family, out of which Madonna-worship arises—yet it horrified him to behold the result, in the shape of an entirely rational woman, all cones and angles, as shown by the notorious Cubist painting of the "Nude Descending the Stair," by Marcel Duchamp.

Furious at the lack of appreciation, the Genius assumed that his mission lay in improving the bourgeois, or at least in exposing and ridiculing him. Shelley was one outstanding example of the missionary-genius. Out of the ranks of aesthetes came some of the bitterest foes of middle-class complacence in the Victorian Age. Burckhardt, the Swiss art-critic, foretold the ultimate triumph of fascist barbarism in Europe, in words of astounding prophetic power. Much akin to him in yearning for the more beautiful life of old Italy and in hatred of the Machine-Age was the English art-critic, John Ruskin. With the passion of an Isaiah, Ruskin denounced laissez faire. "Don't emigrate to China, poison Chinamen, and teach them to make steam-engines," he pleaded, or England will lose her markets. The philosophy of Manchesterism must result in chaos:

Day after day, your souls will become more mechanical, more servile; also you will go on multiplying, wanting more food, and more; you will have to sell cheaper and cheaper, work longer and longer, to buy your food. At last, do what you can, you can make no more, or the people who have the corn will not want any more; and your increasing population will necessarily come to a quite imperative stop—by starvation, preceded necessarily by a revolution and massacre.

Ruskin cast aside the claims of Science and National Economy to solve the riddle. There could be no other outcome but: "Ruin—inevitable and terrible, such as no nation has yet suffered . . . England has to drink a cup which cannot pass from her—at the hands of the Lord, the cup of His fury." Such men as Ruskin and Morris, the aesthetes, were in fact, more pessimistic, more inimical to capitalism than the Marxians. Marxians supposed that, under social control, the machine could bring happiness to mankind. Not so the aesthetes of England who, after many years of effort to reach a compromise, finally arrived at the view that the ideal society, furnishing a basis for true beauty, was attainable only by giving up the machine itself—by accepting the meagerness of the handicraft-agrarian life once more.

Infinitely more bitter than Marx, more akin in gloom to the old Hebrew prophets, was Ruskin. Successively he abandoned the belief that more education for the masses, better design in industry, higher humanitarianism, or even social control of the producing system, would bring the noble life to mankind. Abandoning capitalism, and socialism, and indeed progress itself, he was peering into an ever more chaotic-seeming future when his mind was mercifully darkened, and he died.

THE ARISTOCRATIC FAÇADE

The true memorials of the age were not the châteaux of the opulent, but the giant gilt-and-plaster caravanseries and casinos in the watering-places where the restless, ever-changing circles of the cosmopolitan rich gathered. For all its worship of the Home, it was the Hotel which symbolized a time yearning for permanence, but able to erect only a gaudy façade behind which the guests were forever coming and going.

This façade was achieved in part by the aid of the aristocracy, as so often in the history of the business man before. As the eighteenth-century English philosopher, Hume, discussing "Our Esteem for the Rich," pertinently observed, the sympathetic emotions cannot be aroused in the lowly members of society toward the owners of wealth, if their treasures seem transient. The "passion of loyalty," as he phrased it, is most easily produced by the long-lived, the traditional. And no better and easier way was found in the next century than that he recommended, by buying land and uniting wealth to old families, thereby lending the enchantment of permanence to possessions. The new capitalist, proud as he was of breaking with the past in every other respect, made haste in Europe to take a mellower title; the rising exploiters of mines, like Godulla in Silesia, whose daughter at length was married into the family of the Counts Schaffgotsch, found this especially easy, for mine-ownership has ever been compatible with nobility; financiers and speculators also discovered preference, as usual, like the Siennese financial adventurer, Torlonia, who profited from the confusion of

Italy after Napoleon's invasion, by buying up old palaces and old families, climbing to princely rank.

From this process the American was more or less excluded. Though he might buy the trappings of feudalism in wholesale lots, he could not acquire the feudal distinctions for himself; nor could he plant his palace squarely in the midst of a town with soldiery about it and cannon at the gate, like the château of the Schneider at Creusot. He could not bellow commands from his citadels with quite the roar of autocratic Krupp in Essen. And if he wanted bagpipes with his meals, he had to move across the seas, like Carnegie, to a Scotch castle.

Not altogether devoid of genealogical hankerings, the American frequently turned to look up his ancestors and trace his line, if he could, back via the *Mayflower* to William the Bastard. More often, he was reduced to surrounding himself with pedigreed dogs and cats, as a kind of dumb courtiers. Or he enveloped himself in a mellowed atmosphere by giving money for reconstructions. Colt, for example, went into a veritable frenzy over the Charter Oak at Hartford, though the town's opposition prevented him from making a park around it; meanwhile Colt, with his fortune from arms-manufacture, built a baronial hall, which he called "Armsmear," and married a young relative to a German Junker. He felt that he ought to have a title himself, and acquired one from a good customer, the Sultan of Turkey, and with it a proper coat-of-arms. But he seems to have looked upon his heraldic device as in the nature of an advertisement, for he had it protected from infringement by trade-mark registration.

Though the American himself rarely sought a title—the Astors and Goelets, who moved abroad to climb, were exceptions—or even married one, he was willing enough to finance such ambitions in his daughters. Statisticians have reckoned up the sums transferred in dowries for the daughters of American business men to Europe; in 1898 it was computed that 134 such marriages had carried $176,155,000 to European noblemen; eminent on the list were the two Singer sewing-machine girls, and of course the Vanderbilt and Gould brides. The famous Gould-Vanderbilt rivalry over railroads culminated in a social duello. The former had overreached the latter in railway warfare: when Gould slashed his rates, Vanderbilt bought up Western cattle and shipped them cheaply over his rival's lines. Gould retaliated by shipping his daughter abroad, marrying Anna to a French count. But Vanderbilt almost immediately scored again by uniting his Consuelo to an English duke.

Indirectly therefore—and by seeking presentations at court, especially in the less fussy German States—many Americans in the Gilded Age acquiesced in the general aristocratization of social goals. It is true that in America the break-down of this pretense had already come before the War, around 1910, when the American Croesus, after the Bradley-Martin ball, put his costumes in mothballs and seriously began trying to discover a democratic style for his behavior. But it was already too late for him to do anything to alter the fateful trend in the rest of the world—the restoration of the old martial caste of aristocracy, European *samurai*, whose fortunes he had helped to rebuild, through his daughters' dowries.

The business man not only let the whole tone of society be set by professional arbiters, the aristocrats, but at the same time handed over war and politics to the old groups of experts, the generals, the lawyers and politicians. Only a few business men, and those chiefly in Britain, entered the arena themselves; on the whole, the newly arrived capitalist saw little cause to take over the arduous work of determining policy and administrating programs. The French Revolution had showed sensible men the danger of such exercise of power, and echoes of that earthquake were still reverberating when the fresh revolutionary wave of 1848 gave Europe another scare. From weariness or torpor, from modesty or nervousness, the Victorian business man, after trying his hand for a time, decided to rule by compromise, leaving the terrible and terrifying onus of State management mainly to men accustomed to such burdens.

In such circumstances, the old sociai set-up of the pre-Machine Age was permitted to stand, as a hollow and over-decorated shell, up to the explosion of the World War. The self-made capitalist moved into this vacant structure, much as the Goths in the Dark Ages had encamped in the captured palaces of the Romans. For a long time the edifice promised to stand without repair or enlargement. He did not muster the decision to tear down the aristocratic culture, and lacked the skill in masonry to build a new one—perhaps, indeed, it would have been impossible to build one around jungle law. And in the meantime, an abundant feast was spread which invited him to forget the morrow.

When the business man thus took possession of the societal edifice that had been reared by kings, priests and soldiers, during centuries, he found the masses still enchained by old loyalties. English servants had been trained by dukes and continued to serve the nabobs perfectly —for a time; French valets had been beaten and kicked about by gentlemen into an admirable submission in which they continued. The formal usages of the old régime held together the incongruous groups of the "newcomes," and prevented a social competition as unregulated as the economic. The business man did not envisage a time when this left-over heritage would be used up, when the last vestiges of humility among masses and good form in the upper ranks might be destroyed, by the exaltation of profit as the prime motive of life. So long as he could, he left the façades standing.

The Victorian State therefore, like the interminable rows of semi-detached villas in that age, had an elaborate "Front" of classic or baroque style, which bore scant relation to the plain, utilitarian rear of the structure. And the man himself retired to bosky ambush behind whiskers. As the old Prussian Liberal, Varnhagen, complained, the Revolution had merely cut off the queues at the back; the citizens, still used to slavery, promptly grew them on their chins instead. This period of luxuriant hirsute embellishment was not brought to a close until the middle of the War, in 1916, when soldiers were ordered to shave, that they might get on their poison-gas masks. A major cataclysm was required in Europe before man came out of hiding.

BUSINESS, ARISTOCRACY AND IMPERIALISM

One of the easiest and most slipshod forms of present thinking is the assumption that capitalism and imperialism are exactly synonymous and that business hunger for markets was exclusively to blame for the World War. This view gained popularity as the outcome of many impassioned pleas from English Liberals, such as J. A. Hobson, before the War; Hobson, desiring to warn business of the dangers of imperialist competition, omitted to emphasize other factors in the game. The theory was finally formulated in iron-clad terms by Lenin, who wrote amid the fury of conflict, in 1916, that imperialism was the inevitable "last stage" of capitalism. Before and during the conflict, however, a more comprehensive estimate of what Schumpeter calls the "Sociology of Imperialisms" was hardly possible.

Since the World War the documented researches of German historians have presented a fuller picture of backgrounds and foregrounds of War. Perhaps because feudal relics were so conspicuous in Germany that they could not be ignored, the younger school of writers, Kehr, Hallgarten and Vagts, have been inclined to give a fresh emphasis to non-business institutions and men in the diplomatic conflicts leading up to the World War. In Germany, in neighboring Russia, in Austria-Hungary and Turkey, aggressive movements cannot be explained in simple terms as market-drives; nor was an investors' push, as Eugene Staley indicates, the prime force behind American expansion.

Rather, evidence points to the menace, in Europe, of the old feudal-aristocratic elements in society, with whom business had come to such a social and political compromise. A primordial appetite for land, a feudal lust for extended boundaries, inspired the government of mammoth Russia to a ceaseless outward pressure both on Europe and Asia.

Some business interests were involved, especially oil; but courtiers were the participants in the lumber-company which fomented clashes with Japan. Nor was Russia "saturated" with capitalism; the reverse was true. Her primitive despotism held down the peasants so that they could not consume the goods of industry; her aristocrats, refusing to engage in commerce, persisted in forcing their grain upon Germany, thereby provoking the fierce jealousy of German landed gentlemen.

At the same time, little agrarian Serbia was wrangling with the stubborn backwoods noblesse of Austria-Hungary over the right to ship in grain and pork. This was one of the fundamental quarrels which eventuated in the War—a row not over pig-iron but pigs. For when Serbia touched the match, Russia's noblemen, with a dark will to war, a savage readiness for last extremities, began to mobilize; with Russia's mobilization, it is generally thought, the War "started."

Capitalists in the pre-War era should have had, logically, an eager interest in overthrowing the Romanov dynasty and opening up that gigantic region to exploitation. Yet for various reasons, they could not do so. German financiers, among them the Mendelssohns, did try to penetrate further the Russian State and the idea was pleasant to business men generally in Germany. However, at the instance of Prussian agrarians and high military men, permission for floating additional loans was withheld. This is a striking instance of the danger in the business man's compromise with aristocracy—with the feudal element hindering the capitalization of Russia because it wanted the money for mortgages.

"International finance" has an invidious ring today. Nevertheless it may be argued, plausibly, that capitalism was not international enough in the Edwardian era. English financiers, for example, worked in such close cooperation with the Government that the investments of English funds were diverted to Canada and the colonial lands, and away from the Continent of Europe. Had England formed binding financial ties with France and Germany, she might have put restraints on the war forces developing so near at hand. German Jewish bankers acted as a brake on war, tending to hold both England and America back from the conflict. If the Mendelssohns and others had been in a position to retard Russia also, valuable time might have been gained. Had German finance been allowed to compete with French in Russia, the "encirclement" of Germany would not have been so complete, and the division of Europe into hostile camps would have been more difficult.

It was the governmental control over finance in European countries and the employment of banking power in the interests of diplomatic games which exercised so fatal an effect upon the intercourse of nations. French loans went to bolster up the tottering despotism of the Russian Czars, not solely because of the bankers' thirst for profits. The banks of France were playing the balance of power politics dictated by politicians instead of using the people's savings for strengthening domestic capitalism. Governments in England, France and Germany were all, in varying ways, directing finance according to preconceived notions of national advantage and not for immediate profits alone.

Next to "international finance" in the scale of popular obloquy, come the munitioneers, and certainly they helped prepare the conflict. The German heavy-industrialists had bought so extensively into French munitions-plants that they profited richly by every new French appropriation for armament against Germany. They also supported the naval rivalry with Britain; but in this case, as Kehr pointed out, they formed a deal with the Prussian agrarian Junkers, who upheld a big fleet in return for tariff protection against foreign grain and meat. Munitioneers, without politicians and Junkerdom, would not have been able to jam naval bills through the Reichstag, in the face of opposition from other business interests. The exporters of Germany hated the big fleet appropriations. Business was thus divided within itself, and the very element of capitalism which should have been seeking foreign markets by force, according to the Lenin thesis, was actually conducting a campaign for reconciliation with Britain.

Of course, the widely circulated theory maintains that the munitioneers frightened the masses by war-scares to increase naval and military appropriations. In fact, a number of flagrant instances of this may be found especially in Britain. But the blood-lust of the folk was not merely a response to hired agitators; nor was it cannon-makers alone who whetted imperial cravings. Take, for instance, the comic opera story of Samoa, as related by Vagts. There a merchant firm of Hamburg, the Godeffroys, did have holdings which they wished the German Government to guarantee for them against foreclosure by foreign creditors; they received the promise of financial backing from Bismarck. But the reason he supported the scheme was complex; it was not his care for Samoa; he sought to unite the German folk behind himself by playing on the strings of imperialist nationalism. In the end the Reichstag, expressing the opinion of the average German business man, refused to sanction the Godeffroy-Bismarck plan in its original extreme form.

The French masses were more warlike than the French business man on many occasions, since aggressive warfare was connected popularly with memories of the French Revolution and Napoleon; for a long time bellicosity and radicalism were linked together in France. In Britain the mill-town masses went frantic over both the Crimean War and the Boer War, apparently from the sheer joy of imagining such martial enterprise. The Spanish-American hostilities offer another example of the popular voice outshouting that of big business. Big business in the United States, speaking through Mark Hanna, Platt and Aldrich, was emphatically opposed to so reckless a venture, which seemed to threaten a budding boom, but the roar of the folk, inflamed by Hearst and Pulitzer, was what McKinley heard and heeded. The next dramatic imperialist, Theodore Roosevelt, was a trust-busting foe of big business. Even the so-called "Dollar Diplomacy" was in part the effort of diplomats to be busy, and not solely a response to aggressive exporters.

Imperialism, therefore, was a creed worked out by many sorts of men. Politicians, navalists and soldiers, diplomats and intriguing bureaucrats urged on their diverse interests in the names of Glory, the State, Progress and Carrying Light to Them That Sit in Darkness. Not all business men had accepted imperialism; but they had accepted the continued prominence of such classes, and, having no policy of their own, and unwilling to take full responsibility for all government, they bowed to the prevailing trend. Unable to divine the frightful outcome, or provide a substitute slogan and concept, they went along with the rest, impelled by a half-superstitious faith in the prevision of the State, over-awed by figures who seemed their social superiors, and lured by promises of bigger and better business, forever and ever expanding beyond all dreams of magnitude piled on magnitude.

Then Imperialism led to many serious diplomatic crises. And it did not bring permanent prosperity any more than laissez faire. As imperial governments staked out the backward places of the earth, the chances for new expansion and development proved more limited than had been expected. In primitive places, half-naked workers in paddies and plantations did not enjoy wages that enabled them to buy expensive goods sent out from European cities with a far higher labor standard. A coolie toiling in an Eastern rice-swamp for fifteen cents a day would not buy his shirts from a European cotton-factory where workers were paid two or three dollars a day. Naturally, factories were set up to take advantage of this cheaper labor, but these Eastern centers were soon underbidding those of the West.

In such circumstances, the prime hope of Western business lay in cutting the wages of its employees to starvation levels. However, that drastic operation could not be accomplished by moral suasion, perhaps not even by police force. The frontiers of the earth were closing. There were no more worlds to conquer; and the "backward peoples" not only were unable to buy the flood of Western goods at the prices charged; they were setting up counter-tides. The business of most nations was approaching a low ebb in 1913 and the opening of 1914. Conditions were very bad in America, where there was "severe depression with little activity and extensive unemployment; many failures." England was feeling a decline, notably in the iron and steel industry. Political disturbances aggravated depression in Germany; conditions were not much better in France. There was stagnation in Sweden and paralysis in Canada, dullness in South Africa and Australia, severe trouble in Argentina, slump in Japan and gloom in China. Real panic gripped Italy and the Netherlands.

Broad and deepening lay the shadow around the mechanized and developed world, at the close of this epoch of revelry. But the darkness was densest upon the two countries destined to take the decisive steps toward the World War. Austria had "internal and external political troubles, record emigration," and trade was coming to a standstill. Russia suffered a panic, and was sunk in depression.

At this conjuncture, the activities of warriors, diplomats, governments, financiers and other business men, and the emotions of peoples, flowed together. The world moved as one body from depression to disaster.

PART FIVE

THE BIG BUSINESS MAN

XXVII

GREAT WAR, GROWING MASSES,
BIG BUSINESS AND THE
CLOSED FRONTIERS

THE GREAT WAR outran the previous concepts of the business men, as also of generals, diplomats, bureaucratic place-seekers and the cheering peoples who had stumbled together from the economic crisis into the mighty Worry to End Worries. As it went on, the combat transformed industries, extended governmental control over their methods and often over their profits, and even took the sons of the business men, who had been safely kept at home since burgher-militia were disbanded long ago; and in brief, death and disaster became again immediate concerns of business men, as they used to be in the Middle Ages, when merchants shivered behind their stout walls and debated in Hanseatic conclave the question: "Will war pay?"

This query had been little heard during that long, secure century that lapsed between the fall of Napoleon and the shot at Sarajevo. In the earlier half, it is true, Cobden and Bright had discussed it at length, when they tried to stem the imperialist urges in Britain and prevent the Crimean War. These capitalists who had helped to bring about the industrial revolution were quite sure that they desired peace to complete their work; on concrete grounds, arguing that wars are bad investments and diminish the wealth of mankind, Cobden appealed to Britons. They proved deaf to such crass "materialistic" considerations. He was decried as a sordid profit-taker, impervious to holy sentiments. Tennyson called him an ignoble tradesman, "whose ear is stuffed with cotton" and rang "even in dreams to the chink of his pence." Never, cried the poet, should "Britain's one sole God be the millionaire," and "this huckster put down war!"

Before long the pleas of Cobden and his followers in England were brushed aside, as were those of French sympathizers with Manchester doctrines, such as Jean-Baptiste Say, who fought similar imperialism in their own land. In either country, manufacturers at first dreaded the diversion of energy and wealth to conquest, even of foreign markets;

but their voices were drowned in the tides of nationalist fervor; and armed imperialism brought so many successes that it seemed foolish as well as unpatriotic to question such policies. Talk of war among business men was carried on by other peoples, Swedes, Americans and Germans, and of course, primarily men engaged in trades allied with war-activities, who could not entirely avoid thinking about the matter.

Of them all, Alfred Nobel took the gloomiest view of the future. "The so-called Christian world is still little more than a battlefield," he wrote in 1896, the last year of his life, in a work forebodingly entitled, "Nemesis." He had done as much as anyone living to make it so, this strange wanderer who created dynamite for Russia and then handed it on to Britain and Germany with supreme impartiality. "I am a citizen of the world; my Fatherland is wherever I work and I work everywhere," said Nobel, in words which might have been proudly spoken by Death himself.

Between pride in his own ingenuity and terror at what he had done, Nobel became a pitiable figure, perpetually torn by vainglory and remorse. Early in his career, he advocated in the Swedish journal, *Aftonbladet*, which he had founded, a strong control over armaments: "If there is a branch of production which ought to be strictly national, or at least, jealously controlled by the nation, it is assuredly that." But he could not resist the temptation to spread his "safety powder" to the world. After he had done so, in a spasm of horror, he left his fortune to the cause of Peace. In despairing letters, almost the only ones in which a "self-made" man berates his own product, Nobel confessed himself a failure, without imagination, family, friends, even enemies, "drifting . . . like a purposeless wreck, broken by fate, with no lovely memories of the past, no false but welcome illusions of the future." And in a startling burst of confidence, he, the atheist, declared to a Swedish chaplain: "I am filled with loathing of myself."

One of the rarest phenomena is a really pessimistic business man, and Nobel, the Swedish atheist, belongs to that exclusive category along with the French-American Girard and the German philosopher of gloom, Schopenhauer, a merchant's son and a good investor himself. Such an example of an uneasy conscience would be hard to duplicate among the robust British armament-exporters, the greatest in the world. As for the French business man, that supposedly irrepressible and voluble Gaul, he has actually said less about himself and his plans than almost any other. Much more agitation was going on in business circles in America, where the Scotch iron-master, Andrew Carnegie, was distributing money for peace purposes as eagerly as Nobel, but with an infinite faith in the power of arbitration to stave off trouble, no matter how many iron ships and guns he sold and the nations bought. His speeches on peace were taken somewhat lightly, it is true, and Washington society laughingly declared it worth a Carnegie medal for heroism to listen to one. President Taft joked about the Scotchman's desire to stick his "great red beard" into everything.

Merrier peals greeted the "Peace-Ship" enterprise of Henry Ford who, like Carnegie, made goods with a war-use. How far Ford's desire to pacify the Old World may have coincided with a clear-sighted realization that continued war would not pay, and would not pay him, may be guessed from a graph showing how steadily Ford auto-mobile-production had gone up into 1915, and how swiftly it went back from America's entry into the War until 1919.

While such business men, whose wares were sure of sale either in war or peace, declared the profits of the latter preferable, a third American, Hudson Maxim, repudiated pacific argument. This extraordinary indi-vidual combined the Yankee's love of horseplay with a flaming fantasy akin to that of Jules Verne and indeed, as he boasted, he was the de-scendant of French Huguenots—a Yankee Huguenot, who would not admit a whisper of doubt to interrupt his perpetual "whooperupski" of laughter. Insisting upon the funny side of his inventions, he published gruesome jests in a compendium, "Dynamite Stories," and was furious at persons not readily amused by them. "One of my associates in war-work," he complained, "had a great reputation for ability and effi-ciency, but in reality was a big false alarmski—no damn goodski—a babe in the woods. He had no imagination and no sense of humour at all; and a person without these is essentially a lower animal."

Probably the remorse-ridden Nobel would have seemed the lowest sort of animal to this carefree propounder of whooperupski. None was more eager for America's entry into the War than Hudson Maxim, contributor of many inventions, including a submarine mine and "my multi-perforated smokeless cannon powder," which "was manufactured in enormous quantities by the Du Pont Company for the Allies . . . In dollars-and-cents value, more of it was used than of any other single munition, and it had much to do with our winning. The Du Ponts re-ceived a single check from the Russian Government for sixty million dollars' worth of it." As Maxim insisted, he had done his best to drive America to war, by gratis distribution of his book, "Defenceless America," a hundred thousand copies going to teachers and notables generally, while "eight thousand were placed in guest rooms beside the Bible in leading hotels." The motion picture based on this "Battle-Cry of Peace" was "seen by fifty million people. Probably no other one thing did so much to get the United States into the war as did my book, with that great picture sweeping the country."

Perhaps Maxim was the solitary example of an American business man who exuberantly claimed a prime share in pushing his country into the War; and in all likelihood, he greatly over-estimated the results of his own eloquence, as he certainly did the beauty of his own poetry. It would be difficult to exaggerate the effects of the various inventions of the Maxim family, however, upon heightening the deadliness of that strife; Hudson's smokeless powder and the automatic gun of his brother, Sir Hiram, who won a British title, transformed the battle of the nations into an unforeseen carnage. Naturally, French writers such as Paul Allard hastened to point out the fact that ex-Huguenots, the Maxims, made the War what it was, while another ex-Huguenot family, the Du Ponts, closely allied in business with them, piled up one of the colossal single fortunes in munitions from that conflict—a fact which awakens echoes in French minds of other Huguenots, whose genius was manifested in the provisioning and preparing of armies and navies.

If ex-French families played such a practical rôle in the War, it was also true to tradition that German business men should have produced the most penetrating theoretical works on the subject. In Germany, the conflict between business and the armed State was sharper than in England or France, where industrialists were contented with their achievements and position, or in the United States, where the State was not taken so seriously. Bitter and alarmed to the last, many Germans proved major prophets about the War. The Socialist textile-merchant, Engels, painted a picture of approaching desolation that turned out to be more accurate than his forecasts of contemporary crises. The most brilliant mind of German business circles at a later day, Walter Rathenau, leader of the electrical industry, in 1911, foretold the ruin of nations through war and urged disarmament on the quota basis to save Europe. From the outset, he could see that war must involve a war-economy, at least for Germany; perceiving the economic basis of military strength, he argued with blind generals that a department must be set up to deal with such problems. It was not until the War was many months advanced that generals admitted he was right.

A banker standing between these countries, a German-American, Paul M. Warburg, announced, while the War was still in progress, that it would bring momentous changes to his fellow-business men. In "Government and Business," he insisted that, no matter what party won, neither State nor economy would anywhere emerge unaltered:

> In the State of the future, particularly in Europe after the war, the most efficient government promotion of industries in any lines will be held to exist in actual government ownership . . . More than ever before will States become solid industrial and

financial unions effectively organized for world competition, driven by the necessity of perfecting a system of the greatest efficiency, economy and thrift, in order to meet the incredible burdens created by the war.

WAR AND BUSINESS BIGNESS

How far big business wants and "causes" war, or even profits by war, especially now that war has such revolutionary implications, are matters on which large room is left for debate. The contrary may more easily be maintained: war makes business bigger. From very early times, this trend may be followed. The martial conquests of old Rome, by heaping up tribute in the capital city, provided the basis for the first giant finance-capitalism. The mediaeval Crusades changed consuming habits over Europe and brought riches to Italian cities, making early-capitalist manufacture possible. The wealth stored up in European towns, partly as a result of that impetus, was at length used to offer loans to monarchs, spreading the dynastic wars of the sixteenth century, which formed the modern States. In turn, the States arising from that business-financed strife became the fosterers of bigger businesses. As Sombart has shown for the baroque period, the conflicts of French and German monarchs advanced the size, scope and substance of enterprise: purveying munitions, uniforms, provisions and transport for growing armies and the floating of loans for ever mightier military games helped to lift business from the petty handicraft stage to the large-scale transactions of modern times.

Although Sombart did not choose to illustrate his thesis by references to the New World, examples were abundant there. The years immediately following the American Revolution witnessed the rapid growth of corporations, charters for which had been difficult to obtain under British rule. Before the Revolution there were only a handful of companies in America; within little more than a score of years, 220 new companies had sprung up. The Civil War assisted in swelling business enterprise. Surveying the war-carnival at Washington, Edmund Clarence Stedman, the broker, exclaimed: "You would be astonished to see the *immense* crowd of vulgarians who had got rich off this War, and their grandchildren will be the aristocrats of the future." Although many of the leaders in big business were opposed to the declaration of war on Spain in 1898, the war itself provided a stimulus for business and was followed by an enormous growth of trusts and combines, despite the existing anti-trust acts.

The greatest of wars but carried further this traditional tendency. It was accompanied by the formation of new companies, the consolidation of old concerns, and the establishment of inter-relations on a scale that outstripped anything imagined even by the former titans of business. In Germany this development was easy. There, farmers and petty business men had never been allowed to hamper, hamstring, and harass corporations by anti-trust legislation. On the contrary, the government of Imperial Germany had favored the creation of companies, combinations, concerns, and cartels, seeing in them great weapons for the prosecution of foreign commerce. Nor, despite some grumblings of the common law against combinations in restraint of trade, did Great Britain interfere with the establishment and consolidation of corporations. If business conservatism impeded the process, it nevertheless went forward under the impact of war requirements and post-war opportunities. Although the Wilson administration threatened at the outset to put teeth into the old anti-trust legislation, the intention was forgotten in the heat of the war itself. In fact in 1918 Congress exempted from the provisions of the anti-trust laws all combinations engaged in foreign trade. During the war period and the years immediately following, American corporations reported net profits of more than thirty billion dollars, exceeding the immediate cost of the war to the Government of the United States; 21,000 new millionaires were created by 1919. Under genial Republican administrations lasting from 1921 to 1933, American business men formed still bigger combinations, holding companies, and consolidations—giants more bewildering in their complications and staggering capitalizations than any of the simple trusts, corporations, and combines which had raised populist fury forty years previously.

Although concentration of enterprise was the outcome of war, this is very far from saying that warfare was profitable everywhere and to business as a whole; indeed, to a large degree, this new consolidation was the result of governmental regimentation in the war, since bureaucracies naturally prefer to deal with larger units; while many old firms increased their capital, that of smaller men was drastically wiped away by taxes and inflation, in the warring countries. For small-scale business war brought new threats.

Only of the neutrals, Holland, Sweden, Switzerland, and the United States which did not enter until the last year of war, may it be said confidently that they won more than under peace-time conditions. That was largely because governments not at war did not need to regulate war-profits; such countries enjoyed the rush orders without bearing the burdens imposed on economy by war. This was especially the case with America. Had she rushed in earlier, with her reckless method of spending, she would have stumbled into abysmal depths of debt and disorder, possibly surpassing the chaos of other belligerents. Her swell of golden gains was not checked by the State; because profits were not cut down, wages could be kept high, increasing the general consuming power. These gains, some firms like the Du Pont Company claimed, were exacted from foreign governments, not wrung from American citizens.

The exceptional case of America proves anything but the thesis that modern war benefits business. In previous ages, this might have been maintained of some wars; for then, as Caspary remarks, the running expenses of armies were very largely paid out of land, and the profits won by purveyors were re-invested in land. Thus the American Revolution, to go no further back, was to a large degree financed by throwing Western lands on sale or paying the army with land scrip; the French Revolution was paid for in part by confiscating noblemen's estates and church properties. After conflicts were over, the land still existed, even though in new hands. The Great War, however, for the first time really began to eat up at an unprecedented rate a quite fictitious substance, capital, "imaginary money" as the old English used to call it; this airy figment of confidence could be exploded in a short time, leaving no trace behind. The "war of materials" involved an "immaterial war" quite as destructive.

The costs of the Great War outstripped the wealth of nations; in Germany alone, they mounted to an average of two billion marks a month, whereas the entire new capital-accretions in previous peace years had reached only ten billion *a year*. To be sure, much of this expenditure was paid out to business men, but that was not all a source of profit, for most industries had to bear heavy expenses in transforming plants for war-time use, giving up peace-markets; they had also to subscribe to enormous government loans which re-absorbed the gains as far as possible. No matter what methods were adopted by governments, some part of business, and usually the smaller men, had to suffer. The weakest went to the wall.

Even for munition-makers, in the warring countries, there were deep disappointments. Governments, after they perceived that this was to be a "war of materials," began to clamp down on profits as had never been done before. In the Napoleonic wars, for instance, munitioneers piled up millions without stint, until, in a fit of rage, Napoleon flung someone in jail and picked his pockets to even up things. Now this rough and ready practice would not do any longer; the flow had to be checked at the source. The British were most decided about that, for they determined from the first to pay their way largely by taxation. Less willingly followed the French, and still more reluctantly the Germans who considered profits an essential of civilian "morale," and hoped to recoup by victory.

The most tremendous of wars, accordingly, failed to bring gains to armament-makers in these countries in anything like a proportionately colossal size. Leading works at Skoda, Creusot or Essen reported hardly more than double the net profit in preceding peace years; even allowing for ingenious bookkeeping, this does not indicate fantastic profits in keeping with the scope of warfare, which had brought sixty-six million men under arms. Vickers, held down by English law to 20 per cent of the average net profits of the last two peace years, also lost huge credits extended to European governments and after 1919 for a while verged on bankruptcy. Krupps' suspended dividends from the end of the War to the accession of Hitler. Even in fortunate America, Du Ponts' suspended dividends for two years after peace was concluded. All in all, the experience showed, not that war is good for arms-makers, but that armed peace—or neutrality—is what really pays for them.

If the munitions-makers had their difficulties, other business men had more. Since the British paid for war so extensively out of taxes, the increasing burdens weighed heavily on the middle classes, shrinking average fortunes and hence impairing luxury-trades. More serious was the situation in France and Germany, which had relied on credit to pay their way and after the War repudiated the government debts through inflation and devaluation, crushing the middle classes. The French also lost through the debt-repudiation and wiping out of private enterprise in Russia. The Germans not only suffered by the fall of the mark, but many guessed wrong on some of the gyrations of the French franc and so met total shipwreck.

A tremendous cracking, straining and upheaval of social strata went on under such pressure in ex-belligerent countries. And while many old firms with pre-War standards collapsed, a large proportion of those which took their place were insubstantial. Nothing proved airier than the war-gains of the noisy German-Austrian "Kriegsgewinnler," or, as the Italians called them, "pescecane"—"sharks." These were mostly small fellows, few of them manufacturers, usually jobbers, "go-betweens" for governments who distributed orders for uniforms and the like to little shops, or speculative importers and hoarders of foodstuffs, all without a solid basis beneath them; making a loud splash for a moment, they disappeared. Nor were the dazzling fortunes built in a day like Aladdin's Palace through inflation and attendant speculation more permanent: like magic came and went the riches of the German Stinnes, the Austrian Castiglione and Bosel, Loewenstein of Belgium and Kreuger of Sweden, and the Englishman Hatry. On the whole, it is likely that the best-preserved harvests were reaped by such of the older, well-established houses as had managed to survive the War and its aftermath. But there were fewer of these, and they had become vastly greater than before.

THE BUSINESS MAN ENTANGLED IN CORPORATE COMPLEXITIES

The accumulation of wealth and concentration of capital brought immediately a set of extremely bewildering problems in management, control, ownership and direction to all business men, small as well as great, in every country. The mighty had to struggle with corporate structures of giant size, dwarfing the men who made them, raising ticklish issues of division and delegation of authority, of a self-perpetuating "business bureaucracy," with all its tendencies to stagnation and "ingrowing-pains." The little men were no less enmeshed in associations, ostensibly for their own protection against Big Business, but entangling them in bureaucracies of their own, until they, too, were caught in problems of size. From the depths as well as the heights, therefore, welled up a piteous cry for "business leadership"—something new in the world.

Up to this time, all human enterprises, commercial as well as political, had been of a size permitting personal direction and individual comprehension. If, like the Mongol Empire or Roman capitalism, they were very large, at least the separate parts could be left to themselves. The Eastern emperors merely received the tribute of virtually independent satraps; the Roman capitalist invested his wealth in estates which were almost self-sufficient communities, each able to feed and clothe itself and produce its own tools. How easy management was is evident from the fact that even Roman emperors for a long time after Augustus, still had not committed all their accounts to paper; they and capitalists likewise could rely on the memories of specially trained slaves for a great part of the details.

Much of the extraordinary leadership-ability of the mediaeval men may be accounted for by the pettiness of their undertakings. A burgomaster of Lübeck could see all around his one job or several jobs; he knew his way about in boats and on the battle scene; the function of decision was vested in him personally and behind him stood a tiny cohesive community of 20,000 souls. Perhaps best of all, when he had brought home his few sacks of wool or a shipload of lumber, he could spend the snow-bound winter months in inactivity, snoring and stuffing or perhaps composing a miracle-play for a municipal festival and otherwise recuperating his strength. As far as tastes and income go, he might easily be derided by a village grocer of today, but for sound nerves and bluff self-confidence, and "leadership" generally, he may well be envied by the modern "director" of a billion-dollar corporation.

Some strain on the nervous system, to be sure, has always been brought by the effort to organize activities and calculate profits and risks. This has ever distinguished the business man from other types. No other profession, apparently, equals business in its power to wear man out. Certainly there was no such generic term as the Tired Soldier. Politicians lived to a great age. Priests flourished on meagre diet and flagellation. Farmers bore toil and misfortune, growing stronger. All through the eras of epic carnage and herculean labors, explorers and pioneers kept burly and jolly. Only the effort to organize and calculate has brought forth that strange phenomenon, the Tired Man.

This was to some extent evident even in the dawn of history; as will be recalled, the godlike Odysseus was compared by Homer to a weary trader: starved, spent by a struggle in a sea-storm raised by furious Olympians, crawling on the shore in a state of almost complete prostration, that hero, for a moment, resembled a business man. But, careworn as the merchant appeared to the laughing swordsmen of that and later ages, he still managed to keep up with his enterprises for a long time, and one does not encounter a true modern case of a "nervous wreck" until the seventeenth century.

The first real nervous wreck, produced by over-extension of economic enterprise, would seem to be Wallenstein. That great war-entrepreneur not only hired and led armies but fed and clothed them with the products of his tremendous estates, and so became involved in calculations of profit as well as risk to a degree unknown to previous captains. Worrying incessantly, he became a victim of insomnia, a strange new disease which astonished his contemporaries. Apparently none had seen a man unable to sleep in the midst of uproar before; with amazement they recorded the fact that Wallenstein hated to hear clinking spurs at night and bade his officers wrap them in cloth; that he even objected to roosters and the yowling of the superabundant cats and ordered cat-massacres on a large scale.

Such nervosity was abnormal in that century, though today it might be met with in any over-excited man of affairs, in business or out of it. We have all grown more like Wallenstein, as our life, in the Burckhardt phrase, has "ceased to be a Design and become a Business." We tend to forget, however, the rarity of that phenomenon in bygone times; for Wallenstein remained an exception whose like was seldom seen for two centuries more. The big merchants of Holland in the seventeenth century exhibited no more nerves than an alligator. Nor did the industrialists of France, in Colbert's expanding manufactures; and that is not surprising, for the most stupendous establishments of this *grande industrie*, such as the plant at Abbeville, were not half so complicated as a small-town steam-laundry today.

It is not until the nineteenth century, and in America where the size of business organization far outstripped that in Europe, that the "Tired

Business Man" really appears—the product of a new tension, a greater stimulation and insecurity. By 1870, an English visitor found New York most exhausting: "Everywhere you note how much more hurried and hot is the business fever than in London city. Enter one of the lunch-rooms, you find the merchants seated in rows before the long counters, hastily swallowing their food, and meanwhile chattering loud and fast about the money-market." So shocking had things become in 1903 that another Englishman, a manufacturer, accustomed to the calmer, beef-fed and beer-warmed Britons at home, was full of compassion:

> In Britain the healthy, fresh-faced man is usually the employer, and the weary, sad-eyed man is the employee. In America, the employee is filled with frolic. It is the employer who is tired—just tired, just worn out, just living to work, racked with worry.

This was evened up when the Taylor system of efficiency was introduced, to speed the employees like the business men. The general *tempo* of American business life was then copied on the Continent, as well, where increasing concentration and energy were required to win and keep riches. A fortune might melt overnight if a day were spent beyond reach of cables. Instead of moving slowly forward within a narrow specialty, it was necessary to be in constant communication with many spheres; some French and German directors sat on the boards of thirty or forty concerns, while many American big business men had interests so various that they could not recollect them all—even when they were not on a witness-stand.

Ever swifter methods of transacting business added to the exertion; men began living on fast liners and expresses. Hugo Stinnes was always in motion, on a rapid train specially fitted for his work, bending sixteen hours a day over papers until, with no time to care for his ailments, he abruptly died. Presently, the airplane became a customary adjunct, and the Shoe-King, Bata, attempting a hurried flight between four distant conferences in a single day, fell to his death.

With Stinnes, the limit of one man's strength seemed reached. Except for Thyssen and a few others, he was about the "last American in Germany," one might put it—the last giant individualist who held out against the increasing bureaucratization of enterprise, before which even family-firms like Krupp's succumbed. Citroën in France similarly defied concentration of finance and collapsed without a successor. In America, home of the rugged individualist, only a few old-style entrepreneurs were left who, like Henry Ford, managed a business empire themselves, and a few families, particularly the Du Ponts, who kept dynastic privileges intact. "The one man era" as Frick had foreseen, had closed, and the "community of interest" period had opened. More and more authority was diffused and delegated among a crowd of lesser functionaries, "corporation bureaucrats." Only six per cent of American corporate wealth, it was estimated, remained under the actual management of "owners."

Some "titans" continued, of course, with superlative powers at least theoretically in their command—the fifty or sixty American "lords of creation," as Frederick Lewis Allen called them, the "two hundred families" of France, perhaps as many in Britain, certainly far fewer in Germany, all with wealth and influence beyond estimation. Yet these were no longer like the business commanders of old; they were jockeying with "controls" and intangibles, dealing with assets which consisted not of any material substance but increasingly of credits estimated in currencies "cut loose" from gold. In the corporations locked together under holding companies and other over-arching structures, ownership was widely diffused, at least in the Anglo-Saxon countries, among multitudes of small shareholders, far more ignorant of business than the silent partners in old-fashioned merchant companies. In Britain, shareholders were fewer and better informed than in America, and demanded more consideration; in the United States, managers and directors of companies retained perhaps a freer hand, on the whole, in making decisions, which allowed a quicker movement and a wider swing for business; but these were only gradations in a general tendency.

A further complication in the leadership-situation was introduced by the technique of leaving funds in trust for women and infants yet unborn, which brought a new hereditary principle into play. Before it was devised, a single generation of "gilded youth" might destroy the result of their forebears' labors; now, however, formal control could be vested in feeble and incompetent scions of business royalty who, like late sprigs of the Hapsburg or Romanoff trees, might lack qualifications for command. Nor can they even destroy the empires under their control, for these have become self-perpetuating, like political empires. As Robert H. Jackson, internal revenue counsel, declared before the Senate Finance Committee in Washington, on August 7, 1935:

> It was doubtless true that all a grandfather saved from the fruits of his labor could be spent by a grandson . . . It is not true of large invested fortunes under present conditions. They not only perpetuate themselves, they grow . . . A riotous-living heir to one of our larger fortunes would exhaust himself before he could exhaust the income alone of the estate.

In such circumstances, the very rich easily tended to be mere consti-tutional monarchs, titular sovereigns, entitled to bows and no real power; while the shareholders all too readily became a nameless herd of serfs, bought and sold out or otherwise transferred among feudal vassals without their consent or clear knowledge. The actual work of management fell increasingly to the lot of the business bureaucrats, corresponding to the "mayors" of old royal domains, called "business leaders" by courtesy or by error, but in reality only salaried satraps. Ten to one the man who is regarded as a czar of toothpaste turns out to be merely a majordomo of dentifrices, while he who is looked up to with awe as a monarch of starched collars or a king of tin cans, is merely a grand vizier or chamberlain of those useful commodities.

Tied down by fiduciary responsibilities to a great structure, forced to consider the stockholders, or at least manage them, as well as the board of directors, the position of such a bureaucrat was conducive to anything but "initiative" and "leadership." Caution became his watch-word; he shunned public discussion and risky new enterprises. Corpo-rations, said Justice Brandeis, "are constitutionally unprogressive," or at least slow-moving. In America the gas companies hesitated to touch electricity in its experimental stage, while telegraph interests were afraid of the telephone, and both held aloof from wireless. Similar ar-teriosclerosis was in fact shown earlier by Britain, where even by 1856 the iron-industry had grown so conservative that it could see no use in the processes of the inventor Bessemer or, later, in those of Thomas, and these, accordingly, went to benefit German competitors. By the end of that century, England's pace had slowed down so far that her "leaders" were unready to take up industries founded on advanced chemistry and electricity, to which still-growing Germany turned with such zest. But even in Germany, before the War, the iron-industry was feeling the effects of old age, as witnessed in the curious case of Frau Margarethe Krupp.

Between the last male heir of the Krupp family, with his exceedingly frivolous tastes and entire lack of interest in business, and his domineer-ing and puritanical wife no affinity existed. Each complained of the other to the Kaiser, who long hesitated whether to rebuke the husband or, as the husband begged, commit the wife to an asylum. Just as Frau Margarethe was in fact about to be so confined as a hopeless mental case, the husband came into a scandal at Capri and committed suicide. The same day, his wife, the "invalid," shook off doctors and assuming charge of the Krupp plant, revivified it by her extraordinary leader-ship; recognizing that Essen was now too small, she broke with tradi-tion, transferring some business and building greatly enlarged plants elsewhere, with entire success. Even she, however, at length came up against the hardening caste of bureaucracy, and found it impossible to energize the firm any more. The story of the Krupps is particularly illuminating because it can be traced back to the sixteenth century, when the first visible Krupp, apparently a rebel Protestant, accumulated a fortune by buying up properties of his plague-stricken neighbors; twice has the family fallen into stagnation, and twice been rescued by a dynamic woman. Today, however, not even fresh blood infused in the dynasty can have so radical an effect upon a bureaucratized business.

The tendency of commercial bureaucracies to grow stable and harden is more serious than in a political bureaucracy, for the latter does not have to make money—indeed, nowadays, it is not even expected to balance its budgets. The commercial bureaucracy must "show results" on the ledgers; the great firm must ever be expanding and the "status quo," loved by political bureaucrats, is fatal to it. The problem of selecting and training its members, therefore, becomes still more difficult. In America, both business and politics were once subject to a "spoils-system," and all hands in office, private as well as public, used to fly out of the door as soon as a new director took charge. In both spheres, stability and continuity were introduced by examinations and siftings, even pensions, along civil-service lines. While this eliminated much graft from business, it cut down initiative; it became harder to find men with sufficient push and not too much plunge. More immediate, also, became the problem of loyalty.

Loyalty is easier for a State to demand, because theoretically it remains unaltered; it is far harder to swear fealty to something so vague, and so swiftly changing, as a modern holding company. For this reason there remained much artificiality about the feudal-sounding talk of honor and service in business, designed to win the devotion of white-collar employees, if not of industrial workers also, and the confidence of the public-at-large. At least, in the process, the ruthless "Enrichissez-vous" phraseology of the older individualistic business was replaced, under narrowing constrictions, by the softer language of sacrifice; and, as the Black Prince wore the device, "Ich dien," so the great corporation magnate emblazoned "Service" on his escutcheon.

Much of the rugged individualism of business was rubbed off quickly by these tendencies. A study of 7,351 American "business leaders," published in 1932, showed that about 45 per cent of the men in high positions had attended college. Applying the method to men near the top, Frederick Lewis Allen came to the conclusion that the percentage of college men was 53.8 and that on the heights a still larger proportion had been tinctured with college culture. Thus the old-fashioned two-fisted business man, educated in the university of hard knocks, was passing away, and his place was filled by gentlemen who knew better how to conduct themselves at tea-parties, and could make more graceful rapprochements to politicians when a law was to be drafted, but had not necessarily learned from textbook diagrams illustrating "personnel management" just how to steer a mighty ship through troubled seas.

While the "big business man" was growing effete in his ambiguous position, the little man was not much bolder or surer of his ground. Indeed, though his business stayed the same size, his problems grew, becoming national and even international. Never had small-town petty dealers before been faced by such competitive formations as the modern chain-stores, for instance, or by almost universal monopolies, as in tobacco. Terrified by new giants, they rushed into some sort of combination of their own, especially in Germany and America. In the former, every branch had its "Verein" and "Verband," thoroughly organized and prepared for combat; perhaps there was less efficiency and purpose, on the whole, about the American trade associations, which began to spring up before the War and soon became more numerous and immense after it. The American organizations were, however, "super-colossal"; quite unprecedented was the spectacle they presented of little men, gathering together by the hundreds of thousands, speechifying, applauding, thumping one another and the table, swaying to the rhythm of "pep songs," and endeavoring to keep their courage up with paper hats and tin whistles. They had need of all this autointoxication—meaningless as such revelry might appear to outsiders, it had its profound psychological justification: the little men were closing their ranks, testing their cohesion, partly by rhythmical exercises like warriors of old, in order to give small business a weight and a size that could be pitted against big business.

But they too lost something of rugged individualism in the process of combining to defeat combination. One by one, as local units were absorbed in giant associations, their freedom of motion was likewise hemmed in; the maker of fancy "missy" frocks to retail at $1.98, who had but a single loft-room, was in reality bound down within his association, as the corporation bureaucrat by his vaster structure. Yet there was no help for it: one by one, the soda and syrup men, the laundry men, the ladies' skirt men, the knit underwear men, the fancy feather men, submitted to a loss of pioneer bravado. Some businesses had to organize to support laboratories; others to enforce self-regulation through dinner-table agreements, codes of fair practice, or "trade practice submittals," in which they sought the authorization of the Federal Government. This approach to codes began even before the War and had gone far before the Hoover crack and the Roosevelt New

Deal. The sheet glass and edible oils men had undertaken such reforms of their own accord; so had the macaroni men and the insecticides men.

Greater and more complex with every year grew the strife of businesses, big or bound-together. Retail men were at odds with wholesale men; importers combined against exporters; brick men and lumber men attacked rivals in cement, steel, and aluminum; flour men fought fruit men; sugar struck out at tobacco; silk battled with cotton and rayon, coal with oil, and the movies with the radio. Not all this energy was directed within the ranks of business. A few combinations, like the National Erectors' Association of steel men, called by Fitzpatrick "undoubtedly the most class-conscious and belligerent national association in America today," were formed to keep open shop in industrial plants. Other business interests drew together to influence the public or combat sales-resistance; propaganda appeals were made to "retain confidence" or renew lost faith or prevent anticipated troubles. Advertising men advertised to keep public confidence in advertising. Remarkable campaigns were conducted by railroads, airways, shipping interests, banks, public utilities, presenting their cases, partly to seek and partly to avoid political action.

Since it had never been decided in America how far business may go ethically in influencing political action, a new sort of official was brought into service, the "public relations counselor," a type as characteristic of this age as the corporation bureaucrat. "Public relations" bureaus were opened; specialists in playing on human harpstrings, smooth lobby-lawyers, were engaged to harmonize conflicting interests within business, to awaken public sympathy, to exert pressure on disturbers and legislatures. All the arts of the "trouble-shooter" were perfected and applied. At the apex of this development stood the Chamber of Commerce of the United States, with its thousands of members and its experts seeking to read, express, and enforce the opinions of "business America"—all in the hope of bringing the parts together in some sort of well-lubricated machine, and preventing outsiders from throwing sand into the gear-boxes. But who should steer the mighty contraption? Along what paths should it roll? Neither large business nor small had an answer.

Thus far, small business was acting much like big business; and in seeking to defend rugged individualism, much individualism had to be thrown overboard. A new need for "leadership" was felt, and as rarely met, in the association of local units as in the holding company. The associations tended to stratify, to develop their bureaucracies also; and horizontal leadership was as complicated as vertical leadership. When a lengthy inquiry was made by Edgar L. Hermmance, in 1933, for the purpose of forming trade associations for more effective action, he found most of them inefficient. Three-quarters were pure farce and had no other achievement than convivial conventions; barely ten per cent appeared to be in any shape for a concerted drive.

While the little men were groping about for leaders, the big men were no less dismayed by their own indecision. Even in England, original home of political talent among business men, there were grievous complaints. One British business man, S. S. Hammersley, discussing "Industrial Leadership" in 1925, took his fellows to task for neglecting political action and scorning literary expression. Though the Briton accepted titles and even offices, he apparently regarded them too often as decorations and did not try to win popular allegiance or exert weight in national deliberations on behalf of business. The result was that initiative was left to labor: "Whilst labor has grasped the value of propaganda and has received an immense amount of gratuitous support from organs controlled by capitalism, employers have been too lazy or too careless to strive for a friendly public atmosphere."

Decidedly gloomy, Hammersley doubted the efficacy of such proposed bodies as the Grand National Industrial Council, to bring employers together in a deliberative body; he thought that if capitalists would not take the trouble to speak in the real Parliament, it was not likely that a mock assembly would attract them. A second Briton, Sir Ernest J. Benn, in "Confessions of a Capitalist," thought Pareto's philosophy of the "élite" would bolster up the waning morale. Sir Josiah Stamp recommended preservation of old monuments as a way for business to win back public esteem; while Winston Churchill begged everyone to help "re-establish the moral basis of capitalism."

"The American way" was of course different: it consisted always in a distribution of blanks to blank minds, for a start. A symposium was therefore taken in 1919 among leading industrialists who were asked to tell how "creative statesmanship in industrial relations" could be secured. The colossi declined to suggest any method by which they might be transformed into leaders; no Caesars were made by the committee. The talk went on, nevertheless, at conventions. "Too much, heretofore, has American industry been purely on the defensive," decided the National Industrial Council in 1920. "It is time that they escaped from this apologetic attitude and addressed themselves for a program of constructive aggression." Such bold words were symptomatic of the titans' inferiority-complex. Like the little men, roaring and stamping themselves into delusions of grandeur, the big moguls, solemnly dining in state, discreetly tried to nudge and shove one another into "taking a stand."

Dejected by these failures, a remedy was sought in international conferences by Mr. Thomas J. Watson, head of the International Business

Machines Corporation. Having done more than any other man living to take the thought out of business, by his intricate calculating and other devices, Mr. Watson strove to put it back. He "instituted as the chief motto of the company the challenging single word: 'THINK.' " Over the door of his sales-force school he set up a huge sign, "THINK," and had a smaller sign, "THINK," on the desk before him whenever he lectured on the desirability of ratiocination. It was his hope that business men of all the world, thinking together, would evolve a grand plan. In Paris he led a convention dominated by three enormous signs, the middle one reading, "WELCOME, MR. WATSON, THINK," and those flanking it containing the pregnant word, "PENSEZ." Moving to Berlin, he presided over one of the most all-embracing assemblies of economic experts yet held; this, however, proved to be as full of mutual antagonisms as a similar meeting of politicians, or Left-wing novelists, and achieved nothing solid save the decoration of Mr. Watson by Hitler.

To such gatherings of economic experts, the late German Foreign Minister, Dr. Gustav Stresemann, originally also pinned faith. Perhaps if any statesman has arisen from a business sphere in modern times, it was Stresemann. Convinced of the sacred importance of business, he had defied academic tradition in his youth and, amid the gasps of university colleagues, won a doctorate with a thesis on small beer-bottling establishments in Berlin—the basis of the modest paternal fortune. Entering the Union of Saxon Chocolate Manufacturers as a syndic, he brought about cooperation among candy-men and, growing enthusiastic about the possibilities of combination in the industrial world, turned to political fields, to give them effect. Typically the Berlin pusher, before the War he led in agitation for a big Navy for business purposes. After the conflict with Britain which the naval race helped to bring on, Stresemann awoke with a bad headache. Then he dedicated himself to reconstruction through international cooperation.

Though Stresemann ardently desired to integrate the various parts of German business into a smooth-running machine and set it rolling down world paths, he grew more and more skeptical and embittered by the indifference of the business men behind him. The majority could not be roused from their apathy, or induced to take a stand against the feudal elements in German society which threatened through militarism to prevent economic harmony with the outside world. Only the heavy-industrialists, dreading disarmament, roused themselves—against Stresemann. With a heavy heart, Stresemann admitted at length that harmony would have to be imposed from above, if it were to come at all. Following an international conference at Geneva, he repudiated belief in business leadership:

After all, what can come of a meeting of representatives of opposing interests? One of the maladies of our time is the exaggeration of the importance of industrial experts. These gentlemen who conduct their concerns so impeccably, often fail when they have been asked to deal with larger policies. Europe's future depends on industrial reconstruction but the reconstructing will have to be carried out by politicians and not by leaders of industry.

These were ominous words, uttered several years before the Great Crisis of 1929—like everything else nowadays, the biggest history had known. It was accompanied by widespreading bankruptcies in banks and minds.

THE CRISIS OF FAITH

The psychological effects of crises and depressions form a little-studied phase of history. Those who discuss psychology run the risk of being denounced as Freudians, and those who touch upon pocket-books are banned as Marxians—hence fully respectable people, in this age, refrain from talk about either mind or matter.

Yet connections between the two may be traced, if sketchily, to very ancient times. The Eastward drain of precious metals to Arabia and India, which demanded bullion for their myrrh and pepper, involved most Western peoples in coinage difficulties, from the days of Plato and Pliny to Colbert. This trouble was reflected in sharp denunciation of merchants as caterers to luxurious classes or as monopolists responsible for the strange shrinkage in the purchasing power of money.

Plato thought the good life could be built only by preventing merchants from carrying away gold for purple dye and incense; his fulminations laid a basis for the dislike of business men upon which Aristotle, teacher of Alexander the Great, built by explaining monopolies and advising statesmen to look into the matter. His mighty pupil, however, changed price-levels enormously by other means, as Heichelheim's fascinating little study shows. The seizure of royal treasures in the East by Alexander meant a re-distribution of metals in the West again, with terrific effects on the Greek prices of pigs, wages of day-laborers and interest-rates, speeding up the export of wares and the immigration of Greeks to Egypt and Italy, countries slower to follow the general monetary trend and offering higher wages and better interest-rates.

Although Alexander relieved the money-shortage, Roman thirst for luxury started an even greater flow of metals to the East for silk, pepper and perfume. The air of disapproval shed over trade combinations by Aristotle was not forgotten but revived by Roman law-givers who invented the harsh word "monopoly." While prices rose steadily, Roman political leaders diverted popular wrath by baiting monopolists, as did the great *duce*, Julius Caesar; or putting "teeth" into the trust-busting decrees by a death-penalty clause, like Diocletian in the agony of 301, when all evils of the Empire were laid on "the greediness of some of its citizens, whose shameless and wicked practices, whose insatiable lust of robbery neither rich booty nor abundance of goods could still." When diatribes proved vain, the State took over business, but even this did not remove the source of price-disorder.

As the ebb and influx of precious metals continued to agitate the West—unlike the stable, self-contained East—this was partly responsible for the greater instability (or progress) of Western minds. The East-ward drain continued, but the West made more and more money: by mining, by robbing South American kings as Alexander robbed Persian satraps, or by credit. But money would buy less and less through the centuries, at least of industrial products. The price of bread remained more or less constant, proportionately—a loaf cost about the same in the first Crusade as on the eve of the French Revolution. This meant that men survived on the land, though they cursed and grumbled perpetu-ally against merchants. In cities, however, the laborers were forever pressed for food; and the capitalists themselves, flourish as they might for a time, could not found long-lived dynasties on rents. As d'Avenel points out, a family possessing a capital of 100,000 francs at the begin-ning of Saint-Louis' reign could, with the high rate of interest, gain an income of 10,000 francs. But with a 20 to 1 depreciation in money and a 3 to 1 lowering of interest-rates, the family would bleed to death. By 1400 its capital would be worth only 35,000 francs; in 1600 the scions would have a paltry 417 francs a year, and by 1910, they would own just 1,000 francs, which at 4 per cent would yield 40 francs.

In the West, accordingly, men suffered on the land, but survived; while in the cities, they flourished—and faded. Both were angry all the time and every once in a while flew into a fury, during which it was necessary to heave overboard a king, a church or a class, and have an all-around remittance of debts or change of slogans and beliefs. Up to modern times, however, these welterings in woe were long, slow-swing-ing cycles, providing time for gradual readjustments of minds and social strata. From the 1600's, the quick, sharp pains of industrial cycles and exploding "bubbles" were felt. French cities began to quake period-ically and England, as Scott proves, was subject to fits of gloom every ten years or so from the reign of Queen Elizabeth to the coming of the Steam-Engine.

The Steam-Engine cannot be accused of upsetting a beautiful social equipoise, therefore; indeed it alleviated many of the worst features of depression, making famine and plague less certain and dreadful for industrial regions. But machine-made crises had less psychological alleviation, for various reasons. For one thing, there were fewer institutions to be blamed; it was not so easy to divert economic perplexity by religious revivalism, as in the days of Savonarola, Luther and Cromwell. Also, the masses became increasingly urbanized, stimulated by press and telegraph, and bound together in deliriums of hope and fear. Such spasms came and went more swiftly, bringing ever more neurotic break-downs and rebounds: England, foremost capitalistic country of the world, in the nineteenth century, had almost as many bad years as good ones. Fifty-three years of so-called well-being were offset by forty-seven clouded with depression. Thus, even in the golden age of opportunity, in the land of classic laissez faire, prosperity was far from "normal."

In this ticklish situation, the budding capitalist made a major tactical error. He announced that prosperity was the *natural* condition of man; that evolution *must* lead to ease and comfort, obviously "higher" than toil and trouble; and that misery was no part of the divine scheme. Furthermore, he promised that if he were given a free hand, he could make everybody happy all the time. It is true that these reckless words were uttered in the heat of political campaign, but they could never be effaced from the public mind in England. And everywhere that Manchester machinery went, the credo was also exported, giving encouragement to a universal millennial belief in the forthcoming establishment of the Kingdom of God on earth—a belief which the nineteenth century held in common with the ninth.

Now this was really injecting something quite new into the tormented Western world. Up to that hour, those in authority, whether kings or priests, had taken the utmost care to adapt their doctrines to calamity as much as prosperity—indeed they envisaged trouble rather more than joy. Churches prepared to console the afflicted and told them that poverty was honorable since Our Lord had sanctified it; in times of stress, the people clung tenaciously to the rocks of their faith though they moved from rock to rock. Very cautiously, kings refrained from uttering anything too altruistic: divinely appointed to own the earth and receive submission, as they proclaimed themselves, they offered in return only a promise of a generally benevolent outlook and warm sympathy for those who sacrificed themselves in the royal cause. The advantage of this was that nobody could upbraid a king for deserting his principles; and when he was in danger, many eager martyrs formed a wall around him with their bodies. Even a beggared and throneless Pretender like Bonnie Charlie was adored. The haughtier the monarch, the deeper the protestations before him.

The more idealistic and extravagant capitalist was less foresighted; he had not thought of emergency exits. Whenever the whirl of his machinery slackened, he was to blame; if he broke from his own platform of laissez faire, he was denounced. It did not help him to lead a life more virtuous than that of kings, or to procure greater benefits for the million, at least part of the time. None remembered him in a pinch. No pretty Floras rushed to shelter him from the government, as they rescued Charlie. Instead of being petted in adversity as a dear Pretender, the capitalist was excoriated for his pretense.

Sweet Reason and wise Nature, the abstractions upon which business men called, lost charm the moment stocks fell, as had the image of Fortuna, worshiped by the Renaissance. The progressive disillusionment in Nature's powers, from the crash of 1857 on, may be compared to the wholesale desertion of the Luck-bringer in the sixteenth century when the bottom dropped out of Hapsburg war-loans. Still a sphere of faith yet remained in America, where ideologies changed more slowly because the frontiers were not closed. Up to 1929, the Americans ran on the old assumption that everything business did, however conflicting, must work out well in the end; so leaders got the tariff raised, while urging free trade upon others, and scoured the world for markets, meanwhile pouring out millions in loans to rehabilitate their competitors or erecting branch factories in Canada, Ireland, England and Latin America. And for a time all went well—until America had endangered the vast wealth which she had reaped while avoiding participation in the War for three years.

With money to cast abroad among scrambling *duces* and corporations, the dignitaries of American business were regarded with awed respect abroad: German industrialists crossed the sea to study rationalization and *Fordismus* and returned home convinced that Americans had at last put industry and commerce on a high plateau of permanent prosperity. In their opinion, a "Wirtschaftswunder," an economic miracle, had been performed, and that great day had arrived for which Shakespeare had asked in the Renaissance, when he cried: "Will Fortune never come with both hands full?"

At home as well as in foreign countries, the oracular utterances of Morgan, Mitchell, Baker, Schwab, Grace, Aldrich, Rockefeller, Wiggins, Insull, Dawes, Young, Giannini, and others on the heights, were received with deference. Universities gave them degrees; reporters noted their speeches, weddings and receptions, as events of a "business royalty." But the term was ill-advised. Kings had only said: "Children, be ready to give me the last drop of your hearts' blood, in return, if you are lucky, for a half-smile from Me." Business leaders in America, like Englishmen almost a century before, though with still more exuberance, promised concrete gifts for all their countrymen and for all the world—a universal and everlasting two-car garage civilization. This was not only un-royal. It was injudicious.

For upon what slogans could faith be restored in the business man, after the Great Crash of 1929? The old stock of ideas, lovely mind-tissues woven in Renaissance, Reformation, and Enlightenment, were shockingly used up and that kind of spinning, a petty handicraft, was no longer carried on so readily as of yore. Protestantism, after helping to sanctify and bolster up the self-confidence of individualists for four hundred years, had taken a new turn, largely as a result of the business man's own oratory. After the Crash, ministers gathered in national assembly, declared there was no excuse for poverty any longer; instead of blessing it, like Roman Catholics, or urging the people to seek wealth through work like Calvinists, they deplored the selfishness of those in high places. At the same time, another and still more potent magic, which had given the business man almost the only "romance" he has enjoyed, was dropping away—the enchantment of far horizons.

Economic boundaries had been drawn tighter since the War, with its awakening of nationalism and desire for business independence from Turkey to China. "Backward" nations had begun to manufacture for themselves; Argentina was turning her own leather into shoes and Brazilians were spinning their own cotton. Western people were reduced to quarreling over the remainder, by quotas, bounties, high duties, exchange regulations. It was more and more difficult for business men to acquire "the poetry of motion." Yet in its psychological as well as economic aspects, this shutting of the frontiers was disastrous. From time immemorial, the merchant's prestige had to a large degree depended on his association with perilous exploits in distant climes and his cosmopolitan air; even those who begrudged him his money, envied his experiences. In the public mind, formed by literary men, "color" was associated with Eastern traffic or with "pioneering" in the Far West. Business Boston, for instance, would have appeared utterly monotonous, had it not been for the whiff of sandalwood around her wharves.

This seeping away of slogans, creeds, fictions and romance, is the more serious because Big Business, to a greater extent than small, depends upon credit, another name for faith. In the past, when wealth was visible in the form of ingots or acres, beeves and bales, it could be taken with faint apology or none. In this absurdly-called "materialistic age," however, riches are in the shape of credits which exist, like *Peter Pan's* fairies, only so long as all good children believe in them. And so the business man is caught in a truly poignant predicament: he has created an "age of faith," beyond any known in the world, even while he was using up so much of the world's old stock of faiths.

THE NEW FRAMEWORK AROUND BUSINESS

Out of the wreck of ideas and ideologies in modern times, one survived—that majestic seventeenth-century fiction, the State, in which most people still manage, most of the time, to believe. Whenever business is sore beset, and the public grows incredulous over private credit, it is backed up by Government credit. Then behind banks, shops and factories looms more mightily than ever that mental image, formed by philosophers and historians from Campanella to Treitschke, the State— a figment of the imagination which yet has power to sustain currencies "cut loose from gold," hovering in the dim air like ectoplasmic visions at an international séance.

By the immense expansion of credit in the War and after, the State and Business have been brought into ever closer dependence upon each other's trust; in the War, also, both were forced to cooperate in a new framework of boards and departments. After the War, the two spheres could not be fully separated, for the State had to care for the distressed masses of unemployed by taxing business, while business clung to the State, seeking subsidies, the regulation of "cutthroat competition" and, as the Germans call it, even the "socialization of debts." On an upward turn of the cycle, business men might assume an air of authority toward States—men like Charles G. Dawes and later Owen D. Young, who assisted Central European Powers to order and stabilize their finances; but on a downward curve, as the waters were about to close over Dawes' own bank, the Government of the United States had to throw out a lifeline.

How prodigiously both have grown, the business states within the State, and the political framework which must enclose these bodies or perish, was illustrated as early as 1902 by Ghent's "Benevolent Feudalism." Taking the Steel Corporation of that day, he showed that it then drew yearly net profits double the total revenues of the United States Government when Lincoln was elected. It had then 158,000 employees, a number larger than that on the Government's payroll, if postmasters are excepted, and paid in wages $13,000,000 more than the city budget of Greater New York. Since then, of course, the picture has been vastly magnified. The question becomes—how far will the relationship of these enormous structures diverge in character from such relationships in the past?

To all appearances, the two eras of the patrician-ruler and the individualist are over—the age in which the business man could entirely dominate the State, and the age in which he could almost wholly shake it off. The condition favoring the former was localism: the business man could rule, and rule well, in a small society wholly absorbed in one type of business, but over a huge society basically agrarian, or filled with conflicting kinds of business interests, he has hitherto surrendered to an umpire, for that, essentially, is what a king is. For the second type of relationship—utter independence of the State—a world-wide frontier and a great deal of elbow-room are necessary, and in all history, this has been attained in classic form by one country only, England, and there but for a single generation—1840 to 1880.

In another form of relationship, the State may absorb business, as the Byzantine Empire finally did, or the Babylonian before it. In that case the business organizer becomes the commissar, or, as they called it several millennia ago, at Ur, the *damkar*. This is a form suitable to an Eastern Empire like Russia, until recently still Byzantine in her Church and faith; but it would work less easily among peoples who had experienced a Renaissance and a Reformation.

Or again, a compromise is possible, as in the Augustan Age of Rome or eighteenth-century Europe, when the highest offices were left to an aristocracy, and business exploited, though it did not govern, the State. This possibility must be even more readily discounted, for the War swept away much of that aristocracy and diminished the power of the rest. How much the business man has relied upon aristocracy, in some form or other, he does not generally realize; even in the Middle Ages, when he was most proudly "independent" behind city-walls, he left, after all, the task of subduing and overawing the vast majority of the people, who were peasants, to the feudal chivalry. The old aristocracy always cost the business man much more than it was worth, but it saved him many an embarrassing hour of thought.

Now at last the whole splendid costumery and ideology, developed through the ages around the cult of the soil, has begun to crumble and vanish, withdrawing its magic cloak from the business man. Left solitary upon the heights, the spotlight turned on him, with no plumes and cuirasses to distract the public gaze, he has begun to feel very uncomfortable. Looking about him, he perceives also that a far-reaching revolution has been wrought by the War not only in the heights of the State, but all through it: the masses have been quickened through war-propaganda to greater mobility and hopes. At the same time, they have been torn from agrarian self-sufficiency as never before; no longer can the business man look from his battlements upon the "flat land," the villages and furrowed fields, sure that, whatever happens, he can leave the agriculturalists to their own resources. They can no longer feed and clothe themselves; the proud farmer is as anachronistic as the proud aristocrat. The warrior as well is mechanized and dependent upon high-power industry and the State which mobilizes economy behind him. In these circumstances, the capitalist must "accept the State" as Margaret Fuller "accepted the universe"—"Gad, she'd better," remarked Carlyle.

Although the situation is similar throughout the lands of Western capitalism, it by no means follows that they must all look alike. They did not do so in classic times or in the Middle Ages, in the eighteenth century or the nineteenth. And even today their separate heritages make "high capitalism" appear in very different guises under Fascism, British "Tory Socialism," or the American New Deal.

XXVIII

BUSINESS IN SEARCH OF CREDO
AND CHARACTER

THE ESSENCE OF FASCISM is the elaboration of a "Mythos," woven of legend, history and histrionics, to instil and uphold public faith in the State. From the business man's viewpoint, its advantage is that it saves him the trouble of re-building faith in himself, or examining his own creed and character. It enables him to continue, as he has done for centuries, in cozy obscurity behind the screens and scenes of the State, leaving the problems of government to a bureaucracy and the function of adorning and diverting society to an aristocracy. Under Fascism, government "experts" do the hard work of integrating and planning society for the business man; and the Party "élite" of "heroes" draws away attention from merchants and manufacturers or bankers. Since the Party élite accepts some chosen members of the masses, and elevates them to the heights, it gives the people a rich glow of self-admiration, and in many respects forms a securer foundation for the State than the old abasement before a nobility of birth.

This, accordingly, is the laziest way out of the dilemma of the business man's relation to society in modern times. And, as might be expected, it was tried out first on a grand scale under a warm Southern sun, in commercially backward Italy.

FASCISMO: THE DWINDLING BUNDLE OF STICKS

Obviously, a mythos is easiest to compose in a relic-encumbered land like Italy, where nothing has been experienced like the industrial and religious revolutions which slashed through the history-web in other countries. In Italy it was a simple matter to reach across the centuries to grasp an Etruscan symbol of oligarchy, the Fasces, the bundle of sticks bound together with an axe. A well-read man like Mussolini needed only to recall the case of Cola di Rienzi in fourteenth-century Rome, a plain workingman elevated to dictatorship by rich plebeian merchants thirsting for the overthrow of an insolent feudal aristocracy.

Rienzi glorified his person with the scepter and diadem of the Caesars; casting off Christian customs, to the disgust of the Pope, he reconnected himself with the majesty of Imperial Rome by taking a public dip in the antique bath-tub of Constantine the Great. The difficulty was to find money for such pagan pageantry. Rich merchants refused to contribute. And after the aristocrats had been wrung as dry as possible, it was necessary to squeeze the common people by heavier taxes, although to the last Rienzi talked about Liberty, Peace and Justice. The common people, incited by aristocrats, stormed his palace and slew him as, long before, the Gracchi had been slain.

Except for the end of the story—which might now be avoided with perfected police-systems—the pattern was there for Mussolini. And Italy had not changed so much as other lands since the days of Rienzi, or even the Gracchi. Poor, agrarian, extensively illiterate, largely preserving a pre-capitalist mentality, the people were responsive to the same antique gestures, poses and symbols. Very little "rugged individualism" had developed in the commercial sphere, for Italian business had not followed that trend of Northern Protestant lands. Even before Mussolini, heads of interlocking corporations had already established a kind of corporative state, ended laissez faire and enlisted the government in their service. The Roman Church on the whole favored such development, for her doctrine of "corporatism," elaborated by many theologians in various tongues, is designed to accept big business as a social fact, and embrace it in a stabilized planned society—her ancient dream.

Business accordingly accepted the "strong man," if with misgivings. And for a time he did things pleasing to all business; by daggers and castor-oil he suppressed independent trade unions and prohibited strikes, and forced the "lazzaroni," the children of the sun who preserved an antique distaste for toil, to work as French or Englishmen were compelled by the State to do, centuries before. If by way of compensation he gave employees a formal opportunity to present grievances, he arranged to have disputes adjudicated by tribunals with the proper point of view; these tribunals were surrounded by Fascist party members who saw that order was preserved. Having put down communists, socialists and trade-unionists, Mussolini provided entertainments and engagements for workers after hours, *dopolavoro*, to occupy their minds. All such diversions cost money, involving the maintenance of a huge government bureaucracy filled with Fascist "workers" and "heroes." But though the rich were taxed a little to provide Christmas toys and candy for children, they were not bled for circuses, as in old Rome; most of the money came from indirect taxes borne very largely by the beneficiaries of *dopolavoro*. The workers of the new-old Rome have to pay for their circuses as well as their bread.

According to the splendid theory, business was to be bound together, like the Fascist bundle of sticks, in the corporative State, substituted for the democratic State. But it is impossible nowadays to bind businesses together and retain the same number of sticks—the bundle will be ever dwindling, consisting of ever fewer, ever bigger sticks. This is the one visible result of "corporatism" which is not seriously disputed. The corporative State itself is supposed to be a kind of top holding-concern, under which the diverse branches of economic life are unified. In practice, this is hardly more than guild-romanticism; for business men it involves little more than a set of trade associations such as are familiar to other countries. At no point does the corporative State substitute public ownership for private in business enterprise. But it does further the big-scale private business at the expense of small business—that is the natural trend of all bureaucratization of economy.

The substantial interventions of the Fascist or corporative State in business economy have taken the form of financial aids and subsidies to big business. It has arranged ever higher protective tariffs to benefit special interests in industry and agriculture. Like the Reconstruction Finance Corporation in the United States, it lent public money to banks and concerns on the verge of bankruptcy. It has facilitated the merger of corporations, especially for the purpose of saving weak concerns from going to the wall. When established industries feel the pinch of competition, it forbids the erection of new factories likely to cut profits for those already in existence. When business finds it necessary to cut wages, the corporative State does the job, thus relieving management of the difficulties involved in this painful operation. It votes huge sums to the army and navy, and thus provides profitable "business" for the heavy industries and the purveyors. It is not without justification that a recent writer in the *Economist* declares: "So far, the new Corporative State only amounts to the establishment of a new and costly bureaucracy from which those industrialists who can spend the necessary amount, can obtain almost anything they want, and put into practice the worst kind of monopolistic practices at the expense of the little fellow who is squeezed out in the process."

When, in spite of all such public assistance, a big business enterprise gets into financial troubles, the Fascist State comes to its aid. As Salvemini has put the case: "In order to avert the bankruptcy of the big concerns that were on the verge of ruin, the government created certain public institutes to take over the shares of the rescued companies and to supervise the companies in question until they were again in a healthy condition. Mussolini has described these institutes as 'convalescent homes, where organs that have more or less deteriorated come under observation and receive appropriate treatment.'" In upshot this treatment, as Salvemini shows, merely amounts to this: The government institute holds the shares of the diseased concern, runs all the risks of total loss, and if the concern recovers its health returns the shares to the private holders. So by lending money to corporations and by buying shares in times of stress, the corporative State guarantees the life of big business on terms favorable to itself and at public expense.

And what about all the little business men? In 1934, Mussolini declared that "three-quarters of the Italian economic system, both industrial and agricultural" had received help from the State. But this, as Salvemini points out, "is an exaggeration. He should have said three quarters of the *big* firms engaged in banking, industry, shipping, etc." In support of this statement, Salvemini cites an address by Signor Pirelli: "Beyond the frontiers there has been a misunderstanding of the meaning of one of Mussolini's phrases to the effect that three-quarters of the Italian economic system, both industrial and agricultural, is under the supervision of the State. Almost all the medium-sized and little firms and the great majority of slightly larger firms, with the exception of a few categories, are completely outside the sphere of the State's healing activity." Just what this means for the smaller business men and the great body of Italian people becomes evident when it is remembered that the Fascist State has reduced the proportion of direct taxes and increased the proportion of indirect taxes—from which comes the money to heal big business concerns in trouble. According to careful estimates, the proportions of direct and indirect taxes are the reverse of the system of burden distribution prevailing in Great Britain. What, then, the corporative State has done in Italy so far, whatever the hopes expressed in rhetorical imagery, is to entrench business men engaged in monopolistic enterprises and leave the rest of them to engage in the ordinary struggle for existence under a heavy weight of taxes.

Whenever the little men are squeezed out, however, more weight is won by the oldest social elements in Italy—big landowners and the army and bureaucracy. These, therefore, exercise more and more predominance in the Senate, the one relic of the democratic State which has been salvaged. Thus it would appear that Fascismo has not preserved a status quo for business; instead it has set in motion a process with enormous possibilities, as yet unpredictable; the growing conservatism, the weight of landed wealth, the overwhelming might of the biggest businesses may again bind down economic initiative and formalize Italy, as in the days of Absolutism.

Something of that threat is contained in Mussolini's interesting work, the "Prelude to Machiavelli," in which he denies the whole premise of Florentine individualism: "The individual strives constantly to escape. He strives to disobey the laws, to dodge payment of taxes, and to avoid going to war. Only a few, heroes or holy men, sacrifice their own egos on the altar of the State." Setting his face against the whole trend of modern centuries, in which business individualism has transformed the earth, Mussolini demands "a life in which the individual achieves spiritual existence through self-renunciation, the sacrifice of his particular interests and even through death."

It is true, therefore, that business men for the present may welcome Fascismo, which disciplines labor by crushing individualism, but there may come a time when the loss of individualism in the business sphere itself may be felt. Mussolini's pledge to business in 1934, when he announced for the third or fourth time the creation of the corporative State, was conservative in tone: "We shall proceed with great caution. We are sure of ourselves, because our revolution has a whole century before it." But what if that revolution proceeds at the same rate and in the same direction for a whole century? What if Rome, ancient lover and wielder of concentrated political authority, triumphs once more over her old enemy, the commercial-individualist spirit of Florence— ironically, under the Etruscan symbol of the Fasces?

FIELD-GREY CAPITALISM IN GERMANY

When German business followed the line of the Italian, there was a mighty shout from extremists on Right and Left, that Fascism must be the "inevitable" next stage of capitalist development, the newest and most "modern" turn. This is to ignore the historic relation of German and Italian business—both have been akin, both different from other businesses, and, since the seventeenth century, both have been behind other businesses in their political aspects.

It will be recalled how Italians and Germans sank together in the seventeenth century under petty-Absolutism, because they were unable to combine and formulate a policy of business-burghers. Both "awoke" to nationalism and industrialism very late, in the last quarter of the nineteenth century, within a few years of each other, and under very similar circumstances. Italy was unified under the leadership of the Kingdom of Sardinia-Piedmont, which, around Turin, contained the most active Italian business group; the actual unification, however, though desired by business Liberals, was achieved by a military aristocracy of the small realm. This condition was duplicated in Germany, welded together by the military-agrarians of the Kingdom of Prussia. The fates of the two countries ran parallel through the War and even afterward, when Italy was left feeling "cheated of victory," and Germany was really defeated.

After the War, German business men were stripped of their shipping, industrial, banking, investment and colonial interests abroad. The savings and bond investments of the lower and middle classes were almost wiped out by inflation. Only the heavy industries, the well-organized cartels and concerns, and large enterprises survived fairly well the general wreckage. These interests received the principal benefits from American and other loans poured into Germany after 1923. For several years, unhampered by disruptive anti-trust legislation, they could proceed easily with rationalization, mergers, consolidations and cartelization; the coalition cabinets did not interfere seriously, and for a good while the I.G. dye interests even had a representative in the cabinet.

Could this greater German business now step forth in the political sphere at last? That was the issue. The old feudal-military elements in society were temporarily shocked into retirement from the scene; it was possible for business men to displace the Junkers and control Germany. Nor was this supreme chance ignored entirely: three German men of business perceived the opportunity and offered plans.

Hugo Stinnes had closely worked with the Department of Raw Materials in the War. This experience acquainted him with the possibilities of mobilizing and centralizing the resources of the nation, and showed him the way to take advantage of the inflation which destroyed so many others. Out of the inflation, Stinnes quickly formed his enormous fortune. Realizing that wealth lay in raw materials, he used the depreciating money to stretch his power over iron, steel, electricity, chemicals, banking, and finally over resources in other lands. But as he built up this towering structure, with its incongruously assorted parts, Stinnes dreamed of making it almost co-extensive with the State. He formulated plans for a regional economic regulation in Germany, proposing to divide the land into spheres, each headed by a dictatorial economic expert. This gigantically ambitious scheme of Stinnes, which can only be compared with the vision of Spanish empire entertained by Ouvrard, remained unrealized. When Stinnes died of overwork, his empire crumbled more swiftly than that of Alexander.

At the same time, the younger Rathenau, Walter, was pondering the problem of industry and the State. Perhaps because his parent forced him to give up painting and literature and make a career in business, he regarded business more theoretically than others. Granting that machines could increase the well-being of masses, he insisted that well-being would not solve the governmental question. In antagonism to Henry Ford, Rathenau maintained that material advance would avail little without mental progress: "The transcendant problem is: the growth of the soul; but what is the problem in practice? Certainly it is not: raising the standard of life" alone. Mere enlargement of production without direction is inadequate.

As Minister of Reconstruction and of Foreign Affairs after the War, Rathenau drew near to the center of power. Sketching his plans for an industrial society, with freedom of enterprise assumed and yet combined with some State-socialistic control, the ambitious business man was approaching the chance to realize his schemes, when he was murdered in cold blood, in June, 1922, by an assassin from fanatic circles then being organized by the Army. The Army knew its foes: Rathenau was one and Stresemann the other. When Stresemann died of exhaustion, like Stinnes, in the effort to create a controlled and balanced capitalism in Germany, the Army, looking around, could see no other business foe.

Behind the Army gathered the heavy-industrialists, as they had stood back of the Big Navy before the War. In 1932 Thyssen openly appealed to great industrialists assembled at Düsseldorf to support Hitler's cause. Other businesses undoubtedly provided encouragement and support for the National Socialist movement: a seeker of a cigarette-monopoly, who, in fact, attained much of his desire through Hitler; a piano-maker's wife, Helene Bechstein, afterwards rewarded by an official injunction upon Germans to remember pianos; and two brothers, manufacturers of peroxide, who may or may not have been actuated by the hope of making all Germans blonde again. And in the rear hovered the vague, diminutive shapes of many small business men, representatives of a mediaeval economic order that had managed miraculously to survive in Germany.

As happened in the Cromwellian Revolution in England, little business was brought around to support the militant elements of big business; and the forces back of Hitler were composed, like those behind Cromwell, of many sheep bleating for the destruction of the lions who went along with them. The situation of the little men in Germany was, however, not so very different from that of seventeenth-century England: Germany had not changed so much at the bottom as she had at the top, during her late and furious push to industrialize herself after 1870. In that swift half-century of unfolding, the marvelous technical triumphs of German business blinded most observers to the fact that very little had been altered down below, in the small towns, among the small men. Though German wharves turned out a *Leviathan*, and German factories a Zeppelin, the basis of German business life was still that of the seventeenth century. In the sleepy, wall-ringed country-towns minds like architecture had remained stagnant. Little or nothing had happened at Hamelin since the Pied Piper took all the young blood away. Rothenburg had scarcely altered a façade or an opinion for four or five centuries. No new house, except a post-office, had been erected in Dinkelsbühl since the trade-routes altered, leaving her high and dry in the fourteenth century. The dark battlements of Nürnberg, the chosen seat of Nazi Party demonstrations, enclosed a people still living upon handicrafts, with a handicraftsman's jealousy of machine-age changes, fearful of the large industries blooming around the old city.

Like Italy, Germany still kept an immense heritage of the past, upon which the mythologists of the Fascist movement could play. They were most successful in winning adherents in small towns, as the analyses of votes before Hitler's accession to power have clearly shown. It was in the "stagnant towns," the picturesque show-places, that shop-keepers and craftsmen rallied around the Swastika; in Nürnberg, the crafts were suffering horribly from the competition of advanced machine-production, forced to accept less and less profit; in Nürnberg's hysteria, Streicher flourished. In other towns, which had been sites of garrisons before the War, the merchants missed the money brought by the soldiers, formerly their chief means of subsistence.

Jew-baiting appealed to these small men for almost the same reasons that it attracted them in the Middle Ages—because Jewish entrepreneurs, though not the biggest in the land, were those most immediately in view of the lowest tradesmen and peasants. As analyses of tax-lists have adequately shown, but a small part of German wealth and business was in the hands of Jews—the richest men of Germany were "Aryan" heavy-industrialists and titled landowners, noblemen with mining affiliations. Relatively poor, Jews became cattle-dealers, with whom the peasants came in contact; or they pressed into low-paid professions, like medicine, competing with the sons of the lower middle class. Another branch open to them was the movie-industry where Jews, especially from dramatically-gifted Eastern Europe, won a high place; this brought upon them the antagonism of small-town movie-operators who became one of the most active and vocal groups behind Hitler. And finally, Jews turned to the department-store, which, again, hits hardest the small retailer, the little man. Agitation against department-stores had once proved even in France a part of the pressure for dictatorship; small shopkeepers, enraged by the growth of the "Louvre" and other big stores, supported the laughable would-be dictator, General Boulanger. But France had accepted the big store, at least in Paris; America and England had been won by Wanamaker and Selfridge without an upheaval. Germany, however, received the phenomenon too late; the spread of emporiums like Tietz's and Wertheim's in Berlin coincided with economic difficulties for the small towns.

The small men of Rothenburg and Hamelin did not know anything about big industrial operations in Germany; they neither saw nor clashed with representatives of steel-cartels. Big business, which was almost wholly Gentile, lay far removed from the spheres of their hatred and indeed of their comprehension. The Jews were thus not connected with any vital interest; not only were they the men daily watched by the "menu peuple" and held accountable in every crisis, but they were not rich enough to command help from the great Gentile business men of Germany. They could easily be dispossessed, without causing any serious disturbance to German economic life—as would certainly not have been the case had they been the "masters" they were painted by propagandists.

Yet when all these business interests, little and big, behind Hitler are considered, it is still not possible to explain Hitler's triumph merely as a device of capitalism to secure power. That would be flying in the face of recorded history, which has ever shown business men, as in the American, French or British Revolutions, to be fomenters of rebellion, but not direct and purposeful revolutionists. That German business men were superior to all others in political daring or adroitness is unlikely; to fancy them capable of laying far-sighted plans, operating in a subtle and Machiavellian manner, with profound knowledge of public psychology, is grossly to over-estimate their intellectual parts and indeed their weight in society.

Without the enormous influence of the land and army in Germany, business drive alone would not have carried Hitler across the Constitution to power. And if Junkerdom was able to find a leader in Hitler also, this was, at least in part, the result of an amusing accident. Big landowners of East Prussia, burdened by debts, desired to present an estate to von Hindenburg, the high but poor representative of their caste. They persuaded various industrialists to open their purses and pay the bill. When Hindenburg acquired the estate of his ancestors he soon learned how hard it was to make farming pay and became intensely aware of the woes of big landowners; at last he was ready to break his vow to support the Constitution, letting Hitler into power, even though not elected, in order to prevent a too-sweeping investigation into corruption in East Prussian agricultural subsidies. The latter had threatened to involve the Hindenburg family. One may speculate on what a different course history might have taken had the industrialists presented Hindenburg instead with a shoe-factory. But this is an idle vision, since German business men, whatever their theoretical talents, have not shown equal finesse in practical politics.

Once the Hitler régime began, it exhibited certain features in common with the Italian scheme. Labor was held down with the full force of government authority, an old dream of German heavy-industrialists from the time of von Stumm, who in the 1880–90's openly advocated a militarization of labor as a means of keeping order in factories. The control over labor was in fact elaborated more in Germany than in

Italy, because German labor was far more intelligent and the demands of German industry for skill and speed were much higher. For a time, also, Hitler managed to divert the minds of the "menu peuple," who had been clamoring for debt-reductions, and the break-up of banks and monopolies, by flinging the Jews, who represented a trifling element, to the lions. Like Italian Fascism, German Fascism preserved private ownership of enterprise; indeed there has been a considerable "re-privatization" of enterprises formerly owned by the State and now sold back to individual concerns. As the American economist, Robert A. Brady, has observed, the Fascist State envisages the private owner-ship of productive property and natural resources; it considers basic the conduct of business for profit, and the ownership control of enter-prise. Insofar, the Fascist State has preserved capitalism—but not in a status quo.

Neither in Germany nor in Italy has the effect of Fascism been a "freezing" of the status quo. Indeed, in the former country, the changes undergone by capitalism have been larger and more revolutionary. The amalgamation and concentration of business proceeds at a rapid rate, while the squeezing out and bearing down of little men is concomitant. Under the iron-clad rules of the Nazi State, the big business men, who come closest to the bureaucracy, fare best; the little men, remotely connected through friends of a party friend of a local commissar, are as far as ever from the focus of power. Nor have they won their desires in any considerable degree, except in the dissolution of cooperatives, for department-stores go on, if the Jews are forced out, and the Nazi movie-industry, under ministerial control, is vastly more "tyrannical" in its demands upon the little projectors.

It is even questionable what the results of Fascism will be for big business in Germany. In the pulling and hauling of competing interests, agrarian, military and industrial, capitalists do not have everything their way. If they do not have to haggle with trade union agents, employers still find they cannot hire and fire with unlimited freedom; and they even discover already that the destruction of the old educational stand-ards is diminishing the output of inventive brains for research labora-tories. Their export and import business is controlled to the last degree, save when they are able to make surreptitious shifts among accounts in foreign countries. Under Nazi judges, they hesitate to go to law over contracts. Every month sees the registration of government decrees as arbitrary as orders in Bolshevik Russia, commanding business men to undertake obligations foreign to what they consider the "normal" con-duct of their enterprises—paid for by the "freezing" of wages, almost the only part of the status quo rigidly maintained. A huge internal debt, much of it floating and concealed, gives bankers and industrialists pause as they think of the future—will it be "a thousand years" before the books must be balanced? And will Germany, with her economy directed intensively to armaments, be recaptured by the military lords who have threatened merchants there for the past fifteen hundred years and more?

TORY SOCIALISM IN BRITAIN

Aristocracy in Britain survived the War so well that there was no need to improvise an "élite" in great haste. Somewhat hurt by heavy taxation upon its estates, its ranks were nevertheless bolstered up by the generous bestowal of knighthoods or baronetcies upon the business leaders in steel, beer or ships, in which the Lloyd George cabinet carried on the age-old tradition. Sacrifices made in contribution to party campaign funds were in no wise overlooked; and humble birth was no bar. An especially large group of automobile men, whose plants had been transformed to war-work, were elevated, among them Sir Harold Bowden, made a baronet for war-services; Bettman, born a German, who joined the Labour Party in 1927 and became an M.P.; and Sir Herbert Austin, a farmer's son, grown rich during the War and after it, who transferred the Ford idea to England, produced the "Baby Austin" for the masses, and achieved a title and a seat in Parliament.

The difference between the British and American "way" is well illustrated by the most readily comparable group, that of the automobilemen. In America, Nash, Timken, Sloan, Durant and the rest, who rose from no simpler origins in farm or grocery than the Englishmen, remained in business. One among them, Charles S. Mott of General Motors, indeed announced his intention to enter politics and thus show a model to his fellows—but the voters would not have him. Another, Willys, became ambassador to Poland, the social height to which American business men frequently aspire. But the leader among them all, Henry Ford, railed at contacts between business and government, which he wished to see divorced; he also denounced retired leisure in favor of the gospel of continuous work in harness. Thus he presented the very antithesis to the "British Ford," Austin.

Though admitted to the aristocracy, and assuming some part in local and national politics, the British man of business did not become the open leader during the crisis of 1929. Indeed that crisis did not affect England so profoundly as some other countries, for various reasons. English business has never been like others. It has had immense imperial resources at its command. Having long before rid themselves of wild-cat banks, British financial institutions could weather the storm without a tremor; and in crowded England, they had not been tempted into such speculations in lands and "developments" as have ever beset

American bankers. Having submitted to heavy direct taxation during and after the War to provide old age, sickness, and unemployment benefits, British business men saw their trade steady under the influences of assured mass buying power. Since they had come to fair working terms with trade unions, and had not turned police loose on agitators, they were spared many of the agonies of class-antagonisms which racked societies with less gifts for compromise. And finally, British business men, who started the great game of modern capitalism before any of the rest, had already reached a stage, even before the War, where they were no longer squabbling as fierce competitors, but willing to divide spheres and combine forces; they were prepared, under Stanley Baldwin, for consolidation in the electrical industries, combining private and public ownership, and for various reasonable plans among mining-owners, designed to mitigate economic strife.

If it was an experiment, therefore, to allow the Labor government to steer the ship in the crisis of 1929, it was not a dangerous one. Labor in England had been conciliated by much social legislation and, having encountered a generally calm and judicious temper among employers, had not learned to show teeth; moreover, the impressive front of aristocracy and monarchy remained unbroken, above and before business. Ramsay MacDonald, accordingly, repudiated by Socialists, rewarded by certain business men, served as titular holder of power during the most difficult stage of operations, while Britain "went off gold," and then it was safe to hand back the portfolios to two business men in succession, Stanley Baldwin and Neville Chamberlain.

To explain the British stability solely on the ground of the survival of an aristocracy, is, however, quite inadequate. One of the decisive factors in achieving Britain's social harmony has been the conciliation of labor through Socialistic measures—a relatively benevolent attitude made possible, rather more than Britons or Americans usually realize, at the expense of the natives in distant imperial possessions, exploited instead of English workers, and through the profits of rearmament.

The realization that humanitarianism must accompany high mechanization came from above in England, to a unique degree. It is true that in France and Germany as well, business men stood high in the ranks of Socialist leaders. The German, Engels, failing to find an instrument for social reform in the Church, turned to political agitation, much to the distress of his own family, to whom he seemed a renegade. In industrial Lyons, likewise, Fourier, the hyper-sensitive son of a rich French merchant, was turned against capitalism by a fateful boyhood incident —once, when he told a customer in his father's shop the unfortunate truth about a piece of cloth, he was spanked by the embarrassed parent. Fourier never forgot or forgave the blow, and though he submitted to a business apprenticeship, he used his inheritance to travel abroad, studying the new industrialism, and combating its excesses, like his contemporary, Robert Owen.

An English business man, however, Robert Owen, really promulgated the new word, Socialism, and that, so he argued originally, for the benefit of capitalists. Himself an early entrepreneur, who had watched the most terrible stages of the budding industrial revolution in Manchester, he became convinced that capitalism, for its own sake, must raise the living conditions of the masses, both to obtain greater skill in industry and to increase consumption. At the outset, therefore, Owen started from somewhat the same premises as Henry Ford; and the cotton-spinning plant he developed at New Lanark was a forerunner of the latter's Detroit plant as an experiment in paternalism.

It had occurred to Owen, almost alone in his day, that a sober, literate laboring population could do better work and more of it than drunken and ricket-ridden clod-hoppers. His partners scouted the idea, saying: "Each of your propositions is true individually; but as they lead to conclusions contrary to our education, habits, and practices, they must in the aggregate be erroneous." Nevertheless, Owen soon convinced them through the balance-sheet; after transforming the tipsy, thieving crowd of wretched operatives through cheap food from company stores, schooling, housing, recreation and employment insurance, he made better yarn than his competitors and marked up a profit of £160,000 in four years. The plan set business men talking; thousands of visitors came to observe it in operation and the future Czar of Russia vainly urged Owen to take the job of remaking the mammoth land of Russia.

Owen was for many years the mightiest of propagandists for a reformed capitalism. Incessantly working for temperance, popular education, and a child-labor statute that would prevent children under ten years of age from working more than ten and a half hours a day, Owen encountered the stubborn resistance of his brother-employers. He enraged them even more by organizing the Grand National Consolidated Trades Union in 1834, thus, though an employer, initiating labor movements for the world. And finally, he went abroad as a self-appointed ambassador to the courts of Europe, to preach capitalistic reform, Socialism from above. A patriarchal-looking manufacturer with an eloquent Welsh tongue, he was received by royalty everywhere, although no crowned heads took seriously his proposition that society might be made rich and content by the proper utilization of machinery, by compromise and education, under a socialized capitalism. Following in the footsteps of Cobden, the laissez fairist preacher to the universe, Owen strove to undo Cobden's work.

Enormous and indelible was the impress left by Owen upon capitalist society, even though he himself, despairing of converting his fellows, ventured into ever more utopian experiments and failures and veered away from private enterprise. Before he died, in the crisis-period of 1858, at the age of eighty-eight, he had, however, seen his fellow-capitalists turning more and more to the principle of alleviating the hardships of the competitive system through humanitarianism. A generation later, Chamberlain and Rhodes took up the plea, coupling progress at home with imperialist expansion abroad. And America, impressed by Owen's visits, acquired a labor movement.

How great a share in reformation movements within capitalism has been shouldered by business men themselves is an aspect of modern history seldom dwelled upon, either by capitalists themselves, who grow nervous at the thought, or by their antagonists, who find it simpler to view them as mere enemies of reform. Yet, if they were gathered together, the stories of experimental manufacturers and employers, who foresaw the coming of a more socialized and less competitive capitalism, would show a clear succession, from Fourier, Engels and Owen to William Gregg, Rathenau, Filene and Ford. Above all, the interaction would be observable in the two Anglo-Saxon democracies, where business has taken more initiative than elsewhere toward solving the problems of social adjustment brought by advancing capitalism.

THE CLAY FEET OF THE ECONOMIC MIRACLE IN AMERICA

Promising to "take the government out of business," President Harding relaxed the control of political authority over the economic sphere after the War, more than was possible in other belligerent lands. And though he carried into office a number of business men whose morals and methods proved distasteful to the public, after investigations had revealed them, American democracy saw no ground for change in 1924. Coolidge was as glad to pursue the course of "letting business alone." He had said, "The man who builds a factory builds a temple," and "large profits mean large payrolls." If his successor, Herbert Hoover, was regarded as a "great engineer," his experience had been at the promoting end, and he too believed in the mysterious but beneficent workings of Nature, human and divine. So sure of the future that he predicted the abolition of poverty by the continued application of Republican policies, his assurance was not shaken even by the approach of the storm of 1929. "We have come out of each previous depression," he said in 1931, "into a period of prosperity greater than ever before. We shall do so this time." There had been unwarranted speculation and reckless financing, as he admitted, but these had been merely excrescences on an admirable system. "Our transcendant momentary need is a much larger degree of confidence among our business agencies." The great forces of enterprise remained unimpaired. "Under the guidance of Divine Providence they will return to us a greater and more wholesome prosperity than we have ever known."

But stricken America was more deeply hurt than England, even if not so cleft as Germany. If, as alleged, the American banking system was sound, it had so many wild-cat institutions in its membership that the entire structure rocked in the gale. Small banks had been falling annually before the crash, and as the depression continued, huge metropolitan banks came down in ruins; it was found that many in charge had been engaged, directly or through affiliates and subsidiaries, in investment and stock-market speculations or had financed true gamblers. Reporting on the failure of a great bank in their city a group of distinguished Detroit citizens said: "The committee finds in the list of bad loans many loans that obviously have no other purpose than speculation in the stock market. . . . They were made to clerks, stenographers, bank officers and bank clerks, salesmen, and others [i.e., dummies] whose income was not sufficient to warrant any substantial credit. The committee also finds in the list of bad loans, loans to officers of this bank and officers in other banks which were clearly made to assist or further stock-market speculations." By a searching inquiry into banking practices, the finance committee of the United States Senate unearthed a tangle of speculations, intrigues, and favoritism even touching the highest places. Leading Republicans, Democrats, senators, cabinet officers, executives of corporations, and an ex-president of the United States had been given "cut-ins" by banking houses, that is, allowed to buy stocks at prices lower than those allowed to the investing public. In the gust of fear and remorse that shook America, all businesses were questioned; even Business itself was reviled and former success-worshippers spat on their idol. This psychic upset was swift as that of old Florence under Savonarola, but not so thorough: Americans did not burn their dearest material goods.

More composure remained in New England than in the West; towns in Connecticut, for instance, had not plunged into debt so heavily as newer communities, afflicted with growth-mania. Industries there had developed along conservative and specialized lines, and some had accumulated reserves for troubles ahead. Banks were closer to industry and trade, and not quite so enmeshed in land-speculations as in the West, where echoes of the old realtor-mania still resounded, and fantastic bubbles were still blown, like that of the Van Sweringens for a mighty skyscraper center in Cleveland, without adequate population in sight. But, though relatively stabilized, and content with small-scale standards, even New England was caught in the toils.

With banks closed throughout the country, railroads falling into bankruptcy, dividends passed, factories shutting, a public growling and millions unemployed, American business men were bewildered in the spring of 1933. Leaders among them called upon President Roosevelt in the White House and besought the aid of the Government of the United States. The heads of one great group of companies offered to turn their concerns over to the Government if it would assume responsibility for their solvency and management. In the hour of trial, American heads of great enterprise turned to the State no whit less eagerly than Europeans, promising collaboration in return for financial aid and bureaucratic guidance.

Gladly the National Recovery Act was drafted by business interests, except for the section providing for collective bargaining in labor relations—a section deemed necessary to secure cooperation from labor. In this Act were incorporated certain broad principles which had been expounded by business leaders, such as Gerard Swope, and in a formal report by the national Chamber of Commerce. Its purpose was to stop cutthroat competition, raise prices, stabilize industries, "balance production and consumption," and enforce codes of fair practices in all the great branches of industry and trade. With a whoop and a hurrah, business men fell in line behind blaring bands, with other marching men and women, carrying the banner of the Blue Eagle. While the Government was thus trying to pump up prosperity and stabilize business, it poured hundreds of millions into banks, railways, and other concerns, with a view to keeping them out of bankruptcy. It also borrowed billions, for which no other borrowers were available, and paid out this money to the unemployed, inflating the buying power of the masses to the advantage of merchants and industries. So far business men, if they had misgivings, seemed happy at the prospects.

As the sagging balloon of business slowly filled, business men began to feel secure again in their possessions. They forgot that they had been in trouble in 1933. Indeed, a theory was created to the effect that business had really recovered in 1932 and that the Roosevelt administration was responsible for the banking collapse of 1933. This theory gained credence as the old trust-busters turned their batteries on NIRA and as business recovered assurance. By the time the Supreme Court declared the Recovery Act invalid, business men were roundly denouncing their own child. They did not want the Government to start out on the dissolution of trusts, and they felt strong enough to stand on their own feet. Once more the slogan of individualism was heard in the land. To spread this idea broadcast, a number of big business men financed the Liberty League and launched a campaign against the Roosevelt administration on all fronts. Distinguished lawyers for business concerns challenged all the New Deal laws before the Supreme Court and took delight in seeing one after another knocked out by that eminent tribunal. In language that could not be mistaken, the National Manufacturers' Association, the United States Chamber of Commerce, and other business associations turned their batteries loose on "government interference with business"; that is, all interference except tariffs, subsidies, bounties, loans, and expenditures for manufactured products, especially for the army and navy.

Heartened by the cry of the seer and prophet, Henry L. Mencken, that the Republicans could elect a Chinaman President, the main body of business leaders, branded as "economic royalists" by Roosevelt, appealed to the country in 1936, offering the silent "Coolidge from Kansas," Governor Alfred M. Landon, as the Republican candidate. With almost the entire battery of professional columnists and the preponderance of great newspapers on their side, business men of the Republican school, aided by the Hearst press, assailed the New Deal as Communism, Fascism or anarchy. This bold bid for power was futile. One of the worst political defeats on record was suffered by the first proclaimed business man offered for the Presidency by a major party. Business leaders retired in a disarray worse than any seen in 1800, or after 1828 and 1912.

After their disaster of 1936, business man entered upon the third stage —that of watchful waiting. Perhaps their alarms had been a little hasty. During the campaign Joseph P. Kennedy, a New York stock operator, whom Roosevelt had made head of the Securities and Exchange Commission, had declared that "the business men of America, the beneficiaries of the preserved profit system, should be with Mr. Roosevelt," and that "the wealthy have been the chief beneficiaries of the New Deal policies, as witness the financial pages of any paper." After all, apart from a few extravagant holding companies, business organizations and corporations were still intact. Wealth had not been redistributed. Taxes bore more heavily on consumption than they had in the days of Coolidge. Only a small number of speculative practices had been forbidden by law and, as the Senate committee engaged in investigating railroads demonstrated, good old speculative practices had continued unabated under the New Deal. Two hundred great corporations still controlled about half the business wealth of the country, and a careful inventory would doubtless have disclosed a greater concentration of wealth than had existed in 1928. Yet, though unshaken, American business found itself enclosed within an altered frame, one without a close European parallel.

LOOKING FOR THE AMERICAN WAY

In America, as in every country, the bounds for development have been to a large degree set by historic heritage. It was possible for masquerade purposes to revive the antique in Italy, the mediaeval in Germany, and to perpetuate aristocratic benevolence in England. But the traditions for either Fascism or aristocracy are lacking in America; moreover, the character of business itself there, designed for mass-consumption, forbids the creation of an "élite" on any European model, behind which business men could expect to dwell in modest obscurity, and with a minimum of mental exertion.

Since the American traditions go only as far back as the Enlightenment, while Liberty and Equality, the memory of a Revolution for independence, and of a Civil War to free slaves, are the chief components, distinct difficulties for a Fascist movement are presented. A party might perhaps take power under banners inscribed with the name of liberty, but it would require much ingenuity to proceed from that point, since restless millions could hardly be enchanted forever with mere repetitions of the word. A "mythos" might be constructed, but it does not lie readily at hand. And even if it were pieced together, and fastened upon the multitude by some extraordinary Ministry of Propaganda, there would remain the problems of concentration of industry, brought by the enormous bureaucratization of economy under a Fascism.

American industries are founded, far more than any European, upon catering to ever-rising needs of millions of people. They would not thrive upon producing a few elegant cars, like the German and Italian motor-industries, or the sale of champagne to Party heroes. Nor would armament-programs, the chief prop of such European régimes, be sufficient in America, where heavy industries could rapidly fill all possible needs and then would come to a halt, unable to sell enough abroad to keep themselves running. The tremendous national machine of American economy must be fed by mass-orders, which depend in turn upon mass-prosperity, and, to a very much greater degree than in even a European democracy, upon free speech and good spirits. As Fascism in Europe has worked out, the atmosphere of fear created by censorship has ruined many branches of business, the publishing and newspaper trades, the theatrical and cinema fields; in Europe this may not entail such serious disorganizations of economy, but in America terrible prostration would result if the people were afraid to dine out, speak out, and run around in cars to talk with their friends. As the old Frenchman, Ouvrard, discovered in the Revolution, democracy is good for the paper business; and it is still true: paper-consumption went up in France during the recent crisis, with the gain in public discussion, whereas it went sharply down in Fascist Italy and Germany, with the deepening silence, contrary to previous experiences in depressions.

Perhaps more wistfully than toward Italy or Germany, American believers in the élite-theory look to Britain, and wish to see established in America an aristocracy, which, it is supposed, would bring that sublime security characteristic of the old country. But in the first place, the harmony of Britain is secured by many factors, her armament-industry, her empire, her tradition of benevolence tinged with Christian-Socialism; among these, aristocracy is only a single feature. And in the second place, such an aristocracy of birth, however widened by adoption, cannot be imitated adequately by substituting one of wealth. That was one of the chief delusions of many of the American rich from the times of Hamilton to Hanna and Charles Norman Fay, though based upon an entire misconception of the social function of such a class. If it is to be useful to business, an aristocracy must stand aside from and above business; true, rich men may enter it, upon laying aside their identities as they assume ermine and coronets, but they cannot constitute the aristocracy, if it is to serve as a diversion of public interest. The aristocrat remains honorable even in rags—not so the fourth cousin of the grandson of a railway king who went bankrupt—and it is this which makes him acceptable to the masses; he is above them by virtue of birth, which cannot be questioned, and not by virtue of wealth, which can always be taken and redistributed by envious force.

There is, of course, an excellent and serviceable élite already in America—that of Hollywood, perhaps the best in existence for the purposes of business, for it is composed of men and women who may rise from the common people and receive titles by public acclamation—an aristocracy with an abnormally high turn-over. This amusement-aristocracy has assumed the function of the dukes and *duces* of Europe—that of luxuriously diverting itself in public and diverting others. How much the stars of screen, and for that matter also of sport and radio, have relieved millionaires of public scrutiny, can be realized by re-reading the biographies of men like Stillman, who were pursued by the morbid interest of the fascinated populace, until Mary Pickford and Rudolf Valentino flashed on the horizon. In such an élite, gradually enlarged and diversified by spreading interest in all forms of leisure-arts in America, the people sees itself mirrored and seeks its models. Only at their peril would American business men destroy such a popular-élite through Fascist censorship, or substitute their own persons as "aristocrats" in the gaze of the million.

Thus, no matter what glances the American may cast across the ocean, he finds in reality no guidance in foreign methods. For him there is no well-worn path, conveniently marked, requiring no effort or thought on his part. No precedent can be found for his situation, amid a democratic multitude, still fond of the successful man but ready to jeer at his slightest mistaken antic, and with revolution for its only tradition. Still, by this time, he may look back upon accumulated experience of his own. For generations, turning and twisting within these confines, American business men have struggled to rule or to conform, and have advanced in both. With greater skill than Europeans, they learned to guide consumers; yet, far more profoundly than the latter, they have themselves been molded by popular sentiment.

Scarcely a man in the ranks of American millionaires has entirely defied public opinion. Girard, the cynical Frenchman, flouted the tradition of benevolence as long as he lived, but made amends in his will. Though Russell Sage was similarly attacked for over-frugality, his widow glorified his memory by gifts. Crusty old Astor gave a public library. William K. Vanderbilt built more churches than ever, after his incautious "The public be damned," somewhat annoyed that public.

Whenever a major figure in affairs has run afoul of the public opinion of America, as often happens in fevers of investigation, he has soon found his way to the mourners' bench. Thus one of the most free-tongued of the old-style trust-magnates, H. O. Havemeyer, the Sugar King, was said to have told a committee of the Chicago Civic Federation: "Business is not a philanthropy . . . I do not know enough of your ethics to apply them . . . as a business proposition it is all right to get all out of business that you possibly can." It was not long before he saw the wisdom of taking lessons from a pastor's son, his new secretary, John E. Searles. More recently, "the man with the hardest shell and the softest heart in America," as a biographer called him, George F. Baker, proved a refractory witness in Washington. Called the third richest man in the country in 1926, dominating more corporations than any other individual, he felt and said, "It's none of the public's business what I do." After the effects of that remark had been measured, he became one of the stupendous donors of American history.

The extent of American business gifts, and the variety of their objects, one would imagine to be the easiest thing in the world to discover; one might expect business benevolence, one of the most distinctive features of America, to have its history—such, however, is not the case. To secure such a record is extremely difficult; tucked away in the hidden corners of the dullest biographical compilations are most of the notes of contributions to churches, Sunday schools, universities, charitable and other institutions. It was estimated by Ghent in 1901 that business gifts for educational, religious and public purposes had up to then totaled $107,360,000. But that was before the "trust-busting" era, after which benevolence was so enormously stimulated.

The idea of *richesse oblige* is very old in America; merchants like Peabody and Perkins, who gave relatively large sums to institutions for orphans and the blind, carried on what was really a tradition going back to mediaeval patricians. At first business giving bore the Old World religious stamp; but it became rapidly secularized in America, turning away from churches and colleges to medicine, and more recently to the enrichment of leisure, a thoroughly anti-puritanic concept and hence the one farthest from previous patterns. This story of continuous giving, on a scale unapproached anywhere else in the world, with its sudden spurts at crucial moments, and its branching out into many fields, has yet to be written.

One of the interesting, though long out-dated, attempts to study business giving was made by the *New York Tribune* in the 1890's. Of the 4,047 millionaires in America who were considered, the most notable men among them were very lavish, but the majority gave little or nothing. Thus Cleveland, Ohio, had 68 millionaires of whom 21 were givers; St. Louis had 45, with only 10 generous; in Detroit, the proportions were 12 givers to 42 men; in St. Paul, 7 to 28, in Minneapolis, 14 to 44. This, however, was during a highly complacent era, the time of extreme concentration upon private enjoyment. Not long after this, the deluge of giving began. In leading his fellow-millionaires to generosity, a Scotchman, strange to say, was most prominent. Carnegie rebuked the backward rich, and reminded them in an open epistle to Pittsburghians to practice charity, at least on their death-beds, and not to depart "without leaving behind them some evidence of love and gratitude for the city in which they made their fortunes." The successful had better part with a share of their possessions, said E. H. Gary, Chairman of United States Steel, adding, all this massing of wealth without purpose "must be stopped by the rich themselves, or the public will stop it." One of the most pugnacious of Americans, H. C. Frick, the autocratic steel-man, who had refused to compromise in the Homestead strike, began to hand out great sums to charity, explaining that he wished to spare his daughter the odium of being known as one of the country's chief heiresses.

If the scale of their benefactions distinguished Americans from other business men, so did their writings. In all previous literature, their memoirs and compilations of practical advice had followed a routine line, from the testament of the old Mitsui or the first Medici, and the maxims of Morelli, down to those of Defoe and Sir John Barnard in 1776, author of "A Present for an Apprentice, or a Sure Guide to gain both esteem and an estate, by a late Lord Mayor of London." But the American brought a fresh note into the stream of stereotyped formulations. Not interested in the question of Fortuna, he emphasized laughter instead of luck; moreover, he was not trying to guide the apprentice merely, but also to offer an apology to possible critics. At other periods, if business men justified their endeavors, it was in the face of aristocratic prejudice—here were business men struggling mightily to say something in defense as well as encouragement to the common man.

If Carnegie repeated the sage old saws of Franklin, Savary and Defoe, it was with a new twist, insisting that a great business man was a nation-molder whose fortune was "but a drop in the bucket compared with that he showered upon the State and nation." Turning this way and that in the search for apology, successful men strove to justify their careers by argument or, like Schwab, by disarming anecdote:

> Perhaps the way in which Mr. Carnegie differed from many employers could be illustrated by calling up pictures of two boys about to feast. One says "I have a nice pie. Come and watch me eat it." The other says "I have a nice pie. Come, let's eat it."

Constantly aware of the all-surrounding high atmospheric pressure of public opinion, the Americans were reluctant to lay bare their souls in the manner of Alfred Nobel. Rather they sought to shed individuality, if they had any, to conform to the exacting patterns of American life. This tendency was more marked after the popular storms of the "trust-busting" era; then business men put away flashy waistcoats and embroidered braces and, from the heights to the depths, from the tremendous hog-slaughterers to the simplest salmon-canners, went into quiet suits and quiet manners, with mildly twinkling eyes. They assured biographers that, though "public-spirited," they were averse to public posts, that their hobbies were far from eccentric and their characters, simple and genial, were not distinguished in any particular. At the same time, they surrendered the passion for horse-flesh which has ever been associated with the social climbing of business men into a "horsy" feudal aristocracy; some went so far in their renunciation that they took up cow-fancying instead, as did the banker, James Stillman, who explained: "The more you see of horses the faster you get, but the more you see of cows, the more refined you get." And he was right: a gulf separates feudal fox-chasing England and the bovine calm of bourgeois Holland—the worlds of Landseer and of Paul Potter.

Thus, if business has affected democratic manners in America, the converse is also true: democracy has profoundly refashioned American business character. This process was hastened by a unique college education. No other business man has been subjected to such a training: the German indeed was schooled, but primarily in technical fields, whereas the American was sent to college for social ends, for background and finish, for a tumbling in that rushing river of fraternal activities which makes all the pebbles smooth. In colleges endowed by their parents, young would-be business men studied many a new art, such as "Business Psychology," developed by Hugo Münsterberg, which was supposed to turn out the Masterful, Dynamic Man, a "Large Dimension Worker," by the aid of charts picturing the "Mind of the Business Man," quite unhumorously, as a large zero, upon which plays various arrows representing talents for administration, foreign languages, bookkeeping and so on; if the arrows are ideally equalized, the mind should preserve its pure egg-like formation without a dent.

From these beginnings, however faltering, of a special education for business men, the ingenuity of the mind-molders went on to remarkable discoveries without a parallel in other lands. Never in Europe had there been so much money to be made by telling other men how to make money, or how to please their associates. In America, works on "Making Everybody Rich" and "Strategy in Handling People" poured from the presses; mystics from India preached "Thinking Success Into Business" and the use of yoga in the office. Presently came Napoleon Hill with his "Law of Success in Sixteen Lessons, teaching for the first time in the history of the world, the true philosophy upon which all personal success is built." Together with these experts appeared the "public relations counselor," who could guarantee, for a very adequate compensation, to achieve "personality acceptance," summoning with the wave of a hand and a check, clouds of "ghosts" to write speeches and autobiographies for the bewildered or the taciturn.

A "pleasing personality" was readily achieved by such assistance. But then confusion ensued when some harassed business men asked the corporation lawyer to split up their personalities for taxation purposes, sometimes into as many as sixty-four parts. This was, as Secretary Morgenthau described it, "The creation of a multiple personality in the taxpayer. By this device he ceases to be a single individual and becomes a whole group of people, some of whom are earning money while others are losing it . . . Often he convinces himself that these separate people actually exist. Each one of these imaginary individuals into which the taxpayer divides himself deals and trades with all the other imaginary individuals." The question then became, should such business men as adopted this method, try to acquire sixty-four pleasing personalities? Or should they strive for psychotherapeutic re-integration?

Undoubtedly the character of the American business man, multiple or single, became divergent from European models through such pressure, education, legal exercises and psychological massage. He learned to give magnetic handclasps, to develop his will-power before breakfast, unveil monuments, sway consumers and fascinate prospects. But a vague unrest has filled him for a long time, which no professors and counselors have so far been able to allay—the American wants a creed, more than other business men. And since nobody is able to provide him with one, he has set out in pursuit of it himself. Stumbling along by intuition, he has developed various ideas adapted to his unique environment. Selfridge, the American store-keeper who made two fortunes, one in America and one in England, came in contact with the British aristocracy and began to think about honor and ethics for business, although he largely confused honor with honesty, and carelessly mixed up incompatible commercial with feudal codes. At the same time the shoe-maker, Filene, developed the formula of "Service" to society, one of the most potent ever devised by business men. In working out his thesis, Filene reverted almost to a mediaeval doctrine of the "just price," as the proper goal of business enterprise, with "adequate return" and "just conditions" for labor, and "Ich dien" for the entrepreneur.

Although Selfridge and Filene touched mediaeval fountains in their search for a business honor and creed, and undoubtedly whatever the American business man ultimately finds must bear some relation to the sources of the past, this does not mean that the American will travel a road like any of the Old World. The full study of the thought of American business men and their efforts to adjust themselves to democratic standards, remains as yet unmade; but it is nevertheless apparent that they have departed along trails of their own seeking. And though they may at times hanker after distinctions and the safe solution to social questions offered by aristocratization, as business men have always done, the main tendency has been away from this ancient and well-worn route. The enormous markets presented by the American masses condition the character, and must eventually determine the creed, of American business.

As far as historic record goes, there is no reason to suppose that American business must necessarily imitate any other type; indeed, if business history shows anything, it demonstrates the uniqueness of each people in its economic-social development, despite general trends and universal communication. It is true that history sets no pattern for the future; it will be impossible, in a world crowded with millions upon millions of human beings and with machines, to dream of duplicating the little, and simpler, worlds of the past, when the inhabitants of communities were numbered by hundreds or by dozens. There can be no return to the "horse-and-buggy" days, or to the times of clipper and galleon; and in a sense, there can be no advance either, for with every step away from smallness and simplicity into vastness and complexity, some precious quality must be lost forever, even if new virtues are acquired. Yet, if the bygone periods can present no model for future generations that will save them thought of their own, these previous ages have nevertheless conditioned future thinking in a variety of ways, by eliminating some possibilities and opening others. We never imitate the past—yet we are never emancipated from it.

BIBLIOGRAPHY

IN DEFAULT of an adequate bibliography of business history, a book-list is here presented, necessarily much condensed. Easily accessible sources and standard histories, like those of Mommsen or Ranke, Clapham or Sombart, are omitted. Only works made use of directly or quoted extensively are given. Grateful acknowledgment is due to members of the staff of the Warburg Library, formerly in Hamburg, now in London, for assistance, as well as to my parents and my husband, Alfred Vagts, whose books have been drawn upon.

AMERICAN HISTORICAL ASSOCIATION, Annual Report, 1903. Washington, 1904.

ANDRAL, B. G.: Le triomphe de Pomone. Pau, 1916.

BAASCH, ERNST: Der Einfluss des Handels auf das Geistesleben Hamburgs. Hamburg, 1909.

BAKER, GEO. A.: Bad Habits of Good Society, N. Y., 1878.

BANNISTER, S.: William Paterson. London, 1858.

BAUER, STEPHAN: Der Verfall der metaphorischen Oekonomie. (In: Festschrift für C. Grünberg.) Leipzig, 1932.

BEARD, CHAS. A.: Economic Interpretation of the Constitution of the United States. N. Y., 1913.

BEARD, CHAS. A. and MARY R.: The Rise of American Civilization. N. Y., 1933.

BECHTEL, H.: Wirtschaftsstil des deutschen Mittelalters. Munich, 1930.

BERTALL, C.: La comédie de notre temps. Paris, 1874.

BESANT, WALTER: Fifty Years Ago. London, 1892. Eighteenth Century London. London, 1902.

BEZOLD, F. v.: Das Fortleben der antiken Götter im mittelalterlichen Humanismus. Bonn, 1922.

BIEDERMANN, K.: Deutschland im 18. Jahrhundert. Leipzig, 1875.

BLOK, P. J.: Geschichte der Niederlande. Gotha, 1905-7.

BOURNE, H. R. Fox: English Merchants. London, 1886.

BOWDEN, WITT: Industrial Society in England towards the End of the 18th Century. N. Y., 1925.

BRANDT, P.: Schaffende Arbeit und bildende Kunst. 2 vols. Leipzig, 1928.

BRENTANO, LUJO: Die Anfänge des modernen Kapitalismus. Jena, 1916. Der wirtschaftende Mensch in der Geschichte. Jena, 1923. Geschichte der wirtschaftlichen Entwicklung Englands. 3 vols. Jena, 1928. Das Wirtschaftsleben der antiken Welt. Jena, 1929.

BUCHANAN, DANIEL: Development of Capitalist Enterprise in India. N. Y., 1934.

BUECHER, KARL: Die Entstehung der Volkswirtschaft. Tübingen, 1922.

BURCKHARDT, JACOB: Die Kunstwerke der belgischen Städte. Düsseldorf, 1842.

BURGON, J. W.: Life and Times of Sir Thomas Gresham. 2 vols. London, 1839.

CAPEFIGUE, J. B.: Histoire des grandes opérations financières. 2 vols. Paris, 1855–1856.

CASTILLE, H.: Les frères Pereire. Paris, 1861.

CHILD, SIR JOSIAH: The Great Honour and Advantage of the East India Trade. London, 1697.

CILLEULS, A.: Histoire et régime de la grande industrie en France. Paris, 1898.

CLÉMENT, P.: Jacques Cœur et Charles VII. Paris, 1866. Histoire de Colbert et de son administration. Paris, 1874.

COCHUT, A.: Law, son système et son époque. Paris, 1907.

CORDIER, HENRI: Les Marchands hanistes de Canton. Leyden, 1902.

COURANT, M.: Les commerçants chinois. Revue des deux mondes. Vol. 153, 1899.

COYER, ABBÉ: Noblesse commerçante. Paris, 1756.

CRAVEN, AVERY: Edmund Ruffin. N. Y., 1932.

CRAVEN, W. FRANK: The Earl of Warwick. Hispanic American Review, Vol. X.

CROCKETT, A. S.: Peacocks on Parade. N. Y., 1931.

DAENELL, E.: Die Blütezeit der deutschen Hanse. Hamburg, 1905.

DAHLINGER, C. W.: Pittsburgh, A Sketch of its Early Social Life, N. Y., 1916.

DAIRE, E.: Économistes et Financiers du XVIIIème siècle. Paris, 1843.

DANA, J.: The Man Who Built San Francisco. N. Y., 1936.

DANIELS, G. W.: Early English Cotton Industry. Manchester, 1920.

D'AVENEL, G.: Découvertes d'histoire sociale. Paris, 1910.

DAVIDSOHN, ROBERT: Geschichte von Florenz. Berlin, 1925. Florentiner Welthandel des Mittelalters. (Weltwirtschaftliches Archiv. July, 1929.) Beatrice, Simone und Musciattino de' Bardi. Dante-Jahrbuch, vol. X.

DAYTON, A. C.: Last Days of Knickerbocker Life in New York. N. Y., 1882.

DEFOE, DANIEL: The Anatomy of Exchange Alley. London, 1719. The Complete English Tradesman. 1732. A General History of Trade. 1713.

DICTIONNAIRE DES ANTIQUITÉS. Ed. Ch. Daremberg, E. Saglio, etc. Paris, 1904.

DIES, JEROME: Street of Adventure. Boston, 1935.

DOREN, ALFRED: Die Florentiner Wolltuchindustrie. Stuttgart, 1901. Fortuna im Mittelalter. Berlin, 1924.

DUEVEL, THEA: Die Gütererwerbung J. Fuggers des Reichen. Munich, 1913.

DUMESNIL, R.: Histoire des plus célèbres amateurs italiens. Paris, 1853.

EHRENBERG, RICHARD: Das Zeitalter der Fugger. 2 vols. Jena, 1922. Hamburg und England im Zeitalter der Königin Elisabeth. Jena, 1896. Hans Kleberg. Nürnberg, 1893.

EISLER, MAX: Alt-Delft. Vienna, 1923.

ELIAS, J. E.: Geschiednis van het Amsterdamsche regentenpatriciaat. 's-Gravenhage, 1923.

ELLET, MRS.: Queens of American Society. N. Y., 1870.

ENGEL-JANOSI: Soziale Probleme der Renaissance. Stuttgart, 1924.

ESCOTT, T. H.: City Characters under several reigns. London, 1922.

ESPINAS, G.: Recueil des documents relatifs à l'histoire de l'industrie drapière en Flandre. 3 vols. Brussels, 1906.

ÉTIENNE, L.: Les financiers au théâtre. Revue des deux-mondes. Oct. 15, 1870.

EVELYN, J.: Navigation and Commerce. London, 1674.

FISCH, G.: Nine Months in the U. S. London, 1862.

FITZPATRICK, F.: A Study of Business Men's Associations. N. Y., 1925.

FORBES, BERTIE C.: Men Who Are Making America. N. Y., 1926.

FORTESCUE, J. W.: A History of the British Army. Vol. III. London, 1902.

FOWLER, W. W.: Twenty Years of Inside Life in Wall Street. N. Y., 1880.

Fox, Dixon Ryan: The Decline of Aristocracy in the Politics of New York. N. Y., 1919. A Retrospect for Yorkers. New York History Quarterly, vol. XVIII, No. 1, Jan., 1937.

Fraser, J. F.: America at Work. London. 1903.

Friedlaender, L.: Sittengeschichte Roms. Vienna, 1934.

Gebauer, K.: Geschichte des französischen Kultureinflusses auf Deutschland. Strassburg, 1911.

Gebhart, E.: Origines de la Renaissance en Italie. Paris, 1879.

Génard, P.: Anvers à travers les âges. Brussels, 1888-92.

Ghent, W. J.: Our Benevolent Feudalism. N. Y., 1902.

Grant, A. G.: The Huguenots. London, 1934.

Grattan, T. C.: Civilized America. London, 1859.

Groeythusen, B.: Origines de l'esprit bourgeois en France. Paris, 1927.

Grund, F. J.: Die Aristokratie in Amerika. 2 vols. Stuttgart, 1839.

Habaru, A.: Le Creusot. Paris, 1934.

Halley, R.: Lancashire, its Puritanism and Nonconformity. London, 1869.

Hallgarten, Wolfgang: Vorkriegsimperialismus. Paris, 1935.

Hammersley, S. S.: Industrial Leadership. London, 1925.

Harper, F. C.: Pittsburgh of Today. 4 vols. N. Y., 1931.

Hart, B. H. Liddell: Great Captains Unveiled. London, 1927.

Hasebroek, J.: Griechische Wirtschafts- und Gesellschaftsgeschichte. Tübingen, 1928.

Hauser, Henri: Les débuts du capitalisme. Paris, 1927.

Heckscher, Eli F.: Der Merkantilismus. 2 vols. Jena, 1932.

Heichelheim, F.: Wirtschaftliche Schwankungen der Zeit von Alexander bis Augustus. Bonn, 1930.

Hertz, R.: Das Hamburger Seehandelshaus J. C. Godeffroy. Hamburg, 1922.

Heyck, E.: Florenz und die Medici. Leipzig, 1927.

Heynen, R.: Entstehung des Kapitalismus in Venedig. Berlin, 1905.

Hirsch, A. H.: The Huguenots of South Carolina. Durham, 1928.

Histoire de l'Art, edited by André Michel. Paris, 1912.

Houblon, Lady A.: The Houblon Family. 2 vols. London, 1907.

Hunter, W.: The "Fan Kwae" at Canton. Shanghai, 1911.

Ilgner, K.: Die volkswirtschaftlichen Anschauungen von Antonino von Florenz. Paderborn, 1904.

Jansonius, H.: Some Aspects of Business Life in Early Victorian Fiction. 1926.

Janzé, A. de: Les financiers d'autrefois. Paris, 1886.

Johanet, F.: Autour du monde millionaire américain. Paris, 1898.

Johnston, T.: The Financiers and the Nation. London, 1934.

Joret, C.: Pierre et Nicolas Formont. Paris, 1890.

Kehr, Eckardt: Schlachtflottenbau und Parteipolitik. Berlin, 1930.

Kletler, P.: Nordwesteuropas Verkehr, Handel und Gewerbe im frühen Mittelalter. Vienna, 1924.

Kopp, G. v.: Kaufmannsleben zur Zeit der Hanse. Leipzig, 1907.

Krafft, Hans Ulrich: Denkwürdigkeiten. Göttingen, 1862.

Kraus, J. B.: Scholastik, Puritanismus und Kapitalismus. Munich, 1930.

Krupp: Letters. N. Y., 1930.

Lambert, R. S.: George Hudson. London, 1934.

Langford, J. A.: A Century of Birmingham Life. 2 vols. 1868.

Laspeyres, E.: Geschichte der volkswirtschaftlichen Anschauungen der Niederländer. 1863.

LEBLOND, M.: La société française sous la troisième république d'après les romanciers. Paris, 1905.

LEHR, E. DREXEL: King Lehr. Phila., 1935.

LENZ, F., and UNHOLTZ, O.: Geschichte des Bankhauses des Gebrüder Schickler. Berlin, 1912.

LEROUX, A.: Étude critique sur le XVIIIe siècle à Bordeaux. Bordeaux, 1921.

LEVY, H.: Grundlagen des ökonomischen Liberalismus. Jena, 1912.

LEWINSOHN, R.: Umschichtung der europäischen Vermögen. Berlin, 1925.

LILL, G.: Hans Fugger und die Kunst. Munich, 1908.

MACCULLOCH, J. R.: A Collection of Scarce and Valuable Tracts. London, 1859.

MACLAY, W.: Journal. N. Y., 1927.

MANCHESTER A HUNDRED YEARS AGO, edited by W. E. A. Axon. Manchester, 1887.

MANNHEIM, KARL: Ideologie und Utopie. Bonn, 1929.

MARTIN, A. v.: Soziologie der Renaissance. Stuttgart, 1932.

MARTIN, G. GASTON: Nantes au XVIIIe siècle. Paris, 1931.

MARTIN, GERMAIN: La grande industrie sous le règne de Louis XIV. Paris, 1898.

MARX-ENGELS: Gesamtausgabe. Frankfurt, 1927.

MATHIEZ, A.: The French Revolution. N. Y., 1928.

MAVOR, J.: Economic History of Russia. London, 1925.

MEILHAN, S. DE: Du gouvernement, des moeurs, etc. en France avant la Révolution. Paris, 1814.

MELTZER, O.: Geschichte der Karthager. Berlin, 1896.

MELTZING, O.: Das Bankhaus der Medici. Jena, 1906.

MEREDITH, H. A.: The Drama of Money-Making. London, 1931.

MICHELS, R.: Der Patriotismus. Munich, 1929.

MOLMENTI, P.: Venice. London, 1908.

MORISON, SAMUEL E.: Maritime Massachusetts. Boston, 1921.

MORSE, H. B.: Gilds of China. N. Y., 1932.

MILLER, J. C.: Sam Adams, Pioneer in Propaganda. Boston, 1936.

MUENCH, H.: Adolph von Hansemann. Munich, 1932.

MURRIS, R.: La Hollande au XVIIe et XVIIIe siècles. Paris, 1925.

NAMIER, L. B.: Structure of Politics at the Accession of George III. London, 1930.

NEUMANN, KARL: Rembrandt. 2 vols. Munich, 1924.

NORMAND, C.: La bourgeoisie française au XVIIe siècle. Paris, 1908.

ONCKEN, AUGUST: Die Maxime Laissez Faire et Laissez Passer. Bern, 1886.

OPITZ, M.: Die Fugger und Welser. Berlin, 1930.

PAPILLON, THOMAS: Memoirs. London, 1887.

PASSERINI, L.: Gli Alberti di Firenze. Florence, 1869.

PAUMGARTNER, B.: Briefwechsel. Stuttgart, 1895.

PERSSON, A. W.: Staat und Manufaktur im Römischen Reiche. Lund, 1923.

PERUZZI, S.: Storia del Commercio e dei Banchieri di Firenze. Florence, 1868.

PICOT, E.: Les Italiens en France au XVIe siècle. Bordeaux, 1901.

PINNER, F.: Emil Rathenau. Leipzig, 1918.

PRENTICE, A.: Historical Sketches. London, 1851.

PRESTON, HOWARD W.: Rhode Island's Historic Background. Providence, 1930.

QUIETT, GLENN C.: They Built the West. N. Y., 1934.

RANDALL-MacIvor, D.: The Etruscans. London, 1937.

RENARD, G.: Histoire du travail à Florence. 2 vols. Paris, 1913.

REUMONT, A. v.: Lorenzo de' Medici. 2 vols. Leipzig, 1883.

ROERIG, F.: Mittelalterliche Weltwirtschaft. Jena, 1933.

ROHAN, JACK: A Yankee Arms Maker. N. Y., 1935.

Rooses, M.: Geschichte der Malerschule Antwerpens. Munich, 1882.

Ross, Janet: Lives of the Early Medici. London, 1910.

Roth, J. F.: Geschichte des Nürnbergischen Handels. 4 vols. Leipzig, 1802.

Rouff, M.: Tubeuf, un grand industriel français. Paris, 1922.

Sampson, H.: History of Advertising. London, 1874.

Savary, J.: Le Parfait Négociant. Paris, 1675.

Schaal, Hans: Von Tauschhandel zum Welthandel. Leipzig, 1931.

Schillman, F.: Florenz und die Kultur Toskanas. Leipzig, 1929.

Schlesinger, Arthur M.: Colonial Merchants and the Revolution. N. Y., 1917.

Schoenlank, B.: Soziale Kämpfe vor 300 Jahren. Nürnberg, 1894.

Schmidt-Weisenfels, E.: Geschichte des modernen Reichtums. Berlin, 1893.

Schmoller, G.: Die geschichtliche Entwicklung der Unternehmung. Jena, 1890–1893.

Schuecking, L.: Soziologie der literarischen Geschmacksbildung. Munich, 1923.

Schulte, A.: Geschichte des mittelalterlichen Handels und Verkehrs. 2 vols. Leipzig, 1900. Die Fugger in Rom. Leipzig, 1904.

Schultz, Alwin: Deutsches Leben im XIV und XV Jahrhundert. Vienna, 1892.

Scott, W. R.: Constitution and Finance of English, Scottish and Irish Joint-Stock Companies. 3 vols. Cambridge, 1910–12.

Sée, Henri: L'évolution de la pensée politique en France. Paris, 1925.

Selfridge, H. G.: Romance of Commerce. London, 1923.

Shannon, Fred A. and Gates, Paul W.: articles on the Homestead Act in Am. Hist. Review. Vol. XLI. July, 1936.

Shaw, W. A.: Manchester Old and New. 3 vols. London, 1896.

Simons, A. M.: Social Forces in American History. N. Y., 1911.

Sombart, Werner: Krieg und Kapitalismus. Munich, 1913. Der Bourgeois, Munich, 1913.

Strieder, Jakob: Jacob Fugger der Reiche. Leipzig, 1926. Studien zur Geschichte kapitalistischer Organisationsformen. Munich, 1925.

Swarte, V. de: Samuel Bernard. Paris, 1893.

Takekoshi, Yosoburo: Economic Aspects of the History of the Civilization of Japan. N. Y., 1930.

Temple, Sir W.: Observations upon the United Provinces of the Netherlands. London, 1690.

Thirion, H.: La vie privée des financiers au XVIIIe siècle. 1895.

Train, Geo.: Young America in Wall Street. N. Y., 1857.

Vagts, Alfred: Internationale Finanz und internationale Politik. Europäische Gespräche. Hamburg, 1928. Deutschland und die Vereinigten Staaten in der Weltpolitik. N. Y., 1936.

Voigt, G.: Die Wiederbelebung des classischen Altertums. Berlin, 1893.

Waentig, H.: Wirtschaft und Kunst. Jena, 1909.

Wallace, David D.: History of South Carolina. N. Y., 1934.

Walmsley, H. M.: Life of Sir Joshua Walmsley. Liverpool, 1870.

Wantoch, H.: Magnificent Money-Makers. London, 1932.

Ware, Mary C.: Life of Samuel Hibbert Ware. Manchester, 1882.

Warburg, Aby: Francesco Sassetti's letztwillige Verfügung. Hamburg, 1907. Bildniskunst und florentinisches Bürgertum. Leipzig, 1901. Flandrische Kunst und florentinische Frührenaissance. Berlin, 1902.

Warmington, E. H.: Commerce between the Roman Empire and India. Cambridge, 1928.

Weber, Max: Die protestantische Ethik und der "Geist" des Kapitalismus. Archiv für Sozialwissenschaft. Vol. XX. Zur Geschichte der Handelsgesellschaften im Mittelalter. Stuttgart, 1889.

WEIL, A.: The Navy of Venice. N. Y., 1910.

WEISS, C.: History of the French Protestant Refugees. London, 1854.

WERTENBAKER, THOS. J.: Norfolk. Duke University Press, 1931.

WETTEREAU, J. O.: Letters from Two Business Men to Alexander Hamilton. Journal of Economic and Business History, Vol. III, No. 4. Aug., 1931.

WIRTH, MAX: Geschichte der Handelskrisen. Frankfurt, 1874.

WOERTERBUCH DER ANTIKE, edited by Hans Lamar. Leipzig, 1933.

WOLTMANN, ALFRED: Holbein und seine Zeit. 2 vols. Leipzig, 1868.

ZIMMERMANN, ERICH: World Resources and Industries. N. Y., 1934.

INDEX